THE LOST MEANING OF THE SEVENTH DAY

THE LOST MEANING OF THE SEVENTH DAY

Sigve K. Tonstad

Berrien Springs, Michigan

Andrews University Press
Sutherland House
8360 W. Campus Circle Dr.
Berrien Springs, MI 49104–1700
Telephone: 269-471-6134
Fax: 269-471-6224
Email: aupo@andrews.edu
Website: http://universitypress.andrews.edu

ISBN 978-1-883925-65-9

Printed in the United States of America

17 16 15 14 13 8 7 6 5 4

Library of Congress Cataloging-in-Publication Data

Tonstad, Sigve.
The lost meaning of the Seventh Day / by Sigve K. Tonstad.
p. cm.
Includes bibliographical references and index.
ISBN 978-1-883925-65-9 (hardcover : alk. paper) 1. Sabbath. 2. Seventh-day Adventists--Doctrines. I. Title.
BV125.T66 2009
263'.1--dc22

2009037220

Project Director	Ronald Alan Knott
Project Editor	Deborah L. Everhart
Line Editor	Kenneth Wade
Copy Editor	Deborah L. Everhart
Indexer	Karen Schmitt, Schmitt Indexing
Cover Designer	Tiago Baltazar
Text Designer	Tiago Baltazar
Typesetter	Tiago Baltazar

Typeset: 11/16 Sabon MT

To the memory of Carsten A. Johnsen

CONTENTS

PART FOUR

LOSS AND RETRIEVAL: THE SEVENTH DAY IN THE POST-BIBLICAL ERA

PREFACE

The seventh day is an experience and not only history or theology. On this point, writing from the Jewish perspective, Abraham Joshua Heschel and Pinchas Peli are unsurpassed for their perception and eloquence. On the Christian side, Marva Dawn and Dorothy Bass are calling for a sabbatarian renaissance, seeking to retrieve a lost treasure and a meaning-making resource in our time. To their evocative and imaginative suggestions I will add a glimpse of my own experience.

In the simple and very rural home in which I grew up, life on weekdays was limited to the kitchen. The living room was for reasons of necessary frugality not heated during the week and was *de facto* off limits. But on the Sabbath, the living room opened up and was transformed into a house church or a synagogue, wrapped in the "cathedral in time," as Heschel puts it. The first part of the Sabbath in our home was dedicated to the study of ancient texts. While the study at times was tedious for a restless child, it left a residue of reverence for the ancient texts, inculcating in me the attitude that the Bible is a text worthy of close reading. Moreover, the tediousness was softened by anticipation of the Sabbath dinner, a meal that became renowned among my non-sabbatarian friends, who had a great sense of timing and often showed up when they thought that the study of the ancient texts was over. Between my father, who promoted the study of the texts, and my mother, who cooked such spectacular meals despite our meager resources, there is no doubt that the touch of my mother did the most to lift the prestige of the seventh day.

In Oslo, Norway, where I served as pastor of the Bethel Church for more than a decade in addition to tending a medical practice, I collected many more priceless memories of ministry and fellowship on the seventh day. Whether teaching or preaching, I had the opportunity to try out various interpretations of biblical texts, including perspectives that have been developed further here. I want to thank members and non-members of the Bethel community for our open-ended dialogue, for the sense of being seekers together, and for the sobriety that comes to a reader of the Bible when standing where the rubber meets the road. During these years, no seeker in our community was more in earnest or helpful than my sister Solveig, and no one, not even my mother, surpasses the abilities of my wife Serena to make the Sabbath meal an occasion of enduring memories.

I came slowly and rather late to the academic study of the Bible, but wonderful teachers have cushioned the negatives of my delayed journey. My indebtedness to them will be evident at crucial junctures in this book. To have studied under scholars like E. P. Sanders, Richard B. Hays, Bruce Longenecker, and Richard Bauckham is simply a privilege beyond measure. These mentors may not understand my interest in the seventh day or agree with my conclusions, but my sense of gratitude and indebtedness to them is not for that reason any less.

Among scholars from within my immediate community I owe a lot to the late Robert Darnell, as well as to Ivan Blazen, Jon Paulien, and A. Graham Maxwell.

I would like to express my gratitude to Andrews University Press for accepting my manuscript for publication; and to Debi Everhart, editor of the Press, for her grace, patience, and healing touches on the manuscript throughout the long process that this has been. I also want to thank Ken Wade for his careful editing and helpful suggestions.

In the fourth part of this book, looking at the seventh day in the post-biblical period, I pursue perspectives that might loosely be listed under the heading "separations" or "fractures." Two "fractures" are especially important—the breach between the Christian community and Jewish believers and the separation in the Christian outlook from the body and the earth. I am indebted to my friend and mentor, the late Carsten A. Johnsen, for the basic tenets that enabled the latter disconnection to happen. He taught that the Platonic imprint on the Christian outlook and practice with regard to the material world was a devastating detriment. I have not ceased to share that conviction, and I am unable to stop missing my early mentor. For this reason I am dedicating this book to his memory.

This project has been many years in the making. Even at the beginning, when our two daughters were still young and always present, I had the nagging sensation that their childhood and youth too soon would give way to adulthood and absence. Now, in hindsight, the subject that once cut into time that belonged to my daughters has during the periods of their absence been a source of consolation. Time spent with the subject has in a sense been time spent with them.

Let me try to explain. If I were to suggest the meaning of the seventh day with reference to its opposite, the opposite must first be defined, and the counterpoint to the seventh day is in my view separation. Separation, transience, discontinuity, and absence are all familiar realities in human experience. They describe well the land that lies opposite the territory of the seventh day. The Sabbath, on the contrary, means togetherness instead of separation, permanence instead of transience, continuity instead of disruption, and presence instead of absence. According to my understanding the seventh day touches an area of profound existential need, brought to the surface by life's unremitting separations. Seeing in the seventh day the antidote to separation brings my daughters near in thought even when they are far away, a remedy only to be surpassed by the sabbatarian premise that separation is contrary to God's intent and will come to an end.

It is as the counterpoint to the reality of separation that I now sign off on my study of the seventh day.

ABBREVIATIONS

AB	Anchor Bible Commentary
ANF	*Ante-Nicene Fathers*
BDAG	Greek-English Lexicon of the New Testament and Other Early Christian Literature, ed. W. Bauer, F. W. Danker, W. F. Arndt, F. W. Gingrich
BECNT	Baker Exegetical Commentary on the New Testament
BETL	Bibliotheca ephemeridum theologicarum lovaniensum
BHS	*Biblia Hebraica Stuttgartensia*
Bib	*Biblica*
BSac	*Bibliotheca Sacra*
BZAW	Beihefte zur *Zeitschrift für die alttestamentliche Wissenschaft*
BZNW	Beihefte zur *Zeitschrift für die neutestamentliche Wissenschaft*
CBQ	*Catholic Biblical Quarterly*
CC	Continental Commentary
EKKNT	Evangelisch-katholischer Kommentar zum Neuen Testament
EstBib	*Estudios bíblicos*
GNB	Good News Bible
HBT	*Horizons in Biblical Theology*
HNT	Handbuch zum Neuen Testament
HTR	*Harvard Theological Review*
HUCA	*Hebrew Union College Annual*
ICC	International Critical Commentary
Int	*Interpretation*
IST	Issues in Systematic Theology
JAAR	*Journal of the American Academy of Religion*
JBL	*Journal of Biblical Literature*
JBQ	Jewish Bible Quarterly
JSNT	Journal for the Study of the New Testament
JSNT Sup	Journal for the Study of the New Testament: Supplement Series

JSOT	*Journal for the Study of the Old Testament*
JSOT Sup	Journal for the Study of the Old Testament: Supplement Series
JTS	*Journal of Theological Studies*
KJV	King James Version
MNTC	Moffat New Testament Commentary
NASB	New American Standard Bible
NEB	New English Bible
NICNT	New International Commentary on the New Testament
NIGTC	New International Greek Testament Commentary
NIV	New International Version
NJB	New Jerusalem Bible
NKJV	New King James Version
NovT	*Novum Testamentum*
NovTSup	Novum Testamentum Supplement
NRSV	New Revised Standard Version
NTL	New Testament Library
NTM	New Testament Message
NTS	*New Testament Studies*
NTT	New Testament Theology
OBT	Overtures to Biblical Theology
OTS	Old Testament Studies
PG	Patrologia graeca (edited by J.-P. Migne)
RSV	Revised Standard Version
RTR	*Reformed Theological Review*
SBL	Society of Biblical Literature
SBLDS	Society of Biblical Literature Dissertation Series
SBLMS	Society of Biblical Literature Monograph Series
SBLSBS	Society of Biblical Literature Sources for Biblical Study
SJOT	*Scandinavian Journal of the Old Testament*
SJT	*Scottish Journal of Theology*
SNTSMS	Society for New Testament Studies Monograph Series
TDNT	*Theological Dictionary of the New Testament*, ed. G. Kittel and G. Friedrich
TDOT	*Theological Dictionary of the Old Testament*, ed. G. J.

	Botterweck, H. Ringgren, and H.-J. Fabry
TU	Texte und Untersuchungen
TynBul	*Tyndale Bulletin*
VC	*Vigiliae christianae*
VT	*Vetus Testamentum*
WBC	Word Biblical Commentary
WUNT	Wissenschaftliche Untersuchungen zum Neuen Testament
ZAW	Zeitschrift für die alttestamentliche Wissenschaft
ZNW	Zeitschrift für die neutestamentliche Wissenschaft
ZTK	*Zeitschrift für Theologie und Kirche*

CHAPTER 1

INTRODUCING THE SEVENTH DAY

We do not see our revelatory signs; there is no longer any prophet; and there is no one among us who knows how long.
Psalm 74:9 (translation mine)

The seventh day is like a jar buried deep in the sands of time, preserving a treasure long lost and forgotten. We have only partial knowledge of the factors that caused this jar to disappear, but we are nevertheless in a position to predict what will happen when the treasure is recovered. The seventh day will speak again its native voice of blessing (Gen. 2:1–3). It will illuminate the most basic question of human existence because it exposes the bedrock of what it means to be human. It will not draw back from the most crushing facet of human reality because it is designed precisely to convey God's presence when the sense of God's absence is most keenly felt. This claim, so extravagant at first sight, will seem less pretentious if we pause to recall the origin of the seventh day, the dramatic discontinuity in its story, and the contraction that has asserted itself in its absence.

FOUNDATIONS

God is the primary subject of the seventh day. Just like the Dead Sea Scrolls, preserved for millennia in ancient pottery, the content of the jar must command more attention than the vessel that contains it. When we speak of the lost meaning of the seventh day, therefore, we are speaking of meaning that has been lost concerning God. The seventh day draws attention to a subject more important than itself. Unlike treasures similarly buried, however, the seventh day will not wait for someone to unearth and rediscover its treasure before releasing its blessing. It is in the character of God to make the first move, and He has done so. In our time the seventh day is stirring in the ruins, called forth more by the force of its own enduring commission than by the yearnings of the wasteland underneath which it lies. The whisper of sacred time beckons all who move about under its wide canopy to pause in order to be illumined by its story.[1]

In the Bible the seventh day is marked off as the high point and climax of Creation, enshrining God's presence at the center of human experience (Gen. 2:1–3). When the Israelites emerged from cruel bondage in Egypt, the seventh day was made to stand apart as a sign of freedom and dignity (Exod. 16:1–30). In the Ten Commandments, which cover only the most essential ethical obligations and principles of conduct (Deut. 5:22), the seventh day serves as a bill of rights for all God's creatures, human and non-human alike (Exod. 20:8–11; Deut. 5:12–15). The story that underlies the commandment emphasizes a privilege offered; but even if the connotation of an obligation seems inevitable, imitation of the Creator is the essential point (Exod. 20:11). The seventh day is also singled out as the sign of the divine-human relationship, enjoining the observer to manifest God's ways in human relationships (Exod. 31:12–17). The idea that the seventh day is a passing ordinance intended only for the members of a specific ethnic group, the Jews, is countered by the prophet who makes it the centerpiece of a vision of inclusion (Isa. 56:1–8), a critical ingredient in the future restoration (Isa. 58:12–14), and even a feature of life in the earth made new (Isa. 66:23).

God is the primary subject of the seventh day. When we speak of the lost meaning of the seventh day, therefore, we are speaking of meaning that has been lost concerning God.

In the New Testament the seventh day features so prominently in the healing ministry of Jesus that it defines His service, placing the healing intent resolutely in the foreground (Mark 3:1–5; Luke 13:10–17; John 5:1–9; 9:1–14). In the Synoptic Gospels the death of Jesus is conspicuously timed to coincide with the beginning of the seventh day. He died, they all say, at "three [o'clock] in the afternoon" (Matt. 27:45; Mark 15:33; Luke 23:44). While this might be dismissed as incidental trivia, signifying no more or no less than if it had happened on a Tuesday afternoon or on a Thursday, His death echoes the inimitable hallmark of divine activity. Jesus's death is configured according to the scale of Creation (Gen. 2:1–3), urging the reader of the Synoptic Gospels to view His death as an event that is part of a large, unfolding story. The timing alone sets the person of Jesus within the identity of God, and it heralds the continuity and fulfillment of God's redemptive purpose.

Likewise, in the Gospel of John, where the timing is as meticulous as in the Synoptics (John 19:14, 31), we hear Jesus crying out on the cross, "It is finished!" (John 19:30). These are His very last words. As soon as they have been uttered, Jesus bows His head and gives up His spirit. But these words, too, even more than the timing itself, remind the reader of the climax of Creation in Genesis (John 19:30; Gen. 2:1–3). The words spoken on the cross are taken from the first page of the seventh day, recalling its original configuration and character. As in the Synoptics, this has the effect of placing the person of Jesus within the identity of the one God. The acting subject in Creation is also the acting subject in John's portrayal of Jesus's death. On this point all the four evangelists agree; they all see Jesus's death as an event within a story that began at Creation.

The words spoken on the cross are taken from the first page of the seventh day.

When Revelation rounds off the biblical narrative, the last two chapters read as a virtual mirror image of the story of Creation (Rev. 21–22), the earth restored to the state of which the seventh day was originally the hallowed end-point. All these elements, in the New Testament even more than in the Old, endow the seventh day with a halo of distinction.

This is not the whole story, of course. Another side of the account asserts that the seventh day was buried long ago in an unmarked grave. According to this version, when Jesus appeared on the stage of history, the seventh day was doomed. His life, death, and resurrection made the seventh day obsolete, allowing and even encouraging His followers to choose another symbol to take over its functions. No matter how great its biblical mandate, the story goes, Christianity turned its back on the seventh day, embracing in its place the first day of the week, or nothing at all,[2] to serve as the sign of the new faith.

The present inquiry pursues and prioritizes the meaning of the seventh day, placing the lost *meaning* in the foreground and not only the loss of the seventh day as such. Anticipating where the weight of evidence leads, the character of the seventh day is misconstrued if it is seen as a national or religious marker of identity and not as a theological statement. To the extent that it is part of God's story, it cannot be suppressed indefinitely. It must reassert itself to complete its God-ordained mission; it cannot remain in permanent exile.

The formal elements in this story are easily outlined. They divide into (1) the seventh day in the Old Testament, (2) the seventh day in the New Testament, and (3) post-biblical issues that are raised by the eclipse of the seventh day. These three sections make up the body of the present inquiry. The material issues are more complex, but here, too, we have three main elements. By way of a preliminary measure, they are (1) the alienation between Christians and Jews, (2) the estrangement of Christianity from the material world, and (3) the theological depth that lies at the heart of the seventh day.

DISCONTINUITY

From the very beginning of the Christian era a gap opens up between the Christian community and the Jews. Writing perhaps no later than ten years into the second century CE, the rhetoric of Ignatius of Antioch betrays an unmistakable strain of anti-Judaism.[3] Whether or not Ignatius was attempting to forge a link between Christian belief and Sunday worship, and, conversely, whether or not he was disparaging the seventh day and Jewish belief[4] as many scholars read it,[5] the reality of anti-Judaism in the early fathers of the Christian Church is not contested.

In the ensuing centuries the breach between Christians and Jews grew into a chasm, and the early insinuations of Ignatius were but a mild foretaste of the torrent of abuse that would be heaped on Jews by Christians. The two communities, the worship identity of one being observance of the seventh day and the other observing

Sunday, became alienated, even though both owed their origin to the Hebrew Scriptures and were devoted to the one God. Christian antipathy against the Jews had been unrelenting across the centuries.[6] Martin Luther did not sow the seed of anti-Semitism, but watered it to a devastating effect, hoping, in his own words, to furnish the Christian "with enough material not only to defend himself against the blind, venomous Jews, but also to become the foe of the Jews' malice, lying, and cursing, and to understand not only that their belief is false but that they are surely possessed by all devils."[7] It is no wonder that the architects of the Holocaust sought legitimacy in Luther's combustible rhetoric for their intention to rid the world of Jews.

The character of the seventh day is misconstrued if it is seen as a national or religious marker of identity and not as a theological statement.

Try as we may, it is difficult to conceive of the Holocaust apart from Christian vilification of the Jews. There is a link between the alienation that began at the dawn of the Christian era and what is arguably the greatest human atrocity on record.[8] As a reminder that the Church is more than an innocent bystander in this process, the Jewish New Testament scholar Samuel Sandmel, among countless other examples, recalls the memory of his mother's startled surprise at the ringing of church bells even after the family had moved to the United States because, says Sandmel, "the pogroms in eastern Europe from which my parents fled began with the ringing of church bells."[9] Accepting the intimate connection between symbol and reality, to be explored below in greater depth, the eclipse of the seventh day in Christian belief and practice reveals a facet of the ideology and the forces at work. Very early in this process the Christians adopted a condescending and demeaning rhetoric against the Jews, instigating, from the vantage point of being the stronger group, forced conversions, violent pogroms, confiscation of property, and mass expulsion of the Jews, culminating in the project bizarrely known as "the final solution."

This perspective on the Holocaust demands soul-searching; it compels a review of flawed theological priorities. Even if the ideology in question were not the cause of Christian anti-Semitism, we come face to face with sentiments that proved impotent in the face of the atrocities committed against the Jews. Scholars who see the Holocaust as a watershed event acknowledge the need for the Church to retrace its steps.[10] They are, in fact, searching for a new criterion by which to sift what is truly important from what is less important in the Christian faith. In the words of Old Testament scholar Rolf Rendtorff, "Something went wrong at the beginning."[11] If a redemptive path is found, it cannot at this point redeem the Holocaust. But it may, even at this late hour, set the Church on a path of reconciliation and return. In a deliberate way the present study belongs to this quest, finding in the seventh day a window through which we catch a glimpse of what went wrong.

CONTRACTION

The Bible begins with Creation, but Christian theology has for centuries had other priorities. To Gerhard von Rad the primary story of the Old Testament is the election of Israel, an emphasis that reduces Creation to an afterthought and a mere appendage to the weightier biblical concern of human salvation.[12] "Salvation History" is the key concept and the governing theme in this outlook, in relation to which the story of Creation is only a prologue.[13] Marking a dramatic reappraisal and reorientation, leading Old Testament scholars have begun to see Creation not as prologue but as the premise on which everything else rests. "All factors considered, the doctrine of creation, namely, the belief that God has created and is sustaining the order of the world in all its complexities, is not a peripheral theme of biblical theology but is plainly the fundamental theme."[14] Claus Westermann acknowledges that when theology is detached from Creation, "it must gradually become an anthropology and begin to disintegrate from within and collapse around us."[15] It can hardly be denied that this is what has happened.

The ecological crisis that has forced theologians to retreat from entrenched assumptions and priorities owes to theology itself. Moreover, its source is not found in the Enlightenment, in theories attempting to delineate the evolution of the Bible, or even in the rise of evolutionary theory. These forces are at most the late cresting of a "Christian" tidal wave that had little or nothing to say concerning the body and the earth, all the while holding forth its offer of salvation for the human soul. In the ecological consequences of the contracted Christian interest, the moment of truth has arrived. As noted by Wendell Berry, the separation "of the soul from the body and from the earth is no disease of the fringe, no aberration, but a fracture that runs through the mentality of institutional religion like a geologic fault."[16]

The Bible begins with Creation, but Christian theology has for centuries had other priorities.

In the Hellenistic environment of the times, the Early Church adopted a dualistic view of reality, concentrating on the soul while disparaging the body. Withdrawal from the world, while not the choice of all who professed Christianity, became by the fifth century the ideal for Christians. The ones who most truly lived the devoted life were the monks who, in their wholehearted otherworldliness, left behind the burdens of the body and concern for the earth. One of the early pioneers, Pachomius, reportedly founded eleven monasteries in Upper Egypt, claiming a total of seven thousand adherents before he died in 346 CE. Less than one century later Jerome claimed that nearly fifty thousand monks took part in the annual convention of Pachomius's order alone.

The numbers are less significant than the underlying ideology that disparages the body and thus stands in contrast to the earth-affirming and world-embracing ideology of the Old Testament. The Christian theology that prioritized salvation over Creation in the twentieth century was not a novelty but a continuation of a bias of long duration. When theologians set out to reassess its history, they should not confine their research to Enlightenment influences. Moreover, retracing the steps in search of lost territory cannot be done without encountering the life-affirming ramifications of the seventh day.

THE MEANING OF THE SEVENTH DAY

Given the background of discontinuity and contraction noted above, we may still be in need of an element in contemporary life to which we can compare the seventh day—an analogy that facilitates the leap from the familiar to the unfamiliar. While no modern idea or item fits this need completely, there is a sense in which the role of the flag in modern societies comes close to conveying the function of the seventh day, if not its meaning. Like the flag, the seventh day belongs to, and participates in, an underlying reality. To the extent that this analogy applies, we should resist the eclipse of the seventh day as much as we are likely to resist the replacement of the flag of the nation we love and cherish.

Paul Tillich, the German-born theologian who fled his country for the United States in order to escape the Nazi terror, has clarified the symbolic function of the flag, and, indirectly, the function of the seventh day as a symbol. Tillich makes a helpful distinction between signs and symbols, stating that "signs do not participate in the reality to which they point, while symbols do."[17] Applying this definition to the seventh day, it means that a symbol, whether the flag or the seventh day, cannot be replaced unless there has been a change in the underlying reality. Tillich, though his theology does not have much appeal today, wrote with great insight that "the flag participates in the power and dignity of the nation for which it stands. Therefore, it cannot be replaced except after an historic catastrophe that changes the reality of the nation which it symbolizes."[18]

The history of the flag of the United States has demonstrated this reality in a remarkable way. This history began when a simple entry in the journal of Congress for May 20, 1776, read: "RESOLVED: that the flag of the United States be made of thirteen stripes, alternate red and white; that the union be thirteen stars, white in a blue field, representing a new constellation."[19] The striking symbol expressed the nature and identity of the new member of the family of nations. In the declaration that accompanied the creation of the new constellation, the founding fathers of the United States held "these truths to be self-evident, that all men are created equal, that they are endowed by their Creator with inalienable rights, that among these are Life, Liberty and the pursuit of Happiness."[20]

Not surprisingly, exemplifying the relationship between the symbol and the underlying reality, the Confederacy of seceding southern states, the other side of the American Civil War, marshaled its forces under a new flag, *the Stars and Bars*. By this symbol the Confederates proclaimed the breach to be definitive, confirming, on the one hand, that the flag "cannot be replaced except after an historic catastrophe that changes the reality of the nation which it symbolizes,"[21] and, on the other hand, that flags *are* replaced under such circumstances. And yet there was enough similarity between the two flags to recall the common origin. In reality, the Confederate vision portrayed itself as the most faithful representation of the original ideal, refusing to make any concession to the accusation that it represented a reality that had been compromised and betrayed.

After the war, the flag that came into being when the nation was formed took into itself the unfolding story as the nation was reborn and reunited. The change wrought to the old flag symbol at the time of the Civil War is in this respect one of enrichment, absorbing into itself the hard-won gain of the war and in that way striving to become what the country aspired to be all along. Where the founding fathers are the creators of the new nation, Abraham Lincoln, the person who came to the rescue when the Union and its ideals stood the risk of coming undone, is known to history as the "Redeemer President."[22]

In the present context it is important to note that the redemptive event in the nation's story does not stand in opposition to what was laid down at the time of its creation. As far as the history of the United States goes, the creator in the person of the founding fathers and the Redeemer in the person of President Lincoln are on the same side of the issue. Lincoln does not overturn the work of his forebears; he defines it further and redeems it. Notably, too, he preserves the Union and its embattled flag.

Similarly, the two decisive points in the narrative of the seventh day are Creation and the life of Jesus Christ. The seventh day is originally set apart as the high point of Creation, embodying God's ideal and serving as the symbol of the reality that God represents (Gen. 2:1–3). In the terms of the flag analogy, does Jesus the Redeemer rescue the imperiled ideal of Creation, much as Lincoln, the Redeemer President, rose up to save the Republic? In Lincoln's case the preservation of the Union meant the perpetuation and refinement of the flag. What consequences do the life and death of Jesus have for the seventh day?

When asking whether the seventh day is undone by redemption, the biblical narrative adds an element that is absent in the story of the United States. The New Testament insists that the Person it reveres as the Redeemer is none other than the Creator (John 1:3; Col. 1:16). While Lincoln the Redeemer rescues the work of the founding fathers, he nevertheless stands in a distant relationship to the founding of the Republic. Jesus, on the other hand, unites the Creator and the Redeemer in one person. Are we to conclude that Jesus the Redeemer is the One who terminates the seventh day even though this obligates us to assume that He thereby terminates something that is essentially God's own work?

It is crucial to note that a change in a nation, even a convulsive upheaval, does not *always* lead to a replacement of its flag. Instead, those who hold the flag dear may disagree as to its meaning. In its most extreme version the struggle may involve a tacit betrayal of the professed ideal, and the flag may end up reflecting an ideology quite different from what it was originally intended to express. That is to say, the symbol and its underlying idea may drift apart. This drift knows many subtle versions, as Alexander Solzhenitsyn reminded the graduating class at Harvard University in 1978: "Many of you have already found out and others will find out in the course of their lives that truth eludes us as soon as our concentration begins to flag, all the while leaving the illusion that we are continuing to pursue it."[23]

> ***The seventh day is originally set apart as the high point of Creation.***

Symbols, the flag or otherwise, are not intrinsically self-sustaining in terms of what their adherents take to be their meaning. A symbol may come loose from the ideal it was meant to represent, leaving it as the symbol of an illusion. In the history of the nations and their flags, there are also ideological struggles and conflicts over which ideals the country and its flag should represent. In the New Testament, the frequent and intense disagreement between Jesus and His critics as to the meaning of the seventh day falls into this category. The symbol must in such situations absorb the blows and the pain of the struggle in the hope of prevailing in the end, or it must concede the defeat of the contested ideal, even to the point that the flag ends up as the symbol of alien aspirations and values.

THE CHALLENGE OF THE SEVENTH DAY

For the person who tunes in to the biblical narrative, perceiving and internalizing that something goes wrong at the crossroads between Judaism and Christianity is only a start. There is a more remote beginning in the Bible, a beginning of beginnings, at which, too, something goes wrong (Gen. 3:1–6). What goes wrong conditions the rest of the story. The individual books of the Bible stand apart from each other with distinctive concerns and emphases on many points, but the compositional magnet that guides the tributaries together into one stream is the project of making right what went wrong. The path from Genesis to Revelation takes many twists and turns, but when the story is seen from the vantage point of the end, the curtain of perception lifts. There has been a forward movement all along.

When the story ends in Revelation, the setting reminds us of the beginning in Genesis (Rev. 21–22; Gen. 1–2). The seventh day lays claim to importance because it is commissioned to play a role in this unfolding story from the beginning (Gen. 2:1–3); it is recharged and recommissioned in the New Testament account about Jesus, the new beginning (John 1:1; 5:1–9; 9:1–14); and it retains, at least in one vision of the end, an open-ended lease on life (Isa. 66:23). For this reason the seventh day has a theological message quite apart from the circumscribed role it plays in Jewish-Christian relations. What the seventh day says about God, its theological aspiration, is at least as important as its success or failure at the intersection of Jewish and Christian pathways.

And these two elements, one anchored in theology and the other rising from history, invest the seventh day with a third dimension. In this dimension the seventh day speaks existentially, in the here and now, addressing the person who is looking for meaning in his or her life, speaking to you and to me. These three aspects—history, theology, and existence—form a seamless whole, but the challenge facing the seventh day comes to a head most acutely in the crucible of human existence. Does the seventh day address the questions arising from present human reality in a meaningful way? Is it a meaning-making resource, capable of meeting the challenges of the human quest for purpose and hope in the present?

Even at a time when attention to history is at low ebb, the historical track leading up to the existential questions cannot be covered up. Indeed, the Holocaust gives the message of history its most unremitting existential sting. What is left of the moral order in a world where an event like the Holocaust is permitted to happen? Does any sense remain of a loving God, or of God's existence? Must we concede that the Holocaust puts the notion of meaning to the torch?

Writing one year after World War I, in 1919, William Butler Yeats penned a poem taking stock of the human condition in the wake of what was to date the foremost expression of chaos running riot.

> Turning and turning in the widening gyre
> The falcon cannot hear the falconer;
> Things fall apart; the centre cannot hold;
> Mere anarchy is loosed upon the world;
> The blood-dimmed tide is loosed, and everywhere
> The ceremony of innocence is drowned;
> The best lack all conviction, while the worst
> Are full of passionate intensity.[24]

Meaning is in retreat in this vision; "the falcon cannot hear the falconer," drifting far from the familiar voice, and the center is fast giving way. The next verse turns even more ominous. Vultures are stirring indignantly in the desert, and the sphinx, with a "lion body and the head of a man" and until then a reassuring fixture of motionlessness, "is moving its slow thighs." Before this happens, Yeats appears to despair at humanity's options, looking for some intervention from without to redeem the day,

> Surely some revelation is at hand;
> Surely the Second Coming is at hand.[25]

But then he backs off, drawing comfort instead from the hope that human civilization, despite its ugly setbacks, is on track after all. The child of hope will be born in the slow and sometimes cataclysmic convulsions of earthly life because the outlook that at times seems bleak is nevertheless moving in the right direction. Undeterred by the unsteady and awkward forward movement and the coarse tools at its disposal, Yeats ends up believing—as if by a moment of revelation—that history is on the path of progress.

When Yeats wrote this poem after World War I, the candle of optimism was still flickering in the dark. It is doubtful whether Yeats would have staked his faith on the idea of progress if he had been alive to reconsider his poem after World War II, in the aftermath of the Holocaust. In the poem that we do have, entitled "The Second Coming," Yeats's idea is clearly that the First Coming was a disappointment, an illusion in fact, because "twenty centuries of stony sleep" were only "vexed to nightmare by a rocking cradle."[26]

Dismissing the first journey to Bethlehem as a failure, the Second Coming is in Yeats's imagination nothing but the First Coming by other means, the means being humanity's effort to raise civilization to a higher level.

> And what rough beast, its hour come round at last,
> Slouches towards Bethlehem to be born?[27]

For those who, like Yeats, are disappointed in the First Coming, everything hinges on how the First Coming is understood. How could people claiming allegiance to the First Coming contribute directly and indirectly to the attempt to seek the extinction of the very people whose story is told in the Old Testament? The atrocities of the Christian Era cannot be hidden, but it should not be taken for granted that there is a link to Bethlehem, or, looking beyond the Bethlehem of the New Testament, that human civilization in its current course is about to create a Bethlehem that will not end in a nightmare.

The discontinuity and disruption that happened in the first centuries of the Christian era, exemplified in the Christian repudiation of the seventh day, suggest at least that something went wrong then. Just as Lincoln, "the Redeemer President," saves the Union and determines how the Constitution of the United States should be interpreted, "the Redeemer President" of the biblical story sets out on the larger project of gathering God's alienated sons and daughters (Isa. 56:8). He lays down the terms for how the divine Constitution should be read (Matt. 5:17–18, 21–22, 27–28), and He has the restoration of all things as His goal (Acts 3:21). Discontinuity and disruption are not terms that fit the mission of the biblical Redeemer any more than they describe the mission of Abraham Lincoln.

The concerns that are raised by the discontinuity in the biblical story and the disruption in the community of believers make the story itself an object of scrutiny. Is the human story itself defective and devoid of hope? Only when this question stands front and center has the seventh day found the sounding chamber that allows its voice to be fully heard. The character of the human story, its innermost core, is the question that stands front and center where we find the first mention of the seventh day in the Bible (Gen. 2:1–3). For this reason we cannot begin in the middle or with the questions confronting human beings in the twenty-first century. We must begin with the beginning.

Discontinuity and disruption are not terms that fit the mission of the biblical Redeemer.

ENDNOTES

1. Abraham Joshua Heschel, *The Sabbath: Its Meaning for Modern Man* (1951; repr., New York: The Noonday Press, 1975).

2. D. A. Carson, ed., *From Sabbath to Lord's Day: A Biblical, Historical, and Theological Investigation* (Grand Rapids: Zondervan Publishing House, 1982).

3. Ignatius of Antioch, *To the Magnesians*, in *The Ante-Nicene Fathers,* eds. A. Roberts and J. Donaldson (1884; repr., Grand Rapids: Eerdmans, 1987).

4. Ignatius, *To the Magnesians*, 1:62; J. Rius-Camps, *The Four Authentic Letters of Ignatius, the Martyr* (Rome: Pontificium Institutum Orientalum Studiorum, 1979), 40–51.

5. Willy Rordorf, *Sunday: The History of the Day of Rest in the Earliest Centuries of the Christian Church,* trans. A. A. K. Graham (London: SCM Press, 1968 [orig. German ed. 1962]), 221–222; Robert Sherman, "Reclaimed by Sabbath Rest," *Int* 59 (2005): 43–44. A number of studies contest the inference that Ignatius is straightforward pro-Sunday and anti-Sabbath; cf. Fritz Guy, "The Lord's Day in the Letter of Ignatius to the Magnesians," *AUSS* 2 (1964): 1–17; Samuele Bacchiocchi, *From Sabbath to Sunday: A Historical Investigation of the Rise of Sunday Observance in Early Christianity* (Rome: The Pontifical Gregorian University Press, 1977), 213–218.

6. James Carroll (*Constantine's Sword: The Church and the Jews* [Boston: Houghton Mifflin Company, 2001]) leaves no doubt as to the Christian contribution to what became

the Holocaust, exposing the ideology of leading theologians and the practice to which this ideology led.

7. Martin Luther, *On the Jews and Their Lies*, in *Luther's Works* 47, ed. Franklin Sherman, trans. Martin H. Bertram (Philadelphia: Fortress Press, 1971), 305.

8. According to Malcolm Hay (*Europe and the Jews: The Pressure of Christendom over 1900 Years* [Chicago: Academy Chicago Publishers, 1992], 169), the Nazis inaugurated the first large-scale pogrom in 1938 in commemoration of Luther's birthday.

9. Samuel Sandmel, *Anti-Semitism in the New Testament?* (Philadelphia: Fortress Press, 1978), 155.

10. Irving Greenberg, "The Shoah and the Legacy of Anti-Semitism," in *Christianity in Jewish Terms*, ed. Tikva Frymer-Kensky, David Novak, Peter Ochs, David Fox Sandmel, and Michael A. Signer (Boulder: Westview Press, 2000), 25–48; Tod Linafelt, ed., *Strange Fire: Reading the Bible after the Holocaust* (New York: New York University Press, 2000).

11. Rolf Rendtorff, in remarks at the Society of Biblical Literature Annual Meeting, Philadelphia, November, 2005.

12. Gerhard von Rad, "The Theological Problem of the Old Testament Doctrine of Creation," in *Creation in the Old Testament*, ed. Bernhard W. Anderson (Philadelphia: Fortress Press, 1984 [original publication of von Rad's essay in German, 1936]), 53–64.

13. Normal C. Habel, "Introducing the Earth Bible," in *Readings from the Perspective of the Earth*, ed. Norman C. Habel (Sheffield: Sheffield Academic Press, 2000), 27–28.

14. H. H. Schmid, "Creation, Righteousness, and Salvation: 'Creation Theology' as the Broad Horizon of Biblical Theology," in *Creation in the Old Testament*, ed. Bernhard W. Anderson (Philadelphia: Fortress, 1984 [original German essay published in *ZTK* 70 (1973)]), 111.

15. Claus Westermann, "Biblical Reflection on Creator-Creation," in *Creation in the Old Testament*, ed. Bernhard W. Anderson (Philadelphia: Fortress, 1984), 92.

16. Wendell Berry, *The Unsettling of America: Culture and Agriculture* (New York: Avon Books, 1977), 108.

17. Paul Tillich, *Dynamics of Faith* (New York: Harper & Row, 1957), 41–42.

18. Ibid., 42.

19. Cf. Milo M. Quaife, Melvin J. Weig, and Ray E. Appleman, *The History of the United States Flag* (New York: Harper & Brothers, 1961), 29.

20. From The Declaration of Independence, July 4, 1776, in Bruce Frohnen, *The American Republic: Primary Sources* (Indianapolis: Liberty Fund, 2002), 189.

21. Tillich, *Dynamics of Faith*, 42.

22. Allen C. Guelzo, *Abraham Lincoln: Redeemer President* (Grand Rapids: William B. Eerdmans Publishing Company, 1999).

23. Alexander Solzhenitsyn, *A World Split Apart* (New York: Harper & Row Publishers, 1978), 1.

24. William Butler Yeats, "The Second Coming," in *Poem a Day*, ed. Karen McCosker and Nicholas Alberry (Hanover, NH: Steerforth Press, 1996), 458.

25. Ibid.

26. Ibid.

27. Ibid.

THE MEANINGS OF THE BEGINNING

And on the seventh day God finished the work that he had done, and he rested on the seventh day from all the work that he had done.
Genesis 2:2

A more auspicious beginning for the seventh day than the one that is put forward in the first book of the Bible is hard to imagine: "Thus the heavens and the earth were finished, and all their multitude. And on the seventh day God finished the work that he had done, and he rested on the seventh day from all the work that he had done. So God blessed the seventh day and hallowed it, because on it God rested from all the work that he had done in creation"(Gen. 2:1–3). Accepting that the seventh day makes a spectacular entry, it is well to ask whether the first impression will be sustained once we look more closely at the text, the context, and the meanings that we might infer concerning the seventh day in the Creation account.

FIRST IMPRESSIONS

In the compact verses in Genesis the writer's claims with respect to the seventh day fairly stumble over each other, one assertion surpassing the next, appearing to endow the seventh day with an enchanting aura of distinction. First of all, the writer does not hang the seventh day on nothing, nor is the writer content merely to anchor the seventh day to a great occasion in the maze of human history. Instead, Genesis ties it indissolubly to the foundational event of human and creaturely existence.[1] The seventh day is a feature of Creation; indeed, it is the capstone of Creation and comes forth at the dawn of history as the first signifier of the character and meaning of Creation. Second, this Creation must be understood as an achievement that is the exclusive prerogative of God. It features God's sovereign action, engaged in a pursuit for which there is no corresponding human activity. Third, the seventh day is not introduced accidentally or haphazardly. Rather, the seventh day is an immediate fact of Creation, belonging to it and completing it, a day without which Creation remains in limbo.[2]

The elements of deliberation and purpose are described in two sets of carefully worded pairs. In the first of these pairs, the writer of Genesis states that "on the seventh day God *finished* the work that he had done, and he *rested* on the seventh day" (Gen. 2:2). This is a report of the completion of God's activity without any attribution of significance. In the second pair, Genesis announces that "God *blessed* the seventh day and *hallowed* it" (Gen. 2:3). This reports a specific act concerning the seventh day. Here God marks out the significance of the occasion so as to take the matter of its interpretation into God's own hands. If the first of these pairs is retrospective, the second looks forward, and is an indicator of permanence. By the act of hallowing the seventh day God drives the stake of the divine presence into the soil of human time.

The seventh day is the capstone of Creation and comes forth at the dawn of history as the first signifier of the character and meaning of Creation.

According to the plain reading of the text, the seventh day was given immense prestige from the very beginning. Divine purpose and action are involved in a way that give the seventh day significance far beyond anything situational or temporary. The action of the Creator in the Genesis account brings a degree of distinction to the seventh day that represents a formidable deterrent to denigrating it.

ASSESSING THE TEXT AND ITS CONTEXT

Just as the seventh day in many ways has become an ideological and theological orphan, so the modern world has lost touch with the text describing the beginning. The sense of looking at an alien thought world applies not just to the way scholars have analyzed and dissected the biblical narrative during the past two centuries. What has happened to the perception of the biblical text itself is probably less important than the seismic shift in the worldview of its readers. The modern account of evolution speaks of chance, not purpose; it envisions a process without an agent that initiates, guides, and completes it; and it reflects a view of reality in which the seventh day has no meaningful point of contact.

The text itself has also become an object in motion and not a fixed point. Scholars have scrutinized the first five books of the Bible, probing for its nature and origin. The consensus that gradually emerged—and to some extent still prevails—holds that the first five or six books in the Bible derive from several sources, each with its own unique characteristics and each originating at different periods in history. Scholars have attempted to delineate the multiple layers in the finished composition, much like archaeologists excavating a mound try to identify the various strata left behind by the site's inhabitants. Eventually the nameless authors behind the various textual strata have come to be identified by a single letter of the alphabet.

In this reconstruction, known as "the Documentary hypothesis," at least three hands are seen at work in Genesis, designated respectively as J, E, and P. Behind these letters lie characteristics of the imagined author, and between them, at assorted suture lines in the biblical narrative, scholars see the handiwork of anonymous redactors. J, assumed to be the oldest of the primary sources, is known for his fondness for the divine name Yahweh, and the letter J therefore represents the "Yahwist."[3] E, for his part, knows God primarily as Elohim, and thus is dubbed the "Elohist." P, the more important character in the present context, is seen as a much later person or group with a priestly orientation. In this scheme chronological progression in the Bible story follows a different trajectory and sequence than the composition of the text itself.

As to chronology, the "classic" version, in the view of the influential Old Testament theologian Gerhard von Rad, places the material in the so-called J source at approximately 950 BCE, the E source one or two centuries later, while P is relegated to the time after Israel's Babylonian exile, about 538–450 BCE.[4] Increasingly aware of the complexity and pitfalls of this reconstructive task, however, even von Rad hedges his bets, making the precise timing of the writers less critical, "because they are in every instance only guesses and, above all, because they refer only to the completed literary composition. The question of the age of a single tradition within any one of the source documents is an entirely different matter. The youngest document (P), for example, contains an abundance of ancient and very ancient material."[5]

P is important in the present context because the first mention of the seventh day is frequently attributed to the P source. Then again, P is not all that important, partly because P is no more than a scholarly construction and partly because, even where P is recognized, it is admitted that the alleged P contribution "contains an abundance of ancient and very ancient material."[6] On this logic it is the antiquity of the material, not the role or the time of the mysterious P, that counts.

Other developments tend to lessen further the relevance of these fixtures of Old Testament criticism. A sense of weariness, even futility, has been felt in circles occupied by the pursuit of dating the various parts of the Old Testament. The once neat theory has been shaken by realities that not only affect minor details but many of the underlying assumptions as well. Textual elements once said to belong to one source or period are suddenly found embedded in the wrong layer to the extent that the paradigm threatens to unravel. Such instances have led a few scholars to question the basis for the old theory because the existing scholarly maps are in conflict with the actual textual terrain. Instead of the tendency to see the books of the Bible as a composite of textual fragments welded together into a disparate and incoherent whole, the trend is now to see its unity, or, at the very least, there is a renewed appreciation for the indicators of unity.[7]

In the field of biblical studies the source criticism of the Old Testament, largely a Protestant enterprise, seems to have run its course nearly to exhaustion, doomed equally by a flawed premise and by the fact that it left its proponents with very little to say. Alternative approaches seek to let Scripture speak again in its own voice. Projects useful for the present inquiry are literary approaches that are more attentive to Scriptural narrative,[8] and approaches that treat the Bible as more than a human phenomenon, broadly known as a "canonical" reading of Scripture.[9]

Above all, in the present context, it is indispensable to pay heed to neglected voices of Jewish scholarship. These voices are generally less burdened by the strictures of Protestant critical scholarship. Jewish students of the Old Testament are also somewhat less likely to judge a text on the basis of its alleged source, and the perception of textual unity is thereby more prevalent in Jewish scholarship. M. H. Segal, for instance, counters the source theory by asserting that "with the exception of some unimportant additions, the book of Genesis is a work of a unitary character composed by one author who derived his materials from the living tradition of his day."[10] Another Jewish scholar immersed in Genesis, Umberto Cassuto, finds Genesis to be a thoroughly integrated piece of literature.[11] Based on his analysis of the first chapter of Genesis, Cassuto traces a network of *heptads*, groupings of "sevens," crisscrossing the story of Creation in such a meticulous design that the compositional unity of the story and its relation to the seventh day seem to be two sides of the same coin.[12] Both of these distinctive features—the seventh day and the related groupings of "sevens" in the composition of the first chapter of the Bible—point to compositional unity, setting the biblical account of Creation apart from other ancient attempts to describe the origin of the world.

Projects useful for the present inquiry are literary approaches that treat the Bible as more than a human phenomenon.

While not entirely disparaging of the source hypothesis, Nahum Sarna, who also writes from a Jewish perspective, states that "it is beyond doubt that the Book of Genesis came down to us, not as a composite of disparate elements but as a unified document with a life, coherence and integrity of its own. For this reason, a fragmentary approach to it cannot provide an adequate understanding of the whole."[13]

Crucial to the argument of scholars who divide the text is the notion that the seventh day is not an ordinance of Creation.[14] In a chapter entitled "The Sabbath in the Old Testament," H. P. Dressler claims that "the Sabbath originated in Israel as God's special institution for His people."[15] The Creation link is severed in this interpretation because the Genesis account is thought to refer only to "the seventh day" and not to the Sabbath.[16] Despite the fact that God *sabbathed* on the seventh day in the words of the text (Gen. 2:2), the verbal counterpart to the noun "Sabbath," the term should not, in the view of Dressler, be taken to mean that God made of the seventh day a Sabbath for humanity.[17] Throughout, the tenor of the argument is to see the Sabbath as something other than the seventh day of Creation.[18] Whatever the seventh day may have been, the reasoning goes, the Sabbath is a later idea, an ordinance of Moses and an obligation enjoined only on Israel. Moreover, the weightier mandate of the Sabbath in the Old Testament is said to derive from the commandment in Exodus rather than from the narrative of God's rest at Creation.[19]

The view summarized above is not a conclusion that rides easily on the back of the biblical narrative. For this outlook to prevail, the reader must tear asunder what the text of Genesis sees as a seamless whole. In the primary account there is no wedge between the seventh day and Creation, and the hallowing of the seventh day at Creation cannot be seen as anything other than the consecration of the Sabbath.[20]

The fact that Genesis leads the biblical narrative, not some other book, is as important as the unity of Genesis. "That the Bible begins with Genesis, not Exodus, with creation, not redemption, is of immeasurable importance for understanding all that follows," writes Terence E. Fretheim.[21] The Old Testament takes as its point of departure *human* beginnings, not the beginning of Israel. Israel figures prominently in the project of restoration with which much of the Old Testament is preoccupied, but the first chapters of the biblical narrative have the broadest conceivable scope.

This scope is universal, affirming the value of the earth and all its inhabitants without regard for ethnicity or nationality (Gen. 1:28–30).

Universality is the premise from which the biblical narrative proceeds and the goal to which it leads. Any attempt at narrowing this scope yields a truncated reading. Rolf Knierim speaks cogently against the tendency to take a narrow, Israel-centered view.

> If Yahweh is not, in principle and before everything else, the God of all reality, he cannot be the one and only God because he is not God universal. Yahweh may be Israel's God in oneness and exclusivity, but if he is not Israel's God because he is first of all God of all reality and of all humanity, he is a nationalistic deity or an individualistic idol, one among others, actually a no-god. Without the critical notion of universality, the affirmation of Yahweh's oneness and exclusivity does not substantiate the affirmation of his true deity.[22]

With respect to the earliest mention of the seventh day in the Bible (Gen. 2:1–3), it is now possible to summarize important contextual parameters. These are the unity of Genesis, the priority of Genesis over Exodus, and the fact that Creation underlies the entire account, all of which makes the Bible the story of one God and one indivisible humanity. Seeing the seventh day in this broad context makes it clear that it is not solely an Israelite concern. Umberto Cassuto contends that "Scripture wishes to emphasize that the sanctity of the Sabbath is older than Israel, and rests upon all mankind."[23] So closely is the seventh day linked to Creation that to Jon D. Levenson "the text of the Hebrew Bible in the last analysis forbids us to speak of the theology of creation without sustained attention to the sabbatical institution."[24] The reverse is also true: There is no meaningful theology of the seventh day that does not begin with Creation.

Most remarkable, perhaps, is the growing realization that the seventh day leans on nothing else than the Bible for its origin and meaning. This may be called negative evidence, the silence of other sources. Numerous attempts have been made to detect some kind of seventh day precursor in the languages and ruins of the Near East, but to no avail. On this point there is an unusual degree of agreement among the vast majority of scholars. Roland de Vaux, a leading Roman Catholic authority on the ancient Near East, holds that the seventh day goes back to the very beginning of the religion that we find in the Bible.[25] Brevard Childs notes that "there is general agreement that the Sabbath has very early roots in the tradition."[26] John L. McKenzie concurs that "nothing like it is found elsewhere,"[27] that is, outside the Bible. On the basis of available evidence it does not appear that the other nations of the ancient Near East observed a seventh day. Niels-Erik Andreasen affirms that "so far no Sabbath has been found in extra-biblical sources."[28]

The silence of other records thus leaves the Bible as the main if not the only witness to its origin and meaning, and it is the biblical witness that must guide our appraisal of the seventh day.

In the primary account there is no wedge between the seventh day and Creation, and the hallowing of the seventh day at Creation cannot be seen as anything other than the consecration of the Sabbath.

THE MEANINGS OF THE SEVENTH DAY IN THE CREATION ACCOUNT

Already upon its first entry in the Bible, the seventh day comes endowed with an imposing portfolio of meanings, embodying notions of purpose, power, and personhood—of relationship, love, and presence. It pronounces the word of blessing on human existence, and this word is in itself forward-looking, speaking of things to come that are not yet fully revealed.

A DELIBERATE ACT

The Hebrew Bible says that "on the seventh day God finished the work that he had done" (Gen. 2:2). Those who translated the Old Testament from Hebrew into Greek were so puzzled by this turn in the text that they unceremoniously wrote that "God finished his work on the *sixth* day" (Gen. 2:2, LXX), an editorial twist that goes well beyond the accepted rules of translation. Only a few scholars note the solemnity in the text—and the astonishment that ought to follow. John Skinner writes that the seventh day is introduced "with unusual solemnity and consciousness of language," noting also that "the writer's idea of the Sabbath and its sanctity is almost too realistic for the modern mind to grasp."[29] Aware that the seventh day is a "first" in the Bible and a remarkable first at that, Gordon J. Wenham notes that the seventh day "is the very first thing to be hallowed in Scripture, to acquire that special status that belongs to God alone. In this way Genesis emphasizes the sacredness of the Sabbath."[30]

If the seventh day comes as a surprise, it is only one of a litany of surprises in the biblical account of Creation. Unlike the Babylonian creation epic, the biblical story does not have what scholars call a *theogony*, a story of how the gods came into existence. The biblical account begins with God, prior to whom is nothing. God is the beginner and the One who brings everything else into existence. Cassuto writes that

> [t]hen came the Torah and soared aloft, as on eagles' wings, above all these notions. Not many gods but One God; not theogony, for a god has no family tree; not wars of strife or clash of wills, but only One Will, which rules over everything, without the slightest let or hindrance; not a deity associated with nature and identified with it wholly or in part, but a God who stands absolutely outside of it, and nature and all its constituent elements, even the sun and all the other entities, be they ever so exalted, are only His creatures, made according to His will.[31]

Of the things God brings into existence in the account of Creation, then, the seventh day stands apart, charged with the holiness of the Creator in a solemn, deliberate act and a signature statement of God's purpose.

A DISTINCTIVE PREROGATIVE

God has no beginning, but there is also no beginning without God. When the very first sentence of the Bible declares that "in the beginning God *created*...," the author employs a word with a specific acting subject. The word for "create," *bārā'*, refers to an attribute that is unique to God. In the Old Testament the verb *bārā'* is never used with any other subject than God, and there is no corresponding human activity.[32] Creation is God's trademark, a statement of copyright that need not fear any competition because there cannot be any. By placing the seventh day as the culminating event of creation, the Bible dismisses offhand any notion that nature accounts for itself. Instead, the wonder of Creation reverberates throughout the biblical consciousness from first to last.[33] "And God said," Genesis repeats again and again, indicating that nothing happens apart from the divine agency (Gen. 1:3, 6, 9, 11, 14, 20, 24, 26).

The biblical account begins with God, prior to whom is nothing. God is the beginner and the One who brings everything else into existence.

Other specifics in the Genesis account set it apart from the outlook of other cultures. The sun was the highest deity in Egypt, Babylon, and Assyria, with other heavenly bodies cast in supporting roles. These cultures credited the origin of the world to visible heavenly objects, but the Bible explicitly repudiates this. Heavenly bodies are not introduced until the fourth day (Gen. 1:14–18). "The sun, the moon and the heavenly bodies are what they are only because the Creator has called them into existence. Their very names, Sun (Shemesh) and Moon (Yareah), by which Israel's neighbors designate certain gods, are avoided; instead, they are almost contemptuously described as the greater light and the lesser light," writes Walther Zimmerli.[34] In the Genesis account the heavenly bodies have no personal qualities, and their function is limited to separating day and night as mere instruments.

Creation, then, is the foundational event of human existence. In a seminal book written in the nineteenth century, John N. Andrews drew the line between Creator and creature, writing that the seventh day "keeps ever present the true reason why worship is due to God.... The true ground of divine worship, not of that on the seventh day merely, but of all worship, is found in the distinction between the Creator and his creatures."[35]

A few decades before Andrews's study, the Danish philosopher and theologian Søren Kierkegaard swung his rhetorical axe over the philosophical and theological leaders of his day because they assumed an outsize role for humanity and a lesser role for God. Kierkegaard spoke of "the infinite qualitative difference" between God and human beings, upholding a distinction that is of a similar order as that urged by Andrews.[36] The human side must desist from encroachment into God's domain; it must come to its senses with respect to its limitations; it must talk less and listen more. Picking up on this theme seventy years later, Karl Barth, with an explicit attribution to Kierkegaard, insisted that human beings must come to terms with the fact that "God is in heaven, and thou art on earth." Holding this distinction in the foreground, Barth urged that the relation "between such a God and such a man, and the relation between such a man and such a God, is for me the theme of the Bible and the essence of philosophy."[37] This outlook fits well with the connection between Creation and the seventh day. It is a conclusion firmly within the bounds of the Genesis account. This affirmation, however, does not stand alone.

Creation is God's trademark, a statement of copyright that need not fear any competition because there cannot be any.

A SIGN OF PERSONHOOD

Genesis says that "God finished the work that he had done" (Gen. 2:2), thus highlighting an aspect of this account that is often overlooked. The account reports both a beginning and a completion. Barth notes that "God does not continue His work on the seventh day in an infinite series of creative acts."[38] The cessation and completion are markers of personhood and of a definite purpose. Extending this thought, Jacques Ellul, the prolific French sociologist and theologian, emphasizes an understanding of Creation that attributes more than a causal role to God. A mere causal function does not have the means to stop the process. "A cause cannot cease to be a cause without ceasing to be," writes Ellul. "It must produce its effects to infinity. God is not a cause, then, for we are told that he decides to rest."[39]

This is a striking observation because hardly anything sets the biblical story apart as much as the thought that God *finished* God's work. Let it be that the first steps in Creation could come about in a variety of ways. Could it be completed? It could be started. Could it be stopped? It could begin. Could it be finished? If other explanations might suffice to get a creative process started, the biblical account makes it clear that the process had a purpose in mind and could be halted when that purpose had been fulfilled.

The Bible says that "the heavens and the earth were finished....And on the seventh day God finished the work that he had done" (Gen. 2:1–2). These words make the idea of finishing stand out in bold print. It represents a picture of Creation that has no parallel. The seventh day speaks of a completed work to highlight that God had a definite, limited design in mind. From beginning to end the events of Creation bear the marks of momentous decisions, and the entire narrative is driven by a vigorous sense of deliberation and purpose, exemplified especially in the creation of human beings. "Then God said, 'Let us make man in our image, after our likeness.' So God created man, in the image of God he created him; male and female he created them" (Gen. 1:26–27). Mere chance could not direct creation toward such heights, nor was such a possibility seriously proposed until recently.

Ellul's observation shows that God's personhood lies at the heart of this account. A person is at work. An impersonal power would not be free to terminate the process. The impact of the seventh day stands out more by the fact that God completed God's work than by what was begun. While God's *power* certainly is the implied premise of Creation, the rest on the seventh day serves as an expression of God's personhood more than of God's infinite power.

A RELATIONAL MARKER

The recognition of God's personhood in the Creation account and in the hallowing of the seventh day leads to a fourth inference. The text says that God *sabbathed*. Most English versions say that God "rested" (Gen. 2:2). "Resting," however, conveys an aura of passivity that seems anticlimactic in this context, and it is a word that does not precisely capture the original idea. It has been shown repeatedly that the word "desisted" or "ceased" is a better fit, and either of these words have a richer connotation.[40] A suggestive mental picture is one of arrival: a ship gliding into the harbor after a long voyage, a train coming to a halt at a station. The meaning of ceasing is better appreciated by keeping in mind what went before it. In addition to the transition from activity to quietude, there is the expectancy of one person longing to see the other. If resting has the connotation of a car that has been parked, ceasing shows the moment of arrival itself. In the context of the creation account the ceasing points to the joy of being with someone.

The relational implication of the seventh day is often overlooked, dwarfed by the tendency to prioritize God's power, sovereignty, and majesty as more representative features of Creation. Power and sovereignty are attributes of God, but from God's side it is not power that is projected most forcefully in the institution of the seventh day. When God ceases the work of creating, hallowing the seventh day, we see God coming into an enduring relationship with Creation. "By resting on the seventh day, God is thereby shown to have entered into the time of the created order," says Fretheim.[41] Intimacy threatens to eclipse majesty in this scenario; at the very least we are led to see

God's desire for intimacy in the seventh day to the point that God's awesome power and majesty are veiled and held in the background so as not to intimidate human approach.

There is a need to take this insight a step further because theological tradition has so one-sidedly stressed divine majesty that the relational element is rarely seen. Perceiving the seventh day as a relational marker enriches the theology of Creation, promising to rectify the distortion in which the emphasis on sovereignty implies detachment. Jürgen Moltmann grapples with the neglected side that is brought to view in the seventh day, suggesting that "the God who rests in the face of his creation does not dominate the world on this day: he 'feels' the world; he allows himself to be affected, to be touched by each of his creatures. He adopts the community of creation as his own milieu."[42] Humility does not negate majesty, and the self-emptying intimation in the seventh day does not reduce divine sovereignty to nothing, but humility and self-emptying are nevertheless the bigger surprises, the most unexpected and also the most neglected features baked into the seventh day in the Creation account. As Michael Welker notes, "the creating God is not only the acting God, but also the reacting God, the God who responds to what has been created."[43] The seventh day has an interactive character and intent, too, incarnating God in the ongoing experience of human beings.

God's awesome power and majesty are veiled and held in the background so as not to intimidate human approach.

AN EXPRESSION OF LOVE

God's ceasing on the seventh day calls for a fifth observation that probes into the motive behind Creation and the seventh day. What could be the motive for the seventh day and the great ceremony surrounding its introduction? Karl Barth writes perceptively that the characteristic of God that is revealed "in the rest of the seventh day is His love."[44]

What would lead God to set a limit to creative activity and to mark the occasion by the hallowing of the seventh day? Clearly, if by ceasing the Creator stoops to the level of the creatures because God's love "does not seek its own" (1 Cor. 13:5, NKJV), "is not self-seeking" (NIV), or "never seeks its own advantage" (NJB), one cannot avoid the impression that the love revealed is recognizable even in the currency of contemporary notions of love. The beings whose existence is celebrated in the rest of the seventh day are enormously significant to God. Indeed, "the reason why He refrains from further activity on the seventh day is that He has found the object of His love and has no need for any further works."[45]

This is a staggering thought. On the one hand, God's love thus expressed magnifies human value, showing forth in bold print the worth of human beings to God. On the other hand, the seventh day thus understood brings God's love into focus at Creation, placing love at the front and center of God's character and activity from the very beginning. In the New Testament John makes love the centerpiece of his description of God. "Whoever does not love, does not know God," he writes, "for God is love" (1 John 4:8). In the light of the seventh day at Creation, however, the proposal that "God is love" should not be seen as a late disclosure. Love is God's defining attribute from the beginning. From first to last love is the wellspring from which all other actions radiate and around which all else coalesces.

According to the testimony of Genesis, and as noted in Barth's remarkable statement, what is most important to know about God at Creation is that God is love. The seventh day signifies what is most essential to know about God. Therefore, right from its debut the seventh day is not a peripheral afterthought. God ceases from working in order to enjoy the company of the person God has created, suggesting that the seventh day speaks as much about the value of human beings to God as of God's valuation of human life. What lies in the foreground of the seventh day's first mention in the Bible is God's gift, not human obligation. It is as if we hear God speaking, "I am ceasing on the seventh day not only that you may acknowledge and love me, but in order to make it known that I recognize and love you."

AN AFFIRMATION OF PRESENCE

Where theologians have struggled to agree on a unified theme in the Old Testament, they have often seemed like the blind men attempting to describe the shape of an elephant, each mistaking their part for the most important clue to the whole. While most of the proposals have merit as descriptions of significant themes, the suggestion that the Old Testament favors a theology of presence deserves particular distinction. More than anything else, faith in Yahweh means trust in the divine presence. On this point Edmond Jacob writes that "it is not the idea of eternity which is primary when the Israelites pronounce the name Yahweh, but that of presence."[46] Samuel Terrien holds that "[t]he reality of the presence of God stands at the center of biblical faith."[47] He adds that the divine presence "is always elusive,"[48] but this qualification can be left for later. It is the idea of presence that needs to be noted at this point, partly because it stands in contrast to the prevailing sense of God's absence, but mostly because the reality of God's presence lies at the heart of the divine ceasing on the seventh day.

God ceases from working in order to enjoy the company of the person God has created, suggesting that the seventh day speaks as much about the value of human beings to God as of God's valuation of human life.

In setting the seventh day apart, we do not see God standing at a distance from Creation, winding up the clock and then leaving things to take their own course. The God of the seventh day is a near and present God, a Person who is committed to Creation and One who is involved in Creation up close and personal.[49] Presence is a primary idea because in Genesis history begins with God's presence, and the reality of divine presence is emphatically affirmed in the seventh day.

The universal question—Who are we?—often gets this answer: We are the result of chance, and there is no one there to whom we can turn or to whom we may attribute our existence. Yet the seventh day answers: We are created in the image of God. We are not the product of accident, and we are not "orphans in a world of no tomorrows," as Joan Baez once sang.

A DAY OF BLESSING

The solemn words that confer a unique status on the seventh day in Genesis "contain the idea of selection and distinction."[50] Wenham finds it paradoxical that "the day on which God refrains from creative activity is pronounced blessed," concurring, however, that the blessing on the seventh day makes it a blessing to those who come under its sphere of influence.[51] This is a key point: Skinner explains that "[a] blessing is the utterance of a good wish; applied to things, it means their endowment with permanently beneficial qualities."[52] Viewed in this light, "the Sabbath is a constant source of well-being to the man who recognises its true nature and purpose."[53]

> ***The God of the seventh day is a near and present God, a Person who is committed to Creation and One who is involved in Creation up close and personal.***

Blessing, therefore, stands in the foreground, closely intertwined with God's love and God's presence that are part and parcel of the seventh day. Moreover, "foreground" is meant literally because the seventh day—bringing the full measure of God's presence, love, and blessing—marks the beginning of human existence in Genesis. Barth observes that the seventh day does not come at the end of a week of toil and labor for human beings as though its primary purpose is to offer a measure of respite after days of toil. Rather, since "God's seventh day was man's first,"[54] the seventh day sets life's priority for human beings in the most tangible way. Better yet—and much closer to the point—the seventh day brings to view God's priorities. Seeing that human time "begins with a day of rest and not a day of work,"[55] the spiritual pursuit, living life in a relationship with the Creator that is mutually meaningful, stands out as the primary meaning in life.

Abraham Joshua Heschel, the Jewish theologian, educator, and philosopher, disavows a theology of the seventh day that places it within a utilitarian framework, that is, seeing the seventh day as a day of rest that follows work, allowing the batteries to be charged in order that more work may be done. To our minds rest follows work and is necessitated by work. But "to the biblical mind," writes Heschel, "the Sabbath as a day of rest, as a day of abstaining from toil, is not for the purpose of recovering one's lost strength and becoming fit for the forthcoming labor. The Sabbath is a day for the sake of life."[56] This highlights a notion of blessing to which modern life has become a stranger and one which only a sustained process of rehabilitation will remedy.

A SIGN OF REVELATION

The first seventh day must be seen as an expression of God's view and decision, irrespective of any human response. Skinner writes that the Sabbath "is not an institution which exists or ceases to exist with its observance by man; the divine rest is a fact as much as the divine work, and so the sanctity of the day is a fact whether man secures the benefit or not."[57] He can say this because the text we are exploring is descriptive of what God does, and not explicitly prescriptive as to what human beings ought to do. "The first Sabbath is cosmic, only hinting at what its significance will be to man," says Shimon Bakon.[58] The Genesis account of the seventh day is written in the indicative and there is no imperative attached to it.[59] Whether or not human beings will join God in God's rest can only be anticipated and argued tentatively. Where the seventh day is conceived as a human obligation, it might show how important God is for human life and for the meaning of existence. When, on the other hand, the seventh day is left to speak from the concise scaffolding of its first mention in the text in Genesis, the seventh day tells of the importance of human beings to God, and its primary message is not human duty but divine commitment. In its forward-looking stance, the seventh day embodies the notion of revelation. Indeed, its intent to reveal may be the most important member in its portfolio of meanings even though it is also the most subtle. The forward-looking stance intimates a posture of anticipation, and yet the content of the revelation remains outside the field of vision. God's enduring intention is in view, but it is not fully known.

The Bible says that at the end of the creation week, "God saw everything that he had made, and behold, it was very good" (Gen. 1:31). More is implied in this statement than meets the eye. Perceptive Jewish interpreters see it not only as a description of a perfect state, but also a statement that anticipates disruption.[60] "Very good" is an evaluative statement, where "very" suggests that there might be gradations of good, and "good" indicates awareness of its opposite, of what is *not* good, even of evil. As the story in Genesis soon will show, there will also be an opposing view, expressing the opinion that all is not "very good." The meaning of the seventh day is not fully appreciated unless the dissenting voice, too, is heard. In the garden of bliss where the seventh day is first set apart, there is also a serpent.

The seventh day tells of the importance of human beings to God, and its primary message is not human duty but divine commitment.

ENDNOTES

1. Rolf Rendtorff (*The Canonical Hebrew Bible: A Theology of the Old Testament*, trans. David Orton [Leiden: Deo Publishing, 2005], 13) says that the Creation account describes "an absolute beginning; there is no previous history."

2. Nahum Sarna (Gen*esis* [The JPS Torah Commentary; Philadelphia: The Jewish Publication Society, 1989], 14) states that "[t]he seventh day is the Lord's Day, through which all the creativity of the preceding days achieves fulfillment."

3. The entire enterprise of source analysis has been driven by German Protestant scholarship. In German the "Yahwist" source becomes "Jahwist," and thus the letter J instead of Y.

4. Gerhard von Rad, *Genesis*, 2nd ed., trans. John H. Marks (London: SCM Press, 1963), 23.

5. Ibid.

6. Ibid.

7. One such example is found in Rolf Rendtorff, *Das Überlieferungsgeschichtliche Problem des Pentateuch* (Berlin: Walter de Gruyter, 1977). Rendtorff contends for a unitary but late composition.

8. One example of a "unitary reading" that lets the story speak as it stands is found in *The Literary Guide to the Bible*, ed. Robert Alter and Frank Kermode (London: Collins, 1987). In a highly personal evaluation of source criticism and the "Documentary hypothesis," Pamela Tamarkin Reis (*Reading the Lines: A Fresh Look at the Hebrew Bible* [Peabody, MA: Hendrickson Publishers, 2002], 1–14) argues in favor of a unitary reading along lines that guide the present approach.

9. Brevard Childs has been a leading advocate for a "canonical" approach to Scripture, as in *Introduction to the Old Testament as Scripture* (Philadelphia: Fortress Press, 1979). "Canon" as understood in the present context does not envision an arbitrary collection of texts. Rather, as expressed by Samuel Terrien (*The Elusive Presence: Toward A New Biblical Theology* [New York: Harper & Row, 1978; repr. Eugene, OR: Wipf and Stock Publishers, 2000], 32), "the books of the Hebrew Bible and of the New Testament imposed themselves upon Jews and Christians as the regulating standard of their religious commitment and ethical behaviour. *Canon* was originally not a dogmatic structure imposed from without by institutionalized collectivities but an unspoken force which grew from within the nature of Hebrew-Christian religion."

10. M. H. Segal, "The Religion of Israel before Sinai," *JQR* 52 (1961): 46. Segal concludes that "the book of Genesis embodies the living traditions of Israel in Egypt, and may well be a work of the Mosaic age and of the great prophet and legislator himself" (p. 48).

11. Umberto Cassuto, *A Commentary on the Book of Genesis*, Part I, trans. Israel Abrahams (Jerusalem: The Magnes Press, 1961); idem, *The Documentary Hypothesis and the Composition of the Pentateuch,* trans. Israel Abrahams (Jerusalem: The Magnes Press, 1961). In the latter book Cassuto offers a synopsis of his more extensive work in Italian disputing the main pillars of the Documentary Hypothesis.

12. Cassuto, *Genesis*, 12.

13. Sarna, *Genesis*, xviii. Tamarkin Reis (*Reading the Lines*, 15–26) finds the apparent disparity between what is generally thought to be two stories of creation as analogous to the same story being told from two different perspectives and not necessarily by two different authors.

14. Thus, D. A. Carson ("Introduction," in *From Sabbath to Lord's Day*, 16) states, "We are not persuaded that Sabbath keeping is presented in the Old Testament as the norm from

creation onward." A. T. Lincoln ("From Sabbath to Lord's Day: A Biblical and Theological Perspective," in *From Sabbath to Lord's Day*, 346) confirms that the decision with regard to whether the Bible anchors the Sabbath in Creation "will be of paramount importance to the argument about the relation between Sabbath and Sunday."

15. H. P. Dressler, "The Sabbath in the Old Testament," in *From Sabbath to Lord's Day*, 23.

16. Dressler ("The Sabbath in the Old Testament," 28) faults an interpretation that another eye, differently conditioned and motivated, will see as the most natural. "Unless the reader equates 'the seventh day' and 'Sabbath,' there is no reference to the Sabbath here." Likewise, von Rad (*Genesis*, 60) professes that "nothing at all is said" in the Genesis account of Creation about an enduring Sabbath ordinance. Claus Westermann (*Genesis 1–11*, trans. John J. Scullion [London: SPCK, 1984], 237) claims not to find here "an institution, and not even a preparation for the Sabbath, but rather the later foundation of the Sabbath is reflected in these sentences." These views, I suggest, have more to do with how the text is heard than with what is said.

17. Thus Dressler ("The Sabbath in the Old Testament," 28) states, "There is no direct command that the seventh day should be kept in any way."

18. Ibid., 27–30.

19. Lincoln ("From Sabbath to Lord's Day," 343–412) quite consistently uses "the Mosaic Sabbath" as the preferred designation of the seventh day in his discussion of the subject.

20. As will be explored more in-depth later, the rationale for the Sabbath in the Exodus account of the Ten Commandments is that "in six days the Lord made heaven and earth, the sea, and all that is in them, but rested the seventh day; therefore the Lord blessed the sabbath day and consecrated it" (Exod. 20:11).

21. Terence E. Fretheim, *God and the World in the Old Testament: A Relational Theology of Creation* (Nashville: Abingdon Press, 2005), xiv.

22. Rolf Knierim, *The Task of Old Testament Theology: Substance, Method and Cases* (Grand Rapids: Eerdmans, 1995), 14.

23. Cassuto, *Genesis*, 64.

24. Jon D. Levenson, *Creation and the Persistence of Evil* (Princeton: Princeton University Press, 1994 [1988]), 100.

25. Roland de Vaux, *Ancient Israel*, vol. 2, trans. John McHugh (New York: McGraw-Hill, 1965), 479. de Vaux, accepting the paradigm of source criticism, finds the seventh day in all "layers": "It is mentioned in the Elohistic Code of the Covenant (Ex 23:12), in the Yahwistic Code (Ex 34:21), in the two redactions of the Ten Commandments (DT 5:12–14 and Ex 20:8–10), and in the Priests' Code (Ex 31:12–17), *i.e.* in all the traditions of the Pentateuch" (p. 479).

26. Brevard Childs, *The Book of Exodus* (Philadelphia: Westminster Press, 1974), 414.

27. John L. McKenzie, *A Theology of the Old Testament* (London: Geoffrey Chapman, 1974), 79.

28. Andreasen, *Rest and Redemption*, 23; cf. idem, *The Old Testament Sabbath: A Tradition-*

Historical Investigation (SBLDS 7; Missoula, MT: Society of Biblical Literature, 1972); idem, "Recent Sudies of the Old Testament Sabbath: Some Observations," *ZAW* 86 (1974): 453–469.

29. John Skinner, *A Critical and Exegetical Commentary on Genesis* (ICC; Edinburgh: T. & T. Clark, 1910), 35.

30. Gordon J. Wenham, *Genesis 1–15* (WBC; Waco: Word Books, 1987), 36.

31. Cassuto, *Genesis*, 8.

32. Walther Zimmerli, *The Old Testament and the World,* trans. John J. Scullion (London: SPCK, 1976), 22; cf. Thomas J. Finley, "Dimensions of the Hebrew Word for 'create' (*bārā'*)," *BSac* 148 (1991): 409–423.

33. While scholars agree that the Hebrew *bārā'*, "to create," is only used with God as the subject, there is considerable debate as to the meaning of God's creative activity. Is it creation *ex nihilo*, making the world out of nothing, or does it point to God's ordering of chaos? Levenson (*Creation and the Persistence of Evil*, 3, 47) claims that "we can capture the essence of the idea of creation in the Hebrew Bible with the word 'mastery'" rather than creation out of nothing. This debate has had profound implications for Jewish understanding of the reality of evil, as we shall see in the next chapter.

34. Zimmerli, *Old Testament and the World*, 23.

35. John N. Andrews, *History of the Sabbath and First Day of the Week*, 3rd ed. (Battle Creek: Review and Herald, 1887 [repr., Sunfield, MI: Family Health Publications, 1998]), 515.

36. Søren Kierkegaard, *Practice in Christianity,* ed. and trans. Howard V. Hong and Edna H. Hong (Princeton: Princeton University Press, 1991 [org. Danish version 1848]), 131.

37. Karl Barth, *The Epistle to the Romans*, 6th ed., trans. Edwyn C. Hoskyns (London: Oxford University Press, 1968 [1933]), 9–10. Barth's position on this point is first articulated in the preface to the second edition in 1921.

38. Karl Barth, *Church Dogmatics,* vol. III, part 2, *The Doctrine of Creation,* trans. Harold Knight, G. W. Bromiley, J. K. S. Reid, and R. H. Fuller (Edinburgh: T. & T. Clark, 1960), 457.

39. Jacques Ellul, *What I Believe,* trans. Geoffrey W. Bromiley (Grand Rapids: Wm. B. Eerdmans Publishing Company, 1989), 153.

40. S. R. Driver, *The Book of Genesis* (London: Methuen & Co., 1904), 18; Skinner, *Genesis*, 37. This view is strengthened greatly by etymological considerations. Gnana Robinson ("The Idea of Rest in the Old Testament and the Search for the Basic Character of the Sabbath," *ZAW* 92 [1980]: 42) finds that the root *šbt* "has the basic meaning of 'coming to an end' and in the non-sabbatic context it is never attested in the sense of 'rest from labour.'"

41. Fretheim, *God and the World in the Old Testament*, 63.

42. Jürgen Moltmann, *God in Creation: An Ecological Doctrine of Creation,* trans. Margaret Kohl (London: SCM Press, 1985), 279.

43. Michael Welker, *Creation and Reality,* trans. John F. Hoffmeyer (Minneapolis: Fortress Press, 1999), 10.

44. Karl Barth, *Church Dogmatics*, vol. III, part 1, *The Doctrine of Creation,* trans. J. W. Edwards, O. Bussey, and Harold Knight (Edinburgh: T&T Clark, 1958), 215.

45. Barth, *Church Dogmatics* III.1, 215.

46. Edmond Jacob, *Theology of the Old Testament,* trans. Arthur W. Heathcote and Philip J. Allcock (London: Hodder and Stoughton, 1958), 52.

47. Terrien, *The Elusive Presence*, xxvii.

48. Ibid.

49. Thus Gerhard von Rad (*Old Testament Theology*, vol. 1, trans. D. M. G. Stalker [London: SCM Press, 1975], 148) states: "It would be sheer folly to regard this resting of God's which concluded the Creation as something like a turning away from the world by God; it is in fact a particularly mysterious gracious turning towards his Creation."

50. Skinner, *Genesis*, 38.

51. Wenham, *Genesis*, 36.

52. Skinner, *Genesis*, 38.

53. Ibid.

54. Barth, *Church Dogmatics*, III.2, 457.

55. Ibid., 458.

56. Heschel, *The Sabbath*, 14.

57. Skinner, *Genesis*, 35.

58. Shimon Bakon, "Creation, Tabernacle and Sabbath," *JBQ* 25 (1997): 84.

59. Andreasen, *Rest and Redemption*, 75.

60. Pinchas Kahn, "The Expanding Perspectives of the Sabbath," *JBQ* 32 (2004): 243.

CHAPTER 3

PARADISE LOST

They heard the sound of the Lord *God walking in the garden at the time of the evening breeze, and the man and his wife hid themselves from the presence of the* Lord *God among the trees of the garden.*
Genesis 3:8

We often fail to see things, even important things, until someone else points them out to us. Often what we see is restricted by our expectations, by the things we go looking for, or by our presuppositions. In hindsight, when we have been alerted to look for other things, the overlooked element may stand out as the most striking feature in the picture. This is certainly the case when we consider the context in which the seventh day is endowed with the marks of distinction.

As noted in the previous chapter, the link between the seventh day and Creation has been wrongly called into question. Moreover, where the Creation link is accepted, it is often assumed that the seventh day comes into being at a time when all is well in the world. The seventh day has the Paradise of God as its frame of reference. There appears to be no disharmonious cord in the symphony of Creation, no danger that threatens the peace.

Often what we see is restricted by our expectations, by the things we go looking for, or by our presuppositions.

In reality, however, the impression of tranquility is not the whole picture, and the resultant misconception impairs the full meaning of the seventh day when it is considered from the vantage point of its beginning. What readers of the Bible have come to know as "the Temptation Story"—the story that breaks the state of harmony—is really a story of misrepresentation. It is also the story of the dissonant voice, placing the seventh day in the context of conflict.

THE MISREPRESENTATION STORY

The change that comes about in the state of Creation in the third chapter of Genesis is so dramatic that the contrasts should be carefully marked before probing into the cause or occasion that led to the transformation. Three of the elements in the striking "before" and "after" in the narrative are appreciated in the following excerpts:

BEFORE	AFTER
And the man and his wife were both naked, and were not ashamed (2:25).	Then the eyes of both were opened, and they knew that they were naked; and they sewed fig leaves together and made loincloths for themselves (3:7).
God saw everything that he had made, and indeed, it was very good (1:31).	...cursed is the ground because of you....By the sweat of your face you shall eat bread...; you are dust, and to dust you shall return (3:17, 19).
The LORD God took the man and put him in the garden of Eden to till it and keep it (2:15).	...the LORD God sent him forth from the garden of Eden.... He drove out the man; and at the east of the garden of Eden he placed the cherubim, and a sword flaming and turning to guard the way to the tree of life (3:23–24).

In the scene that we call "before," the man and the woman are naked, but they have no unsettling self-consciousness, and no shame (Gen. 2:25). In the scene designated "after," there is a rush of self-consciousness, a sense of embarrassment and shame, and a scuttle to cover the part of the body that now offends (Gen. 3:7). In the first panel everything is "very good" (Gen. 1:31). In the second panel there is a curse on the ground, there is toil and struggle, and finally death (Gen. 3:17, 19). Originally, human beings are given a home in the Garden of Eden that has all the marks of permanence (Gen. 2:15). After the calamity they are turned out of the Garden of Eden, and measures are taken to prevent their return (Gen. 3:23–24). Moreover, recalling the implications of the seventh day, the "before" state in the Garden of Eden pictures a relationship between the Creator and human beings wherein they meet face to face in confidence, love, and mutual appreciation. Nothing evokes the change—the bone-chilling sense of alienation that comes in the "after" scene—as much as this verse: "They heard the sound of the LORD God walking in the garden at the time of the evening breeze, and the man and his wife hid themselves from the presence of the LORD God among the trees of the garden" (Gen. 3:8). In the echo chamber of the first chapters of Genesis, where the wording is so sparse as to allow each thought to resound many times, the words describing the terrifying estrangement linger long: "I heard the sound of you.....I was afraid....I hid myself" (Gen. 3:10).

Whatever impact this account leaves on modern interpreters, there is no question that it made an impression on subsequent contributors to books in the Bible. In the greatest prophetic vision of the Old Testament, the memory of Paradise Lost is the fixed reference point for the future state for which the prophet is yearning.

> The wolf shall live with the lamb, the leopard shall lie down with the kid, the calf and the lion and the fatling together, and a little child shall lead them. The cow and the bear shall graze, their young shall lie down together; and the lion shall eat straw like the ox. The nursing child shall play over the hole of the asp, and the weaned child shall put its hand on the adder's den. They will not hurt or destroy on all my holy mountain; for the earth will be full of the knowledge of the LORD as the waters cover the sea. (Isaiah 11:6–9)

In this vision Paradise Lost is also Paradise Regained, evoked in the fondest images of peace and harmony. Isaiah's book returns to this theme more than once, sending it off to posterity to become the vision for the promised future state in the New Testament along with the "before" state in Genesis (Isa. 25:6–9; 65:17–25).[1]

In the New Testament, the crisis in Genesis is recalled time and again as the crucial point of reference for its message. We see it in the temptation stories in the Synoptic Gospels, where Jesus seems to retrace the steps of Adam and Eve. As in Genesis, Jesus confronts a tempter who seeks to shake His confidence in God. Unlike Adam and Eve, however, Jesus emerges victorious, refusing to bow to the satanic innuendo (Matt. 4:1–11; Mark 1:12–13; Luke 4:1–13).[2] The contrast is as striking as the similarity, and yet it is the similarity that puts the encounter in the right perspective. Jesus is traversing familiar ground—the ground where the first human beings adopted the serpent's point of view. The echoes of Genesis are meant to enable the reader to revisit the account between the serpent and Eve and thus to gain an appreciation for the scope of Jesus's triumph.

In the Gospel of John, too, no less than in the Synoptic account, Jesus's entire mission has the story in Genesis as its frame of reference. When Jesus refers to His unseen opponent as "a liar and the father of lies" (John 8:44), He is pointing to the deception in Genesis, even calling it "*the* lie." Indeed, when the devil "speaks *the* lie" (John 8:44), he has in mind the lie that stands at the head of the line and the lie that sets the standard. Jesus's mission is to undo the lie and to reverse its consequences. For this reason He casts His own death as the means of setting right what was ruined in the Garden of Eden (John 12:23–33).[3]

The echoes of Genesis are meant to enable the reader to revisit the account between the serpent and Eve and thus to gain an appreciation for the scope of Jesus's triumph.

The apostle Paul has the story in Genesis in mind at the most decisive junctures in his correspondence. In Romans he writes that "sin came into the world through one man" (Rom. 5:12), meaning Adam, "a type of the one who was to come" (Rom. 5:14). Death looms large in Paul's view of reality, and his view in this respect also depends on Genesis (Gen. 2:17; 3:24). "The last enemy to be destroyed is death" (1 Cor. 15:26), Paul writes, signifying that the *last* enemy is also the greatest enemy and the one against which all human remedies come up short. In fact, the juxtaposition of Adam and Jesus, and of death and life, both of which derive from Genesis, are inseparable in Paul's message. To him, the story he has to tell brings the reversal of what happened in the early chapters of Genesis and cannot be understood apart from it. "As in Adam we all die, so in Christ shall all be made alive," he concludes (1 Cor. 15:22).

Nowhere in the New Testament is the story in Genesis more sharply focused than in the book of Revelation. Austin Farrer says of the author of Revelation that "no other New Testament author felt himself called to the same task; no other set himself to capture a visionary experience of the Last Things, by intense and systematic meditation on the whole prophetic tradition."[4] Likewise, Richard J. Bauckham sees John writing "the climax of prophetic revelation, which gathered up the prophetic meaning of the Old Testament scriptures and disclosed the way in which it was being and was to be fulfilled in the last days."[5] Genesis belongs to John's sustained meditation because the first chapters in Genesis are extensively mirrored in the last two chapters of Revelation. The entire biblical narrative folds back on itself, the end recalling and reversing the beginning.

GENESIS 3	REVELATION 21–22
God's presence evoking fear (3:8)	Seeing God's face without fear (22:4)
Curse on the earth (3:17)	No more curse (22:3)
Cut off from tree of life (3:24)	Access to tree of life (22:2)
Returned to dust (3:19)	No more death (21:4)

The examples surveyed above stop short of exploring the weight laid on the story in Genesis in the history of Christianity. However, it is precisely the biblical perspective that invests the Genesis material with significance. Walter Brueggemann, who in many respects is a refreshing iconoclast and creative interpreter of the Old Testament, goes a step too far when he disputes that the story of the alienation in Genesis is a crucial text that lays down the premise for all that follows.[6] Brueggemann asserts to the contrary that the Genesis story "is an exceedingly marginal text."[7] As to the notion that the incident at the tree of knowledge of good and evil in Genesis represents "the fall" in a disastrous and decisive sense, Brueggemann holds that "[n]othing could be more remote from the narrative itself."[8] He also assails the idea that the first chapters in Genesis give an account of how evil came into the world, claiming that "the Old Testament is never interested in such an abstract issue."[9] Finally, dissatisfied with the view that this text reveals the origin of death, Brueggemann states the conviction that "the Bible does not reflect on such a question in any sustained way."[10]

While few interpreters go as far as Brueggemann, his objections are worthy of attention because they force a reassessment of this story in its native context and in its many echoes in other books of the Bible. On all counts Brueggemann's assertions run afoul of the evidence. His characterization of "an exceedingly marginal text" might ring true if the text were measured according to weight or volume, but it goes awry when the qualitative parameters are given their due: the passage from innocence to guilt, from intimacy to alienation,[11] from confidence to fear, from happiness to grief, from life to death, from access to the tree of life to being barred from the Garden. The reader of Genesis is well advised to consider how this story contains the premise for other parts of the biblical narrative, but the reading should begin by heeding the text on its own terms and in its original context. For many, reading the text anew without prejudice, the consequences are likely to be what they are from the perspective of the New Testament.

On the strength of this story we are given the means by which to appreciate the meaning of Jesus's triumph in the temptation stories in the New Testament. Paul's yearning for a second Adam has no meaning apart from Genesis. When he holds death to be "the last enemy," the foremost alien element in human existence (1 Cor. 15:26), his decisive point of reference is the "before" and "after" of the Genesis story, that is, the realization that death was not part of God's original intention and at one point "death will be no more" (Rev. 21:4).

PAYING HEED TO THE DISSONANT VOICE

Between the story of Creation and the devastating sense of loss that is felt as the man and the woman are made to leave the Garden of Eden (Gen. 3:24) lies the story of the dissonant voice (Gen. 3:1–6). This voice is so central to the plot that the entire story collapses without it.

Two texts should be recalled before tuning in to the seditious sentiments voiced in this story, each expressing a point of view that will be shamelessly contradicted.

> God saw everything that he had made, and indeed, it was very good. And there was evening and there was morning, the sixth day. (Gen. 1:31)

> And the LORD God commanded the man, "You may freely eat of every tree of the garden; but of the tree of the knowledge of good and evil you shall not eat, for in the day that you eat of it you shall die." (Gen. 2:16–17)

These texts, the first assessing the setting of human existence and the second laying down the terms under which human beings are to live, prepare for the well-aimed missive of the dissonant voice.

> Now the serpent was more crafty than any other wild animal that the LORD God had made. He said to the woman, "Did God say, 'You shall not eat from any tree in the garden'?" (Gen. 3:1)

The identity of the being that insinuates these charges is not fully delineated in the meager information given in the story of Creation. The more complete picture emerges later, by means of brief installments scattered throughout the Bible.[12] The puzzle is completed in the book of Revelation, where the opposing power is identified as "that *ancient* serpent called the devil or Satan" (Rev. 12:9; 20:2). Jon Levenson points out that the notion of an opposing voice represents a challenge to belief in a sovereign God. The wonder, therefore, is not that the Bible says so little about the opposing power but that it says anything at all. Levenson suggests that the bits and pieces referring to a satanic character in the Old Testament do not speak to his unimportance but to the fact that the story of his rebellion "has been repressed rather than destroyed."[13]

Yearning for a second Adam has no meaning apart from Genesis.

In another example, one of the earliest critics of Christianity, the Middle Platonic philosopher Celsus (ca. 180 CE), lambastes the Christians for holding a view of reality that he considers naïve. The Christians, Celsus complains, "*make a being opposed to God; devil, and in the Hebrew tongue, Satanas are the names which they give to this same being*."[14] Celsus, whose disparaging views of Christianity are preserved in the writings of the Christian apologist Origen (ca. 185–254 CE), finds the Christian position unworthy of God because the Christian outlook envisions a God who performs far below expectations. According to Celsus, it is sacrilege to infer that "*when the greatest God indeed wishes to confer some benefit upon men, He has a power which is opposed to Him, and so is unable to do it*."[15] The Christian position has produced a God who seems weak and ineffective. By proposing the existence of an opposing power that infringes on God's domain, God "*is worsted by the devil*."[16] In Celsus's view, the existence of such a being does not make sense because any attempt to oppose God should easily be held in check by God's power.[17]

But in Genesis we find an opposing power. This power matches the New Testament view that the serpent is Satan in disguise.[18] The character of the opposition manifests itself in what the opponent says. On this point the critic Celsus hits the nail on the head, describing the Christian notion of Satan as a sorcerer that "*proclaims opposing opinions*."[19] Indeed, it is precisely by paying attention to what the serpent says that the demonic character of the opponent becomes manifest. No notion of the demonic could possibly exceed the innuendo that is hurled against God in the Genesis story (Gen. 3:1). When Old Testament scholars reject the view that the serpent in the story represents an exalted being opposed to God, asserting that "the text says nothing about such enmity toward God,"[20] it is fair to ask whether the scholars are listening to what the serpent is saying. If the serpent's words do not qualify as "enmity toward God," one is left to wonder what else needs to be said in order for it to qualify as enmity.

The serpent's first utterance is a case study in subversive efficiency, fully deserving the characterization "*the* lie" that Jesus gives it in John (John 8:44). "Did God say, 'You shall not eat from any tree in the garden'?" (Gen. 3:1). The staggering possibility that the Creator makes it unlawful to eat from *any* tree in the garden transforms the terms of human existence. Two further charges follow (Gen. 3:4–5), but the defenses of the person who first hears it are irreparably shaken by the impact of the first statement.

The momentum in this dialogue belongs from the outset decisively to the serpent. When the woman lamely attempts to correct the misrepresentation (Gen. 3:2), she fails miserably. It is as if we hear her sheepish protest—"No, no, God did not say that..."—drowned out in the noise and wreckage of transformed perceptions and the shattered mental paradigm caused by the first suggestion.

Leon R. Kass states the matter succinctly in the series on Genesis that was broadcast on public television in the United States in the 1990s.

> The serpent asks the Bible's first question and produces the first conversation. He calls into question the goodness of God. Could God be the kind of being Who would put you amidst all these trees and tell you not to eat from any of them? He calls God a liar—"No, you're not going to die," he tells them. He undermines authority and suggests new and attractive possibilities. Once the authority of command or law or custom or instinct is undermined,

> the mind is free to imagine new possibilities. When the text says, "She saw that the tree was good for food," we can see that Eve has already made a judgment about the goodness or badness of the tree. In a sense, she's already tasted of the tree even before reaching for it.[21]

In one of the most astute expositions of this account, R. W. L. Moberly points out how the serpent brazenly puts what God had said on its head.

> God's words had emphasized freedom—the man could eat of every tree with only one prohibited. The serpent makes the prohibition universal. Instead of "You may certainly eat from every tree of the the garden" we have "You shall not eat from any tree of the garden" attributed to God. Why should the serpent say something which, as the woman duly points out, is clearly not the case? Apart from the fact that the serpent thereby engages the woman in debate, the main point lies presumably in the implication of the serpent's words. What matters is not that the serpent's words are obviously false, but that they imply that a total prohibition is the sort of unreasonable prohibition that one might expect from God, who is to be seen as more interested in restriction than in freedom. Such an innuendo is not dismissed simply by pointing out the obvious inaccuracy of the serpent's words.[22]

As noted in these comments, the serpent begins with a falsehood. It does not matter that the serpent has to back off somewhat from the initial misrepresentation. Moberly captures the implication that "a total prohibition is the sort of unreasonable prohibition that one might expect from God."[23] Or, catching a similar thought from a slightly different angle, the initial charge ensures that even a lesser prohibition comes to be seen as unreasonable. Either way the charge opens up a new way of looking at God, shaking their confidence in God's goodness and trustworthiness.

At the heart of this verbal exchange is the question, What kind of person is God? Moberly is certainly right that "God's words had emphasized freedom,"[24] but the serpent construes these terms as deprivation of freedom and an unjustified restriction. Thus, the question of God's motive cannot be avoided. Moberly, again, notes that

> the serpent implicitly attributes a base motive to God for making the prohibition in the first place. The clear implication is that God acted out of fear and envy. Thus the silence about the motivation of the prohibition in 2:17, which in that context was presumed to be for man's good, is given an entirely different slant by the serpent—repression, not benefit, was the reason. It will naturally follow from this that if an unworthy motive underlies the prohibition, then there will be little wrong in disobeying it. It is noteworthy that the serpent never tells the woman to transgress God's prohibition. He simply calls into question both God's truthfulness (by denying his warning) and God's trustworthiness (by impugning his motives) and leaves the woman to draw her own conclusions.[25]

As the dramatic exchange unfolds, it is evident that the force of the initial distortion sets the terms for what follows. Once the initial premise is allowed to fester, no remonstration on the part of the woman is able to hold back the mental implosion.

Dietrich Bonhoeffer gives proof of exquisite listening in his discussion of the encounter between the woman and the serpent.

> "Did God say?" "Yes he did say…but why did he say it?" That is how the conversation continues. "He has said it out of envy.…God is not good but evil, tormenting…be intelligent, be more intelligent than your God and take what he grudges you.… He has said it, indeed you are right, Eve, but he has lied. God's Word is a lie…because you will not die."[26]

As the conversation unfolds, trust is eroded and then lost because the party in whom trust was placed is no longer thought to be trustworthy. What began as an insinuation regarding the benevolence of God gets bolder. In the end the serpent launches a blunt, uncompromising attack on God's credibility. God's "you shall die" (Gen. 2:17) stands against the serpent's alluring assurance, "You will not die" (Gen. 3:4).

Both statements cannot be true. "In these two statements the world gapes asunder for Adam," writes Bonhoeffer. "Statement stands against statement. This is beyond the power of comprehension, for how is he to know what a lie is? Truth against truth—God's truth against serpent's truth...."[27] At this point in the narrative the pendulum swings decisively and fatefully in favor of the serpent. The narrator in Genesis reports that "when the woman saw that the tree was good for food, and that it was a delight to the eyes, and that the tree was to be desired to make one wise, she took of its fruit and ate; and she also gave some to her husband, who was with her, and he ate" (Gen. 3:6).

THE SEVENTH DAY IN THE CONTEXT OF CONFLICT

The suture lines that scholars postulate with respect to the composition of Genesis break up what belongs together, impairing the reader's ability to grasp the whole. To the extent that the stories in Genesis have an etiological thrust,[28] aiming to explain what from the standpoint of the narrator has become present reality, the message of the first chapters of Genesis puts the "very good" of God (Gen. 1:31) and the "not good" of the serpent (Gen. 3:1) front and center of the account. Crucial to the account is its triangular character. It is not only a story of two parties, interested only in God and human beings. A third party is at work, intent on breaking the relationship between God and the human family. The consecration of the seventh day must not be seen in isolation from the reality of conflict that is central to the entire narrative, read as a whole.

God's "very good" will be contradicted in short order by the serpent's "not good," or, if the source critics have their way, the "not good" of the serpent is emphatically contradicted by the "very good" of God. Whichever way one looks at the story, the "very good"↔"not good" polarity lies at the center, submerging the lines of demarcation that have been sacred to scholars.

"God saw everything that he had made, and indeed, it was very good," we read in the story of Creation (Gen. 1:31). The seventh day follows, and its ideology is not in doubt (Gen. 2:1–3). Like the statement immediately preceding it, the seventh day builds on the conviction that the Creator is good and that God's goodness is reflected in every facet of the created order.

But this statement expresses only God's point of view. At this juncture, therefore, it is wise to pay heed to Pinchas Kahn, who sees the seventh day not only looking to the past but even more anticipating future disruption, already aware of the loss.[29] The "not good" of present reality needs to be explained even as the "very good" of God's creation is remembered, and it is already implied in the original field of vision. The opposing voice contests God's assessment, successfully making the case for the "not good" point of view (Gen. 3:1, 6). In fact, the "not good" of the serpent deconstructs the "very good" of God. It cannot be emphasized too strongly, therefore, that the "not good" of the serpent addresses what was originally, by God's judgment, "very good." If, on the one hand, the serpent's misrepresentation occasions the loss of what was by God's judgment "very good," the serpent, on the other hand, wins acceptance for the view that the created order was "not good" in the first place. Genesis thus makes the "very good not good" polarity the key to understanding present reality.

With this insight the seventh day moves beyond the "private" sphere between God and humans to become a "public" issue, too. The opposing voice in the Garden of Eden argues that God is lacking in precisely the virtues that the seventh day affirms. In the triangular drama of Genesis, contradictory and mutually exclusive options are thrown in the face of the first human beings and in the face of the present reader as well. In the context of the "very good not good" polarity, the seventh day belongs decisively in the "very good" point of view and is integral to this view. The text says that God "blessed the seventh day and hallowed it" (Gen. 2:3). This means that God is not secretive about the seventh day or tentative in making it a day of special significance. Blessing and hallowing the seventh day indicate intent: it connotes a proclamation, it sends a message, and it stakes out God's position in the cosmic drama that confronts the reader in the earliest chapters of Genesis. Again, within the "very good not good" polarity, the seventh day signals a commitment on God's part to make good on the "very good" point of view.

Once the decision to eat of the tree has been carried out, the dialogue between the woman and the serpent evolves into a *trialogue*, an exchange involving *three* parties. God addresses the serpent as a distinct, important, and primary character in the conflict. "I will put enmity between you and the woman, and between your offspring and hers; he will strike your head, and you will strike his heel," God declares (Gen. 3:15).[30] This statement does nothing if not to create the expectation that God will intervene in order to negate the serpent's point of view, and the centrality of this expectation is amply affirmed when we steal a glance at the New Testament. Echoing Genesis, Paul tells believers in Rome that "the God of peace will shortly crush Satan under your feet" (Rom. 16:20). Hebrews, in an echo of the same text, explains that Jesus shared in flesh and blood "so that through death he might destroy the one who has the power of death, that is, the devil" (Heb. 2:14). John, similarly transfixed by the account in Genesis, will not explain human sin apart from the role of Satan. In his view, too, "the Son of God was revealed for this purpose, to destroy the works of the devil" (1 John 3:8). And in Luke, in a statement that is best understood as yet another echo of Genesis, Jesus assures His disciples that they are rendered immune from demonic powers. "See, I have given you authority to tread on snakes and scorpions, and over all the power of the enemy; and nothing will hurt you" (Luke 10:19). All of this is further confirmation that the story in Genesis is hardly marginal

The opposing voice in the Garden of Eden argues that God is lacking in precisely the virtues that the seventh day affirms.

to the plot that is worked out in the Bible. The New Testament reading rises from the text by virtue of the content of the text and not by some interpretative sleight of hand. Indeed, the prospect that the relationship between God and humanity will be restored is found already in Genesis, and the restoration, as it must, is configured according to the parameters by which the relationship was broken.

Reading the first chapters of Genesis as a whole, we find that the seventh day is commissioned in a context within which God is misrepresented. The reality of conflict makes the seventh day more significant than if it is seen only in the context of tranquility, apart from the opposing voice. The serpent's charge lessens the likelihood that God will someday give up on the seventh day except at the risk of conceding that the means to defend God's reputation are not there. Keeping the seventh day, as believers are urged to do at various junctures in the biblical narrative (Exod. 20:8; 31:13–16; Deut. 5:12; Neh. 13:22), is from the beginning an ideological and theological commitment. The larger thing needing to be kept—indeed, the thing to be kept more than anything else—is whether the "very good" view that God has invested in the seventh day can be sustained (Gen. 1:31–2:3).

The triangular drama involving God, the serpent, and human beings ends on a stark note in Genesis. Human beings depart from God's presence (Gen. 3:22–24). Ahead lies a road of thorns and thistles, days with sweat trickling down furrowed and aging faces, and a yield that is disproportionate to the effort (Gen. 3:18–19). What awaits human beings at the end of the road matches human beginnings: "You are dust, and to dust you shall return" (Gen. 3:19). This is indeed a story of Paradise Lost.

But the journey also begins with the assurance that the travelers will not make the trip alone. We know this because the seventh day has etched God's presence into human reality. Exclusion from the Garden does not mean the absence of God. It is not an exaggeration to say that the seventh day, while not denying that human beings will return *to* dust, also holds out the hope that human beings will return *from* dust. If the orientation of the seventh day from the beginning oscillates between memory and hope, between the reality of Paradise Lost and the prospect of Paradise Regained, the oscillation of hope is stronger than the oscillation of memory. In its original configuration, the seventh day must be seen as promise as much as memorial. It forecasts that God's "very good" will be sustained, transforming the human experience into a journey of hope. Where the biblical narrative early on strikes the note of alienation and loss, the seventh day, commissioned and underwritten by God, speaks of God's commitment to make right what went wrong.

And yet, hopeful as this is, human redemption is not the whole story. The "not good" of the serpent, as noted, is not spoken from the point of view of present reality. According to the serpent, the terms of human existence were "not good" *before* the thorns and the thistles, in the absence of sweat and toil, and *before* the prospect that human life was cut short by death. In Genesis, it is in the context of the "very good" of God that the "‘not good" of the serpent is proposed, promoted, and believed (Gen. 3:1–6). How can this predicament be resolved, conceding that it will not be sufficient only to turn back the clock to a condition of no thorns and thistles, no disproportion between effort and yield, and no death, when precisely this is the state that was said to be "not good"?

Where the biblical narrative early on strikes the note of alienation and loss, the seventh day, commissioned and underwritten by God, speaks of God's commitment to make right what went wrong.

The Bible will tell a long story of how this is accomplished. According to Genesis, however, the bent of the story is from the very beginning suggested by the seventh day. The face of the seventh day is turned toward the future—toward redemption; and redemption, like the seventh day, will bring a revelation.

ENDNOTES

1. It does not lessen the importance of Isaiah's vision to note that it is a rarity in the Old Testament, as Otto Kaiser (*Isaiah 1–12,* trans. John Bowden, 2nd ed. [London: SCM Press, 1983], 259) quite correctly points out. What is more important is the fact of the vision itself and its subsequent impact. In fact, Kaiser (*Isaiah 1–12,* 260) captures the wonderful understatement in the text, writing that "if the suckling and little child play with the most poisonous snakes, the old enmity between the seed of the woman and the seed of the snake has been removed (Gen. 3.15). Thus the text probably says less than it knows."

2. The brief temptation account in Mark is particularly telling. Mark says of Jesus that "he was with the wild beasts" (Mark 1:13). This statement echoes the lost original state. Joel Marcus (*Mark 1–8* [AB, New York: Doubleday, 2000], 168) notes that the statement in Mark "has the sense of close, friendly association..., and in the OT and later Jewish writings the enmity between human beings and wild animals is regarded as a distortion of the original harmony that existed between them in Eden. In the eschaton, that enmity will be reversed (see Isa 11:6–9) and God will make for humanity a new covenant with the wild animals, so that people may live in peace with them once more (Hosea 2:18). Mark apparently believes that this restoration has now happened in Jesus, the new Adam."

3. See my own "'The Father of Lies,' 'the Mother of Lies,' and the Death of Jesus (John 12:20–33)," in *The Gospel of John and Christian Theology,* ed. Richard J. Bauckham and Carl Mosser (Grand Rapids: Eerdmans, 2008), 193–208.

4. Austin Farrer, *The Revelation of St. John the Divine* (Oxford: Clarendon Press, 1964), 4.

5. Richard Bauckham, *The Climax of Prophecy: Studies in the Book of Revelation* (Edinburgh: T. & T. Clark, 1993), xi.

6. Walter Brueggemann, *Genesis* (Interpretation; Atlanta: John Knox Press, 1982), 41.

7. Ibid.

8. Ibid.

9. Ibid.

10. Ibid., 42.

11. Alan J. Hauser, "Gen. 2–3: The Theme of Intimacy and Alienation," in *Art and Meaning: Rhetoric in Biblical Literature,* ed. D. J. A. Clines, D. M. Gunn, and A. J. Hauser (JSOT Sup 10; Sheffield: JSOT Press, 1992), 20–36.

12. Julian Morgenstern ("The Mythological Background of Psalm 82," *HUCA* 14 [1939]: 29–126) demonstrates how the story of a cosmic rebellion is reflected in Psalm 82 and a number of other Old Testament passages.

13. Levenson, *Creation and the Persistence of Evil,* 136.

14. *Contra Celsum* 6.42. The reference is to the translation by Henry Chadwick (Cambridge: Cambridge University Press, 1965).

15. *Contra Celsum* 6.42.

16. Ibid.

17. For a fuller discussion of Celsus's criticism of the Christian belief in an opposing power and Origen's circumspect rebuttal, see my essay, "Theodicy and the Theme of Cosmic Conflict in the Early Church," *AUSS* 42 (2004): 169–202.

18. To Westermann (*Genesis 1–11,* 237–238), following Vriezen, other options for the identity of the serpent are human curiosity, a mythological being belonging to chaos, a clever animal, or a being belonging to the realm of magic. He rejects the notion that the serpent is Satan in disguise.

19. *Contra Celsum* 6.42.

20. Westermann, *Genesis 1–11,* 238.

21. Leon Kass, "Temptation," in Bill Moyers, ed., *Genesis: A Living Conversation* (New York: Doubleday, 1996), 46.

22. R. W. L. Moberly, "Did the Serpent Get It Right?" *JTS* 39 (1988): 6.

23. Ibid.

24. Ibid.

25. Ibid., 7.

26. Dietrich Bonhoeffer, *Creation and Fall: A Theological Interpretation of Genesis 1–3,* trans. John C. Fletcher (London: SCM Press, 1959), 70.

27. Ibid., 71.

28. von Rad, *Genesis,* 17. The notion that the stories in Genesis are meant to serve the interest of the Israelite cult, as argued by von Rad, is not tenable.

29. Kahn, "The Expanding Perspectives of the Sabbath," 243.

30. Driver (*Genesis, 48*) notes that Genesis 3:15 has long been known as the *Protevangelium,* the first promise of a coming Rectifier, a view that is not in favor among many modern interpreters of the Old Testament. R. A. Martin ("The Earliest Messianic Interpretation of Genesis 3:15," *JBL* 84 [1965]: 425–427) shows that the Messianic interpretation was in vogue as early as the third and second centuries BCE. What is more important is that the leading antagonists in Genesis are defined more and more distinctly, in equal measure, as the biblical narrative unfolds.

CHAPTER 4

IMITATION OF GOD

Abraham obeyed my voice and kept my charge, my commandments, my statutes, and my laws.
Genesis 26:5

There is only one text dealing explicitly with the seventh day in the first book of the Bible (Gen. 2:1–3). The rest of Genesis tells briefly of the departure of Adam and Eve from the Garden of Eden (ch. 3), the murder of Abel by his brother Cain (ch. 4), and then the story of the flood and its aftermath (chs. 6–11), but most of the book is devoted to relating the call and wanderings of Abraham, Isaac, and Jacob, the founding ancestors of Israel (chs. 12–50). Aside from its conspicuous position at the time of Creation, no other overt mention is made of the seventh day in these narratives. But there are intriguing clues. Abraham, for instance, is commended in a way that has implications about the seventh day: "Abraham obeyed my voice and kept my charge, my commandments, my statutes, and my laws" (Gen. 26:5). In this chapter, I propose to decode these clues. Our challenge is to become aware of the features that are implicit rather than explicit in the Abraham story and to see him as a person who profoundly imitated God.

DECODING THE CLUES

Until we hear God say of Abraham that he "obeyed my voice and kept my charge, my commandments, my statutes, and my laws" (Gen. 26:5), little has been said to prepare us for an evaluation of a person's life in these terms. We are unprepared for this assessment because the behavior is evaluated before it is prescribed. Granting that Abraham did obey God's "commandments and laws," he appears to have done so *before* these commandments have been spelled out in any length.[1] We get the impression that Abraham obeyed before he was told to do so, so to speak. Better yet, Abraham shows an appreciation for God's ways that may be described as a person finding himself in wholehearted agreement with God more than as one obeying God.

Christian interpreters of the Old Testament have always been quite unanimous in believing that the moral norms of the Bible were known prior to their solemn proclamation during the time of Moses.

The concept of *natural law* was important in the reasoning of the Protestant reformers. It was also important to Thomas Aquinas (1225–74), who, in turn, was indebted to the Greek philosopher Aristotle (384–322 BCE). *Natural law* refers to the broad areas of common ground in people's ideas of right and wrong. Martin Luther, for one, writes concerning the Ten Commandments that

> it is natural to honor God, not steal, not commit adultery, not bear false witness, not murder; and what Moses commands is nothing new. For what God has given the Jews from heaven, he has also written in the hearts of all men. Thus I keep the commandments which Moses has given, not because Moses gave the commandment, but because they have been implanted in me by nature, and Moses agrees exactly with nature, etc.[2]

Imagine this! According to Luther, there is a need for God, for a lawgiver, but there is no need for Moses because the norms of God are knowable through other venues. Luther's comment bears repeating: "what Moses commands is nothing new."[3] Long before God's finger inscribes the commandments on tables of stone, they are engraved on nature, even on the innate moral constitution of human beings, "written in the hearts of all men."[4] The proclamation of the Ten Commandments at the time of Moses is no great novelty because "Moses agrees exactly with nature."[5]

By the time Luther returns to the subject nearly twenty years after the statement noted above (1543), his anti-Jewish sentiments have become more pronounced. However, while the rhetoric is ratcheted up several notches, the position on natural law sounds the same note.

> For perhaps the Jews will also call the Ten Commandments the law of Moses, since they were given on Mount Sinai in the presence of none but the Jews or the children of Abraham, etc. You must reply: If the Ten Commandments are to be regarded as Moses's law, then Moses came far too late, and he also addressed himself to far too few people, because the Ten Commandments had spread over the whole world not only before Moses but before Abraham

> and all the patriarchs. For even if Moses had never appeared and Abraham had never been born, the Ten Commandments would have had to rule in all men from the very beginning, as they indeed did and still do.[6]

Luther's appeal to natural law is not without its problems, as we shall see later, but his conviction that knowledge of God's will does not begin with Moses or Israel is supported by the weight of evidence. Standards exist even if they have not been formally articulated. In the narrative about Cain's murder of Abel we do not doubt that murder is wrong, despite the lack of any explicit prior commandment against murder (Gen. 4:6–7). Sometime later it is said about people in Noah's time that "the LORD saw that the wickedness of humankind was great in the earth, and that every inclination of the thoughts of their hearts was only evil continually" (Gen. 6:5). Such a statement has no meaning unless we can take for granted that the distinction between good and evil is clear-cut and knowable. Nevertheless, the Bible has yet to break this down to particulars.

> ***Long before God's finger inscribes the commandments on tables of stone, they are engraved on nature, even on the innate moral constitution of human beings.***

If anyone asks which commandments Abraham is said to have obeyed, we have to admit that we do not really know. Judging from the fourfold description in Genesis, we should expect a rather comprehensive list. For instance, since observation of the seventh day is stated explicitly at a later point as one of the Ten Commandments (Exod. 20:8–11), it is not unlikely that the Sabbath was one of the items on the yet unwritten list. But our assumptions about this can only be tentative.

The record of Abraham's life in Genesis and the instances of God communicating with him are not best described as "commandments" or "statutes." Abraham is *called* to leave his ancestral home for an unknown destination (Gen. 12:1), and his obedience on that occasion cannot be said to be in response to a codified law. Late in life he is told to offer his dearly beloved son in sacrifice (Gen. 22:1–2),[7] but this, too, has little to do with someone wishing to conform to a God-given "law" that has universal validity.[8] The early summons to "go forth" and the late call to sacrifice Isaac are so exceptional and situational that it is pointless to turn them into an ethical generalization or codified norm.[9]

PAYING ATTENTION TO SILENCE

If we wish to trace the seventh day from Creation to the time of Abraham, we must take a step further, seeking out the unspoken ideals and implied assumptions in the biblical narrative. Commands are rare exceptions in the case of Abraham. When they do occur, they often do not conform to accepted notions of ethical norms. To the person who demands that the commandments be written on tablets of stone with God's own finger before he or she feels certain what God's will might be, Abraham remains an enigma. Yet it is Abraham who takes precedence throughout Scripture more than Moses, and it is the response of insight and trust implied in Abraham's life that is hailed as the ideal in the Bible (Rom. 4:1ff; Gal. 3:6ff). On the one hand, then, lack of explicit mention of the seventh day in connection with Abraham should not be read as proof that the Sabbath has yet to be revealed. On the other hand, leaving Abraham out of the picture in the chronicle of the seventh day leaves an important part out of the picture.

At this stage we are expected to recognize that Israel's religion begins with Abraham rather than with Moses.[10] When God calls Moses in Egypt, God is "the God of your father, the God of Abraham, the God of Isaac, and the God of Jacob" (Exod. 3:6), and God's appearance in the story is cast in terms of an obligation to the prior promise to Abraham (Exod. 3:15; 6:5). Moses's role belongs in the context of resumption and restoration, not as a beginning without antecedents. "Nowhere do we find the designation of God as the God of Moses," says Segal, and the revelation at Sinai does not proclaim to

Moses "a new and hitherto unknown God, or even a new conception with a new name of God."[11]

Moreover, in the story of Abraham the narratival aspects vastly outweigh what might be called prescriptive or legislative elements. Abraham's life unfolds in a compelling interaction and dialogue with God. Readers of these narratives confront the necessity of attuning their ears to the meaning of silence. The best-known story from Abraham's life is so striking in this respect that it is the lead example in Erich Auerbach's *Mimesis*, an exceptional book exploring how literature to varying degrees is true to life.[12] Even though Auerbach was a literary expert and not a biblical scholar, he finds a telling contrast between the Greek poet Homer and the *Akedah*, the story of Abraham's binding of Isaac in Genesis (Gen. 22:1–18).

Lack of explicit mention of the seventh day in connection with Abraham should not be read as proof that the Sabbath has yet to be revealed.

On the surface a comparison of these two pieces of ancient literature seems to favor the Greek poet by a wide margin. Homer's work is much more elaborate and polished, rich in vocabulary and highly developed in syntax, laying out scenes and people in exquisite and captivating detail. But the first impression of sophistication and superiority is misleading. According to Auerbach, even though "the intellectual, linguistic, and above all syntactical culture appears to be so much more highly developed," the Greek writings "are yet comparatively simple in their picture of human beings; and no less so in their relation to the real life which they describe in general."[13] The story of Abraham's sacrifice of Isaac, while outwardly much more coarse and unpolished, is on closer inspection a much more profound and lifelike description. And it is more profound precisely because of what it does *not* say.

Where Homer strives to bring every thought and feeling out into the open, and where his characters are fully exposed in the dimension of the present, the biblical story has perspective and depth of field that is unattainable and unimagined in the Greek epic. In the moments of silence, the large unfilled spaces in the biblical narrative, the author leaves room for the inner life of his characters to emerge. Auerbach writes that

> the two styles, in their opposition, represent basic types: on the one hand fully externalized description, uniform illumination, uninterrupted connection, free expression, all events in the foreground, displaying unmistakable meanings, few elements of historical development and of psychological perspective; on the other hand, certain parts brought into high relief, others left obscure, abruptness, suggestive influence of the unexpressed, "background" quality, multiplicity of meanings and the need for interpretation, universal-historical claims, development of the concept of the historically becoming, and preoccupation with the problematic.[14]

This observation is especially striking in the stories about Abraham. In these accounts there are implied assumptions, unexpressed thoughts, and the need for interpretation; the text invites the reader to participate and unearth what lies under the surface. The stories demand reader participation, says Tamarkin Reis.[15] The author "rarely tells us what anyone feels or thinks; we must intuit that."[16] Arguments from silence can lead to unprovable assumptions, but failure to explore what is left unsaid is far more risky because it means that the historical and narratival aspects, the continuity of the divine purpose, and the psychological depth of the characters that the text seeks to elicit, are eclipsed. While a Homeric reading of biblical texts is often hailed as the ideal of biblical interpretation, requiring the interpreter to see nothing in the text that is not explicitly stated, this approach fails because biblical texts are not Homeric texts, that is, texts that expose everything neatly on the surface.

Abraham is the biblical character who models the true response to God's ways and ideals, and a number of specifics demonstrate that this point goes beyond literary subtlety. The legacy of Abraham is that of God's friend, and the writers of the Bible seem preoccupied by this designation.[17] The writer of Israel's chronicles speaks of the ancient promise as a gift "to the descendants of your friend Abraham" (2 Chron. 20:7). According to the prophet Isaiah the nation of Israel is "the offspring of Abraham, my friend" (Isa. 41:8). Even a New Testament writer remembers that Abraham "was called the friend of God" (James 2:23).[18]

Most likely the description derives from Abraham's exchange with a heavenly visitor in connection with the cities of Sodom and Gomorrah, described as "one of the most extraordinary stories in the ancestral history, and indeed in the Bible as a whole."[19] As the visitors are about to resume their trip to the ill-fated cities, the leader says rhetorically to himself, "Shall I hide from Abraham what I am about to do?" The answer in the mental dialogue implies the wish or obligation on God's part to keep Abraham informed. "No," the story continues, indicating that God will indeed let Abraham in on what lies ahead, "for I have chosen him…" (Gen. 18:17–19).

"I have chosen him" is the wording of many reputable translations (NASB, NIV, RSV, NRSV) even though there is no reason to eschew the more literal rendering of the text, "I have known him" (NKJV), or even, and still better, "for I know him" (KJV). The connotation of the mutuality and intimacy that is thus implied warrants the reading, "I have known him as a friend."[20] The sensational conversation, justifiably designated as "monumental,"[21] is a two-way communication where both participants are listening, both have something to say, and both take away something from the dialogue. We also get the impression that few people after Abraham aspired to such a relationship with God or even thought it possible. On this occasion, however, we see a meeting of minds between God, who wants Abraham to understand,[22] and Abraham, who is seeking understanding.[23]

It is no wonder, therefore, that Paul and James in the New Testament each look to Abraham as the ideal for believers. Pride of place in the revelation of God's character goes to the delicate and intuitive aspects of Abraham's insight, not to the loud thunder and unambiguous affirmations that come centuries later with the Israelite exodus from Egypt. But this does not mean that Paul is unconcerned about the moral standards proclaimed later. Even a casual reading of Paul's own list of what to do and what not to do shows a great deal of overlapping with the Ten Commandments. Paul, however, for reasons we will explore later (ch. 13), is reluctant to get his ideals from the legislated code. He claims instead that "the works of the flesh are *obvious*" before proceeding to his own list of vices (Gal. 5:19–21). In Paul's view, the values sought in the lives of Christians are "the fruit of the Spirit" (Gal. 5:22), not the product of attempts to conform to laws.

The lack of explicit antecedents to the characterization that Abraham obeyed God's commandments and laws (Gen. 26:5) does not mean that God's will had not yet been disclosed. Whether the subject is the Sabbath or any other commandment, silence implies that there is no need to say anything because the person already grasps the unspoken ideal. A law does not become more binding when it is most detailed and explicit. The opposite could be the case, that is, an ideal has a stronger hold on people when there is no need to mention it. Perhaps "law" has achieved its purpose best when a person conducts his or her life in a spiritual way without being asked to do so. Genesis portrays Abraham as just such a person: a human being who modeled trust in God to such an extent that Paul could call him "the father of all of us" (Rom. 4:16).[24]

Just because the seventh day seems to drop out of sight in Genesis, we should not conclude that it had not yet come into being or that it was no longer there any more than we should assume that the sun has ceased to exist when it lies below the horizon. As far as the human story goes in the Bible, there is no point in time before which the seventh day had not been established. When it reappears in Exodus in connection with Israel's deliverance from Egypt, the texts describing its revival (Exod. 16:1–31; 20:8–11) do not speak of something new but of something that is already there.

Segal points out that "the whole story of the creation of the world in six days in Genesis chapter 1, of which the account of the rest day forms an integral and inseparable part, belong to the patriarchal age, and more explicitly to Abraham himself."[25] Sarna, too, affirms the antiquity of the seventh day, noting specifically that the Sabbath "is assumed to be already established" before the revelation at Sinai. [26] Martin Buber is similarly convinced that the Sabbath "is not introduced for the first time on Sinai, it is there already; the believers are only ordered to 'remember.' However, it is not introduced for the first time even in the wilderness of Sin, where the manna is found. Here, too, it is proclaimed as something which is already in existence."[27] R. W. L. Moberly points to additional evidence for the rabbinic tradition that Abraham "observed *tôrâ* before it was revealed to Moses";[28] indeed, this theme is extensively developed so as to make it understood that "Abraham supremely exemplifies the meaning of living by torah."[29] In the rabbinic perspective it is a matter of course that Abraham's exemplification of the Torah includes the seventh day.

Just because the seventh day seems to drop out of sight in Genesis, we should not conclude that it had not yet come into being or that it was no longer there any more than we should assume that the sun has ceased to exist when it lies below the horizon.

IMITATIO DEI

Against this background we should be reluctant to accept the notion that the seventh day, after its spectacular introduction in the story of Creation, falls on hard times and vanishes from view. What we have seen concerning the meaning of silence in the biblical story suggests quite the opposite, providing warrant for the stupendous claims that are grounded in the figure of Abraham in the New Testament.

A few of these statements deserve a review before moving on. In the Gospel of John, in the course of a heated exchange between Jesus and His Jewish opponents, Jesus asserts that "your ancestor Abraham rejoiced that he would see my day; *he saw it and was glad*" (John 8:56). Where the Jews claim a proud spiritual ancestry anchored in Abraham, invoking this ancestry in order to justify their disdain of Jesus, Jesus makes the exact opposite case. In His contrary version, it is precisely the trust and confidence of Abraham that leads to Jesus. Indeed, Jesus sees Abraham as a prophet whose preoccupation is the day of Jesus, a man who longs to see God's purpose revealed and who does see it in a searing but ultimately gratifying manner.[30] If Jesus's Jewish opponents had demanded to see the chapter and verse upon which Jesus based His claim, they would be convinced only if they were willing to follow Jesus's lead, reading in Abraham's story things that are not explicit in the text.

The New Testament portrays Abraham as one who has internalized the human situation, keenly aware of what is lost and oriented to regaining it (Heb. 11:9–10). Abraham is the most towering witness in Scripture to God's reliability, a man utterly convinced of God's constancy and faithfulness. In the compelling mosaic of his character, his life is focused on God's definitive purpose. The New Testament sees him as a man looking forward "to the city that has foundations, whose architect and builder is God" (Heb. 11:10). The faith for which he is known is predicated on God's faithfulness, trusting that Sarah will have a son when she is too old for conception "because he considered him faithful who had promised" (Heb. 11:11). God's faithfulness remains central even when the author of Hebrews discusses Abraham's willingness to offer up Isaac. In the New Testament perception, Abraham is willing to trust that "God is able even to raise someone from the dead" (Heb. 11:19). If Abraham is faithful to God's command, he is—even on this occasion—responding to One whose commands are not unreasonable and who faithfully keeps what is promised. "Abraham believed in God's faithfulness and confirmed it, as it were, by 'acknowledging' it," writes Rolf Rendtorff, summing up the Abraham narrative in the context of Genesis.[31]

Abraham's trust in God's faithfulness makes him the great model in Paul's correspondence. When Paul attempts to sound the depths of God's love, he can do no better than to recall Abraham's sacrifice of Isaac. The binding of Isaac in Genesis, the *Akedah*, opens the door to understanding the death of Jesus. As the father's agony subsides in Genesis, he receives the commendation, "[b]ecause you have done this, and have not withheld your son… by your offspring shall all the nations of the earth gain blessing" (Gen. 22:16, 18). This sentence takes the measure of his sacrifice and self-giving, bringing to light that the binding of Isaac was a greater trauma to the one binding him than to the one being bound. It is impossible not to hear the echo in Romans, now put forward as a testimony to God's self-giving love: "He who did not withhold his own Son, but gave him up for all of us, will he not with him also give us everything else?" (Rom. 8:32). Here the greatest enigma in the Old Testament is harnessed to serve as the strongest evidence for God's reliability and the ultimate proof of God's self-giving.

Abraham is the most towering witness in Scripture to God's reliability, a man utterly convinced of God's constancy and faithfulness.

In the Aramaic Targum, the earliest running commentary on the Old Testament, the commentator is so impressed by the story of Abraham's sacrifice that he makes Abraham an example for God to imitate. Abraham does not demur at the divine command. Instead, says the Targum, "he suppressed his impulse and asked God to do likewise."[32] On this logic Abraham sets the standard, obligating God to follow in his steps. On this logic, too, Abraham is rewarded at last when Jesus intervenes to redeem Abraham's children.[33]

This view, tantalizing though it be, nevertheless falls short of the New Testament view. It is more accurate to see Abraham prophetically imitating God, enacting in comprehensible human terms God's incomprehensible self-giving. Abraham is enabled to do this because he knows God and has become God's intimate (Gen. 18:16–33). While Abraham gives up his son, he is also a person who gives himself up—as does God in the gift of God's Son. But this disclosure cannot be codified in any meaningful sense; it can only be conveyed in action and narrative, lived out in flesh and blood. It shatters the framework of commandments and laws, and it cannot be engraved on stone.

In Abraham we see a person who understands and responds to God's faithfulness. In the forefront of his faith lies the conviction that God is faithful. Stated in the negative, God is not capricious like the gods of the gentiles, and God's commandments are not unreasonable. Contemporary readings of Abraham in the New Testament are gradually rediscovering the emphasis on God's faithfulness, seeing Abraham's faith as secondary to the Person in whom faith is placed.[34] For Abraham the qualities of the object of his faith, God, matter more than his faith. When he, too, is faithful, he is acting as the supreme imitator of God's faithfulness. Ultimately, Abraham's sacrifice of Isaac, as the rest of his life, is best understood as *imitatio Dei,* an imitation of the faithful God in whom he places his trust.

Given this background, it must be concluded that the omission of the seventh day in connection with Abraham does not mean its absence. Because the Creation account "overtly and covertly...points to the seventh day as the clue to the meaning of creation,"[35] we should rather expect to see God's changeless purpose understood, embraced, and appreciated in Abraham's life. In the single mention of the seventh day in Genesis, the text "depicts the deity as himself observing the commandments to cease from labor on the seventh day and to make it sacred."[36] What God does comes first. This, as Levenson suggests, makes the observance of the Sabbath "a matter of *imitatio Dei.*"[37]

But *imitatio Dei*, imitating God with understanding and devotion, is precisely the essence of Abraham's life. He is stirred by God's example, and his appreciation for God's ways shapes his life. The norm according to which his life unfolds is an example observed more than a response to a commandment spoken. As for the seventh day, it is introduced in Genesis as God's own deed (Gen. 2:1–3). When it comes up again, it is with explicit reference to what God did at the beginning, beckoning the believer to imitate God and to experience God's presence in the present (Exod. 20:11; 31:17; Deut. 5:15). Moreover, when the Jewish people are called upon to be stewards of the seventh day, the Sabbath is not introduced as something new and unknown.

The seventh day prevails on the more compelling strength of God's example.

And then there is Abraham, "the friend of God" (James 2:23) and "the father of us all" (Rom. 4:16), the paradigmatic imitator of God. Awakened to the reality of God's faithfulness, he responds, and by his own life of faithfulness he draws attention to God's trustworthiness. Abraham, the verdict goes, "obeyed my voice and kept my charge, my commandments, my statutes, and my laws" (Gen. 26:5). Although the seventh day is not mentioned, it does not mean that it has disappeared, or that it has yet to appear. Still more important, the leading promoter of the seventh day is not Moses, or Abraham, or even Adam. The seventh day prevails on the more compelling strength of God's example, a sign of the faithfulness of the God of whom Abraham's life is a reflection.

For the one who waits for the explicit command in order to drive home the importance of the seventh day, however, there is no cause for worry. The commandment is bound to come.

ENDNOTES

1. This is one of many places to which scholars will point as examples of later redactional insertions. It is my argument here not only that such a conclusion is unwarranted but that it misses the point of Abraham's life and example as it is discussed later in the Bible.

2. Martin Luther, "How Christians Should Regard Moses," in *Luther's Works* 35, ed. Helmut T. Lehman, trans. E. Theodore Bachmann (Philadelphia: Muhlenberg Press, 1960), 168.

3. Ibid., 68.

4. Ibid.

5. Ibid.

6. Martin Luther, "Against the Sabbatarians," in *Luther's Works* 47, ed. Helmut T. Lehman, trans. Martin H. Bertram (Philadelphia: Fortress Press, 1971), 89.

7. A captive to the story of Abraham's sacrifice of Isaac, the Danish philosopher and theologian Søren Kierkegaard (1813–55) uses it with devastating effect in order to demolish the neatly rational systems of Immanuel Kant (1724–1804) and especially G. W. F. Hegel (1770–1831). Where the latter extols the general over the individual, Kierkegaard finds in the story of Abraham the priority of the individual, and, indeed, "the teleological suspension of the ethical" ("the purposive suspension of the ethical"), a construal that defies any generally available understanding of right and wrong and a stance that can only be understood in starkly relational terms. Kierkegaard's poignant and immensely influential treatment of this story is highly pertinent in the present context; cf. *Frygt og Bæven. Dialektisk Lyrikk* (Kjøbenhavn: C. A. Reitzel, 1843; repr. Søren Kierkegaards Skrifter 4, København: Gads Forlag, 1997); English trans. *Fear and Trembling: A Dialectical Lyric,* trans. Walter Lowrie (Princeton: Princeton University Press, 1941).

8. Cf. Omri Boehm, "The Binding of Isaac: An Inner-Biblical Polemic on the Question of 'Disobeying' a Manifestly Illegal Order," *VT* 52 (2002): 1–12.

9. Sarna (*Genesis*, 150) demonstrates the striking similarity and particularity between the initial and the final call of Abraham.

10. Segal, "The Religion of Israel before Sinai," 41–68.

11. Ibid., 41–42.

12. Erich Auerbach, *Mimesis: The Representation of Reality in Western Literature,* trans. Willard R. Trask (Princeton: Princeton University Press, 1953).

13. Ibid., 13.

14. Ibid., 23.

15. Tamarkin Reis, *Reading the Lines*, 10.

16. Ibid.

17. Bernhard W. Anderson, "Abraham, the Friend of God," *Int* 42 (1988): 353–366.

18. Cf. William Baird, "Abraham in the New Testament: Tradition and the New Identity," *Int* 42 (1988): 367–379.

19. Anderson, "Abraham, the Friend of God," 362.

20. von Rad (*Genesis*, 205) has "I have made him acquainted with me." See also Anderson, "Abraham," 363.

21. Mordecai Roshwald, "A Dialogue Between Man and God," *SJT* 42 (1989): 145.

22. Nathan MacDonald ("Listening to Abraham—Listening to Yhwh: Divine Justice and Mercy in Genesis 18:16–33," *CBQ* 66 [2004]: 25–43) unearths subtleties in the text that show God to be leading Abraham to a deeper understanding of God's mercy rather than the other way around.

23. Anderson, "Abraham," 363.

24. The "fatherhood" of Abraham is in Paul's argument spiritual and not physical, as noted by Richard B. Hays, "'Have We Found Abraham to Be Our Forefather According to the Flesh?' A Reconsideration of Rom. 4:1," *NovT* 27 (1985): 76–78.

25. Segal, "Israel before Sinai," 60.

26. Nahum M. Sarna, *Understanding Genesis: The Heritage of Biblical Israel* (New York: Schocken Books, 1966), 19.

27. Martin Buber, *Moses: The Revelation and the Covenant* (Atlantic Highlands, NJ: Humanities Press International, 1988; first published 1946), 80.

28. R. W. L. Moberly, "The Earliest Commentary on the Akedah," *VT* 38 (1988): 305, n. 16.

29. Ibid., 305.

30. Baird, "Abraham in the New Testament," 370–371.

31. Rendtorff, *The Canonical Hebrew Bible*, 27.

32. John Bowker, *The Targums and Rabbinic Literature: An Introduction to Jewish Interpretation of Scripture* (Cambridge: Cambridge University Press, 1969). In the Targum of Pseudo-Jonathan, Abraham prays that "when the descendants of Isaac, my son, shall come to the hour of distress, you may remember them, and answer them, and deliver them; and that all generations to come may say, 'In this mountain Abraham bound Isaac, his son, and there the Shekina *of the Lord* was revealed to him'" (pp. 225–226). According to a Fragmentary Targum, Abraham prays that "when the offspring of Isaac my son shall come to the hour of distress you may remember for their good the binding of Isaac their father, and absolve and forgive their transgressions, and rescue them from every trouble..." (p. 227).

33. Nils Alstrup Dahl, "The Atonement: An Adequate Reward for the Akedah?" in *Neotestamentica et Semitica: Studies in Honour of Matthew Black*, ed. E. Earle and Max Wilcox (Edinburgh: T. & T. Clark, 1969), 15–29.

34. Cf. Stanley Stowers, *A Rereading of Romans: Justice, Jews, and Gentiles* (New Haven: Yale University Press, 1994), 228. A. Katherine Grieb (*The Story of Romans: A Narrative Defense of God's Righteousness* [Louisville: Westminster John Knox Press, 2000], 52) puts God's faithfulness in the foreground of Paul's understanding of Abraham, arguing that "God's reliability and trustworthiness are known" because of real and observable facts.

35. Levenson, *Creation and the Persistence of Evil*, 100.

36. Ibid., 109.

37. Ibid.

CHAPTER 5

THE SEVENTH DAY AND FREEDOM

You have seen what I did to the Egyptians, and how I bore you on eagles' wings and brought you to myself.
Exodus 19:4

Out of Egypt they came, a nation of slaves, whipped into submission by the taskmasters of Pharaoh. In a well-organized mass exodus the Israelites walk apprehensively past the pyramids and the sphinx.[1] Moses leads the way. After centuries of oppression and suffering they are going to their promised land, free at last.

This is the shorthand version of the well-known story in Exodus. What is less well known is the discovery that God seeks the people's freedom more than they are seeking it themselves. Still less known and harder to grasp is the priority of the seventh day in God's freedom project and the discovery that freedom poses an unexpected challenge for the people to whom it is offered.

SEEKING THEIR FREEDOM

In the Book of Exodus, where the story of Israel's deliverance from Egypt is told, the setting is quite different from Genesis. The serenity of Creation has long since receded from view, yielding ground to the thorns and thistles and the struggle for subsistence that were predicted to be the consequence of distrusting God (Gen. 3:17–18). In Exodus the causes for human sorrow have multiplied. Where the first two chapters of the Bible strike the reader as a world too good to be true, the rest of the Bible is set in the familiar territory of the human condition as it is known today.

As the story is told toward the end of the book of Genesis, the descendants of Abraham immigrate to Egypt during a drought (Gen. 47:4). Initially they are well received, but after two or three generations the host country turns hostile (Exod. 1:8; 6:6–20). The Israelites, as Abraham's descendants will be called, lose their privileges, become marginalized, and are eventually enslaved in the most cruel of ways (Exod. 1:11).

One of the most distressing aspects of the new situation is that the opportunity to worship God is severely restricted. Exodus begins by describing a people in deep distress, yearning for liberty and yet powerless to secure it (Exod. 1:13–14; 2:23). At a critical point the exiled Moses is called to lead the Israelites to a fresh beginning in a new country (Exod. 3:1–17). Pharaoh, however, spares no effort to subvert God's call to "let my people go" (Exod. 6:1–12:33). Against the foot-dragging of the Egyptian leader, God's call to "let my people go" is heard insistently, again and again throughout the story (Exod. 5:1; 7:16; 8:1, 20; 9:1, 13; 10:3–4). Although it is often overlooked, the divinely ordained project has a spiritual aspiration because, in almost every instance when Moses informs Pharaoh of God's determination to "let my people go," he also says "so that they may worship me" (Exod. 7:16; 8:1, 20; 9:1, 13; 10:3; cf. 5:1). Ultimately, God's purpose to set the people free will not be thwarted. Moses prevails despite the machinations of the Egyptian leader (Exod. 12:31–33). The timing, too, is exquisite because the liberation of the Israelites is clearly meant to coincide with the fulfillment of God's prior promise to Abraham (Exod. 12:40–41; Gen. 15:13).

THE PRIORITY OF THE SEVENTH DAY

What is most remarkable is that the first taste of freedom for the Israelites includes a spectacular renaissance of, and re-acquaintance with, the seventh day (Exod. 16:1–36). The exodus from Egypt is a stupendous new beginning that comes, just as in Genesis, with a mandate for the seventh day.

It cannot be too strongly emphasized that the Sabbath is already established; it is not invented at Sinai.[2] Buber points out that the Sabbath "is not introduced for the first time on Sinai, it is there already; the believers are only ordered to 'remember.'"[3] Still more to the point, he notes that the Sabbath "is not introduced for the first time even in the wilderness of Sin, where the manna is found. Here, too, it is proclaimed as something which is already in existence."[4]

The seventh day stands out boldly in the Genesis account of Creation. When the biblical narrative returns to the subject in Exodus, the Sabbath retains the same prominent place in the divine program as at Creation, that is, the status of "first encounter." The seventh day is part of the program of freedom; indeed, it marks the first encounter with freedom in a carefully staged exercise.

Continuity with the prior biblical narrative is striking. God's initiative on behalf of the oppressed Israelites is not featured as though God initiates something new, but because God remembers. The Bible says that the people's "cry for help rose up to God" (Exod. 2:23). In a poignant statement it adds that "God heard their groaning, and *God remembered* his covenant with Abraham, Isaac, and Jacob" (Exod. 2:24). Indeed, "God looked upon the Israelites, and God took notice[5] of them" (Exod. 2:25). Thus, the entire narrative unfolds on the scaffolding of the narrative of Abraham.

It cannot be too strongly emphasized that the Sabbath is already established; it is not invented at Sinai.

As the Israelites journey on foot through the Sinai desert en route to the Promised Land, food is miraculously provided day by day (Exod. 16:14, 31). The name given to the food highlights its novelty, *mān hū* in Hebrew, translated "What is it?" in English (Exod. 16:15, 31).[6] In fact, the Israelites called it "What is it?" bread, learning with time that they could depend upon it and that God was teaching them to trust in God, not Pharaoh.[7]

Following God's instructions, the people went out to collect food for each day's use immediately after sunrise. But they soon learned that the expected relationship between effort and result was strangely attenuated. To their surprise "those who gathered much had nothing over, and those who gathered little had no shortage; they gathered as much as each of them needed" (Exod. 16:18).

Moreover, it was carefully pointed out that the manna should be collected each day for that day only. "Let no man leave any of it till the morning," Moses instructs them (Exod. 16:19). Some, however, did not listen to Moses. They saved the leftovers for the next day. But the manna did not store well. By the next morning "it bred worms and became foul" (Exod. 16:20).

This pattern continued for five days. On the sixth day, however, instructions suddenly changed. The people were notified to gather *twice* the amount for the next day. In fact, according to the timeline implicit in Exodus, practice with respect to the amount of manna that is gathered on the sixth day actually precedes explanation of what will become of the extra manna. "On the sixth day they gathered twice as much food, two omers apiece" (Exod. 16:22). When the leaders report this to Moses, he tells them "tomorrow is a day of solemn rest, a holy sabbath to the LORD" (Exod. 16:23). "Six days you shall gather it; but on the seventh day, which is a sabbath, there will be none" (Exod. 16:26).

What will happen then? Will they go hungry? Will the manna spoil as it did on the other days? The break-up of the pattern challenged the people. The next day, however, they were surprised to discover that the manna "did not become foul, and there were no worms in it" (Exod. 16:24).

God was obviously teaching the Israelites a lesson—a lesson that was less about manna than about the Sabbath, as James W. Sonnenday notes.[8] As they made the transition from slavery in Egypt under a ruler who cared neither about rest nor about their dignity, the character of the Sabbath took on exceptional status. The values conspicuously absent in the imperial system of Egypt are precisely those signified by the freedom of the Sabbath. If the people had a hard time understanding the privilege, it was because they had never experienced a day that was not dedicated to work and the struggle for subsistence. Whatever meager opportunities the Egyptians allowed for rest and fellowship, it is certain that the Sabbath was not one of them.

The lesson is carefully calibrated to highlight the exceptional privilege of the Sabbath. While the food that was miraculously provided each day brought the assurance of divine care, it also reinforced the need for daily effort. It was in the nature of the manna to melt when the sun got hot (Exod. 16:21) and to become foul within a day of storage (Exod. 16:20). On the first Sabbath after their captivity, the old routine persisted. It was time to go to work. Material security had to come the old-fashioned way: It had to be earned. Each sunrise, including the sunrise on the seventh day, was a signal to resume the daily grind. There was no exception, rest, or break. Thus, some people dressed for work and went out looking for manna.

But a new surprise awaited them. "On the seventh day some of the people went out to gather, and they found none" (Exod. 16:27). Clearly, someone was trying to tell them something.[9] Moses explained what was happening, "See! The Lord has given you the sabbath, therefore on the sixth day he gives you bread for two days. So the people rested on the seventh day" (Exod. 16:29–30).

What is the point of this Sabbath magic? A forgotten reality was breaking into their toilsome routine. Along the Nile there was neither Sabbath nor shade. Now the ruthless oppression and the entrenched maze of mindless routine were interrupted by a new pattern that allowed them to straighten their aching backs, lift their heads, and make room for their minds to seek a higher destiny.

The liberating enterprise hit them like a bolt from the blue. No matter how much they had longed for better days, they were not ready for the reality that the Sabbath signified. They had to be reoriented and reconditioned in preparation for living as free men and women. All their reflexes were trained for combat, suspicion, and distrust. They had been puppets in someone else's hand; now they had to think and act for themselves, and they hardly knew what to do. What we are witnessing, says Buber, is "an inchoate, stubborn horde during the transition of that horde from the lack of freedom into a problematic freedom."[10] The Israelites knew competition but not community, coercion but not conviction, the cruel demands of Pharaoh but not the gentle touch of God.[11]

Against this background there can be no doubt that the entire undertaking was predicated on God's desire to restore their freedom and dignity. God explained, "I am the Lord your God, who brought you out of Egypt so that you would no longer be slaves to the Egyptians; I broke the bars of your yoke and enabled you to walk with heads held high" (Lev. 26:13, NIV). Jean Louis Ska states aptly that "God's first gift to Israel is not a land or special institutions but freedom. One could even say that Israel, now out of Egypt and in the desert, has nothing but freedom."[12] Taking freedom to be paramount, the entire project could be called "Operation Freedom."

To those who failed to grasp the privilege offered to them, Moses explained that God "has given you the Sabbath, therefore on the sixth day he gives you food for two days" (Exod. 16:29). They need not record the seventh day in the expense column, as though deprived of a day that could be used to improve their lot in life. The day is *given*; it is not taken away.[13] Their needs would be met even if they did not work that day, and they would not gain anything if they did.[14] This people, reared on self-sufficiency and hard labor, were being shown that a higher power was looking out for them (Exod. 16:30).

THE CHALLENGE OF FREEDOM

There is a deeper truth here as well. Freedom from the constant harassment of the Egyptian masters was a good thing, but that change alone was only a beginning and an opportunity. Neither self-determination nor the prospect of a shorter workweek would make enough difference in itself. The descendants of Abraham needed a new center even more than they needed a change of setting and circumstances. When Moses approached Pharaoh, demanding freedom for his people, he left no doubt as to what was needed to set things right. "This is what the LORD says: Let my son go that he may worship me," he insisted (Exod. 5:22–23; cf. 5:1; 8:1, 20; 9:1, 13; 10:3). The Egyptian taskmasters had trampled on the spiritual dimension of human existence, allowing virtually no opportunity for people to relate to the Unseen. Slavery and abuse were part of the plight, but the heart of the problem belonged to the spiritual realm.

Conversely, the opportunity to know God stood at the center of the newfound freedom, and the Sabbath pointed the way. In Exodus the seventh day is the Ellis Island of first impressions—the Statue of

Liberty rising out of the fog. For those who wondered what life in the new reality would be like, the Sabbath set the tone. It served as the gateway to a life of freedom just as in Genesis it marked the beginning of human existence. In this respect the revival of the Sabbath signals the retrieval of lost meaning at the deepest level. With the rest on the seventh day came a different structure to time and strikingly new priorities. The day on which work was not necessary offered an opportunity to experience the care of the Creator, restoring to them a sense of their original dignity as men and women created in the image of God. They were no longer slaves and mere instruments to further the grandiose and self-aggrandizing aspirations of human masters. Now they were free to think and act for themselves; now their lives mattered as individuals and not as a convenient reservoir of cheap labor. God created human beings for such a life in the first place, and to such a life God was setting them free. En route to the Promised Land the neglected flag symbolizing the divine purpose was raised again, signaling that what they were meant to be could only be found in what God is.

Amazingly, Exodus makes it clear that God, not a place, was the destination of the liberated people. On the one hand, God was the precondition for the freedom they were invited to enjoy, and, on the other hand, God was also the end of its fulfillment. No more than three months after the departure from Egypt, while the Israelites were still living as nomads and far from reaching the goal in geographic terms, the spiritual aim was all but complete. On the eve of the giving of the Ten Commandments, God told the people, "You yourselves have seen what I did to Egypt, and how I carried you on eagles' wings *and brought you to myself*" (Exod. 19:4).

This destination was not a geographic location in the Middle East. Instead, "I...brought you to myself" (Exod. 19:4). In this grand homecoming oppressed people were restored to fellowship with God and to a true conception of God's character. "Here it is especially clear that Israel's stay in Sinai is not only an interim stop, but that for the first time Israel is 'with God' here," writes Rendtorff.[15] If they decided to seek the meaning of freedom in God, their experience and example would become an object lesson to the world, bringing other nations into God's sphere of influence (Exod. 19:5–6).

We have already seen, however, that the divinely commissioned "Operation Freedom" ran into difficulties even among the people who were at the receiving end of the freedom they desired (Exod. 16:27–29). Delays, discontent, and turmoil on the way made the journey from Egypt to Palestine last much longer than necessary. Those who were adults at the time of the exodus never entered the promised homeland (Num. 14:28–34). That privilege fell to a new generation forty years later (Num. 14:31; 32:13; Deut. 2:7). At that time Moses convened the people to review the past before he, too, was laid to rest (Deut. 1:1–5; 32:48–52).[16]

Exodus makes it clear that God, not a place, was the destination of the liberated people.

One of the most striking aspects in this review relates to how large the lesson of the manna loomed in Moses's thinking. "Remember," he says, "how the Lord your God led you all the way in the desert these forty years, to humble you and to test you in order to know what was in your heart, whether or not you would keep his commands. He humbled you, causing you to hunger and then feeding you with manna, which neither you nor your fathers had known, to teach you that man does not live on bread alone but on every word that comes from the mouth of the Lord" (Deut. 8:2–3).

Moreover, the topic in this review and the specific language in Deuteronomy hew close to the story of the manna in Exodus. There, too, the experience was cast as a "test" of a certain order. In Exodus the notion of a test designed and failed frames the entire narrative of the manna and the role it played in returning the Sabbath to significance. As the liberated people worried how they were to be fed and sustained in the desert, God said to Moses, "I am going to rain bread from heaven for you, and each day the people shall go out and gather enough for that day. In that way I will test them, whether they will follow my instruction or not" (Exod. 16:4).

As the story winds down, there is more than a hint that the people failed the "test." "How long will you refuse to keep my commandments and instructions?" God asked Moses when some people set out looking for manna on the seventh day (Exod. 16:28), indicating that the people quite consistently had been disrespectful of the privileges offered to them. They neither understood nor adjusted to the reality of freedom.

But if this was a test, what did Moses or even God expect to learn from it? The story should not be seen as an arbitrary test of obedience, a divinely appointed entrance examination. There is something larger here. Jacques Doukhan notes that in Hebrew concepts have a broader and more fluid range than in Western languages. "The basic idea which is contained in the Hebrew words is concrete and refers to an action and a totality," he writes.[17] What is seen in this story is not the people's action only. Rather, the narrative recounts the people's reaction to God's action. God did not set up a static examination for them to pass or fail. Moses explained that the miracle of the manna came about "in order to know what was in your heart" (Deut. 8:2). In this case "the action and the totality" had to reckon with God's miraculous provisions from day to day and the special arrangement with regard to the Sabbath. God set in motion a process that was designed to transform their view of God and change their priorities.

What, indeed, did they think about God the day the manna fell from heaven in the desert, giving them food that the desert could not provide? How did they see God on the seventh day when no manna was on the ground? What thoughts came to mind when they discovered that only on that day the manna did not spoil? The seventh day was offered to them as a day free of toil, and yet for many people the reflex was still to go out searching for manna. Their behavior demonstrates that freedom posed a challenge.

The daily and weekly manna routine continued for at least forty years. Only during the time of Joshua, when the Israelites were established in the new country and had other means of sustenance, did the manna cease (Josh. 5:12). So in reality the "test" in question was intended to probe their thinking about God after God set them free, led them, and cared for their needs. God set before them a life of freedom and dignity on the assumption that freedom is achievable only in fellowship with the Creator. Indeed, freedom was offered in the context of conflict, against the active resistance of Pharaoh. On this point Exodus is convinced that freedom is only possible because of God's opposition to the forces of exploitation, casting God as the guarantor of freedom.

But how did human beings respond to the privilege thus offered? According to the stated purpose of the test, "what is in your heart" would ultimately be revealed (Deut. 8:2). What was left at the end of the experience therefore brought the questions, How, now, do you see things? What, now, is in your heart? As the narrative unfolds, it is possible to draw out at least four points with respect to the seventh day. First, that Exodus affirms the priority of the Sabbath, staging its renaissance in a manner fully as striking as the first mention of the seventh day in Genesis.

Second, the seventh day in Exodus meets a genuine need. In human experience, the Sabbath rest in Genesis precedes work. In Exodus the seventh day is presented as an arresting interruption of the daily grind. Rest is offered to human beings who desperately need relief from competition, exploitation, and coercion.[18] And the importance of the Sabbath to humans is even clearer when freedom from oppression is given as the reason for the Sabbath commandment in Deuteronomy (Deut. 5:12–15).[19] The Sabbath rest serves as an inviolable boundary marker against the forces of oppression—exploitation by the master of his slave, by the employer of his workers, or even the oppression intrinsic to ideologies that treat human life as mere raw material for pretentious political and material projects. God is on the side of human need in this respect, and the worker's need of the seventh day is to be seen as an inalienable God-given right.

Third, the Sabbath returns in the larger context of freedom and as the most distinctive marker of the experience of freedom. As the people are set free from the dictatorship of Pharaoh, they are not merely exchanging the capricious rule of Pharaoh for the benign dictatorship of God. On the contrary, it is precisely the *kind* of rule that sets the two systems apart—one a system of slavery, the other a system of freedom.[20] This point cannot be emphasized too strongly, recalling that misrepresentation of God's rule regarding freedom is the contested issue in Genesis (Gen. 3:1). "You may freely eat," God says in the Garden of Eden (Gen. 2:16). Here, too, under changed and austere circumstances, comes the message, "You may freely eat," partaking of food generously provided. Still more important, they may eat *and* rest, freely taking advantage of the opportunity to abstain from working (Exod. 16:29).

Exodus affirms the priority of the Sabbath, staging its renaissance in a manner fully as striking as the first mention of the seventh day in Genesis.

Fourth, the resurgence of the seventh day expresses the central Old Testament idea of God's presence. As noted already, the reality of the presence of God stands "at the center of biblical faith."[21] The presence of God certainly lies at the heart of the seventh day in Exodus. I "brought you to myself" (Exod. 19:4), says God, and the reality of God's presence is most noticeable in the Sabbath rest. Important as this is in its native context, it also stands in contrast to the prevailing sense of God's absence in the modern experience.

Later on their journey the Sabbath would be proclaimed as one of the Ten Commandments (Exod. 20:8–11), but the renaissance of the seventh day did not begin at Sinai.[22] It began when the miracle of the manna and the rest of the seventh day put a new possibility before the Israelites. In a final note to posterity, measures were taken to ensure that the status of the seventh day would not depend solely on its rising and falling fortune in Israel. Leaving its stewardship to human discretion was considered too risky because actual Sabbath-keeping might ultimately fall short of safeguarding its meaning. As Nahum Sarna points out, the holiness of the seventh day "flows from God's infusion of blessing and sanctity."[23] Having God as its champion, "its blessed and sacred character is a cosmic reality wholly independent of human initiative. Hence the frequent designation 'a Sabbath of the Lord.'"[24]

Whether or not the Sabbath would be kept at all or whether its meaning would be perverted in the course of time, future generations are given access to a residue of what God had in mind in Exodus. Moses was instructed to "take an omer of manna and keep it for the generations to come, so they can see the bread I gave you to eat in the desert when I brought you out of Egypt" (Exod. 16:32). A measure of about four quarts was put in a jar, and "Aaron put the manna in front of the Testimony, that it might be kept" (Exod. 16:34).[25]

If, to future generations, the Sabbath were to be forgotten or reduced to a formality, the jar of manna would be God's enduring commemorative, an occasion to recall how God for forty years let the manna fall on the ground six days out of seven but set the seventh day apart. From the point of view of this commemorative, the Sabbath is not primarily a commandment written in stone, imposed on people as a test of obedience. It is instead a symbol of God's concern for the oppressed and an expression of God's desire for fellowship with human beings. "I bore you on eagles' wings and brought you to myself" must be seen as the first leg of the homecoming (Exod. 19:4). The second leg is a table set with bread from above and a day free of toil. In this way the special day offered to human beings is in itself a message about the kind of person God is.

ENDNOTES

1. This, of course, is meant figuratively. The most imposing monuments of the great pharaohs were already a thousand years old at the time of the Exodus.

2. Sarna, *Understanding Genesis*, 19.

3. Buber, *Moses*, 80.

4. Ibid. U. Cassuto (*A Commentary on the Book of Exodus,* trans. Israel Abrahams [Jerusalem: The Magnes Press, 1967], 186) notes that in Exodus the Sabbath is a matter already known "although the children of Israel had not yet heard the commandments concerning the Sabbath contained in the Ten Commandments." Here, too, in connection with the manna miracle, "the matter is not reported as a first instruction."

5. The text says literally "God *knew* them," using the same word as is used in Genesis with respect to Abraham, "I have known him" (Gen. 18:19).

6. The English spelling "manna" is derived from the LXX translation.

7. James W. Sonnenday, "Unwrapping the Gift Called Sabbath," *Journal for Preachers* 23 (2000): 40.

8. Sonnenday, "Unwrapping the Gift Called Sabbath," 41.

9. According to Benno Jacob (*The Second Book of the Bible: Exodus,* trans. Walter Jacob [Hoboken, NJ: Ktav Publishing House, 1992], 460), the people "did not understand that the double portion provided on Friday and the omission of the *manna* on the Sabbath constituted an even greater miracle" than the daily provision of manna on the other days.

10. Buber, *Moses*, 135.

11. Sonnenday, "Unwrapping the Gift Called Sabbath," 39.

12. Jean Louis Ska, "Biblical Law and the Origins of Democracy," in *The Ten Commandments: The Reciprocity of Faithfulness*, ed. William P. Brown (Louisville: Westminster John Knox Press, 2004), 155–156.

13. Jacob (*Exodus*, 461) finds here "a declaration of extraordinary importance: the character of the Sabbath was here emphasized as a *gift* of God, so significant that God Himself provided an explanation and then spoke of Himself in the third person in order to provide the greatest dignity to the Sabbath as HIS day."

14. Patrick D. Miller, "The Human Sabbath: A Study in Deuteronomic Theology," *Princeton Seminary Bulletin* 6 (1985): 86.

15. Rendtorff, *The Canonical Hebrew Bible*, 52.

16. Questions regarding the authorship and dating of Deuteronomy are many in scholarly literature; cf. Moshe Weinfeld, *Deuteronomy and the Deuteronomic School* (Oxford: The Clarendon Press, 1972). However, these matters do not materially affect the issue addressed in this chapter, that is, the lesson to be drawn from the miracle of the manna in Exodus except in the sense that Deuteronomy on important points echoes Exodus.

17. Jacques Doukhan, *Hebrew for Theologians* (Lanham: University of America Press,

1993), 58.

18. Sonnenday, "Unwrapping the Gift Called Sabbath," 39.

19. Cf. Timo Veijola, "'Du sollst daran denken, dass du Sklave gewesen bist im Lande Ägypten'—Zur literarischen Stellung und theologischen Bedeutung einer Kernaussage des Deuteronioiums," in *Gott und Mensch im Dialog. Festschrift für Otto Kaiser zum 80. Geburtstag*, ed. Markus Witte (BZAW 345; Berlin: Walter de Gruyter, 2004), 253–373.

20. Buber (*Moses*, 108) notes that the Israelites are "departing from Egypt into freedom," but it is not clear why he prefers to call the move into freedom a move "to Pharaonism." This terminology obscures the contrast, which, fortunately, Buber is careful to point out. God's rule is a just rule and is also the rule of law.

21. Terrien, *The Elusive Presence*, xxvii.

22. Jacob (*Exodus*, 460) expresses the belief—somewhat gratuitously—that "the *manna* only served as preparation for the fourth commandment."

23. Nahum M. Sarna, *The JPS Commentary on Exodus* (Philadelphia: The Jewish Publication Society, 1991), 90.

24. Sarna, *Exodus*, 90.

25. Years later, in the New Testament, this striking arrangement is still noticed when the writer of the book of Hebrews points out that the ark in the Most Holy Place "contained the gold jar of manna, Aaron's rod that budded, and the stone tablets of the covenant" (Heb. 9:4).

CHAPTER 6

A RELUCTANT IMPERATIVE

Remember the sabbath day, and keep it holy.
Exodus 20:8

By the time the seventh day is buttressed by being included in the Ten Commandments and by the tenor of the imperative, it has already accumulated an impressive narrative portfolio in the Bible. Contrary to opinions widely held, however, we should be reluctant to anoint the imperative of the commandments as a more compelling form of persuasion than narrative. While it cannot be denied that the Sabbath will speak with the urgency and authority of the imperative, it is a reluctant imperative. The seventh day does not, as it were, fully trust the often illusory power of the imperative, and it is not willing to be estranged from its narratival roots (Exod. 20:2, 11). If, too, the story of God's faithfulness that is etched into the seventh day expects reciprocity on the human level, the solemn encounter at Mount Sinai casts the human response in form of a sacred vocation (Exod. 19:4-6). It envisions a chain reaction of blessing, forging the Sabbath into a conduit of grace to all creation.

REVISIONING THE CONTEXT

If quantity were a measure of strength, the fulcrum of Sabbath theology in the Bible belongs to the time of Moses. At that point the biblical narrative makes the Sabbath so conspicuous that it seems to be on the crest of a rising tide. Starting with the proclamation of the Ten Commandments at Sinai, the numerous references to the Sabbath give it an aura of prominence that has led many to find in them the benchmark of what the Sabbath is meant to be.[1] These texts overshadow the brief mention of the seventh day in connection with Creation in Genesis. According to this reasoning, the Sabbath is not really established until the matter is stated as a commandment (Exod. 20:8–11).[2] Thus, even among proponents of the Sabbath, people look to the Decalogue as the most unassailable bulwark for their position. Only the commandment carries sufficient punch to frame the issue as an obligation and to end all discussion.

On the other hand, the quantity of Sabbath texts in Exodus may be seen as a measure of weakness rather than strength. Perhaps the emphatic imperative of Mount Sinai catches the seventh day at a low point in its trajectory. Although it has been pointed out that the word "commandment" is absent from the proclamation of the Decalogue at Sinai,[3] the diction has an imperative quality.[4] This is in itself not a good omen because the imperative refers only to a potential action and not to an action that has been actualized.

In a real sense the imperative is louder than the indicative because it is weaker.[5] Its use can express real despair as well as authority, an emergency measure that highlights the chasm between the intent of the person who gives the command and the disposition of the people addressed. The imperative may signify that the person issuing it is serious about his or her intent, but the imperative may actually reveal as much about the hearer as about the speaker. To the extent that this is the case in the form the Sabbath takes at Mount Sinai, we should be prepared to concede that the imperative of the Ten Commandments may not remedy what the indicative of the first Sabbath rest fails to accomplish.

Luther's ambivalent attitude to the commandments, at least his tendency to disparage Moses, is not irresponsible in this connection. He is ready to dispense with the commandments altogether, writing that "if Moses had never appeared and Abraham had never been born, the Ten Commandments would have had to rule in all men from the very beginning."[6] Luther assumes that the divine imperatives are known because they have been inscribed on the human constitution by other means. In this perception God's will and purpose remain constant, but the means instituted to ensure that God's intent will be understood and carried out undergoes a steady evolution. Sinai, therefore, is not an occasion to discover that new commandments are hidden in God's sleeve. Rather, the solemn proclamation restates what have been God's commandments all along, albeit in a more striking measure than before. As Patrick D. Miller says, "the divine command is the character of the divine word at a critical point."[7]

Despite this caveat the great revelation at Sinai must not be disparaged. In their native context the Ten Commandments "are presented as uniquely unmediated, public revelation,"[8] a reminder that should discourage any attempt to belittle them. To Rendtorff, "the Decalogue is very clearly set apart from all the other commandments and laws. It was only this that God spoke in Israel's immediate hearing."[9] While the search for a fulcrum in the Old Testament has yielded conflicting results, there are persuasive reasons to believe that if such a center exists, it is found in the Law, rightly understood, and that this center reflects the basis for human existence.[10] Moreover, the tendency to read the commandments as irredeemable negatives is clearly a mistake. If we appreciate the context, seeing the people coming from slavery to liberty, the commandments are as much a gift as liberty.[11]

Indeed, the Ten Commandments are not fully appreciated apart from the introduction spoken at Sinai: "You have seen what I did to the Egyptians, and how I bore you on eagles' wings and brought you to myself" (Exod. 19:4). This shows that the commandments are given as a consequence and sequel to God's intervention. Miller, again, emphasizes that "[t]hese divine commands are rooted in the prior redemption and grace of God. There is a prior reality and a prior act, and that reality-act is determinative for the divine command."[12] With the prologue as evidence, the commandments, including the Sabbath commandment, "grow out of a shaping narrative, the story of the people's deliverance."[13]

THE GLUE OF COVENANT

There is a formal aspect to the introduction to the Ten Commandments that is easily overlooked, partly because the modern reader needs to be briefed on the background in order to see it and partly because it reflects a convention that is unfamiliar to modernity. Yet this formal aspect plays a key role, making the introduction part and parcel of the commandments. If the Ten Commandments are studied apart from this prologue, a crucial element is lost from view.

In this introduction the key word is "covenant" (Heb. *berît*). This word is "the most comprehensive and the most theologically weighty term for God's attention to humans in the Hebrew Bible."[14] Having spoken of the deliverance from Egypt (Exod. 19:4), God sets the terms for what lies ahead, posing the great "if" of the future relationship: "if you obey my voice and keep my covenant" (Exod. 19:5). Here, too, as with the Sabbath, the notion of covenant is not new. It is the obligation of the already existing covenant that lies at the root of the divine intervention on the people's behalf (Exod. 6:4); God has not forgotten the previous agreement. "I have also heard the groaning of the Israelites whom the Egyptians are holding as slaves, and I have remembered my covenant" (Exod. 6:5).

In the biblical context "covenant" is the glue that holds life together. Everything happens by formalized agreement. No human being can see himself or herself apart from his or her context. Commitment to the covenant is basic to survival of the individual and of society. The modern realization that "no man is an island" was strongly held in antiquity. Many societies in the ancient world made covenants among themselves, and such covenants were understood as essential foundations of a stable society.

According to the seminal study by George E. Mendenhall, covenants made between a conquering ruler and his vassals are known as suzerainty treaties.[15] In the preamble of such a treaty the great king identifies himself, disclosing his title and the extent of his domain. This is followed by a description of the background of the relationship between the ruler and the vassal. The review highlights the benefits bestowed on the vassal by the ruler, amounting to an expectation of future obedience and loyalty in response to favors received in the past. The treaty then has a series of stipulations concerning the relationship between the ruler and the vassal. The latter is expected to pay tribute to the king, answer any call to arms, and appear before him once a year. The vassal is not allowed to enter into treaties with any other nation, speak evil of the king, or behave distrustfully. The suzerainty treaties also make provision for periodic public readings of the covenant, reinforcing its value and obligation in the minds of the people. Chief among the witnesses to the treaty are the gods, including the gods of the vassal state. In this way the treaty becomes a religious obligation. Any violation meets with retribution by the gods. Loyalty to the covenant brings blessings while disloyalty results in curses and calamities.

In the covenant between God and Israel some of the same elements are recognizable. With reference to the suzerainty treaties the prologue to the Ten Commandments takes on added significance because it, too, recounts the benefits that God's intervention has bestowed on the people. The Ten Commandments should therefore not be severed from the prior story of deliverance. The similarities between ancient suzerainty treaties and the biblical account are unmistakable on this point, but the connection is easily overemphasized. While the kings of antiquity posed as great benefactors, the reality was usually quite different. These heads of state ruled by conquest, and they levied heavy tributes on their subject peoples. The much-vaunted benefits to the vassal are mostly political propaganda. History is written and recalled for the sake of aggrandizement of the ruler. In this respect the background of the Israelite covenant is as different as are the stipulations.

God restores the people to freedom, self-respect, and dignity, delivering them from slavery in Egypt. When their experience is recounted, it is more than propaganda. God brings them "out of the house of bondage" (Exod. 13:3, 14; 20:2, KJV) for their own sake. Crucially, the values of the Ten Commandments are not the price they have to pay for benefits received. Rather, the commandments embody qualities that will safeguard life and liberty. It is therefore misleading to represent the commandments as equivalent to the stipulations we find in the suzerainty treaties. In the vassal treaties the favor of the king creates the obligation of gratitude. People obey as a token of gratitude to him—whether or not they feel any gratitude and whether or not the stipulations are meaningful to their quality of life.

By contrast, in God's covenant with Israel the stipulations are an extension of the blessing they receive when God liberates them. Understood in this way, the Ten Commandments are as much a gift from God as is liberty. "And now, O Israel," Moses asks, "what does the LORD your God ask of you but to fear the LORD your God, to walk in all his ways, to love him, to serve the LORD your God with all your heart and with all your soul, and to observe the LORD's commands and decrees that I am giving you today *for your own good*?" (Deut. 10:12–13). The commandments are given for their good, not as arbitrary stipulations, not as a test of their moral resolve, and not as the means by which to gauge their gratitude.[16] In a significant shift, the tendency of Christian theologians to denigrate law as an unmitigated negative is waning, and some scholars urge a recovery of the biblical view of the law as a gift.[17]

The commandments embody qualities that will safeguard life and liberty.

The context of the commandments is the covenant. Any infringement on the covenant threatens the essence of human existence, inviting self-destruction. A number of the observations made by Johannes Pedersen in his classic study of the life and institutions of Israel may need to be scaled back, but his view of the covenant is not one of them. In the Hebrew conception, "one is born of a covenant and into a covenant, and wherever one moves in life, one makes a covenant or acts on the basis of the already existing covenant. If everything that comes under the term covenant were dissolved, existence would fall to pieces, because no soul can live an isolated life....Therefore the annihilation of the *covenant would not only be the ruin of society, but the dissolution of each individual soul.*"[18] Covenant means memory, a recollection of the beginning, and mutuality, commitment to an agreement, and these elements are key ingredients in the fabric of existence. To lose the covenant is to come unhinged from the center. This is the context in which the Sabbath commandment belongs.

THE NARRATIVAL ROOTS OF THE SABBATH COMMANDMENT

The meaning-making intent of the Sabbath commandment is the most conspicuous feature.

> Remember the sabbath day, and keep it holy. Six days you shall labor and do all your work. But the seventh day is a sabbath to the LORD your God; you shall not do any work—you, your son or your daughter, your male or female slave, your livestock, or the alien resident in your towns. For in six days the LORD made heaven and earth, the sea, and all that is in them, but rested the seventh day; therefore the LORD blessed the sabbath day and consecrated it. (Exod. 20:8–11)

Three observations are especially important here. First, when the speaker at Sinai calls out the emphatic "remember," it is evident that prior familiarity with the seventh day is assumed.[19] The thrust is not novelty but recollection. Moreover, the call to remember the day goes beyond concern for the day as such; it cannot be severed from the memory that is intrinsic to the day. At the deepest level the entire commandment has a narratival character: The Sabbath tells a story.

Part of the narrative is found in the introduction, recalling the story of their liberation (Exod. 19:4). But the narratival character and substrate also extend to the content of this commandment. More than any other commandment in the Decalogue, the Sabbath commandment is replete with narrative. If the link to Israel particularizes the Sabbath, the link to Creation generalizes it: It is because God is the Creator of all humanity and all of life that Israel will keep the Sabbath. Or, as Benno Jacob puts it, "Neither Sabbath rest nor the working week could have been accorded any higher honor than for God to serve as the example of both."[20]

God's rest at Creation is the rationale for the Sabbath commandment in Exodus as much as it is the occasion that brings the seventh day into being in Genesis.

> Genesis: "So God blessed the seventh day and hallowed it, because on it God rested from all the work that he had done in creation." (Gen. 2:3)

> Exodus: "For in six days the Lord made heaven and earth, the sea, and all that is in them, but rested the seventh day; therefore the Lord blessed the sabbath day and consecrated it." (Exod. 20:11)

> "It [the Sabbath] is a sign forever between me and the people of Israel that in six days the LORD made heaven and earth, and on the seventh day he rested, and was refreshed." (Exod. 31:17)

The consistency of this theme—God's rest at Creation—is not accidental. Looking at the narratival context of the Ten Commandments in general and at the story-laden content of the fourth commandment in particular, Miller's assertion deserves to be resoundingly affirmed: "Narrative carries the commandments."[21]

Second, the commandments have a rational character. They are not presented as blunt take-it-or-leave-it propositions. On the contrary, the Ten Commandments are argued by an appeal to reason. "One of the primary features of Israelite law, one that appears first in the Ten Commandments," says Miller, "is the presence of motivation clauses that serve as a mode of *divine persuasion*, on the one hand, and the *rationality* of the commandments, on the other."[22]

> The presence of divine persuasion indicates that the commandments cannot be reduced to blind obedience. They are not arbitrary or capricious. Nor does God simply set them out to be obeyed. The one who commands also encourages obedience and seeks to draw forth a positive response from those before whom the commands are set. From the side of God, that is, on God's part, it is not assumed that the rightness of the command

> is self-evident or to be imposed from above. The consent of the commanded people is a true consent of the mind and heart.[23]

This is a remarkable observation. If words like "rationality," "not arbitrary," "appeal to reason," "divine persuasion," and "consent" describe the character of the commandments, they also say a lot about the character of the Commander and the type of relationship God is seeking. For this contention to stand, of course, it must apply to all the commandments. If one commandment is found to be arbitrary, even if only one, the good sense of all the other commandments will not make up the difference. Damage to the reputation of the Commander cannot be avoided if the Sabbath commandment, alone among the commandments, is saddled with the stigma of arbitrariness, as argued by the Roman Catholic Church in one of its most important documents (see ch. 24).[24]

Ultimately, all the commandments reflect the character of God. Any addition or deletion impairs the quality and symmetry of the fabric; thus the charge not to "add to it or take away from it" (Deut. 12:32). Reflecting on the biblical perception of the Decalogue, Brevard Childs comments that it is "consistent in touching only upon those areas of extreme importance for the life of the community."[25] There is no hint that the Sabbath fails to meet this specification. If the contention is valid that the commandments should not be regarded "as being merely timeless principles,"[26] the Sabbath retains its own kind of self-evidence no less than the other commandments, grounded in God's character, intention, and example.

At the deepest level the entire commandment has a narratival character: The Sabbath tells a story.

Third, the Ten Commandments are characterized as complete and comprehensive. "Why does the Decalogue contain these precise commandments, these and none other, no more and no less?" asks Buber.[27] The answer, according to the second rendition of the Ten

Commandments, attributes to the commandments an indivisible, inviolable character. Moses reminds the people that "these words the LORD spoke to all your assembly at the mountain out of the midst of the fire, the cloud, and the thick darkness, with a loud voice; and *he added no more*" (Deut. 5:22).

This negation is striking. Most speakers will be content to rehearse what is said on a given occasion. In this instance, however, the Bible also emphasizes what is *not* said. According to the translation of the King James Version, God "*added nothing*." God "added no more" implies that nothing more needed to be said. The "ten words" embody comprehensive principles to safeguard the relationship between God and human beings, and they cover the most crucial elements for protection of interpersonal relationships and respect for human life. They are, says Miller, "a necessary, sufficient, and comprehensive formulation of the divine will regarding what is obligatory for human existence."[28] Above all, the comment that God "added nothing" reinforces what has already been said concerning the character of the Ten Commandments: There is no unreasonable or arbitrary demand or any item in the divine will that has a trivial or pointless purpose. Completely at odds with the Christian tendency to belittle the Sabbath commandment, the Jewish perspective of Benno Jacob extols it without reserve. Exodus 20:9–12, he says, represents "one of the most blessed and sublime sections of divine legislation, which has shown itself capable of providing incomparable benefits to mankind. Nothing seems simpler than the declaration of a day of rest after six days of work, yet no lawgiver of the ancient world produced this idea. For both Greeks and Romans the Sabbath was inconceivable, and they felt only ridicule and disdain for it. For Judaism it has been an inexhaustible wellspring of blessing for life and belief."[29] Such a verdict goes a long way toward dispelling the idea that the Sabbath represents an unwelcome burden or that it should be undeserving of its place in the Decalogue.

RECIPROCITY AND VOCATION

If the kind of response that is expected in God's covenant is distinct from the suzerainty treaties, it does not mean that no response is called for at all. "Now therefore," says the speaker at Sinai, "if you obey my voice and keep my covenant, you shall be my treasured possession out of all the peoples. Indeed, the whole earth is mine, but you shall be for me a priestly kingdom and a holy nation" (Exod. 19:5–6).

A response to the covenant is expected: The people are to be "a kingdom of priests" (Exod. 19:6, KJV). Now that they are set free, they have the opportunity and the obligation to be mediators of the privilege bestowed on them. Instead of emphasizing the prospect of future nationhood, the prologue to the Ten Commandments puts vocation in the foreground. Liberation does not lead to complacency; the liberated people are called to reciprocate by serving as liberators toward those whom, like them, suffer oppression and deprivation, mediators of the freedom and dignity that are God's gift to all human beings.[30] In fact, in Revelation, the last visionary of the Bible can do no better than to look to the Exodus experience for the pattern God has in mind for all men and women who are thus recipients of freedom. "You have made them to be a kingdom and priests serving our God, and they will reign on earth," John writes (Rev. 5:10). The prologue of the Ten Commandments in Exodus echoes loudly in this affirmation.

Ultimately, all the commandments reflect the character of God. Any addition or deletion impairs the quality and symmetry of the fabric.

Miller characterizes the tenor and ethics of the Ten Commandments as *the reciprocity of faithfulness*: In the Ten Commandments as a whole and in the Sabbath commandment in particular, the story of *God's* faithfulness comes first. Miller's notion of reciprocity is meaningful, but it gets it wrong if human faithfulness is placed in the foreground or if the notion of human faithfulness is construed as though human beings put God in their debt.

> The specifics of keeping covenant on the part of the Lord are less clear than are the specifics of the people's responsibility. But the assumption is clear that the people can count on the Lord's preserving the covenantal relationship with the people; that the people's obedience, that is, their faithfulness, is reciprocated in God's faithfulness. The keeping of the commandments is not an activity that stands by itself. It is part of a relational dynamic, a reciprocity of faithfulness on the part of the partners in the covenant.[31]

Faithfulness is the cornerstone of this reciprocal relationship, and it is based on God's faithfulness. In the covenant that frames the Ten Commandments, God is faithful, the One upon whose faithfulness everything else rests. God's character and reputation are on the line. "Faithfulness," in turn, commands a large conceptual field, encompassing words like "constancy," "stability," and "reliability."[32] These qualities come into even sharper relief when their opposites are laid out: God is not capricious or arbitrarily exacting in the slightest. In this conception of faithfulness, it is inconceivable that God will make demands on God's subjects that are not for their benefit, and it is equally unthinkable that God will renege on what is promised.

"I bore you on eagles' wings and brought you to myself" (Exod. 19:4) lays the groundwork for the new relationship and the new vocation. This part, writes Miller, can be "understood to say something about the character of the commander and to particularize what matters in the identity of the one who commands."[33] What matters in the divine identity is God's faithfulness to God's promise. Only then comes the call for reciprocity and the commission to the new vocation: "Now therefore, if you...keep my covenant, you shall be...for me a priestly kingdom..." (Exod. 19:5–6).

But the notion of reciprocity must not be lightly passed over. Reciprocity is intrinsic to, and explicit in, the fourth commandment.

Even commentators such as Dressler[34] who see no expectation of reciprocity in the account of God's rest at Creation (Gen. 2:1–3) should not need convincing on this point. In Exodus the reciprocity that is implicit in Genesis is made explicit and imperative. According to the model of God's rest at Creation, human beings are to desist from work on the seventh day and thereby enter into God's rest.

Moreover, reciprocity on the human level solicits and commands a chain reaction of blessing to other human beings and even to non-human creatures. This, too, is a reciprocity of sorts because the person who experiences God's faithfulness in the rest of the Sabbath is to extend the privilege to son and daughter, to male and female slave, to the resident alien, even to cattle (Exod. 20:10). The fourth commandment envisions a vocation grounded in reciprocity, triggering an avalanche of blessing that is to make all Creation beneficiaries of the Sabbath. While the Sabbath that emerges from Mount Sinai has added the novelty of the imperative, it has also burnished the currency of blessing.

There is no unreasonable or arbitrary demand or any item in the divine will that has a trivial or pointless purpose.

ENDNOTES

1. See Exod. 20:8–11; 16:22–29; 31:13–17; 35:1–3.

2. Dressler ("The Sabbath in the Old Testament," 28) comments on the Sabbath in the Creation account: "There is no direct command that the seventh day should be kept in any way."

3. Sarna (*Exodus*, 107) notes that the precise Hebrew designation is "The Ten Words."

4. The imperative quality is especially evident with respect to the Sabbath commandment, where the word "remember" comes with the force of "an emphatic imperative"; cf. John I. Durham, *Exodus* (WBC; Waco: Word Books, 1987), 289.

5. According to grammarians, indicative and imperative are the mood of the verb. The mood describes how the action of the verb is related to reality. The sentence, "The man walks," is an indicative because walking is actualized. The statement, "Walk!" is an imperative. But the command to walk does not mean that walking will ensue. Commands, no matter how authoritative, do not make the imperative any more than a potential action.

6. Luther, "Against the Sabbatarians," 89.

7. Patrick D. Miller, "Divine Command and Beyond: The Ethics of the Commandments," in *The Ten Commandments: The Reciprocity of Faithfulness*, ed. William P. Brown (Louisville: Westminster John Knox Press, 2004), 14. I am indebted to Miller for many of the ideas in this chapter.

8. Brown, *The Reciprocity of Faithfulness*, 2. The notion of the Law as unmediated revelation appears to be challenged by Paul in his arguments with the Galatians, but caveats are in order because of the rhetorical intensity of this letter (Gal. 3:19–20).

9. Rendtorff, *The Canonical Hebrew Bible*, 55.

10. Otto Kaiser, "The Law as Center of the Hebrew Bible," in *"Sha'arei Talmon": Studies in the Bible, Qumran, and the Ancient Near East Presented to Shemaryahu Talmon*, ed. Michael Fishbane and Emmanuel Tov (Winona Lake: Eisenbrauns, 1992), 93–103.

11. Marty Stevens, "The Obedience of Trust: Recovering the Law as Gift," in *The Reciprocity of Faithfulness*, 143.

12. Miller, "Divine Command," 20.

13. Ibid., 23.

14. Rendtorff, *The Canonical Hebrew Bible*, 433.

15. G. E. Mendenhall, "Covenant Forms in Israelite Traditions," *Biblical Archaeologist* 7 (1954): 50–76.

16. G. E. Wright, *The Old Testament Against Its Environment* (London: SCM Press, 1950), 59.

17. Marty Stevens, "Recovering the Law as a Gift," 133–145.

18. Johannes Pedersen, *Israel: Its Life and Culture,* vols. I–II (London: Oxford University Press, 1926), 308, italics added.

19. Cassuto (*Exodus*, 245) says here, "*Remember the Sabbath day*, with which you are already familiar."

20. Jacob, *Exodus*, 566.

21. Miller, "Divine Command," 23.

22. Ibid., 25.

23. Ibid., 25–26.

24. *The Catechism of the Council of Trent,* trans. by the Rev. J. Donovan (New York: Catholic School Book Co., 1929), 264.

25. Childs, *Exodus*, 396.

26. Ibid.

27. Buber, *Moses*, 129.

28. Miller, "Divine Command," 15.

29. Jacob, *Exodus*, 569.

30. Miller, "The Human Sabbath," 82, 88; cf. Deut 5:12–15.

31. Miller, "Divine Command," 18.

32. Alfred Jepsen, *Theological Dictionary of the Old Testament*, art. "*'āman*," 1:322–323.
33. Miller, "Divine Command," 19.
34. Dressler, "The Sabbath in the Old Testament," 28.

CHAPTER 7

THE STRENGTH OF TIME

You shall keep my sabbaths, for this is a sign between me and you throughout your generations, given in order that you may know that I, the L*ORD*, *sanctify you.*
Exodus 31:13

Exodus gives the Sabbath broad exposure. There, in the miracle of manna, the seventh day stands out as a day that breaks the cycle of toil for subsistence (Exod. 16:14–31). In the Ten Commandments, the seventh day is placed at the center, and its rationale is explained more fully than any of the others (Exod. 20:8–11). And Exodus takes the Sabbath a notch higher, giving it the status of a sign (Exod. 31:13–17). Continuity with Genesis is evident because the Sabbath, whether as one of the Ten Commandments or as a sign, is anchored in God's rest at Creation (Exod. 20:11; 31:17).

And yet the "sign" passages in Exodus pose a significant challenge, beginning with the connection between the sign and the reality to which it points. In what sense does the sign serve as a mnemonic, the means of keeping memories alive? In what ways does it foster meaning? Even though the analogy between Sabbath and the role of the flag in modern society will help our understanding, we may still find it difficult to grasp the ancient idea of the Sabbath as "the strength of time."

SIGN AND REALITY

The "sign" passages in Exodus outline three affirmations with respect to the seventh day. The first of these affirmations makes it clear that the keeper of the sign is to be a person and a people set apart.

> You shall keep my sabbaths, for this is a sign between me and you throughout your generations, given in order that you may know that I, the LORD, sanctify you (Exod. 31:13).

In the second affirmation, the Sabbath participates in, and encapsulates, the covenant.[1]

> Therefore the Israelites shall keep the sabbath, observing the sabbath throughout their generations, as a perpetual covenant (Exod. 31:16).

The third affirmation relates the sign directly to Creation.

> It is a sign forever between me and the people of Israel that in six days the LORD made heaven and earth, and on the seventh day he rested, and was refreshed (Exod. 31:17).

Confusion with respect to terminology is not easily avoided on this point. Recalling Tillich's distinction between a sign and a symbol, what is called a sign in Exodus really belongs to the category of "symbol." Tillich says that signs, properly understood, "do not participate in the reality to which they point, while symbols do."[2] According to this criterion, the seventh day is no mere sign that is easily changed or replaced. It has the texture of a symbol. As a symbol, it participates intimately in the reality to which it points, bringing this reality to bear on the human experience by very tangible means. Writing long before Tillich, however, Johannes Pedersen emphasizes that the biblical signs "are realities; they are not naked things or facts which are *nothing but symbols* or indications of some underlying element."[3] On this logic neither "sign" nor "symbol" is fully up to the task of describing the meaning of the Sabbath. Rather, the Sabbath belongs to a genre of its own, beyond "sign" and "symbol" as these words are understood in the contemporary context. Nevertheless, when Tillich states that "signs can be replaced for reasons of expediency or convention, while symbols cannot,"[4] he describes a characteristic that indirectly heralds the resilience and perpetuity of the Sabbath.

In the Ten Commandments, the seventh day is placed at the center, and its rationale is explained more fully than any of the others.

In the eyes of many Christian interpreters, the specification that the Sabbath is "a sign forever between me *and the people of Israel*" (Exod. 31:17) makes it tempting to construe the sign as though it only has limited application. Does this qualification mean that the sign is only for Israel? Does the Sabbath as a sign have a restricted reach, or will it embrace all human beings?

Recalling Cassuto's claim that "the sanctity of the Sabbath is older than Israel, and rests upon all mankind,"[5] neither ethnicity nor nationality should be the focus of the reference to Israel. It is better to see it in terms of experience, calling, and vocation. What the seventh day says about God looms larger than what it reveals about human reality. In this respect the meaning of the Sabbath is not easily reduced to an identity marker of a certain group of people as though the Sabbath is their copyrighted trademark. Nationhood and Jewishness are not the central issue. To the extent that the Sabbath signifies a sacred vocation, the critical element in this vocation is to be a witness to God's person and ways (Exod. 19:4–5; Rev. 5:9–10). The people are set apart in order to know God and to make God known. In this sense the meaning of the Sabbath rests primarily on God's faithfulness and on the intent of including others in the same experience. When the Jewish people are delivered from slavery in Egypt, God makes the Sabbath a sign of *theology* before it becomes a cornerstone of anthropology or a boundary marker of sociology. Nothing, the Sabbath is commissioned to say, sets God apart from other masters, ideologies, or objects of worship more than the gift of freedom, and nothing expresses more succinctly the purpose of the Sabbath than that all human beings, Jew or non-Jew, are meant to be free (Lev. 26:13).

What the seventh day says about God looms larger than what it reveals about human reality.

We should therefore hesitate to read the declaration that the Sabbath is "a sign forever between me and the people of Israel" (Exod. 31:17) in a limiting, restricting sense. The very opposite is more persuasive. Israel's vocation is in view, a people set free to be ambassadors of the privilege they have been granted. In this connection the Sabbath is the launching pad for a vision of inclusion. Whether as a sign or as a commandment, the generalizing thrust of the Sabbath remains intact. While the seventh day sign is specific, it is also inclusive and aiming to include; it is particular and precise, and yet it is comprehensive. Sarna's view makes a good beginning of seeing the Sabbath as a sign: "Its observance is a declaration of faith, an affirmation of Israel as a holy nation not inherently but by an act of divine will; that the relationship between God and Israel is regulated by a covenant; and that the universe is wholly the purposeful product of divine intelligence, the work of a transcendent Being outside of nature and sovereign over space and time."[6]

THE SIGN AS MNEMONIC

We have already made the connection between a symbol and the underlying reality in general terms, but the precise biblical idea has yet to be explored. The word "sign," translated from the Hebrew *'ôt*, is associated with a wide variety of mental images, as Carl A. Keller demonstrates.[7] While one of these mental images, indeed, is the flag,[8] it is the revelatory character of *'ôt* that commands the greatest interest in the present context. *'ôt* is a code word for a particular kind of sign, an *Offenbarungszeichen*, indicating a sign that has revelatory intent. Thus understood, the sign "is always to be understood within the framework of a divine disclosure in relation to which the sign steps in as the simplified filling-in and amplification of the revealing word of God."[9] The sign has God as its subject,[10] and the main objective of the sign is to preserve awareness of God and what God reveals.

The sign, then, imparts knowledge and functions as a mnemonic. In fact, Old Testament scholars have shown convincingly that there is such a close connection between knowledge and signs that "to know" means virtually "to accept the certainty of something on the basis of a sign."[11] In the same vein the purpose of *'ôt* and its synonym *zikkārôn* is "to prevent something from being forgotten which deserves to be handed down, and to make it real over and over again."[12] The Sabbath is eminently suitable to fill these roles, whether as the sign that keeps alive the memory of the identity-shaping event of Creation (Gen. 2:1–3; Exod. 20:8–11; 31:17) or by recalling God's gracious intervention in Israel's deliverance from Egypt (Deut. 5:12–15). Above all, the Sabbath sign makes the encounter with God a present reality, cementing relationships and recalling God-given ideals. John I. Durham notes that the purpose "of this sign and the reason it must be kept is that Israel might know Yahweh's Presence by experience, in every generation, and be reminded constantly that only by that Presence are they a people set apart."[13]

As noted in the first chapter, the function assigned to the Sabbath in many respects resembles the role of the flag. The flag, too, is a sign, and it is a sign in the sense of a symbol that participates in the reality to which it points. *Old Glory*, the American flag, came into being in order to cement and commemorate the birth of the new country. This did not happen by an act of God as in the case of the Sabbath, but it did owe to a deliberate and explicit decision on the part of the Second Continental Congress. The flag eloquently symbolizes the nature of the country: a voluntary association of states bonded together in a covenant based on commitment to the constitution. All this makes the flag a fitting analogy to the Sabbath—and a useful one, too, because it helps us realize that symbols of this nature run deep in the consciousness and sense of identity of those who hold it dear. Thus, what Henry Ward Beecher said in 1861 with reference to the American flag has overtones that also extend to biblical symbols. "Our flag carries American ideas, American history and American feelings. It is not a painted rag. It is a whole national history. It is the Constitution. It is the Government. It is the emblem of the sovereignty of the people. It is the NATION."[14]

The flag brings back memories and serves to renew one's commitment to the original idea, a symbolic narrative of past history and present reality. The flag recalls the Declaration of Independence, the Constitution, the sacrifices of the Civil War, or more recent images, such as soldiers raising the flag at Iwo Jima,[15] Neil Armstrong and Edwin Aldrin planting the flag on the moon, or the tarnished but largely intact flag that was salvaged from the ruins of the World Trade Center in New York.[16] Like biblical symbols, the flag functions "to prevent something from being forgotten which deserves to be handed down, and to make it real over and over again."[17] The representative and symbolic aspect of the flag is readily appreciated, too, when people speak of saluting the flag, or of protecting and defending it. Those who salute the flag make a statement of loyalty to the country, and those who "defend the flag" thereby signal their willingness to stand up for the entity which the flag embodies.

The founding fathers of the United States, acting in conformity with international convention, chose a piece of cloth to serve as the national symbol. God, however, acting independently of any known convention, did not choose a specific place or an object to serve as God's special sign. The raw material of the biblical sign is a portion of time. Famously, Abraham Joshua Heschel calls the Sabbath a cathedral in time and "a mine where spirit's precious metal can be found with which to construct the palace in time."[18] Since the Sabbath is cut from the invisible cloth of time, it reaches into life on a deeper level than any external emblem. By setting aside a portion of time each week for special use, God fashions the Sabbath from the stuff of life itself. It requires no effort to find it, and no one can escape its reach. In a remarkable Psalm the writer says that God "has caused his wonderful works to be remembered;...he is ever mindful of his covenant" (Ps. 111:4–5). Remembering and causing to remember suggest a dual role, a two-way function by which God and human beings are both said to remember. By weaving the sign into the web of life, the Sabbath creates a bond between human beings and the Creator that is as enduring as is God.

By setting aside a portion of time each week for special use, God fashions the Sabbath from the stuff of life itself.

THE STRENGTH OF TIME

While abstaining from work has something to do with the Sabbath rest, it is clear that the designation of the Sabbath as a sign invests it with a still deeper mission. It is not the object of the Sabbath only to break the demands of labor as if it represents a stage of development on the road toward the long weekend. Addressing the concern that modern life has trapped people in a rut, the advice is often given to stop and "smell the roses," and to learn to "take one day at a time."[19] But this well-intentioned prescription seeks relief in the fragmentation of life rather than in its wholeness. Days taken one at a time cannot provide the connective tissue of purpose and coherence that the Sabbath pours into human existence.

Life in modern society therefore poses a tremendous challenge to the proper understanding of the Sabbath. A society that has surrendered generational links and a sense of community to fragmentation and individualism must necessarily find itself puzzled by the notion of covenant, of mutually binding agreements, and of the Sabbath. In the orphaned experience of modern life with its emphasis on fragmentation and individualism, the value of covenant is easily corroborated even as it is neglected and negated. "The covenant is not a thing to be dealt with as one pleases," says Pedersen. "It goes deeper than everything else, because it is the presupposition of all life."[20]

While abstaining from work has something to do with the Sabbath rest, it is clear that the designation of the Sabbath as a sign invests it with a still deeper mission.

The Sabbath is embedded in notions of wholeness and mutuality that lie at the heart of covenantal thinking because "the actual sign of the covenant is the sabbath."[21] Participating in the reality to which it points, the Sabbath exemplifies and embodies the meaning of covenant by the story it tells and by the means it represents for bringing its story into the lives of each new generation.

Johannes Pedersen goes so far as to suggest that the Sabbath imparts strength to time and becomes the energizing force behind human existence. There is, says Pedersen, "a deeper and wider motive for the rest on the sabbath day than that pointed out here. It is not the welfare of this worker or the other which is the decisive factor. On the sabbath and other feast days work ceases because these days are holy. *From the force gathered around them the rest of time derives its strength*, therefore all life is dependent on the maintenance of their holiness."[22]

In this perception, the Sabbath is the memorial of the origin and purpose of life and even more the thread by which life hangs because it ensures a foothold for God in the human enterprise. Understood in this way, the Sabbath is not only a day at the beginning of human existence or the seventh day that rounds off the week, the day at the end. Rather, it is the day at the center, as Jewish thinkers came to see it, a day that "permeates every day of the week."[23] As a day that "enters with light and departs with fire,"[24] symbolically and even physically in the Jewish Sabbath experience, it provides for the hallowing of human existence. Life is energized and solemnized not so as to lessen its joy but in order to ensure that life is not diminished and depleted. It is for this reason one may say that without the Sabbath time loses its strength.

Only in this light are we prepared to consider the grave consequence that is envisioned in the "sign" passages if the Sabbath should be ignored or violated. "Six days shall work be done," says the Bible, "but the seventh day is a sabbath of solemn rest, holy to the LORD; whoever does any work on the sabbath day shall be put to death" (Exod. 31:15). Whatever the original reaction may have been to this stark injunction, it is safe to say that it strikes the modern reader as excessive, exaggerated, unduly severe, and probably counterproductive. On the one hand, it appears that the measures suggested vastly exceed the merit of the subject. On the other hand, the gut reaction will be that the subject is poorly served by the measures proposed. It seems out of character with the ideas associated with the Sabbath up to this point suddenly to be saddled with such a disconcerting negative.

Of the reflections that are provoked by this injunction, at least three aspects must be considered with care. First and most important, this text belongs to the "sign" passages in Exodus, and it must be understood within this context (Exod. 31:13–17). The sign, as noted on numerous occasions, is not a thing apart or something in itself. It belongs to an underlying reality, fully signifying that reality. The person who violates the Sabbath commits an offense that involves more than disregarding instructions with respect to a certain day of the week. Given the symbolic and representative function of the sign, the violator turns his back on the entire reality that the sign embodies. For this reason it is not only the *day* that is broken but the underlying reality.

The Sabbath is the day at the center.

In modern terminology and with reference to contemporary penal codes, the crime that is addressed is not that of a person performing illicit work on the seventh day but treason. Durham shows a sound grasp of the subject when he writes that "[d]isregard for the sabbath, either by neglect or by a violation of the strictures concerning it, is disregard for Yahweh: and disregard for Yahweh is disregard for the reason and the possibility of Israel's existence as a people."[25] We cannot understand this except as confirmation that the imperiled idea is vocation and not ethnicity.

What happens to the sign implies honor or dishonor to the reality to which the sign points. The sign has to be carefully guarded; to act carelessly toward the consecrated token risks breaking its mental implication.[26] Violation of the token puts the reality itself in jeopardy.

Second, the modern reader should not rush to give priority to a literal reading. If the expectation of a summary execution of the violator of the Sabbath is unlikely, the violator is nevertheless, in the perception of Exodus, set on a fatal course. The implication of this text need not be, "If you violate the sign, I will execute you," but rather, "If you take no thought for the sign, you will be fatally diminished and deprived." The sign keeps watch over the underlying reality, and the latter will slip away if the sign is belittled.

One cannot read the warning about violation of the sign without recalling the warning regarding the tree of knowledge in the Garden of Eden. In Genesis, human beings are cautioned against eating of the tree, "for in the day that you eat of it you shall die" (Gen. 2:17). In Exodus, people are warned against behaving disrespectfully toward the consecrated sign; "whoever does any work on the sabbath day shall be put to death" (Exod. 31:15). Unfortunately, the force of the echo of Genesis is largely lost in translation. Hidden from view to the English reader is the fact that the stated consequence in both instances is expressed by variants of the same word. In Genesis, the text reads *môt tāmût*, "you shall die," using the simple imperfect (qal) for the main verb and what is called the infinite absolute of the same word for emphasis, signifying the certainty of what will happen. In Exodus, the text reads *môt yûmāt*, translated by the NRSV as "shall be put to death." The verbal stem is the same, and the infinite absolute that is used for emphasis is identical, but the main verb has the inflection indicating causation in the passive form (hophal), "you will certainly be caused to die." Death comes to the violator in both scenarios. Execution is not envisioned in Genesis but death is, and death comes by ever increasing installments of anguish in the form of alienation (Gen. 3:8), recrimination (Gen. 3:12), distress (Gen. 3:16–19), and death itself (Gen. 3:19). In Exodus death is sure to come by the same inevitable logic. In the absence of the sign, time will lose its strength. Human beings will find themselves diminished, estranged, and depleted, justifying the warning, "you will certainly be caused to die," the cause being disregard of the sign and the reality that is the condition of existence.

A third facet of this text shifts the interpretation closer to a literal reading, but this interpretation is cognizant of how the Sabbath is perceived in the book of Exodus. The Sabbath is intended as a sign bursting with meaning, but in actuality the sign is not received or cherished. When the "sign" passages state the case for the Sabbath in such stern terms, it reads like an act of desperation; the warning is the language of despair. What might seem like a cause that is determined to succeed whatever the cost might in reality be a lost cause already, or at least it is feared to be a lost cause. The implied importance of the sign is not exaggerated, and the stated consequence is sober-minded enough, but the rhetoric is mostly reflective of a cause that faces an uphill and almost impossible struggle.

Modern life offers supporting evidence for the notion that neglect of the Sabbath, understood also as alienation from the underlying reality, drains life of its strength. Where the spiritual and generational glue is missing, the sense of roots, of history, and of community is weakened. Centuries ago the purpose of the sign was to let people "know that I, the LORD, sanctify you" (Exod. 31:13). In its most stripped down version the Sabbath stands as a reminder that human beings are not alone in the universe. Life offers more than taking time to smell the roses or taking one day at a time. The thought that the best refuge is to avert one's eyes from anything that looks beyond the moment confronts in the Sabbath a bolder vision. Human beings have been offered another center than themselves. In the words of Terence Fretheim, "The sabbath is thus a divinely given means for all creatures to be in tune with the created order of things. Even more, *sabbath-keeping is an act of creation-keeping*. To keep the sabbath is to participate in God's intention for the rhythm of creation. Not keeping the sabbath is a violation of the created order; it returns one aspect of that order to chaos. What the creatures do with the sabbath has cosmic effects."[27] This is surely a stupendous thought, but it is hardly exaggerated. Is not the absence of "creation-keeping" precisely the reality that is staring at us, people living in the twenty-first century, in the face?

Sabbath-keeping is an act of creation-keeping.

But the Sabbath cannot be destroyed unless God forgets it. Only the One who instituted the Sabbath can rescind its sanctity. Human beings owe more to the reality of which the Sabbath is the sign than we realize. The roses we smell in our hurried lives and the days we take one at a time are all gifts from God—evidence that He remains true to His Sabbath commitment even toward those who fail to respond in kind. "Just as the rainbow automatically appears, so the Sabbath comes back regularly without any human contribution," writes Keller. "The Sabbath is in itself holy time regardless of whether man keeps it because God has sanctified this day for all time. The remaining question for the people is only whether to recognize this holiness and relate themselves to it in their sphere."[28]

Pinchas Peli sounds the same note, writing that "the Sabbath, declared once by God, comes and goes at regular intervals without any human intervention; she cannot be stopped or postponed. It remains up to us, however, to let her in, to receive her properly, to acknowledge that indeed we do have an extra dimension to our being. For, if we are not more than what we are—we are, most likely, less than what we are."[29] Recognizing the meaning of the sign and cherishing it as a treasure, therefore, means "to let her in," opening up to the reality of which the Sabbath is the sign. What is at stake to the writer of Exodus, beyond the threat to vocation, is the fear that time will be bereft of strength, and, as expressed by Peli, that we might become "less than what we are."[30]

ENDNOTES

1. According to F. J. Helfmeyer (*TDOT*, art. "*'ôth*," I:182), the Sabbath "is not explicitly called a 'covenant' sign," but "there can be no doubt that this is its function," as indicated by Exod. 31:13, 17.

2. Tillich, *Dynamics of Faith*, 41.

3. Pedersen, *Israel*, I:169.

4. Tillich, *Dynamics of Faith*, 42.

5. Cassuto, *Genesis*, 64.

6. Sarna, *Exodus*, 201.

7. C. A. Keller, *Das Wort OTH als Offenbarungszeichen Gottes* (Basel: Buchdruckerei E. Haenen, 1946).

8. *TDOT* I:169.

9. Keller, *Das Wort 'oth*, 67.

10. Ibid., 11.

11. *TDOT* I:171.

12. Keller, *Das Wort 'oth*, 64.

13. John I. Durham, *Exodus* (WBC; Waco: Word Books, 1987), 412–413.

14. Keller, *Das Wort 'oth*, 64.

15. The story of the raising of the flag at Iwo Jima is movingly told by James Bradley in *Flags of Our Fathers* (New York: Bantam Books, 2000).

16. I. Michael Heyman, Secretary of the Smithsonian Institution, when asked which is the greatest of the Institution's more than 140 million objects, gives a ready reply. "Of all the questions asked of me, this is the easiest to answer: our greatest treasure is, of course, the Star-Spangled Banner"; cf. Leepson, *Flag*, 59.

17. Keller, *Das Wort 'oth*, 64.

18. Heschel, *The Sabbath*, 8, 16.

19. A twentieth-century view on the meaning of time, offered by a well-known psychologist, also finds the recommendation "to smell the roses" shallow and unsatisfactory; cf. Herbert Rappaport, *Marking Time* (New York: Simon & Schuster, 1990).

20. Pedersen, *Israel*, I:308.

21. Childs, *Exodus*, 541.

22. Pedersen, *Israel*, II:290, italics added.

23. Pinchas Peli, *The Jewish Sabbath: A Renewed Encounter* (New York: Schocken Books, 1988), 94.

24. Ibid., 109.

25. Durham, *Exodus*, 413.

26. Pedersen, *Israel*, I:169.

27. Terence E. Fretheim, *Exodus* (Interpretation; Louisville: John Knox Press, 1991), 230.

28. Keller, *Das Wort 'oth*, 141.

29. Peli, *The Jewish Sabbath*, 90.

30. Ibid.

CHAPTER 8

THE SOCIAL CONSCIENCE OF THE SEVENTH DAY

When will the new moon be over so that we may sell grain;
and the sabbath, so that we may offer wheat for sale?
Amos 8:5

Although Johannes Pedersen says that "[i]t is not the welfare of this worker or the other which is the decisive factor,"[1] this statement must not be taken to mean that concern for the worker is absent from the seventh day. On the contrary, social conscience is inseparably intertwined with its ideology. Subtle and implicit at first, the social and ecological thrust of the seventh day becomes increasingly prominent over time. Indeed, the seventh day must be seen as the launching pad for the most exceptional and ambitious project of social justice in the ancient world. We might even speak of a "sabbathized" vision of reality. As we shall see, the most distinctive prophetic voices of the Old Testament line up behind this vision.

SOCIAL AWARENESS

Already in the Creation account, the raw material for social welfare resides in the imperatives of rest and cessation from labor (Gen. 2:2–3).[2] The rest that marks cessation of God's activity is the pattern according to which human beings will order their lives. Human need may not be apparent at first, but the need is anticipated. When the need appears, the seventh day, originally constituted as a day of rest, is ready to meet it.

What may only be inferred in the Creation account, however, looms large in the Ten Commandments. There freedom from work and from the yoke of exploitation are explicit characteristics of the Sabbath (Exod. 20:10). When the circle is drawn, nothing and nobody lie outside its domain: "you shall not do any work—you, your son or your daughter, your male or female slave, your livestock, or the alien resident in your towns" (Exod. 20:10). The particulars on this list are amazing because no parallels have been found in other cultures. Legislation of this kind in the ancient world prioritizes from the bottom up and not from the top looking down, giving first considerations to the weakest and most vulnerable members of society. Those who need rest the most—the slave, the resident alien, and the beast of burden—are singled out for special mention. In the rest of the seventh day the underprivileged, even mute animals, find an ally. "While this law clearly distinguishes between God and all the creatures," says Jean Louis Ska, "social distinctions within the society are, however momentarily, suspended."[3] In the Deuteronomy version of the Sabbath commandment (Deut. 5:12–15), concern for the slaves and the underprivileged is even more prominent.[4]

SABBATIZING REALITY

The Old Testament concern for social justice does not stop at the Sabbath, but the seventh day must be seen as the generating principle giving rise to other markers that are similarly bent on providing rest for the land and relief for its inhabitants (Exod. 23:10–11; Lev. 25 and 27; Deut. 15:1–11).[5] In the two Sabbath satellites, the Sabbatical Year and the Year of Jubilee, care for the land and concern for those who end up on the losing side of privilege underline the social profile of this triumvirate.[6]

Jewish interpreters are careful to note that the introduction to the most extensive presentation of these ordinances must not be overlooked. When the Sabbatical Year and the Year of Jubilee are spelled out in the book of Leviticus, they refuse to be dismissed as late inventions or as trivial policy. "The LORD spoke to Moses on Mount Sinai," begins the text (Lev. 25:1). To Jewish interpreters, the link to Sinai gives the injunctions weight equal to commandments more highly regarded.[7]

In the rest of the seventh day the underprivileged, even mute animals, find an ally.

What God is said to have spoken to Moses on Mount Sinai includes specific instructions with respect to rest for the land (Lev. 25:1–7) and relief from debt for the poor (Lev. 25:8–24). The land, too, is to enjoy a sabbath configured according to its need. "When you enter the land that I am giving you, the land shall observe a sabbath for the LORD. Six years you shall sow your field, and six years you shall prune your vineyard, and gather in their yield; but in the seventh year there shall be a sabbath of complete rest for the land, a sabbath for the LORD: you shall not sow your field or prune your vineyard" (Lev. 25:2–4).

Taking its pattern from the weekly cycle of six days of work followed by a seventh day of rest, this instruction extends the pattern to a seven-year cycle—six years of work and one year of rest for the land, the Sabbatical Year. The land itself, not only the tenants, are included in the provision of rest.[8] From there this text envisions yet another layer, configured as a multiple of seven seven-year periods, "so that the period of seven weeks of years gives forty-nine years" (Lev. 25:8). This most remote outpost of the seventh day, the Jubilee, unambiguously offers relief from debt and restoration of property lost because of economic hardship at some point during the preceding forty-nine years.[9] "And you shall hallow the fiftieth year and you shall proclaim liberty throughout the land to all its inhabitants. It shall be a jubilee for you: you shall return, every one of you, to your property and every one of you to your family" (Lev. 25:10).

It is not hard to see that this system sets a limit to acquisition of land on the one hand, and, on the other hand, provides a safety net for the person threatened with destitution. Were such an order to be implemented, it would lessen the gap between the rich and the poor. "The land shall not be sold in perpetuity, for *the land is mine*; with me you are but aliens and tenants" (Lev. 25:23). The winners and losers in this set-up are ultimately held to the stipulations imposed by the actual owner, whose intention it is to cushion the distress felt by the loser and thereby make all winners in the long run. If a land-tenant has to forego some of his land because of financial trouble, the land will not be lost for good. Whether buyer or seller, the transaction between them concerns a certain number of harvests, not land as such (Lev. 25:16). In the Year of Jubilee, the land reverts to the original tenant free of charge (Lev. 25:13).

It is said of this chapter in Leviticus that it "is permeated by remarkably concentrated direct address, giving the reader a sense of being in the lecture hall or worship service."[10] The quality of direct address suggests that we are privy to a text that was widely in use at some point. Erhard S. Gerstenberger, to whom I am indebted for the assessment noted above, is nevertheless at a loss to see it as a message that has practical meaning. In his eyes, the stipulations are too peculiar to have any relation to real life. He therefore construes the Sabbatical Year and the Jubilee as fantasies of a priestly writer or group of thinkers who knew nothing about the realities of farming and rural life. "We can imagine," writes Gerstenberger,

> how these priestly tridents arrived at a regulation as abstruse as this sabbatical year for cultivated fields, and why they, behind their lives of theological writing, might have forgotten so completely the realities of daily life. For the prescriptions concerning fallow fields are an abstract edifice either to be understood ideally—this is how life in Israel should be—or that has been preserved in just as theoretical a fashion to an urban congregation that itself no longer has anything to do with actual agricultural labor.[11]

Too many voices within the Old Testament show awareness of, and respect for, these ordinances to accept the view that they are merely the product of city-dwelling desk theologians living far removed from the realities of sowing and reaping. When the prophet Jeremiah predicts that Israel's captivity in Babylon is to last seventy years (Jer. 25:11–12; 29:10), and 2 Chronicles refers to the same period, the seventy-year span is determined according to a certain number of sabbatical years gone by. To the Chronicler, the seventy years of captivity are set apart in order "to fulfill the word of the LORD by the mouth of Jeremiah, until the land had made up for its sabbaths. All the days that it lay desolate it kept sabbath, to fulfill seventy years" (2 Chron. 36:21). In this assessment the ecological and social ripples of the Sabbath institution are taken seriously; the Sabbatical Year was meant to be observed, and its non-observance means that God will fulfill His obligation to the land when the appointed stewards fail to do so.

Even in the book of Daniel there is a distant echo of the Sabbatical Year (Dan. 9:2, 24). Where Jeremiah and 2 Chronicles look to the past and to non-observance of the Sabbatical Year as the rationale for the seventy years of captivity in Babylon (Jer. 25:11–12; 29:10; 2 Chron. 36:21; Dan. 9:2), Daniel's view rises from the same crucible. The seventy years that are allocated for the land to rest and recuperate, reflecting 490 years of non-observance of the Sabbatical Year, are in Daniel configured as a new period of opportunity, another "seventy weeks of years," for Israel to make good on its commission (Dan. 9:24). Whether looking to the past, as in 2 Chronicles, or to the future, as in Daniel, the ideological foundation of these periods relates to the Sabbatical Year, which, in turn, is an offspring of the seventh day.

The specifics of the Sabbatical Year and the Jubilee aside, there should be no doubt as to the ideology involved. Gerstenberger explains that in Leviticus 25 "we find ourselves in a socioeconomic sphere of power relations."[12] "Whether a dream of hope or a utopia that is nowhere, the jubilee is a resolve against a status quo of continued oppression and exploitation of people and creation," says Hans Ucko.[13] Echoing a similar sentiment, Jacob Milgrom sees in the Jubilee a socio-economic mechanism to prevent "the ever-widening gap between the rich and the poor which Israel's prophets can only condemn, but which Israel's priests attempt to rectify in Leviticus 25."[14] The leading motif is social justice, "a vision of hope which seeks to create a society without poverty."[15]

THE PROPHETS, JUSTICE, AND THE SEVENTH DAY

While the Sabbatical Year and the Jubilee are innovations that project the cause of social justice onto a wider screen, social conscience remains intrinsic to the seventh day. Recognizing that there is considerable disagreement among scholars as to whether the Sabbatical Year and the Jubilee were meant to be taken literally, no such doubt has been voiced with respect to the Sabbath. To some of the most distinguished prophets in the Old Testament, the relationship between the seventh day and the cause of social justice is so organic that they repudiate any version of the Sabbath that does not reflect this reality.

The prophetic voices raised on this point indicate that the relationship between social justice and the Sabbath came to be seen in a negative light. In the short version of this development, the Israelites, having escaped the erosive effect of cultural assimilation in Egypt, succumb to cultural pressures in the new country (e.g., Judg. 2:7–10). Flagrant violation of truth and justice not only become standard practice but the standard itself (Isa. 59:14–15). Prophets and messengers are sent in rapid succession, but no amount of exhortation and warning suffice to turn the tide (2 Chron. 36:15–16). Interspersed in the unflattering story of decline, a number of the prophets give a glimpse of how people came to regard the Sabbath, telling the story as though the Sabbath in their eyes is a bellwether issue.

Centuries after Moses is laid to rest, the prophet Amos speaks to fellow citizens who continue to observe the Sabbath and a host of religious festivals, but the observance has no meaning because it is divorced from concern for the poor and the oppressed. Amos sees his countrymen look impatiently toward the setting sun, asking, "When will the new moon be over so that we may sell grain; and the sabbath, so that we may offer wheat for sale? We will make the ephah small and the shekel great, and practice deceit with false balances, buying the poor for silver and the needy for a pair of sandals, and selling the sweepings of the wheat" (Amos 8:5–6).

Impatient to see the Sabbath end, the goal is not merely to get back to work but also to pursue a course of exploitation. Amos charges that the practices of the business community of this time reek with stinginess and profiteering. In order to get his point across, Amos quotes the sentiment of people who are at the receiving end of his message.[16] But the apparent negative view of the Sabbath that is espoused by the people who wish for it to end must be qualified to avoid the impression that the Sabbath is no longer observed. Elsewhere, Amos makes it clear that his fellow citizens are not irreligious or unobservant of the Sabbath and other religious festivals (Amos 4:4–5; 8:5). In some ways they appear truly devout, and their services are carefully planned and spectacularly executed.

What is lacking is the ethical core, the element without which the religious rituals become meaningless and counterproductive.[17] The people come across as crass materialists, riveted by the prospects of the stock market of their day and so preoccupied with their own material prosperity that they have lost the connection between the goodness of God and the well-being of fellow human beings.

> Thus says the LORD: For three transgressions of Israel, and for four, I will not revoke the punishment; because they sell the righteous for silver, and the needy for a pair of sandals—they who trample the head of the poor into the dust of the earth, and push the afflicted out of the way; father and son go in to the same girl, so that my holy name is profaned; they lay themselves down beside every altar on garments taken in pledge; and in the house of their God they drink wine bought with fines they imposed. (Amos 2:6–8)[18]

Amos speaks of people who revel in affluence and luxury while being devoid of social conscience (Amos 4:1). He takes them to task for their opulent, leisurely lifestyle which has been achieved by exploitation of others and indifference to the plight of the poor (Amos 3:15; 6:4–6).

Amos repudiates this brand of religion (Amos 5:21).[19] So does his younger contemporary Isaiah, who is equally determined to extricate the Sabbath from the dishonor of being the symbol of a callous, materialistic, and acquisition-bent orientation. "When you come to appear before me, who asked this from your hand?" asks Isaiah (Isa. 1:12). Anyone inclined to persist in this misconception of religion is asked to desist. "Trample my courts no more; bringing offerings is futile; incense is an abomination to me. New moon and sabbath and calling of convocation—I cannot endure solemn assemblies with iniquity" (Isa. 1:12–13).

Clearly, the people addressed by Amos and Isaiah are not irreligious, but they are sworn to a lifestyle of material gain and personal prosperity at the expense of seeking justice for people less fortunate. In the words of Shaul M. Paul,

> Amos delivered a devastating diatribe against the nation's distorted panacea of the cult—the opium of the masses. For him, as for many of the other classical prophets, cultic zeal could neither engender public weal nor atone for infringements upon the moral law. Ritual can never be a surrogate for ethics. "God desires devotion, not devotions," right more than rite. When the cult became a substitute for moral behavior, it was severely denounced and condemned.[20]

Among things listed in the prophetic indictment are "exploitation of the impoverished and underprivileged" and, no less important, a lifestyle of "pampered prosperity and boisterous banquetry,"[21] both of which are apt summaries of Amos's message, and both of which are incompatible with the intent and spirit of the seventh day.

In the alternative offered by Amos and Isaiah, social justice, not religious ritual, is central. "Even though you offer me your burnt offerings and grain offerings," Amos objects on God's behalf, "I will not accept them; and the offerings of well-being of your fatted animals I will not look upon. Take away from me the noise of your songs; I will not listen to the melody of your harps" (Amos 5:22–23). What is sought, instead, is the costlier currency that delivers the benefits of religion to those most needy. "But let justice roll down like waters, and righteousness like an ever-flowing stream" (Amos 5:24).[22] To Gary V. Smith, this text is "an admonition to change the central focus of worship from the performance of the ritual to the establishment of justice and righteousness."[23]

A FRIEND OF THE POOR

These Old Testament voices do not cast the Sabbath and social justice in opposition to each other (Isa. 58:6–7). They lay bare misconceptions and misguided priorities in Israel's religious outlook, but their argument is not against the Sabbath. Instead, they act on the premise that social justice is a core value of the seventh day. George Adam Smith captures the relationship between the Sabbath and social concerns in Amos: "And, as in every other relevant passage of the Old Testament, we have the interest of the Sabbath bound up in the same cause with the interests of the poor. The Fourth Commandment enforces the day of rest on behalf of the servants and bondsmen....The interests of the Sabbath are the interests of the poor: the enemies of the Sabbath are the enemies of the poor."[24]

In Isaiah, the same chapter that spells out the obligation of social justice (Isa. 58:1–12) calls for a restoration of the seventh day (Isa. 58:13–14). There is no hint that the Sabbath is a matter of mere ceremony that is soon to be eclipsed by right ethical behavior or that the prophet opposes Sabbath observance.[25] Having laid out his program of social justice (Isa. 58:1–12), Isaiah turns to the Sabbath as a matter of course.

> If you refrain from trampling the sabbath, from pursuing your own interests on my holy day; if you call the sabbath a delight and the holy day of the LORD honorable; if you honor it, not going your own ways, serving your own interests, or pursuing your own affairs; then you shall take delight in the LORD, and I will make you ride upon the heights of the earth; I will feed you with the heritage of your ancestor Jacob, for the mouth of the LORD has spoken. (Isa. 58:13–14)

Lest there be any misunderstanding, it is the enemies of the Sabbath that are "the enemies of the poor"[26] in their disrespectful attitude toward the disadvantaged and in their relentless pursuit of upward advancement. Conversely, the Sabbath is a friend of the poor, a refuge from the intrusive claims people make on the lives of fellow human beings. While the witness of Amos and Isaiah offers proof of the social character of the seventh day, it also shows the tension building between this vision and that of a culture attempting to dilute the fierce ethical core of the Sabbath. In this context the prophets are determined to prevent the Sabbath from becoming a shallow feature of folk religion and a ritual deprived of ethical sting.[27]

I have given the people of Amos's day the negative label "crass materialists." But by using such terminology we run the risk of deflecting Amos's message as though it is addressing his time only. It is doubtful that their materialism was any worse than that of the average, upwardly mobile and affluent Westerner who spends his wealth with a sense of entitlement and indifference to those who struggle to make ends meet. We need to put ourselves in the line of the moral indictment that comes down from the prophets. In the witness of Amos and Isaiah we are led to recognize the sober, moral core of the Sabbath, the conviction that the God of the Sabbath seeks the benefit of all human beings and will not settle for advantages merely for the few.

The interests of the Sabbath are the interests of the poor: the enemies of the Sabbath are the enemies of the poor.

Why would religion flourish in tandem with rampant exploitation and injustice? The prophetic view that religious activity and materialistic pursuit are what "you love to do" (Amos 4:5) hints that people have not come to such a state simply by being blind to what is happening. Instead, there seems to be a rationale, a process of deliberation that upholds an unjust status quo even to the point of finding it satisfactory. Amos's call to "let justice roll down like waters" (Amos 5:24) demands a reappraisal of religion and religious priorities, raising social justice higher in the scale of value. In this respect Amos's contemporaries are hardly unique.

In the book *Shantung Compound* Langdon Gilkey tells of his life in a large Japanese internment camp in Northern China during

World War II along with 1,450 other internees of foreign origin, two hundred of whom were Americans.[28] The prisoners are largely left to themselves to organize camp life. They are constantly hungry, and food is a perennial topic of conversation. Then in January 1945 a shipment of 1,550 parcels from the American Red Cross arrives. The Japanese commandant decides to give one package to each inmate, and, since the packages came from the American Red Cross, each American will receive one and a half packages.

God of the Sabbath seeks the benefit of all human beings and will not settle for advantages merely for the few.

But seven young American prisoners protest, arguing that since the packages are from the United States, they should only be distributed to the Americans. Any further distribution should happen at the discretion of the Americans. When pressed to estimate how the parcels should be distributed, it emerges that the voluntary scheme most likely would leave each American with five and a half packages and each of the other internees with one quarter of a package!

This case is argued so passionately that the planned distribution is put on hold for ten days, awaiting its resolution from a higher level of authority. In the meantime the camp erupts in intense verbal and sometimes physical conflict at what the non-Americans view as selfishness. Intense discussions rage throughout the camp, some attempting to justify the action and others heaping scorn on those who instigated it.

Most remarkable to Gilkey, however, himself an American, is the skill with which leading Christians in the group defend the inequitable distribution. These Christians seem the most adept in the art of putting self-serving choices in a positive light, dignifying them with a tincture of theology and moral reasoning that seem impervious to alternative points of view.[29] This skill suggests to Gilkey that Christian theology has equipped people with rhetorical tools honed to the task of justifying injustice to the point of making the fracture between religious practice and social justice seem like a constitutional feature of the Christian mindset.

Generalizing from his own experience in Shantung Compound to the role the Christian religion has played and is playing in the world, Gilkey finds believers unwilling to face the political ramifications of social justice. Since many believers "can never see any connection between the action of government and the morality of that government's citizens," it is no wonder that "they find it impossible to relate morality to the problems of politics," he exclaims.[30]

PUBLIC MORALITY

The message of the prophets sounds the same note, insisting that "private" morality not be allowed to eclipse "public" morality. Mordecai Roshwald, writing in a different context, says that "[p]ublic morality includes individual morality, but adds to it the might of the society and its governing institutions. It assures that the right action is not only a noble *intent* of the individual—which may or may not lead to the desirable results—but the good intent is actually translated into the right, as well as beneficial, *deed*."[31] The Old Testament is fully at home in both arenas, the private and the public, but it might be most easily marginalized in the public sphere.

For the social conscience of the seventh day to stand out in force, magnified by the Sabbatical Year and the Jubilee and driven home by the ceaseless preoccupation with social justice in Amos and Isaiah, it must be appreciated that these institutions are systemic and not merely matters left to personal discretion. The seventh day has a political and economic dimension, as well, a point that should not be missed with respect to the seventh day proper and one that cannot be overlooked in the Sabbatical Year and the Jubilee. This triumvirate represents institutionalized, large-scale interventions that are enacted and brought into being as "political" and constitutional conceptions of justice. In the social and economic sphere the Sabbath sets a limit to work and to exploitation of the worker, ensuring for each person the right to rest. If "[a] man's most sacred property is his labour" because "it is the possession of those who have nothing else,"[32] the Sabbath puts the stewardship of work in a religious frame of reference, to be discharged within God's merciful and protective boundaries.

Likewise, the Sabbatical Year extends the privilege of rest to creation itself, and the Jubilee represents a radical, structural realignment of ownership and property every fifty years. This system imposes a ceiling on the acquisition of wealth, providing a spectacular safety net for the less fortunate and even for the less diligent. Attempting to translate the social character of these ordinances into contemporary terms, they belong in the context of the voting booth and in halls of legislation more than in the context of the offering plate. What is proposed in the Old Testament are large-scale, unprecedented ventures. "See, just as the LORD my God has charged me, I now teach you statutes and ordinances for you to observe in the land that you are about to enter and occupy," Moses tells the people as they are about to take possession of the Promised Land (Deut. 4:5). If the people will put them into practice, the ordinances will prove to their benefit and be a source of wonder to others. "You must observe them diligently," says Moses, "for this will show your wisdom and discernment to the peoples, who, when they hear all these statutes, will say, 'Surely this great nation is a wise and discerning people!'…And what other great nation has statutes and ordinances as just as this entire law that I am setting before you today?" (Deut. 4:6, 8).

In practice, however, it is precisely the exceptional character of these large-scale interventions that becomes the stumbling block. Perhaps we should not be surprised at the Chronicler's report, suggesting that the Sabbatical Year was never observed (2 Chron. 36:21). Ultimately, people opt for less ambitious notions than the ecologically-minded stewardship of the land and less drastic social measures than the Jubilee.

The incident from the Shantung Compound illustrates that social justice is an elusive commodity, easily watered down by legalistic paradigms and pious rhetoric. Amos's vision for social justice is part and parcel of the same ideal, facing similar obstacles. What he faults is the fact that the people of his generation live "a religiously embellished sumptuous life of luxury," they abrogate justice, and they try to compensate for real justice by a "misguided trust in pilgrimages and elaborate worship services."[33]

The bottom line of this subject, of course, cannot be the social conscience of the seventh day. What we are witnessing, in the deepest sense, is God's social conscience. In the ministry of Amos and Isaiah, the human voices bring to light God's priorities, and the abuses they decry speak to conditions God finds intolerable. The Sabbath and the Jubilee are divine interventions aiming to rectify injustice. Ultimately, therefore, the prophetic concern cannot be limited to flawed human practice with respect to the divine ideal. What we see, instead, is a profound misperception and misjudgment of God on the part of human beings.

In the social and economic sphere the Sabbath sets a limit to work and to exploitation of the worker, ensuring for each person the right to rest.

The materialism exposed by Amos and the hypocrisy that is so offensive to Isaiah must not be seen only as moral failure on the human level. The God that people continue to revere in their elaborate religious services is someone other than the God of the seventh day. When the prophet Jeremiah wonders how God seems to lose out to the disgusting gods of the Canaanites, he sounds as if he is fearful that the pagan idols will replace the only true God. But this rhetoric barely conceals the deeper and more subtle concern: People may continue to worship the "true" God, but, investing God with false attributes, they transform their object of worship into an idol. This is the deeper meaning of Jeremiah's lament that "my people have changed their glory for that which does not profit," a telltale characteristic of idol worship in the Old Testament, devotion to which is devoid of benefit (Jer. 2:11).

Confusion about the object of worship clouds people's perception of the Unseen, and the effect of the distorted ideal does lasting damage. Those who worship such idols, warns one Old Testament writer, "*will be like them*, and so will all who trust in them" (Ps. 135:15–18). For Israel, as for all who take the same course, the choice is disastrous. "They followed worthless idols and themselves became worthless," says one who tried to understand the demise of ancient Israel (2 Kings 17:15). In this view a person's perception of his or her object of worship translates into behavior. Where we speak of the social conscience of the seventh day, we are led to recognize God's social conscience as the source of the magnificent enterprises of social justice in the Old Testament. All this is brought together in Ezekiel's review of the events that led to Israel's exile in Babylon. The people, he claims, have "rejected my statutes and profaned my sabbaths, and their eyes were set on their fathers' idols" (Ezek. 20:24).

During the era of the great prophets, as the nations of Israel and Judah increasingly turn to the spiritual and moral values from which their ancestors had been set free in Egypt, the Sabbath appears to be a spent force. Countless follow-up commands and prescriptions have been proclaimed to no avail. At last the situation seems beyond remedy (Hosea 8:12; 2 Chron. 36:15–16). In the trajectory of the Old Testament narrative, the wellspring of untried imperatives is running dry, reinforcing the impression that the predicament is at heart one that will not be resolved by ordinary means (2 Chron. 36:16). Moreover, since Israel's failure is said to derive from her eagerness to assimilate the ways of pagan religions, there is no reason to expect a turn for the better because of influences from outside.

What we are witnessing, in the deepest sense, is God's social conscience.

Hence it is surprising to hear precisely these prophets look to a future day for their hope to come to fruition. Amos speaks of a day when God "will raise up the booth of David that is fallen, and repair its breaches, and raise up its ruins, and rebuild it as in the days of old" (Amos 9:11). In Isaiah, we read that "[y]our ancient ruins shall be rebuilt; you shall raise up the foundations of many generations; you shall be called the repairer of the breach" (Isa. 58:12). Where Amos has made social justice the *sine qua non* of his project, Isaiah, too, puts justice front and center. "Justice is turned back, and righteousness stands at a distance; for truth stumbles in the public square, and uprightness cannot enter" (Isa. 59:14). This is the problem not only toward the end of the book but all through the most remarkable prophetic book in the Old Testament. Likewise, resonating with the need, the one who is to come "will bring forth justice to the nations" (Isa. 42:1); indeed, justice is the gist of the mission. The agent that is to come "will not grow faint or be crushed until he has established justice in the earth" (Isa. 42:4).

Surprising, too, is the fact that the restoration that is to come features the Sabbath in a prominent role. This is baffling in its native context and downright shocking in the light of contemporary theological priorities (Isa. 58:13–14; 56:1–8). In the prophetic vision the seventh day is yet to play a role not only in Israel but on a wider stage. When the outlook seems most hopeless, just as the prophet's voice is becoming hoarse from the futility of persuading his own generation, it is disclosed that God has other means at His disposal.

ENDNOTES

1. Pedersen, *Israel*, II:290.

2. Geraldine Smyth, "Sabbath and Jubilee" in *The Jubilee Challenge: Utopia or Possibility?* ed. Hans Ucko (Geneva: WCC Publications, 1997), 64.

3. Jean Louis Ska, "Biblical Law and the Origins of Democracy," in *The Ten Commandments: The Reciprocity of Faithfulness*, ed. William P. Brown (Louisville: Westminster John Knox Press, 2004), 152.

4. Niels-Erik Andreasen, "Festival and Freedom," *Interpretation* 28 (1974): 281–297.

5. Cf. Rendtorff, *The Canonical Hebrew Bible*, 464–465.

6. Andreasen ("Festival and Freedom," 294) calls the Sabbatical Year and the Jubilee "sister institutions" of the Sabbath.

7. Raphael Jospe, "Sabbath, Sabbatical and Jubilee: Jewish Ethical Perspectives," in *The Jubilee Challenge*, 78.

8. Norman C. Habel, *The Land Is Mine* (Minneapolis: Fortress Press, 1995), 102–103.

9. Habel (*The Land Is Mine*, 104) calls the Jubilee ordinance an "economic amnesty."

10. Erhard S. Gerstenberger, *Leviticus,* trans. Douglas W. Stott (OTL; Louisville: Westminster John Knox Press, 1996), 374.

11. Ibid., 377.

12. Ibid., 374.

13. Hans Ucko, "The Jubilee as Challenge," in *The Jubilee Challenge*, 2.

14. Jacob Milgrom, "Leviticus 25 and Some Postulates of the Jubilee," in *The Jubilee Challenge*, 32; cf. also, idem, *Leviticus: A New Translation with Introduction and Commentary,* vol. 3 (AB; New York: Doubleday), 2145–2212.

15. Robert Gnuse, "Jubilee Legislation in Leviticus: Israel's Vision of Social Reform," *Biblical Theology Bulletin* 15 (1985): 47.

16. John H. Hays, *The Eighth-Century Prophet Amos: His Times & His Preaching* (Nashville: Abingdon Press, 1988), 208; Gary V. Smith, *Amos* (Grand Rapids: Zondervan, 1989), 253; Shalom M. Paul, *Amos* (Hermeneia; Minneapolis: Fortress Press, 1991), 257.

17. Jörg Jeremias, *The Book of Amos,* trans. Douglas V. Stott (Louisville: Westminster John Knox Press, 1998), 147.

18. Readers of Amos have been impressed by his rhetorical skill in putting his audience at ease by first going after the cruelty of the surrounding nations (Amos 1:3–2:5), undoubtedly meeting heartfelt approval on the home front. One can imagine that his listeners were less inclined to applaud when he proceeds to point out similar sins at home, a moral evenhandedness that has never been a recipe for popularity.

19. Cf. George Smith, *Amos*, 184–187.

20. Paul, *Amos*, 2.

21. Ibid.

22. To Hays (*Amos*, 174), justice is "the constant theme of the exhortations of the book."

23. George Smith, *Amos*, 187.

24. George Adam Smith, *The Twelve Prophets*, vol. I, rev. ed. (New York: Harper and Brothers, 1928), 190; see also Page H. Kelly, *Amos: Prophet of Social Justice* (Grand Rapids: Baker Book House, 1972), 116.

25. John N. Oswalt, *The Book of Isaiah. Chapters 40–66* (NICOT; Grand Rapids: Eerdmans, 1998), 508.

26. George Adam Smith, *The Twelve Prophets*, I:190.

27. M. Daniel Carroll R., "'For So You Love to Do': Probing Popular Religion in the Book of Amos," in *Rethinking Contexts, Rereading Texts* (JSOTSup 299; Sheffield: Sheffield Academic Press, 2000), 182.

28. Langdon Gilkey, *Shantung Compound: The Story of Men and Women under Pressure* (New York: Harper & Row, 1966).

29. Gilkey, *Shantung Compound*, 96–116.

30. Ibid., 110.

31. Mordecai Roshwald, "A Dialogue between Man and God," *SJT* 42 (1989): 163.

32. Lord Acton, "The Background of the French Revolution," in Sir (John) Acton, *Essays on Freedom and Power* (Gloucester, MA: Peter Smith, 1972), 235.

33. Jeremias, *Amos*, 3–4.

CHAPTER 9

THE PROPHETIC STAKE IN THE SABBATH

And the foreigners who join themselves to the Lord, *to minister to him, to love the name of the* Lord, *and to be his servants, all who keep the sabbath,...these I will bring to my holy mountain, and make them joyful in my house of prayer;...for my house shall be called a house of prayer for all peoples.*

Isaiah 56:6–7

Much of the Old Testament sees Israel in spiritual and political decline, leading, first, to the conquest of the northern kingdom of Israel by the Assyrians in 722 BC,[1] and culminating, second, in the conquest of the southern kingdom of Judah and the razing of Jerusalem and its temple by the Babylonians in 605–587 BC.[2] When the story of national erosion and subsequent captivity is told in the Old Testament, lack of appreciation for the Sabbath is treated as a telltale symptom of the decline as well as a feature materially hastening the process (Amos 8:5; Isa. 1:12–13; Ezek. 20:24).

And yet the prophets are not about to declare the seventh day a lost cause, invariably at the mercy of its observance or non-observance in Israel. In the most forward-looking view of the Sabbath in the Old Testament (Isa. 56:1–8; 58:13–14; 66:23), at least three significant reconfigurations are taking place. While the Sabbath may be in eclipse in Israel, Isaiah's vision gives it a new and unlimited lease on life, foreseeing and urging a Sabbath renaissance, and investing the expected resurgence with striking eschatological overtones (Isa. 56:1–8).

At the deepest level of this reconfiguration, the focus moves from the human stewardship of the seventh day, a fickle measure even in the best of times, to the question of God's character and reliability. Despite the uncertain outlook for the seventh day in Israel, the prophetic vision maintains the connection between the Sabbath and the most contested affirmations about God. Precisely at the point when the cup of human failure is fast filling, the book of Isaiah cuts the subject of the seventh day to the bone, exposing, as it were, the core meaning of the Sabbath with a clarity and intensity of purpose that is unsurpassed in the Old Testament.

THE SABBATH VISION IN ISAIAH

While the notion that Isaiah has three main divisions (1–39; 40–55; 56–66) is by no means universally accepted,[3] and while this question cannot be held as a major concern in the present context, it is brought to the surface only to show that theories of authorship will not undermine or weaken the impact of Isaiah's Sabbath vision no matter which view of the book's composition is held.

Joseph Blenkinsopp, who leans in favor of dividing Isaiah into three parts, concedes that the presumed third part of the book is too elusive to invite definitive claims with respect to authorship. "Dating the last 11 chapters of Isaiah has not been easy since they refer to no historical events and name no historical individuals," he writes.[4] The absence of historical data leads John Oswalt to conclude that it is the theology of this part of Isaiah that matters.[5] Significantly, the prominence of the Sabbath in this part of the book is not contested.

Caveats with respect to the historical data dovetail with crucial markers of thematic unity and continuity. These markers contradict the notion that the "third" Isaiah is tacked on to the rest of the book as a late addition. Whether we see the author as the historical Isaiah living before the exile (Isa. 1:1; 6:1; 37:5–7) or as a more elusive persona, the ending of Isaiah appears to address a community that is concerned about the preservation of its identity.[6] Who is to be included in the community? Who is to be excluded? Who may hold positions of leadership and influence? These questions are more important than the quest to establish a post-exilic context for the prophet's message, as many scholars have done.[7]

Irrespective of how we imagine the historical setting, the Sabbath emphasis found here is remarkable, affirming both its general validity and universality, applying it to two groups that earlier would have been excluded.

> Happy is the mortal who does this,...who keeps the sabbath (56:2)
> To the eunuchs who keep my sabbaths (56:4)
> And the foreigners..., all who keep the sabbath (56:6)

Here the Sabbath stands out as a vital concern, demonstrated by its threefold mention and by the groups included within its reach. The Sabbath clearly is not relegated to a particular time period or restricted to a select group of people.

First, the prophet anchors his message in God's long-anticipated intervention. "Thus says the LORD: Maintain justice, and do what is right, for soon my salvation will come, and my deliverance be revealed" (Isa. 56:1). This verse alone confirms that the message cannot be limited to a narrow point in time. To the extent that we are to see a point in time, the point must be the end-time, the moment of God's final vindication.

The end-orientation loosens the tie to a specific situation in Old Testament times. To questions lying at rock bottom in human existence, the message is one of hope. God's redeeming intervention will come, and God's deliverance "will be revealed" (56:1). Significantly, too, the content and the language reinforce the sense of finality in the passage. Blenkinsopp notes that "everything in 56–66 is decisively oriented to the future,"[8] a feature that certainly applies to the text concerning the Sabbath.

The end-orientation of the Sabbath vision in Isaiah can therefore not be emphasized too strongly. "Isaiah 56:1–8 opens with an exhortation to practice justice and righteousness *in view of* an imminent divine intervention of salvation and judgment (v. 1). We can read this as an anticipation of early Christian *Interimethik*, that is, ethics in the light of eschatology, a way of living in a world or world order that is about to come to an end."[9]

The end-orientation of the Sabbath vision in Isaiah can therefore not be emphasized too strongly.

If we take this perspective seriously, we must concede that although the seventh day appears to be wilting in the historical arena in the context of Israel's decline, God—through the ministry of the prophet—has great plans for it. The Sabbath is not to be abrogated or put on hold but will instead rise to sustain the despairing believer and contribute to carrying him or her through to the end.

A second feature, only to be briefly noted, is that the Sabbath is introduced in the form of a beatitude. "*Happy* is the mortal who does this, the one who holds it fast, who keeps the sabbath, not profaning it, and refrains from doing any evil," the text continues (Isa. 56:2). "Happy," the word preferred by the NRSV, comes with the connotation of a subjective state, seeing happiness as the conscious experience of the believer. While this view is not to be disparaged, it is likely that the text aims toward an objective evaluation. The person in view is "blessed" (NIV), in a state of privilege whether or not he or she is able to "feel" the blessing. Where the believer and the believer's confidence in God are under siege, the Sabbath becomes a means to prevail.

The enduring character of the Sabbath already established, the passage in Isaiah turns to a third affirmation by specifying the target audience. People who are not native Israelites and who have previously been excluded, or have seen themselves excluded, are invited into the domain of its blessing. Two groups are specifically singled out as beneficiaries of the new policy of inclusion—the eunuchs and the stranger. "To the eunuchs who keep my sabbaths, who choose the things that please me and hold fast my covenant, I will give, in my house and within my walls, a monument and a name better than sons and daughters; I will give them an everlasting name that shall not be cut off" (Isa. 56:4–5). This assures the heretofore stigmatized group unlimited access and full, unqualified membership.

The strangers and immigrants, ethnic non-Jews, are also welcome. "And the foreigners who join themselves to the Lord, to minister to him, to love the name of the Lord, and to be his servants, all who keep the sabbath, and do not profane it, and hold fast my covenant—these I will bring to my holy mountain, and make them joyful in my house of prayer" (Isa. 56:6–7). In a later installment the foreigners are ordained to priestly ministry, a function previously the exclusive preserve of Jews of Levitic descent. "And I will also take some of them as priests and as Levites, says the Lord" (Isa. 66:21). A leading Old Testament theologian points out the novelty of this opening of the doors to the priesthood. "Still more surprising is the final chapter," writes Grace L. Emmerson, "where it is envisaged that some of foreign birth may share even in the service of the sanctuary as priests and Levites."[10] End-orientation and universalism, eschatology and inclusion, go hand in hand because the Sabbath has cosmic significance.[11]

Fourth, Isaiah's vision implicitly disavows the notion that the Sabbath is the peculiar preserve of ethnic Jews. Instead of ethnicity, nationality, and tradition the emphasis is on personal choice. A host of action verbs to this effect dominates the passage. The blessing is extended to those who *keep* (vv. 2, 4, 6), *choose* (v. 4), *hold fast* (vv. 4, 6), or *join themselves* (v. 6), all signifying deliberate intention on the part of the person thus described. As noted by Claus Westermann, "[t]hese verbs make it perfectly plain that membership of the community which worships Yahweh is now based upon resolve, a free affirmation of this God and of his worship. No longer is it thought of in national but in individual terms. The chosen people has turned into the confessing community."[12]

We have not fully sounded the depth of this dramatic reconfiguration unless we broaden it into a fifth observation, one that looks more closely at the community in the light of the traditional criteria of exclusion and the present struggle to come to grips with new boundaries. Isaiah proposes to include people who were previously excluded. On this point the new message is in conflict with the old pattern, setting aside previous practice and precedent. There seems to be a discussion in progress in which we hear voices for and against the inclusion of the new groups, and where the voices speaking *against* inclusion seem to have the better argument.

The polemic in the text may not lie on the surface, but it is not necessary to dig deep to find it. The discussion that is in progress comes to view in the curious formulation, "Do not let the foreigner joined to the LORD say, 'The LORD will surely separate me from his people'; and do not let the eunuch say, 'I am just a dry tree'" (Isa. 56:3). Why would the foreigner and the eunuch express what they are reported to say? Whence the foreigner's apprehension that God "will surely separate me from his people"? Isaiah leaves no doubt that God is behind the initiative of inclusion, but inclusion is not a matter of course. Seeking to maintain the ethnic criterion for belonging, people on the other side of the table are resisting the prophetic initiative.

This suggests that the community in view has a hallowed tradition of exclusiveness. In fact, Isaiah's inclusiveness seems to run directly against the command, "No one whose testicles are crushed or whose penis is cut off shall be admitted to the assembly of the LORD" (Deut. 23:1). The controversial nature of the new vision is easy to spot: Will the community on this point set aside the Mosaic counsel and act against the rules laid down by the founding fathers?

Isaiah also advocates the inclusion of foreigners (Isa. 56:6–7). Again, his vision of inclusion confronts explicit counsel to the contrary. Deuteronomy stipulates that only the children of the third generation of foreigners "may be admitted to the assembly of the LORD" (Deut. 23:8). Walther Eichrodt holds that the result of the heritage of Deuteronomy "did in practice set the nations outside the covenant and taught that this should be regarded as a specifically Israelite privilege."[13] How, then, can Isaiah's vision of inclusion stand a chance, noting that "[t]hese chapters begin and end with an open-hearted generosity towards foreigners which is unmatched by anything else in the Old Testament?"[14] And how can the privilege of the Sabbath become the property of groups previously left outside its sphere?

Marking it as a sixth element in Isaiah's affirmations, the driving force behind the paradigm-shattering reconfiguration is theological. God is redrawing the boundary lines to the specifications of God's own character, saying to those previously stigmatized, excluded, or dispossessed: I welcome you.[15] Casting a net that is so wide that the emerging community deserves to be called something other than "the community of Judaism," Walter Brueggemann is nevertheless correct in saying that the believing fellowship "is to be a community that remembers, cherishes, and preserves the name and identity of those otherwise nullified in an uncaring world."[16] The project of including outcasts has no limit because God aims to embrace everybody, with a special note of hope to individuals and groups previously disenfranchised and ignored. "Thus says the LORD God, who gathers the outcasts of Israel, I will gather others to them besides those already gathered" (Isa. 56:8). This is the God of inclusion speaking, God as the insistent and persistent gatherer, so much so that the verb denoting gathering is said to be "Yahweh's most defining verb, Yahweh's most characteristic activity."[17] In this vision of inclusion, within which the Sabbath is given such a conspicuous role, nothing conveys better the universal intention than the statement, "For my house shall be called a house of prayer *for all peoples*" (Isa. 56:7).

Exposing the theological core, or rather, creating awareness that the core of Isaiah's emphasis is theological, is only the penultimate step in Isaiah's message. There is yet another disclosure, a seventh affirmation in his vision for the end-time community and its faith. What we may call the final and ultimate confirmation focuses on a specific and definite characteristic in God. On this point there is striking convergence between the emphasis in Isaiah's end-time message concerning the Sabbath (56:1–8) and the larger theme of the last eleven chapters of the book (chs. 56–66).

The reader who is prone to take offense at the constellation of the Sabbath and refraining "from doing any evil" (Isa. 56:2) because it seems to place an unimportant point, the Sabbath, alongside a far more weighty ethical imperative, "doing any evil,"[18] need not worry. The alleged "awkward parallelism"[19] is certainly not seen as that by the prophet. To him the Sabbath is not merely an identity marker of his community. Rather, the Sabbath expresses the community's hope in its most essential configuration. Indeed, Isaiah's thrice-repeated sentiment with respect to the Sabbath leaves little doubt that he sees Sabbath observance as vital, but his emphasis belongs in the context of a theological affirmation that is at once comprehensive and specific. Believers are urged to remain faithful and to keep the Sabbath in view of God's imminent intervention (Isa. 56:1–8). However, God's intervention is not a consequence of their confidence as though their trust obligates God to act. On the contrary, the believer's trust is entirely a consequence of God's trustworthiness.[20] "We should be righteous, the writer says, because of the righteousness of God. This point is followed throughout the section: Human obedience should be the natural result of divine *faithfulness*."[21]

It is a mistake to place the believer at the center. The entire project depends on the promise that "soon my salvation will come, and my deliverance be revealed" (Isa. 56:1). Urging confidence in this hope the believing eunuch is encouraged to await the fulfillment of God's promise (Isa. 56:5). Likewise, the foreigner is called to persevere on the strength of the divine pledge, "[t]hese I will bring to my holy mountain, and make them joyful in my house of prayer" (Isa. 56:7). The believer's faithfulness is not the cause of God's intervention but an act of reciprocity that takes God's anticipated intervention for granted. Trusting in God's advent, as it were, the believer hangs on to the Sabbath because the Sabbath has come to be integral to his or her hope.

THE SABBATH AND THE FAITHFULNESS OF GOD

It cannot be emphasized too strongly that God's trustworthiness is not affirmed in a vacuum. Isaiah urges confidence in God at a time when the believer's confidence is tested to the limit. Perhaps nothing is as remarkable in the last part of Isaiah as the way the question of God's faithfulness floats to the surface as the dominant theme. Hope is maintained in a context of hopelessness; confidence in God is affirmed precisely when appearances suggest that God's promises are failing. The rallying cry of the prophetic voice is therefore best appreciated when it is heard in contrast to the dire outlook that seems to rise from the situation itself. "Then whoever invokes a blessing in the land shall bless by the God of faithfulness, and whoever takes an oath in the land shall swear by the God of faithfulness; because the former troubles are forgotten and are hidden from my sight" (Isa. 65:16).

The trouble will not last indefinitely, and the twice repeated affirmation, translated by the NRSV as "the God of faithfulness," becomes something of an identity marker of the community that is in view. In Hebrew there is a ring to this expression that is even more striking, as though *'Elōhê 'āmēn* ("God of faithfulness") is meant to signify God's most defining characteristic. Moreover, *'Elōhê 'āmēn* must not be severed from the verbal form *'āman*, or the closely related nouns *'emet* and *'emûnâ*. Alfred Jepsen notes that "*'emeth* was used of things that had to be tested in order to be reliable,"[22] indicating that "reliability" is the best term for the word *'emet* in English. Its cousin, *'emûnâ*, on the other hand, is "a way of acting which grows out of inner stability, 'conscientiousness.'"[23] Thus, in Jepsen's words, "*'emeth* describes the character of a person on whose words and deeds one can rely," and "*'emunah* denotes the conduct of a person corresponding to his own inner being."[24] Jepsen concludes that

> [w]hen a Hebrew heard the various words derived from the root *'mn*, the basic idea that came to his mind was apparently "constancy." When they were used of things, they meant "continual"; and when they were connected with persons, "reliability."...From "stability" through "reliability," *'emeth* acquires the meaning of "truth," while *'emunah* conveys more the idea of "conduct that grows out of reliability," i.e., "faithfulness."[25]

Rising from Isaiah's rousing affirmation of God's faithfulness, magnified by the accompanying expectation that people previously excluded will also experience God's faithfulness, the prophetic vision in Isaiah culminates on a note the like of which is not found anywhere else in the Old Testament. Minor repairs will not suffice for God's intention to become a reality. A mere local undertaking that will touch the lives of only a few will not do. In keeping with the sweeping and universalistic reach of what is to happen, there is to be a new beginning, and the new beginning will retrace the steps of God's original Creation.[26] *Paradise lost* is to become *Paradise regained*, configured according to the goal of God's original purpose. "For I am about to create new heavens and a new earth; the former things shall not be remembered or come to mind" (Isa. 65:17).

This is not a new emphasis in Isaiah (cf. Isa 11:9), but the prophet makes the vision of *Paradise regained* the capstone of his prediction. Hostility will cease, and alienation will be overcome. "The wolf and the lamb shall feed together, the lion shall eat straw like the ox; but the serpent—its food shall be dust! They shall not hurt or destroy on all my holy mountain, says the LORD" (Isa. 65:25).

In chapter 11, Isaiah configures what is to happen at the end of God's intervention early in the book. When this scenario reappears in the closing chapters, however, it is done with a twist that must not be missed. "The wolf and the lamb shall feed together, the lion shall eat straw like the ox" (Isa. 65:25), the text begins reassuringly. And then, suddenly, unexpectedly, Isaiah calls attention to a creature that will be excluded from the harmony, at least figuratively: "but the serpent—its food shall be dust!" (Isa. 65:25c).

Why the mention of the serpent only to exclude it from the harmony that is to return to Creation? The answer, of course, lies in the Genesis story that is looming large in Isaiah's vision.[27] Only a fraction of the original story is echoed in Isaiah, but the connection is not to be missed. In Isaiah, indirectly, we hear God pronounce the verdict on the serpent: "Because you have done this, cursed are you among all animals and among all wild creatures; upon your belly you shall go, and dust you shall eat all the days of your life" (Gen. 3:14). The serpent's fate does not arise from thin air, a point that is easily seen when we line up the statements next to each other.

Paradise lost is to become Paradise regained, configured according to the goal of God's original purpose.

> "and dust you shall eat all the days of your life" (Gen. 3:14)
> "but the serpent—its food shall be dust!" (Isa. 65:25)

In Isaiah, as in Genesis, the undoing of the serpent is assured. The prophet who sees peace returning to "God's holy mountain" with greater clarity than anyone else in the Old Testament connects the dots to make his vision of the end fold back on the biblical story of the beginning.

From all of this it follows that Isaiah is not defending God's faithfulness against evidence to the contrary in his own time only. His message of hope is anchored in a larger narrative, and he sees harmony restored because the original malicious charge of the serpent has been dealt with. In contemporary English, he might have said that the serpent who at the beginning bit the fruit of the tree of knowledge will, in the end, bite the dust.

THE PROPHETIC SABBATH LEGACY

In the light of the foregoing it no longer seems remarkable that Isaiah's view of the new order concludes with an affirmation of the Sabbath. Just as the Sabbath completes Creation in Genesis (Gen. 2:1–3), it is to be the capstone of the new Creation. And just as the seventh day provides the meeting ground between God and humanity in Genesis, it will do the same in Isaiah's vision of the end. "From new moon to new moon, and from sabbath to sabbath, all flesh shall come to worship before me, says the LORD" (Isa. 66:23).

The tribute that thus concludes the book of Isaiah should be seen as the last word about the Sabbath in the Old Testament. While the history of Israel after the Babylonian Exile will add to the unfolding story of the Sabbath in historical terms, as seen in the book of Nehemiah,[28] the prophetic legacy with respect to the Sabbath in the Old Testament is most developed and most forward-looking in Isaiah. What happens in the historical arena, to be considered in the next chapter, must not be allowed to eclipse the prophetic vision. The eschatological character of Isaiah's Sabbath message has a greater reach than the subsequent status of the Sabbath in Israel. Isaiah remains in a league of his own, espousing a Sabbath ideology that follows a distinct and determined trajectory somewhat apart from the history of Israel.

Speaking of history, Israel appears torn between those who are ready to dilute its distinctives in a mix of secular pursuits, as seen in the beginning of Isaiah (Isa. 1:10–20), and those who argue for a narrow delineation of Israel's identity, as seen toward the end of the book (Isa. 56:1–8). Rejecting both of these options, and the latter option in particular, the terms of the covenant between Israel and God are in Isaiah offered to anyone for the taking. Whatever ambiguity there may have been with regard to the status of non-Jews is removed. God's temple is to be a house of prayer for all the sons and daughters of God (Isa. 56:7), and the Sabbath, God's cathedral in time, is made the property of all nations. Ultimately, "all flesh" will embrace the privilege of the Sabbath (Isa. 66:23). In the prophetic scenario the Sabbath is not a day for the sake of Jewishness but an eternal reference point for humanity.

The serpent who at the beginning bit the fruit of the tree of knowledge will, in the end, bite the dust.

To say that the last word concerning the Sabbath in the Old Testament belongs to Isaiah therefore calls for two final thoughts. If the last word belongs to Isaiah, it does not belong to anyone else, that is, it does not belong to Nehemiah, or to the next historical move or construction. Instead, the prophetic vision takes priority, and it is left to the forward-looking prophetic legacy to safeguard the divine intention concerning the seventh day.

The second idea vows that Isaiah does not merely deliver his message to the doorsteps of the New Testament with no obligation for the latter. On the contrary, his message is the soil in which the New Testament story grows and unfolds. Isaiah articulates some of the most important New Testament themes so clearly that it has been called "the fifth gospel."[29] Paul, the dominant voice in the New Testament, enlists the Old Testament in general and Isaiah in particular in support of his message.[30] Even the word "gospel," the core idea of the New Testament, is crafted along lines laid down in Isaiah.[31] Indeed, if the word "grace" is chosen as the most characteristic and representative term for the message of the New Testament, it, too, owes its roots to Isaiah, and it, too, owing to the emphasis in Isaiah, comes with the meaning that "God's faithfulness is firm, not fickle; it is steadfast, not capricious."[32] What comes to be the end-point in the New Testament, the goal toward which God's intervention is moving, is already the end-point in Isaiah (Isa. 65:17; Rev. 21:1). His message is eschatological and comprehensive, a wall-to-wall vision (Isa. 11:1–9; 65:25), reaching as far as the eye can see.

The Sabbath is not a day for the sake of Jewishness but an eternal reference point for humanity.

But most of all the legacy of Isaiah—with his affirmation of the Sabbath, his vision of inclusion, and his end-orientation—distills the believer's most perplexing concern to its purest essence. To the person whose faith is tested in the crucible of disappointment comes the exhortation to persevere, "for soon my salvation will come, and my deliverance be revealed" (Isa. 56:1). The person who takes this assurance to heart, incorporating this promise in his or her observance of the Sabbath, will not be disappointed.

At this point we touch an undercurrent in the biblical narrative that only occasionally breaks through the crust into daylight. What imperils the believer's confidence is ultimately the outworking of the breach between God and the human family at the beginning. Isaiah forges a link that unites past, present, and future, placing the present situation in a larger context by referring to the cause of the breach as described in Genesis 3, then promising that the blight on creation will be removed: "the wolf and the lamb shall feed together…but the serpent—its food shall be dust!" (Isa. 65:25).

Hope tested to the breaking point turns into hope prevailing and triumphant as those who, in my own translation, "count themselves blessed in the land shall count themselves blessed by the God of faithfulness, and those who make a commitment in the land shall make a commitment on the basis of the God of faithfulness" (Isa. 65:17). This affirmation constitutes the core of the believer's identity in the closing chapters of Isaiah. Acknowledging that this affirmation assigns an enduring and unprecedented priority to the Sabbath, the prophetic legacy of the Old Testament puts the seventh day in the mission of making known the faithfulness of God.

ENDNOTES

1. See 2 Kings 17:1–18; 18:9–10; cf. John Bright, *A History of Israel*, 4th ed. (Louisville: Westminster John Knox Press, 2000), 269–278.

2. See 2 Kings 23:36–25:12; 2 Chron 36:5–21; Dan 1:1; cf. Bright, *A History of Israel*, 324–339.

3. R. E. Clements ("The Unity of the Book of Isaiah," *Interpretation* 36 [1982]: 117–129) contends that the notion of a "school of Isaiah" is promoted without any evidence in support of its existence and then invoked to sustain arguments that depend on the viability of the unproven hypothesis in a circular argument. Rolf Rendtorff ("Zur Komposition des Buches Jesaja," *VT* 34 [1984]: 295–320) also notes the striking indicators of thematic unity in Isaiah. While stopping short of dismissing the traditional critical position on sources, Rendtorff finds the notion of an independent "third Isaiah" quite inconceivable (p. 320). John N. Oswalt (*The Book of Isaiah: Chapters 40–66* [NICOT; Grand Rapids: Eerdmans, 1998], 3–6), taking the three-source hypothesis to be wholly unconvincing, argues that "it is the scholarly understanding of biblical prophecy that needs to be corrected, not the traditional view of the book's authorship" (p. 6).

4. Joseph Blenkinsopp, *Isaiah 56–66: A New Translation with Introduction and Commentary* (AB; New York: Doubleday, 2003), 42.

5. Oswalt, *Isaiah 40–66*, 11, 451–452.

6. Ibid.; Brueggemann, *Isaiah 40–66*, 168.

7. Blenkinsopp, *Isaiah 56–66*, 28–37; Raymond de Hoop, "The Interpretation of Isaiah 56:1–9: Comfort or Criticism?" *JBL* 127 (2008): 671–695.

8. Blenkinsopp, *Isaiah 56–66*, 89.

9. Ibid., 133.

10. Grace L. Emmerson, *Isaiah 56–66* (OTG; Sheffield: JSOT Press, 1992), 55.

11. Bernard Gosse, "Sabbath, Identity and Universalism Go Together after the Return from Exile," *JSOT* 29 (2005): 367.

12. Claus Westermann, *Isaiah 40–66*, trans. David M. G. Stalker (OTL; London: SCM Press, 1969), 313.

13. Walther Eichrodt, *Theology of the Old Testament*, vol. 1, trans. John Baker (OTL; London: SCM Press, 1961), 55.

14. Emmerson, *Isaiah 56–66*, 55.

15. Brueggemann, *Isaiah 40–66*, 165.

16. Ibid., 171.

17. Ibid., 173.

18. Westermann, *Isaiah 40–66*, 310; Blenkinsopp, *Isaiah 56–66*, 135.

19. Westermann, *Isaiah 40–66*, 310.

20. Rendtorff, "Zur Komposition des Buches Jesaja," 313.

21. John N. Oswalt, "Righteousness in Isaiah: A Study of the Function of Chapters 56–66 in the Present Structure of the Book," in *Writing and Reading the Scroll of Isaiah: Studies of an Interpretative Tradition*, ed. Craig C. Broyles and Craig A. Evans (VTSup 70: Leiden: Brill, 1997), 188.

22. Alfred Jepsen, art. *āman*, *TDOT*, 1:313.

23. Ibid., 1:317.

24. Ibid., 1:320.

25. Ibid., 1:322–323.

26. Blenkinsopp, *Isaiah 56–66*, 286.

27. Cf. ibid., 287.

28. The important passages about the Sabbath in Nehemiah are in 9:13–14, 10:31, and 13:15–22.

29. John F. A. Sawyer, *The Fifth Gospel: Isaiah in the History of Christianity* (New York: Cambridge University Press, 1996).

30. Richard B. Hays, *Echoes of Scripture in the Letters of Paul* (New Haven: Yale University Press, 1989), 35, 53; J. Ross Wagner, "The Heralds of Isaiah and the Mission of Paul," in *Jesus and the Suffering Servant: Isaiah 53 and Christian Origins*, ed. W. H. Bellinger and W. R. Farmer (Harrisburg, PA: Trinity Press International, 1998), 193–222. See also C. A. Evans and J. A. Sanders, ed., *The Gospels and the Scriptures of Israel* (JSNT Sup 104; Sheffield: Sheffield Academic Press, 1994).

31. In a study garnering two passages from the last part of Isaiah (Isa. 60:6; 61:1) as well as two from earlier parts of the book (Isa. 40:9; 52:7), Millar Burrows ("The Origin of the Term 'Gospel'," *JBL* 44 [1925], 22) concludes that "we may be quite sure that in these four passages from the Second Isaiah is to be found the main source for the Christian use of the term 'gospel.'"

32. Bernhard W. Anderson, *Contours of Old Testament Theology* (Minneapolis: Fortress Press, 1999), 60.

CROSSROAD AND COUNTDOWN

In those days I saw in Judah people treading wine presses on the sabbath, and bringing in heaps of grain and loading them on donkeys; and also wine, grapes, figs, and all kinds of burdens, which they brought into Jerusalem on the sabbath day; and I warned them at that time against selling food.
Nehemiah 13:15

In chronological and historical terms the last mention of the Sabbath in the Old Testament is found in the book of Nehemiah.[1] Nehemiah occupies a position of prominence as a Jewish official at the Persian court by 445 BCE (Neh. 1:1; 2:1).[2] From this position he receives a mandate to rebuild Jerusalem (2:5), eventually making him the governor of Judah (5:14; 8:9). It is also established that he has passed off the stage by 407 BCE, from which time there is external evidence that a new governor is installed in Judah.[3]

Nehemiah plays a key role in rebuilding Jerusalem and re-establishing Israel as a viable state after the Exile. His account of events includes a host of difficulties that would surely have broken the resolve of a less gifted and determined personality, especially since his commitment to the cause of rebuilding requires him to leave the comforts of life at the Imperial Court in Persia.[4]

But his commitment remains unshaken. Firsthand news from Nehemiah's own brother, describing a country in a state of ruin, does not deter him from embarking on the mission (1:2–3; 2:3). When these reports are confirmed during his own fact-finding investigation (2:12–15), the dismal state of his homeland merely reinforces his resolve (2:17). Intensified opposition from local dignitaries (2:10; 4:1, 7) doesn't discourage him. Whether ridicule (2:19; 4:2–3), physical threats (4:8), conspiracy (6:2), blackmail (6:6–7), or entrapment (6:10–12), however craftily conceived, nothing avails to distract him from his task or lead him to become disillusioned.

Nehemiah comes across as a person of integrity—a devout, courageous, and resolute leader who is able to see through the cunning of his opponents (6:8, 13) and to inspire his own side to persevere (4:6, 14, 23). Citing Nehemiah's diplomatic skill and organizational ability, Jacob M. Myers finds him to be more than just a "building contractor."[5] Ultimately, Nehemiah sees his mission ordained and accomplished by the help of Providence (6:16). What keeps him going is a profound sense of calling, and it is from the sense of a calling accepted and faithfully executed that he seeks a higher commendation (5:9; 13:14, 31).

Nehemiah's promotion of the Sabbath is integral to the spiritual aspiration of his mission. In the ensuing conflict, he resorts to means that go beyond mere persuasion. This puts the Sabbath at a crossroad in his "diary," caught between an ordinance imposed and a privilege received. The long-term effect of his intervention is mixed. For this reason the legacy of his work might best be seen not as an unmitigated success but as a countdown to a new beginning.

NEHEMIAH'S PROMOTION OF THE SABBATH

While the book of Nehemiah abounds with descriptions of trials and threats arising from without, the Sabbath passages tell another quite unrelated story. These passages show that the troubles instigated by people hostile to his mission are matched by problems brewing within. In fact, the rhetoric of his "memoir" leaves the impression that the external threats are less vexing to him than the internal obstacles. Overcoming the hostile machinations of his enemies is sufficient to ensure success in terms of national rebirth, but his criterion for success is not a political measure. Instead, Nehemiah conceives his task in spiritual terms (7:5; 10:1). What he seeks is Israel's spiritual rebirth, the recovery of Israel's spiritual vocation, and the re-inscription of this vocation on Israel's sense of identity (8:2; 9:6–38; 10:28–29).[6]

Viewed in the light of this aspiration, it is easier to understand Nehemiah's distress when the indifference toward the Sabbath manifested by earlier generations reasserts itself among his compatriots (13:15, 17).[7] To his dismay, a number among the new generation of Israelites seem intent on carrying on with their business on the Sabbath as much as on any other day of the week. Instead of contemplating the meaning of the Sabbath in their newfound freedom, people borrow a page from the course taken by their ancestors after the exodus from Egypt (Exod. 16:27): Deciding to forego the Sabbath rest, they dress for work. Nehemiah writes that "in those days I saw in Judah men treading the wine presses on the sabbath, and bringing in heaps of grain and loading them on asses; and also wine, grapes, figs, and all kinds of burdens, which they brought into Jerusalem on the sabbath day" (Neh. 13:15). Surely this is a disappointing turn of events, greatly aggravated by the conviction that disregard for the Sabbath contributed materially to the Exile in the first place (Neh. 13:17–18).[8]

On this point, says Myers, Nehemiah "reflects the dicta of the prophets (Jer 17:19–27; Ezek 20:12–24), who attributed the misfortune of Judah to the violation of the Sabbath."[9] We can only imagine his feelings at the thought that Israel is returning to square one, treating the Sabbath with the same lack of respect as in the days of Amos.[10] It must have seemed to him that they were about to snatch failure from the jaws of victory. In view of the grave crisis, the stern measure—"and I warned them on the day when they sold food" (Neh. 13:15)—deserves a touch of empathy.

If the intimation that Nehemiah is willing to resort to force anticipates the end-game, it does not mean that he will leave other means untried. Relating the incident in first person, he writes that "I remonstrated with the nobles of Judah and said to them, 'What is this evil thing that you are doing, profaning the sabbath day?'" (Neh. 13:17). The verb here is the Hebrew word *rîb*, translated variously as "contended" (KJV, NKJV), "remonstrated" (RSV, NRSV), "reprimanded" (NASB, NJB), or "rebuked" (NIV). It implies a heated exchange, yet he is only *speaking*. "I tried to persuade the nobles of Judah," would be a justifiable translation.[11]

Nehemiah faces a dilemma when the nobles resist his persuasion. They simply signal to the donkeys to continue their way to the marketplace, eager to get on with the day's business. What is Nehemiah to do?

According to Nehemiah's account, he comes up with a plan to stop those who are bent on disregarding the Sabbath. "When it began to be dark at the gates of Jerusalem before the sabbath, I commanded that the doors should be shut and gave orders that they should not be opened until after the sabbath. And I set some of my servants over the gates, to prevent any burden from being brought in on the sabbath day" (13:19). Wright calls this "the second measure taken to enforce the observance of the Sabbath,"[12] an attempt to impose constraints when compliance isn't forthcoming. In this way legislation works to guard the sanctity of the Sabbath.

Neither persuasion nor legislation suffices to keep the merchants at bay, however: "Then the merchants and sellers of all kinds of merchandise spent the night outside Jerusalem once or twice" (13:20). What is Nehemiah to do now? Before considering his next and final step, it is well to be reminded of what will be lost if the desecration of the Sabbath continues. "He was particularly concerned with the religious welfare of the people," says Myers, "because as a student of history and as a realist, he knew that their existence depended on fidelity to Yahweh."[13] To his way of thinking the merchants cannot be allowed to put Israel's sacred calling in jeopardy. Whatever it takes to tame their intransigence seems legitimate. In this situation his last resort, the final, desperate measure, will be force. "Why do you lodge before the wall?" he asks before spelling out the consequences: "If you do so again I will lay hands on you" (13:21).

What persuasion and legislation failed to do is accomplished by the use of force, the measure of last resort. "From that time on they did not come on the sabbath," says Nehemiah (13:21). This ends the matter, at least on the surface, apparently ensuring that the Sabbath from henceforth will not be threatened by the intrusion of commercial interests.

THE SABBATH AT A CROSSROAD

Since this text in Nehemiah marks the last explicit mention of the Sabbath in the Old Testament, it is legitimate to ask whether it also draws up the future trajectory of the Sabbath and, if so, what direction it maps out other than making sure that the Sabbath has a future. Nehemiah's intervention on behalf of the Sabbath happens *ad hoc*, dictated by the need of the moment.

What matters to him is the restoration of Israel and the recommitment of the returning exiles to their spiritual calling. Convinced that the Sabbath is part and parcel of that vocation, he cannot allow the project to slip on this point.

It may seem unfair to demand of such a person that he should pause in order to test the legitimacy of his approach by scrutiny of the means employed. Must he, too, reckon with the possibility that means may be used that is actually inimical to the defined objective?

Any cause that needs legislation and coercion to win can be problematic. One possibility is that these measures, once used, establish precedent and may become permanent. A second risk is that individuals who will not be swayed by persuasion may only be deterred by legislation and subjugated by coercion. They are not truly won over and may in fact simmer with antagonism under the appearance of conformity. Third, the means that are deemed justified in the interest of advancing the good cause may also be claimed by causes less worthy. It follows that the worthiness of the cause does not confer legitimacy on the means. If the "good" cause authorizes the use of dubious means, it opens the door for the same means to be appropriated by a variety of causes, ideologies, and projects.

In the light of such concerns, it is possible that Nehemiah's deployment of force is a step too far, that it sets a dangerous precedent, and that it represents a pyrrhic victory in the form of present gain at the cost of future loss. The fact that his opponents are in the wrong does not mean that he is justified in taking any course of action in order to outflank them.

It is not possible to draw firm conclusions in the case of Nehemiah. We can hope that he does not irreparably antagonize his opponents, imagining instead that after a period of reflection they come to be happy and willing Sabbath observers themselves.

And we can construe his authorization of force to mean that he does not intend to change his opponents' opinion, but merely to safeguard the peace and tranquility that will allow others to enjoy the privilege of Sabbath peace undisturbed by commerce. In this construct he is not imposing his values on them but protecting the values and priorities of others from infringement. His intent, then, is to restrict and not to coerce.

Nevertheless, the Sabbath stands at a crossroad in the book of Nehemiah. After the Exile the Sabbath is barely limping along, requiring stark measures in order to regain a foothold. More significant, perhaps, Nehemiah's project also stands in contrast to the prophetic legacy of Isaiah. Isaiah espouses ideology and a pastoral concern while Nehemiah is a political leader and a man of action. Isaiah argues his vision against a hallowed tradition (Isa. 56:1–7). Nehemiah, by contrast, appears to side with tradition, fearful that "the old-time religion" will lose out (Neh. 9:26–29; 13:18). Isaiah presents a vision of inclusion (Isa. 56:7–8) whereas Ezra and Nehemiah see their group's identity threatened and in need of protection by separation (Neh. 9:2; 13:2). "When the people heard the law, they separated from Israel all those of foreign descent," Nehemiah says without apology (13:3). With the benefit of hindsight, it is on this point that the difference between the two emphases seems most striking, and this point becomes the contested ground in the history of the Sabbath that is yet to unfold. In Isaiah "the chosen people" gives way to "the confessing community,"[14] emphasizing personal choice rather than ethnicity or nationality as the basis for belonging. Nehemiah, on the other hand, envisions a national entity composed of people with the same ethnic background that is to carry forward the work of God. Where Isaiah sees "a house of prayer for all peoples" (Isa. 56:7), Nehemiah pursues the less risky proposition of a house of prayer for the Jews only.

The strength of the comparison between Isaiah and Nehemiah relies in part on the impression that there is a difference between their emphases, but it also builds on evidence that Israel's subsequent history lines up better along the lines of Nehemiah's approach than along the Sabbath ideology of Isaiah. As future generations are embroiled in a struggle not unlike Nehemiah's, the defenders of the faith resort to similar tactics.

The New Testament reveals a Jewish nation that had adopted a pattern of exclusion and resorted to coercion regarding Sabbath observance. "Look, your disciples are doing what is not lawful to do on the sabbath" (Matt. 12:2; cf. Mark 2:24; Luke 6:2), Jesus's critics inveigh against Him in the Synoptic witness. The Gospel of John says that "the Jews started persecuting Jesus, because he was doing such things [healing] on the sabbath" (John 5:16); indeed, "for this reason the Jews were seeking all the more to kill him" (5:18).

Preserving one's identity is not an easy task in a sea of hostile forces. Greek culture makes its presence felt in the Near East even prior to the conquest by Alexander the Great. Upon Alexander's death in 323 BCE the region is at the mercy of the Hellenistic rulers who divide his empire between them.[15] Greek becomes the language of the region, at least of the educated classes. Association with the Hellenistic overlords offers unprecedented opportunity for upward mobility for aristocratic and educated Jews. This group actively encourages assimilation, being willing to water down the peculiarities of Jewish tradition in order to bring it more in line with the more cosmopolitan tenets of Hellenism. Whether Hellenistic influences make significant inroads on Jewish outlook and practice, as Martin Hengel suggests,[16] or whether the emerging Judaism successfully weathers the storm of these influences, as Louis Feldman reads the evidence,[17] there can be no doubt that preservation of identity is a critical concern.

Where Isaiah sees "a house of prayer for all peoples," Nehemiah pursues the less risky proposition of a house of prayer for the Jews only.

The *Hasidim*, meaning the pious ones, actively resist the forces attempting to dilute Jewish distinctives (1 Macc. 2:42).[18] The internal Jewish tensions finally come to a head when the Seleucid king Antiochus IV Epiphanes (175–163 BCE) launches an attempt to eradicate the Jewish religious distinctives by force (1 Macc. 1:1–61). At that point those who wish to remain faithful to tradition take up arms under the leadership of Mattathias and his sons (1 Macc. 2:1–30). Despite the superior forces of the Seleucids, the uprising, under the leadership of Mattathias's son Judas Maccabeus ("the hammer"), succeeds to an amazing degree (1 Macc. 3:1–25; 3:38–4:35). Antiochus's brazen scheme is brought to naught (1 Macc. 6:1–16). Jewish worship is restored in the Temple (1 Macc. 4:36–59), and the Jews, led by the emerging Maccabean powerhouse, are able to carve out a measure of political independence that will last until the Romans overrun Judah one hundred years later, in 63 BCE.

But political independence does not, as many hoped, translate into restoration of Jewish religious identity. The Jewish Hasmonean rulers overreach their mandate, assume illegal prerogatives, and corrupt Jewish institutions.[19] Despite the Indian summer of Jewish political independence, the struggle to preserve the national soul continues. In fact, the voices vying for influence in the religious realm are shaped as much during the time of national independence as during the times of foreign occupation.[20]

On the basis of the available evidence, the struggle for Jewish identity and against assimilation begins with Nehemiah's effort on behalf of the Sabbath. His struggle, in turn, is inspired by the conviction that the Exile was the result of compromise with foreign and "pagan" influences. The struggle receives a further boost following Antiochus's attempt to assimilate the Jews by force more than two hundred years later. But the quest for religious authenticity is fueled to even greater intensity during the years following Antiochus's debacle.[21] The Pharisees, one of the groups vying for influence according to the New Testament account, emerge during this time, tracing their roots to the Hasidim in the period of the Maccabean revolt, perhaps even to people who spearheaded the reform efforts during the time of Ezra and Nehemiah.[22] To these religious leaders, living at the dawn of the Christian era, preservation of identity remains the central concern. In ideological terms the Pharisees are believers in coercion,[23] and they subscribe to a national, collective aspiration.

Preservation of identity stands as the most pressing concern in the eyes of the religious leaders that are in the foreground in the gospels, too, and in the voices we hear arguing against Paul in his letters in the New Testament. Even the politically ascendant class, the Sadducees, argue their case against Jesus by invoking nationalist concerns (John 11:48–50). The book of Acts reports that Paul's arrest was triggered by the suspicion that Paul's companion Trophimus, a Gentile, had been allowed into an area that was off limits to anyone but Jews (Acts 21:27–30). Most revealing of all is Paul's account of Peter's failure of nerve in Antioch, drawing back from table fellowship with Gentile believers in Jesus for fear of antagonizing leading Jewish believers from Jerusalem (Gal. 2:11–14). These examples and others like them[24] confirm that the issue of identity is a paramount concern, put to the test precisely as others come knocking on the door, asking for entrance.

A NEW PERSPECTIVE

The New Testament evidence on this point has caught the attention of leading scholars to the point that it has been called a "New Perspective."[25] According to the "old" perspective, Judaism at the time of Jesus was a religion of "works," seeking God's favor by human effort. This view, many scholars now believe, is incorrect. Judaism is not to be seen as a religious system that believes in salvation by works. According to the "New Perspective," it is simplistic and unfair to portray the situation as though Jewish teachers at the time of Jesus are crudely promoting an ideology of human merit to the exclusion of divine grace. But if salvation by works is not the chief project of the Pharisees and other opponents of Jesus, what is?

Generations of scholars have emphasized that the Jewish religious sentiment inclines toward salvation by works, and that the conflict between Jesus and the Pharisees, and between Paul and Judaism, as noted, is principally a conflict between salvation by human works and salvation by grace. This view sees Paul offering salvation as a gift while his opponents, representing Judaism, believe that one has to earn it.

E. P. Sanders, one of the leading scholars to challenge the traditional view, finds this representation of Judaism misleading, one-sided, and downright wrong.[26] His own investigation claims to discover a grace-centered Judaism at the time of Jesus and Paul. Sanders concludes that "fundamental to Jewish piety was the view that God's grace preceded the requirement of obedience and undergirds both the life of Israel and also the entire universe."[27] With few exceptions, Sanders claims, Jewish literature shows that "obedience maintains one's position in the covenant, but it does not earn God's grace as such. It simply keeps an individual in the group which is the recipient of God's grace."[28] In this scenario, the keeping of the Sabbath, for instance, is not intended to earn God's favor but is a response to favor already received. On the whole, Sanders's view of the evidence has been hailed as a landmark, the essential feature in the "New Perspective," and a view that must be reckoned with.[29]

But if the conflict between Jesus and the Pharisees, or between Paul and Judaism, does not revolve around the question of grace versus works, what is the problem? Is the notion of belief in the same divine grace a chimera, partly caused by a more shallow view of the divine standard in Judaism, as when Sanders admits that "no rabbi took the position that obedience must be perfect"?[30] Is this suspicion confirmed by his admission that some rabbis, while not claiming perfection, "had a hard time thinking of what commandment they might have disobeyed?"[31] Should one take his observation that "the principles behind the sacrificial system, or its religious significance, are nowhere discussed" to mean that in Judaism such understanding was considered unimportant—people were merely going through the motions of religion without grasping the meaning of what they were doing?[32] Is it legitimate to extrapolate backwards to this time Jacob Neusner's comment about the later Mishna, a principal component of the canon of Judaism, to see in the Judaism of Jesus's time a similar and rarefied detachment from reality? Neusner describes the Mishna "as if people sat down to write letters about things they had never seen, to people they did not know—letters from an unknown city to an undefined and unimagined world: the Mishna is from no one special in utopia, to whom it may concern."[33] Does the New Testament reflect only Jesus's encounter with fringe elements in Jewish society and not with the representative mainstream?[34] Or should one settle for Sanders's most sweeping assertion? "In short," writes Sanders, "this is what Paul finds wrong in Judaism: it is not Christianity."[35]

It is hardly persuasive to make the distinction between Judaism and Christianity hinge on so little, as has been pointed out.[36] Sanders's own explanation is more helpful than the supposition that the only defect in Judaism is that it is not Christianity. The crux has to do with preferential treatment of the Jews. Israel's election implicitly would leave the rest of humanity in limbo, creating an untenable barrier between the "in" group and those on the outside. Such a view implies that God is arbitrary, and it invites a spirit of complacency and pride in the favored group. For that reason, writes Sanders, when Paul criticizes Judaism "he does so in a sweeping manner, and the criticism has two focuses: the lack of faith in Christ and the lack of equality for the Gentiles."[37]

If we identify preservation of identity as the most urgent priority of the Jewish religious leaders, the dots connect across the centuries, and we are in a better position to appreciate what is at stake with respect to the Sabbath. Stirrings within Judaism in the form of proselytism fail to overcome the tendency to exclusivity.[38] One does not need to negate altogether the traditional view that Jesus and Paul are up against people who believe in salvation by works in order to maintain that the other breaking point, the more representative and telling difference, is their view of the Gentiles. "Lack of equality for the Gentiles," as Sanders points out,[39] is a crucial ingredient, and this feature defines the boundary between the elect and the non-elect, the in-group and those on the outside, better, say, than the traditional notion that Jews in the time of Jesus are bent on earning salvation by their works.[40] What they seem to do, whatever may be the case with respect to faith versus works, is to cultivate an exclusivist ethos. Within this framework, the Sabbath becomes a mark of distinction between those who are chosen and those who are not.

But this also closes the circle back to where we began this chapter, with Nehemiah and the effort to engrave a sense of identity and vocation on the consciousness of his compatriots. Measures are taken after the Exile to protect Jewish identity against secular and pagan influences. Despite their benign intent, the end result is to lessen Israel's tendency to conform to other nations, at least in the circles that rub shoulders with Jesus and Paul. The Babylonian captivity, the Maccabean uprising, the subsequent disappointment with the Hasmoneans, and finally the heavy hand of Roman hegemony leave the people more receptive to the influence of the religious leadership.[41] Over time the guardians of piety win a measure of support for their resolve not to copy the religious practices of their neighbors or return to the moral chaos of the past. To a degree unimaginable in the days of Nehemiah, they succeed in placing the Sabbath at the vanguard of this cause.

COUNTING DOWN TO A NEW BEGINNING

While the new religious and political consensus at the time of Jesus took the importance of the Sabbath for granted, experience had shown that the actual observance of the Sabbath could not be left to individual discretion. Steps were taken to ensure that the seventh day not be trampled upon again. At the dawn of the Christian era the rabbinic project of protecting the Sabbath had come a long ways, giving the Sabbath the status it was denied prior to the Exile. But the emerging Sabbath emphasis had a narrow scope compared to the outlook of the prophet Isaiah (Isa. 56:1–7). Where the latter envisioned an inclusive outreach to all people, the Pharisees sought separation.[42] While it may be true that "Judaism in the Land of Israel proceeded from a position of strength and confidence,"[43] it was a confidence that found itself threatened and bewildered in the face of the humanity of Jesus and the inclusive vision of Paul. The brand of Judaism that confronted Jesus appears to be a movement in retreat, closing the doors to the outside, determined to preserve the blessings of the Sabbath for itself while excluding the Gentiles.[44]

The defensive character is also reflected in the minute regulations applied to the keeping of the Sabbath. The elaborate regulations aimed for completeness, as if to prescribe a definitive cure for the spiritual failure of the past. From a status of neglect the Sabbath was raised above other days to become the flag of Judaism, the symbol of the nation, and "an essential feature of Jewish identity."[45] At last the nation seemed about to internalize the importance of the Sabbath, showing at least some willingness to march to its drumbeat.[46] In the Damascus Rule, representing the more extreme Essene community and said to date from 100 BCE, we read that "no man who strays so as to profane the Sabbath and the feasts shall be put to death; it shall fall to men to keep him in custody. And if he is healed of his error, they shall keep him in custody for seven years and he shall afterwards approach the Assembly."[47]

If prophecy in the voice of Isaiah makes the message of inclusion and the affirmation of God's faithfulness to all the Sabbath legacy of the Old Testament (Isa. 56:1–7), delivering it to the door of the new era, history forges an alternative and competing ideal in the form of a message of exclusion, and, to a lesser extent, a vision of human rather than divine faithfulness. It is the latter ideal that wins out. The Sabbath arrives on the shore of the New Testament as a truncated spiritual resource. Though its prestige seems to have increased, it is much diminished from its original inclusive and world-embracing meaning. By enacting a series of detailed Sabbath laws, the advocates of the Sabbath ended up living in a world of sharp and inviolable demarcations between the elect and the rest of humanity.

It behooves us to acknowledge that we are looking at a complex world with many moving parts, secular and religious. Our sources are limited, and what is only a part is easily mistaken for the whole. Moreover, our understanding of the time prior to the destruction of Jerusalem in 70 CE is often distorted by a tendency to extrapolate backwards in time from the Judaism that emerged after Jerusalem's destruction, as if nothing changed. For instance, exemplifying the risk of mistaking a part for the whole, readers of the New Testament are prone to get the impression that the Jews at the time of Jesus were eagerly waiting for the Messiah to come, as the Synoptic source makes it appear.[48] Other sources from this period indicate that "the concept of the Messiah was only of peripheral interest to later Second Temple Judaism."[49] Donald Harman Akenson states that in "the contemporary texts—the Dead Sea Scrolls, the Apocrypha, and the Pseudepigrapha—Messiah was at most a minor notion in Judahism around the time of Yeshua of Nazareth. Most of the Chosen People were not awaiting the Messiah."[50]

The brand of Judaism that confronted Jesus appears to be a movement in retreat, closing the doors to the outside, determined to preserve the blessings of the Sabbath for itself while excluding the Gentiles.

Alternatively, it is possible that the preaching of John the Baptist and other events preceding the public ministry of Jesus created new facts on the ground in the form of a messianic expectation that is not captured by other sources. Better yet, the notion that the Messiah comes because he is *needed* and not because he is *expected* does justice to the biblical evidence without doing violence to the extrabiblical sources. In light of known confounders, however, it is important to state clearly what is not in doubt: The Sabbath appeared to be a marker of Jewish identity *before* the destruction of Jerusalem fully as much as it would assume that role in Judaism when the latter was deprived of its national and political foundation. The messianic expectation, while certainly not absent in the New Testament documents, is beyond dispute in the rabbinic sources, and it is conspicuously linked to the Sabbath. In the rabbinic vision people are waiting for a new initiative, for someone to make the first move. "Rabbi Johanan said in the name of Simeon ben Yochai: 'If Israel were to keep two Sabbaths according to the laws thereof, they would be redeemed immediately.'"[51] Rabbi Levi claimed no less with regard to the Sabbath: "If Israel kept the Sabbath properly even for one day, the son of David would come. Why? Because it is equivalent to all the commandments."[52]

Within this outlook the Sabbath is the mark of a distinct ethnic group, implicitly and sometimes explicitly promoting the idea that human beings are not equal in God's eyes. It is theoretically possible for non-Jews to become part of the elect, but Jewish and Pharisaic practice tends toward exclusion.[53] Instead of pointing to the God of all, the constricted Sabbath vision points to the God of the few. Instead of seeing the seventh day as a sign of God's faithfulness, the prevailing sentiment aspires to place human faithfulness in the foreground. Instead of setting the stage for the Gentiles to be gathered in to the knowledge of the one God (Isa. 56:8), there is confusion concerning God's intent. Instead of adding up the record of human failure, there still lingers the illusion that the ball is in the human court, and that victory will depend on a human initiative. In the emerging rabbinic theology of the Sabbath, human beings need to make good on their end of the deal before God will do His part. "If Israel kept the Sabbath properly even for one day, the son of David would come," Rabbi Levi would say after the fall of Jerusalem.[54]

The expectation that Israel would keep the Sabbath properly for a single day, as envisioned by Rabbi Levi, followed by the assumption that success on the part of Israel in this regard would bring the coming of the Messiah, certainly highlights the importance of the Sabbath within the rabbinic outlook. From the perspective of the New Testament, however, Rabbi Levi turned out to be mistaken as much with respect to timing as to the stipulated prerequisite. The New Testament shows that even before the rabbinic genius came to see things this way, the Son of David had quietly arrived.

Instead of pointing to the God of all, the constricted Sabbath vision points to the God of the few.

ENDNOTES

1. Chronological assertions must reckon with divergent views of the composition of the Old Testament. Nevertheless, even by the criteria of the most radical views on this subject, it is not easy to contest the view that Nehemiah's contribution is late. The texts explicitly dealing with the Sabbath are Neh. 9:13–14; 10:31–32; and 13:15–22.

2. According to Bright (*A History of Israel*, 379), the date of Nehemiah's career "extended (Neh. 2:1) from the twentieth year of Arxtaxerxes I (445) until (Neh. 13:6) sometime after that of the king's thirty-second year (433)."

3. *The International Standard Bible Encyclopedia*, rev. ed. (Grand Rapids: Wm. B. Eerdmans Publishing Co., 1939), art. "Nehemiah."

4. Bright (*A History of Israel*, 374–376) notes the rising fortunes of the Jewish Diaspora communities in the Persian Empire, a development that would put the incentive to leave in competition with the incentive to stay.

5. Jacob M. Myers, *Ezra·Nehemiah: Introduction, Translation and Notes* (AB 14; New York: Doubleday, 1965), lv.

6. Cf. Wright's monograph (*Rebuilding Identity*), where the notion of rebuilding identity is seen to constitute the gist of Nehemiah's mission and of the book that bears his name.

7. While Wright (*Rebuilding Identity*, 221–242) wants to figure out the "redaction history" of Nehemiah, taking various layers of redaction for granted, he does not contest that the Sabbath is a chief concern in what he considers to be the earliest version.

8. Derek Kidner, *Ezra and Nehemiah* (TOTC; Downers Grove, IL: Inter-Varsity Press, 1979), 130–131.

9. Myers, *Nehemiah*, 215.

10. H. G. M. Williamson, *Ezra, Nehemiah* (WBC 16; Waco: Word Books, 1985), 395.

11. Wright, *Rebuilding Identity*, 223.

12. Ibid., 224.

13. Myers, *Nehemiah*, 215.

14. Westermann, *Isaiah 40–66*, 313.

15. The political history of this period is told in depth by Peter Green in *Alexander to Actium: The Historical Evolution of the Hellenistic Age* (Berkeley: University of California Press, 1990), especially pp. 435–452, 497–524.

16. Martin Hengel, *Judaism and Hellenism*, 2 vols., trans. John Bowden (London: SCM Press, 1974).

17. Louis H. Feldman, *Jew and Gentile in the Ancient World: Attitudes and Interactions from Alexander to Justinian* (Princeton: Princeton University Press, 1993).

18. Victor Tcherikover, *Hellenistic Civilization and the Jews* (Philadelphia: The Jewish Publication Society of America, 1959; repr. Peabody, MA: Hendrickson Publishers, 1999), 78, 125–126, 196–230.

19. When Jonathan, the younger son of Mattathias and the successor of Judas Maccabeus, usurps the high priesthood in 152 BCE, effectively assuming the beguiling messianic mantle of priest and king, the stage is set for alienation between the ruling Hasmonean party and the Pharisees; cf. Hengel, *Judaism and Hellenism*, I:175–180, 306; Louis Finkelstein, *The Pharisees: The Sociological Background of Their Faith*, vol. 2 (Philadelphia: The Jewish Publication Society of America, 1946), 619; Tcherikover, *Hellenistic Civilization and the Jews*, 254–262; Bright, *A History of Israel*, 458–464; Green, *Alexander to Actium*, 522–524.

20. Tcherikover, *Hellenistic Civilization and the Jews*, 256–257.

21. Feldman, *Jew and Gentile in the Ancient World*, 420.

22. Hengel, *Judaism and Hellenism*, I:175–180.

23. One piece of evidence, as Tcherikover (*Hellenistic Civilization and the Jews*, 256) points out, is that the Hasmonean rulers were in the Pharisees' good favor when the former carried out the forcible Judaization of the population in Palestine (1 Macc. 3:1–9).

24. See also the story of Peter's dream and the acceptance of the Gentile Cornelius in Acts 10:1–48.

25. The term "New Perspective" was first used by James D. G. Dunn in 1982, and it has stuck since; see the essay "The New Perspective in Paul," in Dunn's book, *Jesus, Paul and the Law* (Louisville, KY: Westminster/John Knox Press, 1990), 183–206.

26. E. P. Sanders, *Paul and Palestinian Judaism* (Minneapolis: Fortress Press, 1979); idem, *Paul, the Law and the Jewish People* (Minneapolis: Fortress Press, 1983); idem, *Jesus and Judaism* (Philadelphia: Fortress Press, 1985); idem, *Judaism: Practice and Belief 63BCE–66 CE* (London: SCM Press, 1992).

27. Sanders, *Judaism*, 275.

28. Sanders, *Paul and Palestinian Judaism*, 420.

29. Despite the impact of "the New Perspective," a number of scholars are reluctant to yield ground; cf. Peter Stuhlmacher, *Revisiting Paul's Doctrine of Justification by Faith: A Challenge to the New Perspective* (Downers Grove: InterVarsity Press, 2001). In a companion essay in Stuhlmacher's book, Donald A. Hagner ("Paul and Judaism. Testing the New Perspective," 75), himself a critic, calls Sanders's contribution "a Copernican revolution in Pauline studies."

30. Sanders, *Paul, the Law and the Jewish People*, 28.

31. Sanders, *Paul and Palestinian Judaism*, 176.

32. Ibid., 80.

33. *The Mishna: A New Translation,* ed. and trans. by Jacob Neusner (New Haven: Yale University Press, 1988), xiii.

34. Sanders (*Paul and Palestinian Judaism*, 426) writes that "the possibility cannot be completely excluded that there were Jews accurately hit by the polemic of Matt. 23, who attended only to trivia and neglected the weightier matters. Human nature being what it is, one supposes that there were some such. One must say, however, that the surviving Jewish literature does not reveal them."

35. Sanders, *Paul and Palestinian Judaism*, 552.

36. Dunn ("New Perspective," 187) claims that Sanders fails to follow through on his own findings. "The Lutheran Paul has been replaced by an idiosyncratic Paul who in arbitrary and irrational manner turns his face against the glory and greatness of Judaism's covenant theology and abandons Judaism simply because it is not Christianity."

37. Sanders, *Paul, the Law and the Jewish People*, 155.

38. George Foot Moore, *Judaism in the First Centuries of the Christian Era: The Age of the Tannaim*, vol. 1 (Cambridge: Harvard University Press, 1927–1930), 323–324. Paula Fredriksen ("Judaism, the Circumcision of Gentiles, and Apocalyptic Hope: Another Look at Galatians 1 and 2," in *The Galatians Debate*, ed. Mark D. Nanos [Peabody, MA: Hendrickson, 2002], 239–241) argues that the evidence for Jewish missionary outreach is flimsy, that conversions were generally initiated at the request of the Gentile, and that the reported population growth cannot be used as evidence for conversions or for active proselytism.

39. Sanders, *Paul, the Law and the Jewish People*, 155.

40. On the point of "national righteousness," "nationalist presumption," or "ethnocentrism" many scholars have come to agree with Sanders; cf. respectively, N. T. Wright, "The Paul of History and the Apostle of Faith," *TynB* 29 (1978): 65; James D. G. Dunn, "The Justice of God: A Renewed Perspective on Justification by Faith," *JTS* 43 (1992): 14; Bruce W. Longenecker, *Eschatology and the Covenant: A Comparison of 4 Ezra and Romans 1–11* (Sheffield: Sheffield Academic Press, 1991), 228.

41. Finkelstein, *The Pharisees*, II:619.

42. Hengel (*Judaism and Hellenism*, 306) points to the tendency towards segregation as the occasion for Antiochus's militant anti-Semitism.

43. Feldman, *Jew and Gentile in the Ancient World*, 420.

44. Feldman (*Jew and Gentile in the Ancient World*, 288–449), as noted, does not quite dispel the impression of exclusivity despite documenting acceptance of proselytes.

45. Robert M. Johnston, "The Rabbinic Sabbath," in *The Sabbath in Scripture and History*, ed. Kenneth A. Strand (Washington, DC: Review and Herald Publishing Association, 1982), 71.

46. Sanders, *Judaism*, 209–211; 236–240. Sanders notes that Jewish Sabbath observance was attractive in the eyes of many Gentiles and enticing to some in the Christian community at the end of the fourth century.

47. Geza Vermes, *The Dead Sea Scrolls in English*, 3rd ed. (London: Penguin Books, 1987), 96.

48. Cf. Mark 15:43; Matt 11:2–3: Luke 2:25–38: 3:15; 7:18–19; 23:50–51.

49. Donald Harman Akenson, *Saint Saul: A Skeleton Key to the Historical Jesus* (Oxford: Oxford University Press, 2000), 40.

50. Akenson, *Saint Saul*, 41.

51. *The Babylonian Talmud*, art. Shabbath 118b, ed. Rabbi Dr. I. Epstein (London: The Soncino Press, 1961), 582. Rabbi Simeon ben Yochai (c. 100–160 AD) was one of the greatest disciples of Rabbi Akiba (c. 50–135 AD), the father of the Mishna.

52. *The Midrash*, vol. III, *Exodus Rabbah* XXV.12, ed. H. Freedman and Maurice Simon, trans. S. M. Lehrman (London: The Soncino Press, 1939), 315.

53. Sanders, *Judaism*, 270.

54. *Exodus Rabbah* XXV.12.

CHAPTER 11

THE SABBATH AND THE HEALING MINISTRY OF JESUS

Now it was a sabbath day when Jesus made the clay and opened his eyes.
John 9:14

All of the gospels go out of their way to anchor the life of Jesus in the unfolding story of God's faithfulness in the Old Testament. To Matthew, emphasizing the connection to Israel's founding eminences, Jesus is "the Son of David, the son of Abraham" (Matt. 1:1). To Luke, highlighting the human bond and the universal reach, Jesus is the "son of Adam," who, in turn, was the "son of God" (Luke 3:38). In the Gospel of John, pushing the horizon to infinity, the story begins with Jesus's preexistence (John 1:1). John, of course, does not thereby intend to downplay the humanity of Jesus. It is precisely the preexistence of Jesus that endows His humanity with the potential to dispel the darkness with regard to human misperception of God. Of Jesus's genuine humanity there is no more doubt in John than in the other gospels. "And the Word became flesh and lived among us, and we have seen his glory, the glory as of a father's only son, full of grace and truth," says the Prologue in John (1:14).

All the gospels, too, make the healing ministry of Jesus *on the Sabbath* a major emphasis and a subject fraught with far-reaching consequences. The healings are important in their own right, but the Sabbath healings stand apart because they give rise to heated controversy. The controversy escalates to the point that it triggers the decision on the part of His most determined opponents to silence Jesus by force (John 5:18; 7:1, 15–24). While all the gospels tell this story to varying degrees, it is most fully developed in the Gospel of John. In this gospel the Sabbath healings constitute the backbone of the entire plot. Jesus heals on the Sabbath, plunging ahead even though He is aware that His opponents are vehemently against it (John 5:16; 9:16). The Sabbath healings, in turn, become flashpoints for controversy with regard to His identity (5:17–18; 8:31–59). John, however, is not content merely to place Jesus within the identity of God (1:1). The high Christology of this gospel serves *theology*. What Jesus is and

All the gospels make the healing ministry of Jesus on the Sabbath a major emphasis.

does are intended to reveal what God is like. We miss the point of the Sabbath healings, and many readers are indeed prone to miss it unless we see the movement from the identity of Jesus to the character of God (5:19–20; 10:37–38; 14:8–9).

HEALING ON THE SABBATH

Among the many passages dealing with the Sabbath in John, none is more striking than Jesus's healing of the paralytic at the pool of Bethzatha.

> Now in Jerusalem by the Sheep Gate there is a pool, called in Hebrew Beth-zatha, which has five porticoes. In these lay many invalids—blind, lame, and paralyzed. One man was there who had been ill for thirty-eight years. When Jesus saw him lying there and knew that he had been there a long time, he said to him, "Do you want to be made well?" The sick man answered him, "Sir, I have no one to put me into the pool when the water is stirred up; and while I am making my way, someone else steps down ahead of me." Jesus said to him, "Stand up, take your mat and walk." At once the man was made well, and he took up his mat and began to walk. (John 5:2–9)

John tells the story in brief, matter-of-fact strokes, yet providing just enough detail to allow each stage of the miracle to sink in: The man has a chronic, disabling illness. For thirty-eight years he has hoped for healing. One single venue, as later manuscripts spell it out, seems open to him (5:4), but the man always ends up disappointed (5:7). Then Jesus appears. Hope is kindled. With Jesus's command comes a sense of empowerment, the ability to do what is commanded. Suddenly, strangely, the paralytic responds to the command, gets up, and walks!

Even now, years later, the man's recovery leaps from the pages of the New Testament in a way that commands attention. We are therefore caught completely off guard by the implications of the next sentence, charged as an unexpected negative: "Now that day was the sabbath" (5:9).

The same sequence of events is repeated on a later occasion (9:1–7).[1] Jesus sees a man blind from birth. At first the blind man seems to be nothing more than "a mere object of curiosity and theological speculation" (9:2).[2] But Jesus sees him as something more: "Neither this man nor his parents sinned; he was born blind so that God's works might be revealed in him," He says to His disciples (9:3). When Jesus had said this, "he spat on the ground and made mud with the saliva and spread the mud on the man's eyes, saying to him, 'Go, wash in the pool of Siloam' (which means Sent). Then he went and washed and came back able to see" (9:6–7).

Here, too, John leaves much to the imagination. It is left to the reader to relive the years that the blind man spent in darkness and then to perceive the sparkle in the man's eyes—the stunned exuberance of coming from darkness into the light. John is focused elsewhere, on the storm clouds gathering on the horizon. The trouble that lies ahead is vaguely anticipated by doubts as to the man's identity and the need to verify that a miracle has taken place (9:8–21). These soundings are harbingers of conflict, a forewarning of the outrage that will ensue should it be established that a man blind from birth has had his eyesight restored on the Sabbath. Everything adds up to the realization that John relates the miracle for some other reason than to report the healing as such.

As John tells the story, the man is reduced to a bystander. Even though it is all about him—*he* is the blind man, and it is *he* who has had his eyesight restored—his opinion seems to carry little weight. In the torrent of conflicting opinions no one pays attention to him. The NRSV captures well the dynamic of the present tense in Greek, "He *kept* saying" (9:9), indicating thereby that his attempt to get a word in edgewise was virtually ignored.

Rather than rejoicing with the healed man, however, the guardians of proper Sabbath conduct turn the event into a trial. A determined effort is underfoot to quell the man's exuberance, and, if possible, to cast doubt on the veracity of the healing. Failing that, the next step must be understood as a tightening of the screws, moving the case to another forum that is likely to be even more hostile. "They brought to the Pharisees the man who had formerly been blind" (9:13). Then, only then, does John reveal the flashpoint in the story, the element that explains the fierce opposition: "Now it was a sabbath day when Jesus made the clay and opened his eyes" (John 9:14).

THE SABBATH HEALINGS AS THE SUBSTRATE OF CONTROVERSY

A wonderful thing has happened, but the body language of Jesus's critics loudly states that people in the audience had better restrain their sense of wonderment. Under normal circumstances they should be crowding around the restored cripple excitedly, showering him with questions: How does it feel to walk again after thirty-eight years? They should descend on the blind man like reporters at a press conference: What is it like to see for the first time?

This is not what happens. "It is astonishing that the Jews are unmoved by the miracle, either at this point or in what follows," says Ernst Haenchen.[3] The spirit of awe and gratitude that might be expected is drowned out by the narrator's explanatory remark that it happened on the Sabbath (5:9; 9:14). All of a sudden the air is chilled by a logic that takes no joy in what has taken place. Harsh interrogation and unyielding criticism pursue the healed and the healer. The critics have no eye for the point of view of the recipients of the miracles. Their reaction is conditioned by the timing, and the sentence, "Now that day was a sabbath" (5:9) transforms the passage. It "is no longer soaring aloft on the wings of hope" but has "plummeted to the ground with a decided thud," says Karen Pidcock-Lester.[4]

Much of what is happening in this clash of outlooks is implicit in the text. Herman Ridderbos is certainly correct in advising that "in order to understand a story like this one must know the enormous significance of the sanctity of the sabbath for the Judaism of that day (and thereafter)."[5] Until the question of timing is introduced, the fact that Jesus healed on the Sabbath, the accounts are mere stories, worth telling, perhaps, but it is not clear what their "plot" is. "Plot," in turn, is more than a certain sequence of events because the "plot" furnishes the hinge of the story. The hinge in these stories relates to the Sabbath. "This is the point of the story for John [in ch. 5], as also at 9:14 where Jesus healed the blind man," says J. H. Bernard.[6]

Two details, one in each of these chapters, are giveaways that make the sensitive issue stand out clearly. In the story of the paralytic, the red flag in the account is the mat. In the story of the blind man, it is mud. Jesus throws down the gauntlet by publicly ignoring Jewish Sabbath regulations. Two of the thirty-nine prohibitions in existence specifically dealt with carrying a pallet and kneading dough.[7] Jesus flaunts one prohibition by asking the man to carry his mat away with him (5:8) and the other prohibition by preparing a mixture of mud and putting it on the blind man's eyes (9:6). John emphasizes this by repeating that "it was a sabbath when Jesus *made the mud* and opened his eyes" (9:14), and, in the man's firsthand account, "the man called Jesus made mud, spread it on my eyes and said to me" (9:11), and, again, in his answer to the Pharisees, "He put mud on my eyes" (9:15). The mat and the mud aside, acts of healing were only permitted if life was in danger.

But the Sabbath healings are deliberate actions of Jesus. He does not stumble into these conflicts by accident. We are not likely to hear Jesus say: "If I had known they would get so upset, I would not have done it." Time and again John informs his readers that Jesus understands the implications of His actions (6:6; 13:1, 3). Moreover, the crippled man first, and the blind man later, could have been healed on another day. Alternatively, Jesus could have performed these healings more discretely. At the very least He could have refrained from using mud when healing the

Jesus throws down the gauntlet by publicly ignoring Jewish Sabbath regulations.

blind man, and He could have instructed the paralytic to come back after sundown to pick up the mat.

Jesus's healing activity on the Sabbath is not unique to the Gospel of John.[8] While the Sabbath miracles stand out less conspicuously in the Synoptics, there, too, they are so numerous as to make them a characteristic feature of Jesus's ministry (Matt. 12:10–14; Mark 1:21–27; 3:2–6; Luke 13:10–17; 14:1–6). Mark, in characteristic shorthand, shows that there is nothing subtle about the way He conducts one of His healings—no hint that Jesus in the rush of controversy fails to anticipate the indignation that will come.

> And he entered the synagogue, and a man was there who had a withered hand. And they watched him, to see whether he would heal him on the sabbath, so that they might accuse him. And he said to the man who had the withered hand, "Come here." And he said to them, "Is it lawful on the sabbath to do good or to do harm, to save life or to kill?" But they were silent. And he looked around at them with anger, grieved at their hardness of heart, and said to the man, "Stretch out your hand." He stretched it out, and his hand was restored. The Pharisees went out, and immediately held counsel with the Herodians against him, how to destroy him. (Mark 3:1–6)

Here, as much as in the Gospel of John, Jesus proceeds despite the bristling objections of the onlookers. Mark's comment that "they watched him, to see whether he would heal him on the sabbath" (Mark 3:2) indicates that they know the answer. Jesus will heal the ailing person, and He will heal him even if the person has a chronic illness that does not demand instant attention. Moreover, He will heal even though He knows that it will get Him into trouble. In all the instances of healing on the Sabbath that are recorded in the four Gospels, Jesus's healing on the Sabbath is characteristic of His ministry.[9] The healings are carried out as a matter of principle. Jesus will not make concession to potential objections.

The acts of healing on the Sabbath are an area of common ground between the Synoptics and John, undercutting the speculative argument that the Sabbath controversies in John look to a time after the time of Jesus for their generative locus. John did not write the story of a sectarian community subsequent to Jesus, as Rudolf Bultmann proposed,[10] cleverly camouflaging it as the story of Jesus.[11] Richard J. Bauckham dissents persuasively from the notion of a sequestered "Johannine community" and from the implied corollary that John reveals a community turned in on itself, as though John is describing the history of the community for the community's own consumption.[12] Instead, there is a coherent and connected line "from the way the Gospels addressed their first readers…to the way the Gospels have been read ever since."[13] Jesus, not the community, is at the center of these narratives. With respect to the healing ministry of Jesus on the Sabbath, John's account must be read as stories about Jesus and His time rather than as a window on "the Johannine community," the very existence of which is eroding.[14]

The Sabbath healings are deliberate actions of Jesus.

The conflict that follows hard on the heels of Jesus's healing ministry on the Sabbath, therefore, is a conflict between Jesus and His contemporary critics. No sooner has the paralytic set off with his mat than he is stopped by "the Jews,"[15] who are quick to bring their objections to bear on him. They say to him, "It is the sabbath; it is not lawful for you to carry your mat" (5:10). They make it clear that Jesus has crossed a red line, having stirred up feelings of antagonism that will not be easily appeased. "Therefore," says John, "the Jews started persecuting Jesus, because he was doing such things on the sabbath" (5:16). Focus is maintained on this event in subsequent encounters; thus, Jesus "did not wish to go about in Judea because the Jews were looking for an opportunity to kill him" (7:1). When He nevertheless shows up in Jerusalem, the healing is still in view, with His opponents' hostile intent simmering under the surface despite their denials to the contrary (7:19–20).

> Jesus answered them, "I performed one work, and all of you are astonished. Moses gave you circumcision (it is, of course, not from Moses, but from the patriarchs), and you circumcise a man on the sabbath. If a man receives circumcision on the sabbath in order that the law of Moses may not be broken, are you angry with me because I healed a man's whole body on the sabbath?" (John 7:21–23)

The moral argument claims the high ground of self-evidence: If it is permitted to circumcise, it must be allowed to heal. There might even be a slight barb in the comparison between the mutilation implied in circumcision and the making whole of a man's body. Whether or not this is the case, John describes an intense see-sawing battle for hearts and minds. Andrew Lincoln argues nicely that the Gospel is dominated by the lawsuit motif in the form of charges, counter-charges, presentation of evidence, weighing of evidence, and the passing of a verdict.[16] Alternatively, Martin Asiedu-Peprah contends that we are not witnesses to a full-fledged three-way trial but to juridical controversy between two parties according to a pattern found in the Old Testament.[17] His model assumes that the point of the Sabbath controversies is to persuade Jesus's opponents and bring them to see Him for who He truly is. While this may be true, it seems more likely that the stories have an implicit *trilateral* thrust, a contest involving *three* parties. There is a judge in the proceedings in the Gospel even though the judge sits outside the story, in the person of the reader.[18]

Where, on the one hand, the interrogation of the man is meant to disestablish that a miracle has taken place (9:8–15, 18–23), and, failing that, to impugn the character of Jesus (9:16–17, 24–34), the answers by the man born blind to the aggressive questioning backfire on every count. The account establishes, on the other hand, the identity of the man (9:9, 20), as well as the fact of his healing (9:13, 21). As to verdict, it cannot be anything other than that the Healer must be a man of God (9:25, 30–33).

THE SABBATH HEALINGS AND THE IDENTITY OF JESUS

Healing on the Sabbath is offensive and fraught with risk, but Jesus's comment on the meaning raises the risk to a new level. Retracing our steps in the narrative, the Jews say to the paralytic who is walking about, "It is the sabbath; it is not lawful for you to carry your mat" (5:10). Perhaps, by itself, the act of healing on the Sabbath would be tolerable, triggering persecution temporarily, as it does (5:16), but without leaving lasting animosity. When, however, Jesus answers them, "My Father is still working, and I also am working" (5:17), all bets are off. Indeed, the discussion ascends to a different sphere altogether as "witnessed by the violence of the reaction."[19] Not only has Jesus violated the sanctity of the Sabbath as they see it, but He aggravates the conflict a thousandfold first by defending His action and then by defending it by claiming to be imitating God. "For this reason the Jews were seeking all the more to kill him," says John, "because he was not only breaking the sabbath, but was also calling God his own Father, thereby making himself equal to God" (5:18).

John's "all the more" is important, signifying that while violation of the Sabbath is considered a serious offense, Jesus's claim to intimacy with God creates an additional aggravation. In fact, imitation *of* God and intimacy *with* God understate the full scope of His claim. While there is imitation and and intimacy, Jesus sets His own identity *within* the identity of God, "making himself equal to God" (5:18). The question of Jesus's identity is now paramount. "In claiming the right to work even as his Father worked, Jesus was claiming a divine prerogative," says Raymond Brown.[20]

Jesus's claim to be God's special envoy and the consternation generated by this claim align the Sabbath healings with some of the most distinctive emphases in the Gospel of John. Disclosing the identity of Jesus step by step, beginning with a series of allusions to Genesis, John never strays from the message that Jesus's relationship with God goes beyond imitation and intimacy, as already noted.[21]

John builds his theme to a crescendo until Jesus's death proves to be the means by which Satan is defeated and the alienation between human beings and God overcome (12:20–33).

Indeed, John's story echoes Genesis and will not be fully understood unless this connection comes to the surface. "The Gospel of John begins like the first book of the Bible. This is of the utmost importance," writes Günter Reim in his in-depth study of John's use of the Old Testament.[22] Reim points out that John not only elicits the memory of Genesis but also shows that the events of Jesus's life continue the story in Genesis, linking the Creator in Genesis to the Logos in John's Gospel. Likewise, Brown is convinced that the parallel between the Prologue of John and Genesis is easily seen.[23] Bultmann concurs that "it would be hard for the Evangelist to begin his work with 'in the beginning' without thinking of 'in the beginning' of Gen. 1:1."[24]

Moreover, the Prologue in John (1:1–18) is suffused with phrases recalling the Genesis account of Creation. Genesis imagery also sounds the themes of John, such as the antinomy of "light" and "darkness" (1:4–5, 9), the emphasis on "glory" (1:14), and the importance of "truth" (1:14, 17). The negative member of these early signals, "darkness," strives against the "light" in John (1:5) and is directly related to the Genesis narrative of the fall (Gen. 3:1–6). As an exchange that still reverberates with the commotion raised by Jesus's healing of the paralytic, Jesus says to His critics, "You are from your father the devil, and you choose to do your father's desires. He was a murderer from the beginning and does not stand in the truth, because there is no truth in him. When he lies, he speaks according to his own nature, for he is a liar and the father of lies" (John 8:44).

This is a huge giveaway. The "liar and the father of lies" points to the serpent's dissembling and outright lie in Genesis (3:1, 4).[25] According to John, Jesus's mission is to undo the damage done by "the father of lies." It is also significant that Jesus refers to "*the* lie," not a falsehood in a general and nonspecific sense, indicating not only the magnitude of the falsehood that was circulated but also its primacy and importance to the story in John.

"Darkness" is attributed to the activity of a personal being, given aliases like "ruler of this world," "Satan," and "Devil."[26] These identifications drive home the identity of the actual opponent in the story. That opponent is not "the Jews" but "the father of lies" (8:44), and it is against the activity of an opponent thus conceived that Jesus's intervention is aimed.

What, however, can Jesus do in order to overcome an enemy whose chief weapons are lies and misrepresentation? John does not speculate as to what the options might be because he knows what God's remedy is: Jesus is the Revealer. This is the point at which the question of Jesus's identity moves beyond the notions of imitation or intimacy, and it could well begin with a reflection on Bultmann's quest for the central message of the Gospel.

Jesus's mission is to undo the damage done by "the father of lies."

Bultmann probes insistently for what he calls the second great riddle of the Gospel, John's "*controlling outlook, his basic conception.*"[27] Bultmann's answer is emphatic: Jesus is the Revealer, the messenger who brings revelation through words and deeds.[28] Speaking in the context of the healing of the paralytic, Jesus does the works that the Father has given Him (5:19), and He speaks the words that He has heard from the Father (7:17–18; cf. 8:28; 12:49–50).[29]

Bultmann, however, insisted that Jesus as Revealer was more important than what He revealed: "The author [John] is only interested in the That of the revelation, not for the What," Bultmann says ingeniously.[30] But the Gospel opposes this separation. W. C. van Unnik shows that the Gospel is just as concerned about the content of the revelation as about its agent.

> Stress is not laid upon the element of wonder in itself, but upon the revelation of Jesus' glory (2,11). Bultmann says that

> [his deeds] do not accredit Jesus because they require faith. That does not seem like a right conclusion. To be sure, they require faith, but for John it was important that they were done and that it was impossible to deny that they had been done. They are proofs which can be accepted in a completely earthly manner (6,27) or rejected altogether or accepted for what they were: the works of God.[31]

Crucially, with the healing of the paralytic and the blind man on the Sabbath, the miracles authenticate the agent (5:36; 10:25; 14:10–11), and they testify to the character of the One who has sent Jesus (5:36; 9:4; 10:25, 32, 37–38; 14:10–11; 15:34). The identity of the agent and the purpose of His coming into the world are indissolubly linked. The Revealer in the Fourth Gospel is revealing the character of God, and the content of this revelation is especially important because it is set in a context where God's character has been misrepresented.

In fact, the prestige of the Sabbath makes the point of Jesus's identity, and the question of Jesus's identity puts His healing ministry on the Sabbath in the clearest light. When Jesus claims that "my Father is still working, and I also am working" (5:17), the Jews in the audience are not slow to grasp the implication. Jesus, as they correctly hear it, has placed Himself within the identity of God, "making himself equal to God" (5:18).

THE SABBATH HEALINGS AND THE CHARACTER OF GOD

Jesus is the Revealer in John, and the truth He reveals is contrasted repeatedly with its opposite: falsehood. In the Prologue, Jesus is "full of grace and truth" (1:14) and the one who brings "grace and truth" in a way not achieved by Moses (1:17). "Truth" is on the line throughout the entire Gospel. True worshipers are to worship the Father "in spirit and in truth" (4:23–24); John the Baptist "testified to the truth" (5:33); and the disciples of Jesus "will know the truth," and the truth will make them free (8:31–32).

As noted already, these claims are made in the context of conflict. The opponent in the cosmic drama "does not stand in the truth because there is no truth in him" (8:44). Jesus, on the other hand, tells the truth (8:45). In one of the most pointed "I am" sayings in John, Jesus is the embodiment of truth, saying, "I am…the truth" (14:6). The Spirit that is to continue Jesus's mission undiminished is "the Spirit of truth" (14:17; 15:26; 16:13). "Sanctify them in the truth," Jesus says in His parting prayer, framing it as His legacy, will, and testament (17:17, 19). When Pilate inquires about His credentials, Jesus can do no better than to respond with the ringing, "For this I was born, and for this I came into the world, to testify to the truth" (18:37).

Bultmann shows that the most common antonym of *alētheia*, "truth," is *pseudos*, "lie."[32] We have seen that where "the truth" is set in pointed opposition to "the lie," we are in the realm of John's intensely personified dualism *and* in the territory of the Genesis narrative of the fall (8:44). Even when we hear Jesus respond to Pilate's query, His answer is best heard within the echoing chamber of the story of the misrepresentation in Genesis. The cause for which Jesus has come into the world, "*that I should bear witness to the truth*" (18:37, NKJV), is not referring to a philosophical quest for ultimate reality, nor is it a statement concerning human ignorance of God in a generic sense. Instead, the truth at issue stands in contrast to the active promotion of falsehood, linked to the brazen proposition of "the father of lies" (8:44).

Like truth, "glory" is an ever-present theme in John. "Glory," however, is a challenging word because we do not use it in everyday speech. We may need help to get the connotation of this important word right. Words that fall in the range of "glory" (*doxa*) are "splendor," "grandeur," or "radiance." In the context of John, less literal terms are better. I incline toward a less luminous word like "character," understood in the sense of "praiseworthy character." John, in his Prologue, will then say, "We have seen his praiseworthy character, the praiseworthy character as of a father's only son, full of grace and truth"

(1:14, translation mine). The "glory" that has been seen is "glory" in a definitive and ultimate sense, "the glory as of a father's only son" (1:14). When Jesus turns water into wine at the wedding in Cana, His first sign, He "revealed his glory," now understood as "praiseworthy character," with the result that "his disciples believed in him" (2:11). This qualification, seeing the miracle as a manifestation of "glory," should also be extended to the healing miracles. As in the case of the blind man in John 9, Lazarus's illness is not a disaster but an occasion for glory to become manifest; "it is for God's glory, so that the Son of God may be glorified through it" (11:4; cf. 9:3). "Glory" is not a human construct, or rather, the human construct of glory does not fit Jesus's conception (5:41, 44; 7:18; 8:44, 50).

To be sure, the early glimpses of "glory" are only preliminary. Only with the approaching death of Jesus does the "glory" theme in John move into high gear, heralded by the announcement, "The hour has come for the Son of Man to be glorified" (12:23). "Praiseworthy character" falls short at this stage, but "glorified" is hardly up to the task either. Perhaps "vindicated" or "exalted" do somewhat better. In this part of John, Isaiah's Servant Songs are present through hints and whispers that suffuse John's message.[33] In Isaiah, too, the concept of "glory" is to be understood as glory of a different order. The "glory" that is in view is a self-emptying and self-denying quality (12:24);[34] it is not self-serving, and it does not seek its own advantage. According to the antecedent in Isaiah, the Servant "shall prosper; he shall be exalted and lifted up, and shall be very high [LXX: 'shall be highly glorified']" (Isa. 52:13). When we ask how this will manifest itself, Isaiah shows the Servant marred in His appearance (Isa. 52:14), "a root out of dry ground," a man without "form or glory," having "nothing in his appearance that we should desire him" (Isa. 53:2). Needless to say, these are challenging paradoxes. John, and before him Isaiah, is asking to see a "praiseworthy character" in a person that to the naked eye and to the natural human perception seems devoid of anything worthy of praise.

While the translators of the Bible have given little thought to helping the modern reader hear these echoes, John comes to the rescue when he gives an explicit attribution to Isaiah: "Isaiah said this because he saw his glory and spoke about him" (12:41). Like Isaiah's audience we, too, are left speechless (52:15), the faculties of comprehension shattered by the thought that He of whom it is said, "he had no glory" (53:2), does have "glory" but His "glory" is absence of glory on human terms, belonging to a different currency.

As with "light" confronting "darkness" and "truth" facing "falsehood," "glory" stands in counterpoint to a quality that has been denied. The One whose character and reputation are at stake, ultimately, is God. G. B. Caird tells us that Jesus brings God's "glory" to light, meaning that it has been hidden, perhaps even smeared. "When Jesus speaks and acts, it is the Father speaking and acting in him."[35] Jesus's suffering has a revelatory quality, bringing to light glory that has always been present.

Echoing Genesis, John shows Jesus to be involved in Creation (1:3). The relation is so intimate as to conflate the identity of the Logos and God (1:1–2). So it is with Jesus the Revealer. "Whoever has seen me has seen the Father," Jesus tells the last holdout who has yet to see the connection (14:9). If "the lie" that is spoken by the "father of lies" is falsehood directed against the character of God, it can only be refuted by one who shares the divine identity. This Person can say as no mere human being can ever say, "I am...the truth" (14:6). If God's "glory" is misrepresented and misperceived, the problem is rectified by the only One who can make God known (1:18; 14:6–9). "Revelation," "truth," and "glory" all come to a head in the lifting up of Jesus on the cross. This moment of ultimate disclosure is also the moment of reconciliation, Jesus drawing all people to Himself (12:32).[36] On the terms of the Gospel of John, at least, it is highly appropriate, as does J. Terence Forestell, to say that salvation is revelation.[37]

Once the relation of Jesus to God is established, it is possible to appreciate more fully what the healing ministry of Jesus says about

God. Jesus's insistence on healing on the Sabbath is best understood when we see the Sabbath not as the prized possession of the Jews but as God's signature statement. In effect, Jesus is delivering on the original commitment invested in the seventh day at Creation.

To suggest that Jesus actually "broke the sabbath," as his critics do (5:18), is to assume, wrongly, that they have grasped its meaning. "If, as is often claimed, the evangelists aimed at inculcating...Christian doctrine such as annulment of the Sabbath legislation...they did a pitiful job which falls far short of proving their alleged thesis," Geza Vermes aptly observes.[38] In the Gospel of John Jesus is not guilty as charged. Following the healing of the paralytic "the Jews persecuted Jesus because he did this on the sabbath" (5:16). Like Jesus, His critics invoke the memory of creation as the basis for Sabbath holiness, but their idea of the Sabbath derives from a distorted picture of reality. The distortion hails back to a distant time when all was well in the world. In the serenity and perfection of God's rest at Creation, as their still picture has it, something is missing: Where is God in the face of *present* need and suffering?

Being *present*, and responding to *present* reality, constitutes the essence of Jesus's idea of the Sabbath. At creation God's commitment to humanity is described by God's rest, but the reality of disease and death calls for a different Sabbath message. Resting in the face of crying needs implies remoteness and indifference. God is not like that, for God is not remote; God is *present*. This message, written on the Sabbath from the beginning, is still the message of the Sabbath, and Jesus delights to point it out. No matter how shocking the thought, Jesus defends His actions by the ultimate criterion: "My Father is *working* until now, and I am also working" (5:17, translation mine). Prioritizing the notion of presence, *working* takes precedence over *resting*. God is, as it were, hard at work to make right what is wrong.

Some scholars have suggested that Jesus based His Sabbath behavior on a view already widely accepted in Judaism.[39] This view falls far short of doing justice to Jesus's frequent Sabbath miracles because it assumes that the miracles say not more about God than what was commonly held to be the case. In John, however, Christology is the scaffolding for what Jesus brings to light about God and not an end in itself.[40] Jesus belongs within the divine identity, but the aim is less to show who Jesus is and more to represent what God is like. "If I am not doing the works of my Father, then do not believe me," Jesus says in the Gospel before proceeding to prioritize the question of God's character over the question of His status. "But if I do them, *even though you do not believe me*, believe the works, so that you may know and understand that the Father is in me and I am in the Father" (10:37–38). In other words, Jesus's works, including His acts of healing on the Sabbath, are to become their view of God whatever their view of Jesus. He is willing to remove Himself from the picture in order that His works, hypothetically separated from His person, might shape their view of God. Jesus is God in this Gospel, but if one message is more important, it is to show that God is like Jesus.

It is highly appropriate to say that salvation is revelation.

For this reason Jesus does not explain His actions by an idea that is already in wide currency among the Jews, as scholars tend to see it. What He says, and the shock that follows, can only be understood by viewing it in terms of something they do not know. The Jewish religious system that is reflected in the Sabbath conflicts reduces God to a distant player in human affairs. Beyond keeping the universe on course, no initiative seems imminent on God's part. The Sabbath has come to epitomize the stalemate, anticipating the view that "if Israel kept the Sabbath properly even for one day, the Son of David would come."[41] And yet there is Jesus in their midst explaining that "the very works that I am doing, testify on my behalf that the Father has sent me" (5:36).

Nothing in the prevailing theology of the time has prepared people for Jesus.[42] As to His work, He appeals to His knowledge of the Father. As to the correct understanding of the Father, He is pointing to Himself. Jesus's Sabbath activities are not accounted for by God's ordinary work. Maintenance of the created order will not suffice when the created order is threatened by dissolution, and when human beings are in the thrall of disease and death. Rather than waiting for human beings to break the deadlock by impeccable Sabbath observance, Jesus brings the Father's compassion to view on the Sabbath. In the words of G. Campbell Morgan, "There can be no rest for God while humanity is suffering."[43] Jesus cannot wait till the next day because He is magnifying the original message of the Sabbath in the context of human suffering. Ministering to the person in need, reaching out to heal and to restore, lies at the heart of the divine character and mission.

From now on events accelerate in John's Gospel. The end is rapidly approaching, anticipated by what must be seen as a watershed statement temporally and ideologically. "My Father is working *until now*" (5:17), emphasizing a temporal horizon, suggests that the completion of Jesus's work is not far away. After healing the blind man, Jesus declares that "night is coming when no one can work" (9:4). Heading into the final week of His ministry, He points to the lengthening shadows, reminding them that "the light is with you for a little longer" (12:35).

The timing that is such a critical feature of the Sabbath healings is maintained till the end. On the cross, the script of this Gospel retraces the steps of the Creation account. As the Sabbath draws near, Jesus's life is fast ebbing. At that point His voice rings out in a final announcement, "It is finished!" (19:30).

These words, a single word in Greek, signify completion, not the end in an absolute sense. It is significant to hear Jesus cry out "it is finished" at that specific point in time. The resurrection and Sunday morning will come, but Jesus will not wait to say "it is finished" until then. He has reasons to say it at that point in time, on Friday night. The Sabbath that is about to begin is not a theological no-man's land.[44]

The Greek expression in John 19:30 is the word *tetelestai*, a word that must not be orphaned from the Creation parentage.[45] In the Genesis account, when "the heavens and the earth were finished," the Greek translation of the Old Testament chose the same term, *sunetelesthēsan* (Gen. 2:1; cf. 2:2). If we keep the ear close to the ground, listening to the distant Old Testament echo, the connection cannot be missed. John is appropriating the language of the Creation account, specifically the language heralding the inauguration of the first Sabbath.[46] As Creation culminates in the Sabbath rest, the work of making right what is wrong comes to completion (19:31–34). The relationship between the Revealer and the revelatory intent of the Sabbath is here at its zenith. In John's story, where attention to detail is everything,[47] the timing cannot be more precise, the scene more poignant, or the message more persuasive.

Ministering to the person in need lies at the heart of the divine character and mission.

"Finished." This is the key word, deserving to stand alone because it is a word that brings together all the parts of the story. "What God had begun by the Word in the days of Creation, God finished by the Word in the days of the Redemption," says Ethelbert Stauffer.[48] God has kept the commitment embodied in the seventh day.

From henceforth the meaning of the Sabbath must be viewed through the lens provided by the life and death of Jesus the Revealer.

ENDNOTES

1. R. Alan Culpepper (*Anatomy of the Fourth Gospel: A Study in Literary Design* [Philadelphia: Fortress Press, 1987], 139) demonstrates how the two Sabbath healings in the Gospel of John parallel each other, the Sabbath serving as the contested issue.

2. Guillermo Cook, "Seeing, Judging and Acting: Evangelism in Jesus' Way: A Biblical Study on Chapter 9 of the Gospel of John," *International Review of Mission* 87 (1998): 390.

3. Ernst Haenchen, *John 1: A Commentary on the Gospel of John,* trans. Robert W. Funk (Hermeneia; Philadelphia: Fortress Press, 1984), 246.

4. Karen Pidcock-Lester, "John 5:1–9," *Int* 59 (2005): 62.

5. Herman Ridderbos, *The Gospel According to John,* trans. John Vriend (Grand Rapids: Eerdmans, 1997), 187.

6. J. H. Bernard, *A Critical and Exegetical Commentary on the Gospel According to St. John*, vol. 1 (ICC; Edinburgh: T. & T. Clark, 1928 [repr. 1993]), 232.

7. *The Mishna*, art. *Shabbat* 7:2; Eduard Lohse, art. "*sabbaton,*" *TDNT*, 7:26–28.

8. The fact that all the Gospels describe Sabbath healings and ensuing controversy strongly supports the case for authenticity, anchoring these stories in the context of Jesus's ministry; cf. Marcus Borg, *Conflict, Holiness and Politics in the Teaching of Jesus* (New York: Edwin Mellen Press, 1984), 145–162; Craig S. Keener, *The Gospel of John: A Commentary*, vol. 1 (Peabody: Hendrickson Publishers, 2003), 645.

9. Lesslie Newbigin (*The Light Has Come: An Exposition of the Fourth Gospel* [Grand Rapids: Eerdmans, 1982], 63) points out that "one fifth of all the material in the four Gospels is concerned with the healing of physical disease." In John, a disproportionate share of this relates to healing on the Sabbath.

10. Rudolf Bultmann, "The New Approach to the Synoptic Problem," in *Existence and Faith: Shorter Writings of Rudolf Bultmann*, ed. Schubert M. Ogden (London: Collins, 1964), 42–43. The essay was originally written in 1926. Leading Johannine scholars have adopted this view in one form or another; cf. D. Moody Smith ("Johannine Christianity: Some Reflections on Its Character and Delineation," *NTS* 21 [1975]: 230); R. Alan Culpepper, *The Johannine School: An Evaluation of the Johannine-School Hypothesis Based on an Investigation of the Nature of Ancient Schools* (Missoula, MT: Scholars Press, 1975); John Ashton, *Understanding the Fourth Gospel* (Oxford: Clarendon Press, 1991), 160–198. Ashton admits that it is troubling for this hypothesis to end up with such diverse places as Ephesus, Antioch, or Alexandria.

11. In a very influential book, J. Louis Martyn (*History and Theology in the Fourth Gospel* [New York: Harper & Row, 1968]) reads John as though the story of the "Johannine community" is particularly prominent in the Sabbath controversies.

12. Richard J. Bauckham, "For Whom Were Gospels Written," in *The Gospels for All Christians: Rethinking the Gospel Audiences*, ed. Richard J. Bauckham (Edinburgh: T & T Clark, 1998), 9–48; idem, *The Testimony of the Beloved Disciple: Narrative, History, and Theology in the Gospel of John* (Grand Rapids: Baker Academic, 2007), 9–31, 113–123.

13. Bauckham, "Gospels," 47.

14. Richard Burridge (*What Are the Gospels? A Comparison with Graeco-Roman Biography* [SNTS 70; Cambridge: Cambridge University Press, 1992]) argues convincingly that the gospels conform to the genre of ancient biography or *bioi*; see also, by the same author, the more popular, *Four Gospels, One Jesus?* (London: SPCK, 1994).

15. The question as to who should be seen behind John's broad and general term "the Jews" favors the religious leaders of his time; cf. Urban C. Von Wahlde, "The Johannine 'Jews': A Critical Survey," *NTS* 28 (1982): 33–60.

16. Andrew T. Lincoln, *Truth on Trial: The Lawsuit Motif in the Fourth Gospel* (Peabody: Hendrickson, 2000).

17. Martin Asiedu-Peprah, *Johannine Sabbath Conflicts as Juridical Controversy* (WUNT 2. Reihe 132; Tübingen: Mohr Siebeck, 2001), 8–9, 13–38. The author assumes a community-setting post-70 CE as the occasion for the Gospel, weakening its theological utility.

18. Asiedu-Peprah (*Johannine Sabbath Conflicts*, 34–38) operates within the surface parameters of the story when he emphasizes the bilateral character of the conflict, but the implicit premise of the proceedings is nevertheless that there is a third party, a "judge" in the person of the reader. Yet reader persuasion is paramount in Asiedu-Peprah's model.

19. Brown, *The Gospel According to John,* I:217.

20. Ibid.

21. Rudolf Bultmann ("Die Bedeutung der neuerschossenen mandäischen und manichäischen Quellen für das Verständnis der Johannesevangeliums," *ZNW* 24 [1925]: 102) turned out to be mistaken in many of his assumptions with respect to the Gospel of John, but the emphasis on Jesus as the Revealer is one insight that cannot be improved upon; cf. see also John 5:36; 9:4; 10:25, 32, 37–38; 14:10–11; 15:34.

22. Günter Reim, *Studien zum alttestamentlichcn Hintergrund des Johannesevangeliums* (Cambridge: Cambridge University Press, 1974), 99.

23. Brown, *The Gospel According to John*, I:4.

24. Rudolf Bultmann, *The Gospel of John: A Commentary,* trans. G. R. Beasley-Murray, R. W. N. Hoare, and J. K. Riches (Philadelphia: The Westminster Press, 1971), 20.

25. Reim, *Hintergrund des Johannesevangeliums*, 98.

26. David E. Aune, "Dualism in the Fourth Gospel and the Dead Sea Scrolls: A Reassessment of the Problem," *Neotestamentica et Philonica. Studies in Honor of Peder Borgen*, ed. David Aune, Torrey Seland, and Jarl Heenning Ulrichsen (Leiden: Brill, 2003), 287.

27. Bultmann, "Verständnis der Johannesevangeliums," 102.

28. Bultmann's interpretation in this respect is endorsed by Ashton (*Understanding the Fourth* Gospel, 497), and it is also affirmed by Marianne Meye Thompson (*The God of the Gospel of John* [Grand Rapids: Eerdmans, 2001], 140), albeit with a different emphasis.

29. Bultmann, "Verständnis der Johannesevangeliums," 102.

30. Ibid., 146.

31. W. C. van Unnik, "The Purpose of St. John's Gospel," in *Studia Evangelica* I, ed. Kurt Aland, F. L. Cross, Jean Danielou, Harald Riesenfeld, and W. C. van Unnik (Berlin: Akademie-Verlag, 1959), 401–402.

32. Bultmann, art. "*alētheia*," *TDNT*, 1:238.

33. Cf. Isa 42:8; 49:3, 5; 52:13; 53:2.

34. G. B. Caird, "The Glory of God in the Fourth Gospel: An Exercise in Biblical Semantics," *NTS* 15 (1969): 276. Margaret Pamment ("The Meaning of *doxa* in the Fourth Gospel," *ZNW*

74 [1983]: 12) shows that *doxa*, the Gospel's concept of glory, "is used with associations not of power, but of selfless generosity and love."

35. Caird, "The Glory of God in the Fourth Gospel," 271.

36. Cf. Tonstad, "The Father of Lies, 'the Mother of Lies' and the Death of Jesus," 193–208.

37. J. Terence Forestell, *The Word of the Cross: Salvation as Revelation in the Fourth Gospel* (Rome: Biblical Institute Press, 1974).

38. Geza Vermes, *The Religion of Jesus the Jew* (Minneapolis: Augsburg Fortress, 1993), 13; cf. also Keener, *John*, I:641–645. According to Moody Smith ("John," 105), "John clearly believes that Jesus does not violate the Sabbath law."

39. Bultmann, *The Gospel of John*, 246; cf. also Leon Morris, *The Gospel According to John* (Grand Rapids: Eerdmans, 1971), 309. Lohse, art. "*sabbaton*," *TDNT*, 7:27; Brown, *The Gospel According to John*, I:217; Asiedu-Peprah, *Johannine Sabbath Conflicts*, 209.

40. Even though she does not take it as far as one might wish, Marianne Meye Thompson (*The God of the Gospel of John* [Grand Rapids: Eerdmans, 2001]) deserves credit for seeing the Christology of John subservient to its theology (see esp. pp. 239–240).

41. *Exodus Rabbah* XXV.12.

42. As Hengel (*Judaism and Hellenism*, I:307) has shown, the loss of freedom after 63 BC was felt acutely because foreign rule was felt to interfere with obedience to the law. For that reason many hoped for a repetition of the "Maccabean miracle," meaning a new military triumph.

43. George Campbell Morgan, *The Gospel according to John* (New York: Fleming H. Revell, 1933), 91.

44. A rare exception in this respect is Alan E. Lewis (*Between Cross and Resurrection: A Theology of Holy Saturday* [Grand Rapids: Eerdmans, 2001]), whose attention to the theological implications of the day between Friday and Sunday, the day when the body of Jesus lies in the grave, is unprecedented and noteworthy even if it does not follow the narrative of the Gospel of John.

45. Cf. Reim, *Hintergrund des Johannesevangeliums*, 99.

46. The notion that Jesus has come to *finish* God's work is prominent in John (4:34; 17:4; 19:30), as is the notion that His relation to the Sabbath is revelatory of *God's* work (5:17, 36); cf. Keener, *The Gospel of John*, 2:1148; cf. also Roland Bergmeier, "ΤΕΤΕΛΕΣΤΑΙ: John 19:30," *ZNW* 79 (1988): 282–290.

47. It is fascinating that the *absence* of order in Mark, usually considered the primary and paradigmatic Synoptic witness, was a matter of awareness already in the Early Church. According to Eusebius, Papias said in the second century that "Mark...wrote down carefully, *but not in order*, all he remembered of the Lord's sayings and doings"; cf. *Eccl. Hist.* 3.39.15.

48. Ethelbert Stauffer, *Jesus and His Story,* trans. Richard and Clara Winston (New York: Alfred A. Knopf, 1970 [1959]), 141.

CHAPTER 12

THE SABBATH AND THE GREATEST COMMANDMENT

And ought not this woman, a daughter of Abraham whom Satan bound for eighteen long years, be set free from this bondage on the sabbath day?
Luke 13:16

According to Matthew, the person who steps forward to ask Jesus the far-reaching question, "Teacher, which commandment in the law is the greatest?" is a Pharisee (Matt. 22:36). The identity of the questioner is crucial because the popular stereotype sees the "Pharisees" as self-righteous, exclusivist, and thoroughly confused about what is important. How do we size up the questioner in this exchange, realizing that we may deal with the member of a group that has been wrongly stereotyped? How do we hear his question? And how does the Sabbath fare in relation to the quest for the greatest commandment in the law?

SIZING UP THE QUESTIONER

The New Testament features Pharisees that seem to conform to this negative stereotype. In the parable of the two worshipers in Luke, Jesus specifically designates one of the two people in the story a Pharisee, on His way to the temple to pray (Luke 18:10). Luke even explains that the parable was addressed "to some who trusted in themselves that they were righteous and regarded others with contempt" (18:9). In the parable this Pharisee stands aloof "by himself," and his prayer reeks with self-satisfaction, "God, I thank you that I am not like other people" (18:11).

But did such a Pharisee exist? It seems more likely that Jesus is creating a cartoon character in which a stance that *tends* toward exclusiveness and moral superiority is deliberately exaggerated in order to make a point. In the currency of the cartoonist, the crooked nose is drawn more crooked and the bushy eyebrows are exaggerated. We recognize the character, and we get the point, but we do not look at the cartoon as though it is a precise portrait of the person in question.

In Matthew, Jesus brings a litany of charges against the Pharisees that further bolster the stereotype (Matt. 23:13–35).[1] Where the Pharisee in the example in Luke is smug and self-satisfied, the Pharisees in the Matthean account are unable to sift the trivial from the important, concentrating on minor things at the expense of weightier matters. "Woe to you, scribes and Pharisees, hypocrites! For you tithe mint, dill, and cummin, and have neglected the weightier matters of the law: justice and mercy and faith. It is these you ought to have practiced without neglecting the others. You blind guides! You strain out a gnat but swallow a camel!" (Matt. 23:23–24).

Moreover, the Pharisees are more concerned about keeping up appearances than about integrity of character and the inner life. "Woe to you, scribes and Pharisees, hypocrites! For you clean the outside of the cup and of the plate, but inside they are full of greed and self-indulgence. You blind Pharisee! First clean the inside of the cup, so that the outside also may become clean" (Matt. 23:25–26).

Scholars have tried a host of approaches to these sayings, wishing to lessen their sting. One approach is to insist that these statements cannot be authentic sayings of Jesus.[2] Graham Stanton says that the denunciation of the scribes in Matthew, ch. 23, whatever their background, "does not excuse them," noting that Christians rightly "feel acutely embarrassed by them and by the way they have been used by some in earlier generations to fuel anti-Semitism."[3] Lloyd Gaston, taking an even more radical view, claims that it was Matthew who taught the church to hate Israel.[4] For him this means that where the handiwork of the redactor Matthew is evident, it should no longer be part of the Christian Canon.[5]

Other interpreters, reluctant to excise these texts from the New Testament or to concede that they are out of character with Jesus, look for less radical remedies. The possibility that parables and sayings of Jesus may be rhetorical exaggerations has already been mentioned. John Bowker finds evidence of diversity within the Pharisaic movement and suggests that the "Pharisees" in these texts are real, but they are extremists and not representative of mainstream Pharisee ideology.[6] Moreover, the picture of the Pharisees in the New Testament is not uniformly negative. The apostle Paul had a Pharisaic upbringing and training (Phil. 3:5; Acts 23:6; 26:5), and his mentor Gamaliel is portrayed in the book of Acts as a model of reason, tolerance, and nuance (Acts 5:34–39).[7] Moreover, if these statements are sayings of Jesus, we do not know *how* they were spoken. The seven woes in Matthew end on a note of utter sadness, Jesus expressing the wish "to gather your children together as a hen gathers her brood under her wings," yet coming up short (Matt. 23:37). Given that there is no harshness in this utterance, it is possible that the harsh-sounding sayings should be read differently from the way they are often perceived.

There may be a tendency to feel smug, to emphasize minor issues of form over major issues of fairness, to look better on the outside than on the inside, and to prescribe more than to perform.

Of the options that remain, the one that is most difficult is to see less distance between us and the "Pharisees," admitting that now, too, especially in religious communities, there may be a tendency to feel smug, to emphasize minor issues of form over major issues of fairness, to look better on the outside than on the inside, and to prescribe more than to perform. If read with circumspection, therefore, as J. A. Sanders suggests, the New Testament will not be the story about them but about us. A right reading "will someday bring us to see that the Bible, as canon and as parable, is ultimately not about Jews and non-Jews in any of its parts, but reflects normal, human protagonists and antagonists in many kinds of situations on this rapidly shrinking globe."[8] Much may be gained if we adjust to seeing the Pharisees this way.

HEARING THE QUESTION

"Teacher, which commandment in the law is the greatest?" asks the Pharisee in Matthew (22:36), or, as in Mark, "Which commandment is the first of all?" (Mark 12:28). Jesus's answer reveals that this is not a question He takes lightly. He says in reply, "The first is, 'Hear,

O Israel: the Lord our God, the Lord is one; you shall love the Lord your God with all your heart, and with all your soul, and with all your mind, and with all your strength.' The second is this, 'You shall love your neighbor as yourself.' There is no other commandment greater than these" (Mark 12:29–31).

The exchange between the Pharisees and Jesus proceeds according to the standard rules of rabbinic inquiry. It reveals that the Pharisees are people in search of perspective on their values; they are capable of distinguishing between the greater and the lesser. Jesus's answer is the conclusion at which they also have arrived. Seeking the foremost principle from which the rest of the law can be deduced, they, too, are aiming to unearth bedrock. Jesus's response, quoting Scripture, takes no one by surprise (cf. Deut. 6:5; Lev. 19:18). The scribe in Mark affirms as much, answering, "You are right, Teacher; you have truly said that 'he is one, and besides him there is no other'; and 'to love him with all the heart, and with all the understanding, and with all the strength,' and 'to love one's neighbor as oneself,'—this is much more important than all whole burnt offerings and sacrifices" (Mark 12:32–33).

On this question, at least, Jesus and the Pharisees seem to be in agreement, and the subject on which they agree is the most important subject of all. Mark's account concludes on a note of warmth, a flash of mutual recognition. "You are right," says the scribe, and Jesus, returning the compliment, rejoins, "You are not far from the kingdom of God" (Mark 12:32, 34).

Despite the amicable character of this exchange, it is worthwhile to examine it more closely. How are we to understand the duality of Jesus's answer, explicit in Matthew and readily agreed to by his partner in the dialogue, "On these *two* commandments hang all the law and the prophets" (Matt. 22:39)? Specifically, how are we to avoid the point that the second commandment is seen as "the second most important commandment" (12:31) as the *Good News Bible* translates Mark? Indeed, how are we to avoid the impression that to love the neighbor, important as that is, is not as important as "the greatest and first commandment" (Matt. 22:38)? If the Pharisees prove themselves less adept at meeting the demands of "the second most important commandment," at least they can take comfort in the fact that they put first things first. In their outlook there is a way to love God that makes allowance for caring less about people. Religion can flourish even though there is no appreciable benefit to humanity. So what if human need is neglected as long as God gets His due!

The notion that Jesus is espousing two great commandments, prioritizing them in order of importance, must therefore be questioned. The "second" commandment is second only in order of sequence.[9] It is not second in importance, or independent of the first, or optional. Matthew makes this point more explicit since he has Jesus say that "the second is like it" (Matt. 22:39). It is second but has the same weight and quality, "just as great as this one,"[10] and "both qualify as 'the greatest' imperative."[11] Jesus, drawing on familiar Old Testament texts, is merely spelling out the implications of loving God in terms of human relationships.

The unity of the two commandments is substantiated in the letters of Paul. If, in Matthew, the two commandments stand as "a summary of the Decalogue,"[12] and if it is true that "we imitate what we love, so to love God is to imitate the One whose love is catholic,"[13] there is no way to drive a wedge between these two commandments. Paul, in Galatians and Romans, does not hesitate to declare that the law can be summarized in *one* principle rather than two. After reviewing some of the Ten Commandments he asserts in Romans that "whatever other commandment there may be, are summed up in this *one* rule: 'Love your neighbor as yourself.' Love does no harm to its neighbor. Therefore love is the fulfillment of the law" (Rom. 13:8–10).

In Galatians, Paul is even more pointed, writing that "the entire law is summed up in a *single* command: 'Love your neighbor as yourself'" (Gal. 5:14). The variant from Jesus's answer to the Pharisee is remarkable in that, in Mark and Matthew, "the greatest and first commandment" is the premise for the second commandment (Matt. 22:38). In Paul's argument, however, the first commandment is subsumed in the second, becoming virtually invisible. Paul's concern is embodied in the second commandment, "summed up in a single command" (Gal. 5:14). This is the litmus test and the ultimate quality check in the religion of which Paul is the leading promoter.

Paul's contribution to this subject is found within the context of a much wider discussion of the function of the law. Under the heading of newness (Gal. 6:15; Rom. 6:4; 2 Cor. 5:17), Paul believes that what other religious projects at best can describe or demand, the good news will deliver. No matter how these statements are interpreted and qualified, they promise a benefit to human relationships and to the believer's fellow human being. This is one point that cannot be eroded.

Ernest De Witt Burton is appropriately surprised that Paul, having spent so much effort cutting the law down to size, then turns around to give "as the reason for their serving one another that thus they will fulfil the whole law."[14] But one should not assume that Paul introduces a contradiction or even a new turn in his argument. The ethical outcome must be seen as the destination to which his message is leading all along (Gal. 5:6; 6:15; 1 Cor. 7:19). Again, accepting that Paul is constraining the law, urging that the law can prescribe but not deliver (Rom. 7:7, 12–13), he nevertheless returns to it. Also voicing surprise, Richard N. Longenecker wonders whether Paul, "having made such a great show of throwing out the law through the front door," instead sneaks it in through the back door.[15]

This, of course, makes Paul seem incoherent and self-contradictory, and worse, it restores dignity to the law that his prior argument has taken away. E. P. Sanders tries to solve this problem, beginning with the proposal that when reading Paul we must distinguish between his reasons and his arguments, Paul's reasons being a deeper current than the situational and rhetorical character of his arguments.[16] If one builds on this scaffolding, Paul's line of thought is coherent and even quite conventional with respect to the law. He does not see the law as the means of "getting in" to the believing community, but it remains in force as the means for "staying in," albeit qualified and modified to accommodate the Gentile mission.[17] Longenecker, following Stephen Westerholm, walks the fine line that Christian believers do not do the law, but they fulfill it;[18] "Galatians 5:14 is not itself a command to fulfill the law but a statement that, when one loves one's neighbor, the whole law is fully satisfied in the process."[19] Paul's argument, then, is not an argument from law but an argument from love.[20] Fulfillment of the law cannot be evaded even though it happens "apart from law" (Rom. 3:21) and by means other than law.

Few commentaries match J. Louis Martyn's attempt to get under the skin of Paul's reasoning in Galatians.[21] Martyn is exceptionally attentive to nuances in the text, and he is daring in his interpretations, trying out options that might deter more conventional interpreters. But his approach is not without pitfalls. If we accept that there is a situational aspect to Paul's argument, it advises caution on our part because our view of the situation is incomplete. If, too, we accept that Paul's rhetoric at times is highly charged, a "literal" reading of Paul can lead to misunderstanding. Martyn lives close to the edge, eager to reproduce an authentic, living Paul, and yet he runs the risk of further inflaming Paul's metaphors when they actually need to be cooled by interpretation. Sanders's suggestion that we need to distinguish between Paul's reasons and his arguments is useful on this point lest we construct a Paul who is more intent on titillating scholars than nurturing new believers. Paul's rhetoric soars at times, but in the end there is an earthy, ethical sobriety in Paul to which modern interpreters rarely do justice.

Paul, who is determined to yield no ground to the law even when he points out unacceptable behavior, presents the Galatians with a "vice list" of his own that is easily correlated with the Ten Commandments. But Paul will not get his standard from there (Gal. 5:19–21). To him, the fifteen vices listed are "works of the flesh," and they "are obvious" (Gal. 5:19), needing no law for them to be seen as inappropriate and unworthy. And although he is against "works of the law" (Gal. 2:16; 3:2, 5, 10, 12) as a requirement for winning God's favor, the Galatians will ignore his vice list to their eternal peril; "I am warning you, as I warned you before: those who do such things will not inherit the kingdom of God," he says solemnly (Gal. 5:21). When he turns to his "virtue list," it can also be loosely correlated with the Ten Commandments, but Paul persists in avoiding any code. His prized virtues are "the fruit of the Spirit" (Gal. 5:22), and "the fruit of the Spirit," conceived as a bulk shipment of qualities, "is love, joy, peace, patience, kindness, generosity, faithfulness, gentleness, and self-control" (Gal. 5:22–23). And then, having said this, Paul comes up with yet another mysterious twist in his view of the law.

Why, we must ask, does Paul make the statement, "There is no law against such things" (Gal. 5:23)? Is he implying that the law is such an unmitigated negative that the most flattering thing he can say about it is that it is not opposed to these virtues? If Paul needs to relate the virtues to law, surely the statement should be that "the law is *for* these things." But, as noted by F. F. Bruce, Paul will not say this because he "does not simply mean that the nine virtues which make up the fruit of the Spirit are not forbidden by law; he means that when these qualities are in view we are in a sphere with which law has nothing to do."[22] Holding his list of virtues up to the Ten Commandments, as Paul does in Romans (Rom. 13:6–10), we must concede that we see a difference. Where the Ten Commandments speak of not stealing (Exod. 20:15), Paul speaks of generosity, and where the commandment prohibits murder (Exod. 20:13), Paul promotes gentleness and self-control. He has, as Bruce notes, moved beyond the sphere of law to a level where law is unable to go.

Nevertheless, what is fulfilled and brought to completion is the law, sharply focused "in a single commandment" (Gal. 5:14). Moreover, Paul, the former Pharisee, takes the intent of the law to be most clearly manifest in how we relate to our fellow human beings.

Martyn comments in detail on the meaning of the verb *plēroō* in this passage, to "fill" or "fulfill," on the use of the perfect tense, and on the subject that is concealed in Paul's use of the passive.[23] On the first point he argues that *plēroō* is better read as "bringing something to completion" than to "fulfill." He takes the perfect to follow the usual sense as "the present state of affairs that is the result of past action."[24] This leads us to ask whose action is in view. Taking this a step further, in a novel reading, Martyn finds the acting subject by rephrasing the sentence in the active voice. He argues that the subject must be Jesus: "For *Christ has brought the Law to completion* in one sentence: 'You shall love your neighbor as yourself.'"[25]

Prioritizing Jesus as the acting subject over the performance of the believer restores to the law the prestige that Paul's prior argument has taken away. His grudging attitude toward the law is suddenly gone because Jesus reconfigures the law in a stunning way. The code is not let in through the back door after being turned away at the front door. Rather, everything happens at the front door now that the code is swallowed up by its living embodiment in Jesus. Stating this in terms that have been used in the case of Abraham in the Old Testament (ch. 4), what leads the way again is narrative, not legislation. Only in the lived life of Jesus do we learn what the law's intent is; the life of Jesus alone does justice to the law. Story takes precedence over law, and it is by attention to the story that the believer's life is transformed (2 Cor. 3:18). Moreover, it is arresting to hear Paul say that "Christ has brought the law to completion *in one sentence*" because the one sentence that reveals the character of the law, is this: "You shall love your neighbor as yourself" (Gal. 5:14). Ministry for others of the kind that is revealed by Jesus is now seen to be the character of the law, and, indirectly, the character of God.

What triggers the dispute in the gospels and what remains at the center in Paul's letters are the life and actions of Jesus. When the questioner in Mark moves in to test Jesus, "seeing that he [Jesus] answered them well" (Mark 12:28), it might seem that Jesus is proving

Himself to be the sharper intellect or the keenest reader of Scripture, but these are secondary matters. It is Jesus's ministry to the needy that sets Him apart, serving as the matrix of subsequent conflict (Matt. 9:10–13; 11:18–19; Luke 15:1–2). Paraphrasing Matthew and Mark, the Pharisees seem to have the edge in terms of keeping "the greatest and first commandment" (Matt. 22:38) while Jesus excels at keeping "the second most important commandment" (Mark 12:31, GNB). Needless to say, however, confidence at having performed well at the greatest commandment does not prove anything because, in this conflict, excelling at the "first" commandment has become a smokescreen to cover up what happens at the level of the "second" commandment. We see this clearly in the discussion of the greatest commandment in Luke because there, unlike in Matthew and Mark, the scribe tries to back away from the implication of Jesus's answer by asking, "Who is my neighbor?" (Luke 10:29).

THE GREATEST COMMANDMENT AND THE SABBATH

Jesus's embodiment of the greatest commandment is nowhere more apparent than in His attitude toward the Sabbath. If one looks at the thirty-eight times the Sabbath is mentioned in the four gospels in connection with something Jesus said or did,[26] the message is always a perfect exemplification of the compassion that Jesus makes to be the heart of the law. The religious devotion that His critics promote as the highest priority, sometimes offering it as a substitute for compassion, conflicts with Jesus's order of priorities. All is put on graphic display in one of Jesus's Sabbath healings in Luke.

> Now he was teaching in one of the synagogues on the sabbath. And just then there appeared a woman with a spirit that had crippled her for eighteen years. She was bent over and was quite unable to stand up straight. When Jesus saw her, he called her over and said, "Woman, you are set free from your ailment." When he laid his hands on her, immediately she stood up straight

> and began praising God. But the leader of the synagogue, indignant because Jesus had cured on the sabbath, kept saying to the crowd, "There are six days on which work ought to be done; come on those days and be cured, and not on the sabbath day." But the Lord answered him and said, "You hypocrites! Does not each of you on the sabbath untie his ox or his donkey from the manger, and lead it away to give it water? And ought not this woman, a daughter of Abraham whom Satan bound for eighteen long years, be set free from this bondage on the sabbath day?" (Luke 13:10–16)

This story is a case in point on the respective priorities of the religious community and Jesus. In the foreground we see the woman, "bent over and…quite unable to stand up straight" (Luke 13:11). She comes to Jesus's attention unsolicited as if to show that His eye, like a magnet, is drawn to those who are ailing. The woman responds to His healing touch, straightens her back, and breaks out in gratitude (13:13).

But here, as in the Gospel of John, the main focus of the story is the reaction to Jesus's act of healing. The leader of the synagogue is not happy at what is taking place. "There are six days on which work ought to be done," he says (13:14). Recalling that the Ten Commandments hang on the double commandment of love to God and love to the neighbor (Matt. 22:37–40), we are led to believe that it is love for God that makes him solicitous for the Sabbath. Obedience to God dictates a kind of observance of the Sabbath that puts human misery on hold. Moreover, it is *human* misery that is left to run its course because those who criticize Jesus allow human beings to be treated with less compassion than their donkeys (Luke 13:15). Jesus's critics lack the intuitive compassion that is the mark of genuine love. Indeed, it is precisely on the level of intuition that Jesus and His critics stand apart because Jesus responds to a need on the spur of the moment, with a need-sensitive spontaneity that would be diminished if He needed to think through what course to pursue.

Before healing a man with the withered hand, another story of Sabbath healings in Luke, Jesus asks, "Is it lawful on the Sabbath to do good or to do evil, to save life or to destroy?" (Luke 6:9, NKJV; cf. Mark 3:1–6). This is a strange question. Why does Jesus phrase His question in the form of the antinomy "to do good or to do evil...to save life or to destroy" except to expose the inadequacy of the underlying paradigm? Surely no one in His audience will propose that it is lawful "to do evil" on the Sabbath! Surely, too, no one is tempted to defend the view that it is *un*lawful to "do good" or "to save life." The audience concedes as much when, according to Mark, they remain silent (Mark 3:4).

This means that Jesus operates more within a framework of healing than in a framework of law. His actions have a spontaneous character; they are intuitive as much as they are imitative. In fact, when defending His course of action, He finds a precedent in what His critics are doing on the Sabbath. To any of them it is intuitive and self-evident to "untie his ox or his donkey from the manger and lead it away to give it water" (Luke 13:15). They do not need to investigate whether it is "lawful" before deciding to feed the hungry animal. Similarly, supposing that a sheep falls into a pit, "will you not lay hold of it and lift it out?" (Matt. 12:11). The notion of a prescription for or against these interventions is superfluous, overridden by a spontaneous and intuitive awareness of need. Jesus defends His Sabbath healings by drawing His argument from His critics' own practice.

Jesus's embodiment of the greatest commandment is nowhere more apparent than in His attitude toward the Sabbath.

Everything that Jesus affirms in His responses is an implicit corrective to misguided convictions and a rebuke to a defective moral intuition. When Jesus calls the bent-over woman a "daughter of Abraham" (Luke 13:16), making her a person of distinction, His critics' implicit corollary is to see her as a nameless loser on the fringes of society, a citizen of the land God gave to Cain. When He treats her case as a matter of urgency, intent on intervening on her behalf immediately and without delay, the leader of the synagogue is indignant because he moves within a set of priorities that are fixed, knowing no need and no emergency that merits interference with the pattern (13:14). The leader apparently believes that interventions of this kind ought to happen on another day (13:14).

The duration of her suffering is mentioned twice in the short passage, first when she is introduced (13:11) and the second time when Jesus justifies His intervention (13:16). Translators struggle to convey the exclamatory flavor of the second mention of the eighteen years, "eighteen *long* years" being one way of rendering the common Greek word *idou*, "behold" (NIV, NASB, NRSV). Perhaps the New King James Version succeeds better on this point, inserting a pause and an emphatic call to "think of it": "So ought not this woman, being a daughter of Abraham, whom Satan has bound—think of it—for eighteen years, be loosed from this bond on the Sabbath?" (Luke 13:16, NKJV). The eighteen years have been registered by Jesus who knows that they have been long years and who makes the length of the years and not just the number of years His reason to intervene.

But His rationale also brings out the incongruity of her plight. The woman is "a daughter of Abraham," an endearing description that rings with entitlement, and she is also a person "whom Satan has bound" and thus one who has been deprived of her blessings. No description could better highlight what is at stake in the eyes of Jesus. We do not hear Him say, "Stuff happens," treating her fate dismissively and the price some people have to pay for living in a disordered and messy world. To the extent that she is proof of a disordered state, she is the victim of Satan. This is an additional incentive for Jesus to drive back the forces of darkness and restore her to health.

On this point at least some interpreters see Jesus within the frame of reference of Creation, and the pieces fall into place when it is recognized that the Sabbath is "the designated day for the liberation of Creation."[27] In fact, grasping the greater theme of Luke-Acts,

Jesus's ministry cannot be explained apart from the assumption that it is His mission to heal all Creation of its damage. The most far-reaching term for this in Luke is the Greek word *apokatastasis*, the gist of which is restoration. Having begun the work of restoration during His earthly sojourn, the risen Jesus "must remain in heaven until the time of universal restoration [*apokatastasis*] that God announced long ago through his holy prophets" (Acts 3:21). *Apokatastasis* and its verbal counterpart *apokathistēmi* (Mark 3:5; 8:25; 9:12; Luke 6:10) have the connotation of "restoring everything to perfection," taking it back to the starting point, indeed, changing it "to an earlier good state or condition."[28]

We are now in a position to draw some conclusions, beginning with the exchange between Jesus and the Pharisee concerning the greatest commandment in the law. Jesus's answer portrays love to God and love for one's fellow human beings as inseparable. If one side is emphasized over the other, even as we hear it from Jesus, it is the second commandment because it is on this point that the religious priorities contemporary to Jesus fall short (Matt. 22:39). The same thrust is found in Paul, who, in Romans, makes all the commandments come together in the one commandment to love one's neighbor (Rom. 13:9), but who also, in Galatians, sees the full range of this commandment brought to completion in Jesus (Gal. 5:14). Seeing the commandment embodied in Jesus, Paul transforms law into narrative so as to make the living embodiment lead the way instead of law.

Jesus's ministry cannot be explained apart from the assumption that it is His mission to heal all Creation of its damage.

But what becomes of the Sabbath in this scenario? It rises to the highest level in its course because it highlights the meaning of the greatest commandment. Whereas Jesus's critics make the Sabbath the inspiration and alibi for their indifference to human need, for Jesus the Sabbath and awareness of human need are indissolubly linked.

The Sabbath is the pledge of God's healing, restoring presence. "The sabbath was made for humankind, and not humankind for the sabbath," says Jesus (Mark 2:27). The greatest commandment and the Sabbath, united in living narrative, converge in concern for others and awareness of human need.

When we read Jesus's justification for His course of action in this light, the points of emphasis stand out distinctly. His statement to people in the synagogue in Galilee should be read in two stages, like this, my own literal translation merely reinforcing the good work of the New King James Version: "This woman, being a daughter of Abraham, whom Satan has bound—think of it—*for eighteen years,* must she not be loosed from this chain?" This is the first stage, and the emphasis on the many years of suffering and the necessity of healing her (*ouk edei lutēnai*) should not be toned down. The second stage is this, grasping that Jesus is exposing not only a moral intuition in disrepair but also a defective view of the Sabbath: "This woman, being a daughter of Abraham, whom Satan has bound—think of it—for eighteen years, must she not be loosed from this chain *on the Sabbath*?" (Luke 13:16).

The greatest commandment and the Sabbath, united in living narrative, converge in concern for others and awareness of human need.

ENDNOTES

1. W. D. Davies and Dale C. Allison (*A Critical and Exegetical Commentary on the Gospel According to Saint Matthew*, vol. 3 [ICC; London: T. & T. Clark, 1997], 307) show that in the context of Matthew the seven woes on the Pharisees are distinctive in form but not in content; "the woes constitute a climax, not a novum."

2. Davies and Allison (*Matthew*, III:308), reflecting the idea of a post-Jesus "community of Matthew," note that these sayings show the bitterness felt by "a Jewish-Christian group estranged from its mother community."

3. Graham Stanton, *The Gospels and Jesus* (Oxford: Oxford University Press, 1989), 78.

4. Lloyd Gaston, "The Messiah of Israel as Teacher of the Gentiles," *Int* 29 (1975): 25–40.

5. Rosemary Radford Ruether (*Faith and Fratricide: The Theological Roots of Anti-Semitism* [New York: The Seabury Press, 1974], 116) takes this approach to even greater lengths.

6. John Bowker, *Jesus and the Pharisees* (Cambridge: Cambridge University Press, 1973), 6–42.

7. Cf. Peter J. Tomson, "Gamaliel's Counsel and the Apologetic Strategy of Luke-Acts," in *The Unity of Luke-Acts*, ed. J. Verheyden (BETL 142; Leuven: Leuven University Press, 1999), 585–604.

8. J. A. Sanders, in the foreword of *Anti-Semitism and Early Christianity*, eds. Craig A. Evans and Donald A. Hagner (Minneapolis: Fortress Press, 1993), xvii.

9. Davies and Allison, *Matthew*, III:243.

10. BDAG, art "*homoios*."

11. Davies and Allison, *Matthew*, III:243.

12. Ibid., 245.

13. Ibid., 244.

14. Ernest De Witt Burton, *A Critical and Exegetical Commentary on the Epistle to the Galatians* (ICC; Edinburgh: T. & T. Clark, 1921; reprinted 1959), 294.

15. Richard N. Longenecker, *Galatians* (WBC; Dallas: Word Books, 1990), 241.

16. Sanders, *Paul, the Law and the Jewish People*, 4. Sanders's view of Paul is on this point not without merit.

17. Ibid., 93–122.

18. Longenecker, *Galatians*, 242–243.

19. Stephen Westerholm, "On Fulfilling the Whole Law (Gal. 5:14)," *Svensk exegetisk årsbok* 51–52 (1986–87): 235; idem, *Perspectives Old and New on Paul*, 329.

20. Longenecker, *Galatians*, 243.

21. J. Louis Martyn, *Galatians: A New Translation with Introduction and Commentary* (AB; New York: Doubleday, 1997).

22. F. F. Bruce, *The Epistle to the Galatians* (NIGTC; Grand Rapids: Eerdmans, 1982), 255.

23. Martyn, *Galatians*, 486–490.

24. Ibid., 489.

25. Ibid.

26. The total number is greater, but on several occasions the Sabbath is mentioned to specify a point in time in other respects.

27. Karl Löning, "Gottes Barmhertzigkeit und die pharisäische Sabbat-Observanz. Zu den Sabbat-Therapien im lukanischen Reisebericht," in *Das Drama der Barmherzigkeit Gottes*, ed. Ruth Scoralick (Stuttgarter Bibelstudien 183; Stuttgart: Verlag Katolisches Bibelwerk, 2000), 223.

28. BDAG, art. "*apokathistemi*" and "*apokatastasis*."

CHAPTER 13

PAUL AND THE CRISIS IN GALATIA

You are observing special days, and months, and seasons, and years.
Galatians 4:10

Explicit references to the Sabbath are extremely rare in the letters of Paul (Col. 2:16), and even implied references are few (Gal. 4:10; Rom. 14:5). Despite the scarcity of Sabbath material, Paul's influence has dwarfed that of the Gospels with respect to the Sabbath. The earliest impetus toward the Sabbath's eclipse is often traced to him.[1] Two of Paul's assumed Sabbath references will be reviewed in separate chapters, the first one implicit in Galatians 4:10, the second usually thought to be explicit in Colossians 2:16. We will turn to Galatians first. Our task is simplified by fresh insights into the letters of Paul that we will review before proceeding to consider the "special days" in the letter. This text, in turn, must be illuminated by the most conspicuous affirmations in Galatians, the most important of which is Paul's way of telling the story of God's faithfulness.

UNDERSTANDING PAUL

In addition to the "New Perspective" discussed earlier (ch. 10),[2] we must acknowledge a number of valuable insights that facilitate our understanding of Paul's letters. The first of these insights is that Paul wrote letters, not gospels. This distinction would seem trite if not for the fact that it is a difference that has *not* been observed. Paul's letters have been read as though they were gospels. While the gospels assume an open-ended and indefinite readership addressing *all* Christians,[3] the implied reader of the letter is by contrast a defined, limited group or person. At one time Adolf Deissmann even went so far as to assert that Paul's letters are "genuine, confidential letters, not intended for the public or for posterity" but meant to be read by "the addressees only."[4] While this may be an overstatement,[5] it is true that the content of a letter is defined by the situation of those addressed.

Paul wrote letters, not gospels.

In a ground-breaking study of Paul, J. Christiaan Beker calls the situational determinant the *contingency* of Paul's letters. Beker writes that theologies of Paul often tend to forget that Paul's thought "is geared to a specific situation and that his arguments cannot be divorced from the need of the moment."[6]

Rather than accepting this, there has been a tendency on the part of interpreters to play down the particularity of the letters "in order to save Paul's authority for the church universal."[7] Paul's letters have been read as though they are addressing all Christians without the need to account for the situation of the original addressees as though "Paul's theology was bequeathed to subsequent generations as revealed doctrine."[8] Galatians is a case in point because, as J. Louis Martyn notes, reading this letter "is like coming in on a play as the curtain is rising on the third or fourth act."[9] This realization calls for great sensitivity in reconstructing the setting of the letter, and it imposes stricter limits on the conclusions reached.

A second insight, no less important, is the need to recognize the underlying narrative in Paul's letters. As argued by Richard B. Hays in yet another pivotal study of Paul,[10] we must not approach the letter as though it is an independent statement, complete in itself. Prior knowledge of the gospel message is assumed because Paul is writing to established churches, most of which he founded himself.

This view of Paul's letters is a far cry from older scholarship. To Albert Schweitzer, one of the characteristics of the letters is precisely the absence of an underlying narrative. "So far as possible he [Paul] avoids quoting anything from the preaching of Jesus, or, indeed, mentioning it at all," Schweitzer contends. "If we had been dependent on him for our knowledge, we should not have known that Jesus spoke in parables, preached the Sermon on the Mount, or taught his disciples the Lord's Prayer."[11]

We are, of course, not solely dependent on the letters of Paul for knowledge of Jesus, and the original recipients were even less so. The story that in Schweitzer's view is missing is not left out, but it is implicit rather than explicit. Contrary to Schweitzer, Hays sees the narrative undercurrent of the letter as one of the keys to its interpretation.[12] Paul's train of thought becomes much clearer if we recognize the subtle narrative elements and the highly allusive character of the text. For instance, Paul writes that "when the fullness of time had come, God sent his Son, born of a woman, born under the law" (Gal. 4:4). This sentence is bursting at the seams with narrative, each element in the sentence representing a narrative panorama of its own while also serving as flash points for a story well known because it had been told and elaborated on a previous occasion.[13]

Whence the notion of "the fullness of time"? Whence the idea that God "sent his Son"? Whence the woman? These ideas and concepts are not presented in Paul's letters to the Galatians for the first time, and their persuasive force derives in large measure from their familiarity. The story that is vouchsafed in this manner finds common ground with the story that is told in the Gospels. "When the fullness of time had come," Paul writes in the declarative cadence of the familiar rehearsal (Gal. 4:4). But his is the lesser voice, here a mere echo of the greater voice of Jesus as recorded, for instance, in the Gospel of Mark: "The time is fulfilled, and the kingdom of God has come near; repent, and believe in the good news" (Mark 1:15). Paul's compressed story assumes the larger story of the Gospel and will spring no surprises on the reader other than to ensure that no other gospel is invented (Gal. 1:6–7).

The story is not left out, but it is implicit rather than explicit.

Paul, needless to say, is not quoting the Gospel of Mark. His letters antedate Mark and the other Gospels. But Paul does not need to quote Mark because he can allude to the "Gospel of Paul," meaning the story of Jesus that he has told to the recipients of his letters on previous occasions. The notion that Paul is a man of propositions rather than a storyteller, as suggested by Beker,[14] or that he is an interpreter of stories rather than the person who tells the story, as in Hays's nuanced version,[15] interjects an unnecessary dichotomy. Even if it were true that Paul prefers proposition to narrative or that he would rather interpret the story than tell it, he cannot derive persuasive propositions apart from the story, and he cannot interpret the story without first telling it.

"It was before your eyes that Jesus Christ was publicly exhibited as crucified!" Paul reminds the Galatians in one of the most powerful flashbacks to his prior telling of the story (Gal. 3:1). As Hays demonstrates, "Jesus Christ crucified" is a densely packed allusion to a larger story and itself the most riveting image.[16] When, therefore, Paul writes that the crucifixion happened "before your eyes" (Gal. 3:1), he does not suggest that the Galatians were present in Jerusalem at Jesus's crucifixion. Their presence is figurative; through the ministry of Paul the Galatians witnessed the crucifixion in Jerusalem some twenty years after the actual event.[17] Indeed, judging from what Paul expects this allusion to accomplish in the context of his letter, we ought rather to infer that Paul's telling of the story was extensive and second to none, the canonical Gospels not excepted. Even as to telling of the gospel story, Paul may have been "the best there was."[18]

To recognize the narratival character of Paul's letters, as leading scholars now urge,[19] frees the letters from the narrow propositional constraints traditionally imposed on Paul. Moreover, where the voice of Paul, as perceived in Christian dogma, is heard over the voice of Jesus in the Gospels, the relationship should be reversed. The message of Jesus in the Gospels, addressing all Christians in an open-ended readership, takes precedence, and the voice of Paul, addressing specific situations in named churches, will not dilute or invalidate the Gospel narrative. Applying this insight to the Sabbath, we should be reluctant to accept that the affirmation of the Sabbath that we find in the Gospels will be disaffirmed by Paul in his letters.

As a third insight, the letters of Paul are not simple monologues. They are conversations with many voices, at times carrying forth at high and heated pitch.[20] The first voice is what Paul says in the written word of the letter. The second voice is Paul's actual voice, echoing in the letter at crucial points and filling out what is not stated in the letter (Gal. 3:1; 1 Cor. 15:1–3; 2 Thess. 2:5).

The more challenging task, however, is to recognize the voices of Paul's opponents in the letters, and along with them the voices of the people Paul seeks to persuade. Martyn aptly describes Paul's partners in this dialogue as "voices one can hear from offstage."[21] In Galatians alone there may be as many as five conflicting voices, not counting the voice of Paul.[22] The task of the interpreter is to pay attention to these voices and to try to hear what they are saying. For instance, when Paul asks, "Who has bewitched you?" he is addressing church members in Galatia who have been bewildered by Paul's opponents (3:1). When, however, he argues from Scripture that a certain text in the Old Testament "does *not* say, 'And to offsprings' (plural), as of *many*; but it says, 'And to your offspring' (singular) that is, to *one* person" (Gal. 3:16), we should read his rebuttal as an answer to his opponents. *They* are arguing for "offsprings" (plural) as the correct reading.[23]

> ***Even as to telling of the gospel story, Paul may have been "the best there was."***

In fact, Paul's rhetoric has the tenor and immediacy of one who expects his opponents to be present at the reading of the letter. This means that he is not only aware of what the opponents have been saying but also anticipates what they will say. The letter attempts to silence the opponents by anticipating their arguments.[24] What must be admitted, however, and what is not sufficiently admitted by many commentaries, is that while we must listen for the voices from offstage, we cannot be entirely sure what they are saying.

A fourth insight, this one also promoted by Richard Hays, urges that interpretations of Paul's letters must pay more attention to his use of the Old Testament.[25] The novelty on this point is not that Paul counts on Scripture to corroborate his own testimony; no one denies Paul's copious references to the Old Testament.[26] It is rather that when Paul reads the Old Testament, he is far more sensitive to the original context of his quotations and allusions than scholars generally have been willing to grant.[27] His own voice interprets and amplifies the Old Testament, but the Old Testament voice is not sublimated.[28] The Old Testament partner fills in the broad narrative framework of the letter, that is, the voices of the Old Testament blend with Paul's preached message in person and with his written word of the letter. As we shall see below, differing views of the role of the Old Testament in Paul's letters yield conflicting conclusions.

The fifth and final insight may in the present context be the most important because it restores to Paul's letters the apocalyptic character that interpreters have ignored for generations. In 1960, Ernst Käsemann asserted that "apocalyptic was the mother of all Christian theology."[29] Thus extending the hand of recognition to apocalyptic, the door was opened to reckon with such motifs as the vindication of God, universalism, cosmic dualism, and, even more to the point, to see these emphases in the letters of Paul.[30] These elements balance concern for human salvation with God's apparent failure to deal with the reality of evil (theodicy), they shift the focus from an individualistic preoccupation to a cosmic-universal concern, and they make awareness of the cosmic powers loom at least as large as awareness of human sin. Apocalyptic, long dismissed as an insignificant tributary, is actually "the main stream" in the New Testament.[31] Paul is not an exception in this respect. Beker concludes that "Paul is an apocalyptic theologian with a theocentric outlook,"[32] and not, as in the old paradigm, a person who is unfazed by the radical notions of apocalyptic and a thinker who has Christ rather than God at the center of his thought.[33] Amid the diverse situations that are addressed in Paul's letters, we should therefore see the apocalyptic hub as "the coherent center of Paul's gospel."[34] When Paul in Galatians says that Christ "gave himself for our sins to set us free from the present evil age" (1:3–4), his thought is shaped by the apocalyptic notion of the two ages, the present *evil* age and the age to come, and by the notion that Christ brings deliverance from the cosmic powers that hold sway in the present age. When he says that he did not receive the gospel "from a human source, nor was I taught it, but I received it through a revelation of Jesus Christ" (*di' apokalupseōs Iēsou Christou*), he is highlighting that the gospel was *apocalyptically* revealed; it came to him by God's direct in-breaking, shattering all his prior conceptions (1:11–12). Indeed, the message he preaches, often presented as though it meets human criteria for "good news," must be reconfigured according to an apocalyptic conception that makes it precisely the opposite. "The gospel I preach is *not* what human beings normally have in mind when they speak of 'good news,'" Paul insists (1:11).[35]

Paul's rhetoric has the tenor and immediacy of one who expects his opponents to be present at the reading of the letter.

As we turn to the Galatians' observance of "special days" (4:10), we must be attuned to all the foregoing elements: the situational parameters of this letter, its underlying narrative, its myriad voices, the Old Testament echoes, and, above all, the cosmic-universal aspiration of its apocalyptic vision.

OBSERVING SPECIAL DAYS

Paul writes disapprovingly to the Galatians that "you are observing special days, and months, and seasons, and years" (4:10). Taken by itself this text will not disclose its meaning to the contemporary reader. We must therefore begin by delineating the options that are suggested by the text. Is Paul, first of all, referring to a Jewish or a pagan calendar?

On the one hand, Paul is writing to Gentile converts whose baggage includes undesirable elements that must be abandoned. But they are also under siege by teachers who wish them to adopt circumcision, a Jewish marker of identity. Scholars tend to see the Jewish element as most decisive, assuming that the "days, and months, and seasons, and years" refer to sacred occasions in Judaism, and that the "days" in question refer to the Sabbath.[36]

An alternative view sees the "days, and months, and seasons, and years" as part of a more complex picture.[37] Paul is writing to the Galatian churches at a time when they, prompted by false teachers, are debating whether to adopt the practice of circumcision, but they have not yet made the decision.[38] While most scholars seem to believe that the Galatians are eager to adopt circumcision, Troy W. Martin finds evidence for quite the opposite. He urges that we should examine Paul's accusations and not his arguments in order to come to grips with the actual issue.[39] According to the first of the two main accusations, the Galatians are under pressure to accept a Law-oriented gospel that includes circumcision (1:6–9). According to the second accusation, and the more important of the two, the Galatians are counting the cost, basically concluding that "it isn't worth it," and are therefore on the verge of "turning back" (4:8–11). Indeed, Martin proposes that "the Galatians are so reticent to become circumcised that they prefer to return to their paganism instead."[40]

Greek aversion toward circumcision enhances the plausibility of Martin's reconstruction.[41] Psychological inferences and textual evidence are additional reasons for giving this option a serious hearing. In fact, the immediate context of Paul's warning against "days, and months, and seasons, and years" (4:10) pictures them turning back to their former pagan ways. "How can you *turn back* again to the weak and beggarly elemental spirits? How can you want to be enslaved to them again" (4:9)? Reading this literally, "turning back" for a Gentile would not mean to turn to Judaism, and the practices to which they would then be turning could not be Jewish calendrical elements.

Moreover, assuming that Paul is trying to counter the impact of the false teachers, it seems strange that he is not using Jewish expressions such as "sabbath," "new moon," "Passover," and the like.[42] Given that the time list in Galatians "is completely compatible with pagan time-keeping systems,"[43] the scenario on this point is not that the Galatian believers are about to adopt a Judaized version of Christianity. It is rather that the opposite is happening. Deterred by the false teachers' insistence on circumcision, they are giving up on Paul's gospel altogether, reverting to their former state of subservience to the hostile elements and rhythms of the cosmos (4:3). In this construct Paul is fighting a war on two fronts. On the one hand, he is hoping to persuade them not to submit to the circumcision-message of the false teachers. On the other hand, he is nudging back those who are tempted to revert to their pre-gospel ways. According to this reconstruction of the Galatian setting, Paul is not addressing the issue of Sabbath observance at all.

When Paul upbraids the Galatians for "observing special days, and months, and seasons, and years" (4:10), a comprehensive calendrical system seems to be in view. If the Sabbath is part of this list despite the non-Jewish terminology that is used, it belongs to a gamut of items that is far more extensive than observance of the seventh day. Again, assuming that the Sabbath represents the "days" on this list, the "months, and seasons, and years" would presumably include the rest of the Jewish calendar, such as the Passover, the Feast of Tabernacles, and even occasions such as the Jubilee. If this is what Paul has in mind, drawing his list from the agenda of his opponents, it is truly remarkable that he does not use the Jewish terms.

Christ brings deliverance from the cosmic powers that hold sway in the present age.

Again, if the Sabbath is part of a Judaizing agenda, it is merely one item in a wide-ranging package. Paul's repudiation of this package and its underlying mentality is unquestionable, but this does not automatically shed light on which of the meanings or practices he rejects.

While the role of the Sabbath in the Galatian context remains unclear, some of Paul's opponents clearly believe that new believers must be circumcised in order to enjoy full acceptance into fellowship (2:12; 5:2, 6, 11; 6:12–13). Of this there is no doubt, and this demonstrates the Jewish character of the opponents' program. With respect to circumcision Paul is adamant: New believers need not be circumcised. A decision to be circumcised is a dead end and the path to sure spiritual loss. "I, Paul, am telling you that if you let yourselves be circumcised, Christ will be of no benefit to you" (5:2), he declares with a degree of vehemence that the opposing teachers will be hard pressed to match.

Martyn is probably right when he reads Paul's rhetoric as a biting sarcasm. Paul's view of what the Galatians are up to is conceived in the most graphic and literal terms, "ending with the flesh" (3:2). "Are you Galatians really so foolish as to think that, having begun your life in Christ by the power of his Spirit, you can now move on to perfection by means of a severed piece of flesh?"[44] "Ending with the flesh" means that the initiation rite to membership in the new community would involve a surgical procedure on the male genitals, leaving a heap of human foreskin as the material proof that the gospel was fully accepted. Even though Paul was himself "circumcised on the eighth day" according to Jewish tradition (Phil. 3:5), his message is incongruous with this outcome.

Any reading of the circumcision issue in the Galatian churches will conclude that circumcision has come to an end in the context of Paul's Gentile mission. Before accepting that the Sabbath falls under the same judgment,[45] we must take a critical look at how Paul construes his message in relation to the Old Testament.

PAUL'S AFFIRMATIONS IN GALATIANS

Even though Galatians is occasioned by the activity of false teachers who have arrived in the wake of his ministry, Paul was there first, and markers of his initial message are scattered throughout the letter (Gal. 3:1; 4:19; 6:14). These markers go a long way toward establishing his most essential emphases. Powerful and evocative allusions to Paul's prior preaching are found throughout the letter (3:1; 4:6, 13–14). Among these allusions the expression "Jesus Christ crucified" is particularly striking because, as suggested by Hays, it "stands for the whole story and distills its meaning."[46]

The claim that "Jesus Christ crucified" (3:1) captures the whole story means not only that Paul's message is a story rather than a doctrinal statement. *This* story is a story of a different kind. For Paul, who by his own admission "advanced in Judaism" beyond people of his age (1:14), the most searing facet of his autobiography is the fact that his commitment to "Judaism" (*ioudaismos*) did not lead to Jesus and definitely not to "Jesus Christ *crucified*."[47] In the ashes of his shattered world "Jesus Christ crucified" will rise to become the uncontested foundation and focus of his faith and preaching. Martyn's translation gives greater force to what happened, that is, to *how* it happened. "For I did not receive it from any human being, nor was I taught it," Paul says; "it came to me by God's *apocalyptic* revelation of Jesus Christ" (1:12).[48] Again, in Martyn's translation, "when it pleased him [God] *apocalyptically* to reveal his Son to me, in order that I might preach him among the Gentiles, I immediately kept to myself, not asking advice from anyone" (1:15–16).[49]

If "Jesus Christ crucified" is an expression that "stands for the whole story and distills its meaning,"[50] Paul is heralding an unexpected novelty on the level of content (what was revealed) as well as on the level of appropriation (how he was made aware of it). It is the singularity of what is revealed that leads Paul to picture the law as inferior to, and subsequent to, God's promise to Abraham (3:15–19).[51] Taken literally, he seems to suspend the entire history of Israel when arguing that the promise was made to Abraham and "his seed" (singular), not to "his seeds" (3:16, NKJV). This seemingly trivial detail has enormous consequences. "Seeds," referring to many, encompass the entire history of Israel. "Seed," on the other hand, referring to one, has one single individual in mind. Paul emphasizes a point rather than a line; the text "does not say, 'And to offsprings,' as of many; but it says, 'And to your offspring,' that is, to one person, who is Christ" (3:16).

Apocalyptic is in; the established order is out (1:12, 16). The Spirit is in; "works of law" are out (3:2–5); Abraham is in (3:6–9); Sinai is out (4:21–31). The promise is in; the law is out (3:16–19). The single "seed" is in; plural "seeds" are out (3:16). Circumcision is out, but so, surprisingly, is "uncircumcision," either option inimical to Paul's message (5:2–3, 6; 6:15). Above all, "Jesus Christ crucified" is in, towering above any other point of reference. Galatians provides the most compelling warrant for what Beverly Roberts Gaventa calls "the singularity of the Gospel."[52] Paul's message refuses any comparison that will make "Jesus Christ crucified" blend into the woodwork of ordinary conceptions of religion, even if the religion is that of Paul the Pharisee prior to his experience on the road to Damascus.

Jesus Christ "publicly exhibited as crucified!" (3:1). The exclamation mark in the NRSV is entirely appropriate. We almost sense the astounded buzz in Paul's voice as though he has stumbled upon the scene for the first time. When Hays says that this expression "stands for the whole story and distills its meaning,"[53] we are expected to see more than the crucifixion scene itself. "The whole story" can only be grasped if we see it as God's story. Paul's use of the perfect passive "crucified" (*estaurōmenos*) is meant not only to convey the result but also to recall the events leading up to the result; that is, where the perfect tense puts the completed action into sharp relief, it does not leave behind the events and the context that culminated in the completed action. A larger story is implied right down to the grammar of the expression. God is not absent from the choreography of the "public exhibition" that is thus distilled. This is God's story, God revealed in Jesus, and nowhere more fully revealed than in the public display of Jesus on the cross.

This is God's story, God revealed in Jesus, and nowhere more fully revealed than in the public display of Jesus on the cross.

Where the apocalyptic character of Paul's message suggests discontinuity, a drastic turn that wreaks havoc with expectations, his message is continuous with the deepest layers of the Old Testament. The reference to "Jesus Christ and God the Father" in the opening sentence of Galatians (1:1) can refer to no other God than the God of the Old Testament. In Romans and 1 Thessalonians, Paul calls his gospel "the gospel of God" (Rom. 1:1; 15:16; 1 Thess. 2:2, 8–9), indicating that God is not only the source but also the subject of his message. Paul's gospel in Galatians thus takes for granted "the continuity provided by the consistent identity of the one God" (3:20)."[54] "But when the fullness of time had come, God sent his Son, born of a woman, born under the law," Paul says in a synopsis of the story he has told the Galatians while with them in person (4:4), with no need to explain which God he has in mind. Christ, the singular seed of Abraham (3:16), is also the promised seed of Adam, "born of a woman" (4:4). The expression that in Galatians "stands for the whole story and distils its meaning"[55] is therefore a story that can only be understood within the context of the biblical narrative.

"It is precisely within history, in the person of a son of woman, in the person of one crucified, that God reveals the end of history's distinctions between and among peoples," Beverly Roberts Gaventa observes.[56] But this observation, looking at the story of Jesus from the point of view of its result, must not lose sight of the fact that God's story in the Bible has from the beginning no other goal. It is ground lost that is being restored. Profound, if selective, continuity dots Paul's message, providing crucial links to God's story in the Old Testament. In Galatians continuity rests primarily on Abraham (3:6–9, 14), on the promise given to Abraham "four hundred thirty years" before the law (3:16–18), and on the character of Abraham's trust in God (3:9). Assuming that Paul had a choice among many Old Testament characters, he has no better model than Abraham for the kind of outlook he wishes the Galatians to adopt (3:9, 14, 18).

If, therefore, we ask for the meaning that is distilled by the expression "Jesus Christ crucified," there is no better explanation than God's faithfulness. "Jesus Christ crucified" is the riveting, eye-catching focal point in God's story which drives home the reality of

God's faithfulness. In Galatians (and Romans) divine faithfulness looms larger than human faith; Paul's concern moves God's action into the foreground rather than the human response to God's action. Traditional readings of Paul's faith-language see Paul contrasting human works and human faith, repudiating the first while approving the latter (2:15–21; 3:10–14). The revised reading, by contrast, urges that the phrase *pistis Christou*, usually translated as "faith in Christ,"[57] is better translated "the faithfulness of Christ."[58] *Pistis* can mean "faithfulness" as well as "faith," and Old Testament antecedents favor "faithfulness."[59]

If we ask for the meaning that is distilled by the expression "Jesus Christ crucified," there is no better explanation than God's faithfulness.

The evidence that challenges precedent[60] on this point comes chiefly in the way *pistis Christou* echoes the Old Testament. Abraham, whose story is recalled in the "proof" section of Galatians (3:6–9), lived much of his life under the cloud of a promise unfulfilled (Gen. 15:1–6), and yet his entire life was predicated on the conviction that God is faithful. Indisputably, when the Old Testament puts the stamp of approval on Abraham, it is grounded in Abraham's recognition of God's reliability rather than in Abraham's faith, if it were possible to detach the latter's faith from this grounding.

The witness of Habakkuk, one of the Old Testament voices that echoes in Galatians (3:11), also sounds the message of God's faithfulness. The Old Testament prophet looks in horror at a world where injustice and cruelty run rampant, leading him to despair in the face of God's apparent non-action. "O Lord, how long shall I cry for help, and you will not listen? Or cry to you 'Violence!' and you will not save? Why do you make me see wrongdoing and look at trouble? Destruction and violence are before me; strife and contention arise. So the law becomes slack and justice never prevails. The wicked surround the righteous—therefore judgment comes forth perverted" (Hab. 1:2–4).

In its native Old Testament context, Habakkuk's plea is "the passionate prayer of a desperate man," sounding the note of "moral outrage and perplexity."[61] The source of the perplexity is God's apparent *un*-faithfulness, the appearance of a disintegrating moral order. When he takes up his position eagerly awaiting "what he will say to me, and what he will answer concerning my complaint" (Hab. 2:1), there can be no doubt that the backdrop is God's seeming failure to make things right in the world.

The question in Habakkuk, therefore, is first of all a theodicy question that finds human reality so disconcerting that God's faithfulness is on the line. Second, the expectation in Habakkuk, the response to his question, is to wait for something to happen that will put trust in God's faithfulness on a secure footing. "For there is still a vision for the appointed time; it speaks of the end, and does not lie. If it seems to tarry, *wait for it; it will surely come*, it will not delay" (Hab. 2:3). The "it" that seems to tarry cannot be construed as anything other than God's action in the world; the "it" that will surely come is not human faith but proof of God's faithfulness. Third, in the LXX, the likely source of Paul's reference to Habakkuk, God's faithfulness is explicitly at the heart of the affirmation. "The righteous shall live by my faithfulness" (Hab. 2:4, translation mine).[62]

Taking stock of the passage in its original context, Hays asserts that "parties on all sides of the debate have been surprisingly content to assume that Paul employs the passage as a proof text for his doctrine of justification by faith with complete disregard for its original setting in Habakkuk's prophecy."[63] Indeed, says Hays, "when Paul quotes Hab. 2:4, we cannot help hearing the echoes—unless we are tone-deaf—of Habakkuk's theodicy question."[64]

This assessment plays out in the context of Paul's use of Habakkuk in Romans. Hays is somewhat reluctant to make the same point when Paul invokes Habakkuk in Galatians (3:11).[65] His reluctance in this regard is judicious, but caution goes too far if it leads to the assumption that Paul has no interest in Habakkuk's theodicy question when he writes to the Galatians. "If it seems to tarry, wait for it; it will surely come, it will not delay," Habakkuk is told (Hab. 2:3), concluding, as he must, that God will bring something to bear on the disarray that fuels his perplexity and indignation. Everything hinges on the "it" that will come, repeated four times in one single sentence in Habakkuk. Paul's message in Galatians is precisely that God has intervened in the fullness of time, sending forth his son (Gal. 4:4). Habakkuk's distinctive voice has not been silenced or subverted.

In Galatians, Paul follows through on this line of reasoning by giving *pistis* the texture of an event, aligning it with Habakkuk's expectation that something will happen, the mysterious "it" that "will surely come" (Hab. 2:3). "Now before faith (*pistis*) came, we were imprisoned and guarded under the law until faith would be revealed," says Paul, as translated by the NRSV (3:23). The valence of *pistis*, occurring here in two instances in the same verse, does not hail trust in God as the innovation that has burst upon the scene. *Pistis* is shorthand for an event and not for the stance of the believer; it is what is believed rather than the act of believing that is the focus of Paul's attention. Translations that better convey Paul's intent might be "before the message came," "before Christ came," or even, grasping that *pistis* is shorthand for a larger story, "before [God's] faithfulness was demonstrated," especially in view of the fact that the last part of the verse says that *pistis* "would be revealed" (3:23). Hans Dieter Betz, in a clean break with precedent, thus notes that *pistis* "describes the occurrence of a historical phenomenon, not the act of believing of an individual."[66] Martyn takes the emphasis on an occurrence still further.

It is what is believed rather than the act of believing that is the focus of Paul's attention.

> Here we see that, in Paul's mouth, the verb *apokalyphthēnai*, "to be apocalypsed" means more than its literal equivalent, "to be

> unveiled." It is not as though faith and Christ had been all along standing behind a curtain, the curtain then being at one point drawn aside, so as to make visible what had been hidden. To explicate the verb *apokalyphthēnai*, Paul uses as a synonym the verb *erchomai*, "to come on the scene." And the result is startling, for it shows that Paul's apocalyptic theology—especially in Galatians—is focused on the motif of invasive movement from beyond.[67]

Habakkuk, we recall, was assured that something would happen, veiling it as the enigmatic "it" (Hab. 2:3). Now, from the vantage point of Galatians, it has happened. The "it" has been revealed; it has burst upon the scene. And the prophetic "it" has addressed the problem head on, revealing the faithfulness of God. The same logic necessarily applies in verse 25; "now that *pistis* has come" should be understood as a shorthand expression for a larger story, at the heart of which is the account of God's faithfulness. The far-reaching consequences of the revised reading are readily appreciated in the following comparison.

PISTIS CHRISTOU AS "FAITH IN CHRIST"	PISTIS CHRISTOU AS "FAITHFULNESS OF CHRIST"
We ourselves are Jews by birth and not Gentile sinners; yet we know that a person is justified not by the works of the law but through faith in Jesus Christ. And we have come to believe in Christ Jesus, so that we might be justified by faith in Christ, and not by doing the works of the law, because no one will be justified by the works of the law (2:15–16, NRSV).	We, who are Jews by birth and not "Gentile sinners," knowing that a man is not set right by works of the law but through the faithfulness of Jesus Christ, we, too, put our trust in Christ Jesus in order that we might be set right by the faithfulness of Christ, and not by works of the law (2:15–16).

PISTIS CHRISTOU AS "FAITH IN CHRIST"	PISTIS CHRISTOU AS "FAITHFULNESS OF CHRIST"
I have been crucified with Christ; and it is no longer I who live, but it is Christ who lives in me. And the life I now live in the flesh I live by faith in the Son of God, who loved me and gave himself for me (2:19–20, NRSV).	I have been crucified with Christ; and it is no longer I who live but Christ who lives in me. And the life I now live in the flesh I live by the faithfulness of the Son of God, who loved me and gave himself for me (2:19–20).
But the scripture has imprisoned all things under the power of sin, so that what was promised through faith in Jesus Christ might be given to those who believe (3:22, NRSV).	But the scripture imprisoned all things under [the power of] sin so that what was promised might be given through the faithfulness of Jesus Christ to those who believe (3:22).

The revision of Paul's faith-language, as seen in the column on the right, provides a lucid, sensible reading that strips away awkward redundancy while retaining the echo of the Old Testament voices. The translation also shows that Paul is not contrasting human *faith* and human *works*, castigating the latter. What holds priority in Paul's happens on God's side, not the human side. His emphasis is on the faithfulness of God that has come to light in Jesus.[68]

The whole story that is distilled in the public exhibition of "Jesus Christ crucified" is more than a drama that can be grasped within a human frame of reference. Paul's story assumes knowledge of a conflict that exceeds the boundaries of the human story (Gal. 1:4; 1 Cor. 2:7–8). Scholars who perceive the cosmic sweep of God's redemptive intervention are advocating a shift away from legal terminology that has long dominated the interpretation of Paul.[69] Martyn' s new translation of Galatians replaces "justified" with the word "rectified" as a better rendition of the scope and intention of the Greek verb *dikaióo* because Paul's notion of "justification" is more comprehensive than what a strict legal framework is able to convey. As evidenced in my own translation above, what must be "set right" exceeds a legal concern. The antinomy Paul presents is not between works and faith, or between doing and believing, as the traditional view has it. It is between law and "the faithfulness of Christ" as the basis for righting what has gone wrong. According to Martyn, "the subject Paul addresses is that of God's *making right what has gone wrong*."[70]

It is hard to improve upon Martyn's choice of words on this point. Not only does his terminology open up to the contemporary reader a scope of "what has gone wrong" to include the role of angels and powers other than human beings. It also envisions that what God will set right includes non-human creation and the entire cosmos. In the cosmic-universal framework of Paul's message God's faithfulness confounds demonic charges to the contrary (2 Cor. 11:3), human beings are set free from the dominion of cosmic powers (Gal. 1:4), and God's faithfulness promises relief to the groaning and suffering of non-human creation (Gal. 6:15; Rom. 8:19–22).[71]

From this vantage point other key terms in Galatians must be seen in a new light. The terms *hosoi ex ergōn nomou* (3:10) and *hoi ek pisteōs* (3:7, 9), usually translated "those who are doing the works of the law" and "those who believe," pitting "works" and "faith" against each other, are delivered from their captivity to a legal and propositional framework. These terms are best understood as shorthand expressions of identity, defining one group whose identity is "derived from [God's] faithfulness" (*hoi ek pisteōs*; 3:7, 9) and another group whose identity is "derived from observance of the Law" (*hosoi ex ergōn nomou*; 3:10).[72] "Identity" and sense of identity cut to the core of the drama that is playing out in the churches in Galatia, one group building its sense of identity on its commitment to observing the Law, brandishing circumcision as the mark that proves the genuineness of their profession. In Paul's eyes, however, what begins with "Jesus Christ crucified" cannot end with the surgical removal of male foreskin (3:1–3), and the message of God's faithfulness in Jesus cannot accommodate an emphasis that sets up human faithfulness, or even human faith, as the main focus.

Paul is, in fact, carefully laying the groundwork for a vision of inclusion. The physical mark of circumcision on those who are "of the works of the law" also sets up a boundary marker, the underlying message of which is separation from other people or groups. A parallel example has been found at Qumran, where the community used the expression "works of the law" to indicate their commitment to scrupulous observance of Old Testament ordinances.[73] "We have separated ourselves from the multitude of the people," says the writer of the scroll.[74] In the Galatian context, "works of law" coupled with circumcision have the same connotation of separation, nullifying what in Paul's message points in the opposite direction. Paul, like Isaiah before him, pursues a vision of inclusion (Isa. 56:1–7). The wall of separation must come down, and the estranged human family must be gathered into one (Eph. 2:14). In the new paradigm, "there is no longer Jew or Greek, there is no longer slave or free, there is no longer male and female; for all of you are one in Christ Jesus" (Gal. 3:28).

Paul is carefully laying the groundwork for a vision of inclusion.

Daniel Boyarin, looking at Paul from a Jewish perspective, cannot be faulted for choosing this text as his exhibit A in Paul's transformed and transforming vision.[75] Boyarin is mistaken, however, in assuming that Paul's vision is grounded in Greek universalism, in the philosophical quest for the "universal man," and thus in a view that is inimical to Judaism.[76] Paul's understanding of the character of God determines his view of inclusion, not universalism according to a Greek construct. It is the apparent or implied exclusion of the Gentiles, not Jewish particularity as such, which must be rectified. Paul eschews exclusion but not particularity; he decries discrimination but not differences. His main mission is to affirm that there is no "face factor" (*prosōpolēmpsia*) with God (Rom. 2:11). In the translation of the NRSV, preferential treatment is out of character with God, for "God shows no partiality" (Rom. 2:11; Gal. 2:6; Eph. 6:9).

Contrary to Boyarin's critique, Paul's conviction is grounded in theology, not in philosophy. If, as in Boyarin's version, Paul comes across as a *radical* Jew, he is radical not because he allows other ideologies to shape his thought and to dilute his Jewishness, but because he digs into the deepest layers of his Jewish heritage and the source that feeds it. The exclusion that has been overcome is an exclusion that was never intended. Paul is not less Jewish when he proclaims the inclusion of the Gentiles without the requirement of circumcision. In E. P. Sanders's words, "God always intended this—he proclaimed it in advance to Abraham—and his will is uniform and stated in Holy Writ."[77]

What Paul brings to bear on the reader in Galatians, therefore, is above all a new view of God, combining the most profound insight with the most unrestrained exclamation. Guiding his reader to the top of the mountain, or, in his own terminology, agonizing once more in labor pains until they get the point (4:19), Paul moves toward his deepest and most comprehensive affirmation by an argument from the Galatians' prior experience.[78] "And because you are children," he writes, "God has sent the Spirit of his Son into our hearts, crying, 'Abba! Father!'" (Gal. 4:6; cf. Rom. 8:15). In this way Paul draws his most powerful argument from the mouths of those he seeks to persuade, recalling, as this text does, the believer's baptismal experience. But he also takes full advantage of the narrative that underlies the exclamation, "Abba! Father!" Believers in Jesus, whether in Galatia or in Rome, "did not receive a spirit of slavery to fall back into fear" (Rom. 8:15). Biblically, anthropologically, and existentially *fear* is the most succinct description of the human condition. And fear thus conceived draws its most terrifying power from the demonic misrepresentation of God. As stated in the Genesis story, at the point where the human beings have their first bitter taste of accepting the serpent's view of God, "I heard the sound of you in the garden, *and I was afraid*" (Gen. 3:10).

All this is set right in Paul's message to the Galatians. Human beings who said, "I heard the sound of you..., and I was afraid" and who, because they were afraid, "hid themselves from the presence of the LORD God" (Gen. 3:8), are not afraid any more and no longer feel the need to run away from God's presence (Rom. 8:15). No transformation is more evocative than to hear lips that previously could only say, "I was afraid," now exclaim, "Abba! Father!" God's apocalyptic revelation in Jesus, the public exhibition of "Jesus Christ crucified," has transformed the believer's outlook. Fear is out; trust is in. Martyn's view that the apocalyptic dimension entails an "invasive movement from beyond" and not only the removal of the curtain in order to "make visible what had been hidden,"[79] is to the point, but it must not overshadow that God has not revealed anything other than what God is (Gal. 3:23; Rom. 16:25–26; 1 Cor. 2:6–10; Eph. 3:9; Col. 1:26). God's faithfulness thus revealed is from henceforth the center of the believer's new identity. As Douglas J. Moo notes, "in crying out 'Abba, Father,' the believer not only gives voice to his or her consciousness of belonging to God as his child but also to having a status comparable to that of Jesus himself."[80] The believer has not only become the adopted and obedient son of the Father, but he has also adopted Jesus's view of the Father. "Abba! Father!"' should for this reason be seen as the end-point of Paul's affirmations in Galatians and, as it were, the view from the top of the mountain.

THE SABBATH IN GALATIANS

On the basis of the foregoing we are in a position to draw a few tentative conclusions. First, as we have seen, the list of "special days, and months, and seasons, and years" in Galatians 4:10 may refer to a pagan calendar. In that case Paul's letter provides a window on the local Galatian drama as the Galatians argue among themselves whether to adopt the circumcision-message of the teachers or return to their own traditions and its pagan calendar. In this view there are high stakes for those involved, but the conflict has little direct bearing on Paul's view of the Sabbath.

Second, if the list refers to elements in the Jewish calendar, we have reason to wonder why these elements are described in uncharacteristic non-Jewish terms. At the core of the Judaizing interpretation is the notion that devotion and subservience to "the elemental forces of the world" (*ta stoicheia tou kosmou*; 4:3) is no less a problem in the Jewish legacy than in the pagan tradition.[81] Going "forward" into a Judaized version of Christianity, as Paul's opponents have it, is to Paul nothing else than to go back to essential tenets of paganism and to an equally debilitating form of enslavement (4:9). When push comes to shove in this scenario, paganism and the Judaizing ideology are two of a kind, equally subservient to the *stoicheia*, "the weak and beggarly elemental forces" (4:9; cf. 4:3).[82] For the same reason the observance of "special days, and months, and seasons, and years" (4:10), now ostensibly promoted within a Judaizing paradigm, has the same function as the observance of the calendrical occasions that were part of the Galatians' attempt to please and appease "the elemental forces of the cosmos" in their pagan past (4:3).[83]

"Abba! Father!"' should be seen as the end-point of Paul's affirmations in Galatians and the view from the top of the mountain.

This view is conceivable not only because it is held by many scholars but also because the law, as Paul argues against his opponents, is truly unable to produce the virtues it promotes. His opponents harbor unrealistic expectations with respect to the law, thinking that there is such a thing as a law "that could make alive" (3:21), all the while producing evidence to the contrary (6:13). Any negative allusion to the Sabbath, if that is what we have, must therefore be understood in the context of the activity of the false teachers. Paul's rejection focuses less on the specifics of their program than on the tenor of their outlook. The teachers make observance of the law the basis for the believer's sense of identity (3:2, 5), they want to make a good showing in the flesh (6:12), they demand circumcision in order to avoid persecution (5:11; 6:12), they fail to keep the law despite insisting on conformity to its precepts (6:13), and they boast about those who have been successfully proselytized (6:13).[84] Again, assuming that the "days" refer to the Sabbath as one ingredient in a Judaizing endeavor (4:10), Paul's opposition reflects less what the Sabbath represents and more what it has come to mean within the comprehensive package promoted by his opponents. The context is so thoroughly polemicized that we must think twice before we extrapolate its message to a non-polemical context. Beker notes that the blistering rhetoric puts both sides under tremendous strain as Paul battles the Judaizers because, "in the process of radicalizing their position, he radicalizes his own."[85] Thus Galatians may tell us what Paul thinks about the Sabbath in the context of the activity of his opponents, but it is not thereby representative of what Paul thinks about the Sabbath or even the best place to launch such an inquiry.

And yet, as the third point, Galatians sizzles with affirmations that lie close to the meaning of the seventh day even though its polemic makes it impossible to identify them as such. Paul drives the spade into the deeper layers of the Old Testament narrative until it hits the rock on which the entire narrative rests. He prioritizes Abraham over Moses (3:17); he finds in Abraham not only a person who believes in God but one who prefigures God's faithfulness in his own person (3:15–17);[86] he places the entire notion of covenant in the category of promise (3:18);[87] he cuts Sinai down to size (3:19); he exults in the assurance that God's *pistis* (faithfulness) has been revealed in Jesus (3:23, 25); he even makes the audacious claim that Hagar, the non-Jewish slave woman in Genesis who was *not* the mother of the Israelites, "is Mount Sinai in Arabia and corresponds to the present Jerusalem" (4:24–25).

But Paul does not invent a new God. The God whose faithfulness is on display in the public exhibition of "Jesus Christ crucified" is the Creator who put His reputation on the line when God "blessed the seventh day and hallowed it" (Gen. 2:3). Just as the seventh day in its original configuration draws attention to what takes place on God's side in the divine-human relationship, Paul's most trenchant affirmation in Galatians is relentless in its focus on what God is doing (3:2; 4:4). He chips away at the ethnocentric disposition of Judaism and its sociology of exclusion with such fervor that he has no less a person than Peter on the ropes (2:11–14). However, he does not thereby do injury to the seventh day when the seventh day is seen as the commitment of the God *of* all human beings *to* all human beings. At its deepest layer, where the spade hits the rock, the Sabbath is a statement from God to the human family and not a preserve of the Jews or a boundary marker denoting Jewish identity. Narrative trumps law in Paul, but even on this point the Sabbath is not diminished because in its original configuration it belongs to the realm of narrative (Gen. 2:1–3). Indeed, when the Sabbath appears reluctantly in the context of law "four hundred thirty years" after Abraham (3:17), it insists on taking along its inaugural narrative (Exod. 20:11). The cosmic-universal scope of Paul's message embraces all creation. How can God, Paul asks, possibly be "the God of Jews only? Is he not the God of Gentiles also? Yes, of Gentiles also" (Rom. 3:29). Indeed, God is no less the God of non-human creation, too, the latter confident that God will prove faithful to it, as well (Rom. 8:19–23). Lesser points of reference are all brushed aside, circumcision as much as uncircumcision, as when Paul exclaims, "For neither circumcision nor uncircumcision is anything; but a new creation is everything!" (6:15).

Paul thrives in the deepest layers of the biblical story, supplemented heavily by the message of revelation and inclusion in Isaiah,[88] but there is no layer below which there is no Sabbath. Creation theology and the apocalyptic theology of Galatians are seamlessly united at the source: God is the subject of both. The apocalyptic message tells God's story, casting it as the story of God's faithfulness to all human beings and to all creation, and yet in this respect saying nothing other than what must be inferred from the story of creation and the consecration of the seventh day (Gen. 2:1–3). The inclusion of the Gentiles is not a novelty or an unexpected turn in God's story but a reality that is intrinsic to the beginning of the story and therefore deserving of all the vehemence that Paul unleashes on views to the contrary. Above all, the revelatory character of apocalyptic, dramatic, sudden, and final is preceded and anticipated by the revelatory intent of the seventh day, as though they in every important respect share the same DNA. What has been revealed is what was promised (Gal. 3:22). The beloved "Abba! Father!" of Galatians and Romans (Gal. 4:6; Rom. 8:15) is precisely the God who declared the revelatory intent when "God blessed the seventh day and hallowed it" (Gen. 2:3).

Fourth, if it needs to be said, Paul's dizzying put-down of the law in Galatians (3:19–26; 4:21–31; 5:2–4) does not lead to ethical nihilism. The tenor of his message is not that less will be attempted because less must be achieved. Those who let the flesh run riot "will not inherit the kingdom of God" (5:21). But God's remedy against "the desires of the flesh" (3:3, 5:16–17, 24) and "the elemental spirits of the cosmos" (4:3, 9) is not found in the category of law. The crucifixion of Jesus reaches into human existence as a liberating force that breaks their power; "those who belong to Christ Jesus have crucified the flesh with its passions and desires" (5:24). Theology and ethics come together in "a recapitulation of the life-pattern shown forth in Christ."[89] Jesus's death on the cross signals the end of the old age; "the world has been crucified to me, and I to the world" (6:14), and the demise of the enslaving powers mark the beginning of a life that draws strength from the Spirit, not from the law (5:16, 25). At last there is relief, an effectual remedy; at last the forces that keep human beings "from doing what you want" (5:17) have met their match. To "live by the Spirit" means for Paul a possibility that no law is able to achieve or even to define (5:16, 23).[90]

Nevertheless, even Paul has a law hidden in his sleeves. "Bear one another's burdens, and in this way you will fulfill the law of Christ," he says as the letter to the Galatians winds down (6:2). "The law of Christ," recognized as an allusion to the life and teaching of Jesus,[91] is the new benchmark. This phrase is crucial and more specific than a general endorsement of the principle of love, and it lies closer to the Law of Moses than what many interpreters have thought.[92] When Christ enters the picture the law sheds whatever the negative connotation of an unrealized imperative might be because the law has become an embodied reality. Putting the pieces together, Graham Stanton argues that "the law of Christ" *"is the law of Moses redefined by Christ, with the 'love commandment' and 'carrying the burdens of others' as its essence; it is fulfilled by Christ in his own self-giving love."*[93] If Christ in this way transforms law into narrative, he does not thereby, as the Gospel narratives show, relegate the Sabbath to oblivion.

Finally, Paul's affirmations are not situational although the false teachers are a dominant voice in the letter to the Galatians. God is neither remote from human affairs, as Habakkuk felt, nor is there partiality in God's dealing with humanity, as the line of demarcation between Jew and Gentile long made it appear. The revelation of God's love in "Jesus Christ crucified," the faithfulness of God, and "the law of Christ" apply beyond the boundaries of the Galatian controversy, addressing the human plight quite apart from the few knowns and the many unknowns of this letter. To the extent that we come to terms with these affirmations, we might be ready to entertain the possibility that Paul, better than anyone else, has explained the lost meaning of the seventh day.

We might be ready to entertain the possibility that Paul, better than anyone else, has explained the lost meaning of the seventh day.

ENDNOTES

1. This is certainly the implication of Rordorf's influential study *Sunday*, especially pp. 118–139.

2. The "New Perspective," as noted in chapter 10, holds that Paul in some of his letters confronts ethnocentricity rather than legalism, as traditionally understood; cf. Sanders, *Paul and Palestinian Judaism*. For an evenhanded review, see Brendan Byrne, "Interpreting Romans Theologically in a Post-'New Perspective' Perspective," *HTR* 94 (2001): 227–241.

3. Bauckham, "For Whom Were Gospels Written," 9–48; see also Martin Hengel, *The Four Gospels and the One Gospel of Jesus Christ*, trans. John Bowden (London: SCM Press, 2000).

4. Adolf Deissmann, *The New Testament in the Light of Modern Research* (London: Hodder and Stoughton, 1929), 23–24.

5. The letter to the Colossians was also to be read out loud in the church at Laodicea (Col. 4:16).

6. J. Christiaan Beker, *Paul the Apostle. The Triumph of God in Life and Thought* (Philadelphia: Fortress Press, 1980), 25.

7. Ibid.

8. Ibid., 28.

9. Martyn, *Galatians*, 13.

10. Richard B. Hays, *The Faith of Jesus Christ: An Investigation of the Narrative Substructure of Galatians 3:1–4:11* (SBLDS 56; Chico: Scholars Press, 1983; [repr. Grand Rapids: Eerdmans, 2002]), 33–117.

11. Albert Schweitzer, *The Mysticism of Paul the Apostle*, 2nd ed., trans. William Montgomery (Baltimore: Johns Hopkins University Press, 1998 [orig. London: A. & C. Black, 1931]), 173.

12. Hays, *The Faith of Jesus Christ*, 33–117.

13. According to Jerome Murphy-O'Connor (*Paul: A Critical Life* [Oxford and New York: Oxford University Press, 1997], 24), Paul arrived in Galatia in September 46 CE. He spent two winters there (46–48 CE), allowing him ample time to cover the story of Jesus and its interpretation in depth.

14. Beker, *Paul the Apostle*, 352–353.

15. Richard B. Hays, "Is Paul's Gospel Narratable?" *JSNT* 27 (2004): 217–239.

16. Hays, *The Faith of Jesus Christ*, 196.

17. According to Bruce W. Longenecker (*The Triumph of Abraham's God* [Edinburgh: T. & T. Clark, 1998], 62), "Paul's Christian instruction to gentile converts included some synopsis of Jesus' own life of obedient sonship to God, complete with Aramaic soundbites."

18. E. P. Sanders's characterization that Paul was "the best there was" may apply across the board of his many skills and activities; cf. *Paul* (Oxford: Oxford University Press, 1991), 12. The task of retrieving the narrative substructure of Paul's thought is still in its infancy in

contemporary scholarship, and still a ways away from the Early Church tradition that Luke, "the companion of Paul, recorded in a book the Gospel preached by him [Paul]"; cf. Irenaeus, *Against Heresies* 3.1.1 (written ca. 175–185 CE).

19. Bruce W. Longenecker, ed., *Narrative Dynamics in Paul* (Louisville: John Knox Press, 2002).

20. .Cf. Hans Dieter Betz, *Galatians* (Hermeneia; Philadelphia: Fortress Press, 1979), 14–25.

21. Martyn, *Galatians*, 14.

22. Michael Barnes, "Paul, Context and Interpretation: An Interview with E. P. Sanders," *Journal of Philosophy and Scripture* 2 (2005): 37–42.

23. Scott W. Hahn ("Covenant, Oath, and the Aqedah: Διαθήκη in Galatians 3:15–18," *CBQ* 67 [2005]: 79–100) shows that Paul's insistence on a singular "seed" of Abraham is not contrived but follows from the *Aqedah* story in Genesis 22.

24. J. Louis Martyn, "Events in Galatia: Modified Covenantal Nomism versus God's Invasion of the Cosmos in the Singular Gospel: A Response to J. D. G. Dunn and B. R. Gaventa," in *Pauline Theology*, vol. I, ed. Jouette M. Basler (Minneapolis: Fortress Press, 1991), 160–163.

25. Richard B. Hays, *Echoes of Scripture in the Letters of Paul* (New Haven: Yale University Press, 1989); idem, *The Conversion of the Imagination: Paul as Interpreter of Israel's Scripture* (Grand Rapids: Eerdmans, 2005).

26. See, e.g., Craig A. Evans and James A. Sanders, ed., *Paul and the Scriptures of Israel* (JSNT Sup 83; Sheffield: JSOT Press, 1993).

27. William Sanday and Arthur C. Headlam (*A Critical and Exegetical Commentary on the Epistle to the Romans* [ICC; Edinburgh: T. & T. Clark, 1902; reprinted 1992], 289) claim that "the Apostle does not intend to base any argument on the quotation from the O.T., but only selects the language as far as being familiar, suitable, and proverbial." In their eyes "there is no stress on the fact that the O.T. is being quoted," that "the Apostle carefully and pointedly avoids appealing to Scripture," and that "no argument is based on the use of the O.T." This view is quite typical of how scholars have tended to see Paul's use of the Old Testament.

28. Hays, *Echoes of Scripture*, 36–42.

29. Ernst Käsemann, "Die Anfänge christlicher Theologie," *ZTK* 57 (1960); translated by W. J. Montague as "The Beginnings of Christian Theology," in *New Testament Questions for Today* (Philadelphia: Fortress Press, 1969), 102. As Beker notes (*Paul the Apostle*, xiv), "the designation of apocalyptic as the coherent center of Paul's theology runs counter to a long tradition of theological resistance to all things apocalyptic."

30. J. Christiaan Beker, *Paul's Apocalyptic Gospel* (Philadelphia: Fortress Press, 1982), 14–15; cf. also idem, *Paul the Apostle*, 136–137.

31. Klaus Koch, *The Rediscovery of Apocalyptic,* trans. Margaret Kohl (London: SCM Press, 1972), 14.

32. Beker, *Paul the Apostle*, 328.

33. For a review of the range of Paul's apocalyptic language, see Martinus C. de Boer, "Paul, Theologian of God's Apocalypse," *Int* 56 (2002): 21–33.

34. Beker, *Paul the Apostle*, 28; see also pp. 136–137.

35. This is Martyn's translation (*Galatians*, 178); see also idem, "Apocalyptic Antinomies in Paul's Letter to the Galatians," *NTS* 31 (1985): 410–424.

36. J. B. Lightfoot, *St. Paul's Epistle to the Galatians* (London: Macmillan and Co., 1876), 171–172; Burton, *Galatians*, 232–234.

37. Dieter Lührmann, "Tage, Monate, Jahrezeiten, Jahre (Gal. 4,10)," in *Werden und Wirken des Alten Testaments*, ed. Rainer Albertz, Hans-Peter Müller, Hans Walter Wolff, and Walther Zimmerli (Göttingen: Vandenhoeck & Ruprecht, 1980), 428–445; Troy Martin, "Pagan and Judeo-Christian Time-Keeping Schemes in Gal 4.10 and Col 2.16, " *NTS* 42 (1996): 105–119.

38. Troy W. Martin, "Apostasy to Paganism: The Rhetorical Stasis of the Galatian Controversy," *JBL* 114 (1995): 437–461; repr. in *The Galatians Debate: Contemporary Issues in Rhetorical and Historical Interpretation*, ed. Mark D. Nanos (Peabody, MA: Hendrickson, 2002), 73–94; idem, "Whose Flesh? What Temptation? (Galatians 4.13–14)," *JSNT* 74 (1999): 65–91; idem, "The Covenant of Circumcision (Genesis 17:9–14) and the Situational Antithesis in Galatians 3:28," *JBL* 122 (2003): 111–125.

39. Martin, "Apostasy to Paganism," 79.

40. Martin, "The Covenant of Circumcision," 120.

41. Martin, "Apostasy to Paganism," 77; cf. also Paula Fredriksen, "Judaism, the Circumcision of the Gentiles, and Apocalyptic Hope: Another Look at Galatians 1 and 2," *JTS* 42 (1991): 532–564; repr. in *The Galatians Debate*, 235–260.

42. Martyn, *Galatians*, 414.

43. Martin, "Time-Keeping Schemes," 111.

44. Martyn, *Galatians*, 294.

45. Ibid., 414–418.

46. Hays, *Faith of Jesus Christ*, 197.

47. Beverly Roberts Gaventa, "Galatians 1 and 2: Autobiography as Paradigm," *NovT* 28 (1986): 309–326.

48. Martyn, *Galatians*, 3, 97–105, 144, emphasis added.

49. Ibid., 4, 157–159, emphasis added.

50. Hays, *Faith of Jesus Christ*, 197.

51. Martyn, "Events in Galatia," 171.

52. Beverly Roberts Gaventa, "The Singularity of the Gospel: A Reading of Galatians," in *Pauline Theology*, vol. I, 153–156.

53. Hays, *Faith of Jesus Christ*, 197.

54. Martyn ("Events in Galatia," 174) emphasizes discontinuities in Paul, but on this point

he is quick to affirm continuity.

55. Hays, *Faith of Jesus Christ*, 197.

56. Gaventa, "The Singularity of the Gospel," 158.

57. Martin Luther (*Vorlesung über den Römerbrief 1515/16* in *Ausgewählte Werke* [Munich: Chr. Raiser Verlag, 1957], 132) consistently and decisively reads *pistis Christou* as "faith in Christ."

58. In Galatians the most important texts are Gal. 2:16; 2:20; 3:22. In Romans the most important passage is Rom. 3:21–26; cf. also Phil. 3:9. The bibliography on this point is vast and will be limited to a few references; cf. Gabriel Hebert, "'Faithfulness' and 'Faith,'" *RTR* 14 (1955): 33–40; George Howard, "The 'Faith of Christ,'" *ExpT* 85 (1974): 213–214; Hays, *Faith of Jesus Christ* (probably the most pivotal study to date); Stanley Stowers, *A Rereading of Romans* (New Haven: Yale University Press, 1994), 194–213; Martyn, *Galatians*, 246–280; Gaventa, "The Singularity of the Gospel," 157–158; Sigve Tonstad, "πίστις Χριστοῦ: Reading Paul in a New Paradigm," *AUSS* 40 (2002): 37–59; Douglas Harink, *Paul among the Postliberals: Pauline Theology beyond Christendom and Modernity* (Grand Rapids: Brazos Press, 2003), 17, 25–65; Hung-Sik Choi, "ΠΙΣΤΙΣ in Galatians 5:5–6: Neglected Evidence for the Faithfulness of Christ," *JBL* 124 (2005): 467–490.

59. Bultmann (art. "*pistis*," *TDNT* 6:174–82) demonstrates that *pistis* in classical Greek carries the meaning of "reliability," "trustworthiness," *and* the stance toward one whose trustworthiness is above question, that is, "confidence" or "trust." The Old Testament conditioning of *pistis* is crucial, but Old Testament and Hellenistic usage merely expands the scope and direction of meanings that are already intrinsic to the Greek term. According to Ian G. Wallis (*The Faith of Jesus Christ in Early Christian Traditions* [SNTSMS 84; Cambridge: Cambridge University Press, 1995], 1–23), lexical evidence for pre-New Testament use of *pistis* in the Septuagint and in Hellenistic Jewish Literature favors the notion of "faithfulness" rather than "faith." Bultmann (*TDNT* 6:204) admits that *pistis* in the New Testament "can mean both 'faithfulness' and 'trust,'" but he claims that "it is seldom used in the former sense," that is, as "faithfulness." This view is no longer tenable. The conceptual realignment with respect to New Testament usage of *pistis* negates much of his assertion that the New Testament concept of faith diverges significantly from the Old Testament.

60. For a review of the precedent, see Gerhard Kittel, "πίστις Ἰησοῦ Χριστοῦ bei Paulus," *Theologischen Studien und Kritiken* 79 (1906): 419–436.

61. Francis I. Andersen, *Habakkuk: A New Translation with Introduction and Commentary* (AB 25; New York: Doubleday, 2001), 123, 125.

62. Defenders of the view that *pistis Christou* should retain the meaning "faith in Christ" argue, among other things, that this is the translation that is least contaminated by a theological agenda even though this option is equally in need of, and even more indebted to, a theological framework; cf. Barry Matlock, "Detheologizing the ΠΙΣΤΙΣ ΧΡΙΣΤΟΥ Debate: Cautionary Remarks

from a Lexical Semantic Perspective," *NovT* 42 (2000): 1–23; idem, "Even the demons believe": Paul and πίστις Χριστοῦ," *CBQ* 64 (2002): 300–318; idem, "PISTIS in Galatians 3.26: Neglected Evidence for 'Faith in Christ'?" *NTS* 49 (2003): 433–439; idem, "The Rhetoric of πίστις in Paul: Galatians 2.16, 3.22, Romans 3.22, and Philippians 3.9," JSNT 30 (2007): 173–203.

63. Hays, *Echoes*, 39.

64. Ibid., 40.

65. Hays, *The Faith of Jesus Christ*, 140.

66. Betz, *Galatians*, 176, n. 120. Francis Watson, who vigorously defends the view that *pistis Christou* should be translated "faith *in* Christ," takes issue with the notion of revelation (and *pistis*) as an event; cf. "Is Revelation an 'Event'?" *Modern Theology* 10 (1994): 383–399; idem, *Paul and the Hermeneutics of Faith* (London and New York: T. & T. Clark, 2004), 127–163.

67. J. Louis Martyn, "The Apocalyptic Gospel in Galatians," *Int* 54 (2000): 254.

68. Martyn, "Events in Galatia," 165.

69. The traditional Protestant or "Lutheran" interpretation holds that "declare righteous" should be the preferred translation of *dikaióo*; cf. Stephen Westerholm, *Perspectives Old and New on Paul: The "Lutheran" Paul and His Critics* (Grand Rapids: Eerdmans, 2004), 261–296.

70. Martyn, *Galatians*, 250. In the dense passage in Romans 3:21–26, the *locus classicus* for the traditional interpretation of "justification by faith," Robert Jewett (*Romans: A Commentary* [Hermeneia; Minneapolis: Fortress Press, 2006], 268–294) eschews the term "justifies" in favor of the less technical "set right" (3:22) and "makes righteous" (3:26).

71. Sigve Tonstad, "Creation Groaning in Labor Pains," in *Exploring Ecological Hermeneutics*, ed. Norman C. Habel and Peter Trudinger (Atlanta: Society of Biblical Literature, 2008), 141–150.

72. Martyn, *Galatians*, 5–6. See also Choi, "ΠΙΣΤΙΣ in Galatians 5:5–6," 467–490.

73. James D. G. Dunn, "4QMMT and Galatians," *NTS* 43 (1997), 147–153.

74. Dunn, "4QMMT and Galatians," 147.

75. Daniel Boyarin, *A Radical Jew: Paul and the Politics of Identity* (Berkeley: University of California Press, 1994), 3, 22–23.

76. Boyarin, *A Radical Jew*, 13–38.

77. Sanders, *Paul, the Law and the Jewish People*, 162.

78. Sigve Tonstad, "The Revisionary Potential of 'Abba! Father!' in the Letters of Paul," *AUSS* 45 (2007): 9.

79. Martyn, "Apocalyptic Gospel," 254.

80. Douglas J. Moo, *The Epistle to the Romans* (NICNT; Grand Rapids: Eerdmans, 1996), 502.

81. Martinus C. de Boer, "The Meaning of the Phrase τὰ στοιχεῖα τοῦ κόσμου in Galatians," NTS 53 (2007): 204–224.

82. Ibid., 209–216.

83. Ibid., 217.

84. Charles B. Cousar, *A Theology of the Cross: The Death of Jesus in the Pauline Letters* (OBT; Minneapolis: Fortress Press, 1990), 139.

85. Beker, *Paul the Apostle*, 57.

86. Hahn, "Covenant, Oath and the Aqedah," 88–92.

87. James D. G. Dunn, "Did Paul Have a Covenant Theology? Reflections on Romans 9.4 and 11.27," in *The Concept of the Covenant in the Second Temple Period*, ed. Stanley E. Porter and J. C. R. Roo (Leiden: E. J. Brill, 2003), 287–307.

88. Richard Hays, "Paul's Hermeneutics and the Question of Truth," *Pro ecclesia* 16 (2007): 128–129).

89. Hays, "Christology and Ethics," 280.

90. Bruce, *Galatians*, 255.

91. Burton, *Galatians*, 329.

92. Graham Stanton, "What Is the Law of Christ?" *Ex auditu* 17 (2001): 47–59.

93. Ibid., 56; emphasis his.

CHAPTER 14

THE RIDDLE OF "SABBATHS" IN COLOSSIANS

Therefore do not let anyone condemn you in matters of food and drink or of observing festivals, new moons, or sabbaths. These are only a shadow of what is to come, but the substance belongs to Christ.
Colossians 2:16–17

If the dilemma that confronts the reader with regard to the Sabbath in Galatians is complex, it becomes daunting when we turn to the letter to the Colossians. In an in-depth study of the situation in Colossae, Clinton E. Arnold admits that the task of reconstructing the situation "is comparable to filling in the gaps of a 5,000 piece mosaic while possessing only 150 tiles and not knowing exactly where many should be placed!"[1] Hardly anyone disputes that the letter to the Galatians is written by Paul, but there is at least some uncertainty as to whether the subject of the Sabbath is addressed in that letter. In contrast, the vast majority of interpreters believe that the letter to the Colossians addresses the Sabbath, but many scholars doubt the letter is written by Paul. If these doubts are allowed to stand, it means that Paul's explicit contribution to the New Testament view of the Sabbath is minuscule.

Fortunately, there is no compelling reason to question whether the apostle Paul is the author of Colossians (Col. 1:1, 23; 4:18).[2] As to the Sabbath, the author of the letter tells the Colossians not to let "anyone condemn you in matters of food and drink or of observing festivals, new moons, or sabbaths (*sabbatōn*)" (Col. 2:16).[3] At first glance this would seem to settle the question as to whether the Sabbath is addressed. Moreover, the statement seems to cast the *sabbata* in negative terms. Colossians appears to address the subject of the Sabbath, indicating that the Colossians should not yield ground to critics who hold that they need to keep the Sabbath, observe other festivals, and practice certain restrictions with respect to food and drink. According to this reading of the letter, Paul weakens the status of the Sabbath as a Christian ordinance.

> ***The vast majority of interpreters believe that the letter to the Colossians addresses the Sabbath.***

But there are other ways to understand this text. While (1) the view that the *sabbata* in Colossians refers to the Jewish Sabbath remains viable, featuring agitators who are pushing a Judaizing agenda, it has also been suggested (2) that the *sabbata* in Colossians refers to something other than the seventh-day Sabbath; (3) that Paul is referring to the Sabbath but is *affirming* the Sabbath observance of the Colossians rather than decrying it; (4) and that the *sabbata* in Colossians refers to sabbaths that have lost their Jewish character, now referring to religious observance that is carried over into a non-Jewish set of beliefs. Each of these options deserves careful scrutiny. As with Galatians, however, the most important concern must be to understanding Paul's affirmations in Colossians.

COLOSSIANS AND THE SABBATH

The notion that Paul is defending the Colossian Christians against criticism on the part of Jews or Judaizing Christians has a long-standing tradition. This view takes it for granted that Paul is speaking of the Jewish Sabbath, and the "*sabbatōn*" belong to a Judaizing agenda. F. C. Baur argued this view in the nineteenth century,[4] and it remains resilient. In Baur's evolutionary model,[5] Paul everywhere seeks to counter and to overcome Judaizing influences with a message that entails a higher level of religious development. The problem in Colossae, as in Galatia, is the attempt to impose Jewish observances on Gentile believers in Jesus.

The pitfall of this view is the tendency to assume that Paul's opponents held the same beliefs in most or all of the churches he addresses. Increasingly aware of this potential fallacy, scholars recognize that attempts to resolve the difficulties in Paul's correspondence must take into account the particulars in each letter. With an eye on Baur's one-sided approach, Jerry L. Sumney seeks a method by which to characterize and identify Paul's opponents in each letter. Sumney makes it his first point that we run afoul of the evidence if we read Paul's letters as a homogenous group.[6] We cannot assume that he addresses the same type of opponent in each letter because of evident diversity in the letters. Each letter must speak for itself. The shadowy figures that move about in the letters are not all Judaizers, or, if they are Judaizers, then this conclusion must be sustained by convincing support in the letter in question.

Sumney takes great care to sift through the available evidence and to rank it in terms of importance. Explicit statements constitute the first level of evidence, followed by allusions in didactic and polemical contexts, and then by less certain allusions as a third and less reliable level.[7] Applying this method, Sumney categorizes a number of statements as explicit, including the reference to *sabbata* in Colossians 2:16.[8]

In a tone much more subdued than in the letter to the Galatians, Paul urges the Colossians to "see to it that no one takes you captive through philosophy and empty deceit, according to human tradition, according to the elemental spirits of the universe, and not according to Christ" (Col. 2:8).[9] This statement is best seen as the framework within which the concern of Colossians belongs. Apparently, the integrity of the church is threatened by a worldview that seeks to appease fate and hostile powers by asceticism and "harsh treatment of the body" (2:23). In practical terms the opponents are promoting a litany of strict guidelines about food, drink, and religious festivals. A possible excerpt of their list of slogans says simply: "Do not handle! Do not taste! Do not touch!" (2:21).

The difficulties in Paul's correspondence must take into account the particulars in each letter.

Does the evidence in Colossians point to a Jewish agenda? In order to come to terms with Paul's opponents in this letter, the interpreter must address the texts that are most significant and about which there is, fortunately, a fair degree of consensus.

Heeding the challenge in Colossians, Christian Stettler thus returns with a view that is close to the traditional opinion.[10] He argues, correctly, I believe, that Colossians "does not oppose a group within the Colossian church."[11] Indeed, it seems quite certain that Paul nowhere in the letter speaks of an apostasy or even of "any dissent between himself and the Colossian Christians."[12]

But Paul is concerned about "philosophy and empty deceit" that are in the air, philosophy "according to human tradition, according to the elemental spirits of the universe, and not according to Christ" (2:8). Would Paul credibly describe a Judaizing program in this way? Would Jews see themselves in such terms? Stettler argues in the affirmative, claiming that while Jewish *Christians* hardly would refer to their teaching as "philosophy," it is possible that Hellenistic Jews may have done so.[13] When he has dealt with this hurdle to seeing Jewish agitation behind the philosophy in Colossians, the identity of the *sabbata* in Colossians 2:16 is not much of a problem. According to Stettler, it follows that "the regulations mentioned in Colossians 2:16 are those of the Torah of Moses."[14] It follows, too, as he sees it, that the Colossian Christians are under siege from members of the local Jewish synagogue, who deny validity to the Christians' belief because they fail to adopt the Jewish features that would certify the authenticity of the Christians' profession. "According to 2:16–17a," says Stettler, "the Christians at Colossae are condemned by the local synagogue because they do not keep those regulations of the Torah which are most crucial for Jewish identity, namely the laws about idolatry and purity..., the Jewish festivals and the sabbath."[15]

In this reconstruction it is not deemed necessary to invoke other candidates for the concerns voiced in the letter even though the reference to "philosophy and empty deceit" (2:8) seems to invite other options or a mix of options. Moreover, and contrary to what might be expected, circumcision, the most contentious issue in Galatians, is not featured as a defining issue in the Colossian controversy. Nevertheless, Stettler sees no need to entertain options other than Jewish opponents. All the particulars in Colossians may in his view be accounted for by seeing the opponents as Torah-observing Jews.[16] This view, affirming the attitude of traditional Christian interpretations, takes the most negative view toward the question of the *sabbata* in Colossians.

A simpler option holds that Paul is addressing something other than the Sabbath in Colossians, focusing on the term that is used rather than on the context. Proponents of this view argue that the third member of the phrase "festivals, new moons, or sabbaths" (2:16) merely refers to the foregoing members. While the enumeration of "festivals (*heortē*), new moons (*neomēnia*) or sabbaths (*sabbata*)" (2:16) may signify movement from annual to monthly to weekly observances in a pattern reflecting Old Testament antecedents,[17] it has been suggested that the phrase in Colossians derives from the literary device of "inverted parallelism," moving "from annual to monthly and then back to annual."[18]

Support for this construction may be found by relating Paul's statement in Colossians to Hosea 2:11, "I will put an end to all her mirth, her festivals, her new moons, her sabbaths, and all her appointed festivals." In a book-length work that examines many other linguistic factors pointing to a non-weekly Sabbath interpretation, Ron du Preez argues that this verse in Hosea represents not only an inverted parallelism but "an augmented inverted parallelism";[19] the sabbaths in question, like the festival that begins the foursome members on the list, are the *annual* sabbaths of the Jewish liturgical year (cf. Lev. 16:31–32). In other words, the *sabbata* in Colossians refer to "*ceremonial/cultic sabbaths*, and not the weekly seventh-day Sabbath."[20] This reconstruction finds support in Paul's argument that the "festivals, new moons or sabbaths" are said to be "a shadow of what is to come" (Col. 2:16–17), and it accepts the *shadow* vs. *reality* construct that is common in other interpretations. According to the Christian view of the Jewish liturgical calendar, a number of special annual occasions in the Jewish system were intended to prefigure the coming of Christ. These occasions are also designated *sabbata* (Lev. 16:31–32). To the extent that Jesus is the reality prefigured by these ordinances, reverence for the shadow sets up a competing point of reference. Overlapping somewhat with Stettler's interpretation above, "nobody asks for the shadow, however great it is, once the reality has come."[21]

The *contextual* parameters of the sabbath question in Colossians are elusive, as du Preez points out.[22] As is evident in the view suggested above, the text rather than the context sets the tone for the interpretation. Whether the acknowledged complexity provides warrant for short-circuiting the contextual challenge is far from settled, however. The appeal of this approach is its simplicity; the drawback is that it is unlikely to persuade unless it engages the issues that are addressed in the letter.[23] It is characteristic of other proposed interpretations of the *sabbata* in Colossians to take on this challenge.

The two views reviewed so far are very different, one bypassing the demand to consider the context, the other taking a view of the context that seems to ignore markers that point to a non-Jewish and more complex set of problems. Remarkably, a third view argues that Paul is not faulting the Colossians for adopting practices that are irrelevant; he is, in fact, affirming them in what they are doing. Troy W. Martin's interpretation thus breaks radically the mold established by earlier studies of the *sabbata* in Colossians.[24] Adopting the main tenets of Sumney's criteria for how to identify Paul's opponents, Martin's translation of Colossians 2:16–17 is particularly intriguing. Respecting the grammatical nuances in the text and the structure of the sentence, he argues, first, that Paul is not setting up a contrast between "shadow" (*skia*) and "reality" (*sōma*) despite the fact that leading translations and commentaries prefer this view, as noted below.

Paul is not faulting the Colossians for adopting practices that are irrelevant.

> These are only a shadow of what is to come, but the substance belongs to Christ (NRSV).
>
> These are a shadow of the things that were to come; the reality, however, is found in Christ (NIV).
>
> These are only a shadow of what was coming: the reality is the body of Christ (NJB).

Rather than contrasting *shadow* and *substance* (NRSV) or *shadow* and *reality* (NIV, NJB), Martin argues that the contrast in Paul's argument must pay closer heed to the relationship between the last part of the sentence, "the body of Christ" (2:17), and the first part of the sentence, "let no one judge you" (2:16). *Sōma* is figurative, but it is not figurative in contrast to *skia*. The phrase "the body of Christ"(*sōma tou christou*) means just that, "the body of Christ," relating to the first part of the sentence as an equal. Since this phrase does not have a verb, it looks to the first part of the sentence to supply the verbal element. That verb is *krinein*, which carries the meaning *dividing, selecting, deciding, discerning, determining, valuing, assessing,* and *judging.*[25] All these meanings are relevant in the present context. "Let no one judge [*krinein*]," Paul writes, but "[let everyone discern (*krinein*)] *the body of Christ*" (2:16–17).[26] As Martin argues, "[t]he verb κρινέτω (*krinetō*) determines the action that is forbidden by the first member and then enjoined by the second member of this antithesis."[27]

Where traditional translations see Paul urging the Colossians to be steadfast in the face of criticism of practices they are *not* observing, Martin's translation finds quite the opposite. Paul urges the Colossians not to be deterred by criticism of practices they are in fact observing, meaning festivals, new moons, and *sabbata*. His quarrel is not with a system he deems invalid but with a system that serves a purpose.

> Although he recognizes the absence of ultimate reality in the Christian time-keeping system, the Colossian author still argues for its validity because of its relationship to the ultimate reality. He exhorts the Colossians not to submit to the critique that their time-keeping scheme is useless, tyrannical or illusory. He urges them to ignore the accusation that the practice of festival, new moon and Sabbaths propagates false hopes and expectations about the future. He admonishes the Colossians, "Let no one critique you by your eating and drinking or in respect to your feast, new moon or Sabbaths which practices are a shadow of

> things to come but let everyone discern the body of Christ by your eating and drinking or in respect to your feast, new moon, or Sabbaths" (Col. 2.16–17). Instead of being on the defensive end of a poignant critique, the author encourages the Colossians to take the offensive and proclaim Christ to the critics by their Christian practices.[28]

The practices that are critiqued in the letter are the practices of the Colossian Christians. They are not the practices of Paul's opponents. These opponents are indeed trying to take the Colossians captive "through philosophy and empty deceit" (2:8), and it is precisely for this reason that they attack the Colossian practice.

Taking this interpretation to the level of real historical options and probabilities, Martin suggests that the critics in Colossae are Cynics, given that the type of criticism matches what is to be expected from a Cynic point of view.[29] The distinctive contribution of Martin's study, then, is to see actual Sabbath-keeping in Colossians, and to affirm it.

A fourth option returns to the view that Paul is criticizing practices among the Colossians, but he is not against them because they are Jewish or of a Judaizing kind. This view looks at features in the letter that are not easily explained within a Judaizing paradigm. Where traditional studies saw a Judaizing intent on the part of Paul's opponents, Martin Dibelius broke new ground when he emphasized the Gnostic rooting of the "philosophy" in Colossians.[30] His study opened the gates to other views of the opponents in Colossae, and most interpretations now see a non-Jewish constellation at work, often with an admixture of ideas and practices that have a Jewish flavor. According to F. F. Bruce, writing in the days when there was as yet no in-depth study of how to identify Paul's opponents in a given letter, the deviant teaching of the Colossians fused a local variety of Judaism with a philosophy of non-Jewish

The distinctive contribution of Martin's study, then, is to see actual Sabbath-keeping in Colossians.

origin—an early and simple form of Gnosticism.[31] This "Judaism" is a far cry from the stalwart orthodoxy Paul encounters elsewhere, and it generally had a bad name among Jews. Evidence for blurred boundaries between religious groups in terms of belief and practice has not been hard to find. Bruce, for instance, cites an example from Colossae of a Jewish lady who could be both "honorary ruler of the synagogue and priestess of the imperial cult."[32]

Other studies reveal a similar shift in opinion. Eduard Schweizer concludes that even though there are Jewish elements in the Colossian "movement," it does not sail under the flag of the Mosaic Law but under that of a "modern" philosophy.[33] Even "the written code" (2:14) referred to in the letter has more in common with Pythagorean rules than with the Mosaic Law. Eduard Lohse finds the observance of the Sabbath and other sacred days among the Colossians to rest upon their understanding of the elements of nature rather than on the Old Testament. "When these days are singled out and carefully kept, the course of nature is followed as determined by the movement of the stars," according to the Colossian view of reality.[34] Lohse argues that the requirement to observe festivals, New Moon, and Sabbath is not based on the Old Testament or on the Ten Commandments. Instead, the obligation derives from "the basic principles of this world" (2:8). To the Colossians, these principles determine the course of the stars and lay down the order of the calendar. Since human beings are subject to the elements of the world through birth and fate, they must submit to them by observing ascetic dietary rules and set times. "The philosophy makes use of notions taken over from the Jews," concludes Lohse, but "these have been recast in the furnace of syncretism, subjected to the elements of the world to become vehicles for their expression."[35]

The possibility that the Colossians observed a sacred calendar for the sake of the "elemental spirits of the universe" (2:8) must be distinguished from the keeping of the Sabbath in the Old Testament, where it is evidence of conformity to God's law. Peter O'Brien suggests that "Paul is not condemning the use of sacred days or seasons as such; it is the wrong motive involved when the observance of these days is bound up with the recognition of the elemental spirits."[36]

This view of the Colossian predicament has been developed further by Clinton E. Arnold's in-depth investigation entitled *The Colossian Syncretism*. Arnold shows that the tenets of Paul's opponents at Colossae are quite different from the views he confronts in his letter to the Galatians. For one thing, there is no mention of "the works of law," and no polemic against circumcision.[37] This leads him to conclude that the leaders of the Colossian "philosophy" are Gentiles. Arnold writes that "the environment was characterized by a significant level of religious syncretism. There was a fair amount of borrowing from cult to cult. There was also a strong tendency for the newer religions to assimilate features of the older local religions."[38]

Whether the opponents in Colossae were Gnostics (Dibelius), Platonists and Pythagorean (Schweitzer), Cynics (Martin), adherents to tenets of folk religion (Arnold), or people who pushed "a distinctive blend of popular Middle Platonic, Jewish, and Christian elements that cohere around the pursuit of wisdom," as argued in-depth by Richard DeMaris,[39] the common denominator of these options is what they were *not*, and they were not primarily Jewish. The quest for their exact identity may elude us, as Sumney concludes with a touch of nihilism,[40] but the sum of these studies go a long way toward eliminating the notion that Judaizing opponents constitute a single, definable, and adequate account for the conflict in Colossae. The possibility that the *sabbata* in Colossians refers to something other than the seventh-day Sabbath cannot be ruled out, and we must also take seriously the possibility that Paul speaks affirmatively of Colossian Sabbath-keeping, as argued by Martin. The weightiest evidence, nevertheless, seems to favor a composite explanation. The

The common denominator of these options is what they were not, and they were not primarily Jewish.

fourth option therefore invites a further look at the broader message of Colossians.

THE SABBATH AND THE MESSAGE OF COLOSSIANS

Even though the "festivals, new moons, or sabbaths" are terms originating in Jewish practice, they do not have the same significance to the Colossians as in the Old Testament.[41] According to Joachim Gnilka, the Colossians are not interested in the festivals and the Sabbath because they rehearse the Old Testament narrative or because they prefigure salvation. Times and seasons are expressions of "the order ruled by the cosmic powers that hold sway over the birth, death, sicknesses, and destiny of humanity."[42]

When this crucial difference between the meaning of the Sabbath in the Old Testament and that of the Colossians is overlooked, it leads to unwarranted and misleading conclusions. Paul's emphasis cannot be divorced from its historical context or from the specific problem it seeks to correct. Contrary to the Colossian outlook, the Sabbath in the Old Testament hardly rests on a "hollow and deceptive philosophy" based on "human tradition and the basic principles of this world" (Col. 2:8, NIV).

More than in Galatians, Paul is concerned about Creation and the beginning of the world, and no less than in Galatians, he is eager to point out what has been done to set right what has gone wrong. Two distinctive emphases come together in this letter, the first presenting Christ as the Creator (1:15–17) and the second presenting Christ as the one who has overcome the "principalities and powers" (2:15). Both emphases have a bearing on the Sabbath.

CHRIST AS CREATOR

In Colossians, Paul envisions Creation and the work of restoration as indivisible, held together in the same person. Christ, Paul insists, is not only the Savior but also the Creator. In one of the most highly developed statements on the divinity of Jesus in the New Testament, Paul writes that "he is the image of the invisible God, the first-born of all creation; for in him all things were created, in heaven and on earth, visible and invisible, whether thrones or dominions or principalities or authorities—all things were created through him and for him. He is before all things, and in him all things hold together" (1:15–17).

This passage includes Christ in the one God of Israel. Christ is not merely exercising delegated authority. As Richard Bauckham has shown, the creation of *all things* is characteristic of Jewish monotheist rhetoric.[43] Paul signifies it with an array of Greek prepositions, each of which covers an aspect of divine causality that now belongs to Christ. Creation is *from* him, *through* him, and *to* him, placing Christ within the divine relationship to all things. He is, as this terminology has been understood, the *efficient* cause, the *instrumental* cause, and the *final* cause of all that exists. Just as in the Old Testament the verb *bārā'*, to "create," is a verb that can only have God as its subject; the New Testament portrayal of Christ as Creator can only mean that Christ is included in the divine identity. "Creation, axiomatically, was the sole work of God alone," says Bauckham.[44] It is on the platform of Christ's role as Creator that Paul built the case for Christ's work as redeemer. The God who creates and redeems is the same Person, and Christ is that Person. His supremacy in Creation is the basis for healing the blight that affects all Creation.

> ***Paul is concerned about Creation and the beginning of the world, and is eager to point out what has been done to set right what has gone wrong.***

But this is more than a striking and convenient argument for the pre-existence and the divinity of Christ. In Colossians, Creation is the reference point for redemption. Paul sees Jesus as the firstborn of Creation (1:15) and the firstborn of the dead (1:18). His role as Creator expresses His mandate, but it also evokes Creation as the state to which all things must be restored. By Christ's triumph Creation is to come back to itself. Creation and redemption belong to an indivisible whole. The clinching argument for its indivisibility and the evidence for its success come together in the same agent: Christ as Creator *and* Restorer.[45] When Jesus walked about on earth as a human being, Paul is saying, He asserted and regained dominion over all the territory that He brought into existence in the beginning.

Paul claims that through Christ "God was pleased to reconcile to himself all things, whether on earth or in heaven, by making peace through the blood of his cross" (1:20). The meaning of the reconciliation can be expressed in better everyday terms. Paul uses the Greek word *apokatallassō*, and the *Louw-Nida Lexicon* explains that this word signifies "to reestablish proper friendly interpersonal relations after these have been disrupted or broken." It also elaborates that "the componential features of this series of meanings involve (1) disruption of friendly relations because of (2) presumed or real provocation, (3) overt behavior designed to remove hostility, and (4) restoration of original friendly relations." The scope of what happened comes through in the translation of the *Good News Bible*. Paul says that through the Son "God decided to *bring* the whole universe *back* to himself" (1:20, GNB). This translation conveys the meaning of Paul's term much better than the more technical language used in other translations. Restoration of a previously friendly, but subsequently broken relationship comes to be the meaning of what Christ accomplished by His death on the cross.

But Paul also introduces a puzzling disclosure that has baffled interpreters if it has not been overlooked altogether. As we go over the ground again, this time choosing the translation of the New English Bible, we see Paul writing that "through him God chose to reconcile the whole universe to himself, making peace through the shedding of his blood upon the cross—to reconcile all things, whether on earth or in heaven, through him alone" (1:20, NEB).

The puzzling and often overlooked element is mentioned twice in this text. According to Paul, what transpired in the particularity of the cross is meant to have a cosmic impact. It has to do with "the whole universe," and the peacemaking mission is intended to heal estrangement "whether on earth or in heaven." This description gives rise to at least two questions. The first is to determine what had gone wrong that could be made right by means of the death of Christ on the cross. Before attempting to answer this question, it is important to admit that Jesus's death on the cross will always surpass the ways we seek to explain it. E. P. Sanders suggests that "Paul's thought did not run from plight to solution, but rather from solution to plight,"[46] requiring the reader to admit that when our perception of the problem is held up to the light of the solution, we fall short on both counts. Colossians describes a problem, and it does hold forth Christ as the solution, but it should not be assumed that the description of the problem adequately prepares for the solution.

By Christ's triumph Creation is to come back to itself.

The second question relates to how we are to understand the cosmic sweep in Colossians, the suggestion that there was also something in heaven needing to be made right. In Colossians these questions are so closely related that the purpose of Christ's death on the cross cannot be separated from its impact on "the whole universe."

EXPOSING PRINCIPALITIES AND POWERS

Paul writes that the believers have been rescued "from the power of darkness" (1:13), under whose sway they were "estranged and hostile in mind" (1:21). He recalls their submission to "the elemental spirits of the universe" (2:8, 20), "the rulers and authorities" (2:15), the leader of whom is designated in Ephesians, closely to Colossians, as "the ruler of the power of the air" (Eph. 2:2). These, to be sure, are metaphors for the power of Satan and his deceptive activity. Arnold is correct when he asserts that "these beings are evil and hostile to the purposes of God."[47] Moreover, they should not be seen merely as "emanations from a high god or even as impersonal forces."[48]

Recalling Sanders's suggestion that Paul's logic often runs from solution to plight,[49] this could be one such instance. Christ is clearly presented as the solution. While we are not left guessing as to what the problem is, Christ is a solution that surpasses the human ability to define the problem. Although the terminology is general and bent to accommodate the Colossians' background, in the Colossian context we hear allusions to the story of the fall in Genesis, the satanic agency, the sinister method of evil, and Satan's spurious charge, portraying God as capricious and arbitrary (Gen. 3:1). And we see the result not only among the Colossians, who have become "estranged and hostile in mind" (Col. 1:21), but also throughout the entire universe.

Christ's death on the cross cannot be separated from its impact on "the whole universe."

The full text of the divine solution in Colossians is therefore worth pondering. "Having disarmed principalities and powers," Paul writes, "He made a public spectacle of them, triumphing over them in it [the cross]" (Col. 2:15, NKJV). Here, too, a more graphic translation better describes what is seen transpiring. On the cross Christ "stripped off the clothing" of the principalities and powers, leaving the agencies of evil naked and publicly disgraced. God does not annihilate His opponent, but God exposes him for what he is. On the cross the accusations that were made against God boomerang back on the evil one. Jesus, who is stripped naked and exposed on the cross, actually strips the evil one of his clothing, leaving him exposed and stripped of power. If we return to the conventional plight-to-solution mode, Jesus comes as the solution to the plight as the plight is defined by the biblical narrative. Only now are we able to do justice to Paul's careful alignment of creation and redemption in Colossians and rise on its wings to grasp the healing impact of the cross on the whole universe, "whether on earth or in heaven" (1:20).

When Paul tells the Colossians not to let anyone "condemn you in matters of food and drink or of observing festivals, new moons, or sabbaths" (2:16), allowing the possibility that the Sabbath is in view, it is best understood as a commentary on the syncretism he confronts. This background helps resolve the enigmatic comment that "these are only a shadow of what is to come, but the substance belongs to Christ" (2:17).[50] If, as many scholars believe, Paul plays on the contrast between "shadow" (*skia*) and "body" (*sōma*), the imagery must not be pressed too far. It works best to see "shadow" as something unreal and "body" as the reality.[51] Paul is urging the Colossians to discard other points of reference than Christ. His point, then, is that "these things are a mere shadow of what must be; the reality [belongs to] Christ" (2:17)[52] Indeed, the expression "what is to come" (*tōn mellontōn*), suggests an experience that is not yet in their possession.[53]

But if the *sabbata* in the Colossian syncretism seems to reflect negatively on the Sabbath, the sweeping affirmations in Colossians speak precisely to the reality of which the biblical Sabbath is the sign. In this sense the theological affirmations of Galatians and Colossians arrive at the same destination. These letters, each in their own way, hold up Jesus as the means by which humanity's misperception of God will be overcome. In Colossians, the alienation that is overcome runs through the entire cosmic order. Paul insists on the unity of Creation and redemption because Christ's mandate in redemption is anchored in Creation. The demolition of the "principalities and powers" by Christ's death on the cross (2:15, KJV) heals the estrangement that affects the whole universe because the One dying on the cross reveals God.

It sounds almost too simple to state that Paul's theological affirmations in Galatians and Colossians run on parallel tracks with what the seventh day affirms about God. Anticipating, as we must, that the Christian Church will move away from the Sabbath, Paul's message of fulfillment and his story of God's faithfulness are not the soil in which we should expect discontinuity. If the seventh day is the sign of Creation, will some other day be the sign of redemption? The answer must be that such a change is inconceivable unless there has been a breach in the identity of God. If the Sabbath is the day of the Creator, will the Redeemer have another symbol?

On many points we are hampered by our limited ability to sort out the situation to which Paul is speaking. Two conclusions nevertheless are possible. In Colossians as a whole, the *sabbata* do not come straight from the Old Testament or from a simple Judaizing opponent. The traditional view is defective on this point. Even more important, we see Paul proclaiming that Christ the Restorer is also Christ the Creator, the one in whom "the whole fullness of deity dwells bodily" (2:9; cf. 1:19). Creation and Restoration will not be torn apart because Restoration proves the faithfulness of God. A clear-cut and definitive account of the *sabbata* in Colossians may be out of reach, but the weightiest affirmations of this letter are the ones of which the Sabbath is the sign.

If the Sabbath is the day of the Creator, will the Redeemer have another symbol?

ENDNOTES

1. Clinton E. Arnold, *The Colossian Syncretism* (Grand Rapids: Baker Books, 1996), 228.

2. See Peter T. O'Brien, *Colossians* (WBC; Waco: Word Books, 1982), xli–xlix; Arnold, *The Colossian Syncretism*, 6–7; Christian Stettler, "The Opponents at Colossae," in *Paul and His Opponents*, ed. Stanley Porter (Leiden: Brill, 2005), 169. Michael Prior (*Paul the Letter-Writer and the Second Letter to Timothy* [JSNT Sup 23; Sheffield: Sheffield Academic Press, 1989]) reviews in-depth the criteria used by scholars to determine Pauline authorship as part of his own investigation into the authorship of Second Timothy. He finds many of the methods used seriously flawed, urging that closer attention should be paid to the implications of co-authorship, the use of secretaries, and the great variety of situations addressed by the letters. His own conclusion is that Second Timothy, a letter often considered to be non-Pauline, not only is authentic but may in view of single authorship and its private character reflect Paul as much or more than the "authentic Paulines" as they are traditionally seen.

3. The triad is asymmetric because the first two members are singular whereas the reference to "sabbaths" (*sabbatōn*) is the genitive plural of *sabbaton*. In the following, the nominative

plural *sabbata* will be preferred.

4. F. C. Baur, "Die Christuspartei in der korintischen Gemeinde, der Gegensatz des petrinischen und paulinischen Christentums in der ältesten Kirche, der Apostel Petrus in Rom.," *Tübinger Zeitschrift für Theologie* 4 (1831): 61–206; idem, *Paul the Apostle of Jesus Christ, His Life and Work, His Epistles and His Doctrine*, 2 vols., trans. Eduard Zeller (London: Williams and Norgate, 1876 [repr. Eugene: Wipf and Stock, 2003]).

5. Baur's model is thoroughly influenced by Hegel's idealized notion of historical progress.

6. Jerry L. Sumney, *Identifying Paul's Opponents: The Question of Method in 2 Corinthians* (JSNT Sup 40; Sheffield: Sheffield Academic Press, 1990), 8–42; idem, *"Servants of Satan," "False Brothers" and Other Opponents of Paul* (JSNT Sup 188; Sheffield: Sheffield Academic Press, 1999), 1–32, 188–213; idem, "Studying Paul's Opponents: Advantages and Challenges," in *Paul and His Opponents*, ed. Stanley E. Porter (Leiden: Brill, 2005), 7–58.

7. Sumney, *Identifying Paul's Opponents*, 110–111.

8. Sumney, *Servants of Satan*, 190–191. Other important texts listed are Col. 2:4, 8, 16–18, 20–23 (explicit references); 1:9–10, 22–23; 2:2–3; 3:1–2 (allusions); 1:12–14; 2:9–10, 13–15 (affirmations); cf. *Servants of Satan*, 188–213.

9. While Paul refers to "the elemental spirits of the world" in Galatians (4:3) and to "the elemental spirits of the universe" in Colossians (2:8), the semblance of common ground takes on very different meanings in the respective letters.

10. Stettler, "The Opponents at Colossae," 169–200.

11. Ibid., 174.

12. Ibid.

13. Ibid., 177.

14. Ibid., 179, 182.

15. Ibid., 193.

16. Ibid., 196.

17. Richard E. DeMaris, *The Colossian Controversy: Wisdom in Dispute at Colossae* (JSNT Sup 96; Sheffield: Sheffield Academic Press, 1994), 56. Relevant passages in the LXX are Hos. 2:13; 1 Chron. 23:31; 2 Chron. 2:3; 31:3.

18. Kenneth A. Strand, "The Sabbath," in *Handbook of Seventh-day Adventist Theology*, ed. Raoul Dederen (Hagerstown, MD: Review and Hearald, 2000), 506.

19. Ron du Preez, *Judging the Sabbath: Discovering What Can't Be Found in Colossians 2:16* (Berrien Springs, MI: Andrews University Press, 2008), 85–128, especially pp. 95–107.

20. Ibid., 125.

21. Stettler, "The Opponents at Colossae," 182.

22. du Preez, *Judging the Sabbath*, 1–16.

23. The range of options as to potential opponents in Colossians must even reckon with the possibility that there were no opponents; cf. Morna D. Hooker, "Were There False Teachers in

Colossae?" in *Christ and the Spirit in the New Testament: In Honour of C. F. D. Moule*, ed. B. Lindars and S. Smalley (Cambridge: Cambridge University Press, 1973), 315–331.

24. Troy W. Martin, "But Let Everyone Discern the Body of Christ (Colossians 2:17)," *JBL* 114 (1995)" 249–255; idem, *By Philosophy and Empty Deceit: Colossians as Response to a Cynic Crititque* (JSNT Sup 118; Sheffield: Sheffield Academic Press, 1996).

25. Friedrich Büchsel, art. "*krinō*," *TDNT* 3:922–923.

26. A similar use of *krinein* is found in Rom. 14:13.

27. Martin, "But Let Everyone Discern the Body of Christ," 253.

28. Martin, *By Philosophy and Empty Deceit*, 133–134.

29. Ibid., 206.

30. M. Dibelius, "The Isis Initiation and Related Initiatory Rites," in *Conflict at Colossae*, ed. F. O. Francis and W. A. Meeks, rev. ed. (SBLSBS 4; Missoula, MT: Scolars Press, 1975), 61–121.

31. F. F. Bruce, *Paul: Apostle of the Heart Set Free* (Grand Rapids: Eerdmans, 1977), 413.

32. F. F. Bruce, *Commentary on the Epistle to the Colossians*, in *The New International Commentary on the New Testament* (Grand Rapids: Eerdmans, 1957), 166.

33. Eduard Schweizer, *Der Brief an die Kolosser* (EKKNT 12; Neukirchen: Benziger Verlag, 1976), 121.

34. Lohse, *TDNT*, art. "*sabbaton*," 30.

35. Eduard Lohse, *Die Briefe and die Kolosser und an Philemon* (Gottingen: Vandenhoeck & Ruprecht, 1968), 170–171.

36. Peter T. O'Brien, *Colossians, Philemon* (WBC; Waco: Word Books, 1982), 139.

37. Arnold, *The Colossian Syncretism*, 233.

38. Ibid., 310.

39. DeMaris, *The Colossian Controversy*, 16–17.

40. Sumney, "Studying Paul's Opponents," 51–58.

41. Arnold, *The Colossian Syncretism*, 215.

42. Joachim Gnilka, *Der Kolosserbrief* (Freiburg: Herder, 1980), 146; see also Arnold, *Colossian Syncretism*, 215.

43. Richard J. Bauckham, *God Crucified: Monotheism and Christology in the New Testament* (Carlisle: Paternoster Press, 1998), 31–32.

44. Bauckham, *God Crucified*, 36.

45. The notion that the Creator and the Redeemer is the same person is not unique to Colossians. It is implicit in Jesus's assertion in Mark that "the son of man is Lord of the sabbath" (Mark 2:28); in John with the claim that "all things were made through him, and without him was not anything made that was made" (John 1:3); in First Peter where Jesus "was destined *before the foundation of the world* but was made manifest at the end of the times for your sake" (1 Pet. 1:20); in Revelation, where Jesus is portrayed as "the Lamb that was slain *from the creation of the world*" (Rev. 13:8); and in Hebrews, where the connection between

creation and redemption explicitly incorporates the meaning and purpose of the seventh day (Heb. 4:3–4).

46. Sanders, *Paul and Palestinian Judaism*, 443.

47. Arnold, *The Colossian Syncretism*, 255.

48. Ibid.

49. Sanders, *Paul and Palestinian Judaism*, 443.

50. Harold Weiss (*A Day of Gladness: The Sabbath among Jews and Christians in Antiquity* [Columbia, SC: University of South Carolina Press, 2003], 134–136), following Troy Martin, also contests on syntactical grounds that the contrast in Colossians is between *skia* ("shadow") and *sōma* ("body").

51. Gnilka, *Kolosserbrief*, 147.

52. Gnilka (*Kolosserbrief*, 148) also suggests that the *soma* alludes to the church.

53. Martin, "But Let Everyone Discern the Body of Christ," 249, n. 1.

CHAPTER 15

THE REST THAT REMAINS

So then, a sabbath rest still remains for the people of God; for those who enter God's rest also cease from their labors as God did from his.
Hebrews 4:9–10

Chronologically speaking, the last explicit mention of the Sabbath in the New Testament is found in the book of Hebrews, a unique piece of writing that is better described as a sermon than as a letter.[1] It is the most polished piece of literature in the New Testament;[2] Luke Timothy Johnson calls it "one of the most beautifully written, powerfully argued, and theologically profound writings in the New Testament."[3] This "sermon" promptly brings up the Sabbath (Heb. 4:1–11), using it as an integral part of its overall message. The message, in turn, addresses people who are at risk of giving up. In order to reignite their resolve, Hebrews pulls out the "family album," so to speak—reviewing pictures of a long line of people, "an immense cloud of witnesses" (12:1),[4] who did not give up (11:4–40). At the end of the line, towering above the rest, stands Jesus. He, too, faced the temptation to give up (5:7; 12:2–3). Hebrews places the faithfulness of Jesus within the larger context of God's faithfulness, and in this book, too, the strongest incentive not to give up is the conviction that God is faithful (10:23).

While the affirmation of God's faithfulness is not unique to Hebrews, the sabbatarian emphasis is distinctive and conceptually demanding. We might say that the sermon draws a triangle: one corner marked "future," the second corner "past," and the third corner "present." The "future" refers to a promise unfulfilled and not yet in the possession of those who have staked their lives on it (11:10, 13–16, 39–40). The past looks to a work completed—indeed, a work "finished at the foundation of the world" (4:1–4). And what of the "present"? In Hebrews the "present" concentrates on a sabbatarian message, described as "a sabbath rest" that "still remains for the people of God" (4:9).

TO WHOM IT MAY CONCERN

Hebrews poses a unique challenge because there is no agreement among scholars as to authorship, audience, or occasion. Some have even suggested that Hebrews is the work of a woman, perhaps Paul's valued co-worker Priscilla (Acts 18:2, 18, 26; Rom. 16:3; 1 Cor. 16:9; 2 Tim. 4:19).[5] Even though there is much we do not know about the original audience, however, we know enough to benefit, and we know enough to say that we do not really need to nail down the specifics. The author exhorts the reader not to give up. We fairly hear the voice of the preacher, again and again, speaking directly to the listener with an immediacy that suggests a face-to-face encounter: "let us take care" (4:1); "let us...make every effort" (4:11); "let us hold fast" (4:14; 10:23); "let us go on" (6:1); "let us run with perseverance" (12:1); "let us then go to him" (13:13). Sometimes solemn, sometimes encouraging, and always with great feeling, the author wants the reader to persevere. "If one element serves to focus the overall paraenetic [exhortative] program of Hebrews it is the exhortation to be faithful," says Harold W. Attridge.[6]

A speaker who urges his audience not to give up would hardly say that unless he or she considered it a real possibility that people might give up or were actually doing so. Since little knowledge is available regarding the original context and situation, Hebrews becomes a message "to whom it may concern." The person to whom this message is addressed is one who is tempted to let go of his or her faith, whether for reasons of hardship or for reasons adding up to the possibility that the foundation of his or her commitment is not holding up.

HEBREWS AND THE IDENTITY OF JESUS

Perseverance is the take-home message of Hebrews, but human perseverance and faithfulness are not grounded in themselves. Hebrews presents a cascade of faithful witnesses that run through the sermon from start to finish. The ultimate witness in this cascade is Jesus (12:1), appearing at the far end of "a cloud of witnesses" consisting of famous and lesser known names from the Old Testament (3:1–6; 11:4–40). These witnesses lead up to His witness, and yet they also make His witness stand in a category of its own. Emphasizing continuity as well as distinctiveness, the sermon weaves a remarkable tapestry. The testimony of the witnesses points in the same direction, but the witness of Jesus is one of a kind.

Hebrews wastes no time getting to the most important subject, the question of Jesus and His identity. "In the past, God spoke at many times and in many ways to the fathers in the prophets. In these final days, he has spoken to us in a son, whom he has made heir of all things, through whom also he created the universe," reads the opening passage (1:1–2).[7] Even though some of the force and polish is lost in translation,[8] the main points are preserved. The speaker makes a distinction between past and present, casting the present as "these final days." We see God's ongoing communication with the human family, but a contrast is drawn that prioritizes God's revelation in Jesus. Other elements in the opening sentence enhance the contrast; in the past God has spoken through the prophets, but now God has spoken "in a son." The superiority of the "son" over other human beings through whom God has spoken must not be in doubt. Not only is the son "made heir of all things," but He is also the one through whom God "created the universe" (1:2). The testimony of Jesus stands apart from any other witness. It carries the weight of one who belongs to the identity of God.

The ultimate witness in this cascade is Jesus, appearing at the far end of "a cloud of witnesses" consisting of famous and lesser known names from the Old Testament.

Hebrews speaks at length about the identity and character of Jesus. Jesus is greater than the angels (1:4–14). He is greater than Moses (3:1–4). Moses was a servant in someone else's house (3:5), but Jesus is "a son over his own house" (3:6). Jesus is also a greater priest, of a different order than the priests from the tribe of Levi (7:1–25); He is "a high priest forever according to the order of Melchizedek" (6:20; 7:17).

The question of being, spelling out the identity of Jesus as one who bears "the radiance of [God's] glory and the imprint of [God's] fundamental reality" (1:3),[9] is not the whole story. The force and quality of Jesus's witness depend as much on His character as on His identity. Clarity with regard to Jesus's identity brings enormous prestige to Jesus, of course, but it is a two-way street. The radiance of His life bears the imprint of God's "fundamental reality," and yet access to the divine reality is now through Jesus. God's "fundamental reality" is encountered in the fully human reality of Jesus. As human beings "share flesh and blood, he himself likewise shared the same things" (2:14); indeed, "he had to become like his brothers and sisters in every respect" (2:17). The concept of faithfulness that is so important in the sermon presents Jesus as a human being whose faithfulness models faithfulness for others. "Because he himself was tested by what he suffered, he is able to help those who are being tested," says Hebrews (2:18). Human beings may at times despair and be in tears, and so was Jesus (5:7). The tapestry of faithfulness demonstrates an unbroken thread from the faithfulness of Jesus to human perseverance because the human experience of Jesus compasses the experience of ordinary human beings.

And yet Hebrews does not make Jesus's faithfulness grow only in the soil of His humanity. As we have seen already, there is more to the identity of Jesus than that of an exceptional human being. Jesus is the "merciful and faithful high priest" (2:17). Moses, too, "was faithful" (3:2, 5) "to testify to the things that would be spoken later" (3:5), but Christ "was faithful over God's house as a son" (3:6). Never slack in connecting Jesus's faithfulness and the believer's hope, Hebrews quickly adds that "we are his house if we hold firm the confidence and the pride that belong to hope" (3:6).

HEBREWS AND THE FAITHFULNESS OF GOD

All threads meet in the passage that in some interpreters' eyes epitomize the entire sermon.[10] "Let us hold fast to the confession of our hope without wavering, for he who has promised is faithful" (10:23; cf. 11:11). All the faces and facets of faithfulness and the "cloud of witnesses" that are yet to come (11:4–40) rest on the foundation of God's faithfulness. Attridge states that "[t]he basis for maintaining a confession of hope is that God is 'faithful.'"[11] Jesus has this in common with the "immense cloud of witnesses": He, too, staked His life on the faithfulness of God. But His life is nevertheless in a category of its own. God's faithfulness is attested by the faithfulness of Jesus in all its configurations. "The author shows forth Jesus as one who fully trusts in God (2:13a; cf. 5:7) as well as one who faithfully reflects God to humanity (1:3; 7:25; 9:24)," says Todd D. Still.[12]

Hebrews has yet fully to unfurl the background against which God's faithfulness in Jesus is affirmed. When Hebrews quotes the Old Testament prophet Habakkuk (10:37–38; cf. Hab. 2:2–4), it becomes clear that the affirmation of God's faithfulness is most needed when believers are weighed down with the sense of God's absence or with the sense of an inexplicable delay. We have not been far off the mark by believing that a speaker who makes "perseverance" his watchword must be speaking to a situation where there are strong inducements to give up, and we will not be surprised when he or she, facing such a situation, finds in Habakkuk a reason for comfort.

The affirmation of God's faithfulness is most needed when believers are weighed down with the sense of God's absence or with the sense of an inexplicable delay.

Habakkuk's voice is heard widely in the New Testament,[13] and we hear him again here: "For yet 'in a very little while, the one who is coming will come and will not delay; but my righteous one will live by faith. My soul takes no pleasure in anyone who shrinks back'" (Heb. 10:37–38; Hab. 2:3–4).

The Hebrew text of Habakkuk differs from the Greek translation that is used in Hebrews. Where the Hebrew text of Habakkuk says that "my righteous one shall live by his faithfulness," suggesting a Messianic connotation (Hab. 2:4, *BHS*),[14] the Greek text says that "the righteous shall live by my faithfulness" (Hab. 2:4, LXX). "My" is dropped before "righteous," but the pronoun is changed from the third to the first person, that is, from "*his* faithfulness" to "*my* faithfulness." In the Greek translation of Habakkuk, the faithfulness upon which the believer's hope rests is the faithfulness of God. In Hebrews, however, the phrase becomes ambiguous because "my" goes with "righteous one" and not with "faith(fulness)."[15] It is debatable whether the possessive "my" has been transposed in the sentence or whether it should also be inferred in the last part of the clause to read, "but my righteous one shall live by [my] faithfulness," a solution that resonates well with the Greek text of Habakkuk as well as with the context in Hebrews. What is not debatable, however, is that the affirmation in Hebrews rests on the rock of God's faithfulness. According to Attridge, "[t]he passage from Habakkuk, with its assurance of God's ultimate and decisive intervention into human affairs and its call for fidelity in the face of that eventual intervention, is particularly apt as a message for Jews or Christians with apocalyptic expectations who were troubled by the delayed arrival of the final act in the eschatological drama."[16]

As for Habakkuk so for the listeners to the sermon found in Hebrews: There appears to be a delay in the fulfillment of God's promise. Hope is growing dim, or, to a similar effect, the apparent delay draws the believer to other attractions.

But Hebrews has a different vantage point than Habakkuk. He could only see faintly, as a promise, the surpassing witness of Jesus. Hebrews admits that "we do not yet see all things put under [Jesus]" (2:8, NKJV) because we are still buffeted by temptation, injustice, or the glamour of the cities of this world. Jesus came, but things have not improved as expected; the hope is not fulfilled. Nevertheless, the pain is softened by what we do see, and "we do see Jesus" (2:9). The challenge is to keep on seeing Jesus, looking to Him who is "the pioneer and perfecter of our faith, who for the sake of the joy that was set before him endured the cross, disregarding its shame, and has taken his seat at the right hand of the throne of God" (12:2).[17]

This verse is crucial, and it looks in two directions. Jesus is the one who fully models faithfulness. Attridge says correctly that "the 'faith' [*pistis*] that Christ inaugurates and brings to perfect expression is not the content of Christian belief, but the fidelity and trust that he himself exhibited in a fully adequate way and that his followers are called upon to share."[18] And yet more must be said. Hebrews has not invested so much space and energy on the question of the identity of Jesus for nothing. Jesus is the cornerstone and capstone of the whole story; He is the one who makes God's faithfulness beyond doubt. The second affirmation is as important as the first because the most vexing question of human existence, in Habakkuk as in Hebrews and beyond, centers on the question of God's faithfulness.

THE REST THAT REMAINS

Why, in the context of its unremitting affirmation of God's faithfulness, does the sermon bring up the seventh day (4:4)? Why, while urging perseverance and faithfulness to the hope that depends on God's faithfulness, does the sermon turn to the Sabbath (4:9)?

The subject comes up immediately following the mention of God's faithful servant Moses and the faithfulness of Jesus (3:1–6). While Jesus is greater than Moses, Moses's testimony helps us understand what Jesus offers. A new exodus is underway, patterned upon the promise of deliverance from Egypt and the offer to enter God's rest (3:7–18). In the Old Testament story the Israelites experience God's faithfulness, but they do not reciprocate. Hebrews brings together seminal incidents in Israel's wilderness experience, quoting Psalm 95. The bottom line at the end of the forty years in the wilderness is that the people haven't learned to trust God, and as a result "They shall not enter my rest" (Heb. 3:11; Ps. 95:11; cf. Num. 14:23, 28–30).

The specific language is important because Hebrews does not say that "they cannot enter my *land*." It is "my *rest*" that is important, not "my land." In the Exodus story, too, people come to God (Exod. 19:4) and to God's rest (Exod. 16:22–30) before coming to the land. When Hebrews says that "they were unable to enter because of unbelief" (3:19), the emphasis is more on the people's self-imposed exclusion from God's rest than from the Promised Land.

The Sabbath is introduced at this point to shed light on the meaning of "my rest" (3:11; 4:3). The reference to Israel's wilderness wanderings gives way to an allusion to Genesis. Here the reference point for God's faithfulness is no longer Israel's experience after leaving Egypt but a point further back in time. The sermon describes Israel as excluded from God's rest even though "his works were finished at the foundation of the world" (4:3). This is both a reference to Creation, taken from the passage in which the Sabbath rest is instituted in Genesis (Gen. 2:1), and a reminder that the subject is still God's faithfulness.[19] Having determined that the believer's hope in Hebrews rests on God's faithfulness, it now appears that God's faithfulness is part and parcel of the message of the Sabbath. "For somewhere he has spoken about the seventh day in these words: 'And on the seventh day God rested from all his work,'" Hebrews continues (4:4, NIV).

Philip Edgecumbe Hughes notes that the "seemingly vague *somewhere* which introduces this Genesis quotation…is used here to signify a text that is well known."[20] The Sabbath is introduced as a well-known theme that gives the overriding argument more force. Moreover, the reference to the Sabbath is entirely positive, as Hebrews in general tends to be toward the Old Testament. As Richard Hays points out, "[a]t no point does Hebrews suggest that the [Old Testament] is legalistic, that it leads to self-righteousness, that its moral laws are in any way inadequate, or that its conception of God stands in need of correction."[21]

The reference to the Sabbath is entirely positive, as Hebrews in general tends to be toward the Old Testament.

Hebrews goes on to recall those who forfeited entry into the Promised Land because of distrust. Even those who enter the land under the leadership of Joshua fail to arrive at the promised destination. "For if Joshua had given them rest, God would not speak later about another day," says Hebrews (4:8), indicating that the entire project that began when Israel left Egypt still awaits completion. In fact, non-arrival and non-entry are mapped out in a series of verses repeating the fact (3:18–19; 4:1, 3[x2], 5–6, 10–11). This compositional feature "is a stunning example of repetitive texture giving thematic coherence to a passage, but even more significantly serving the ideological agenda of an author," says David A. deSilva.[22] Israel never truly arrived at the experience to which God wanted to lead them.

The completion of the journey to the Promised Land, when it comes, is described with reference to the Sabbath. "So then, a sabbath rest still remains for the people of God; for those who enter God's rest also cease from their labors as God did from his" (Heb. 4:9–10). The author could have written that "a *rest* [*katapausis*] still remains for the people of God," but instead, invoking a term that is found only this once in the Bible, the author writes that "a *sabbath* rest [*sabbatismos*] still remains" (4:9). The rest that is envisioned rises from the substrate of the Sabbath, going all the way back to Creation. The striking feature, of course, is that the Sabbath surfaces in the sermon as part and parcel of its message.

It might be sufficient to ascertain that Hebrews supports the connection between the Sabbath and the faithfulness of God. This means, on the one hand, that the Sabbath is a beacon to God's faithfulness and, on the other hand, that God's faithfulness inevitably compasses the Sabbath.[23] Reliability is the essence of God's faithfulness. Hebrews invokes the Sabbath as a way of highlighting God's reliability and constancy. "As both etymology and later attestations indicate, it is not simply a synonym for rest, but designates more comprehensively sabbath observance," says Attridge.[24]

From the point of view of human experience, the assertion that "a sabbath rest [*sabbatismos*] still remains for the people of God" (4:9) is suggestive. *Sabbatismos* is a new configuration in the Bible, a step beyond the familiar horizon. If, as noted above, the mention of the Sabbath conjures up a well-known subject, and if the true experience of the Sabbath rest never materialized in Israel, it is primarily the meaning of this rest that is at stake in Hebrews. The Sabbath rest "still remains" because it has not yet come to fruition in the experience of the believer. Hebrews gives us a ladder by which to come into possession of the promised experience.

There are at least three rungs on the ladder toward the experience to which Hebrews wants the reader to rise. The statement that God's work "was finished from the foundation of the world" is not hyperbole (4:3) and appears elsewhere in the New Testament.[25] In what way or what sense was God's work finished?

On this point Hebrews looks beyond the narratival and historical facts that are first apparent. With the naked eye we see the work of creation brought to completion on the seventh day in the Genesis story (Gen. 2:1–3), but with the inner eye Hebrews sees ultimate deliverance and restoration ensured even in the original intention of the seventh day. This aim was not executed, but it was intended; it was not implemented, but it was assured. Hebrews reveals that the gospel of redemption was already present in the Creation account, enshrined in the notion of God's rest in the face of a *completed* work. When Hebrews turns to the distant past in order to put the message of God's faithfulness on the firmest footing possible, it sees the present and the future enshrined in God's rest at Creation.

Hebrews invokes the Sabbath as a way of highlighting God's reliability and constancy.

On the horizontal axis the sweep of Hebrews is comprehensive—from the outer edge of the past all the way back to "the foundation of the world" (4:3) and from there all the way in the opposite direction to the outer boundary of the future. This is the second rung of the ladder. Christ, "having been offered once to bear the sins of many, will appear a second time, not to deal with sin, but to save those who are eagerly waiting for him" (9:28). All is not finished and complete. While the people on its long list of Old Testament witnesses all had faith and were faithful, they did not see their hope materialize any more than the believer in the present.

> All of these died in faith without having received the promises, but from a distance they saw and greeted them. They confessed that they were strangers and foreigners on the earth for people who speak in this way make it clear that they are seeking a homeland (11:13–14).

> But as it is, they desire a better country, that is, a heavenly one. Therefore God is not ashamed to be called their God; indeed, he has prepared a city for them (11:16).

> Yet all these, though they were commended for their faith, did not receive what was promised (11:39).

In these passages the attention is on the future, and the emphasis is on non-fulfillment, non-entry, and on a day that is yet to come. This is also the experience and outlook of Hebrews and its audience. "For here we have no lasting city, but we are looking for the city that is to come" (13:14). The Sabbath of the past reaches across the ages to clasp hands with the Sabbath of the future. The apparent tension between fulfillment that is assured by God's promise and non-fulfillment that is evident in the believer's experience is overcome because the Sabbath embodies the fulfillment of all. "Hebrews posits a symmetry in the activity of God," writes Koester. "If God's work culminated in a Sabbath rest at the dawn of time, Hebrews assumes that God's work will culminate in a Sabbath rest at the end of time."[26]

The eschatological leaning of Hebrews cannot be overemphasized. All the enlisted witnesses in the sermon are testimony as much to a hope unfulfilled as to the certainty of its fulfillment. "Yet all these, though they were commended for their faith, did not receive what was promised, since God had provided something better so that they would not, apart from us, be made perfect" (11:39–40). Without the future fulfillment the believer's hope will be suspended.

And yet, despite the make-it-or-break-it role of eschatology, the third rung on Hebrews' ladder speaks to an experience in the present. The Israelites had the door thrown open to them in their own time in the Old Testament, but "they were unable to enter because of unbelief" (3:19). This is the paramount lesson in Hebrews. Failure to enter then entails the risk of failure to enter now, in the present, as in the insistent urging of Hebrews:

The Sabbath of the past reaches across the ages to clasp hands with the Sabbath of the future.

> Therefore, as the Holy Spirit says, "Today, if you hear his voice, do not harden your hearts as in the rebellion, as on the day of testing in the wilderness, where your ancestors put me to the test, though they had seen my works for forty years" (3:7–10).
>
> As it is said, "Today, if you hear his voice, do not harden your hearts as in the rebellion" (3:15).
>
> again he sets a certain day—"today"—saying through David much later, in the words already quoted, "Today, if you hear his voice, do not harden your hearts" (4:7).

Today is the hinge of the sermon's concern and the hub of the wheel. When Hebrews says that "a sabbath rest still remains for the people of God" (4:9), it holds out an experience that is available in the present. It points the way, too, explaining that "those who enter God's rest also cease from their labors as God did from his" (4:10). Johnson sees this as a promise to have "a share in God's own way of existing."[27]

"But in what sense does God speak of 'my rest'?" asks Bruce. "Does it simply mean 'the rest which I bestow' or does it also mean 'the rest which I myself enjoy'?"[28] And he answers his own question unequivocally, "It means the latter: the 'rest' which God promises to His people is a share in that rest which He Himself enjoys."[29] Bruce thinks that the rest which "is reserved for the people of God is properly called a 'sabbath rest'—a *sabbatismos* or 'sabbath keeping'—because it is their participation in God's own rest."[30]

It is not easy to make the move from past to future and then to the present, the latter culminating in the ringing call to enter "*today*" (3:7, 15; 4:7). In an intriguing study, Hays characterizes the sermon as a "self-consuming artifact,"[31] attributing the notion to Stanley Fish's book, *Self-Consuming Artifacts*.[32] Fish describes two kinds of sermons. One kind "satisfies the needs of its readers" because it attempts no more than "to mirror and present for approval the opinions its readers already hold."[33] This kind of communication "tells the reader that what he has always thought about the world is true and that the *ways* of his thinking are sufficient."[34]

The other kind of sermon, however, "requires of its readers a searching and rigorous scrutiny of everything they believe in and live by."[35] This type of literature or sermon "does not preach the truth but asks that its readers discover the truth for themselves, and this discovery is often made at the expense not only of a reader's opinions and values, but of his self-esteem."[36] If the audience feels flattered and affirmed by the first type of sermon, it feels humiliated and bewildered after the second type. Moreover, there is a therapeutic undercurrent in the second type; its modus is "less one of speaker to hearer, or author to reader than of physician to patient."[37] It invites the readers "to reconsider the terms—to rethink what they thought about reality, particularly about the relation between Israel's God and self-satisfying religion."[38]

Most significant, however, is not the fact that the sermon assumes that the views and convictions of its audience need overhauling. The greater surprise is the realization that the sermon thinks the same about itself; it does not wish to draw attention to itself or to see itself as an adequate and final solution. "A self-consuming artifact signifies most successfully when it fails," says Fish, "when it points away from itself to something its forms cannot capture."[39] In the case of Hebrews, as Hays applies this insight, the sermon enables the reader to see beyond it, leading "the reader beyond its own rhetoric to an encounter with the living God."[40] The author, whether Paul, Priscilla, or someone else, leads the reader by way of the Sabbath to know the faithfulness of God, and beyond, consuming itself in the endeavor to point the way to the rest that "still remains for the people of God" (4:9). In the triangle of Hebrews, past, present, and future are a seamless whole, and the temporal horizon of the sermon definitely looks to a point in the future for the fulfillment of the believer's hope. But the starting point of the Sabbath rest envisioned in Hebrews is "today" (3:7–10, 15; 4:7).

The starting point of the Sabbath rest envisioned in Hebrews is "today."

ENDNOTES

1. William Johnsson (*In Absolute Confidence: The Book of Hebrews Speaks to Our Day* [Nashville: Southern Publishing Association, 1979], 13–15) neatly summarizes the arguments for seeing the book as a sermon. More recent scholarship has not altered this view of the book's genre.

2. Luke Timothy Johnson, *Hebrews: A Commentary* (NTL; Louisville: Westminster John Knox Press, 2006), 8–9.

3. Johnson, *Hebrews*, 1.

4. The translation is that of Harold W. Attridge (*A Commentary on the Epistle to the Hebrews* [Hermeneia; Philadelphia: Fortress Press, 1989], 354).

5. Cf. Craig R. Koester, *Hebrews: A New Translation with Introduction and Commentary* (AB; New York: Doubleday, 2001), 45. Pauline authorship remains a possibility but not with the certainty suggested by the King James Version, "the Epistle of Paul the Apostle to the Hebrews."

6. Attridge, *Hebrews*, 22.

7. The translation is taken from Johnson (*Hebrews*, 63).

8. The opening sentence of Hebrews extends over four entire verses in Greek, which are not easily broken down into good English. Attridge (*Hebrews*, 35) offers a translation that

goes a long way toward preserving the flavor of the original sermon without compromising clarity. "Having spoken of old in multiple forms and multiple fashions to the fathers through the prophets, in these final days God has spoken to us through a Son, whom he established as heir of all things, through whom he also created the universe, who, being the radiance of his glory and the imprint of his fundamental reality, bearing all things by his powerful word, having made purification for sins, took a seat at the right hand of the Majesty on high, having become as far superior to the angels as he has inherited a name more excellent than they" (Heb. 1:1–4).

9. Translation modified from Attridge (*Hebrews*, 35).

10. Johnsson, *In Absolute Confidence*, 25; cf. also Philip Edgecumbe Hughes, *A Commentary on the Epistle to the Hebrews* (Grand Rapids: Eerdmans, 1977), 414; Attridge, *Hebrews*, 289.

11. Attridge, *Hebrews*, 289.

12. Todd D. Still, "*Christos* as *Pistos*: The Faith(fulness) of Jesus in the Epistle to the Hebrews," paper presented at the Conference on Hebrews and Christian Theology, University of St. Andrews, July, 2006, p. 8.

13. Note key texts like Rom. 1:16–17; Gal 3:11; 2 Thess 2:3–12; Rev 6:10.

14. Richard B. Hays, "'The Righteous One' as Eschatological Deliverer: A Case Study in Paul's Apocalyptic Hermeneutics," in *Apocalyptic and the New Testament: Essays in Honor of J. Louis Martyn*, eds. Joel Marcus and Marion L. Soards (JSNT Sup 24; Sheffield: Sheffield Academic Press, 1989), 191–215.

15. See note by Attridge (*Hebrews*, 303).

16. Attridge, *Hebrews*, 303.

17. Ibid., 22.

18. Ibid., 356.

19. Thus Koester (*Hebrews*, 277) states, "Those addressed by Hebrews were facing an issue that, from the author's point of view, had to do with God's faithfulness."

20. Hughes, *Hebrews*, 159.

21. Hays, "'Here We Have No Lasting City': New Covenantalism in Hebrews," Conference on Hebrews and Christian Theology, St. Andrews, Scotland, July 19, 2006, p. 5.

22. David A. deSilva, *Perseverance in Gratitude: A Socio-Rhetorical Commentary on the Epistle "to the Hebrews"* (Grand Rapids: Eerdmans, 2000), 153.

23. Herold Weiss, "'*Sabbatismos'* in the Epistle to the Hebrews," *CBQ* 58 (1996): 685.

24. Attridge, *Hebrews*, 130; cf. also F. F. Bruce, *The Epistle to the Hebrews* (NICNT; Grand Rapids: Eerdmans, 1964), 74.

25. Matt. 13:35; 25:34; John 17:24; Eph. 1:4; 1 Pet. 1:20; Rev. 13:8; 17:8.

26. Koester, *Hebrews*, 279; cf. also Bruce, *Hebrews*, 78; deSilva, *Perseverance in Gratitude*, 163.

27. Johnson, *Hebrews*, 122.

28. Bruce, *Hebrews*, 73.

29. Ibid.

30. Ibid., 77.

31. Hays, "New Covenantalism in Hebrews," 20–26.

32. Stanley Fish, *Self-Consuming Artifacts: The Experience of Seventeenth-Century Literature* (Berkeley: University of California Press, 1972). Fish discusses Plato's *Phaedrus*, Augustine's *On Christian Doctrine*, and examples from the seventeenth-century authors Donne, Herbert, Bunyan, and Milton.

33. Fish, *Self-Consuming Artifacts*, 1.

34. Ibid.

35. Ibid.

36. Ibid., 1–2.

37. Ibid., 2.

38. Hays, "New Covenantalism in Hebrews," 25.

39. Fish, *Self-Consuming Artifacts*, 4.

40. Hays, "New Covenantalism in Hebrews," 23.

CHAPTER 16

FROM SABBATH TO SUNDAY

The stream of divine life in its passage from the mountain of inspiration to the valley of tradition is for a short time lost to our view, and seems to run under ground.
Philip Schaff

The Sabbath amasses an immense portfolio of meaning in the Old Testament, with one meaning towering above the rest. Whether as narrative, commandment, or promise, the weekly Sabbath affirms the reliability of God. Neither the broad portfolio of meaning nor the specific focus on God's faithfulness is diminished by Jesus or by the writings of the New Testament. In light of the message that is thus centered on the faithfulness of God, we should not expect the Church to abandon the seventh day.

History springs a surprise on the student in this respect. The religion that receives its name from Jesus Christ does not retain the Sabbath. In this and the following chapters, glimpses of this history and its attendant ideology will be reviewed. This, of course, is not an easy task. It is insufficient merely to unearth the fact of Sunday's ascent at the expense of the Sabbath. The penchant to consider the Sabbath and Sunday apart from their respective portfolios of meaning introduces a distortion that is alien to the character of the subject. When the Sabbath goes into eclipse, it is necessary to ask questions like the following: What happened to its portfolio of meaning? Did Sunday assume the massive portfolio? Could the meanings hitherto invested in the Sabbath realistically be outsourced to another entity?

Whether as narrative, commandment, or promise, the weekly Sabbath affirms the reliability of God.

When we define the task this way, the subject necessarily becomes much larger. For instance, the Christian outlook will adopt a view of the human person, the earth, and of non-human creation quite different from the outlook that belongs to the seventh day. It truncates the subject to trace the fate for the Sabbath without also pursuing the loss of these meanings, or, to see it from the opposite direction, without looking at forces and "meanings" that proved inimical to the survival of the Sabbath. While our aspiration in this respect must be modest, almost on the level of bullet points and suggestions for further inquiry, the subject is more fairly served by highlighting some items that belong to the Sabbath's portfolio of meaning than by proceeding as though there is no portfolio to consider.

A COMPLEX PICTURE

Sunday's eclipse of the Sabbath comes early, at least by the witness of some well-placed sources,[2] and the eclipse has generally been seen as inescapable and nearly total. Describing the notion of inevitability tongue-in-cheek, David Flusser says that it was "clear from the beginning that the Sabbath could not be accepted as a Christian holiday, as it was—and is—one of the central phenomena of the Jewish 'legalism.'"[3] This verdict takes it for granted that Judaism was at heart legalistic, and that all Christians saw Sabbath observance as legalism. If that is true, it seems strange that the Sabbath was partially observed by Christians as late as the fourth century.[4]

But was the issue legalism? Conceding that the New Testament exposes a conflict between Jesus and Jewish religious leaders of His day, the issue is better described as a problem of exclusivity than as legalism.[5] The idea that the Sabbath is a burden is not supported by the biblical evidence, and it is simplistic to assume that the Sabbath was perceived as a yoke in the Jewish experience.[6]

We must also ask whether Jewish Sabbath observance represented God's intent. In the ministry of Jesus God's intent is to be revealed (John 5:17–19). The intent thus revealed with respect to the Sabbath takes precedence over Jewish ideals and practice in Jesus's day. Indeed, while Christian scholarship and church tradition see and accept discontinuity between Christianity and Judaism, there has been little willingness to consider the possibility of discontinuity between Jesus and Christianity.

The eclipse of the Sabbath should *not* be treated as a foregone conclusion. Earlier studies have been hampered by facile views of uniform practice in the Christian community, and, as to the origin of Sunday, by extrapolating later practice backwards to New Testament texts. These texts hardly hold up under the weight made to rest on them.[7] Gerard Rouwhorst sees scholarship on early Christianity slowly coming to realize that early Christianity must be seen as a diverse and complex phenomenon in which the influence of Judaism was felt to varying degrees, and in important places was barely felt at all.[8] Just as it falls to the victor to write the history of what happened, the victor "remembers" the past in a way that gives preferential treatment to evidence that favors his or her stance.

The bias of history written from the point of view of the victor has been felt to the full in the Christian view of Jewish belief. Only now, at the beginning of the twenty-first century, do we see large-scale studies trying to correct misrepresentations of the Jewish legacy and to temper Christian triumphalism.[9] And yet even the most earnest effort in this respect finds it hard to rid itself of this very triumphalism. As a case in point, noting that Paul remained a Jew after coming to faith in Jesus, one contributor to the study referenced above holds that Paul "had a *relaxed* attitude to the observance of days and feasts."[10] The metaphor suggests that the subject is a matter of indifference and that those who are not "relaxed" have missed the point. It seems more likely that the person who has "a relaxed attitude" is the evangelical author in the twenty-first century, attributing his own attitude to Paul. Taking a casual stance toward the subject assumes that Judaism is a legalistic religion because it does not take a relaxed attitude toward the Sabbath. In view of these and other potential sources of bias, it might be wise to withhold judgment as to whether Paul was similarly detached.

Conversely, but equally telling as to how rhetoric reveals the stance of the victor, Jewish Christians who refused to give up the observance of the Sabbath, like the Ebionites, are characterized as "fanatical" whereas converts from paganism who were attracted to the Sabbath are dismissed as "superstitious."[11]

We may nevertheless give three elements the status of facts. Despite evidence of continued Sabbath observance in the church for several centuries, as in Syria, Egypt, and Ethiopia, it is indisputable that the trend is lopsided in favor of Sunday from the middle of the second century CE.[12]

Second, the rise of Sunday remains shrouded in mystery. In an early study, Selby Vernon McCasland predicted that "[t]he obscurity surrounding the origin of a weekly celebration of Sunday as the chief day of worship in the early church will probably never be fully removed."[13] This sentiment has stood the test of time. "Nowhere do we find any evidence which would unambiguously establish where, when and why the Christian observance of Sunday arose," Willy Rordorf writes thirty years later.[14] New and valuable insight into the life of the early Church has come to light, but on this point little has changed. "Every attempt to find an explication for the origins of Christian Sunday necessarily remains speculative," Rouwhorst concedes in his review of scholarship at the beginning of the new millennium.[15]

Third, there is scant evidence that the change from Sabbath to Sunday involved a wrenching decision in the Early Church. Manuscript evidence demonstrates points of ambiguity and complexity that were previously unrecognized.[16] Rouwhorst believes it "very likely that in the first Christian communities the Sabbath observance became time and again a matter of discussion," counting on passages in the letters of Paul to support this view.[17] Nevertheless, the relative lack of controversy is remarkable. Theologians in the second century debate a host of issues, but the Sabbath is not one of them. As the Church increasingly embraces Sunday, the Sabbath sinks into oblivion almost unnoticed, unaccompanied by prior decision or even significant deliberation.[18] This shift can no longer be treated as inevitable, but the ease with which it appears to have happened cries out for a broader accounting.

As the Church increasingly embraces Sunday, the Sabbath sinks into oblivion almost unnoticed.

THE END OF JEWISH INFLUENCE

What transpired in the minds of Christians in the second century as they gradually abandoned the Sabbath remains obscure, but we do have some evidence. "But Sunday is the day on which we all hold our common assembly because it is the first day on which God, having wrought a change in the darkness and matter, made the world; and Jesus Christ our Savior on the same day rose from the dead,"[19] Justin Martyr writes near the middle of the second century, in one of the earliest records of Sunday's eclipse of the Sabbath. And in *The Epistle of Ignatius to the Magnesians*, Ignatius, bishop in Antioch in the first decade of the second century, writes that "those who were brought up in the ancient order of things have come to the possession of a new hope, no longer observing the Sabbath, but living in the observance of the Lord's Day, on which also our life has sprung up again by Him and by His death."[20] The "old" must give way to the "new" because the old order was temporary and inferior. Ignatius speaks of an emerging identity, one ingredient of which is that his community is no longer "observing the Sabbath."

Apparently the Jewish connection is severed. Additional factors showing increasing distance between Jews and Christians, including diminished Jewish influence in the Christian community, confirm this impression. This holds true especially with respect to what transpired in Jerusalem and at Rome.

In Jerusalem, where the Christian community must have included mainly believers from a Jewish background, the two Jewish uprisings against the Romans, in 66–70 and again in 132–135 CE, had devastating consequences. Not only did the religious leadership have to relocate, but the first war decimated the Jewish population.[21] This reduced the influence of the Jewish-Christian community within the wider Christian movement. After ruthlessly crushing the Bar-Kokhba revolt (132–135),[22] the Roman government imposed harsh restrictions on the Jews throughout the empire. Both Jews and Jewish customs were banned in the new city the Romans built on the ruins of Jerusalem.[23]

Inevitably, church leadership fell to Gentile Christians, accelerating the move away from anything perceived to be "Jewish." The gulf between Jews and Gentiles in the church widened. Oskar Skarsaune says that in Israel, "possibly more than anywhere else, Jewish and Gentile believers in Jesus were living apart from each other. There were probably no mixed communities in the land."[24] Thus, on the one hand, Jewish Christians did not have to adapt their lifestyle in order to enjoy community with Gentile believers, and, on the other hand, Jewish influence on the Gentile Christian community was almost non-existent.

Rome is another case in point. Samuele Bacchiocchi argues that the change from Sabbath to Sunday did not originate in the community of Jewish Christians in Jerusalem, but in Rome.[25] Roman influence may be overstated in the sense that there is no church decision on record that allows a positive statement to this effect. There is, however, evidence that the Church of Rome early on lost its sense of a Jewish connection. In *1 Clement*, an early Christian document originating in Rome no later than very early in the second century, there is no sense of either indebtedness to or conflict with Judaism. "Thus *1 Clement* seems to reflect a situation in the Roman church when there was no living memory of a conflict with the Jewish community (almost 50 years earlier), and probably no direct contact with the synagogues. The heritage from the synagogues had been 'domesticated' and taken for granted, but its source seems to have been forgotten," says Reidar Hvalvik in a detailed study.[26]

This is astonishing because there is ample evidence that the Roman church originated within the Jewish community.[27] How members in this community became Christians is not known, but it must have happened early—so early, in fact, that the Jewish connection is the only one plausible. What is more remarkable, however, is that by the turn of the century, the context of *1 Clement*, Jewish elements and awareness of Jewish roots seem obliterated. "So directly is the Old Testament applied to the Church that the author betrays no awareness of a radical new beginning, a new covenant established by Christ; no awareness of the deep disruption between the Christian community and Jewish people," says Skarsaune of the sentiment expressed in *1 Clement*.[28] Indeed, in the Christian community in Rome, the Sabbath is degraded to an anti-Jewish day of fasting.[29]

If ambiguity is precluded in the Christian community in Rome early in the second century, evidence from other areas in the Roman Empire tells a different story. Casting a broad net, scholars recognize pervasive Jewish influence on Christian worship practices such as the reading of Scripture and the Eucharist.[30] But there is also evidence in selected sources of a lingering affection for the Sabbath long after the issue appears to be resolved for Christians in Rome and elsewhere. In the seventh book of the Apostolic Constitutions, dating from the end of the fourth century, polemics against the Sabbath are absent; indeed, the Sabbath narrative of the Old Testament is fondly rehearsed.[31] Imagine hearing this prayer recited in a Christian Church toward the end of the fourth century!

> Lord, almighty, you created the world through Christ
> and set apart the Sabbath to remember this
> —because on it you rested from (your) works
> —for meditation on your laws,
> and you ordained feasts for the gladdening of our souls,
> so that we may be reminded of the Wisdom created by you (7.36.1).
>
> You gave them the Law of ten oracles
> clearly expressed by your voice and written by your hand.
> You commanded (them) to keep the Sabbath,
> not giving a pretext for idleness but an opportunity for piety,
> for the knowledge of your power, for prevention of evil (7.36.4).
>
> For the Sabbath is rest from creation,
> the completion of the world,
> the seeking of laws,
> the thankful praise to God for (those things) which were
> given to men (7.36.5).[32]

The blessings in this document correspond to the Jewish Sabbath blessings, the order is the same, negative references to the Sabbath from the earlier document on which the Apostolic Constitutions is patterned have been omitted, and a specific Sabbath blessing has been inserted.[33] Indeed, the document includes what is best seen as a later interpolation, its polemical tone awkward in a prayer, to the effect that the believers must not overestimate the Sabbath at the expense of Sunday.[34]

> All of which [what has been affirmed concerning the Sabbath]
> the Lord's day surpasses,
> pointing to the Mediator himself,
> the Lawgiver, the Cause of resurrection,
> the Firstborn of all creation,
> God the Word and a man born of Mary,
> the only begotten without a man,
> the one who lived a holy life;
> who was crucified under Pontius Pilate
> and died and rose from the dead.
> The Lord's day was commanded by you, Master,
> to offer thanks for all (these) things (7.36.6).[35]

From the vantage point of the original version, there can be little doubt that the resounding affirmation of the Sabbath is primary, and that the prayer from the beginning sees Christ in the Sabbath narrative. In the version available to us, Sunday is said to surpass the Sabbath, but the passage seems strained; it has a me-too flavor, a Johnny-come-lately, indicative of later polemics.

Rouwhorst suggests two possible explanations for the exceptionally positive attitude toward the Sabbath on the part of some Christians. One possibility is that they "wanted to remain faithful to the oldest ritual tradition they had received from the first missionaries."[36] Faithfulness in this respect may have been facilitated by relative isolation from the rest of the world. The other possibility is that the Christians in question "were more acquainted and familiar with Jewish liturgical traditions than those living in other areas."[37] In any event, the Christian affirmation of the Sabbath seems to be rooted in a deep stratum that is respectful of the Jewish legacy.

It is against the background of the resilient appeal of Jewish practice that we must understand the attempts on the part of leading Christians to diminish the allure of the Jewish system. In contrast to the situation at Rome, when leaders of the Church in Asia Minor launch a frontal assault on Jewish belief and practice in the fourth century, it indicates an ongoing relationship and enduring points of contact that the Christian leader finds troubling. John Chrystostom (347–407), archbishop of Constantinople, is determined to wean Christians from their regard for anything Jewish and to end the connection between the Church and the synagogue.

There can be little doubt that the resounding affirmation of the Sabbath is primary.

While still in Antioch, in 386, John Chrystostom began a series of sermons against Christian "Judaizers" that would become an enduring reservoir of Christian invective and hostility against the Jews. The sermons must be understood in their context—one part of which is to recognize that their disparagement of the Jews is possible only where the attitude they represent has been long in the making. But the context also speaks of ongoing and friendly relations between Christians and the Jewish synagogue. Christians were attending the synagogue, fellowshipping with the Jews on the Sabbath, and participating in Jewish religious festivals.[38] John would not mince words in his determination to end the connection.

"Many, I know, respect the Jews and think their present way of life a venerable one" (*Jud.* 1.3.1) even to the point of considering the Jews "as more trustworthy teachers than their fathers" (*Jud.* 3.6.6), he says, clearly implying that Christians who are thus disposed are holding the Jews in undeservedly high esteem.[39] The rhetoric quickly becomes more inflammatory. Christians in John's audience are lambasted because "you observe with them [the Jews] the fellowship of the festivals, you go to their profane places, enter their unclean doors, share in the table of demons" (*Jud.* 1.7.5).[40] Little is held back here; the religious gatherings of the Jewish community in Antioch are now "profane places," "unclean doors," even "the table of demons." Indeed, his aim is announced from the start in his first sermon.

> Another very serious illness calls for any cure my words can bring, an illness which has become implanted in the body of the Church....What is this sickness? The festivals of the pitiful and miserable Jews are soon to march upon us one after the other in quick succession: the feast of Trumpets, the feast of Tabernacles, the fasts. There are many in our ranks who say they think as we do. Yet some of these are going to the festivals and others will join the Jews in keeping their feasts and observing their fasts. I wish to drive this perverse custom from the Church right now (Jud. 1.1.4; 1.1.5).[41]

His intent thus stated, John proceeds to deliver his goods, blow by intentionally painful blow. He deploys the metaphor of disease and sickness, as shown in the example above; he calls the Jews "wild beasts" bent on destroying the flock (*Jud.* 4.1.1); he impugns them for impiety and drunkenness, meaning the impiety that is implicit in their belief and drunkenness as a way of demeaning their practice (*Jud.* 8.1.1).[42]

In reality, there are no wild beasts in sight, no Jew intending to prey on the Christian community or even to influence it. As Wilken notes, "it is not likely that the Jews were pursuing the Christians; indeed it was the Christians who were willingly seeking out the Jews."[43] John's rhetoric does not reflect reality; it is rhetoric aiming to create a new reality, sowing seeds of disparagement and hostility against the Jews, perhaps even reflecting the Christians' newfound position of strength by the fact that the emperor Theodosius just at that time proclaimed Christianity the official religion of the Empire. Toward this end, operating within the rules of rhetoric of his day, John effectively deploys "half-truths, innuendo, guilt by association, abusive and incendiary language, malicious comparisons, and in all, excess and exaggeration."[44] The most deadly weapon was yet to come because John would not be content to describe the Jews of Jesus's day as "Christ-killers." Time, place, and situation are swept aside by the rhetorical avalanche; the "Christ-killers" are in their midst in the form of the person of the Jewish believer and in the form of the Jewish synagogue (*Jud.* 1.5.1).

There is no evidence that John Chrysostom meant to unleash violence against the Jews, but hints of a tendency in this direction have been found in his day.[45] To Wilken, indeed, to anyone, this should not come as a surprise. In view of the hate-filled rhetoric, "surely something of this charged and emotive language must have passed into the attitudes of the people toward one another and their relations with one another."[46]

With regard to the Sabbath, there can be no doubt that the conflict between Jews and Christians accelerated the Sabbath's loss of prestige. When Sunday was substituted for the Sabbath, it was the visible sign of Christianity's abandonment of Judaism, or, more precisely, "the sign of the end of the determining influence of Jewish Christians on the Christian faith."[47]

Other factors were also working in favor of a move away from practices perceived to be Jewish. When the emperor Constantine came to power, the Christian community enjoyed a change of fortune with wide-ranging consequences. All of a sudden the Christians achieved privileges traditionally reserved for pagans.[48] It became easier to take the step of joining the church. Constantine's predecessor Diocletian (284–305) took upon himself the dignity of a god in order to try to strengthen people's devotion to the imperial power.[49] Constantine also used religion, in his case Christianity, to bolster his power, taking the role of divinely appointed vice-regent.

There can be no doubt that the conflict between Jews and Christians accelerated the Sabbath's loss of prestige.

By then Sunday had had both pagan and Christian proponents for centuries. Through the influence of Mithraism, beginning at least one hundred years prior to Christianity, the notion of Sunday sacredness was spreading all the way to Rome.[50] Gaston

H. Halsberghe shows that "from the early part of the second century A.D., the cult of *Sol Invictus* was dominant in Rome and in other parts of the Empire."[51] The sun cult persisted longer and had a greater influence than historians and philologists have granted. Significantly, Halsberghe notes that the cult was second only to the influence of the eclectic Neo-Platonic school, another influence that could only accelerate the trend away from the earth-affirming view of reality that dominates the Old Testament. During the rule of Constantine the sun cult reached extraordinary heights. Following his conversion it waned gradually, leaving a permanent imprint on European culture, one example of which is Christmas.

Along with sun worship came the planetary week and a special day dedicated to the sun, dies solis, or Sunday. Jürgen Moltmann suggests that March 3, 312, be considered the "birthday" of Sunday as a state day of rest, referring to a letter from the emperor Constantine to the official A. Helpidius bearing that date. In this letter, the emperor urged that "all judges, townspeople and all occupations should rest on the most honourable day of the sun."[52] This helps to explain the rapidly rising trajectory of Sunday. Unfamiliar with the Old Testament and unimpressed by the way the message about Jesus was received in the synagogue, the Church, now adjusting to the overtures of the state, found it easy to replace the Sabbath with the day of the sun. Without much effort the latter was remodeled into a memorial to the resurrection. What better day than that, and what better way since Sunday was already held in high esteem by the Romans?[53] It is doubtful that Sunday could have taken hold so extensively without the prior conditioning. In view of the widespread influence of the sun cult there is no basis for Oscar Cullmann's assertion that Sunday is "a specifically Christian festival day."[54]

LESS TANGIBLE FORCES

The foregoing has examined evidence that is available "above ground," beginning with the uncontested fact that the Christian

Church left the seventh day behind and grounded in the conviction, held less widely,[55] that the change from Sabbath to Sunday marked a profound change. But other factors must have come into play as well. Even historians who have grappled with this era have found it necessary to invoke hidden factors, or at least to acknowledge that we are studying the working of forces that are elusive and obscure. Philip Schaff, looking at the transition from the apostolic age to the second century, expresses a view that captures the striking change even though many will no longer accept his premise.

> The hand of God has drawn a bold line of demarcation between the century of miracles and the succeeding ages, to show, by the abrupt transition and striking contrast, the difference between the work of God and the work of man, and to impress us the more deeply with the supernatural origin of Christianity and the incomparable value of the New Testament. There is no other transition in history so radical and sudden, yet so silent and secret. The stream of divine life in its passage from the mountain of inspiration to the valley of tradition is for a short time lost to our view, and seems to run under ground.[56]

Schaff's convictions are less widely accepted today, but the view of this once highly respected Protestant historian deserves a hearing. When he compares the New Testament to literature immediately succeeding it, he sees "a bold line of demarcation," an "abrupt transition and striking contrast," indeed, a transition so drastic that "there is no other transition in history so radical and sudden." And yet he cannot tell us how it happened because the change is "silent and secret," like a stream disappearing underground.

Above ground we see a rift between Christians and Jews; we see Christian anti-Judaism increasing, and we see Christians "no longer observing the Sabbath, but living in the observance of the Lord's Day."[57] Above ground, the Jewish connection disappears abruptly, as evidenced by *1 Clement*, leaving even the scholar puzzled.[58] Above ground, we hear the voice of John Chrysostom, interpreting Paul in

Galatians to the effect that Paul urges them "to scorn the sabbath" (*Jud.* 3.3.1),[59] and calling heaven and earth to witness against the members of his church in Antioch that if any of them "share in the Sabbath, or observe any other Jewish ritual great or small," he considers himself guiltless of their blood (1.8.1).[60] That something is changing, viewing this period from the vantage point of the results, is also evident when Peter Brown writes that the conversion of Constantine in 312 "might not have happened—or, if it had, it would have taken on a totally different meaning—if it had not been preceded, for two generations, by the conversion of Christianity to the culture and ideals of the Roman world."[61] Nevertheless it is change that exceeds the explanatory power of the factors operating "above ground."

The notion of factors operating "below ground" is closely related to the idea that the Sabbath carries a portfolio of meanings. If, for instance, a member of this "portfolio of meanings" is ill matched to the changing reality, it might also endanger the entity that holds the portfolio. It is not farfetched to look for less tangible factors to drive the move away from the Old Testament Sabbath. Underneath the surface, as it were, a gulf has been opening between the outlook of the Old and the New Testament and the worldview of leading Christians in the second century that disables the Sabbath as much or more than anti-Jewish sentiment. We must therefore open up to the possibility that a new symbol emerges because the Christians' perception of reality—the very foundation ground of their understanding of the world—is changing. Indeed, it is misleading to divide the forces that are driving the eclipse of the Sabbath into forces operating below ground and above ground when one of the forces of change is the ground itself.

ENDNOTES

1. Philip Schaff, *History of the Christian Church,* vol. 2 (New York: Charles Scribner's Sons, 1910; Grand Rapids: Eerdmans, 1970), 7.

2. Ignatius, *To the Magnesians* 8:10, *ANF* 1:62–63; Justin Martyr, *First Apology*, 67, *ANF* 1:186.

3. David Flusser, "Tensions Between Sabbath and Sunday," in *The Jewish Roots of*

Christian Liturgy, ed. Eugene J. Fisher (New York: Paulist Press, 1990), 143.

4. Ibid.

5. Sanders, *Paul, the Law and the Jewish People*, 155; Fredriksen, "Judaism, the Circumcision of Gentiles, and Apocalyptic Hope," 239–241.

6. Gerard Rouwhorst, "The Reception of the Jewish Sabbath in Early Christianity," in *Christian Feast and Festival*, ed. P. Post, G. Rouwhorst, L. van Tongeren, A. Scheer (Louvain: Peeters, 2001), 243; cf. also Isidoro Kahn, "Jewish Sabbath" in *The Jewish Roots of Christian Liturgy*, ed. Eugene J. Fisher (New York: Paulist Press, 1990), 121–129.

7. A case in point is Ernest Haag's use of 1 Cor. 16:2; Acts 20:7; and Rev 1:10; cf. *Vom Sabbat zum Sonntag: Eine bibeltheologische Studie* (Trier: Paulinus Verlag, 1991), 174–180.

8. Gerard Rouwhorst, "Continuity and Discontinuity Between Jewish and Christian Liturgy," *Bijdragen, tijdschrift voor filosofie en theologie* 54 (1993): 72–83; idem, "Jewish Liturgical Traditions in Early Syriac Christianity," *VC* 51 (1997): 72–93; idem, "Liturgical Time and Space in Early Christianity in Light of Their Jewish Background," in *Sanctity of Time and Space in Tradition and Modernity*, ed. A Houtman, M. J. H. M. Poorthuis, J. Schwartz (Leiden: Brill, 1998), 265–284; idem, "The Reception of the Jewish Sabbath in Early Christianity," 223–266; idem, "The Reading of Scripture in Early Christian Liturgy," in *What Athens Has to Do with Jerusalem: Essays on Classical, Jewish, and Early Christian Art and Archaeology in Honor of Gideon Foerster*, ed. Leonard V. Rutgers (Leuven: Peeters, 2002), 307–331; idem, "Table Community in Early Christianity," in *A Holy People: Jewish and Christian Perspectives on Religious Communal Identity*, ed. Marcel Poorthuis and Joshua Schwartz (Leiden: Brill, 2006), 69–84.

9. An earnest and impressive study in this respect is *Jewish Believers in Jesus: The Early Centuries*, ed. Oskar Skarsaune and Reidar Hvalvik (Peabody: Hendrickson, 2007).

10. Donald A. Hagner, "Paul as a Jewish Believer—According to His Letters," in *Jewish Believers in Jesus: The Early Centuries*, ed. Oskar Skarsaune and Reidar Hvalvik (Peabody: Hendrickson, 2007), 145, emphasis added.

11. C. Mosna, *Storia della domenica dale origini fino agli inizi del V secolo* (Roma: Analecta Gregoriana, 1969), 182–188; quoted in Rouwhorst, "The Reception of the Jewish Sabbath," 231.

12. Kenneth A. Strand, "A Note on the Sabbath in Coptic Sources," in *The Early Christian Sabbath*, 16–24; Samuele Bacchiocchi, "The Rise of Sunday Observance," in *The Sabbath in Scripture and History*, ed. Kenneth Strand (Washington, DC: Review and Herald, 1982), 142.

13. Selby Vernon McCasland, "The Origin of the Lord's Day," *Journal of Biblical Literature* 49 (1930): 65.

14. Rordorf, *Sunday*, 177. Rordorf's study is an apology for Sunday.

15. Rouwhorst, "The Reception of the Jewish Sabbath in Early Christianity," 253.

16. David A. Fiensy, *Prayers Alleged to Be Jewish: An Examination of the Constitutiones Apostolorum* (Chico: Scholars Press, 1985).

17. Rouwhorst, "The Reception of the Jewish Sabbath in Early Christianity," 245.

18. Carsten A. Johnsen, *Day of Destiny: The Mystery of the Seventh Day* (Loma Linda, CA: The Untold Story Publishers, 1982), 103.

19. Justin Martyr, *First Apology,* 67.

20. Ignatius, *Magnesians* IX.1.

21. Oskar Skarsaune, "The History of Jewish Believers in the Early Centuries—Perspectives and Framework," in *Jewish Believers in Jesus: The Early Centuries*, ed. Oskar Skarsaune and Reidar Hvalvik (Peabody: Hendrickson, 2007), 756.

22. Isidore Epstein, *Judaism* (London: Penguin Books, 1959), 117–119; Shmuel Safrai, "The Jews in the Land of Israel," in *A History of the Jewish People*, ed. H. H. Ben-Sasson (Cambridge: Harvard University Press, 1976), 330–333.

23. Epstein, *Judaism*, 118; S. Safrai, "The Jews in the Land of Israel," 334; Lee I. A. Levine, "Judaism from the Destruction of Jerusalem to the End of the Second Jewish Revolt: 70–135 C.E.," in *Christianity and Rabbinic Judaism: A Parallel History of Their Origins and Early Developments*, ed. Herschel Shanks (Washington, DC: Biblical Archaeological Society, 1992), 125–149.

24. Skarsaune, "The History of Jewish Believers in the Early Centuries," 758.

25. Bacchiocchi, *From Sabbath to Sunday*, 165–212.

26. Reidar Hvalvik, "Jewish Believers and Jewish Influence in the Roman Church until the Early Second Century," in *Jewish Believers in Jesus: The Early Centuries*, ed. Oskar Skarsaune and Reidar Hvalvik (Peabody: Hendrickson, 2007), 211; cf. also Rouwhorst, "Continuity and Discontinuity," 75.

27. Hvalvik, "Jewish Believers and Jewish Influence in the Roman Church," 179–187.

28. Oskar Skarsaune, "The Development of Scriptural Interpretation in the Second and Third Centuries—Except Clement and Origen," in *Hebrew Bible/Old Testament: The History of Its Interpretation*, vol 1.1, *From the Beginnings to the Middle Ages (Until 1300)*; ed. Magne Sæbø (Göttingen: Vandenhoeck & Ruprecht, 1996), 381–382.

29. Kenneth A. Strand, "The Sabbath Fast in Early Christianity," in *The Early Christian Sabbath*, 9–15.

30. Sofia Cavaletti, "The Jewish Roots of Christian Liturgy," in *The Jewish Roots of Christian Liturgy*, ed. Eugene J. Fisher (New York: Paulist Press, 1990), 7–40; Rouwhorst, "The Reading of Scripture in Early Christian Liturgy," 305–331; idem, "Table Community in Early Christianity," 69–70.

31. Rouwhorst, "Jewish Liturgical Traditions in Early Syriac Christianity," 81; Apostolic Constitutions (VII.23.2; VII.36.1.5, VIII 33.2).

32. Fiensy, *Prayers Alleged to Be Jewish*, 75, 77, 79.

33. Rouwhorst, "Jewish Liturgical Traditions," 81.

34. Ibid., 85–87.

35. Fiensy, *Prayers Alleged to Be Jewish*, 79.

36. Rouwhorst, "Jewish Liturgical Traditions," 84.

37. Ibid., 84–85.

38. Robert L. Wilken, *John Chrysostom and the Jews: Rhetoric and Reality in the Late 4th Century* (Berkeley: University of California Press, 1983), 75.

39. The references are taken from Paul W. Harkins's translation, *Saint John Chrysostom: Discourses against Judaizing Christians,* The Fathers of the Church: A New Translation 68 (Washington, DC: The Catholic University of America Press, 1979), 10, 68.

40. *John Chrysostom: Discourses against Judaizing Christians*, 28.

41. Ibid., 3–4.

42. Wilken, *John Chrysostom and the Jews*, 116–120.

43. Ibid., 118–119.

44. Ibid., 116.

45. Ibid., 123.

46. Ibid.

47. Moltmann, *God in Creation*, 294.

48. Already by the end of Constantine's century, a bishop could command a salary five times that of a public physician and equal to that of the provincial governor; cf. Wilken, *John Chrysostom and the Jews*, 6–7.

49. Martin P. Nilsson, *Imperial Rome* (New York: Schocken Books, 1962), 90.

50. McCasland, "The Origin of the Lord's Day," 76–82.

51. Gaston H. Halsberghe, *The Cult of Sol Invictus* (Leiden: E. J. Brill, 1972), 167.

52. Moltmann, *God in Creation*, 294.

53. McCasland ("The Origin of the Lord's Day," 80–81) contends plausibly that the veneration of Sunday in Mithraism prepared the way for Sunday observance in Christianity in conformity with "the general psychological principle which underlies all syncretism."

54. Oscar Cullmann, *Early Christian Worship* (Philadelphia: The Westminster Press, 1953), 11.

55. Cf. S. R. Llewelyn, "The Use of Sunday for Meetings of Believers in the New Testament," *NovT* 22 (2001): 207.

56. Schaff, *History of the Christian Church,* II:7.

57. Ignatius, *Magnesians* IX.1.

58. Hvalvik, "Jewish Influence in the Roman Church," 211; Rouwhorst, "Continuity and Discontinuity," 75.

59. *John Chrysostom: Discourses against Judaizing Christians*, 54.

60. Ibid., 31–32.

61. Peter Brown, *The World of Late Antiquity* (London: Thames and Hudson, 1971), 82.

IRRECONCILABLE DIFFERENCES

Hellenism was…the pervading and invading mind-set of the millions who must in the main have been quite unconscious of the tidal forces bearing them along.
G. H. C. MacGregor and A. C. Purdy [1]

If anti-Judaism is one of the forces driving the eclipse of the Sabbath, operating mostly above ground, Hellenism is the ground itself. Indeed, at the time when Christianity comes into existence, Hellenistic culture is the air people breathe, the ground upon which people walk, and the conceptual framework within which they do their thinking. It refers to what we call "culture."

"Culture," in turn, is an invisible fact of life that resists being captured and analyzed. A person's culture is as much a part of the eyes that see as of what is seen. Like eyeglasses through which we see the world, "culture" makes it hard to see our own thoughts. Hellenism is not hidden from view because it runs below ground, but it is hidden because no one is able to see it.[2] With respect to the Sabbath, Hellenism does not only represent a challenge but also, at least in the non-Jewish context, an irreconcilable difference.

THE CHALLENGE OF HELLENISM

"Hellenism was in the very air breathed by the men of the first century," it has been said; "it was the *Zeitgeist,* comparable to our modern "scientific spirit" and perhaps no better understood by the average man; it was the pervading and invading mind-set of the millions who must in the main have been quite unconscious of the tidal forces bearing them along."[3] Hellenistic culture had left its mark on the Jewish society even before Jesus's birth. In fact, the notion of a distinct division between Hebrew and Greek worlds of thought in this era needs to be modified.[4] Cultural influences do not arrive in packages or travel in straight lines from one group to another. Greek language, philosophy, and culture arrived in the Near East ahead of Alexander the Great in the fourth century BC.[5] Even with Alexander its arrival "was incidental rather than conscious or deliberate."[6] Its momentum and appeal were almost irresistible. As early as the third century BC it was necessary to produce a Greek translation of the Old Testament in the Jewish community of Alexandria because Hebrew had become a foreign tongue even to the resident Jews.[7]

There are varieties of thought within Hellenistic culture,[8] but in relation to Christianity Plato's influence is preeminent. His voice echoes and reechoes in the writings of the early fathers of the Christian Church. Crucially, they do not hear Plato as an alien voice.[9] They read him fondly, greeting Socrates as a Christian before Christ and as a martyr on the lines of the martyrs of the Old Testament.[10] To the mind of Justin Martyr, the worldview of Plato is compatible with that of the Old Testament. What is good in Plato owes to Plato's indebtedness to the ancient Jewish legacy."For Moses is more ancient than all the Greek writers. And whatever both philosophers and poets have said concerning the immortality of the soul, or punishments after death, or contemplation of things heavenly, or doctrines of the like kind, they have received such suggestions from the prophets as have enabled them to understand and interpret these things," Justin writes in his *First Apology*.[11]

The Old Testament as the source of Plato's thought? Prophets teaching the immortality of the soul? Socrates a Christian before Christ? Is this a triumph of the imagination, or is it better recognized as a colossal failure of perception? When scholars today look at the amalgamation of worldviews taking place during this period, they acknowledge the chasm that separates the worldview of the Old Testament from that of Plato. But Justin and many fathers in the Church were unable to see the gap.[12] The Old Testament affirmation of history, the earth, and the body is in the second century reconfigured according to the outlook of Plato, whose preoccupation is precisely to decry history, the body, and the earth. The true seeker of truth, Socrates says in his farewell discourse, "would like, as far as he can, to be quit of the body and turn to the soul";[13] he gets rid, "as far as he can, of eyes and ears and of the whole body, which he conceives of only as a disturbing element, hindering the soul from the acquisition of knowledge."[14] These are not sentiments that are easily reconciled to the tenor of the Old Testament.

By contrast, beginning with the first book, the Bible hails the creation of the earth and the fashioning of humans as material beings (Gen. 2:7). The prophets envision the redemption of the earth, conceiving human existence always as earthy and embodied existence (Isa. 65:17–19; 66:22; Rev. 21:1). With respect to materiality the New Testament even exceeds the Old. In the Old Testament God creates human beings in God's image (Gen. 1:27–28), but in the New Testament "the *Word* became flesh" (John 1:14). The divine solution is not to abolish flesh, as Plato urges at every turn, but to assume flesh and thus to redeem human beings. John piles on the very thing that Plato wants to escape, using the word "flesh" (*sarx*) in order to convey the materiality of his message. On the cross Jesus dies a real death, His executioners subjecting the event to stark physical verification (John 19:33–34). John's materiality continues undiminished when the reality of Jesus's resurrection is put to the test by the doubting Thomas (John 20:27).[15] John Ashton deplores "the crudity of the images that have been evoked" in John's resurrection portrayal,[16] and, in a statement that deserves commendation for its honesty, he exclaims, "How difficult it is not to see John as the kind of thinker one would like him to be!"[17]

The divine solution is not to abolish flesh, as Plato urges at every turn, but to assume flesh and thus to redeem human beings.

How difficult, indeed, identifying the materiality of John's Gospel as the offending element! And how different this conception from Plato, and from the Platonic version of Christian belief in the church fathers! Socrates speaks of death as liberation, the moment when the soul is released from its imprisonment in the body and freed to pursue truth unimpeded by bodily distractions.[18] The prospect of drinking the hemlock leaves him unperturbed. In his farewell address, the tone is casual and often interrupted by laughter. "So really," Plato quotes Socrates as saying, "if we're ever to have clean knowledge of anything, we must get rid of the body and observe the things themselves with the soul itself."[19] Step by step Plato, through the voice of Socrates, leads his conversation partners to accept that the soul is immaterial and immortal, the godlike part of the human being that exists before birth and lives on after death. Moreover, permeating the outlook of the teacher (Socrates) and the student (Plato) alike, the particularity of human existence finds itself pushed to the side by the teacher's wild goose chase for unattainable and irrelevant definitions and by the student's vision of an unseen, immaterial reality as the ultimate state of existence.[20]

THE PRISM OF PHILO

Plato's views are not transmitted to the Christian Church in a straight line. It is an irony of history and testimony to the transforming power of Hellenism that the connecting link and leading instrument of mediation is Jewish. Philo (20 BC–40 AD), a wealthy scholar living in Alexandria, and "one of the most remarkable literary phenomena of the Hellenistic world,"[21] serves as the bridgehead between Plato and the Christian fathers. Philo's life overlaps in part the lives of Jesus and the apostle Paul. His role can hardly be overestimated because his interpretation of the Old Testament sets the tone for the way the fathers in the Church will read it. In addition, Philo in his own personal biography embodies Hellenism.[22]

As he rewrites the Jewish scriptures in the context of Platonic philosophy, Philo wants to prove to his fellow Jews that the two systems are compatible. Perhaps more accurately, he seeks to demonstrate to the outside world that the Jewish scriptures are philosophically as sophisticated as the best in Greek thought.[23] The particularities and peculiarities of Jewish teaching and practice did not fit the Hellenistic mindset, inducing Jewish thinkers even prior to Philo to take the first steps to recast the Old Testament in a Platonic pattern.[24]

No one, however, is as important as Philo, and no one is as successful.[25] In Philo's view Plato is a follower of Pythagoras, and Pythagoras is a follower of Moses, and Moses is the father of philosophy. Moreover, the philosophy of which Moses is the father is precisely the Middle Platonism espoused by Philo.[26] Philo's project of reinterpretation is unmatched for its audacity. By means of allegorical interpretation the narratives of the Old Testament are transformed until they echo Plato. At the same time Plato is perceived as one working under divine inspiration. Philo brings together the outer extremes of two interpretive worlds, claiming verbal inspiration for the Old Testament source and yet throwing the door wide open to the interpreter to pursue multiple meanings. "There never was a more exaggerated theory of inspiration; and there could not be a stronger justification for the interpreter's license," Folker Siegert says of Philo's ability to pull one rabbit after another out of the hat, the rabbit being an embellished form of Platonism and the hat the Old Testament.[27]

Peder Borgen writes that "Philonic Judaism was the result of a Hellenization which was as complete as possible for a group which retained throughout its loyalty to the Torah."[28] This view understates the reality because Philo, by deploying allegory without restraint,[29] finds the Old Testament to support the pre-existence of the soul, the immortality of the soul, and the soul's glorious liberation from the body at death. "[A]fter living long," he says, the immaterial soul of the worthy person "passes away to eternity, that is, he is borne to eternal life."[30] Death, in Philo as much as in Plato, is liberation. If Philo, a Jewish thinker, comes to the conclusion that in Plato we hear the voice of Moses, we are not surprised that Justin Martyr in the second century and the church fathers of Alexandria in the third century have few reservations with respect to embracing Philo's approach to the Old Testament.

Justin seems to be aware of Philo, being even more emphatic than Philo in claiming an organic relationship between Moses and Plato.[31] But this is a moot point. A native reading of the Old Testament hardly seems to be an option for Justin. Etienne Vacherot, in his large history of the interaction between early Christianity and Hellenism, concludes that Justin's thought "is the philosophy of Plato applied in an ingenious manner to Christian dogma."[32] More recently, W. H. C. Frend is equally emphatic, stating that Justin "never grasped the essential incompatibilities between Platonism and Christianity."[33]

IRRECONCILABLE DIFFERENCES

Did these "essential incompatibilities" contribute to the eclipse of the Sabbath? The question cannot be answered directly because it is not addressed in these terms by the church fathers. It must be answered indirectly by casting a wider net than what is commonly done. The Platonic influences on Christian thought are not exactly subtle, and they certainly lead to a shift away from the biblical affirmation of physical reality. Not only is Hellenism the ground itself, "the tidal forces" bearing people along,[34] and not only is Hellenism the soil, but it is also soil that is unfriendly to Judeo-Christian particularity. Philo wanted to remove the embarrassment that these particularities generated in Greek eyes. The Hellenizing influence, as noted by John Howard Yoder, came in addition to the fact that "mainstream Christianity has been resolutely anti-Jewish" since the middle of the second century C.E."[35]

The Platonic influences on Christian thought are not exactly subtle, and they certainly lead to a shift away from the biblical affirmation of physical reality.

Anti-Judaism as such is not the issue here. The issue, instead, is the character of the biblical witness and, above all, the biblical affirmation of the body and the earth. When Justin explained that his community held its common assembly on Sunday because that is the day on which God "wrought a change in the darkness and matter," and the day when Jesus Christ "rose from the dead,"[36] the wider context of a conversion to Hellenistic thought cannot be left out of the account. What emerges is a bleached version of human reality, deprived of color and connection to the earth all the way down to its roots. The discontinuity that comes to view is not a line of demarcation between Judaism and Christianity, but between the worldview of the New Testament and that of the early Church. The adoption of the Platonic outlook becomes part of the fabric of Christianity to the extent that not until the twentieth century, if then, would theologians appreciate the Church's accommodation of Platonism as an irreconcilable difference.[37]

In the writings of Clement of Alexandria (d. about 215) and Origen (ca. 184–254), the most prominent apologists of the early church, the ambiguity and reserve that are evident in the writings of Justin Martyr are absent, and there is even less awareness of a conflict between biblical and Platonic thought than there is in Justin's writings.[38] According to Origen, the creation of the world is not an expression of God's original plan but a remedial solution to the problem of sin. "God therefore made the present world and bound the soul to the body as a punishment," he writes.[39] The physical world and the flesh-and-blood reality of the body are so fraught with materiality that in his view they cannot be part of God's original intent. "For if all things can exist without bodies, doubtless bodily substance will cease to exist when there is no use for it," Origen writes in one of his clearest statements on the subject.[40] He struggled with the subject again and again, presenting his view as tentative and yet logically necessary. "If therefore these conclusions appear logical," he says, "it follows that we must believe that our condition will be at some future time incorporeal; and if this is admitted, and it is said that all must be subjected to Christ, it is necessary that this incorporeal condition shall be the privilege of all who come within the scope of this subjection to Christ."[41]

Materiality and corporeality are inimical to Origen's mindset, as incompatible with the divine intention as within the thought-world of Plato. "Thus," concludes Origen, "it appears that even the use of bodies will cease; and if this happens, bodily nature returns to non-existence, just as formerly it did not exist."[42] Interpreters of Origen may have misunderstood his method, but the Platonic imprint on his understanding of reality is unambiguous. "To Plato he owes his whole bent of thought," writes R. P. C. Hanson, "his whole tendency to see all tangible and temporary phenomena as mere ephemeral symbols of a deeper, permanent, invisible reality, a tendency which shows itself throughout all his work, as much in his theory of the pre-existence of souls as in his treatment of historical events, of sacraments and of eschatology."[43]

Origen can only do so much to overcome the distance between two worldviews that are incompatible; he cannot succeed except by letting go of the New Testament distinctive. "The result showed, once again, the immense difficulty of fitting a revealed religion based on Scripture into a philosophic framework based on Plato," writes Frend.[44] Where Justin Martyr shows confusion concerning the soul's autonomy from the body, the later fathers think uncritically in terms of the immortality of the soul. Neither Clement nor Origen ties individual identity to the body, thus downplaying belief in a literal resurrection. In the fourth century Augustine weighs in with a dualistic anthropology that is so unequivocal and definitive as to make it almost unthinkable that the first Christians ever believed anything else.[45] Frend writes that "nothing could be more opposed than the Jewish and Greek views of God, of creation, of time and history, and of the role of humanity in the universe,"[46] and yet the church fathers set out to bridge the gap, deeming the effort a success because they did not see a gap in the first place.[47] "Through the door that they opened," writes Werner Jaeger, "Greek culture and tradition streamed into the church and became amalgamated with its life and doctrine."[48]

It is in the context of the swirling current of Hellenistic influences that the Sabbath is lost. The stream of this influence is subterranean in the sense that it is easier to make the case for the reality of profound change than to describe its nature. We are left to map out the course of the stream on the basis of where it disappears from the surface to where it emerges again in broad daylight. Looking at the subject from the vantage point of portfolios of meaning, the seventh day does not fit into the Platonic negative perception of the material world. For Justin, a vestige of creation, light, is retained in the Christian symbol, being sufficiently elusive to resonate with the Platonic view while the physical world itself lies awkwardly outside the shrinking field of vision.[49]

ABSENCE OF GRACE

In the mind of Origen, the Old Testament affirmation of the Sabbath is turned on its head. Like the body, the Sabbath is perceived as a punishment. He looks to Scripture to prove this view, choosing the story of the manna in Exodus to make the case. "Because it is evident from the Scriptures that on the Lord's day God rained manna from heaven, and on the Sabbath He rained none down," Origen asserts, "the Jews may understand that even then our Lord's day was preferred to the Jewish Sabbath, that even then [it was] shown that on their Sabbath no grace of God would descend from heaven for them, and [that] no heavenly bread, which is the word of God, would come down for them."[50] All of a sudden the day that is given as a special blessing is transformed into a deprivation in Origen's transforming rhetoric. The gift has become a sign of deprivation and a sign of absence of grace. From the soil of this text, so acutely unpromising to his outlook, Origen will claim that "even then our Lord's day was preferred to the Jewish Sabbath."[51] A more complete and wholehearted inversion of the original story can hardly be imagined! Nevertheless, this is how, under the influence of Plato and Philo, one of the greatest of the church fathers read the Old Testament.

The seventh day does not fit into the Platonic negative perception of the material world.

As a symbol no longer in line with the changing perception of reality, the Sabbath ceases to play a role in the Christian community, leaving a vacuum that will grow larger with time. The revised gospel is promising escape from creation, not its restoration—the abolition of the material world, not its healing. At that time few among the early Christian apologists seemed to realize that the Old Testament is indispensable to a correct understanding of Christ, or that "the Old Testament prophecies run to Christ, as tidal rivers to the sea."[52] As the scope of God's dominion is fractured, believers will be increasingly at a loss regarding how to relate to the world or whether to relate to it at all.

Behind the tension between Jews and Christians, a profound transformation of thought has taken place. On the shifting foundation of Hellenism the material world is neglected to an extent never contemplated by Plato. It is as if the Christians, standing only a step away from Marcion and his repudiation of materiality in the second century, also are bent on abandoning the world.[53] Jesus is seen more as the Savior of the soul than as the Creator of material reality and the fashioner of the body. This is the changed reality, and the Sabbath simply does not fit the shrunken and ill-adapted harness. Under the conditioning of Hellenism, the ancient symbol is doomed, but not only because of anti-Jewish sentiment. The underlying view of reality has been transformed by irreconcilable differences between the biblical affirmation of the body and the earth and the Platonic yearning to be rid of both.

The observer who is left to ponder the causes of the transformation may never have the means to study the process up close and in detail. We should seek the reason for this apparent shortcoming in the character of the problem and not in the absence of evidence. The sources are not silent on the most important points. The connections are there, and the voices we hear are not whispering. We realize that the ground is shifting, and with it the conceptual groundwork. And while the causes may seem elusive, the consequences will be written in banner headlines and bold print.

ENDNOTES

1. G. H. C. MacGregor and A. C. Purdy, *Jew and Greek: Tutors unto Christ* (Edinburgh: The Saint Andrew Press, 1959), 143.

2. Schaff, *History of the Christian Church,* II:7.

3. MacGregor and Purdy, *Jew and Greek*, 143.

4. See Martin Hengel, *The "Hellenization" of Judea in the First Century after Christ* (London: SCM Press, 1989), 1–6; James Barr, *The Semantics of Biblical Language* (Oxford: Oxford University Press, 1961 [repr. Eugene, OR: Wipf and Stock, 2004]), 1–45.

5. Cf. Arnaldo Momigliano, *Alien Wisdom: The Limits of Hellenization* (Cambridge: Cambridge University Press, 1990 [orig. 1975]), 74–96.

6. Peter Green (*Alexander to Actium*, 312–335), apparently in order to capture the fact that Hellenism was both elusive and dramatic, characterizes its spread as "the dog that barked in the night."

7. Cf. Mogens Müller, *The First Bible of the Church: A Plea for the Septuagint* (JSOT Sup 206; Sheffield: Sheffield Academic Press, 1996).

8. John Boardman, Jasper Griffin, and Oswyn Murray, ed., *Greece and the Hellenistic World* (Oxford: Oxford University Press, 1986 [repr. 1992]); Robin Lane Fox, *The Classical World: An Epic History from Homer to Hadrian* (London: Allen Lane, 2005); cf. Roy Porter, *Flesh in the Age of Reason: How the Enlightenment Transformed the Way We See Our Bodies and Souls* (London: Penguin Books, 2004), 28–43. The pages refer to the chapter "Religion and the Soul."

9. John Dillon (*The Middle Platonists 80 B.C. to A.D. 220*, rev. ed. [Ithaca: Cornell University Press, 1996]) traces in detail how core ideas of Plato were preserved and modified, and, eventually, appropriated by leading Christian theologians.

10. Justin Martyr, *Second Apology* 10; *ANF* 1:354–355; cf. Sara Parvis and Paul Foster, ed., *Justin Martyr and His Worlds* (Minneapolis: Fortress Press, 2007).

11. Justin Martyr, *First Apology* 44; *ANF* 1:323.

12. Frend, *The Rise of Christianity*, 237. Even Barr (*Semantics of Biblical Language*, 10–13), wisely, does not appear to challenge crucial areas of difference such as the contrast between the static and the dynamic, exemplified in the Old Testament preoccupation with history; the contrast between abstract and concrete; and the contrast in the conception of the human person.

13. Plato, *Euthyphro, Apology, Crito, Phaedo,* trans. Benjamin Jowett (New York: Prometheus Books, 1988); quotation is from *Phaedo*, 77.

14. Plato, *Phaedo*, 77.

15. Porter (*Flesh in the Age of Reason*, 19) aptly captures this detail in his discussion of the materiality of the Gospel story.

16. Ashton, *Understanding the Fourth Gospel*, 512.

17. Ashton, *Understanding the Fourth Gospel*, 512.

18. Plato, *The Phaedo*, trans. Raymond Larson (Wheeling, IL: Harlan Davidson Inc., 1980).

19. Ibid., 62.

20. I. F. Stone, *The Trial of Socrates* (New York: Anchor Books, 1989), 68–89; see also Plato, *Timaeus and Critias*, trans. H. D. P. Lee (Middlesex: Penguin Books, 1971).

21. Dillon, *The Middle Platonists*, 139.

22. Dillon (*The Middle Platonists*, 140–141) shows that Philo was steeped in Plato's works, had a full basic Greek education, and did not know Hebrew.

23. Ibid., 139–183; cf. Werner Jaeger, *Early Christianity and Greek Paideia* (Cambridge: Harvard University Press, 1961), 30–31; Philo, *Legum Allegoriarum*, ed. G. P. Goold, trans., F. H. Colson and G. H. Whitaker, vol. I (Cambridge, MA: Harvard University Press, 1929), 55–107.

24. Folker Siegert, "Early Jewish Interpretation in a Hellenistic Style," in *Hebrew Bible/Old Testament: The History of Its Interpretation*, ed. Magne Sæbø, vol. 1 (Göttingen: Vandenhoeck & Ruprecht, 1996), 141–162.

25. Dillon (*The Middle Platonists*, 143) calls Philo's achievement a *tour the force* in the history in the thought.

26. Dillon, *The Middle Platonists*, 143–144.

27. Siegert, "Early Jewish Interpretation in a Hellenistic Style," 171.

28. Peder Borgen, *Philo of Alexandria: An Exegete for His Time* (Leiden: Brill, 1997), 3.

29. According to Dillon (*The Middle Platonists*, 142, 162–163), Philo is indebted to Stoic allegorizing, doing to the Old Testament what the Stoics had done to Homer.

30. Philo (*QG* 1.16), quoted in Dillon, *The Middle Platonists*, 177.

31. Michael Slusser, "Justin Scholarship—Trends and Trajectories," in *Justin Martyr and His Worlds*, 15; Bruce Chilton, "Justin and Israelite Prophecy, in *Justin Martyr and His Worlds*, 81; cf. also Erwin R. Goodenough, *The Theology of Justin Martyr* (Amsterdam: Philo, 1968 [orig. 1923]).

32. Etienne Vacherot, *Histoire critique de l'ecole d'Alexandrie*, 3 vols. (L'édition Paris, 1846–51; Amsterdam: Adolf M. Hakkert, 1965), I:229.

33. Frend, *The Rise of Christianity*, 237.

34. MacGregor and Purdy, *Jew and Greek*, 143.

35. John Howard Yoder, *The Jewish-Christian Schism Revisited*, ed. Michael G. Cartwright and Peter Ochs (Grand Rapids: Eerdmans, 2003), 147.

36. Justin Martyr, *First Apology*, 67.

37. Oscar Cullmann, *The Immortality of the Soul, or the Resurrection of the Dead?* (London: The Epworth Press, 1958). When Cullmann, in his Ingersoll lecture at Harvard University in 1955, proposed that the New Testament does not teach the immortality of the soul, he was denounced for betraying a fundamental Christian belief.

38. Henry Chadwick, *Early Christian Thought and the Classical Tradition* (Oxford: Clarendon Press, 1966); *Clement of Alexandria,* trans. G. W. Butterworth (Cambridge, MA: Harvard University Press, 1919); Origen, *Homilies on Genesis and Exodus,* trans. Ronald E. Heine (Washington, DC: The Catholic University of America Press, 1982), 61–69. The most thorough and nuanced treatment of Origen's exegesis is probably Karen Jo Torjesen, *Hermeneutical Procedure and Theological Method in Origen's Exegesis* (Berlin: Walter de Gruyter, 1986).

39. *Origen on First Principles,* trans. G. W. Butterworth (London: Society for Promoting Christian Knowledge, 1936; Gloucester, MA: Peter Smith, 1973), I.8.1.

40. *On First Principles*, II.3.2.

41. Ibid., II.3.3.

42. Ibid.

43. R. P. C. Hanson, *Allegory and Event* (London: SCM Press, 1959), 361.

44. Frend, *Rise of Christianity,* 376.

45. Saint Augustine, *The Immortality of the Soul,* trans. John J. McMahon (New York: Fathers of the Church, Inc., 1947).

46. Frend, *The Rise of Christianity*, 368.

47. Frend (*The Rise of Christianity*, 374) is no doubt correct in asserting that despite the influence of Plato on Origen, "emotionally Origen was a Christian through and through."

48. Jaeger, *Early Christianity*, 35.

49. Justin Martyr, *First Apology*, 67; Ignatius, *Magnesians* IX.1.

50. Origen, *Homilies on Exodus,* Homily VII, Chap. V.

51. Ibid.

52. H. H. Rowley, *The Rediscovery of the Old Testament* (Philadelphia: The Westminster Press, 1946), 21.

53. Cf. E. C. Blackman, *Marcion and His Influence* (London: SPCK, 1948), 66–97.

CREATION DISAFFIRMED

The bubonic plague was caused by a parasite carried by rats, but European medicine in the Middle Ages did not know that.

Norman Cantor[1]

In the Old Testament the Sabbath revels in its bond to the earth, stretching the canopy of sacred time over the world and all created life (Gen. 2:1–3). The "Sabbath outposts" of the Sabbatical Year (Lev. 25:2–4) and the Jubilee (Lev. 25:10) confirm the earth-affirming character of sabbatarian ideology. When the New Testament, in Acts, recalls "how God anointed Jesus of Nazareth with the Holy Spirit and with power; how he went about doing good and healing all who were oppressed by the devil" (Acts 10:38), it is an apt summary of how Jesus's concern for human beings was an all-out embrace of the material world and an immersion in bodily reality.

But the melody of Christ and His Creation was silenced in the Christian Church early in its history. Disparagement of the Sabbath, as in the writings of Origen, went hand in hand with repudiation of the body and neglect of the earth. While the Christian civilization of the Middle Ages was the result of many influences, one of them was the Christian view of the body. If attention to nature ground almost to a halt, it was owed in part to the fact that the ideological framework to value nature was lacking.[2] In the following discussion, albeit sketchy, I will attempt to show that estrangement from Creation and ignorance of this world are related to the Sabbath, coming to a head in the calamity known as the Black Death.

The Sabbath revels in its bond to the earth, stretching the canopy of sacred time over the world.

ESTRANGED FROM CREATION

Belief in the immortality of the soul was a key factor in the Christian estrangement from the material world. As this idea germinated within the context of the Christian belief in a final judgment, the fate of the soul became the overriding concern. In the Socratic version, the soul's immortality became an argument for the soul to accept that in the long run goodness is the only viable option. The soul, realizing that it cannot die, "has no refuge or salvation from evil except to become as good and intelligent as it possibly can," Socrates argued.[3] Souls that miss the goal in this life get to try a do-over in successive lives until at last they accede to Socrates's view and become as good and intelligent as possible.

In the Christian view, however, the soul does not get a second chance. Fate is fixed at death. To the extent that choices play a role in the salvation of the Christian's immortal soul, he or she must get it right the first time around. Moreover, earthly life is brief and uncertain. Eternity, on the other hand, is as real as death, and, in the medieval experience, close at hand. In this outlook earthly matters were unimportant—no more than "stage accessories and costumes and rehearsals for the drama of Man's pilgrimage through eternity," according to Lewis Mumford.[4]

This view led to a diminished interest in nature because concern for the body brings no apparent spiritual benefit. The body is only the prison of the soul; why explore it? Life in this world is brief compared to eternity; why bother to understand it? The earth has no place in God's ultimate reality; why study it? That the Christian version of the Platonic view was not derived from the New Testament did not seem to arouse concern. Thus the groundwork was laid for a millennium of indifference toward the body and the natural world. With time this outlook resulted in unprecedented helplessness in matters of health and disease.[5]

People not only lacked rudimentary understanding of health and hygiene. As has been documented, they did not take the kind of interest in the physical world that could lead to insight.[6] It was a Platonized version of Christian belief that furnished the ideas on which medieval society was built.[7] Furthermore, religious institutions kept a tireless vigil to ensure conformity to this outlook.[8]

For centuries, ignorance, uncertainty, and premature death were the lot of ordinary people. Devastating epidemics swept the Christian civilization again and again. It is as if medieval civilization experienced the fulfillment of the visions of John in the book of

Revelation. "I looked and there was a pale green horse! Its rider's name was Death, and Hades followed with him; they were given authority over a fourth of the earth, to kill with sword, famine, and pestilence, and by the wild animals of the earth" (Rev. 6:8). For the medieval person the take-home message was to look to God for consolation, expecting the rewards of the future life to compensate for the miseries of the present.

By the middle of the fourteenth century conditions were ripe for grief on a grander scale than ever. The calamity, remembered as the Black Death, was also emblematic of the medieval disaffirmation of Creation, and, as more than an accidental afterthought, of the Christian attitude toward the Jews.

THE BLACK DEATH AS PARADIGM

The story of the Black Death brings together—and brings to a head—the unsustainable ideology and prejudices of medieval Christianity. Sensing disaster, the harbormasters of Messina tried to quarantine the Genoese fleet that arrived at the docks in October 1347. They prevented the crew from coming ashore, but not the rats and the fleas.[9] Within days the Black Death raged throughout the city.[10] It was to become "the most lethal disaster of recorded history."[11] The pandemic swept across Europe. By 1351 agents of the pope calculated the number of dead in Christian Europe at 23,840,000, an estimated one third of the population.[12] By the end of the century the population of Europe was reduced to nearly one half of the pre-plague level.

The calamity was accentuated by psychological trauma and social alienation. "I pass over the little regard that citizens and relations showed to each other," Boccaccio wrote from his place of refuge in the church that still stands across from the railway station in Florence, "for their terror was such, that a brother even fled from his brother, a wife from her husband, and, what is more uncommon, a parent from his own child."[13] An unnamed observer lamented that "there was no love, no faithfulness, no trust. No neighbour would lend a helping hand to another. One brother had forsaken the other, husbands had forsaken their wives, parents their children, children their parents."[14]

People were filled with a sense of impending doom. It seemed as if the final judgment was upon them and that the last plagues were being poured out, unmixed with mercy. Against the backdrop of the imagery of the Apocalypse the plague could be nothing less than God's final reckoning with humanity. Stunned by what he saw, Petrarch, another of the great Florentine writers of that time, confided that "the whole world seemed about to perish."[15]

The story of the Black Death brings together—and brings to a head—the unsustainable ideology and prejudices of medieval Christianity.

The scope and magnitude of the disaster are more easily appreciated than its nature. In general, however, historians of medicine have looked to the prevailing Christian view of the world as a contributing factor; the unfathomable disaster could not be attributed to accident. Thus, Paul Diepgen shows that theology served the great misconceptions of the time because of the one-sided emphasis on the hereafter and the extremely deficient understanding of the physical world.[16]

Other scholars have reached similar conclusions. Johannes Nohl accounts for the absence of even rudimentary insights by the fact that the universities of that time were under the jurisdiction of the Church,[17] which was suspicious of discovery and novelty. Compared to theology, medicine was seen as a secondary science. The aim of this inferior study was only the care of the physical, transitory organism, a pursuit far less important than caring for the soul. Thus medieval understanding was hamstrung by its own most basic belief.

Edward Neufeld compared the hygienic conditions of medieval Europe with the public health measures in ancient Israel and found the latter to be greatly superior. He, too, suggests a connection between the underlying view of life and the mastery of disease. Of particular interest is his observation that "the understanding of sanitation all over the ancient Near East seems, in fact, distinctly higher than that of early and even late Middle age Europe, where the body was not a thing to be safeguarded, but rather something to be subjugated and controlled."[18] The combination of belief in the immortality of the soul, magnified by the church's suppression of dissent, led medieval people to be estranged from Creation.

The lesson of the Black Death is that those who choose to ignore the material world are liable to suffer the consequences. As the epidemic raged across Europe, insult was added to injury, the injury being estrangement from nature and the insult being an unchecked rage against the Jews. In an ironic twist of logic the Christians of Europe held the Jews responsible for the plague.[19]

In the present context the "Jewish" aspect of the Black Death is important because it also reveals Christianity's attitude toward the Old Testament. As suspicion is fomenting against the Jews, Philip Ziegler notes a Jewish practice that at one and the same time protects and incriminates this group.

> The Jews, with their greater understanding of elementary hygiene, preferred to draw their drinking water from open streams, even though these might often be farther from their homes. Such a habit, barely noticed in normal times, would seem intensely suspicious in the event of the plague. Why should the Jews shun the wells unless they knew them to be poisoned and how could they have such knowledge unless they had done the poisoning themselves?[20]

This conspiracy theory, grounded in prejudice and superstition, was but the beginning. According to Ziegler, suspicion was elevated to the level of proof, and the Jewish connection was treated as axiomatic. Proof of sorts was achieved in September 1348, when Jews in Chillon, France, confessed to poisoning wells. News of the Jewish confession was quickly published abroad.

Balavignus, a Jewish physician, was the first to be racked. After much hesitation, he confessed that the rabbi Jacob of Toledo had sent him, by the hand of a Jewish boy, a leather pouch filled with red and black powder and concealed in the mummy of an egg. This powder he was ordered, on pain of excommunication, to throw into the larger wells of Thonon. He did so, having previously warned his friends and relations not to drink of the water.[21]

Others soon added their confessions while under torture.[22]

As the epidemic claimed victims among Jews and Christians alike, mobs of Christians instigated massacres of Jews in the most highly cultured cities in Europe. Zürich voted in 1348 "never to admit Jews to the city again."[23] Even before the epidemic reached the city, two thousand Jews were murdered in Strasbourg.[24] On a rising crest of prejudice the Jews had been expelled from England as early as 1290, from France a few decades later, and they were banished from much of the remainder of Western Europe within the century following the Black Death.[25] Ziegler calls the massacre "exceptional in its extent and its ferocity"; "it probably had no equal until the twentieth century set new standards for man's inhumanity to man."[26]

The lesson of the Black Death is that those who choose to ignore the material world are liable to suffer the consequences.

This is what happened in the Christian Europe that was estranged from Creation, out of touch with Old Testament insights, and seething with prejudice against the Jews. For all of these reasons the Black Death deserves to be seen as an event that brought the unsustainable logic of the Christian Middle Ages to an inevitable turning point.

THE BLACK DEATH AS TURNING POINT

Christian anti-Judaism and the Platonic preoccupation with the soul in medieval Christianity shadowed each other closely throughout the Middle Ages and beyond as though linked by an invisible chain.

Ziegler writes that medieval culture was conditioned for defeat at the hand of the *Yersinia* bacillus because it was ignorant of nature and the body.[27] What happened in the harbor of Messina in 1347 was a necessary but not a sufficient cause for the ensuing epidemic. Alexander Solzhenitsyn catches the mood when he says that "[t]he Middle Ages came to a natural end by exhaustion, having become an intolerable, despotic repression of man's physical nature in favor of the spiritual one."[28] In the Black Death the intellectual and spiritual foundation of the medieval world, with its repression of the body and the earth, was tested and found wanting.

Henry Sigerist, writing as a medical historian, insists that medicine "cannot flourish when the underlying philosophy is mystical, as was the case in the Middle Ages."[29] He perceived an indissoluble relationship between the underlying worldview of a culture and its adaptation to that world because hygiene and medicine are also part of the general learning of a period and reflect its general outlook on life. Hans Zinsser, a pioneer in typhus research, argues that diseases have changed the course of history more than armies and generals—perhaps, too, more than philosophers and theologians. [30]

An idea or mindset cannot give birth to disease, but it can enable or disable in the struggle against it. The medieval idea of the body and the earth had a paralyzing impact because it did not offer any incentive to improve people's lot in this life. Conversely, a catastrophic event may pass a devastating verdict on an idea. The Black Death did just that to the Middle Ages. Ziegler concludes that if "one were to seek to establish one generalisation...to catch the mood of the Europeans in the second half of the fourteenth century, it would be that they were enduring a crisis of faith. Assumptions that had been taken for granted for centuries were now in question, the very framework of men's reasoning seemed to be breaking up."[31] Robert S. Gottfried reaches a similar conclusion, describing the Black Death as a crisis in which "deep-rooted moral, philosophical, and religious convictions were tested and found wanting."[32]

But the Christian context of the Black Death needs to be moved into the foreground in order to appreciate the full force of the paradox. Medieval culture was steeped in the images of Jesus Christ. Paradoxically, Jesus came to the world as the great physician. Judged by the portraits in the Gospels, Jesus was a person who broke the shackles of disease and suffering because they were matters of the highest priority in His mission. Indeed, it is precisely the fact that Christianity, in the words of Roy Porter, "implicated itself utterly in the dilemmas and dramas of the flesh" that gave the Christian message much of its original appeal.[33] Moreover, Jesus's concern for human well-being, emphasizing that this includes the *physical* well-being of ordinary men and women, must be understood within the context of His indivisible view of Creation and the body. The Creator, appearing in human form (John 1:14), had come to set right what was damaged (John 10:10). On this point Jesus continued and carriesd forward what was also a dominant concern in the Old Testament (cf. Isa. 42:1–9), a mission that cares for the body and the earth.

The medieval idea of the body and the earth had a paralyzing impact because it did not offer any incentive to improve people's lot in this life.

This image was lost by the Middle Ages. For centuries knowledge of the natural sciences remained in the undisturbed freeze-frame in which the great thinkers, mathematicians, and physicians of ancient Greece left it. Nature lay unclaimed and unattended, unleashing her lethal weapons at irregular intervals. Famine and epidemics held sway as though ordained by God as discipline. In the medieval mindset no one had cause for complaint. On the one hand, belief in the divine order lay behind the most senseless calamity. Whatever happened only served to underscore the existing system. On the other hand, as seen in the treatment of the Jews during the Black Death, a more visceral and less submissive impulse on occasion broke through to the surface. In this scenario disease was not ordained by God; it was the consequence of the wicked intent of Jews who stubbornly resisted the conformity that was the prized value of the Middle Ages. Sabbath observance was only the most visible signifier of this non-conformity.

In this fractured state, to which the outlook of the Church was a chief contributor, the Church was also the sole source of comfort. With the exception of the Jews, every human being was a lifelong child of the Church, helped along from baptism to death by sacraments and rituals that covered every phase of life and all experience. Medieval people had no way to know that the faith which sustained them through the vicissitudes of life also tied their hands from the pursuit of survival and security. It took an event out of the ordinary to crack the old order and to bring it down. The Black Death served as the straw that breaks the camel's back.

By ruthless logic the survivors and coming generations would ask if the failure of Christian culture symbolized the failure of Christianity itself. Barbara Tuchman perceives the agony of the question that is bound to follow.

> If a disaster of such magnitude, the most lethal ever known, was a mere wanton act of God or perhaps not God's work at all, then the absolutes of a fixed order were loosed from their moorings. Minds that opened to admit these questions could never again be shut. Once people envisioned the possibility of change in a fixed order, the end of an age of submission came in sight; the turn to individual conscience lay ahead. To that extent the Black Death may have been the unrecognized beginning of modern man.[34]

As the medieval edifice crumbled, the world began looking to new stewards that would serve human need with greater care than the Church had done. Other sources of insight beckoned with new appeal. If, at least with respect to the Christian view of the body, the Middle Ages can be described as a period that emphasized God apart from the world, or even as God *against* the world, what would happen when this age came to an end? The age of faith was ending, its end helped along by the Black Death. The bath water was about to be thrown out. What now of the baby?

ENDNOTES

1. Cantor, *The Civilization of the Middle Ages*, 482.

2. Even though Peter Brown prioritizes the early Christian view of sexuality in his book *The Body and Society: Men, Women, and Sexual Renunciation in Early Christianity* (New York: Columbia University Press, 1988), he provides an excellent introduction to the Christian attitude toward the body.

3. Plato, *Euthyphro, Apology, Crito, Phaedo,* trans. Benjamin Jowett (New York: Prometheus Books, 1988); quotation is from *Phaedo*, 77. Reincarnation and transmigration of souls are implied in the Platonic view.

4. Lewis Mumford, *Technics and Civilization* (New York: Hartcourt, Brace & World, 1934), 29.

5. R. W. Southern, *Western Society and the Church in the Middle Ages* (Middlesex: Penguin Books, 1970); see also Fredrick B. Artz, *The Mind of the Middle Ages: A Historical Survey A.D. 200–1500* (Chicago: The University of Chicago Press, 1953); Jacques Le Goff, *Time, Work, and Culture in the Middle Ages,* trans. Arthur Goldhammer (Chicago: The University of Chicago Press, 1980); idem, *Medieval Civilization*; Norman F. Cantor, *Inventing the Middle Ages* (New York: Quill William Morrow, 1991); idem, *The Civilization of the Middle Ages.*

6. Frend (*The Rise of Christianity*, 746), documenting the rise of the monastic movement in the fifth century, shows withdrawal from the world to be the Christian ideal.

7. Artz, *The Mind of the Middle Ages*, 100.

8. LeGoff (*Medieval Civilization*, 170) describes how medieval Christianity was bent on eradicating the memory of pagan antiquity as well as suppressing dissenting belief arising in its own time. See also Peter Brown, *Authority and the Sacred: Aspects of the Christianization of the Roman World* (New York: Cambridge University Press, 1999).

9. The most widely accepted theory is that the epidemic was caused by the bacterium *Yersinia pestis* inhabiting fleas on the backs of rats. In view of the rapid spread of the disease some scientists have proposed another or an additional agent that accounts better for rapid human-to-human transmission, possibly anthrax; cf. Norman F. Cantor, *In the Wake of the Plague: The Black Death and the World It Made* (New York: Harper Perennial, 2002), 11–25.

10. Robert S. Gottfried, *The Black Death: Natural and Human Disaster in Medieval Europe* (New York: The Free Press, 1983), xiii. It took some time to find a name that did justice to the memory. The name "Black Death" apparently does not come into common usage until the end of the fifteenth century; cf. I. Reichborn-Kjennerud, "Black Death," *The Journal of the History*

of Medicine, 3 (1948): 359–360.

11. Barbara Tuchman, *A Distant Mirror* (New York: Ballantine Books, 1978), xiii.

12. Gottfried, *The Black Death,* 77, xiii. Nohl, referring to the same investigation by Pope Clement VI, puts the number at 42,836,486; Johannes Nohl, *The Black Death: A Chronicle of the Plague,* trans. C. H. Clarke (New York: J. & J. Harper, 1969), 17.

13. Giovanni Boccaccio, *The Decameron,* trans. Leopold Flameng (London: Arthur W. Murray, 1888), 19.

14. Nohl, *The Black Death,* 30.

15. Petrarch, *Epistolae Familiares,* quoted in James Harvey Robinson, *Petrarch: The First Modern Scholar and Man of Letters* (New York: Haskell House Publishers Ltd., 1970), 147.

16. Paul Diepgen, *Die Theologie und der ärtzliche Stand. Studien zur Geschichte der Beziehungen zwischen Theologie und Medizin im Mittelalter* (Berlin-Grunewald: Dr. Walther Rothschild, 1922), 2.

17. Nohl, *The Black Death,* 73.

18. Edward Neufeld, "Hygiene Conditions in Ancient Israel (Iron Age)," *Biblical Archaeologist* 34 (May, 1971): 45.

19. Anna Foa, *The Jews of Europe after the Black Death,* trans. Andrea Grover (Berkeley: University of California Press, 2000), 7–22.

20. Philip Ziegler, *The Black Death* (London: Collins, 1969), 100.

21. Ziegler, *The Black Death,* 102; see also Cantor, *In the Wake of the Plague,* 147–167.

22. Ziegler, *The Black Death,* 102.

23. Ibid., 103.

24. Ibid.

25. Foa, *The Jews of Europe after the Black Death,* 9.

26. Ziegler, *The Black Death,* 108.

27. Ibid., 275.

28. Solzhenitsyn, *A World Split Apart,* 49.

29. Sigerist, *Civilization and Disease,* 161.

30. Hans Zinsser, *Rats, Lice and History* (Boston: Little, Brown and Co., 1934 [repr. London: Macmillan, 1985]), 150.

31. Ziegler, *The Black Death,* 279.

32. Gottfried, *The Black Death,* 163.

33. Porter, *Flesh in the Age of Reason,* 19–20.

34. Tuchman, *A Distant Mirror,* 123.

CHAPTER 19

LORD OF LESS

So the Son of Man is lord even of the sabbath.
Mark 2:28

A fractured view of reality dominated Christian thought from the second century onward. If, as Frend asserts, "nothing could be more opposed than the Jewish and Greek views of God, of creation, of time and history, and of the role of humanity in the universe,"[1] the leading Christian voices of the second and third centuries saw neither the differences nor the consequences. The church fathers adopted what is essentially a Platonic view of the world and the body despite the fact that they saw themselves struggling to preserve a distinctive Christian outlook. None of the church fathers lifted a finger on behalf of the Sabbath. One, however, stirred into action in defense of the biblical view of Creation.

That person was Tertullian, the North African scholar and apologist who died circa 225 CE.[2] His legacy supports the proposition that there is a correlation between a person's view of the material world and the prospects of science and health. The backward glance to Tertullian shows a unique facet of the struggle to develop a specific Christian understanding of the world. Even he, the most earth-affirming of the church fathers, accepted a fracture in Creation, and even he adopted an interpretation of the Old Testament that left the Sabbath out in the cold. Tertullian's valiant effort on behalf of the material world did not save medieval Christianity from a one-sided preoccupation with the soul and the hereafter. If Christ in the medieval outlook was Lord mostly of the soul, it would not be easy to reclaim the body and the earth for Christ. Indeed, when the Enlightenment raised doubts about the basic medieval assumptions, the scope of the lordship of Christ threatened to be reduced to nothing.

THE CASE OF TERTULLIAN

Tertullian was a rare exception among the church fathers. His writings show a man who is aware of conflicting outlooks, and he frames the issue as a conflict between Greek and Hebrew views of reality. His perception and strategy are exemplified in the memorable question, "What indeed has Athens to do with

Jerusalem?"[3] In a number of his polemic treatises he discusses the relationship between the Bible and Greek philosophy and between the Platonic view of the soul and the Christian view of the body. The struggle is evident; he was afraid that Christianity would lose its distinctive message.

To Tertullian, the notion of the immortality of the soul needed no defenders because that was part of most systems of belief. In fact, belief in the immortal soul was not a distinctive *Christian* doctrine or even a Christian doctrine at all. "There is no need, I suppose, to treat of the soul's safety," Tertullian writes, "for nearly all the heretics, in whatever way they conceive of it, certainly refrain from denying *that*."[4] The body, on the other hand, was badly in need of a spokesperson. Tertullian spared no effort in spelling out what he meant by *body* even when the subject was the body of Christ. "*I mean* this flesh," he writes with characteristic emphasis, "suffused with blood, built up with bones, interwoven with nerves, entwined with veins, *a flesh* which knew how to be born, and how to die, human without doubt, as born of a human being."[5]

Contrary to the view of thinkers like Origen, Tertullian maintained that the soul, too, is material, insisting that the substance "which by its departure causes the living being to die is a corporeal one."[6] This conclusion, he claims, is readily appreciated by observing the soul's impact on the body. "It is the soul which gives motion to the feet for walking, and to the hands for touching, and to the eyes for sight, and to the tongue for speech—a sort of internal image which moves and animates the surface. Whence could accrue such power to the soul, if it were incorporeal?" asks Tertullian in what today could be seen as a description of the function of the human brain.[7] He disputes the notion of the soul's pre-existence, maintaining that soul and body are both "conceived, and formed, and perfectly simultaneously, as well as born together; and that not a moment's interval occurs in their conception, so that a prior place can be assigned to either."[8]

Yet even for Tertullian, the soul could be separated from the body as the actual seat of human identity, capable of surviving death. In this respect the soul has priority over the body. "But the operation of death is plain and obvious," he claims; "it is the separation of body and soul."[9] On this point Athens has far more to do with Jerusalem than Tertullian otherwise seemed prepared to accept. "I may use, therefore, the opinion of Plato, when he declares, 'Every soul is immortal,'" Tertullian writes approvingly.[10]

Tertullian's anthropology bears fruit in a wealth of insight into the natural sciences. Extolling his insights, Adolf Harnack writes that "with regard to scientific and medical knowledge all the other church fathers stand far behind Tertullian."[11] This unstinting verdict is attributable to the fact that Tertullian believed in the importance of the body, he thought that the soul is material, and he was a zealous defender of the doctrine of the resurrection of the body.

Tertullian's view is a lesser fracture than the one endorsed by the other church fathers, but even in his writings "Athens" was encroaching on "Jerusalem." Tertullian, too, split the body from the soul, and, accepting that the soul is immortal, he gave priority to the soul. He was also vulnerable on other points. His strident temperament and his Montanist sympathies[12] energized one another so as to make him quite incapable of nuance, insensitive to subtleties in the biblical story, and, above all, less capable of self-criticism. A legal scholar by profession, Tertullian sought the specific command that would move him with respect to the Sabbath. Unable to find the requisite command in Genesis, Tertullian relegated the Sabbath to an inferior and strictly Jewish domain.

> Therefore, since God originated Adam, uncircumcised and inobservant of the Sabbath, consequently his offspring also, Abel, offering Him sacrifices, uncircumcised and inobservant of the Sabbath...Noah also, uncircumcised—yes, and inobservant of the Sabbath—God freed from the deluge. For Enoch, too, most righteous man, uncircumcised and inobservant of the Sabbath,

> He translated from this world; who did not first taste death, in order that, being a candidate for eternal life, he might by this time show us that we also may, without the burden of the law of Moses, please God.[13]

For Tertullian, the Sabbath was part of "the Law of Moses"; it did not deserve to be a part of God's law. The passage reveals Tertullian's hermeneutical blinders. Even though the seventh day looms large in the Genesis account of Creation (Gen. 2:1–3), the Sabbath of the Creation narrative does not set any precedent and does not obligate Adam because there is no commandment attached to it. The commandments to which Tertullian will respond must either be explicit in the biblical text or obvious from nature, and the Sabbath of "the Law of Moses" falls short on both counts. "I contend that there was a law unwritten, which was habitually understood naturally, and by the fathers was habitually kept," says Tertullian,[14] but the Sabbath is not part of the foundational terms of human existence.

Nevertheless, Tertullian should be credited as one who sees the fork in the road even if he cannot point the way consistently in one direction. He, too, is a child of his times, unable to see that his own struggle for the unity of Creation, for the wholeness of the human person, and for the contrast between Jerusalem and Athens should be welcoming to the seventh day.

A FRACTURED DOMINION

In light of this struggle, it may be said that the leaders and Pharisees who rejected Jesus in His time understood many things better than the church fathers. Jesus's most persistent critics actually grasped the scope of one of His most far-reaching claims, "So the Son of Man is lord even of the sabbath" (Mark 2:28).

The impact of this assertion in Jewish ears at the time of Jesus is likely to be lost on modern readers. William H. Willimon notes that "we are no longer shocked" at Jesus's claim, indicating that we would be if only we understood what the claim involves.[15] To Christ's initial listeners the Sabbath ordinance reaches back to the beginning of recorded time and to the most solemn human encounter with the Creator (Gen. 2:1–3; Exod. 31:18; Deut. 5:26). "The Sabbath, built into the very order of creation, was the foundation of Israel's identity."[16] When Jesus claimed lordship over the Sabbath, therefore, He was not merely making a statement about the seventh day. He declared Himself to be the Creator and Lord of the entire Creation.

Jesus's most persistent critics actually grasped the scope of one of His most far-reaching claims, "So the Son of Man is lord even of the sabbath."

Jesus makes it clear that He understood His listeners' high regard for the Sabbath and the stupendous nature of His claim. "So the Son of Man is lord *even* of the sabbath," He says, making "even" the pivotal word in the sentence (Mark 2:28). He agreed with His opponents as to the status of the Sabbath and the implications of His lordship; in fact, He exploited their understanding to remove all doubt as to who He was. They thought, and He would not deny it, that He had made the highest claim possible and asserted the most exalted authority. If Jesus is lord *even* of the Sabbath, then, as the statement implies, everything in life belongs to His domain and is subject to His care and authority.

To many readers of the New Testament the ramifications of this statement have been lost to the point that they read it as though Jesus was asserting His lordship merely to consign the Sabbath to the scrap heap of history. This misreading of the incident is unfounded. The issue "is christological rather than antinomian," as Willimon notes, a clash "not over the rules but over *who* rules."[17] Jesus places the implication of His lordship in direct proportion to the importance of the Sabbath. Only because the Sabbath signifies a matter of supreme importance can His claim to be the Lord of the Sabbath serve as the springboard for His own identity and mission. Rather than trivializing the Sabbath, it is the other way around: On the strength of the self-evident and accepted importance of the Sabbath, Jesus launches the most far-reaching claim with respect to His own identity and dominion.[18]

At one level the Sabbath controversies in the New Testament show Jesus staking out His territory in the world, marking off the boundaries of His domain. When the circle of His lordship is drawn, everything is within the circle. Jesus is Lord *even* of the Sabbath because He is Lord of Creation, of the earth, and of all of history. He is Lord of the present and the future of human destiny, of individuals and of nations. In the book of Revelation, Jesus speaks in the first person as the "I am" of the Old Testament: "I am the Alpha and the Omega, the first and the last, the beginning and the end" (Rev. 22:13; cf. 21:6). It is a lordship that breathes healing and wholeness; it cannot be divided because it is a seamless whole.

It is implicit in Jesus's lordship of the Sabbath that human existence and reality itself are inseparable from the physical world. In point of fact, the material world is God's handiwork and the actual domain of Jesus's lordship. In His reference to the Sabbath Jesus takes His listeners to the outer limit of that of which He is Lord, claiming the earth and life and existence itself as His domain. Marcion in the second century deprecates the physical world as the work of an inferior god. Origen extols some form of immateriality as the original and ultimate form of existence, dispensing with the physical world. Even Tertullian allows a fissure in Creation that casts a shadow over the material world. What these theologians belittle, Tertullian much less than the others, Jesus regards as indispensable and indivisible. Moreover, where these theologians have no use for the Sabbath, Jesus makes the Sabbath the supreme marker of all of which He is Lord.

It is in this sense that the Jews who first heard Jesus make His claim to be the Lord even of the Sabbath understood its ramifications better than Christians who read it later. When Christians thought

On the strength of the self-evident and accepted importance of the Sabbath, Jesus launches the most far-reaching claim with respect to His own identity and dominion.

their cause better served by abandoning the Sabbath, a huge territory was ceded from Christ's domain as though unworthy of His attention. In medieval Christianity Christ was lord of the soul only. The light of His life did not extend to nature and the body or to issues crucial to survival and quality of life in this world. Theologians made no attempt to reclaim the lost ground for their Lord, striving instead to prove that nature and the body have no permanent place in the kingdom to come, while at the same time the Church pursued political power and worldly aggrandizement at almost any price.

A PERSISTENT FRACTURE

When the connection between the Sabbath and the underlying worldview is seen as a motion invisibly linked, it does not stop with the split view of human life in early Christianity. From the fifteenth century onward, says Lewis Mumford, it is as if

> men lived in an empty world: a world which was daily growing emptier. They said their prayers, they repeated their formulas; they even sought to retrieve the holiness they had lost by resurrecting superstitions they had long abandoned: hence the fierceness and hollow fanaticism of the Counter Reformation, its burning of heretics, its persecution of witches, precisely in the midst of the growing "enlightenment." They threw themselves into the medieval dream with a new intensity of feeling.[19]

Nostalgia for the past would not stall the wheel of change at that moment in time. The gilded fog that was medieval civilization's preoccupation with the hereafter was lifting, and the contours of the present world were rising into view. A final blaze of religious fervor was insufficient to revive the existing order.[20] The Church, once in a position to demand unquestioning submission to her dogmas, had lost control. People no longer believed without reservation in the hereafter, and some were even questioning whether the soul exists at all.

The new outlook that came with the disintegration of the old cannot be understood apart from its historical antecedents. Key elements in the lead-up to the Enlightenment were the dualist view of reality, the millennial neglect of the physical world, and the traumatic collapse of this order. As waves lapping the shores of a distant continent, far away from the winds that set the waves in motion, the lingering effects were felt and absorbed in the new world order, in its this-worldly orientation, its materialistic outlook, its rejection of a spiritual reference point, and even in its sense of emptiness.

Here and there, also in scraps and pieces, lay evidence that the collapse of the old order lacked the influences that might heal the fractured view of the world. We see the defect in the concerns of the Protestant Reformation, which had little or nothing to say about the body and the earth. While the Reformation sought to reclaim a lost biblical perspective, the Reformers persisted in taking the immortality of the soul for granted, and the Reformation owed some of its impact precisely to the continued one-sided emphasis on saving the soul. With respect to the way of salvation Luther may have been a disciple of Augustine and the apostle Paul, but with respect to his understanding of the world he remained a child of Augustine and Plato. In the teachings of the Church the separation of the soul from the body and from the world continues to hold sway.[21] Christendom divided into separate camps over the authority of the Bible and the way of salvation, but with respect to the soul there was no division, and there was no sense of the magnitude of the territory that has been lost.

For instance, when René Descartes (1596–1650) drew a line of demarcation between the mind and the operation of nature, he was merely giving the time-honored division of matter and mind a new lease on life.[22] "Am I not myself at least a something?" Descartes asks rhetorically. "But already I have denied that I have a body and senses. This indeed raises awkward questions. But what is it that thereupon follows? Am I so dependent on my body and senses that without them I cannot exist? Having persuaded myself that outside myself there is nothing, that there is no heaven, no Earth, that there are no minds, no bodies, am I thereby committed to the view that I also do not exist?"[23] Descartes came to certainty on this point by eliminating potential pitfalls in human perception, accepting that "our senses sometimes deceive us,"[24] as they do; that people "commit logical fallacies" that cast doubt on their conclusions, which is true; that since our dreams seem real but are fictitious, who can be sure that what seems real in the waking state truly is the way we perceive it?[25] How can a person have certainty about anything? "But I noticed, immediately afterwards, that while I thus wished to think that everything was false, it was necessarily the case that I, who was thinking this, was something. When I noticed that this truth, 'I think, therefore I am' was so firm and certain that all the most extravagant assumptions of the skeptics were unable to shake it, I judged that I could accept it without scruple as the first principle of philosophy for which I was searching."[26]

Jesus makes the Sabbath the supreme marker of all of which He is Lord.

Awkward as the argument is by Descartes's admission, its conclusion is razor sharp. True to a hallowed Christian tradition he would affirm selfhood apart from the body. The self that exists is not itself fraught with materiality or dependent upon mind or body. "I think, therefore I am,"[27] is a statement that immortalizes Descartes, but it also lends new energy to the division between the soul and the body, or, in more modern terminology, between the thinking "self" and the human organism.

But why did Descartes say this at all? Why would he say it at that particular time in history? Why, indeed, would anyone wish to make a case for selfhood apart from the body after the Black Death? Why would he, paraphrasing Roy Porter, disinherit almost the whole of Creation "in a single intrepid stroke"?[28] And why, too, would this statement be hailed by many as a ground-breaking insight?

The reason, of course, is that three hundred years had passed between the Black Death and the time of Descartes. The medieval period was already a distant memory. By this time the world was moving full steam toward the Enlightenment, heady with the sense of change and discovery. If we wish to keep up, we must fast forward because the context of Descartes's dictum is not the medieval period, much less the sense of betrayal that the Black Death inflicted on the medieval ideal.

Historians of science often place the birth of modern science in the year 1543, less than two hundred years after the Black Death and a full one hundred years before Descartes speaks to the subject of "the thinking self" and the body. The year 1543 is chosen as a landmark because it witnesses the publication of the twin monuments of natural science and medicine: *De Revolutionibus* by Copernicus and *De Fabrica* by Andreas Vesalius.[29] Copernicus wrote a groundbreaking book about the universe, Vesalius a spectacular work on human anatomy. Both works were signs of the times, the first harvest of the new and determined orientation toward life in this world and part of the foundation on which modern society would build its impressive edifice. These books were also signs that the balance of power was shifting. Theology would no longer be dominant, or even philosophy. The new era belonged to science, to the exploration of the universe, and to investigation of the body and the earth in ways unimaginable during the medieval period. Before Descartes in 1637 made the statement that earned him a place in history, luminaries like Galileo Galilei (1564–1642),[30] Johannes Kepler (1571–1630),[31] William Gilbert (1544–1603),[32] and William Harvey (1578–1657)[33] had made discoveries that transformed the understanding of the universe, the earth, and the body. Waiting in the wings in Descartes's century were scientists like Robert Boyle (1627–1691) in chemistry, Christian Huygens (1629–1695) in optics, Thomas Willis (1621–1675) in anatomy and physiology, and Isaac Newton (1642–1727).

Descartes was addressing the new paradigm, not the questions raised by the Black Death. As scientific inquiry was seizing the initiative, it was implicit almost from the beginning that the endeavor would threaten the framework of faith. If the hallmark of the old order resided in the absence of materiality, the defining characteristic of the new order was precisely the opposite: materiality, seeking answers to the questions of human existence exclusively from the body and the earth. Although it was faintly evident at the outset, science stood in an adversarial relationship to the traditional outlook; from the point of view of the Christian framework and tradition it was an unwanted child. Its subject matter, nature and the body, had been orphaned in the early Christian view of Creation, and the unwanted child did not seek to win the affections of the parent that severed the tie. So marked was the neglect of the body in the Christian era, in fact, that Vesalius's modest proposal for his work on anatomy was only to recover lost ground in the sense of reclaiming knowledge that was once held. To this effect he qualified the aspiration of his own effort "so that if it did not achieve with us a greater perfection than at any other place or time among the old teachers of anatomy, it might at least reach such a point that one could with confidence assert that our modern science of anatomy was equal to that of the old."[34] His modesty may have had strategic motives, not wishing to stir up hostility, but by "the old teachers of anatomy" Vesalius looked to people who had preceded him by almost 1,500 years. Nothing of significance had happened in his field in the interim.

Descartes perceived, rightly, that the one-sidedness of the new order had in it the impending doom of the soul and belief in the hereafter. How, in a purely materialistic outlook, could such beliefs be sustained? In the context of his time Descartes set out to draw a line that the behemoth of science would not be able to cross, securing an area that in some sense would be off limits to natural science.

To this end he, and others that followed, saw no other option but to revive and revitalize the idea that the human self is independent of the materiality of the body and therefore by definition inaccessible to the tools of scientific inquiry. They did not realize that the separation of the soul from the body cannot be the cure, recalling merely its dismal record during the medieval period; it cannot be the cure because it is the disease.

While believers in the wake of the Black Death still professed Jesus as Lord as if nothing had happened, there is no doubt that the tide had turned. The hereafter no longer seemed as real as before. Soon daring thinkers would posit the soul as a figment of the imagination, undermining the established premise for belief in life after death. Since the Christian faith early on let go its stake in the natural world, and the soul no longer could be taken for granted, the unspoken question was not far away: Christ is still Lord, but of what?

The unspoken question was not far away: Christ is still Lord, but of what?

From the vantage point of the modern world the law of unintended consequences has brought the dreaded answer into full view. The One who had not been recognized as Lord of the Sabbath, or, hewing closer to the words of Mark, the one who has not been recognized as Lord "*even* of the Sabbath" (Mark 2:28), would be recognized as the Lord of nothing.

ENDNOTES

1. Frend, *Rise of Christianity,* 368.

2. Ibid., 348–351; cf. also Eric Osborn, *Tertullian, First Theologian of the West* (Cambridge: Cambridge University Press, 1997), 3–11.

3. Osborn, *Tertullian,* 27–29.

4. Tertullian, *On the Resurrection of the Flesh* II, in *The Ante-Nicene Fathers,* eds.

Alexander Roberts and James Donaldson, vol. III, trans. Peter Holmes (Edinburgh: T & T Clark, repr. Grand Rapids: Eerdmans, 1989), 547.

5. Tertullian, *On the Flesh of Christ* V, in *Ante-Nicene Fathers* III, 525.

6. Tertullian, *A Treatise on the Soul* V, in *Ante-Nicene Fathers* III, 185.

7. Tertullian, *Treatise on the Soul,* VI. Murphy ("Human Nature," 25) calls an integrated, indivisible view of the human person "nonreductive physicalism."

8. Tertullian, *Treatise on the Soul* VI, in *Ante-Nicene Fathers* III, 185.

9. Tertullian, *Treatise on the Soul* LI, in *Ante-Nicene Fathers* III, 228.

10. Tertullian, *Resurrection* III, in *Ante-Nicene Fathers* III, 547.

11. Adolf Harnack, *Medizinisches aus der ältesten Kirchengeschichte* (Leipzig: J.C. Hinrichs'sche Buchhandlung, 1892), 78.

12. The Montanist movement of the late second and early third centuries was characterized by apocalypticism, asceticism, and rhetorical militancy (Frend, *The Rise of Christianity,* 253–256).

13. Tertullian, *An Answer to the Jews,* II, in *Ante-Nicene Fathers,* 3:153.

14. Ibid., 3:152.

15. William H. Willimon, "Lord of the Sabbath," *Christian Century* 108 (1991): 515.

16. Ibid.

17. Ibid.; Robert A. Guelich, *Mark 1–8:26* (WBC 34A; Nashville: Thomas Nelson Publishers, 1989), 128–130.

18. According to William L. Lane (*The Gospel According to Mark* [NICNT; Grand Rapids: Eerdmans, 1974], 120), the passage sets forth "Jesus' true dignity."

19. Mumford, *Technics and Civilization,* 45.

20. Cf. Charles Mackay, *Extraordinary Popular Delusions and the Madness of Crowds* (London: Richard Bentley, 1841 [repr. New York: Harmony Books, 1980]), 477–515.

21. Berry, *The Unsettling of America,* 142.

22. Murphy, "Human Nature," 6–8.

23. René Descartes, *Meditations on First Philosophy,* in Monroe C. Beardsley, *The European Philosophers from Descartes to Nietzsche* (New York: Random House, 1960), 33.

24. René Descartes, *Discourse on Method and Related Writings,* trans. Desmond M. Clarke (London: Penguin Books, 1999 [first published 1637]), 24.

25. Descartes, *Discourse on Method,* 24.

26. Ibid., 24–25.

27. Ibid., 24.

28. Porter, *Flesh in the Age of Reason,* 65.

29. I. Bernard Cohen, *Revolution in Science* (Cambridge, MA: Harvard University Press, 1985), 105–125, 485–488.

30. Galileo Galilei is recognized for his work on the motion of bodies, set forth in the small publication entitled *De Motu* around 1590. In 1633 Galileo was condemned to house arrest for

the rest of his life for his support of the Copernican view of the universe.

31. Johannes Kepler, following in the steps of Copernicus, published *Mysterium Cosmographicum* in 1596, *Astronomia Nova* in 1609, and the seven-volume *Epitome Astronomiae* in 1621.

32. William Gilbert published *De Magneta* in 1600, establishing the standard work on electrical and magnetic phenomena.

33. In 1628 William Harvey published *De Motu cordis,* a groundbreaking study on the heart and the human circulation that was the basis for all modern research on the heart and blood vessels.

34. Cohen, *Revolution in Science,* 487.

A FRIENDLY WITNESS

God saw everything that he had made, and indeed, it was very good. And there was evening and there was morning, the sixth day.
Genesis 1:31

There is a built-in reflex in the notion of the Sabbath to resist the assertion that the world is the product of chance and to dismiss the idea that there is an adversarial relationship between faith in God and the witness of nature. As to the former, the Sabbath story begins on the note that "*God* created the heavens and the earth" (Gen. 1:1). This speaks of a personal beginning, of purpose and not of chance, and it points to God as the Creator of nature. Marcion's peculiar attempt to absolve the God of the New Testament from all responsibility with respect to the created order finds no support in the Bible.[1]

Instead, the Bible is utterly enthralled with the greatness of the material world. "God saw everything that he had made, and indeed, it was very good" (Gen. 1:31). And nature reciprocates, proclaiming, "You, God, are very good" (Ps. 19:1–14; 92:1–6; 104:1–23), or as in other psalms, "the earth is satisfied with the fruit of your work" (Ps. 104:13), and "all your works shall give thanks to you, O LORD" (Ps. 145:10).[2] In this scenario nature is not a hostile witness, and the study of nature will not lead to conclusions that are hostile to belief in God. Moreover, contrary to the view of the leading philosopher of the Enlightenment, there is no need to "abolish knowledge," as though nothing less would be required in order to salvage belief. Within a sabbatarian framework, the relish for the particularities of nature and history is undimmed.

THE WITNESS OF NATURE

Personhood, purpose, and presence combine as Creation comes to a climax with the institution of the Sabbath. "And on the seventh day God finished the work that he had done, and he rested on the seventh day from all the work that he had done" (Gen. 2:2). In all that follows, the indissoluble link between the Creator and Creation is assumed. The poet laureate of the Old Testament treats the connection as self-evident, an inexhaustible supply of praise to God. "The heavens are telling the glory of God, and the firmament proclaims his handiwork" (Ps. 19:1).

According to the biblical story, whether in prose or poetry, the relationship between the Creator and Creation lies like an open book before all who live in the world. "Day to day pours forth speech, and night to night declares knowledge," declares the poet (Ps. 19:2), confident that the witness of nature not only guards the memory of the Creator but also provides a minute-by-minute update of God's sustaining presence in the world. In the poetic perception there is no voice, yet all may hear. "There is no speech, nor are there words; their voice is not heard; yet their voice goes out through all the earth, and their words to the end of the world" (Ps. 19:3–4). The message pulsates wordlessly throughout the entire created order as a subliminal intuition held in trust by all. In this outlook there cannot be any separation between the Creator and the world. Should such a breach arise, it will not be because of intrinsic disparity between the message of the Bible and the evidence of nature. The alienation must be forced upon the relationship by outside forces, by a failure of ideology as in the early Christian disparagement of the body and the earth, by unfamiliarity, or by a breach in the human perception.

Personhood, purpose, and presence combine as Creation comes to a climax with the institution of the Sabbath.

All these factors play a role in the impact of modern science on society. Science shook established notions about the world, but the explanation need not be that the fingerprints of the Creator have disappeared from the earth. The Bible contests such a conclusion, counting on nature to corroborate its testimony.

Nevertheless, in the aftermath of the Black Death and the Renaissance, the early discoveries of science appeared to weaken the case for faith in God. This trend accelerated greatly with the publication of Isaac Newton's *Principia* in 1687. Karl Popper says that hardly anyone living today can imagine the impact of this book when it first appeared.[3] At last it seemed that humanity had arrived at real, certain, and demonstrable knowledge. On the horizon lay the possibility of absolute truth and the promise of a new account of reality.

Despite the exhilaration following Newton's discoveries and despite the fact that Newton himself was a firm believer in God and an avid interpreter of Bible prophecy, *Principia* introduced a view of the world that seemed to leave less to do for God. The new insight suggested the reality of infinite space and infinite time, leaving the idea of a beginning in time in doubt. More serious still, it created the impression that all events are mechanically determined. These assumptions left little room for individuality, for God, and for the notion of a moral purpose.[4] According to the new perception, nature appeared to dispense with its Creator as though the evidence of nature is indifferent to the question of God's existence.

This was followed by earnest efforts to rescue faith in God from science and from a purely scientific reading of the physical world. Descartes, as we have seen, saw his work as an important contribution in this effort. Others would follow, equally alarmed by the implications of allowing science to operate without any constraints and equally determined to set a limit to science so as not to jeopardize belief in a higher order.

ABOLISHING KNOWLEDGE

Like Descartes before him, the German philosopher Immanuel Kant (1724–1804) recognized the imminent demise of the old order. He set out to demonstrate that science can no more describe the ultimate reality of the universe than philosophy can prove the reality of the soul. In an argument whose obscurity is only surpassed by its impact, Kant insisted that the observer must not think that he is dealing with the thing he observes as it really is. What is available is only the thing as it appears to the observer. Things in themselves are unknowable, because "things in themselves" are not, as Kant saw it, in space and time.[5] We immediately recognize that this is similar to

Plato's and Descartes's ideas. In this respect Kant does not propose anything new.

But Kant goes a step further, wishing to pinpoint more precisely the boundary between science and belief. Since the scientific investigation of nature seems to leave no role for God, such investigation cannot be the answer. In Kant's system general truths must be independent of experience, clear and certain in themselves.

> It is only the principles of reason which can give to concordant phenomena the validity of laws, and it is only when experiment is directed by these rational principles that it can have any real utility. Reason must approach nature with the view, indeed, of receiving information from it, not, however, in the character of a pupil, who listens to all that his master chooses to tell him, but in that of a judge, who compels the witnesses to reply to those questions which he himself thinks fit to propose.[6]

Kant is saying that the most important knowledge is not knowledge derived from experience or from the investigation of nature, but *a priori* knowledge, truth that precedes experience. The mind of the observer, rather than the nature of the evidence, guides a person to an understanding of general truths.

The tone of the statement is even more striking. Kant does not want his observer to walk about as a pupil, naïvely rummaging about in nature as the humble recipient of nature's discretionary disclosures. On the contrary, he insists that the observer should assume the stance of a judge, compelling nature to testify. Kant does not say so explicitly, but his rhetoric suggests that the observer's presuppositions must lead the way; indeed, he takes for granted that the observer will not listen to "all that his master [nature] chooses to tell him." Thus faith and ethics will be saved. In his own estimation Kant, by shifting the emphasis to the subjective element, removed faith to where the critical eye of science could not reach it.

Kant was on the battlefield waging war—not on science as such, but on the assumption that scientific investigation poses a threat to faith. He made no attempt to contest the assumption itself, retreating instead to what was to him the unassailable fortress against which no discovery would prevail. His self-described Copernican revolution consisted in showing that "in knowing, it is not the mind that conforms to things but things that conform to the mind," he explained.[7] "I must, therefore, abolish *knowledge*, to make room for *belief*."[8]

Proceeding with this task, Kant passes a generous verdict on the effort. He envisions that by putting "knowledge" in its place, he is conferring "an inestimable benefit on morality and religion, by showing that all objections urged against them may be silenced for ever by the Socratic method, that is to say, by proving the ignorance of the objector."[9] Proving people's ignorance is what Socrates did in Athens, and this is what Kant proposed to do during the Enlightenment. "For, as the world has never been, and, no doubt, never will be, without a system of metaphysics of one kind or another, it is the highest and weightiest concern of philosophy to render it powerless for harm, by closing up the sources of error."[10]

Even on the basis of the meager evidence reproduced above, it is clear that Kant intended to "save" religion. Descartes tried to salvage religion by re-commissioning the separation of the soul from the body. Kant's theory opened a second fracture: the separation of the observer from the world. Subsequent thinkers would modify this view or add to it, but their contributions are secondary developments compared to the strong and steady current of the Kantian movement, flowing ever wider and deeper as the acknowledged axiom of all mature philosophy, as Will Durant expansively describes it.[11] From Kant's point of view his initiative was meant to protect religion from science and the evidence of nature. In actuality, the rescue operation solidified the notion that science represented a threat to faith, all the while widening the breach between the Christian faith and the external body of evidence to which it belongs.

In the years to follow many boats would set sail on the widening Kantian waterway, some more aware than others that Kant's aspiration to place religion on a secure footing bought security at a high price. Friedrich Nietzsche (1844–1900) predicted that the influence of Kant would one day "take the form of a creeping and destructive skepticism and relativism."[12] To the German poet and dramatist Heinrich von Kleist (1777–1811) the sense that Kant had destroyed his faith in the value of knowledge was devastating. Deeply shaken by the experience, von Kleist wrote that "it is impossible for us to decide whether that to which we appeal as truth is in truth the truth, or whether it merely seems to us so....If the sharp point of this thought does not pierce your heart, do not smile at one who feels wounded by it in the holiest depth of his soul. My highest, my only aim has fallen to the ground, and I have none left."[13]

THE OBSERVER AND THE WORLD

In the biblical story of Creation, the division between the observer and the world does not exist. Originally there is no antagonism between them, no suggestion that things appear to the observer as something other than what they are. "I must, therefore, abolish *knowledge*, to make room for *belief*,"[14] Kant declares, offering retreat from the external world as his remedy even though, within the biblical view of reality, the remedy addresses a problem that is unknown to the biblical view. In the original biblical perspective, the earth and its occupants interact in a state of harmony (Gen. 1:31). In this framework a person has the capacity to perceive and understand reality. What is seen reflects what is really there, and the observer is not estranged or excluded from that which he or she observes.

This relationship is illustrated by an inconspicuous sentence in the Creation story. "So out of the ground the Lord God formed every beast of the field and every bird of the air, and brought them to the man to see what he would call them; and *whatever the man called every living creature, that was its name*" (Gen. 2:19). In a low-key and unassuming way, this text affirms the broad mandate. Human beings are empowered to describe the world.[15] This exercise must not to be seen as a naming game in which the human being develops an arbitrary taxonomy for all of God's creatures. In the deepest sense the *name* expresses the fundamental characteristics of its subject. For this reason the naming of animals profoundly implies a commission to comprehend the world. A system of communication is developing in which the observer comprehends, and comprehension is manifested in communication. Words and reality correspond. The words that are used to describe the world correspond to the reality that has been comprehended. In this system the human mind is not haphazardly imposing itself on the external world. When Genesis says that "*whatever the man called every living creature, that was its name*" (2:19), it is not to be seen as though God is willing to abide by the result of the unrestricted mandate no matter how bizarre the consequences. It is rather that human beings have the capacity to carry out the assignment successfully. "That was its name" signifies that the outcome is representative of the character of the subject. At Creation God endowed the human mind with the means to figure out what the world is like and to know God through God's created works. The world of Creation lay open as a limitless source of insight into the character of God.

This view is not contrived or invalidated even in the context of the twenty-first century. Neurological science has shown that the human brain to some extent dedicates specific areas for specialized functions down to amazing minutiae of perception and comprehension. In a sense the anatomical makeup of the brain with its distinctive loci of function and comprehension reads as a carefully crafted processing facility of outside input, certainly exceeding anything envisioned by Kant. For instance, the neurologist Oliver Sacks reports a case illustrating that the slightest injury to the brain can open up huge deficits in a person's comprehension. In *The Man Who Mistook His*

The world of Creation lay open as a limitless source of insight into the character of God.

Wife for a Hat, Sacks tells of a man who suddenly is unable to recognize faces, any face, in fact, even the face of his own wife.[16] Otherwise the patient seems perfectly normal. There is no evidence that his eyesight is affected because he identifies objects with ease and precision, and no other dysfunction is detected. It is only when the patient gets up to put on his hat that the subtle impairment is exposed. He cannot see the face of his wife; he mistakenly thinks that what he sees is a hat, reaching in the direction of her face in the belief that it is his hat. The patient, a professor of music, has suffered a small injury to the visual cortex at the back of his brain. This injury makes it impossible for the brain to organize and reconstitute the human face from the electrical impulses and the packets of chemicals that mediate normal visual input. In the context of the Kantian concern, the human brain is structured to comprehend reality, and it flails in the dark when the link between the brain and the outside world is interrupted.

In the Bible, too, comprehension is a problem, but the problem does not break down along the lines that are so vexing to Descartes or Kant. The biblical view conceives the problem in ethical and perceptual terms under the notion of "sin." This notion derives from a Greek word that means "to miss the mark" (*hamartia*), and will, in the present context, accommodate the English expression "to miss the point." Sin profoundly distorts the harmony between the earth and the observer on two levels. As to the external world, nature is damaged to the point that it no longer reflects the character of God consistently. The evidence from nature becomes ambivalent, contradictory, even misleading. If the observer believes that everything before him reflects the character of God, he or she risks forming an opinion of God that misses the mark. Nature alone no longer serves as a reliable point of reference to distinguish between what is of God and what is not.

A change also happens in the mind of the observer. Sin diminishes the human capacity to perceive what is there. Human reason no longer inclines toward God and truth (1 Cor. 2:14). The first scene after the fall shows the breach between God and human beings.

Before the breach, the human family welcomed God with expectation and joy. Now, after the breach, "they heard the sound of the Lord God walking in the garden in the cool of the day, and Adam and his wife hid themselves from the presence of the Lord God among the trees of the garden" (Gen. 3:8, NKJV). All of a sudden human beings look apprehensively at God across a great divide, a divide that will widen as humans drift further and further from insight that once was self-evident.

In this predicament outside help is needed. It is impossible for human beings to bring coherence to the confusing signals of the world, and the problem is aggravated by the fact that each person approaches the task with diminished capacity. Studying the world as it is now will not be sufficient because the world, in the biblical view of reality, is under the blight of sin. Nature, observation, and experience cannot solve the riddle. Creation itself is moaning under the dominion of an alien power (Rom. 8:19–22). "Cursed is the ground because of you," God declares of the adversarial relationship that has come to exist between human beings and nature. Nature will not disclose itself to human beings as before or bend to human wishes. "Thorns and thistles it shall bring forth to you," God warns, not because thorns and thistles belong to God's idea, but as proof that something is interfering to distort the original design (Gen. 3:17).

Nature alone no longer serves as a reliable point of reference to distinguish between what is of God and what is not.

The observer needs information as to how things turned out this way, a vantage point from which to view the world. In the biblical perspective human finitude is not acknowledged by admitting that we do not know anything with certainty along the lines proposed by Socrates or Kant. Instead, the remedy is God's redemptive intervention. Human finitude is acknowledged by willingness to listen when God speaks, and God has spoken (Heb. 1:1).[17] Nothing expresses the biblical remedy better than the prophetic insight, "Morning by morning he makes my ear alert to listen like a disciple" (Isa. 50:4, NJB). The answer is not in the mind itself but in the gift of hearing and in a person's willingness to listen. "The Lord God has opened my ear, and I was not rebellious, I did not turn backwards," says Isaiah (50:5).

Theologians call this "special revelation," and the content of revelation is the comprehensive story that is found in the Bible. Indeed, "story" is an appropriate term, and the story includes the seventh day. In fact, the Sabbath is itself a *raconteur*, a storyteller, giving a compressed version of the terms of human existence, a reliable and faithful witness to what God has done and an open door to the experience of God's presence.

Even revelation, however, is not enough. If special revelation is needed to compensate for the distorted witness of nature, special illumination is required to make up for the diminished capacity of the observer because special revelation is easily missed or ignored. It cannot be otherwise, says Paul, because "the natural man does not receive the things of the Spirit of God, for they are foolishness to him; nor can he know them, because they are spiritually discerned" (1 Cor. 2:14, NKJV). In a still more noteworthy passage in the Gospel of John, Jesus compares the workings of the illumination that must come from without to the workings of the wind. "The wind blows where it chooses, and you hear the sound of it, but you do not know where it comes from or where it goes. So it is with everyone who is born of the Spirit" (John 3:8). In other words, a redemptive power is directly at work to effect the illumination that is needed, elusive and invisible. Its existence is ascertained by its effect, but the spiritual agency is publicity-shy and will not be pinned down as to its origin or its mode of operation.

Kant's offer to "abolish knowledge to make room for belief" runs contrary to the tenor of the biblical witness because it posits "knowledge" as a threat to belief when knowledge, properly configured, sustains belief. Kant is understood to have thought that time and space are qualities of reason rather than qualities of the world.[18] They are "all in the head," as it were, determining the mould of all perceptions, and irremediably subjective. This complicates a relationship that in one respect, at least, is much simpler in the Bible, and it is exemplified in the Sabbath. No Sabbath is conceivable apart from time and space, meaning that time and space are realities of the external world. By consecrating the Sabbath God sets a mark on the nature of the world, commissioning human beings to relate to reality according to the way it is created. In such a world it is still possible to know with certainty even though that knowledge is partial and imperfect (1 Cor. 13:9).

THE PRESTIGE OF PARTICULARITY

In Kant's system of generalities the Sabbath is a discordant particularity. The seventh day is neither a category of the human mind nor an *a priori* insight, and neither does it rise self-evidently from nature. Standing as a towering peak in the landscape of perception, it represents a voice from without, bringing illumination from without. The seventh day seals the relationship between the Creator and the world, opposing efforts to drive a wedge between the two. "So God blessed the seventh day and hallowed it, because on it God rested from all the work that he had done in creation" (Gen. 2:3) is a statement that cements the work of God and the voice of God into the human experience.

The particularity of the Sabbath is an ill fit in the Kantian system of general truths because it rolls out the welcoming mat to the irreducible particularities that make up much of the biblical narrative. Acceptance of particularities, in turn, is part of its portfolio of meanings. Neither Kant's general truths nor the principle of analogy, as advocated in the twentieth century by Ernst Troeltsch (1865–1923),[19] is adequate for the task of sifting true claims from false. This principle holds that the likelihood of an event having occurred is proportional to its regular occurrence, but it has no place for the singular event. The principle of analogy frowns, too, on what to the Bible is dearest of all, the *unrepeatable* event. The Sabbath keeps vigil over the latter category, an unapologetic particularity playing host to a feast of hope for the irreducible particularities and unrepeatable events that are the Bible: Abraham's sacrifice of Isaac (Gen. 22:1–14); the burning bush of Moses (Exod. 3:1–5; Acts 7:30); the birth of a child to a woman who had yet to experience intimate relations with a man (Matt. 1:18, 25; Luke 1:31–35); the exceptional life and death of that child as a grown man, reported in the New Testament as a singular, unrepeatable event (Rom. 6:10; Heb. 7:27; 9:26; 10:10; 1 Pet. 3:18); and the resurrection of that person from the dead (Acts 2:24; 10:40; 13:30; Rom. 10:9; 1 Cor. 15:4; Gal. 1:1; Rev. 1:18).

Kant, addressing his own view of science, wanted to "abolish knowledge to make room for belief." A similar view was adopted by Rudolf Bultmann, one of the most influential New Testament scholars of the twentieth century. Speaking in the spirit of Kant, Bultmann tried to dissociate Christianity from the remaining vestige of contact with the external world.

> Radical demythologization is the parallel of the Pauline-Lutheran doctrine of justification apart from works of the law by faith alone. Or rather, it is its consistent application in the sphere of knowledge. Just as the doctrine of justification, it destroys all man's false security and all false longing for security, whether that security rests on his good behaviour or on his validating knowledge. The man who will believe in God must know he has nothing in his hand which he might believe, that he is, as it were, up in the air, and can demand no proof for the truth of the word addressing him.[20]

Faith, as Bultmann defines it, should not be corroborated by any particularity in history. The witness of the New Testament is in this view not primarily a witness to events that happened but stories told to elicit faith quite apart from the content of the stories. Looking back to the perspectives we have studied in the Old and the New

Testaments, the focus in this outlook is human faith and not divine faithfulness. By such radically contrived disclaimers, the biblical witness has, like the man traveling from Jerusalem to Jericho, fallen into the hands of robbers (Luke 10:30), and, even more than the victim in Luke's story, the witness has had its bones broken and is fractured to the marrow.

Contrary to this view, the New Testament makes "room for knowledge" because its message is the raw material for belief. The treasure comes in "clay jars" (2 Cor. 4:7), and the person who accepts it, seeing "in a mirror, dimly," says of himself or herself, "Now I know only in part" (1 Cor. 13:12). But while knowledge is partial and illumination incomplete, the witness is nevertheless crucial. "But just as we have the same spirit of faith that is in accordance with scripture—'I believed, and so I spoke'—we also believe, and so we speak," Paul writes (2 Cor. 4:13). He is tireless in proclaiming what has happened in his own time because he is convinced of its validity and importance. "But how are they to call on one in whom they have not believed?" he asks with concern. "And how are they to believe in one of whom they have never heard? And how are they to hear without someone to proclaim him?" (Rom. 10:14). In this paradigm knowledge cannot be abolished as though its abolition will benefit belief. On the contrary, the knowledge of which he speaks is the source and sustainer of belief. The apostle seeks the listening ear, confident that "faith comes from what is heard, and what is heard comes through the word of Christ" (Rom. 10:17).

Even now, despite the distortions of sin, nature has not ceased to reveal God, as the writers of the Bible tell it. The poet who writes that "the heavens are telling the glory of God, and the firmament proclaims his handiwork" (Ps. 19:1) is not describing a point of view that is possible only for one who has limited knowledge of the operations of the world. In the silent witness of nature he discerns the hand of the Infinite. Nature does not tell the whole story, but the teachable observer has other information to fill in the gaps to make the picture consistent with itself. In the New Testament, the apostle Paul is convinced that God is not a marginal inference from the witness of nature. "Ever since the creation of the world his invisible nature, namely, his eternal power and deity, has been *clearly* perceived in the things that have been made," he writes (Rom. 1:20).

That was the conviction when the human ability to explore nature was limited. Will anyone corroborate this line of reasoning when the prejudices of the Middle Ages are exposed and a new era brings unknown mysteries to light? Creation made a spectacular impression at the distance from which the ancient sages observed it. Is the close-up view a disappointment? Should people feel less inclined to praise the Creator after William Harvey's discovery of the circulation in the seventeenth century, Rudolf Virchow's description of the cell two centuries later, or by the unraveling in our time of the complex universe that inhabits each cell? Should the joy inspired by a pre-Copernican sunrise lessen after the discovery of photons and the relationship between matter and energy? Are the heavens, when observed through the telescope, no longer telling the glory of God? Has the time passed for seeing in nature "a conscious, intelligent, planning, controlling, and presiding Creator," as Charles Spurgeon claimed to see it?[21]

Despite the distortions of sin, nature has not ceased to reveal God.

For many people in the twenty-first century the answer to these questions has been negatively conditioned by the troubled relationship between Christianity and the physical world. Alien ideas embedded in the matrix of the Christian tradition set up an antagonism between science and faith that at times seems beyond healing. It is remarkable that one of the most lucid observations in this respect came from the scientist who is often thought to have done great injury to the cause of belief. Charles Darwin (1809–1882) had been deeply affected by the idea of an immortal soul and its traditional fallout, eternal punishment. He saw it as an idea offensive to reason. Describing his slow and reluctant rejection of Christianity, Darwin confided that "I can indeed hardly see how anyone ought to wish Christianity to be true; for if so the plain language of the text seems to show that the men who do not believe, and this would include my Father, Brother and almost all my best friends, will be everlastingly punished."[22] Darwin's view of "the plain language of the text" is problematic, but the entrenched notion of the immortal soul is clearly there to haunt him. Choosing the words that he felt this doctrine deserves, he added emphatically, "And this is a damnable doctrine."[23]

> ***In the biblical perspective there is no hostility between the Creator, the Sabbath, the body, and the earth.***

The Sabbath, itself an enthusiastic particularity, is a bosom friend of the particularities in the biblical witness and a friend of the witness of nature. The biblical concern is not to rise up to defeat science because science, deployed within a framework that is aware of the ambiguous message of nature and of human limitation, serves the cause of the Creator. Silencing science is tantamount to turning against a friendly witness. "Knowledge" does not need to be downgraded. In the biblical perspective there is originally no split between nature and observer, and no hostility between the Creator, the Sabbath, the body, and the earth.

ENDNOTES

1. Brown, *The Body and Society*, 90.
2. Cf. Walter Brueggemann, *The Message of the Psalms: A Theological Commentary* (Minneapolis: Augsburg, 1984), 28–31.
3. Karl Popper, *Conjectures and Refutations* (London: Routledge and Kegan, 1963), 93.
4. A. D. Lindsay, in the "Introduction of Immanuel Kant," *Critique of Pure Reason,* trans. Norman Kemp (London: J. M. Dent & Sons Ltd, 1934), xi–xii.
5. Kant, *Critique of Pure Reason*, 3.
6. Ibid., 10–11.
7. Cohen, *Revolution in Science*, 240. It is a moot point that Kant himself never referred to

this change as a *revolution*. He clearly considered his own contribution on the same level as that of Copernicus.

8. Kant, *Critique of Pure Reason*, 18.

9. Ibid.

10. Ibid.

11. Will Durant, *The Story of Philosophy* (New York: Pocket Books, 1953), 253.

12. Friedrich Nietzsche, *Tracts Against the Times*, quoted in Karl Popper, *The Open Society and Its Enemies*, vol. 2 (London: Routledge, 1966), 382.

13. Ibid.

14. Kant, *Critique of Pure Reason*, 18.

15. Fretheim (*God and the World in the Old Testament*, 56–58) and others are certainly on solid ground in claiming Gen. 2:19 as a text showing human autonomy, allowing human beings to shape the future, but he puts too little emphasis on human capacity to get it right.

16. Oliver Sacks, *The Man Who Mistook His Wife for a Hat and Other Clinical Tales* (New York: Harper & Row, 1970), 8–22.

17. See Nicholas Wolterstorff, *Divine Discourse: Philosophical Reflections on the Claim that God Speaks* (Cambridge: Cambridge University Press, 1995).

18. For a helpful note on this subject, see Popper, *Conjectures and Refutations*, 179.

19. Ernst Troeltsch (*Zur Religiösen Lage, Religionsphilosophie und Ethik* [Tübingen: Verlag von J. C. B. Mohr (Paul Siebeck), 1913], 729–753) proposed that the probability of an occurrence is proportional to its conformity to normal human experience. Claims of exceptional occurrences are by definition suspect; they are, in fact, impossible.

20. Quoted in Peter Stuhlmacher, *Historical Criticism and Theological Interpretation of Scripture*, trans. Roy A. Harrisville (London: SPCK, 1979), 64.

21. Charles H. Spurgeon, *The Treasury of David*, vol. 1 (Grand Rapids: Guardian Press, 1976 [orig. 1870–1885]), 305 (commentary to Psalm 19).

22. *The Autobiography of Charles Darwin* (New York: W. W. Norton & Company, 1969), 87.

23. Ibid.

CHAPTER 21

FROM CREATION TIME TO CLOCK TIME

Then God made two great lights: the greater light to rule the day, and the lesser light to rule the night.
Genesis 1:16

Although the transition from "creation time" to "clock time" has received little attention, it remains one of the greatest transformations in human history. Taking place toward the end of the Middle Ages, the birth of "clock time" was to transform life in ways as profound and universal as any idea or discovery that constitutes the modern world. Gradually, in increments and spurts, the office of keeping time is transferred from the clocks of nature, the sun and the moon, to the mechanical clock. By now commonplace to the point of making it nearly impossible to conceive what life was like without it, the invention of the mechanical clock marks a turning point in civilization. David Landes calls it "one of the great inventions in the history of mankind—not in a class with fire and the wheel, but comparable to movable type in its revolutionary implications for cultural values, technological change, social and political organization, and personality."[1]

Control of time confers the prerogative to set priorities and to determine what is important. This is the true challenge of "clock time" and its most seductive temptation. "Clock time" takes a human measure of what comes first in life, but it is precisely the human measure that has, against all expectations, proved problematic. How could it be, far into the era of "clock time," that the human measure would seem to be *de*-humanizing? How could *human* control of time become a threat to civilization, a testimony to the limits of human autonomy? These questions, as we shall see below, invite the prospect of retrieving the blessing of "creation time."

CLOCK TIME

Before the mechanical clock day and night were under the dominion of the rotation of the earth around its own axis. With the invention of the clock control of time was wrested away from nature to create a new awareness of time and a different sense of destiny. Somewhere between the Middle Ages and our own time the symphony of nature died down, and the ceaseless humming and insistent drumbeat of machinery took over.

The mechanical clock is a vigilant master because it reinforces the objective reality of time despite its continuing subjective quality.[2] People continue to experience periods of pain and sorrow as drawn-out, never-ending hours. Waiting time feels like time that lasts forever. Happier moments quicken the pace of time's passing. Suddenly "time flies," and in the most exuberant experiences the sense of time passing lets go completely. It was, we say, as if "time ceased to exist."

The clock holds all people and all experience firmly in time's objective reality. By gradual increments of conquest the clock forges human society into an image of itself. It is the prototype machine, overseeing life everywhere and at all levels. Human beings cannot originate or extend time, but we can organize and improve it. Time cannot be changed, but it can be harnessed. As Mumford observes, "the clock is not merely a means of keeping track of the hours, but of synchronizing the actions of men."[3] In that sense the clock has created the conditions for the industrial society and is itself its first and most successful product.

After paving the way for mass production, the clock has taken up a slumberless watch to monitor and ensure its continued success. "The clock, not the steam-engine, is the key machine of the modern industrial age," Mumford writes perceptively. "For every phase of its development the clock is both the outstanding fact and the typical symbol of the machine: even today no other machine is so ubiquitous."[4] More than in the era of "creation time," time has become a commercial commodity. Landes argues that the mechanical clock "made possible, for better or worse, a civilization attentive to the passage of time, hence to productivity and performance."[5] Not only does the clock mark a decisive breakthrough for technology, but it also signals a new era of European leadership and power. Carlo Cipolla tells of a galley that left Venice in the summer of 1338, bound for the East. As a conspicuous item among its cargo, the galley carried a clock.[6] This was probably a mechanical clock that was part of a bold business venture on the part of the trader Giovanni Loredan, who hoped to sell the clock in Delhi. "No chronicler took notice of the event in those days and modern historians scarcely mention it in their writings. Yet that was a fateful event. Europe had begun to export machinery to Asia," says Cipolla.[7]

As the supremacy of time was transferred from nature to a machine, the clock set the tone for what life would be like in the new era. Human beings have to conform to the new routine. Industrial and technological society breaks down the boundaries formerly set by night and day and the fluctuations of the seasons. The machine cannot be turned off; it must produce its product "around the clock" and to the full of its capacity. The worker, in turn, must be there on the assembly line to tend to the machine. In this way the worker becomes an extension of the machine, acquiescing to its terms. Eventually it yields a truism: "Time is money"—even though the converse cannot be true. Money is not time.

At first the clock represented human conquest of nature. In the course of time it has been revealed that the inventor achieved this mastery by putting himself under the dominion of a machine with rigid demands of its own. Like the ungovernable broom in Goethe's poem about the sorcerer's apprentice, a spectacular invention defies the dictates of the hapless inventor.

In an unexpected twist the clock has come to express not only humanity's dominion over creation but also our alienation from it.

In an unexpected twist the clock has come to express not only humanity's dominion over creation but also our alienation from it. Where city clocks once tolled with the promise of liberating technology, portable watches now spur executives and employees to meet deadlines, make appointments, and be "on time." Clock time symbolizes the atomization of existence, the severance of the moment from the past and the future. It brings precision to life but is silent about life's purpose; it reminds of duty but not of destiny; it dictates work but not rest; it promotes productivity, and it has made it appear that productivity is the purpose of existence. Under the clock's accounting recreation time is characterized as "time off." What kind of time, then, is work, and what does the notion of "time off" suggest about the relative value of the two divisions?

THE GRIP OF CLOCK TIME

The productivity made possible by the clock has been a stunning success. Nevertheless, in the downstream effect of mass production and unlimited consumption, the seeds of society's undoing have been sown. As ecological disaster threatens life on a fragile earth, people wonder whether civilization can survive. It is not necessary to be an alarmist in order to agree with former vice president Al Gore, who says that the earth is in the balance.[8] Human domination over nature is boomeranging. It is clear that human beings are not above Creation, as the most enthusiastic scientists and philosophers after the Renaissance once imagined.

In his early book *Amerika*, Franz Kafka makes a tantalizing case for seeing Western civilization as something other than what it is reputed to be.[9] Karl Rossmann, the main character in *Amerika*, arrives in New York with other immigrants under the welcoming gaze of the Statue of Liberty. In a foretaste of *Kafkaesque* eeriness, the new country provides encounters that have biblical overtones. Karl, who has come in search of life, liberty, and the pursuit of happiness, ends up as a menial hotel employee in a suburb of New York that Kafka mysteriously calls *Rameses*.

Rameses is an allusion to the Bible, the name of a city in the book of Exodus.[10] It is shorthand for oppression and slavery, evoking the story of Israel's hardship in Egypt. As the situation of the downtrodden people is getting increasingly precarious, the Exodus narrative says that the Egyptians "set taskmasters over them to oppress them with forced labor. They built supply cities, Pithom and Rameses, for Pharaoh" (Exod. 1:11). When this allusion appears in Kafka's book, the sensitized eye is supposed to remember the biblical story. On his way to opportunity and affluence, young Karl ends up in what is the biblical epitome of slavery.

The historical *Rameses* was an Egyptian city built for human aggrandizement by slave labor of the most exploitative kind. "The Egyptians became ruthless in imposing tasks on the Israelites," says the Bible (Exod. 1:13). Dominance led to exploitation, the dominant group pursuing its own interest at the expense of the less fortunate and disempowered. Egyptian prosperity was bought at the expense of the misfortune of someone else. In this context God intervenes to set the Israelites free (Exod. 5:1).

The original exodus story in the Bible is the story of the deliverance of an oppressed people. God is determined to lift the yoke off the shoulders of the deprived, the downtrodden, and the downcast. Pharaoh's recalcitrance, be it ever so determined, will not prevail. Thus we hear the steady and rising demand, "Let my people go!" And thus we hear the stated *telos*, the purpose of the remarkable intervention—"so that they may worship me" (Exod. 7:16; 8:1, 20; 9:1, 13; 10:3). In a real sense, the ensuing struggle is a conflict over the management of people's time. God resists the priority set for the Israelites by the Egyptian despot. The latter's version of "clock time" is demeaning, and God, who prevails in the conflict, delivers the people in order that they may regain control of their time and discover that human time is best protected by a higher Master.

The slaves struggling in the merciless heat of the city that the author of Exodus calls *Rameses* are called to priorities very different from the ones set by the slave masters, over the objections and active resistance of the masters (Exod. 5:1–2). They achieve liberty at last, and their first taste of freedom, as we have seen (ch. 5), marks a return to creation time and to the Sabbath (Exod. 16:22–26). Just as it is in the nature of allusions to leave the thought incomplete, this one beckons the reader to finish it. If Kafka's whispered allusion to *Rameses* is heeded, modern civilization, especially the industrialized world that still claims the afterglow of a Christian legacy, has come full circle to the Exodus story. Rameses is now the city of which all people are citizens, derailed from life's real purpose and trapped in a trajectory that will end in defeat. It is as if the Creator speaks again to the modern masters of clock time and productivity, "Let my people go" (Exod. 5:1). Not only has the freedom that was promised by the invention of the mechanical clock turned into a new kind of slavery, but impending ecological disaster exposes the underlying premise of misguided priorities, excess, and exploitation. Arnold Toynbee summarizes the problem and the challenge:

> For the last 200 years, we have given priority to the maximization of material wealth, regardless of the price in human suffering and in the wrecking of the natural environment from which our wealth has been extracted by the modern device of mechanization. From now on, we shall have to give priority to the re-humanization of human life and to the conservation of what we have left of our natural environment, whatever the cost....[11]

RETRIEVING CREATION TIME

Clock time, then, often sets priorities that dehumanize life. Perhaps "dehumanizes" is a misleading term, and perhaps, for the same reason, it will not suffice only to re-humanize human existence. Compared to the priorities set by the Creation time and the Sabbath, it is better to say that the clock "de-theologizes" life by removing God from the reckoning of time, and, from the vantage point of this insight, to ponder the prospect of "a religious counter-revolution."[12] Contemporary human existence plays out under the mastery of the clock, captive to the priorities of which the clock is the leading instrument. In the process, writes Neil Postman,

> we have learned irreverence toward the sun and the seasons, for in a world made up of seconds and minutes, the authority of nature is superseded. And thus, though few would have imagined the connection, the inexorable ticking of the clock may have had more to do with the weakening of God's supremacy than all the treatises produced by the philosophers of the Enlightenment; that is to say, the clock introduced a new form of conversation between man and God, in which God appears to have been the loser. Perhaps Moses should have included another Commandment: Thou shalt not make mechanical representations of time.[13]

Such a commandment does not exist, but there is a commandment about time that meets the need (Exod. 20:8–11). The Sabbath has the power to overturn distorted priorities. In the biblical perspective the Sabbath interrupts the routine of clock time and the obligation of work by calling all creation to a day of rest according to the great clock of nature. As daylight fades every Friday night, "from evening to evening" (Lev. 23:32), the Sabbath breaks the cycle of business and the struggle for subsistence. At the setting of the sun, clock time yields to Creation time in order to respond to a higher summons, mediated by the clock of Creation. Human priorities, set by the clock and the necessity of working, come face to face with God's generous provision. Every human being is entitled to abstain from work and to lay aside projects in order to rest. As a means to keep track of time the clock is unsurpassed, but the mastery of time belongs to "the two great lights, the greater light to rule the day and the lesser light to rule the night," appointed as time-keepers long ago by the Creator (Gen. 1:16). For this reason the hours of the Sabbath begin at the gentle tolling of nature's ruling light, not at an arbitrary hour defined by the mechanical clock (Lev. 23:32).

The clock "de-theologizes" life by removing God from the reckoning of time.

The Sabbath sets another goal than productivity as the measure of human life. God's neglected provision establishes human dignity on its own spiritual footing, calling for respect and humility in the human stewardship of creation. "In the sabbath stillness men and women no longer intervene in the environment through their labour. They let it be entirely God's creation," writes Jürgen Moltmann.[14] But this limitation cannot be construed as a deprivation. On the contrary, it is the absence of the limitation that is truly threatening. "Without the Sabbath quiet, history becomes the self-destruction of humanity," Moltmann warns, implicitly urging a retrieval of resource for healing.[15] "Through the seventh day rest, history is sanctified with the divine measure and blessed with the measure of a true humanity."[16] God has put a limit on work, not in order to trivialize human accomplishment, but because human enterprise apart from God is ending in failure. It does not require the wisdom of a prophet to read the writing on the wall.

The ecological debacle of Western civilization gives a fresh reason to reconsider the Sabbath. In the depleted reserves of the earth's environment the story of the prodigal son is recapitulated on a grand and global scale (Luke 15:11–32). Like the son who first demands his inheritance, determined to strike out on his own away from home and free of any restraining input, the human enterprise has celebrated the illusion of complete and limitless autonomy. But now the party is drawing to a close, and nature's dwindling resources confront the profligate ways of humanity with the discovery that the inheritance is spent. We live in the era of consequences, of ecological bills coming due, and of crisis.

In the face of this crisis the appeal of the Sabbath is obvious. Addressing a culture that values production and prosperity above all else, the Sabbath represents a sphere of silence made all the more striking because the rhythm of society does not make room for it. It is chiseled into the bedrock of existence by the Creator, but only the eye of faith can empower it to set limits on human activity. In the absence of a natural foothold in the world the Sabbath becomes a practical countermeasure to secularism, a wordless occasion to train one's vision on the higher reality. Thus, as Marva Dawn urges perceptively, "[t]o return to Sabbath keeping is not nostalgia. Rather, it is a return to the spiritual dimension that haunts us. In an age that has lost its soul, Sabbath keeping offers the possibility of gaining it back....In contrast to the technological society, in which the sole criterion of value is the measure of efficiency, those who keep the Sabbath find their criteria in the character of God, in whose image they celebrate life."[17]

Between the divinely offered privilege and the most profound perception of human need that are its original idiom, the enticing whisper of the seventh day may still be heard among louder voices now calling attention to it. And yet the louder calls, even though they are voices of lesser stature, also carry their message with power and emotion. If the seventh day in its original configuration bears a message of human limitations, the louder voice now addresses the toxic consequences of human self-importance, confronting the addicting illusion that everything must fall into line with the priorities enforced by clock time. In this setting keeping the Sabbath is "an act of prophetic resistance,"[18] a resetting of priorities away from self-interest in the area of work and recreation alike. For the same reason the Sabbath is aptly perceived as a time for *No*, a time to turn one's back on the illusion that production and consumption are the primary purpose of existence. In this sense the Sabbath is the launching point of a disciplined journey in the direction of a center other than oneself.[19] The prophet had his finger on the pulse of modernity when he wrote,

The Sabbath has the power to overturn distorted priorities.

> If because of the sabbath, you turn your foot
> From doing your own pleasure on My holy day,
> And call the sabbath a delight, the holy day of the LORD honorable,
> And honor it, desisting from your own ways,
> From seeking your own pleasure

> And speaking your own word,
> Then you will take delight in the LORD,
> And I will make you ride on the heights of the earth;
> And I will feed you with the heritage of Jacob your father,
> For the mouth of the LORD has spoken. (Isa. 58:13–14, NASB)

The pointed contrasts in this prophetic valuation must not be missed. Beginning with the contrast between self-centered pursuit and concern for the common good (Isa. 58:1–12), the ancient sabbatarian vision draws out stark opposites as to how human beings relate themselves to time. Decrying the life preoccupied with pursuing "*your own* ways," "seeking *your own* pleasure," and "speaking *your own* word," the prophet urges his reader to recognize that the self-important and self-preoccupied life will diminish the self and lead to the dissolution of human community. His remedy, of course, is the Sabbath, promoting it as the means by which to reconnect to God, to history, to community, and to the earth and thus to combat the disconnections of Sabbath-less existence.

Speaking from the ruins of the failed stewardship of clock time and its legacy of exploitation, the Sabbath protects against a purely human dictate. It holds out the promise of liberty to the oppressed and overworked; indeed, it reaches out to calm and contain even the restless scheming of the oppressor. Self-importance and the delusion of absolute autonomy, perhaps the most resistant human addictions, can find in the Sabbath a remedy. In the story of the seventh day there is an end to work and a call to heed the summons of Creation time because, in the beginning, God "rested on the seventh day from all the work that he had done" (Gen. 2:2).

And then, too, breaking into the whisper of Creation time, as we shall see and hear, there is the uninhibited wailing of the voice of the earth.

ENDNOTES

1. David S. Landes, *Revolution in Time* (Cambridge, MA: The Belknap Press, 1983), 6.
2. Some of the greatest minds in history have tried to pin down time without success, proving

Augustine right that everybody knows what time is but nobody is able to explain it; cf. *Time,* ed. Jonathan Westphal and Carl Levenson (Indianapolis: Hackett Publishing Company, 1993).

3. Mumford, *Technics and Civilization,* 14.

4. Ibid.

5. Landes, *Revolution in Time,* 7.

6. Carlo M. Cipolla, *Clocks and Culture* (New York: W. W. Norton & Company, 1978), 13.

7. Ibid.

8. Al Gore, *Earth in the Balance* (London: Earthscan Publications, 1992).

9. Franz Kafka, *Amerika,* trans. Edwin Muir (New York: New Directions, 1946); also published as *The Man Who Disappeared (Amerika),* trans. Micheal Hofmann (New York: Penguin Books, 1996).

10. Robert Alter (*The Pleasures of Reading in an Ideological Age* [New York: W. W. Norton & Co., 1996], 121–123) uses *Rameses* as an example of a single-word allusion to the Old Testament in modern literature.

11. Arnold Toynbee, "The Religious Background of the Present Environmental Crisis," in *Ecology and Religion in History,* 146.

12. Toynbee ("Religious Background," 146–147), whose perception of the cause of the problem is less persuasive than his view of its seriousness, envisions "a religious counter-revolution" along lines quite different from the ones mandated by a sabbatarian perspective.

13. Neil Postman, *Amusing Ourselves to Death* (New York: Penguin Books, 1985), 11–12.

14. Moltmann, *God in Creation,* 277.

15. Ibid., 139.

16. Ibid.

17. Marva J. Dawn, *Keeping the Sabbath Wholly* (Grand Rapids: William B. Eerdmans, 1989), 50.

18. Willimon, "Lord of the Sabbath," 515; cf. also Barbara Brown Taylor, "Sabbath Resistance," *Christian Century* 122 (2005): 35.

19. Gregory S. Cootsona, "A Time for No," *Perspectives* 17 (2002): 24.

CHAPTER 22

THE LOST VOICE OF THE EARTH

For the earnest expectation of the creation eagerly waits for the revealing of the sons of God.
Romans 8:19, NKJV

The Sabbath confers God's blessing on all of creation (Gen. 2:1–3: Exod. 20:8–11). Human beings are not the only beneficiary. But the voice of the earth and of non-human creation has gone missing, suppressed and marginalized by an outlook centered on human well-being only. In light of the Bible, a retrieval of the Sabbath is genuine only when it reflects the scope of the original blessing—when it hears the lost voice and the silent yearning of non-human creation and the earth.

INTERDEPENDENCE

In the creation account God confers an almost identical blessing on animal and human life.[1]

> God blessed them [sea creatures and birds], saying, "Be fruitful and multiply and fill the waters" (Gen. 1:22).
>
> God blessed them [human beings], and God said to them, "Be fruitful and multiply, and fill the earth" (Gen. 1:28).
>
> So God blessed the seventh day and hallowed it (Gen. 2:3).

In this three-fold way, Genesis announces that there is a purpose for nature and all its inhabitants. Non-human creation comes into possession of a God-ordained bill of rights, receiving the "word of empowerment" that is intrinsic to the blessing.[2] Non-human creation, too, is subject to the blessing that means, in the words of Claus Westermann, "a silent advance of the power of life in all realms."[3]

This discovery calls for a redirection of interpretation and a drastic reconfiguration of priorities. Of the three explicit blessings in the Genesis account of Creation, the human mandate on the sixth day and the blessing of the seventh day receive a fair measure of attention while the equally weighty and identically worded blessing on non-human creation is rarely noted.

The relatedness of human beings and the earth is profoundly anchored in the wording of Genesis 2: "the LORD God formed man [*'ādām*] from the dust of the ground [*'ădāmâ*], and breathed into his nostrils the breath of life; and the man [*'ādām*] became a living being" (Gen. 2:7). In this outlook human beings are made of the same material as the earth; they share, in the most literal sense, *common ground*.[4] The connection, here captured at the level of the raw material of each, is striking. Carol Newsom writes that "there is no more telling indication of the intrinsic relatedness of things than the similarity of words."[5]

The Sabbath plays a unifying role in this story of wholeness and interconnections. In the cosmic sweep that is the prelude to its introduction, "the heavens and the earth were finished, *and all their multitude*" (Gen. 2:1). Non-human beings, the earth, and the entire created order are included in the bird's-eye appraisal that heralds the blessing of the seventh day.

The objection might be raised that the Creation account, by commissioning humans to "have dominion over the fish of the sea and over the birds of the air and over every living thing that moves upon the earth" (Gen. 1:28), appears to give humans preference. The text has been used to justify carelessness toward non-human creation. But a closer reading of the text and its context will show that there is no mandate for exploitation. Human beings are created in the image of the God who gave the first blessing to non-human creation (Gen. 1:27). This creates the expectation that human beings will act toward non-human creation in the posture of blessing. Moreover, the notion of dominion is best understood in the sense of working, tilling, and keeping, not exploitation (cf. Gen. 2:5, 15).[6] As Barr points out, the Genesis account does not even envisage the idea of human beings "using the animals for meat and no terrifying consequences for the animal world."[7]

The Sabbath confers God's blessing on all of creation.

In Exodus, too, and specifically in the Sabbath commandment, the tenor of blessing on non-human creation continues. Animals are named as beneficiaries of the Sabbath alongside human beings (Exod. 20:10).

It is within this framework that the ecological dimension of the biblical message belongs. The threat of global warming and imminent environmental collapse are surely compelling reasons to tend to the consequences of modern civilization, but from the point of view of the Bible an "environmental" concern does not constitute an adequate frame of reference for the relationship between human beings and the earth. As Kathryn Greene-McCreight argues,

> [t]he Christian cannot speak of the "environment" or "environmental issues," for creation cannot be reduced to the environment. If creation is loosed from the narrative framework of the Bible, we are left with absolutely no warrants to care for the created order. This is largely why we are in the "environmental" crisis in which we find ourselves. In public discourse, creation has in fact been loosed from its biblical narrative framework. The only warrant that the secular world gives us to care for the "environment" is a thinly veiled version of self-concern: our children will suffer unless we change our habits. Divorcing creation from redemption leaves us alone in the world with our own only companion. The message of ecologists is far more powerful when framed in terms of the biblical narrative: the waters we pollute and the land we poison were created by the One who made, reconciles, and redeems us.[8]

To the extent that self-concern is the reason for increased interest in the "environment," it misses the mark. There is a better reason to care for nature because the earth and non-human creation are under God's blessing, "with the rights and privileges thereunto pertaining." From the point of view of the Bible, interest in non-human creatures and the earth is not motivated by an ecological state of emergency but by recognition of the dignity and the rights of the rest of the created order. The ecological paradigm is too narrow because, as Matthew Scully concedes, this is a problem that "confronts us with questions of conscience."[9]

The call for urgent redress is nowhere more piercing than in the example of suffering of pigs, turkeys, and chickens that lead the line of victims of modern factory farming in the Western hemisphere. These creatures, each in its own distinctive animal voice,[10] testify that the relationship between human and non-human creation has become unhinged and intolerable. Having witnessed the abuse firsthand at a factory farm and numbed by the sight of freedom-loving animals trapped helplessly between stress and despair, Scully is forced to say that the abuse taking place "is not the worst evil we can do, but it is the worst evil we can do to them."[11] The relationship has become crudely and purely exploitative, entirely oblivious to the notion of God's blessing on non-human creation.[12] How is it, one must ask, that the blessing pronounced on the animal world on the fifth day of Creation has nowhere been ignored as much as in countries that claim a Christian legacy? How is it, too, in the present quest for lost meaning, that disregard for God's blessing on the seventh day may be exceeded only by disrespect for God's blessing on non-human creation? Instead of blessing, a system of systematic cruelty and exploitation is now slowly coming to light.[13]

The violation of non-human creation, perpetrated with impunity on an unprecedented scale, is oblivious to the intimate interdependence between human life and the rest of creation.[14] In the biblical perception, the earth is given a voice that cannot be ignored. Nature is not only *aware*, but it cares deeply about how life is lived. When Israel takes possession of Canaan, they displace a people whose customs are said to have offended nature to such an extent that "the land vomited out its inhabitants" (Lev. 18:25). Confident that the land will keep a watchful eye on the new tenants, the Israelites are warned not to pursue the same course. Otherwise, the land "will vomit you out as it vomited out the nations that were before you," they are told (Lev. 18:28). The earth is capable of responding with gratitude and generosity or with disgust and inhospitality, depending on the treatment by her occupant.

Significantly, the mood of the land is described as a reliable barometer of the inhabitants' spiritual and moral condition.

Lawlessness and social injustice send ripples of disharmony throughout all creation, registered faithfully on the Richter scale of nature's tortured soul. After a series of examples of such injustice, the prophet Hosea claims that because of people's cruelty, "the land mourns, and all who live in it waste away; the beasts of the field and the birds of the air and the fish of the sea are dying" (Hosea 4:3).[15] "How long will the land mourn, and the grass of every field wither?" asks Jeremiah well over a century later, pained by the same connection between ethics and ecology (Jer. 12:4). The means to abuse nature on a large scale did not exist when this was spoken, but the indivisible unity of creation is seen by the perceptive eye. "Were you angry with the rivers, O LORD? Did you rage against the sea when you rode with your horses and your victorious chariots?" asks the prophet Habakkuk (Hab. 3:8). Clearly the answer is no, but the convulsions of the earth reflect the violation of the moral order and humanity's short-sighted stewardship.

Nature is not only aware, but it cares deeply about how life is lived.

Times of revival and reform bring relief to the land, proving that nature is capable of happier emotions. Longing for such a moment to come, Isaiah prophesies that "the desert and the parched land will be glad; the wilderness will rejoice and blossom. Like the crocus it will burst into bloom; it will rejoice greatly and shout for joy" (Isa. 35:1–2). He sees nature keeping a pained but expectant vigil, cheered by the cause of spiritual reform and in brighter moments exulting that "the mountain and hills will burst into song before you, and all the trees of the field will clap their hands" (Isa. 55:12). Confident of a response, he calls on the choir of creation to be part of the celebration:

> Sing for joy, O heavens, for the LORD has done this;
> shout aloud, O earth beneath.
> Burst into song, you mountains,
> you forests and all your trees. (Isaiah 44:23, NIV)

In reality such festive moments exist more in prophetic dreams than in actual life. The course of history seems to be caught in a downward spiral, and the will to break loose is lacking. Spurned as pessimists and alarmists by their contemporaries, the prophets recognize in the local situation a crisis with global overtones, linking current events to the end of time. From the spiritual cause to the physical and material consequences they see the world moving toward ruin.[16]

> The earth dries up and withers,
> the world languishes and withers,
> the exalted of the earth languish.
> The earth is defiled by its people;
> they have disobeyed the laws,
> violated the statutes
> and broken the everlasting covenant.
> Therefore a curse consumes the earth;
> its people must bear their guilt.
> Therefore the inhabitants are burned up,
> and very few are left.[17] (Isaiah 24:4–6, NIV)

To the prophet Jeremiah the order of the universe is disintegrating right before his eyes. Since the terms of life have been violated, nature cannot be held on course. Beyond the imminent but limited disaster, a vision of final dissolution is rising, returning the world to the chaos prior to creation.[18]

> I looked at the earth,
> and it was formless and empty;
> and at the heavens,
> and their light was gone.
> I looked at the mountains,
> and they were quaking;
> all the hills were swaying.
> I looked, and there were no people;
> every bird in the sky had flown away.
> I looked, and the fruitful land was a desert;
> all its towns lay in ruins
> before the LORD, before his fierce anger. (Jer. 4:23–26, NIV)

The echoes of the creation account in Genesis resound like peals of thunder in this prophecy. Once again the earth is formless and void. The lights of the heaven are extinct. All the inhabitants are gone. Time is thrown into reverse as the end reversely recapitulates the beginning. This vision "of the creation returning to chaos is unparalleled in prophetic literature—or, for that matter, in any literature ancient or modern," says Jack R. Lundbom.[19] But the prophecy is not to be read as a vindictive prediction or as stark retribution. On the contrary, what happens affirms the reality of interdependence, the bond that exists between human and non-human creation. The earth mourns in Hosea, because, says Melissa Tubbs Loya, "[a]s the necessary result of Israel's crimes, Earth *must* mourn."[20] What happens is the inevitable result of following misguided priorities and unsustainable pursuits.

In the New Testament, too, Jesus describes a state of increasing disorder in the world. He predicts "signs in sun and moon and stars, and upon the earth distress of nations in perplexity at the roaring of the sea and the waves, men fainting with fear and with foreboding of what is coming on the world; for the powers of the heavens will be shaken" (Luke 21:25–26). These upheavals are not arbitrary judgments designed to instill fear in the inhabitants of the earth. In the biblical scenario they express the earth's revulsion at the abuse that has been perpetrated on its surface. At last the earth can no longer conceal her terrible secrets. Impartially and faithfully, as seen by Isaiah, "the earth will disclose the blood shed upon her, and will no more cover her slain" (Isa. 26:21).[21] Just as the land "vomited out" the inhabitants, the whole earth rebels to turn the human master out of his or her dominion. In the final uprising nature itself seems consumed by the effort, going down in a purging conflagration that puts an end to the long night of terror (2 Pet. 3:10).

HEARING THE VOICE OF THE EARTH

The "Christian" contribution to the plight of non-human creation, either by neglect or by deliberate abuse, has been so incriminating that

Christianity, in the eyes of some scholars, is largely to blame for the world's ecologic crisis. This is hardly the whole story. Whatever guilt the Christian culture of the West has incurred by inflicting damage on nature, the cause is principally found in the departure of Christianity from the biblical idea. It is not a biblical idea that "no item in the physical creation had any purpose save to serve man's purposes," as Lynn White claimed in a much celebrated essay.[22] If Christians have failed to speak up on behalf of nature, the explanation must be sought in the loss of the biblical view of Creation and not in the biblical view itself. To suggest that "by destroying pagan animism, Christianity made it possible to exploit nature in a mood of indifference to the feelings of natural objects"[23] betrays gross ignorance of the true Judeo-Christian idea of Creation as it is found throughout the Bible and institutionalized in the weekly Sabbath. The warning that "we shall continue to have a worsening ecologic crisis until we reject the Christian axiom that nature has no reason for existence save to serve man"[24] hits wide of the mark. A more appropriate counsel will instead call for a return to the original biblical affirmation of the worth of non-human creation. Indifference to nature surely cannot be described as a "Christian axiom."[25]

Neglect of Creation and a relentless anti-sabbatarian bias are constants in the Christian enterprise. Beginning, as we have seen, with the Christian repudiation of materiality, its disdain for the body, and its ceaseless preoccupation with the fate of the soul, the material world was for centuries banished to neglect. Then, with the awakening of the Enlightenment and the Industrial Revolution, the Church acquiesces to an era of exploitation of nature's finite resources. On this point Lynn White's savage critique of the environmental consequences of Christian theology is warranted; it does become a near-axiom that "nature has no reason for existence save to serve man."[26]

Indeed, reducing Creation to a subsidiary concern is not an accident but an articulated emphasis of leading theological voices of the twentieth century. No less a person than Gerhard von Rad argues that Creation is only the prologue to the history of salvation that in his eyes is the controlling theme of Scripture.[27] It is, moreover, a prologue that was added once the rest of the story was in place, and thus it is virtually an afterthought.[28] Acceptance of this outlook leaves Christian theology bereft of the means to play a role in the care and protection of the earth, fulfilling the critique voiced by Claus Westermann: "Once theology has imperceptibly become detached from Creator-Creation, the necessary consequence is that it must gradually become an anthropology and begin to disintegrate from within and collapse around us."[29]

Neglect of Creation and a relentless anti-sabbatarian bias are constants in the Christian enterprise.

The Sabbath occupies the center of this conceptual and relational context. In any project to make up for past neglect and to rectify the consequences of misplaced priorities, the Sabbath is primed to play a leading role. Any turn of heart that is sensitized to non-human creatures and to the earth will also be welcoming to the Sabbath.

THE YEARNING OF THE EARTH

A revealing passage confirms that for the New Testament, the totality of Creation remains within the purview of God's redemptive intent. In Romans, Paul turns the pulpit over to nature, writing that "the whole creation has been groaning as in the pains of childbirth right up to the present time" (Rom. 8:22).[30] "For the creation waits with eager longing for the revealing of the sons of God; for the creation was subjected to futility, not of its own will but by the will of him who subjected it in hope; because the creation itself will be set free from its bondage to decay and obtain the glorious liberty of the children of God" (Rom. 8:19–21). The imagery is striking and evocative. Non-human creation is groaning in labor pains; it waits with eager longing; it is conscious of its own transitoriness and unworthy state. Paul resorts to the Greek word *mataiotēs*, translated "futility," a word that carries with it the distant drumbeat of the wisdom literature in the Old Testament, the "vanity of vanities" that the ancient wisdom seeker pronounced on his failed quest for meaning (Eccles. 1:2ff.). In the context of Paul, this "futility" means that nature does not relish the burdensome role assigned to her. As the reading of the *Good News Bible* puts it, "creation was condemned to lose its purpose" (Rom. 8:20).

As is so often the case in Paul's letters, there is a prior narrative coming into play in the passage. "For we know that the whole creation groans and labors with birth pangs together until now" (Rom. 8:22). "We know" indicates that Paul is reaffirming a known story and theme.[31] The perspective of nature writhing in the pain of childbirth, even the groans of nature, belongs to the outlook of the first Christian believers. To the extent that this outlook is eclipsed, it represents a lost treasure, a contraction of the Christian vision, and a spiritual hearing loss.

In the underlying narrative the Old Testament enters conspicuously into the picture. "For the creation was subjected to futility, not willingly, but because of Him who subjected it in hope," Paul says (Rom. 8:20, NKJV). There is virtual unanimity among scholars that Paul in this text alludes to the Genesis story of the Fall.[32] "Cursed is the ground because of you," God says to Adam in Genesis (Gen. 3:17), indicating consequences to nature because of the choice made by humans. Genesis implies that from henceforth there will be discord in the relationship between human beings and nature. The prediction that the ground shall bring forth "thorns and thistles" indicates that nature will be less pliant to human stewardship (Gen. 3:18), and it is also a case in point for Paul's contention that creation "was subjected to futility" (Rom. 8:20).

Scarred, defaced, and ruined, in the end the earth finds no consolation except in the Creator. This is the way the end is envisioned in the New Testament, suggesting that the call to step back from the brink has not been heeded. And yet Paul's singular perception of the relationship between God and the world has an unexpected twist. Creation waits for God to intervene, but its waiting has matured a profound and patient insight into God's ways. Creation does not only wait for *God*; "all of creation waits with eager longing for God *to reveal his sons*" (Rom. 8:19, GNB). Nature suffers in the service of God's redemptive purpose. It is subservient to the higher goal, a reliable participant in the design of bringing healing and restoration to human beings. While the restoration of nature follows the restoration of people, the one is unthinkable without the other.

> The LORD created the heavens—
> he is the one who is God!
> He formed and made the earth—
> he made it firm and lasting.
> He did not make it a desolate waste,
> but *a place for people to live in.* (Isaiah 45:18, GNB)

Nature keeps a vigilant watch for "the revealing of the children of God" because the believers offer hope even though they may be few in number, and they offer hope because their existence is proof of a greater hope. A secret, implied reciprocity is in view. Nature will accept as children of God those who "demonstrate their sonship by exercising the kind of dominion that heals rather than destroys,"[33] and the children of God will give nature a foretaste of the relief that is to come. God's three-fold blessing remains in force. As Philip Esler perceives the context of Romans, nature swells the ranks of the believers because it is "aligned with, and supportive of, the tiny minority constituting the Christ-movement."[34] Believers will acknowledge the blessing that rests on non-human creatures, and they will hear in earth's yearning an echo of their own deepest longing (Rom. 8:22–23). The earth, too, aggrieved and devastated under human dominion, is secure in the confidence that God's blessing has not been

God's blessing has not been revoked from non-human creatures, from human beings, or from the Sabbath.

revoked from non-human creatures (Gen. 1:22), from human beings (Gen. 1:28), or from the Sabbath (Gen. 2:1–3).

ENDNOTES

1. Wenham, *Genesis 1–15*, 24; Fretheim, *God and the World*, 106.

2. Fretheim, *God and the World*, 50.

3. Claus Westermann, "Creation and History in the Old Testament," in *The Gospel and Human Destiny*, ed. Vilmos Vajta, trans. Donald Dutton (Minneapolis: Augsburg Publishing House, 1971), 30.

4. Carol Newsom, "Common Ground: An Ecological Reading of Genesis 2–3," in *The Earth Story in Genesis*, ed. Norman C. Habel and Shirley Wurst (Sheffield: Sheffield Academic Press, 2000), 60–72.

5. Newsom, "Common Ground," 63.

6. Barr, "Man and Nature," 63–64.

7. Ibid., 62–63.

8. Kathryn Greene-McCreight, "Restless Until We Rest in God: The Fourth Commandment as Test Case in Christian 'Plain Sense' Interpretation," in *The Ten Commandments: The Reciprocity of Faithfulness*, ed. William P. Brown (Louisville: Westminster John Knox Press, 2004), 234–235.

9. Matthew Scully, *Dominion: The Power of Man, the Suffering of Animals, and the Call to Mercy* (New York: St. Martin's Press, 2002), xi.

10. This according to Isaac Bashevis Singer's perception in his short story "The Slaughterer" in *The Collected Stories of Isaac Bashevis Singer* (New York: Farrar, Straus and Giroux, 1996 [first publ. 1953]), 209.

11. Scully, *Dominion*, 289.

12. Scully (*Dominion*, x) states, "[w]hen a quarter million birds are stuffed into a single shed, unable even to flap their wings, when more than a million pigs inhabit a single farm, never once stepping into the light of day, when every year tens of millions of creatures go to their death without knowing the least measure of human kindness, it is time to question old assumptions, to ask what we are doing and what spirit drives us on."

13. Cf. Charles Patterson, *Eternal Treblinka: Our Treatment of Animals and the Holocaust* (New York: Lantern Books, 2002); Gail A. Eisnitz, *Slaughterhouse: The Shocking Story of Greed, Neglect, and Inhumane Treatment Inside the U.S. Meat Industry* (New York: Prometheus Books, 2007).

14. Cf. Melissa Tubbs Loya, "'Therefore the Earth Mourns': The Grievance of Earth in Hosea 4:1–3," paper presented at the annual Society of Biblical Literature meeting in Washington, DC, November, 2006; Laurie J. Braaten, "Earth Community in Joel 1–2: A Call

to Identify with the Rest of Creation," *HBT* 28 (2006): 113–129.

15. Hans Walter Wolff (*A Commentary on the Book of the Prophet Hosea* [Hermeneia; Philadelphia: Fortress Press, 1974], 68), crediting K. Koch and F. Horst, says that "the judgment results not from the direct actions of Yahweh himself, but from an 'organic structure of order,'" within which everything reciprocally affects everything else, also describing it as a "synthetic view of life."

16. Walter Brueggemann, *Isaiah 1–39* (WBC; Louisville: Westminster John Knox Press, 1998), 192; Norman J. Charles, "A Prophetic (Fore)Word: 'A Curse Is Devouring the Earth (Isaiah 24.6)," in *The Earth Story in the Psalms and the Prophets*, ed. Norman C. Habel (Sheffield: Sheffield Academic Press, 2001), 123–128.

17. Joseph Blenkinsopp (*Isaiah 1–39: A New Translation with Introduction and Commentary* [AB; New York: Doubleday, 2000], 352) sees in the diminution of the world's population "the annulment of the creation command to increase and multiply."

18. Cf. Walter Brueggemann, *A Commentary on Jeremiah: Exile and Homecoming* (Grand Rapids: William B. Eerdmans, 1998), 59; Shirley Wurst, "Retrieving Earth's Voice in Jeremiah: An Annotated Voicing of Jeremiah 4," in *The Earth Story in the Psalms and the Prophets*, ed. Norman C. Habel (Sheffield: Sheffield Academic Press, 2001), 172–184.

19. Jack R. Lundbom, *Jeremiah 1–20: A New Translation with Introduction and Commentary* (AB; New York: Doubleday, 1999), 356.

20. Tubbs Loya, "Therefore the Earth Mourns," 11.

21. Thus, as John D. W. Watts notes (*Isaiah 1–33* [WBC; Waco: Word Books, 1985], 342), "*[T]he land* will apparently be called as a witness. It will no longer serve to *cover up* for the people's guilt in all the murders and acts of violence that have transpired."

22. Lynn White, Jr., "The Historical Roots of Our Ecological Crisis," *Science* 155 (1967): 1205, reprinted in *Ecology and Religion in History*, 15–31.

23. White, "Ecological Crisis," 1205.

24. Ibid., 1207.

25. Cf. Richard Bauckham, "Joining Creation's Praise of God," *Ecotheology* 7 (2002): 45–59.

26. White, Jr., "Ecological Crisis," 1207.

27. von Rad, "The Theological Problem of the Old Testament Doctrine of Creation," in *Creation in the Old Testament*, 53–64.

28. Habel, "Introducing the Earth Bible," 27–28.

29. Claus Westermann, "Biblical Reflection on Creator-Creation," in *Creation in the Old Testament*, 92; see also in the same volume, H. H. Schmid, "Creation, Righteousness, and Salvation: 'Creation Theology' as the Broad Horizon of Biblical Theology," 102–117.

30. For a more extensive discussion of this passage, see my "Creation Groaning in Labor Pains," in *Ecological Hermeneutics*, ed. Norman Habel (Atlanta: Society of Biblical Literature, 2008), 143–151.

31. James D. G. Dunn, *Romans 1–8* (WBC; Dallas: Word Books, 1988), 410.

32. C. E. B. Cranfield, *A Critical and Exegetical Commentary on the Epistle to the Romans*, vol. 1 (ICC; Edinburgh: T. & T. Clark, 1979), 413; Dunn, *Romans 1–8*, 470; Joseph A. Fitzmyer, *Romans: A New Translation with Introduction and Commentary* (AB; London: Geoffrey Chapman, 1993), 505; Grieb, *The Story of Romans*, 80; Edward Adams, "Paul's Story of God and Creation: The Story of How God Fulfils His Purposes in Creation," in *Narrative Dynamics in Paul*, ed. Bruce W. Longenecker (Louisville: John Knox Press, 2002), 28–29.

33. Robert Jewett, "The Corruption and Redemption of Creation: Reading Rom. 8:18–23 within the Imperial Context," in *Paul and the Roman Imperial Order*, ed. Richard A. Horsley (Harrisburg: Trinity Press International, 2004), 46.

34. Philip Esler, *Conflict and Identity in Romans: The Social Setting of Paul's Letter* (Minneapolis: Fortress Press, 2003), 262.

CHAPTER 23

CREATION AND THE NEW CREATION

Listen, I will tell you a mystery! We will not all die, but we will all be changed, in a moment, in the twinkling of an eye, at the last trumpet.
1 Corinthians 15:51–52

The fact that "Genesis and Revelation provide a creational bracket for the Bible"[1] means more than that these books, like the frame of a picture, call attention to the scenes within the frame while not being part of the picture. Genesis and Revelation are not mere bookends. Creation in Genesis and the new creation in Revelation belong together, enhancing and clarifying each other. The middle and the ending of the story are incomprehensible apart from the beginning, and the beginning pointedly prefigures the ending. "And behold, it was very good," says Genesis (1:31, NASB), and we can say no less of the ending that is found in Revelation. It is of an ending that is "very good" that the Sabbath is the climax, and to such an ending it looks forward. The memory that is enshrined in the Sabbath is the substrate of hope, and the hope that dwells in its bones cannot disappoint memory.

> ***Genesis and Revelation are not mere bookends. The memory that is enshrined in the Sabbath is the substrate of hope, and the hope that dwells in its bones cannot disappoint memory.***

For this very reason, the reason of hope, the Sabbath and creation are indissolubly linked. It takes more than memory for the story to end well. It takes a notion of creation that counts on acts that are out of the ordinary, truly "acts of God," and a view of the new creation that surpasses memory. From the point of view of the ending of the story, the subject of creation must be treated gingerly, with tip-toeing reverence, if it expects to come to terms with a vision of the new creation that magnifies and intensifies the memory of the old even more than it recapitulates it.

CREATION AND NEW CREATION AS FRAMEWORK

Memory and recapitulation are all over the place with echoes of Genesis in the book of Revelation. In Genesis God creates "the heavens and the earth" (Gen. 1:1). In Revelation John sees "a *new* heaven and a *new* earth" (Rev. 21:1). In Genesis the created order comes under a curse (Gen. 3:17), but in Revelation "there shall be no more curse" (Rev. 21:3, NKJV). In Genesis human beings are alienated from God, running away from God's presence in fear (Gen. 3:10). In Revelation's view of the earth made new, "God lives among human beings" (Rev. 21:3, NJB). Alienation is nowhere to be found. Fear and misapprehension are overcome; "they will see his face, and his name will be on their foreheads" (Rev. 22:4).

At the center of the "old" earth in Genesis is the tree of life, located "in the midst of the garden" (Gen. 2:9). In Revelation, the tree of life is there, and still in the middle (Rev. 22:2). Denial of access to the tree of life encapsulates the loss in Genesis (Gen. 3:24). Access to the tree of life epitomizes the privilege in Revelation (Rev. 2:7; 22:14). For human beings, bruised and broken, access to the tree of life is crucial because "the leaves of the tree are for the healing of the nations" (Rev. 22:2). The presence of the tree of life in both depictions strengthens the impression that the "new" earth in important respects is the "old" earth reclaimed and restored.[2] If Genesis describes Paradise Lost, Revelation describes Paradise Regained.

Allusions to Isaiah complement the allusions to Genesis in Revelation.[3]

> For I am about to create new heavens and a new earth; the former things shall not be remembered or come to mind (Isa. 65:17).

> Then I saw a new heaven and a new earth; for the first heaven and the first earth had passed away, and the sea was no more (Rev. 21:1).

These texts resonate more deeply when we pay attention to the character of Old Testament allusions in Revelation. In Revelation, there is "a pattern of disciplined and deliberate *allusion* to specific Old Testament texts," says Richard Bauckham.[4] The allusions, moreover, are not haphazard; they are "meant to recall the Old Testament context."[5] Although John's allusions are mere fragments and flashes of Old Testament texts, he wants the reader to see the whole in instances where he only supplies the part. In visual terms Revelation is a panorama of the cosmic conflict between good and evil from beginning to end. The Old Testament allusions, carefully deployed, yield a comprehensive story with the strictest economy of words.

Reading Isaiah's vision of the new creation broadens the picture, aligning the end of all things in the New Testament with the beginning of all things in the Old Testament even more closely. "For as the new heavens and the new earth, which I will make, shall remain before me, says the LORD; so shall your descendants and your name remain. From new moon to new moon, and from sabbath to sabbath, all flesh shall come to worship before me, says the LORD" (Isa. 66:22–23).

The aspiration of Isaiah's vision is also universal and inclusive, urging the restoration of creation and inclusion of all peoples in a grand sabbatarian vision (Isa. 56:1–7).[6] The vision of the new creation retains the universal scope; "*all* flesh shall come and worship before me, says the Lord" (Isa. 66:23). Revelation alludes specifically to this text, too, slightly reworded, "All nations will come and worship before you" (Rev. 15:4). The non-mention of the Sabbath in Revelation does not leave it out because it is fully in character with Revelation's allusions to mention a mere fragment of a text and yet to intend the entire Old Testament passage to come into view. For this reason the Sabbath of Isaiah's vision, as in the Genesis creation account, belongs undiminished within Revelation's view of the new earth.

The "creational bracket" is also crucial to the plot playing out in the Bible.[7] Those who sing God's praise in Revelation sing not only because *they* have prevailed in the struggle against the "ancient serpent, who is called the Devil and Satan, the deceiver of the whole world" (12:9; cf. 20:2). The fervor of the singing is a measure of the conviction that *God* has prevailed. The "ancient serpent," of course, is the serpent of the Genesis narrative (Gen. 3:1). By projecting this character on the screen, the "creational bracket" of Genesis and Revelation pinpoints the issue in the cosmic conflict all the way down to the subversive, discordant voice. As the "ancient serpent" sees it, God's ways are not "just and true." The resounding affirmations in Revelation cannot be fully appreciated unless they are held up to the voice of accusation.[8] Indeed, the affirming voices can do no less than to persist in their endeavor "day and night without ceasing" (Rev. 4:8) because they are aware that the voice of accusation is tirelessly at work "day and night" (12:10). The voice of accusation, in turn, reverberating with the accusation brought against God in the first book of the Bible, is only fully overcome in the last book.

Revelation spills over with the consciousness of an ongoing story that will not be complete until it locks arms with the beginning, and the consciousness of the beginning is bursting at the seams precisely in the passage in Isaiah that is Revelation's quarry for what is to come. "The wolf and the lamb shall feed together, the lion shall eat straw like the ox; but the serpent—its food shall be dust! They shall not hurt or destroy on all my holy mountain, says the LORD" (Isa. 65:25). What might seem gratuitous and unwarranted to the unsensitized ear will appear deliberate, purposeful, and resonant with meaning once the ear gets attuned to the biblical narrative. Isaiah is describing the new creation, but he cannot help bracket the subversive agent with the abrupt and emphatic interjection: "but the serpent—its food shall be dust" (Isa. 65:25). This detail is not lost on Revelation, where John tirelessly keeps the focus on "the ancient serpent" (Rev. 12:9; 20:2). The story will not end until the issue raised by the accusation has been resolved, only then throwing the door open to the healing of all creation.

And yet, as the drama comes to a close, the prospect for the new creation appears daunting. Can illness, death, grief, and devastation be reversed?

Human reality puts the notion of creation to the test all the way down to its most essential meaning: It is because God is the Creator that there is hope. God of the first Creation and the first Sabbath rest is also God of the New Creation and the ultimate Sabbath fulfillment. When the God of Revelation says, "Behold, I make all things new" (Rev. 21:5, KJV), it has meaning because God, as the first and last books of the Bible see God, is the One who brings all things into existence (Isa. 40:26; 42:5; 45:12; John 1:3). Within the "creational bracket" of Scripture, it is no more remarkable that human beings will live again than that human beings came into existence at all; the reality of human life is itself no more a matter of course than the resurrection from the dead. The prospect for a new creation seems daunting because it *is* daunting, and yet it is no more daunting than causing human life to arise from the "dust of the ground" in the beginning (Gen. 2:7).

God of the first Creation and the first Sabbath rest is also God of the New Creation and the ultimate Sabbath fulfillment.

Revelation holds together the first and the last, "the first heaven and the first earth" with "a new heaven and a new earth" (Rev. 21:4), because its notion of first and last, of "old" and "new," of beginning and end, is grounded in the same person.

> "I am the Alpha and the Omega, the beginning and the end" (21:6; cf. Isa. 44:6; 48:12).
>
> "I am the first and the last" (1:17).
>
> "These are the words of the first and the last" (2:8).
>
> "I am the Alpha and the Omega, the first and the last, the beginning and the end" (22:13).

In Revelation God will be who God is in Genesis; God will be the Omega because God is the Alpha; God will be the last because God is the first; God will be the end because God is the beginning. Revelation's hope rests on the strength of the identity between first and last. "Death will be no more; mourning and crying and pain will be no more," says John (21:4). "The first things" will pass away (21:4), but the God who is the first and the last will not (1:5, 17; 2:8; 22:13).

The New Testament does not speak of the future hope in vague generalities. "Write this, for these words are trustworthy and true," God says in Revelation (21:5). Surpassing even the witness of Revelation, Paul describes the believer's hope with a degree of specificity that is unmatched anywhere in the New Testament.

"IN THE TWINKLING OF AN EYE"

The New Testament specifies what lies ahead for human beings and the earth in such pointed language that it must take precedence over Old Testament notions of God's creative activity. Paul goes further than anyone else on this point. He is not content merely to affirm that creation one day "will be set free from its bondage to decay" (Rom. 8:21). In 1 Corinthians he provides an expansive, detailed account of the hope that creation shares with believers. Paul, of course, does not operate entirely on his own or in a vacuum. His message must be understood within the context of an apocalyptic expectation.[9] "Listen, I will tell you a mystery!" he writes to the Corinthians. "We will not all die, but we will all be changed, in a moment, in the twinkling of an eye, at the last trumpet. For the trumpet will sound, and the dead will be raised imperishable, and we will be changed" (1 Cor. 15:51–52).

The most remarkable feature in this description is its detailed mode, the fact that Paul "now explains both the manner and the time of the transformation," says Hans Conzelmann.[10] And Conzelmann is right; the details of the description put a lot on the line. In 1 Corinthians Paul describes the resurrection as a sudden, instantaneous occurrence. The transformation of the living and the resurrection of the dead are cast as twin events that depend on the same divine reality. God as Creator undergirds Paul's confidence, the in-breaking of creative power against which even death will not stand. The fact that the exclamation, "Where, O death, is your victory? Where, O death, is your sting?" (1 Cor. 15:55) echoes the Old Testament (Hosea 13:14) does not diminish its force, partly because Paul takes the Old Testament saying where it hardly dares to tread and partly because any antecedent, if it exists, cannot diminish it.[11] For him, "the saying that is written will be fulfilled" (1 Cor. 15:54), bolstered incontrovertibly by the resurrection of Jesus (1 Cor. 15:3–8). For this reason he is able to declare with confidence, "Death has been swallowed up in victory" (1 Cor. 15:54; cf. Isa. 25:8).[12]

The "what" and the "how" should not be dismissed as unimportant or incidental in a text that takes both to such lengths as Paul does in 1 Corinthians.[13] While he specifies only the mode of what will happen to the believer "at the last trumpet" (1 Cor. 15:52), it is understood that the power that works transformation in the living believer is also what effects the resurrection of the dead.

WHAT	HOW
"we will all be changed"	"in a moment, in the twinkling of an eye"
"the dead will be raised imperishable"	"in a moment, in the twinkling of an eye"

Paul's detailed description in 1 Corinthians is unsurpassed on this point, presenting the "what" and the "how" as seamless, inseparable, and mutually interdependent realities. Indeed, the assertion that "the dead will be raised imperishable" is bolstered by the logic that it must happen and can happen in no other way except "in the twinkling of an eye."

The connotation of a sudden, instantaneous event is also described in detail in 1 Thessalonians, most likely Paul's first letter and the oldest document of the New Testament. "For the Lord himself, with a cry of command, with the archangel's call and with the sound of God's trumpet, will descend from heaven, and the dead in Christ will rise first" (1 Thess. 4:16). Again, as Paul will later write to the Corinthians, it is more than an ordinary day at the office when the new creation comes into existence. "[T]he sound of *God's* trumpet" is to be heard, just as in 1 Corinthians, which refers to "the *last* trumpet" (1 Cor. 15:52).[14] Moreover, when Paul envisions the resurrection taking place "with a cry of command, with the archangel's call" (1 Thess. 4:16), he hews close to the message to the Corinthians. What redeems human beings depends on an event that is no mere rite of passage (1 Cor. 15:52). In both letters, we see Paul linking the resurrection and the second coming of Jesus,[15] and, as an element that is still more important for our understanding of how the New Testament configures the Christian hope, we see the new creation taking place out of nothing. With reference to Paul's statement in Romans (4:17), Gottfried Nebe observes that "God the creator summons things that are not yet in existence as if they already existed."[16] In Paul's view no less than in Revelation, "*creatio ex nihilo* and resurrection of the dead are connected with one another on the basis of the greatness and power of God."[17]

Paul is able to speak this way only because the hope of which he speaks is *his* hope, too, the bedrock of assurance for his own life and mission.[18] "Behold, I tell you a mystery!" is an exclamation generated from the depth of personal discovery and assurance, not soaring rhetoric aimed at correcting people who are confused. It is also implied that he is rehearsing a dear and familiar story. His description of the resurrection begins with the reminder that "I handed on to you as of first importance what I had in turn received" (1 Cor. 15:3), meaning that the final fulfillment of the believer's hope comes as the climax of a story told previously. The expectation of what will happen "in a moment, in the twinkling of an eye" and the reminder that "the trumpet will sound" suggest a rehearsal or a repetition that would "not be in place unless Paul were seeking to appeal to an established statement."[19]

Conzelmann's comment gives the dramatic and instantaneous character of the Christian expectation full exposure.

> Paul indeed underlines the note of instantaneity: "it [the trumpet] sounds, and..." This signal is the end. The customary conceptions of time must now fail. There now follows the resurrection and the transformation—in *one* act: there is no advantage and no disadvantage.[20]

> The concentration of everything into a single instant expresses the miraculous character of the new creation, the note of contingency.[21]

Paul's view of the new creation is predicated on his faith in God as the Creator, seen through the lens of apocalyptic. Its conception depends on God as the One "who gives life to the dead and calls into existence the things that do not exist" (Rom. 4:17).[22] The New Testament configuration of God as Creator is neither contrary to the Old Testament conception nor a corrective to it. And yet the New Testament goes where the Old Testament rarely ventures—confronting head on the reality of human transience and death. In this sense the New Testament notion of creation is forged in the crucible of death and extinction to a degree that is unknown in the Old Testament. And yet, while it may be said that the New Testament claims no more on God's behalf than what God is able to deliver (Isa. 46:8–10), it claims what God *must* deliver for the hope of a new creation to have any meaning (1 Cor. 15:17–19). This becomes acutely clear when the prospect of a new creation is set against the New Testament conception of the human person.

"THE DEAD SHALL BE RAISED INCORRUPTIBLE"

We are back, inevitably, to the notion that human existence is *bodied* existence. The future life is not ensured because of the immortality of the soul. There is no back door, no loophole, and no "plan B" in this vision. The future life depends entirely on the resurrection of the body. Paul's argument with the Corinthians on this point is particularly striking because it takes place in a cultural context that needed no convincing as to the hope of an afterlife. *That* hope is to Paul a fiction, and the immortality of the soul is definitely not the basis for *his* hope. Significant credit belongs to Rudolf Bultmann for his rediscovery, so contrary to tradition, that in New Testament thought a human being does not *have* a body (*soma*) but *is* a body.[23] The paradigm shift thus introduced is more striking when held up to the enduring dualist conception of the human person throughout centuries of Christian thought. In the traditional conception, a human being is conceived of as a material body that has an immaterial and immortal soul (cf. chapter 17). The soul survives death while the body, because it is material, is subject to death. This idea, so entrenched in the mentality of institutional Christianity, is not what Paul is proposing. What he has in mind lies closer to what Oscar Cullmann shared with his audience in a lecture at Harvard University in 1955, when he showed that immortality of the soul and resurrection of the body originally were thought to be mutually exclusive, only to find himself stunned by critics accusing him of betraying a cornerstone of Christian belief![24]

It is impossible to appreciate what the New Testament says about the resurrection and the new creation unless the materiality of human existence is taken for granted.[25] Paul singles out death as "the last enemy" (1 Cor. 15:26) because death, humanly speaking, means the irrevocable cessation of human existence. When death is at last annihilated in Revelation, it happens with the implication that death is "the last enemy" and the ultimate threat to God's creation. "Death and Hades" must finally let go of their victims (Rev. 20:13–14). It is Jesus's foremost distinction to be able to say of Himself, "I am the first and the last and the living one. I was dead, and see, I am alive forever and ever, and I have the keys of Death and Hades" (Rev. 1:17–18). And yet this statement, taking the measure of Jesus to its outermost extreme, is also an acknowledgement of death's magnitude.

Acknowledging the materiality of human existence, Paul affirms that the future hope depends on a Creator who is able to create instantaneously and out of nothing. Restoration of the dead cannot happen by a process playing out over time, and it will not happen by any power residing within nature. The trumpet must sound from above and from without, signaling a singular, exceptional intervention. The dead will be raised "in the twinkling of an eye" because no other way is open to passage (1 Cor. 15:52). With the reality of death Creation is back to Ground Zero. God must do at the new creation what God is said to have done when "God formed man from the dust of the ground, and breathed into his nostrils the breath of life; and the man became a living being" (Gen. 2:7), only on the larger scale envisioned in Paul's apocalyptic vision. Many voices in the New Testament are joined around this theme, but Paul says it best, speaking to us with trembling in his voice and in the familiar diction of the King James Version, "the dead shall be raised incorruptible" (1 Cor. 15:52, KJV). In my imagination he repeats it, shifting the emphasis for our benefit: it is the *dead* that shall be raised; "the dead shall be *raised*," and then, trailing off as if in deep thought, the last word of the sentence lingers long: "*incorruptible*" (1 Cor. 15:52, KJV). The believer's hope is not disappointed. Plato has been proven wrong. Materiality and incorruptibility are not incompatible entities. The King James Version and Händel's *Messiah* let this word be the last, and we should take care not to miss its shattering import.

"O DEATH, WHERE IS YOUR STING?"

By now it is obvious that the believer's hope in the New Testament is configured according to specfications that are not readily available in the marketplace of contemporary ideas. On the one hand, the New Testament vision is no more than it must be for the believer's hope to stand a chance. On the other hand, its vision perceives creation and the new creation as a seamless whole. It hardly needs to be said that the theory of human evolution, whether as paradigm or in its specifics, cannot deliver the vision that ends in the new creation. Even if we believe that the Old Testament story of Creation was never intended to compete against scientific approaches to the origin of life, we must concede that there is nothing in the "scientific" outlook on which to base belief in a life beyond the grave.

"Creation-as-process" is a stranger to the hope of a new creation. Grappling with these issues, many people seek harmony between the biblical story and science by concluding that science tells us what happened, and the Bible tells us that God was behind it. For the person who, in the name of scientific rigor, finds it necessary to dismiss the Old Testament story of Creation as a singular event in time, the gain to scientific thinking will be short lived because the New Testament hope depends precisely on the kind of singular event that a "scientific" conception of reality deems impossible. For the new creation to materialize there must be another account of reality.

The theory of human evolution, whether as paradigm or in its specifics, cannot deliver the vision that ends in the new creation.

For Paul, as Conzelmann notes, "[t]he concentration of everything into a single instant expresses the miraculous character of the new creation, the note of contingency."[26] Whatever we assume with respect to the mode of creation in the Old Testament, the New Testament configures the new creation as a singular, instantaneous event. As we ponder this prospect, we are expected to acknowledge that in a material conception of human life, nothing else than an instantaneous intervention has any meaning.

On this point, perhaps, the modern reader feels that he or she has escaped the ashes of the Old Testament view of creation only to be thrown into the fire of the far more demanding account in the New Testament. The six days allotted to the process of creation in Genesis seem laughable from the vantage point of contemporary notions of life's origin (Gen. 1:1–31), but six days are a long time compared to what the New Testament will allow for the new creation to come to pass. If the New Testament message takes priority and holds its ground, it is not because it is more accommodating to "scientific" accounts of reality.

What has become a stumbling block to the modern mind—the singular event—is in the Bible the cornerstone of hope. Belief in creation, conceived as radically as in the letters of Paul, cannot be the problem because it is the solution; it cannot be a liability to faith because it is the basis for it. Against the reality of death nothing will avail except for the Lord to descend from heaven "with a cry of command, with the archangel's call and with the sound of God's trumpet" (1 Thess. 4:16). Nothing within human beings can bring the dead back to life, and nothing within nature can restore creation to health. If there is any hope for all those who died believing in God's faithfulness even though "none of them received what had been promised" (Heb. 11:39), it depends entirely on the intervention that will come to pass "in a moment, in the twinkling of an eye, at the last trumpet" (1 Cor. 15:51–52). Paul's close-up view of *how* this will happen is not an affront to human reason, but rather a realistic account of what must take place if the hope that is held out in the New Testament is to become a reality.

If there is any hope for all those who died believing in God's faithfulness, it depends entirely on the intervention that will come to pass "in a moment, in the twinkling of an eye, at the last trumpet."

In Paul's vision of Creation the distance between Old Testament narrative and New Testament apocalyptic is almost undetectable. It is, in fact, non-existent because *vindication* lies at the core of the apocalyptic view.[27] What Paul espouses in regard to the new creation is through and through, too, a sabbatarian view of reality, the conviction that God is not leaving creation in the lurch. Paul's direct speech in his resurrection homily is telling because his language reflects the reality of conflict. Someone is there at the other end, poised and eager to defeat human beings and God's intent. The prospects for faith are precarious. It almost seems as if the enemy will be able to pull off his goal to thwart God and God's purpose for creation. Almost, that is, but not quite, because Death itself, now capitalized and personified, must bite the dust. Only when we hear it against this background are we able to appreciate the force of Paul's direct speech, "Where, O death, is your victory? Where, O death, is your sting?" (1 Cor. 15:55). And, lest we forget, only when we allow ourselves to be drawn into Paul's view of reality will the inadequacy of other views be fully exposed.

What will happen at the end and the means by which to achieve that end go hand in hand. Paul's hope for the future leans on the premise of the instantaneous event, indeed, on the assurance that his premise is already secure (1 Cor. 15:21–22). Urging belief in a new order that will come about "in a moment, in the twinkling of an eye" is not wishful thinking but in every way consistent with what the Creator has done in the past (Ps. 33:6–9).

The Sabbath is not missing in this vision. Greene-McCreight says that "Christians cannot separate logically or conceptually creation from redemption. It is the created order that will be redeemed, and which God chooses to crown in the sanctification of the Sabbath."[28] Moltmann echoes the same sentiment, urging that "[o]n the sabbath the redemption of the world is celebrated in anticipation."[29] But no modern voice surpasses that of Paul; certainly no one comes close to the earthy realism and the sabbatarian premise that permeate his proclamation of the new creation, his insistence on putting the constituent ingredients of the New Testament hope to the test. The dead will be raised "in a moment, in the twinkling of an eye" (1 Cor. 15:52), and the earth, too, will be delivered from the lip service that has etched deep furrows of despair across its aging surface. The entire created order, reconfigured as the new creation, "will be set free from its bondage to decay and will obtain the freedom of the glory of the children of God" (Rom. 8:21). If in this sense the end recapitulates the beginning, it might be that views of the beginning must be reconfigured in the light of what Paul and other voices in the New Testament say about the end. The specificity of the promise intensifies the memory of what God has done in the past, and the certainty of the memory establishes the promise of what God will do in the future. Creation belongs to the portfolio of the Sabbath as memory and hope. What was "very good" at the beginning (Gen. 1:31) must be vindicated; it must become "very good" before the blessing of the seventh day itself will find rest. Death is the last enemy, indeed (1 Cor. 15:26), the name of the darkness that claims the future of all human beings. When, however, memory and promise are refracted through the prism of the Sabbath, hope is writ large (Isa. 65:17; 66:22–23; Rev. 21:4). Creation has come home to itself in the new creation.

ENDNOTES

1. Fretheim, *God and the World in the Old Testament*, 9; cf. also Elke Toenges, "'See, I am making all things new': New Creation in the Book of Revelation," in *Creation in Jewish and Christian Tradition*, ed. Henning Graf Reventlow and Yair Hoffman (JSOTSup 319; Sheffield: Sheffield Academic Press, 2002), 138.

2. Leonard L. Thompson (*The Book of Revelation: Apocalypse and Empire* [Oxford: Oxford University Press, 1990], 85) translates the word *kainos* ("new") as "renewal."

3. David Mathewson, *A New Heaven and a New Earth: The Meaning and Function of the Old Testament in Revelation 21.1–22.5* (JSNT Sup 238; Sheffield: Sheffield Academic Press, 2003), 33–36.

4. Richard Bauckham, *The Climax of Prophecy: Studies in the Book of Revelation* (Edinburgh: T. & T. Clark, 1993), xi.

5. Ibid.

6. Gosse, "Sabbath, Identity and Universalism," 359–370.

7. Cf. Sigve K. Tonstad, *Saving God's Reputation: The Theological Function of* Pistis Iesou *in the Cosmic Narratives of Revelation* (LNTS 337; London and New York: T. & T. Clark, 2006).

8. Cf. Klaus-Peter Jörns, *Das hymnische Evangelium. Untersuchungen zu Aufbau, Funktion und Herkunft der hymnischen Stücke in der Johannesoffenbarung* (Gütersloh: Gütersloher Verlagshaus Gerd Mohn, 1971); idem, "Proklamation und Akklamation: Die antiphonische Grundordnung des frühchristlichen Gottesdientes nach der Johannesoffenbarung," in *Liturgie und Dichtung*, ed. H. Becker and R. Kaczynski (Sankt Ottilien: EOS Verlag, 1983), 187–208.

9. Martinus C. de Boer, "Paul and Jewish Apocalyptic Eschatology," in *Apocalyptic and the New Testament: Essays in Honor of J. Louis Martyn*, ed. Joel Marcus and Marion L.

Soards (JSNTSup 24; Sheffield: Sheffield Academic Press, 1989), 169–190.

10. Hans Conzelmann, *1 Corinthians: A Commentary on the First Epistle to the Corinthians*, trans. James W. Leitch (Hermeneia; Philadelphia: Fortress Press, 1975), 291.

11. Martinus C. de Boer, *The Defeat of Death: Apocalyptic Eschatology in 1 Corinthians and Romans 5* (JSNTSup 22; Sheffield: JSOT Press, 1988), 127.

12. De Boer (*The Defeat of Death*, 127) accounts for the variance in Paul's version from the text in Isaiah 25:8.

13. It is disappointing that de Boer (*The Defeat of Death*) and Joost Holleman (*Resurrection and Parousia: A Traditio-Historical Study of Paul's Eschatology in 1 Corinthians 15* [NovTSup 84; Leiden: E. J. Brill, 1996]), despite book-length doctoral investigations, have little or nothing to say concerning this feature.

14. Conzelmann (*1 Corinthians*, 291) notes that the trumpet has an apocalyptic connotation and that "the *last* trumpet" connotes "not the last in a series of trumpet blasts, but the eschatological one"; cf. also Friedrich, art. "*salpinx*," *TDNT* 7:87–88.

15. Holleman, *Resurrection and Parousia*, 204.

16. Gottfried Nebe, "Creation in Paul's Theology," in *Creation in Jewish and Christian Tradition*, ed. Henning Graf Reventlow and Yair Hoffman (JSOTSup 319; Sheffield: Sheffield Academic Press, 2002), 116.

17. Nebe, "Creation in Paul's Theology," 119.

18. Stephen C. Barton, "The Epistles and Christian Ethics," in *The Cambridge Companion to Christian* Ethics, ed. Robin Gill (Cambridge: Cambridge University Press, 2001), 65.

19. Conzelmann (*1 Corinthians*, 291), crediting Johannes Weiss.

20. Conzelmann, *1 Corinthians*, 291.

21. Ibid.

22. According to Nancy Duff ("The Significance of Pauline Apocalyptic for Theological Ethics" in *Apocalyptic and the New Testament*, 281), "apocalypse" "also means the 'invasion' of God's grace into the world, an invasion that brings into existence what was not there before (Rom. 4.17)."

23. Rudolf Bultmann, *Theology of the New Testament*, vol. 1, trans. K. Grobel (London: SCM Press, 1952), 195–196.

24. Cf. Cullmann, *The Immortality of the Soul, or the Resurrection of the Dead?*

25. Cf. Jack H. Wilson, "The Corinthians Who Say There Is No Resurrection of the Dead," *ZNW* 59 (1968): 90–107; see also N. T. Wright, *Surprised by Hope* (London: SPCK, 2007).

26. Conzelmann, *1 Corinthians*, 291.

27. Beker, *Paul's Apocalyptic Gospel*, 14–15; cf. also idem, *Paul the Apostle*, 136–137.

28. Greene-McCreight, "Restless Until We Rest in God," 234–235.

29. Moltmann, *God in Creation*, 276.

THE LOST MEANING OF THE SEVENTH DAY

Can a woman forget her nursing child, or show no compassion for the child of her womb? Even these may forget, yet I will not forget you.
Isaiah 49:15

As we acknowledge that the seventh day has more than one meaning, as others have done,[1] and recognize that more than one of its meanings are endangered, it might seem odd to condense this concern into a singular issue, eschewing for a moment the lost meanings (plural) in order to highlight the lost meaning as if it comes down to one. This is a considered decision, warranted not so much by the fact that the Sabbath was abandoned by the Christian Church as by the reason given for supplanting it.[2] The drift away from the Sabbath may early on have been due to voiceless, subliminal factors. In the course of time, however, the Church registers that the Sabbath has been supplanted, and it becomes necessary to come up with a reason. This chapter addresses the content and quality of the stated reason, and, as more than an aside, the struggle to come to terms with the essential character of the Sabbath.

UNDERSTANDING ARBITRARINESS

Change can take place in the absence of awareness or intent, and the decline of the Sabbath can be conceived in such terms. Eventually, however, the Church will find a reason that justifies the eclipse, and its reason will relate to the assumed meaning of the seventh day. Gradually the Sabbath came to be seen as an *arbitrary* institution.

"Arbitrary" is therefore an important word with respect to the Christian view, its use conforming to the pocket Webster definition that something is arbitrary when it is "not regulated by fixed rule or law," is "despotic," "capricious," or "unreasonable." Arbitrariness thus strikes a dissonant cord in any relationship, and the dissonance is not any less if it is found to exist in God's relationship to human beings. If God is arbitrary when instituting the Sabbath, and if "arbitrariness" points to an order that is "unreasonable," "capricious," or even "despotic," it is a good thing to have the arbitrary element removed.

These issues are not fully defined or vocalized in the first centuries of Christianity, but leading Christan voices as early as the second century seem convinced that it is no loss to Christian faith and practice to dispense with the Sabbath. As we have seen, Justin Martyr spoke in defense of Sunday observance in the middle of the second century,[3] and Sunday became the official day of rest in the empire two centuries later. At that point, however, Sunday keeping seemed to owe its status more to what people were doing than to why they were doing it. Theologians like Jerome and Augustine dealt with the subject at some length, but the theological underpinnings of Sunday observance remained fragmentary for centuries.[4] To the ordinary citizen the chief rationale for Sunday keeping may have been that it is not the Sabbath, that is to say, that Sunday observance set Christians apart from the Jewish community. This assumption is strengthened by the fact that the Council of Laodicea in 360 C.E. explicitly legislated against Judaizing practices, one of which is resting on the Sabbath.[5] While Sunday in important respects comes to occupy the position once held by the Sabbath, it is not settled whether Sunday has the same grounding or carries the same portfolio of meanings.[6]

Like many unresolved questions that simmered under the surface for centuries, the Sabbath got a measure of official attention when leaders of the Roman Catholic Church faced the crisis presented by the Reformation. What thus became known as the Counter-Reformation was in many respects a process of coming to self-awareness as much as an initiative to manage the impact of the Protestant movement. One of the fruits of the Catholic effort was a large and comprehensive catechism on church doctrine known as the *Catechism of the Council of Trent* (1566).[7] This catechism speaks at length about the Sabbath. Rather than attributing the change from Sabbath to Sunday to an accidental departure from the teaching of the Bible, the catechism uses the substitution to illustrate the mandate of the Church. In this catechism the Church does not see itself as a victim of ideas and currents beyond its conscious control. Neither anti-Judaism nor Hellenism features in the Church's account. Instead, the Church owns up to what happened, casting itself as an active promoter of the change: "the Church of God has in her wisdom ordained that the celebration of the Sabbath should be transferred to the Lord's day."[8]

This idea was not invented *ad hoc* in the sixteenth century. It echoes Eusebius (260–339), who expressed similar sentiments more than one thousand years earlier. Eusebius was a great admirer and contemporary of the emperor Constantine and the author of the first and most influential history of the early church.[9] As bishop of Caesarea he wrote in a comment on Psalm 92 (Psalm 91 in LXX) that "all that was prescribed for the Sabbath, we have transferred to the Lord's Day, inasmuch as it is the most important, the one which dominates, the first and the one which has more value than the Sabbath of the Jews."[10] Eusebius seems to accept the notion of a "portfolio of meanings" along the lines we have explored with respect to the Sabbath. His notion of "transfer" is intriguing because it assumes that the portfolio can be transferred unimpaired. Not to be missed, too, is his condescending view of the Sabbath, described as "the Sabbath of the Jews." The "transfer" that is implied can only mean that the entire portfolio of meanings has been entrusted to a more able entity.

At the Council of Trent the view expressed by Eusebius received the status of official church doctrine. In a tone of self-assurance the *Catechism of the Council of Trent* explains

> why Christians observe not the Sabbath, but the Lord's day. The point of difference is evident: the other commandments of the Decalogue are precepts of the natural law, obligatory at all times and unalterable, and hence, after the abrogation of the Law of Moses, all the commandments contained in the two tables are observed by Christians, not however because their observance is commanded by Moses, but because they accord with the law of nature and are enforced by its dictate: whereas this commandment, if considered as to the time of its fulfillment, is not fixed and unalterable, but is susceptible to change, and belongs not to the moral but ceremonial Law. Neither is it a principle of the natural law: we are not instructed by the natural law to worship God on the Sabbath rather than on any other day.[11]

The wording of the answer makes it clear that discussion of this issue had been going on for some time before the *Catechism* was written. No matter what we think of the reasons that are given, it is evident that the framers worked hard to get it right. In the brief passage the *Catechism* invokes the concept of "natural law" three times in addition to speaking of "the Law of nature" once. "Natural law," the argument goes, carries the weight of moral law and cannot be changed or set aside. All the commandments of the Decalogue belong to the category of "natural law" except one.

The exception is the Sabbath commandment, which "is not fixed and unalterable, but is susceptible to change." The Sabbath is not "a principle of the natural law" because it has no basis in the nature of things as they are open to us: "we are not instructed by the natural law to worship God on the Sabbath rather than on any other day." Moreover, to the extent that Christians concern themselves with the rest of the Ten Commandments, they do so not because the Commandments are part of the Law of Moses but because they belong to the realm of "natural law."[12]

In its attempt to relegate the Sabbath to the inferior category of ceremonial law,[13] the Catechism appeals to a notion that has had a long and laborious evolution in Roman Catholic tradition. Thomas Aquinas (1224–1274), who was again indebted to the Greek philosopher Aristotle (384–321 BC) and to early Christian writers,[14] elaborated the concept in the thirteenth century in the most decisive and enduring way. "Natural law," as it is to be understood in his writings, "is the theory that there are certain non-gainsayable truths about what we ought and ought not to do. These truths are described as principles known per se."[15] Aquinas further believed that human reason has the capacity to recognize moral law, reflect on it, and impress it on himself or herself.[16] On

The Sabbath is not "a principle of the natural law" because it has no basis in the nature of things as they are open to us.

these grounds it is easy to see where the explanation in the Catechism is coming from and where it is going with respect to the Sabbath.

Natural law, understood as a principle or as an emanation from nature, has little or nothing to say about the Sabbath. The other commandments hold their ground because they conform to the moral imperative of nature as they were perceived in the sixteenth century. Indeed, several of the commandments are hailed as valid all over the world in ways that support the argument.[17] In most societies, perjury runs contrary to the social fabric and the legal code as a matter of course. Murder is considered a crime in all civilized countries. Theft, too, meets with condemnation in societies that do not look to the Ten Commandments for guidance. Even the ethics of sex and family reflect an unwritten standard that is recognized all over the world. With respect to many of the Ten Commandments there is hardly any disagreement as to their relevance.

A similar consensus does not exist with regard to the Sabbath. It cannot appeal to an implied norm in society because there is no innate sense in human beings to perceive that among the seven days of the week, the Sabbath stands apart. Neither human reason nor the prompting of conscience designates the seventh day for special honor. According to the norm of natural law the Church seems justified in the claim that the Sabbath can be abolished or its sanctity transferred to a day deemed to be better suited.[18] Thomas Aquinas, for his part, believed that a day of rest belongs to the realm of natural law but not resting on a specific day of the week.

But how valid is the concept of natural law when it comes to deciding between right and wrong, or how useful is it as the means by which to assess the quality and validity of God's commandments? Philosophically, on closer inspection, the notion loses much of its initial appeal. Lord Acton tells the story of the Athenian philosopher Carneades, who came to Rome in the year 155 BC on a political mission. During his stay Carneades was persuaded to deliver two public lectures in order to give the Romans a taste of Greek thought.

"On the first day he discoursed on natural justice. On the next, he denied its existence, arguing that all our notions of good and evil are derived from positive enactment. From the time of that memorable display, the genius of the vanquished held its conquerors in thrall," writes Acton.[19]

The implication of the performance is obvious. As the master of Greek dialectics that he must have been, Carneades on the first day made a compelling case in favor of natural law. The Romans went home that night believing that perceived realities in nature must be the basis of law. But the sentiment created by the first lecture vanished once the arguments against it were presented. Philosophy, logic, and the actual practice of civilized societies prove the issue to be far more complex so as to make the entire concept of natural law of dubious value.[20]

Natural law becomes a less persuasive notion when we realize that tenets of behavior thought to derive from the nature of things often are culturally conditioned. Philosophers have argued for the justice of slavery based on natural law, and Christians have bolstered the argument from nature with the claim that the Bible supports it. Thomas Aquinas, observing the ways of nature such as the king bee among bees, concludes that "in nature, government is always by one."[21] This, of course, means that monarchy is the best form of government if nature's instruction is to be heeded. Aquinas does not find support for democracy on the basis of natural law. He also decries religious freedom, believing the death penalty to be the dictate of nature for heresy. One Aquinas scholar says that the idea of religious freedom "was completely alien to his thought."[22] Conceptions of "natural law," then, are not above cultural conditioning,[23] and attempts to derive what ought to be from the way things are open to tremendous pitfalls.

Just as the notion of natural law figures prominently in the Christian view of right and wrong, it comes back time and again as the Church's reason for giving up the Sabbath. Stipulations not grounded in natural law are by implication arbitrary not only in the sense that they may be altered or abolished. They also raise the question as to whether they bring anything good. Rejection of the Sabbath is nourished by the belief that it does not bring a benefit to human life, at least not a benefit that is tied to a specific day of the week. It is the alleged absence of benefit, or the absence of sufficient benefit, that leaves the Sabbath vulnerable. These are among the elements that have reduced the Sabbath to "a time-bound application of a timeless principle," as Calvin describes it,[24] or at worst to "a stern commandment" for Jews only, according to Luther's less generous view.[25]

If we allow Webster's definition of "arbitrary" to color the word, it implies that God might be "despotic," "capricious," and "unreasonable." Luther's suggestion that we are faced with "a *stern* commandment" diminishes the Sabbath along these lines, proving that in this respect, at least, there is no conflict between the German reformer and the Roman Catholic Church. While the Reformation calls the teachings of the Church into question on a number of points, restoration of the Sabbath is not on Luther's agenda. Arbitrariness of the kind implied in Luther's comment calls God's character into question as much as the sentiments expressed in the *Catechism of the Council of Trent*. An arbitrary intent, if that is what we have, inevitably casts a shadow over the one who thus exercises his or her authority.

Rejection of the Sabbath is nourished by the belief that it does not bring a benefit to human life.

When we resist the tendency to separate the Sabbath from its portfolio of meaning in general, and from its *basic* meaning in particular, it becomes easier to see that more is at stake than what the long neglect of the subject might have led us to believe. "How could the seventh-day Sabbath be abolished when it was based on a pattern of work and rest established at creation by God himself?"[26] asks Lyle D. Bierma in a discussion of the Sabbath in the theology of one of the lesser-known Reformers. How could it, indeed? The confidence with which the Roman Catechism deploys the notion of natural law vastly exceeds the merits of the concept. Luther's view of the Sabbath as "a stern commandment" is not the Reformer at his best, but it is honest and to the point. Even though Luther hardly intended it that way, his view connects well to a subject larger than the seventh day itself. According to the Bible, the suspicion of arbitrariness on the part of God lies at the core of the story of good and evil (Gen. 3:1). This, it turns out, is also the issue that comes to a head in connection with the Sabbath.

THE LIMITS OF "NATURAL LAW"

Beginning in Genesis, the Bible shows that a voice has been heard above and beyond nature. That voice is the voice of God, disclosing matters that do not arise from nature itself (Gen. 2:17). In the account of "the Fall" in Genesis, human beings face a choice that will not be resolved by an appeal to nature (Gen. 3:1). When the subversive power tries to lead human beings to distrust God, it counts on the charge of arbitrariness to drive the wedge of distrust into the divine-human relationship. Moreover, nature seems to support the serpent's insinuation. The woman, taking a careful look at the tree, "saw that the tree was good for food, and that it was a delight to the eyes, and that the tree was to be desired to make one wise" (Gen. 3:6). There is nothing in nature to help her—nothing that makes it a matter of course that she is well advised to stay away from this particular tree. On the contrary, the tree is beautiful and enticing. Under the spell of the serpent's suggestion, it is as if the tree beckons her to make her judgment as to what is beneficial or detrimental according to the evidence of nature (Gen. 3:6).

The insinuation that God is arbitrary calls the quality of God's command into question.[27] In the serpent's view the command is repressive; it is, as in Luther's terminology, "a stern commandment." While at face value the serpent appears to promote the well-being of human beings, his real aim is to defame God. If the commandment truly is arbitrary, the Commander must be, too. This sets up a predicament with few solutions if lasting damage to the reputation of the Commander is to be avoided. Either it must be demonstrated that God is not the source of the commandment, or it must be shown that the commandment is not what the serpent makes it out to be. A hypothetical third option, that the command is arbitrary and that arbitrariness, if provable, does no harm to God's reputation, is not an option from the point of view of the serpent. The premise of the story is precisely that if arbitrariness is proven, the damage is done and the serpent's mission accomplished.

As to the first option, the serpent knows that the authorship of the commandment is above question (Gen. 2:16–17). This expectation is confirmed when the woman admits that the tree is indeed fraught with a prohibition (Gen. 3:2). The first option eliminated, therefore, the second possibility becomes the crux of the temptation. All eyes are, as it were, on the quality of God's command.

Is the prohibition not to eat of the tree of knowledge arbitrary, all other options considered? This question requires some reflection before it is answered. What is certain even to a passing glance is that the woman eats of the tree partly because nature fails to tell her what to do. She knows the prohibition and has rehearsed it (3:2–3), but when she looks at the tree, she sees nothing to deter her from going ahead (3:6). Nature is silent. Nothing in the appearance of the tree alerts her to danger. Having considered the matter carefully, "she took some and ate it. She also gave some to her husband, who was with her, and he ate it" (3:6).

"Natural law" is of no help, failing decisively in humanity's first test of the principle. In the language of Carneades, the choice between right and wrong in this case falls within the category of "positive enactment" rather than natural law. Adam and Eve choose to act contrary to God's "positive enactment." They do it because they have been persuaded that legitimate moral law runs on parallel tracks with natural law, and they do it because, as theologians later articulate it, they have come to see an ordinance that is not based on "natural law" as arbitrary.

Why, nevertheless, does God give the commandment regarding the tree of knowledge in the first place? Why would God give *any* command, including the commandment to show reverence for the seventh day, if nature lacks the means to drive the point home? The issue underlying these questions is not merely whether God's ordinances should be considered binding and unalterable regardless of how they appear to human reason. Here the deeper concern deals with the quality and purpose of God's ordinances. Are they for the good of human beings? Do they serve a purpose, or do they contain elements that are incomprehensible to the point that it is fair to call them arbitrary?

In the Garden of Eden, as noted above, the critical choice does not revolve around *what* God has said, even though the serpent's insinuation calls for a clarification (3:2). The crux of the discussion relates to *why* God had said it.

The crafty insinuation at the beginning emphatically makes the point. "Did God really say, 'You must not eat from any tree in the garden?'" (3:1). There can be no doubt that the intent behind the insidious misquote is to portray God as exacting and arbitrary. As Moberly notes, "God's words had emphasized freedom" (Gen. 2:16),[28] but the serpent sees only deprivation, twisting the idea of freedom to its exact opposite. One might say that the notion of natural law is a human idea, making its debut in the Garden of Eden, but the suggestion that God's command is arbitrary is truly satanic. When the turn comes to the book of Revelation, the bits and pieces in the puzzle all converge on "that ancient serpent, who is called the Devil and Satan, the deceiver of the whole world" (Rev. 12:9; 20:2). The campaign of the Devil, a word that is appropriately translated "Mudslinger," owes its success to misrepresentation of God. What is intended as a benefit to human beings, even as an expansion of freedom, is construed as a privation. When the woman evaluates the proposition, taking nature as her point of reference, she concludes that the serpent must be right.

How does this add up? We are led to conclude, first, that the quality of God's commands is the central issue in the conflict that plays out in the beginning pages of the Bible. The serpent misconstrues the intent of the command for the purpose of smearing the character of the Commander. It is implicit that this charge, if true, damages God's standing. Second, despite its prestige in the history of the Church, the notion of natural law is of little use. This notion presupposes a perception of right and wrong that is as exhaustive as God's, making light of the fact that human beings are *not* God; we are created, subject to law, and dependent on God for direction even before our reasoning powers were impaired by sin and misperception. On the whole, too, the notion of natural law misreads the range and intent of God's commands, proving to be even more damaging to theology than it is to ethics.

Third, the conflict that comes to view in connection with the tree of knowledge in the Garden of Eden is in every way reminiscent of the kind of discussion that has been so damaging to the Sabbath. Despite the fact that neither command is a tenet of "natural law," they are, each in its own way, singular and highly conspicuous commands. Whether as narrative or as commandment, the Sabbath is no less intriguing than the command concerning the tree of knowledge; indeed, each is primed to draw attention to the reality and intent of the divine command. In this respect Luther's careless denigration of the Sabbath as "a stern commandment" echoes the serpent's suggestion that there are commands that should not have been given. The negative slant in Luther's outlook is pervasive. The Sabbath commandment hardly deserves to claim God as its author; it is more indebted to "Moses" than to God, and its negative character is underwritten by the allegation that it is "imposed" (although on the Jews only).[29] Luther has less zeal on behalf of Sunday than the

Roman Catholic Church and is less concerned about what "the Church of God has in her wisdom ordained,"[30] but the difference is one of degree and not of kind.

We miss the most important point, however, if the foregoing has led us to believe that the Roman Catholic Church, Luther, or other Protestant Reformers belittle the Sabbath because all are opposed to anything that smacks of arbitrariness. Nothing could be farther from the truth. To the greatest lights in the history of Christianity, whether Augustine,[31] Luther,[32] or Calvin,[33] the most sacred doctrine is the sovereignty of God. Each in his own distinctive way, surpassing his predecessor in chronological order, takes an almost perverse delight in harnessing the alleged arbitrariness of God in his advocacy of God's sovereignty. No doctrine is more offensive in their eyes than suggestions that infringe on God's sovereignty, and no weapon is deemed more effective than to brandish the alleged arbitrary character of God's will. Luther deploys the supposedly arbitrary character of the Sabbath purely for rhetorical reasons, having no objections to the notion that God is arbitrary in other areas. Indeed, divine arbitrariness is a cornerstone in Luther's theology, exceeded only by the even greater status that this notion has achieved in the Calvinist tradition.[34]

Whether as narrative or as commandment, the Sabbath is no less intriguing than the command concerning the tree of knowledge.

The quest for the basic meaning of the Sabbath, therefore, already complex and self-contradictory, is further complicated by yet another surprise. Not everyone goes along with the view that the Sabbath should be abandoned, but the charge that the Sabbath is arbitrary is accepted virtually across the board. Where the Roman Catholic Church and leading Protestants argue that the Sabbath is changeable because it is arbitrary, defenders of the Sabbath concur that it is arbitrary, but they do not agree that it should be changed. "Why, then, should a man keep the Sabbath?" asks one who thinks that it should be kept. "To the Christian there is only one reason, and no other," he answers, "but that reason is enough: God has spoken. The Sabbath commandment rests definitely and solely on a "Thus saith the Lord," and has no ground in nature, as such. It is for this reason that God makes the Sabbath His sign and test."[35]

The writer quoted above seeks to turn the alleged arbitrariness of the Sabbath to its advantage, arguing that the Sabbath should be kept precisely because it is *not* enjoined by nature. The ideology of the Sabbath, at rock bottom, is in his eyes that it should be kept because God said so, no other explanation being necessary.

Attempting to come to grips with the basic meaning of the Sabbath, Matitiahu Tsevat argues that while there are social and ecological benefits associated with Sabbath keeping, these do not reflect its primary meaning and purpose.[36] Even the two versions of the Ten Commandments, where reasons for the Sabbath are specified (Exod. 20:8–11; Deut. 5:12–15), fail to get to the heart of its character.[37] Instead, the Sabbath is at its best and most true to its basic character when no reasons are given for it other than that it should be kept.[38] Its intention, says Tsevat, is

> to fill time with a content that is uncontaminated by, and distinct from, anything related to natural time, i.e., time as agricultural season or astronomical phase....That content, displacing the various ideas and phenomena associated with natural time, is the idea of the absolute sovereignty of God, a sovereignty unqualified even by an indirect cognizance of the rule of other powers. As man takes heed of the sabbath day and keeps it holy, he not only relinquishes the opportunity of using part of his time as he pleases but he also foregoes the option of tying it to the secure and beneficial order of nature. The celebration of the sabbath is an act completely different from anything comparable in the life of ancient Israel. The sabbath is an isolated and strange phenomenon, not only in the world but also in Israel itself.[39]

Tsevat is certainly correct in calling the Sabbath "an isolated and strange phenomenon," but is it really true that its most important meaning "is the idea of the absolute sovereignty of God"? A closely related statement, written from a Christian point of view, seeks the basic meaning of the Sabbath precisely in its alleged arbitrariness.

> In an arbitrary manner God appointed that on the seventh day we should come to rest with His creation in a particular way. He filled this day with a content that is "uncontaminated" by anything related to the cyclical changes of nature or the movements of the heavenly bodies. That content is the idea of the absolute sovereignty of God, a sovereignty unqualified even by an indirect cognizance of the natural movements of time and rhythms of life. As the Christian takes heed of the Sabbath day and keeps it holy, he does so purely in answer to God's command and simply because God is his Creator.[40]

Let it be that the Sabbath "is an isolated and strange phenomenon," but is it arbitrary in the sense that Tsevat and others suggest? Is divine arbitrariness the default position in theology, the rising tide that lifts all ships, including the ships that have the Sabbath as part of their cargo? It is a bold proposition. But boldness here plays close to the edge of recklessness, advancing a position that should not be accepted as a matter of course. We do well to explore whether the source of this view is to be found in ideologies that are alien to the meaning of the Sabbath.

"CAN A WOMAN FORGET?" (ISA. 49:15)

A nuanced definition of terms and context may soften the impression that the search for the basic meaning of the Sabbath has brought into view options that are polar opposites, but it will not make the issue go away. Not only is it evident that the Church has singled out the alleged arbitrariness of the Sabbath as its weak point, the vulnerable element that justifies the substitution of the Sabbath for Sunday. It is more perplexing that defenders of the Sabbath have chosen to turn the alleged arbitrariness of the Sabbath into its strong point, urging that it is precisely by virtue of its arbitrariness that the Sabbath is equipped to execute its mission in the world. When the nuances have been made, and the scriptural evidence has been reviewed once more, therefore, we might uncover a tremendous cache of lost meaning.

Nuance helps because the statement that God appointed the Sabbath "in an arbitrary manner"[41] carries a different connotation if we revise it to say that God instituted the Sabbath in a *contingent* manner. Contingency and arbitrariness are related in the sense that they are entirely grounded in the will of the one who executes the action. But they are not the same because "arbitrariness" implies that the person behind the action is asserting his or her authority to no apparent benefit other than to have one's authority recognized. "Contingency," on the other hand, leaves the question of intent open. A contingent action need not have the intent of driving home a person's authority. A host of other options are open to account for it.[42]

In defective human terms the contingency of the Sabbath belongs in the same category as parents who celebrate the birthday of a beloved child or to the fond marking of a wedding anniversary. These celebrations are not arbitrary because they are anchored in real historical events, but they are contingent in the sense that there is no law to obligate that they be observed. The initiative is entirely in the mind of the parent or the spouse. More importantly, they do not have an arbitrary intent as if the celebration of the birthday is meant to drive home the truth of parental sovereignty, or, in the case of the wedding anniversary, as if the celebration primarily seeks to reinforce the legal contract of marriage.

The Bible offers many pictures that counter the suspicion of arbitrariness. God is not a person to whom one should ascribe arbitrariness even if sovereignty is a defining attribute of God. "See," exclaims the prophet, "I have inscribed you on the palms of my hands; your walls are continually before me" (Isa. 49:16). This text projects the attributes of care and kindness, seeking to draw the one to whom this is spoken with the assurance that she or he is welcome rather than by the assertion of sovereignty. And then this, as a better analogy for the depth of the divine memory that is expressed and institutionalized from Creation in the Sabbath rest, "Can a woman forget her nursing child, or show no compassion for the child of her womb? Even these may forget, yet I will not forget you" (Isa. 49:15). This text undergirds beautifully Carsten A. Johnsen's suggestion that the contingency of the Sabbath has in it not only the element of reaching out to touch but of "total contact."[43] In Isaiah's terms, God is the Divine Mother seeking not the occasional touch but the healing and sanctifying embrace of her broken child. The picture is one of close contact, even skin contact, and it is not a picture that looks to "arbitrariness" or to "sovereignty" as the words that best describe what we are seeing.

According to *Dies Domini*, too, God's response to human beings and to Creation "is a 'contemplative' gaze which does not look to new accomplishments but enjoys the beauty of what has already been achieved."[44] There is contingency in the "contemplative gaze" because it is a freely chosen action, but there is no arbitrariness, no intent for which "arbitrariness" is an appropriate characterization. On a still higher note, it is said that in order to reach "the heart of the 'shabbat' of God's 'rest,' we need to recognize in both the Old and the New Testament the nuptial intensity which marks the relationship between God and his people."[45] The recipient of the Sabbath blessing, therefore, finds himself or herself in the emotional territory of the marital relationship as well as in the relation between the mother and her child.

Such focal images make it awkward to call on the notion of sovereignty in order to explicate the basic meaning of the Sabbath. The inadequacy of this notion looks still more flawed when it is held up to the light of the controversy over the character of God that unfolds in the Bible. The God who blesses and sanctifies the seventh day does not come across as an arbitrary Person in any of the ordinary meanings of this word. God has the good of human beings at heart. He does not set aside a day of rest in order to publish abroad His sovereignty, nor is there any capricious rationale in the choice of the seventh day. As we have seen, the indicative of God's rest in the Creation story precedes the imperative of the commandment. Even in the context of the Ten Commandments, "the commandment urges that something be remembered" before decreeing that something be done.[46]

What is to be remembered sets a priority for the meaning of the Sabbath that can be clearly expressed. In its original configuration in Genesis, the Sabbath speaks primarily about the value of human beings to God and only secondarily about God's importance to human beings. God invests the Sabbath with His presence, promise, and blessing before there is any mention of the expected human response.

While it is bold and creative to make the alleged arbitrariness of the Sabbath into a positive feature, it is hazardous to the cause for which the Sabbath is a symbol. On the premise that the controversy between good and evil in the biblical narrative revolves around the question of whether or not God is arbitrary, it is difficult to appreciate how God will be vindicated from the charge that God is arbitrary under a symbol that proves God's arbitrariness. Moreover, if the alleged arbitrary feature of the Sabbath is made to be its most fundamental characteristic, it leaves a residue of arbitrariness on God's reputation. By choosing this line of reasoning, defenders of the Sabbath may be winning the battle for the Sabbath at the tremendous cost of losing the war concerning the character of God. Less is gained by keeping the Sabbath because those who reject it and those who defend it are in agreement with regard to the larger question. To both groups arbitrariness is part of the Sabbath, perhaps even the bottom line of its meaning. Defending the Sabbath by accepting the argument that it is arbitrary looks increasingly like an ill-conceived idea that founders on the shoals of its implied premise.

God invests the Sabbath with His presence, promise, and blessing before there is any mention of the expected human response.

The scriptural roots of the seventh day lead into an entirely different theological landscape. Contrary to the view of Tsevat and many others, this landscape has narrative rather than law as the primary source in the quest for the meaning of the Sabbath. It greets the Sabbath more as a privilege than as an obligation, seeing it more as a token of divine faithfulness than as a test of human obedience. Reciprocity on the human level is expected, but the response of obedience will not come in the form of obedience to an arbitrary command.

It almost seems like the view of God that the serpent presented in the Garden of Eden has become an axiom of theology even though the entire message of the Bible counters the charge. What if the truth instead is that there is no arbitrariness in God? And what if the Sabbath is itself the most striking proof of this counterclaim? Where the biblical narrative is allowed to lead the way, the origin of the Sabbath is no more arbitrary than anyone's birthday and no more contrived than the Fourth of July. Scholars and theologians on both sides of the issue have succeeded in proving that the Sabbath is not a tenet of natural law, but it does not follow, as many assume, that it thereby is arbitrary. In fact, it might even belong in the category of *natural*, as something that is comprehensible and intrinsic to the purpose for which it exists. By love's logic the Sabbath needs no elaborate explanation or defense: It is time solemnly prioritized for the loved one and a sign of faithfulness to the loved one that will not be rescinded.

Arbitrariness is not intrinsic to the Sabbath despite the status that the notion has achieved. The source of this outlook is quite likely found in "the idea of the absolute sovereignty of God,"[47] but this view is not what grows most naturally in the native soil of the Sabbath. It is rather a notion that has been imported to, and imposed on, the Sabbath from systems of thought that have singled out "sovereignty" to be the most representative word about God. Leading thinkers in the history of the Church disparage the Sabbath because it does not agree with their notion of "natural law," but they are more than eager to embrace arbitrariness when it suits their cause. The Sabbath is abrogated because of its alleged arbitrariness only to be replaced by a view of God that takes arbitrariness to unimaginable heights in Christian theology. The influence of this outlook still haunts the Sabbath even among those who affirm its enduring value.

It is now possible to see that the *meaning* of the seventh day has been compromised even more than the seventh day itself. The Sabbath—and its meaning—is lost because people look in the wrong direction: to ethical necessity, natural law, or divine sovereignty, issues lying on the fringes of the horizon of the Sabbath, if not elements from another theological solar system. The biblical Sabbath has a distinctly different frame of reference, vigilantly guarding against the charge that God's rule is tinged with an arbitrary intent. Indeed, the many in the Christian tradition who came to see the Sabbath as a dispensable feature in the divine will, pointing out that it fails the test of "natural law," may have missed the point badly. "Natural law" may suffice for ordinary notions of morality, but it falls short as a measure for goodness that exceeds necessity.

By love's logic the Sabbath is time solemnly prioritized for the loved one and a sign of faithfulness to the loved one that will not be rescinded.

According to the biblical idea, the Sabbath does not primarily seek the acknowledgement of the absolute sovereignty of God, arbitrarily exercised.[48] In distinction from views that place necessity, law, or sovereignty at the center, the Sabbath expresses God's self-giving love, before which all the usual measuring sticks of moral quality fall short. In the unlikely event that a woman should forget her nursing child, finding no image more compelling, God's faithfulness is of a different and enduring order, says the prophet Isaiah. "Even these may forget, yet I will not forget you" (Isa. 49:15). This, more than sovereignty, is the raw material that shapes the basic character of the seventh day and the place to look for its lost meaning.

ENDNOTES

1. In the apostolic letter of Pope John Paul II entitled *Dies Domini*, proclaimed on May 31, 1998, five broad meanings are assigned to Sunday as a day of worship and rest, each the spawning-ground for a host of derivative meanings: *Dies Domini* ("Day of the Lord"), *Dies Christi* ("Day of Christ"), *Dies Ecclesiae* ("Day of the Church"), *Dies Hominis* ("Day of Humanity"), and *Dies Dierum* ("Day of Days"). These meanings lie close to meanings that have been explored here in relation to the seventh day, in which the meanings have a firmer grounding and from which they receive an indisputable mandate.

2. Some interpreters and historians have grappled with the issue as it confronted the Protestant reformers. Lyle D. Bierma ("Remembering the Sabbath Day: Ursinus's Exposition of Exodus 20:8–11," in *Biblical Interpretation in the Era of the Reformation*, ed. Richard A. Muller and John L. Thompson [Grand Rapids: Eerdmans, 1996], 273) writes that "more than any other section of the Decalogue, the Fourth Commandment is fraught with hermeneutical difficulties. Why, for example, is this the only one of the commandments that was neither repeated in the New Testament nor literally kept by the early Christian church? How could the seventh-day Sabbath be abolished when it was based on a pattern of work and rest established at creation by God himself?"

3. Justin Martyr, *First Apology* 67; cf. Ignatius, *Magnesians* IX.1.

4. In the teachings of Augustine "the Sabbath commandment is singled out as precisely the one commandment that Christians are not to take literally." Moreover, Augustine "never based Christian observance of Sunday on the Sabbath commandment"; cf. R. J. Bauckham, "Sabbath and Sunday in the Medieval Church in the West," in *From Sabbath to Lord's Day*, ed. D. A. Carson (Grand Rapids: Zondervan, 1982), 301.

5. Bauckham, "Sabbath and Sunday in the Post-Apostolic Church," 261.

6. *Dies Domini* IV.60.

7. *The Catechism of the Council of Trent,* trans. by the Rev. J. Donovan (New York: Catholic School Book Co., 1929).

8. *Catechism of the Council of Trent*, 267.

9. Eusebius, *The History of the Church,* trans. G. A. Williamson (London: Penguin Books, 1989).

10. Eusebius of Caesarea, *Commentaria in Psalmos* 91, *PG* 23, 1172. The reference to the Sabbath as "the Sabbath of the Jews" is noteworthy. The idea of "transfer" is maintained in more recent expressions on the subject within the Roman Catholic Church. According to *Dies Domini* IV.63 (1998), the Christians, as proclaimers of liberation, "felt that they had the authority to transfer the meaning of the Sabbath to the day of the Resurrection."

11. *Catechism of the Council of Trent*, 264.

12. Martin Luther ("How Christians Should Regard Moses," 172–173) takes a similar view. "Thus we read Moses not because he applies to us, that we must obey him, but because he

agrees with the natural law and is conceived better than the Gentiles would ever have been able to do."

13. The idea that the Sabbath is a temporary, ceremonial ordinance is not easily supported by the Ten Commandments. If it is possible to make a distinction on the basis of the Old Testament, the Sabbath is not in the ceremonial category. The Ten Commandments were written by the finger of God and placed within the Ark of the Covenant (Exod. 32:15; 34:28; 40:20). The ceremonial ordinances were written on scrolls by Moses and placed next to the ark (Deut. 31:24–26). In the New Testament the distinction between moral and ceremonial law is submerged in the greater question of God's grace and human merit (Gal. 3:10–25).

14. Lincoln ("From Sabbath to Lord's Day," 380) finds already in Tertullian the idea that only what is in character with natural law truly belongs in the Decalogue.

15. Ralph McInerny, "Ethics," in *The Cambridge Companion to Aquinas*, ed. Norman Kretzmann and Eleonore Stump (Cambridge: Cambridge University Press, 1993), 212.

16. Thomas Aquinas, *Summa Theologica* I, 94, art. 1–6; see also F. C. Copleston, *Aquinas* (London: Penguin Books, 1955), 219–242.

17. C. S. Lewis (*Mere Christianity* [New York: Macmillan, 1960; orig. 1943], 17–39) uses the evidence for a generally recognized moral code to great advantage in his argument for Christianity.

18. Cf. *Dies Domini* IV.63 (1998).

19. Lord Acton, *Essays in Freedom and Power*, 68.

20. The concept of natural law still plays a central role in Roman Catholic thought. The Church's prohibition, not only against abortion, but also against the use of contraception, has its basis in the notion of natural law. But it is hard to be consistent, and the law requiring priestly celibacy no doubt has another basis.

21. Thomas Aquinas, *The Governance of Rulers*, ch. 2, quoted in Paul E. Sigmun, "Law and Politics," in *Cambridge Companion to Aquinas*, 220.

22. Sigmun, "Law and Politics," 221; cf. *Summa Theologicae* IIaIIae.11.3.

23. The apostle Paul, too, tries to derive a norm from nature as he sees it in his day, but his argument was no doubt more persuasive in its original cultural setting than it has been subsequently (1 Cor. 11:14–15).

24. Bierma, "Remembering the Sabbath Day," 279.

25. Luther, "How Christians Should Regard Moses," 165. Peter Hirschberg ("Martin Luthers Haltung zu Shabbat und Sonntag im Horizont des Jüdischen Shabbatsverständnisses," *Luther* 69 [1998]: 81–100), arguing on behalf of the obvious and necessary benefits of a day of rest in the Bible and in human experience, finds Luther's understanding of the subject deficient. For Luther, the Sabbath is for the Jews only, and his shallow grasp of Jewish Sabbath observance borders on the comical. To the extent that the Sabbath rest has merit, it owes to "nature" and not to God, a rhetorical move that further diminishes the Sabbath. Contrary to Luther,

Hirschberg sees the Sabbath grounded in human need and in God's promise of rest.

26. Bierma, "Remembering the Sabbath Day," 273.

27. For a further discussion, see Sigve Tonstad, "The Message of the Trees in the Midst of the Garden," *JATS* 19 (2008): 1–16.

28. Moberly, "Did the Serpent Get It Right?" 6.

29. Luther, "Against the Sabbatarians," 91.

30. *Catechism of the Council of Trent*, 267.

31. Augustine's view represents a break with the convictions of his predecessors with regard to freedom, persuasion, and non-coercion, coinciding with the changing political fortunes of his time; cf. Elaine Pagels, "The Politics of Paradise: Augustine's Exegesis of Genesis 1–3 Versus That of John Chrysostom," *HTR* 78 (1985): 67–99.

32. Luther's most sustained contribution to this subject is the book prized by himself above any other in his voluminous authorship, *The Bondage of the Will,* trans. J. I. Packer and O. R. Johnston (New York: Fleming H. Revell, 1957). Luther was responding to Erasmus, who had roused Luther's ire by his advocacy of free will. The weakness of Erasmus's position does not vindicate Luther's view, as when he goes out of his way not to allow any interpretation that aims at explicating difficulties in the Bible. For Luther the best explanation is the sovereignty of God (cf. *The Bondage of the Will*, 314–316).

33. In his discussion of why some people have been devoted to damnation and others to eternal salvation apart from any choice of their own, Calvin writes that "God's will is so much the highest rule of righteousness that whatever he wills, by the very fact that he wills it, must be considered righteous. When, therefore, one asks why God has so done, we must reply: because he has willed it. But if you proceed further to ask why he so willed, you are seeking something greater and higher than God's will, which cannot be found"; cf. *Calvin: Institutes of the Christian Religion*, vol. 2, ed. John T. Mc Neill, trans. Ford Lewis Battles (Philadelphia: The Westminster Press, 1960), 949.

34. Calvin, *Institutes* II:920–964. Karl Barth (*Church Dogmatics* IV.3, 431) writes of Job's suffering that Job should serve God "with no claim that His [God's] rule should conform to some picture which he [Job] has formed of it." God "does not ask for his [Job's] understanding, agreement or applause. On the contrary, He simply asks that he should be content not to know why and to what end he exists, and does so in this way and not another." God is accountable to nobody, and certainly not to sinful human beings; cf. R. Scott Rodin, *Evil and Theodicy in the Theology of Karl Barth* (IST 3; New York: Peter Lang, 1997), 2–3.

35. M. L. Andreasen, *The Sabbath* (Takoma Park, Washington, DC: Review and Herald Publishing Association, 1942), 29.

36. Matitiahu Tsevat, "The Basic Meaning of the Biblical Sabbath," *ZAW* 84 (1972): 447–459.

37. Tsevat ("The Basic Meaning of the Biblical Sabbath," 447–448) sees the "ethiotetic" rationale of the Sabbath commandment as secondary.

38. Tsevat ("The Basic Meaning of the Biblical Sabbath," 452–454) prioritizes Leviticus 23:3 as the text that exhibits the Sabbath in its primary form.

39. Ibid., 458.

40. Cf. also Raoul Dederen, "Reflections on a Theology of the Sabbath," in *The Sabbath in Scripture and History*, ed. Kenneth A. Strand (Washington, DC: Review and Herald Publishing Association, 1982), 302.

41. Ibid.

42. Johnsen (*Day of Destiny*, 26–36) shows that the contingency of the Sabbath exemplifies God's freedom while also embodying the most literal meaning of the Latin word *contingere*, meaning to "touch," and, better still, showing forth God's insistence "on touching us *altogether*."

43. Ibid., 35.

44. *Dies Domini* I.11.

45. Ibid., I.12.

46. Ibid., I.16.

47. Dederen, "Reflections on a Theology of the Sabbath," 302.

48. Tsevat ("The Basic Meaning of the Biblical Sabbath," 455), despite his eagerness to strip the Sabbath of any rationale except for the assertion of sovereignty, nevertheless succeeds in giving the notion of sovereignty an excellent rationale. "There is, therefore, nothing incongruous nor bold in the conclusion that every seventh day the Israelite is to renounce dominion over time, thereby renounce autonomy, and recognize God's dominion over time and thus over himself."

CHAPTER 25

THE SABBATH AND THE IMPERIAL IDEAL

I do not call you servants any longer, because the servant does not know what the master is doing; but I have called you friends, because I have made known to you everything that I have heard from my Father.
John 15:15

The combination of anti-Judaism, Hellenism, and alleged lack of theological merit diminished the Sabbath in the Church, as we have seen. What happened on the other side of the equation, the side of Sunday, however, is not merely a rise in fortune that is proportional to the Sabbath's decline. Already in the early stages of the Sabbath's eclipse, Sunday must be seen as a potential rival and a factor that hastened the decline of the Sabbath. In this process imperial promotion of Sunday plays a significant role. Beginning in the fourth century the imperial dimension was more than an incidental aspect of the rise of Sunday in the Roman Empire. This is an aspect that also has profound theological implications, shaping people's view of God.

IMPERIAL RULE

The emperor wields power in a manner that is consonant with his title. He is the *imperator*, defined as "the ruler answerable to none."[1] The nature of this form of government can be summarized by way of pithy contrasts. The emperor rules by decree, not by persuasion; he governs by command, not by consent; he relies on force, not on consensus or popular acclaim. The relationship between the emperor and his subjects is that of master and subject, the former issuing orders and the latter obeying them. There is no built-in mechanism of accountability in the imperial system of government except for riots and assassinations.

Beginning only a short time after Constantine's accession to the imperial office and his conversion to Christianity, the arm of the state quickly began to make itself felt in the affairs of the Church. "The Church," says A. H. M. Jones, "had acquired a protector, but it had also acquired a master."[2] The new master was a ruler answerable to none.

Constantine's advocacy of Sunday was legislative. Reaching beyond the Christian framework and connotation, Constantine decreed that "all judges, townspeople and all occupations should rest on the most honorable day of the sun."[3] In this formulation the

Christian connection was conspicuously left out of the picture. The emperor pressed the injunction instead "under its old astrological and heathen title, *Dies Solis*, familiar to all his subjects, so that the law was as applicable to the worshippers of Hercules, Apollo, and Mithras, as to the Christians."[4] No mention was made of Christ or the resurrection of Christ. It is as *Dies Solis* that the ordinance was expected to resonate.

What was in the mind of the emperor will never be fully known, but it is clear that he was venturing into the realm of religion. The deed must speak for itself where a statement of intent was lacking, but a statement of implied intent would eventually follow. It came from the pen of Constantine's uncritical propagandist Eusebius. He placed the intitiative in the context of Constantine's ambition to rid the world of "hatred of God," writing admiringly that "the blessed prince labored to make all men do this, as it were making a vow, to make all men little by little religious."[5]

The emperor is the imperator, defined as "the ruler answerable to none.

"The blessed prince" Constantine approached the task with a sense of calling, "as it were making a vow," says Eusebius. The religious aspiration was freely admitted; the goal was "to make all men… religious." This could not happen overnight; it would have to happen "little by little." Eusebius singles this out as the key element in the strategy. Legislation would facilitate the task, and Sunday observance was one of the practical means by which to achieve it. In the eyes of this head of state, the government was offering a helping hand to the Church. By God's providence Constantine, as the head of the secular authority, was now the leading agent for the Christianization of the world.[6] From that time onward the citizens of the empire were to have access to the blessings of Christianity with less effort on their part. It was to be delivered to their door as a gift of the state.

To the delight of the Church, Constantine and his sons placed religion in the foreground when they, in Eusebius's approving view, made it their very first action "to wipe the world clean from hatred of God."[7] The rhetoric of "wiping clean" gives room for pause because of the evident imperial connotation. What is there to stop a ruler that is answerable to none, considering the means at his disposal? The sense of the high calling and the confidence in his means loomed large already in the emperor's threatening posture toward the Donatists, who were at the receiving end of imperial threats not because they were unbelievers but because they did not conform to the certified view. "What higher duty have I in virtue of my imperial office and policy than to dissipate errors and repress rash indiscretions and so to cause all to offer to Almighty God true religion, honest concord and due worship?" Constantine asked.[8] This piece of self-understanding, justifying the intolerance by the emperor's sense of infallibility, explains what was in store for the Donatist dissenters. They would "pay the penalty which their mad and reckless obstinacy deserves."[9] The end result not only made Christianity the religion of the state and the emperor the chief sponsor of Christianity, but it also ensured close imperial supervision over what Christians would do and believe.

The exuberance with which Eusebius, as a man of the Church, greeted the politics of the empire has more than passing interest. As bishop and historian he founded the political philosophy of the Christian state, taking his ideals almost unabridged from the Roman Empire. It is Eusebius's wholehearted approval and not only his description of what happened that should attract attention. Neither the flaws of the Roman system nor the potential risks involved in this apparent victory of good over evil seemed to trouble him.[10] On the one hand, there was the risk of domination of the Church by the state, leading to loss of freedom. On the other hand, there was the risk of hypocrisy and spurious conversions, leading to loss of integrity. Eusebius, speaking for the Church, seemed oblivious to these dangers. To him and his contemporaries the prospect of a Christian state meant the ultimate triumph of Christianity, no further concern being necessary. The universal church became Roman by joining its interests to those of the state, eventually acquiring the seat of power of the ancient empire. With this merger came the opportunity to adopt civil legislation in the interest of religion, as Constantine did when he made Sunday legislation the pioneering feature of his program of religion and statecraft.

But "legislation" as such was not the only resort of the new way of Christianity. What happened was not legislation by an elected body of representatives where the legislators represented the diversity and the will of the people. This was legislation by imperial decree. In the empire the will of one man was binding on the many. Constantine did not change the imperial system of government after converting to Christianity, and the Church of his day acquiesced to the imperial will as a matter of course. Constantine's decrees were those of an autocrat, and the arm of the Christian state would, before long, become more intrusive than the pagan state aspired to be.[11] Whether by the pagan emperor, the Christian emperor, or the Christian pope in the Middle Ages, the supreme authority resided in a single human being who expected unquestioning submission to his will.[12] As radical as it may have seemed that the empire was embracing Christianity, it was also clear that Constantine "intended neither to abandon his predecessor's scheme of policy[13] nor to renounce the fascinations of arbitrary authority," says Lord Acton.[14]

IMPERIAL THEOLOGY

The imperial structure of government, with a supreme ruler answerable to none, became etched into the structure of the Church. It was a similarity in more than name when the Roman pontiff inherited from the emperor the title of *Pontifex Maximus*, the highest priest in the pagan cult, and the Church adopted the pattern of the imperial system of government. "The idea that western society had to recognize the predominance of a sharply defined, clerical élite, as the emperors had once recognized the special status of members of the Roman Senate, was the basic assumption behind the rhetoric and ceremonial of the medieval papacy: like the last glow of evening, the late Roman senator's love of *Roma aeterna* had come to rest on the solemn façade of papal Rome," says Peter Brown.[15]

This assessment has far-reaching ramifications for church structure and policy, of course, but it is more important that the imperial framework and mindset are deposited on the structure and texture of Christian theology. As to the former, the papal office acquires the status implicit in the original imperial title. The pope, too, was a ruler accountable to none. His word, too, had the force of law apart from the consent of his constituents. Like the pattern of the imperial government, the bishop of Rome became the *pater patriae*, whose authoritative role took on an autocratic character just as in the empire.[16] In the Christian state soldiers gave way to doctrines and armies to dogmas, but the arbitrary and imperial way of exercising authority continued undiminished.[17]

The imperial model came to be reflected in society's perception of God. By inference God was the ultimate despot, the One whose decrees must be obeyed without questioning, and the ruler who was accountable to none. Indeed, to complete the fusion of the two, as in the medieval period, the Christian emperors first and the popes later executed their offices according to what was assumed to be a divine pattern. If, in a chronological reconstruction of this development, the imperial model bequeathed its legacy to theology, it fell to theology to provide the warrant for imperial government.

Sunday was absorbed into this constellation of theology and governance, not as an incidental feature but as one of the means of promoting it. In the program "to make all men little by little religious,"[18] each citizen of the empire was to be a child of the Church. In order to accomplish this all men were made to walk in step, conforming to the rhythm of the same invisible drummer. Sunday had the backing of the emperor, rising on the strength of the imperial will. The arbitrary nature of the imperial will was crucial to its success and to the subsequent dominance of Christianity in the

Western world. Eusebius's glowing version may be exaggerated in the sense that the influence of Christianity in his day was still lagging behind the universality he envisioned. But he defined the ideal and the means by which to achieve it. Universality was from that time not only seen as the goal but also as the norm. In the empire of Constantine, the narrow road leading to life (Matt. 7:13–14) widened sufficiently to give room for everybody. Within five decades the road of Christianity was the only road left. Attempts to take other roads were treated as crimes against the state. Couched in the worthy intent of turning people toward God, Christians "were to use every means of persuasion: flattery and battery alike."[19] "Silencing, burning, and destruction were all forms of theological demonstration," says Ramsay MacMullen. When it was over, only Christians were left, Christians of one persuasion only.[20]

The main issue, therefore, is not that the imperial pattern was reproduced in the hierarchal structure of the Church. Historically, the imperial system was adopted because it was the pattern of the state, but theologically it was accepted as *God's* way. God was perceived as the ultimate *imperator*. If consent and accountability were missing in human society, it is justified because these elements were also absent in the heavenly government on which the earthly rule was modeled. When the constellation of Church and state resorted to legislation, coercion, and persecution, it justified it as God's method. A church that issued dogmas, laws, and anathemas in God's name obeyed a god that was thought to rule by imperial decree. If the earthly representative seemed dictatorial, the Christian state was merely conforming to the ways of its own imperious master. To say that "[t]he Church gave unto God the attributes which belonged exclusively to Caesar"[21] is therefore more than a clever play on words. It is very much true to what happened.

God was perceived as the ultimate imperator.

NON-IMPERIAL THEOLOGY

It may be true that the conversion of the emperor might not have happened unless it had been preceded by "the conversion of Christianity to the culture and ideals of the Roman world."[22] But this assessment assumes a lesser conversion than the one that actually happened. The problem is not only that historians overestimate the depth of Constantine's conversions; it is rather that we underestimate the Christian ideal. Nowhere is the New Testament distinctive more staggering than in Jesus's words, "I do not call you servants any longer, because the servant does not know what the master is doing, but I have called you friends, because I have made known to everything that I have heard from my Father" (John 15:15).

The imperial system had nothing in common with this declaration. No one in the Christian empire thought of God in such terms. In one sweeping statement Jesus appeared to set aside all the accepted notions of the proper relationship between master and servant, not to speak of the relationship between human beings and God. The governing authority threw itself open to scrutiny, so to speak. "I have made known to you everything" is a non-imperial ideology, a statement of empowerment for the disciple and of accountability for the master. *This* ruler is not a ruler answerable to none. Jesus does not relinquish authority, but His authority travels the road of transparency. In Jesus's view trust and secrecy are mutually incompatible.

We read this in the Gospel of John, the Gospel that is most tightly linked to the book of Genesis and most single-mindedly dedicated to proving that Jesus reveals the character of God. "Whoever has seen me has seen the Father," Jesus said in this Gospel (14:9). Stating it first in the negative, "no longer" means a repudiation of established practice, a departure from what is expected and entrenched. Following through with the positive statement, Jesus heralded a new era. But the novelty must not be overstated precisely because of the echoes of Genesis in John. There is an antecedent to His outlook. We should read Jesus's statement as though He was reading from the script of Creation, pulling the script of the seventh day from the ashes of misapprehension and forgetfulness. The anti-imperial flavor of Jesus's mission mirrors the anti-imperial connotation of the seventh day at Creation. Neither the notion of accountability nor that of transparency is a novelty. Already in Genesis, God came to human beings in the mode of empowerment and not as an imperial figure. The statement that God "rested on the seventh day from all the work that he had done" sets the terms for the future relationship as much as it reflects on what had been achieved (Gen. 2:2). When Genesis says that "God blessed the seventh day and hallowed it" (Gen. 2:3), it means that God was inviting human beings into His sphere, investing the relationship with high and enduring expectations (Gen. 2:3). "I have called you friends, because I have made known to you everything that I have heard from my Father," Jesus says (John 15:15), as if setting up a stunning and unprecedented ideal. And yet what is this but a forgotten meaning of the seventh day?

The anti-imperial flavor of Jesus's mission mirrors the anti-imperial connotation of the seventh day at Creation.

What is the ideology of the seventh day, its primary and original meaning, but a statement hewing close to the words of Jesus in John? What is the seventh day but sacred territory of mutuality and reciprocity generously carved out by the Creator? And, taking the question to the most basic level, what is the seventh day except a statement of intent on God's part, showing God to be not only the sovereign God but also "the reacting God, the God who responds to what has been created?"[23] The Master who speaks in the context of the seventh day is also the Master who listens, and He listens with such abandon that the distinction between Master and disciple is no longer the best way of describing the relationship. "I have called you friends," spoken in the perfect tense and thus revealing a completed action, should not only be read as an ideal that has been actualized in the relationship between Jesus and His disciples. It is also the distant memory of the Sabbath at Creation. There, too, in the Sabbath blessing, we hear the Logos of John speaking, "I have called you friends."

Lesslie Newbigin writes aptly that the difference between the servant and the friend revolves around the question of comprehension. "Their obedience, therefore, will not be the uncomprehending submission of the slave.... Therefore, their obedience will be the eager, intelligent obedience of those whose master is also the one who has made them his friends."[24] This comment projects the success of God's intent, and yet it is the intent that needs to stand in the foreground in case it might be compromised by lack of reciprocity on the part of the disciple. To be a servant means less privilege, but it also means less responsibility. The servant might decide to trade the privilege so as to diminish responsibility. The imperial ideal, we read in a source more ancient than the gospels, owed its success to the yearning to be commanded on the part of the subject as much as to the sovereign's determination to command. "A law should be brief, so that the unskilled may grasp it more easily. Let it be like a voice from heaven; let it order, not argue. Nothing seems to be more pedantic, more pointless than a law with a preamble. Advise me, tell me what you want me to do; I am not learning, I am obeying."[25]

What is the seventh day but sacred territory of mutuality and reciprocity generously carved out by the Creator?

In the first part of this statement, we hear the imperial voice. Its ideal is to order, not to argue or explain. There should be no preamble, no rational context for the command that might lessen the imperial authority and thus appear to empower the subject. In the second part of the statement, the subject is speaking, enthusiastically acquiescing to the imperial policy. "Tell me what you want me to do," and then, in effect, saying, "I do not want to understand, I want to obey." This is the imperial ideal, articulated in the empire but also adopted and actualized in the history of the Christian Church. It stands in contrast to everything we hear Jesus say and everything enshrined in the intent of the seventh day. The latter is *not* a statement that has an imperial intent, *not* the voice of one commanding and the other obeying orders, *not* the instrument of a sovereign who rules with disdain for the opinion of his subjects, and *not* the ordinance of an authority who will be answerable to none. If, as envisioned here, the Sabbath belongs to the anti-imperial framework that we find in Jesus, and if Jesus is reading from the script of Creation, the Sabbath that rises from the ashes must be cleansed of the residue of imperial ideology that sticks to it, too. In the historical home stretch of the Sabbath narrative, the Sabbath, revived and refocused by the life and teaching of Jesus, yearns to return to its anti-imperial roots in Creation, inching ever closer to its own beginning and to itself.

"Taken together," says Niels-Erik Andreasen, "the Old Testament heritage and the New Testament gospel have proved exceedingly heavy burdens for the first day to carry."[26] This suggests that the shoes left behind by the seventh day are too large for the first day to fill—that the Church underestimated the Sabbath and had unrealistic expectations as to the notion of "transfer." And this problem comes in addition to the imperial contribution to the rise of Sunday and the imperial imprint on Christian theology that have shaped the habits, structures, and thought patterns of the Christian world. It is a background that saddles Sunday with an ideological disposition from which it will not easily be extricated quite apart from the question of whether Sunday could adequately take over the portfolio of meanings originally belonging to the Sabbath.

But the seventh day presents a challenge to the imagination that is not eliminated by these affirmations. Andreasen, having questioned the adequacy of the institution preferred by the Church, adds that "the sabbath *lifts them both with ease,* bringing blessings to man and a message about redemption in Jesus Christ."[27] This statement is defensible within the context where it is found, but the phrase "with ease" sounds too sanguine. It is easier to agree that the first day buckles under the weight placed upon it by the Old and the New Testaments than to affirm that the Sabbath lifts the burden "with ease." Or, recalling the imperial legacy, it is easier to agree that the imperial legacy causes Sunday to buckle under this weight than to predict the success of the Sabbath. History, even the history played out in the pages of the Bible, suggests otherwise on the point that matters most. The story of the Sabbath, too, is a story of lost meanings and a history within which the imperial ideal is an ever-present threat. In the script of Creation and the blessing of the Sabbath, culled from the ashes in the Gospel of John, we stumble across a staggering thought whether we see it from the point of view of the Composer or of the recipient. The Sabbath and its meaning are endangered species. On this logic it will come as less of a surprise to discover that the last book of the Bible distills the cosmic conflict into a confrontation of signs.

ENDNOTES

1. Nicholas Purcell, "The Arts of Government," in *The Roman World*, ed. John Boardman, Jasper Griffin and Oswyn Murray (Oxford: Oxford University Press, 1986), 163.

2. A. H. M. Jones, *Constantine and the Conversion of Europe* (Toronto: The University of Toronto Press, 1978 [orig. 1948]), 107.

3. Moltmann, *God in Creation*, 294.

4. Schaff, *History of the Christian Church*, vol. III, 380.

5. Eusebius, *The Life of Constantine*, Book IV, ch. XVIII.

6. Ramsay MacMullen (*Christianizing the Roman Empire A.D. 100–400* [New Haven: Yale University Press, 1984], 43–51) documents that Constantine paid public honors to the sun long after his conversion to Christianity.

7. Eusebius, *The History of the Church*, X.9.9.

8. Jones, *Constantine and the Conversion of Europe*, 103.

9. Ibid.

10. S. L. Greenslade, *Church and State from Constantine to Theodosius* (London: SCM Press, 1954), 10.

11. Frend, *The Rise of Christianity*, 505.

12. As the best known example of papal absolutism, in the year 1075, Pope Gregory VII claims the authority to depose emperors and the right to "absolve subjects of unjust men from their fealty." Here the tenor is thoroughly imperial; cf. *Dictatus Papae* (1075), in Brian Tierney,

The Crisis of Church and State 1050–1300 (Englewood Cliffs, NJ: Prentice-Hall, 1964), 49.

13. Constantine's immediate predecessor was Diocletian (284–306), the instigator of the last large-scale persecution of Christians, an able but ultimately sorry figure who harnessed religion in order to bolster the prestige of the imperial office, hoping thereby to save the empire.

14. Lord Acton, *Essays on Freedom and Power*, 82.

15. Brown, *The World of Late Antiquity*, 135.

16. If one accepts the thesis of the Roman Catholic theologians Raymond E. Brown and John P. Meier (*Antioch and Rome* [London: Geoffrey Chapman, 1983]), a strong and explicitly hierarchal system of church government was well in place in the leading churches of Antioch and Rome by the beginning of the second century, as reflected in the writings of Clement of Rome and Ignatius of Antioch. Already at such an early date the overseer of the church assumed the posture more of a ruler than a servant.

17. Frend, *Rise of Christianity*, 505.

18. Eusebius, *The Life of Constantine*, Book IV, ch. XVIII.

19. MacMullen, *Christianizing the Roman Empire*, 119.

20. Ibid.

21. A. N. Whitehead, *Process and Reality* (Cambridge: Cambridge University Press, 1929), 485.

22. Brown, *The World of Late Antiquity*, 82.

23. Welker, *Creation and Reality*, 10.

24. Newbigin, *The Light Has Come*, 202–203.

25. *Posidonius*, vol. 2, ed. I. G. Kidd (Cambridge Classical Texts and Commentaries; Cambridge: Cambridge University Press, 1988), 654.

26. Andreasen, *Rest and Redemption*, 104.

27. Ibid., italics added.

CHAPTER 26

CONFRONTATION OF SIGNS

Also it causes all, both small and great, both rich and poor, both free and slave, to be marked on the right hand or the forehead, so that no one can buy or sell who does not have the mark, that is, the name of the beast or the number of its name.

Revelation 13:16–17

This book began on the note that symbols are important conveyors of meaning, and on this note it now draws to a close. "Genesis and Revelation provide a creational bracket for the Bible,"[1] we have observed, but the creational bracketing is not the only similarity between the outermost books of the Bible.[2] These books also occupy common ground by giving symbols broad exposure. Genesis does it by introducing the seventh day at the very beginning of its story, setting it up as a symbol that expresses the divine intent (Gen. 2:1–3). Revelation follows suit by raising the role of symbols to a more urgent pitch than at any time in the biblical narrative (Rev. 13:16–17; 14:9–11). Indeed, Revelation allots to symbols the prerogative to signify what is at stake, making the conflict between good and evil come down to a confrontation of signs. To come to terms with Revelation's message on this point, it is necessary to explore the parameters of the confrontation that unfolds in its pages and from there to decipher what we are calling a "confrontation of signs."

COSMIC CONFLICT

In order to have a confrontation, there has to be more than one party. Anton Vögtle states succinctly that God "is not the only one who is at work in this world—as the Apocalypse makes so abundantly clear."[3] This is the first and most important premise of Revelation's story. It would not be a sensational observation except for the fact that few are making it. Most critical interpretations pay little attention to the actual scope of the conflict that lies at the heart of Revelation's story.[4] Temporally, John's story aims to reveal reality in its dimensions of past, present, and future (1:19).[5] Spatially, his vision looks beyond the earth and human reality. The "someone-other-than-God" who is at work in this world is ultimately a non-human adversary. When the veil is removed in Revelation, no sentence reaches further than the statement, "And there was war *in heaven*" (12:7). Revelation bears witness to a cosmic conflict.

To many scholars, the Roman Empire is the other power that is at work in Revelation.[6] These scholars cast a net that is too small when held up to the aspiration of Revelation's symbols. It is not necessary to deny references to the Roman Empire or to eschew an imperial connection (Rev. 13:1–2; Dan. 7:2–7) as long as we do not conclude that these referents fully match the force of Revelation's symbols. In temporal terms, the war in heaven recalls a primordial event as this event is depicted in the poems of Isaiah and Ezekiel (Rev. 12:7–9; cf. Isa. 14:12–19; Ezek. 28:12–20).[7] In spatial terms, John time and again points to a star that fell from heaven (Rev. 8:10; 9:1, 11; 12:7–9), thus sketching the heavenly origin of the Destroyer that now wreaks havoc on the earth. When he sees Satan thinly disguised in the figure of "the ancient serpent" (Rev. 12:9; 20:2), he infers that humanity has fallen under the spell of a demonic power and its misrepresentation of God (Gen. 3:1–6). When he leaves Satan alone on the stage at the end of the drama (Rev. 20:2), having carefully removed the two collaborators that in the eyes of many interpreters guarantee the Roman connotation (Rev. 19:20), John lets the reader know that in his eyes, at least, the enemy that is his chief concern is a non-human power.[8]

Revelation bears witness to a cosmic conflict.

John's copious allusions to the Old Testament put meat on the bones of this story. In Isaiah, the prophetic ear hears "the Shining One" say in his heart, "I will ascend to heaven; I will raise my throne above the stars of God;...I will make myself like the Most High" (Isa. 14:13–14). The characters and plot that we find in Isaiah and Genesis carry over into Revelation. As noted earlier (ch. 3), John was writing "the climax of prophetic revelation,"[9] and not until the last book of the Bible is the plot at the beginning resolved. The studied and meticulous complexity of John's composition, his pervasive use of Old Testament allusions, and the sweep of his vision testify to his aim of exposing the origin and character of evil and carrying this story forward until evil is no more (1:19; 21:4). John does not leave the reader in the belief that the Roman Empire itself exhausts the character of evil or to assume that when the Empire is curtailed, evil itself will be run into the ground.[10] It is within the context of a longstanding conflict with a cosmic scope that we must understand the confrontation of signs.

CONFRONTATION OF SIGNS

According to Revelation's depiction of the end, human beings are given the choice between two signs. These signs, in turn, represent the two sides in the conflict. The subversive side is determined to put its "mark" (*charagma*) on its followers. The mark has a representative function; it has "the name of the beast or the number of its name" (13:17). It is to be placed "on the right hand or the forehead" (13:16), indicating that the mark is to define the bearer in a decisive way. The project has a universal aspiration, aiming to include "both small and great, both rich and poor, both free and slave" (13:16). Grave sanctions await those who refuse to be marked. In its kindest version, "no one can buy or sell who does not have the mark" (13:17). At its most severe, the power that instigates this project causes "those who would not worship the image of the beast to be killed" (13:15).

The other side in the conflict also has a sign. The end is put on hold, says the angelic guide, "until we have marked the servants of our God with a seal on their foreheads" (7:2–3). Those who receive this mark have the name of the Lamb "and his Father's name written on their foreheads" (14:1). A person can have "the mark" or "the seal" but not both.

In the short version, there can be no doubt that a confrontation of signs is central to the message of the last book of the Bible. In fact, the inadequacy of the Roman Empire view becomes acute precisely with respect to the confrontation of signs. Nero, the focal image that in many interpretations belongs at the center of John's prophecy, is an insufficient "end" in temporal terms as well as with respect to what appears at the end. James L. Resseguie is spot on when he asks, "In what way is Nero the consummate opponent of Christ?"[11] The Roman interpretation also faces the problem of non-fulfillment with respect to the signs in Roman times. No interpreter denies that the signs are important, but many will admit that they are at a loss to know what they represent. Among the four options listed in David Aune's encyclopedic commentary, three refer to imperial practices: (1) "to the tattooing of slaves, soldiers, or the devotees of a particular deity"; (2) "as a reference to Roman coins used to buy and sell commodities"; (3) "as a reference to imperial seals."[12] George Eldon Ladd covers some of the same ground, explaining that "the word for 'mark' was used for brands on animals," and "was also a technical term for the imperial stamp on commercial documents and for the royal impression on Roman coins."[13] In this view he follows the conclusion of the influential study by Adolf Deissmann, who equates the technical word *charagma*, translated "mark," with "the name of the imperial seal, giving the year and the name of the reigning emperor, and found on bills of sale and similar documents of the 1st and 2nd centuries."[14]

There can be no doubt that a confrontation of signs is central to the message of the last book of the Bible.

For none of the options listed above, however, is there a credible historical fulfillment of what "the mark of the beast" might be in Roman terms. Ladd admits that "we know of no ancient practice which provides adequate background to explain the mark of the beast in historical terms," or "historical situation associated with emperor worship which explains this prophecy."[15] The absence of a persuasive historical referent is quite devastating, given that interpreters are confident that the Roman Empire is in view, and especially when we are aware that the signs lie at the heart of the conflict in Revelation.

These difficulties disappear when the reality of a cosmic conflict is allowed to explain the imagery in Revelation. The disproportion between God's story and the story of the Roman Empire, as the latter is often understood, ceases to be a problem because God's ultimate opponent is a non-human power. The eschatological horizon remains intact because Revelation aspires to describe the final showdown between God and God's non-human opponent. Non-fulfillment in Roman times is precisely what we should expect concerning a confrontation that is neither adequately described as Roman nor a thing of the past. In light of the "creational bracket" that unites Genesis and Revelation, the biblical narrative, more than the historical situation contemporary to John, must guide the reader. Looking beyond the Roman horizon, the two stories that come to a head in the confrontation of signs in Revelation are God's story and the story of "the ancient serpent."

GOD'S STORY

God's story has no beginning and no ending, but the part of God's story that begins in Genesis ends in Revelation. Revelation's allusions to Genesis extend to the very core of the battle that rages at the center of its narrative, featuring the same main characters (Gen. 3:1–15; Rev. 12:1–17). The serpent, the medium that in Genesis sows the seeds of distrust in the mind of the woman (Gen. 3:1–6), has in Revelation become "the *ancient* serpent," also known as "the devil and Satan, the deceiver of the whole world" (Rev. 12:9).[16] In Genesis, we see misrepresentation turning into distrust, distrust maturing into alienation, and alienation ripening into fear (Gen. 3:1, 6, 8, 10). In Revelation, the misrepresentation is exposed, the alienation is overcome, and fear is banished (Rev. 22:3–4).

Genesis supplies the raw material for the most salient aspects of the story in Revelation. In Genesis, God tells the serpent that the woman's offspring will bring an end to its hegemony (Gen. 3:15). In Revelation, "the woman" is ready to give birth (Rev. 12:1–2).[17] In Genesis, the woman is told to expect increasing "pangs in childbearing; in pain you shall bring forth children" (Gen. 3:16). In Revelation, the woman is "crying out in birth pangs, in the agony of giving birth" (Rev.

12:2).[18] The child that is a promise in Genesis has become a reality in Revelation (Gen. 3:15; Rev. 12:5). "But her child," says Revelation, "was snatched away and taken to God and to his throne" (Rev. 12:5). The fleeting glimpse notwithstanding, the attentive reader will know what it means. God has prevailed in the conflict.

To John, however, it is the *way* God prevails and not only the reality of victory that is the heart of his story. John sees a throne in heaven, and someone is sitting on the throne (4:1–2). A sealed scroll is then introduced, reminiscent of the scroll presented to the prophet Ezekiel in the Old Testament (Rev. 5:1; Ezek. 2:9–10). The scroll represents the problem that must be solved, and a mighty angel asks in a booming voice, "Who has what it takes to open the scroll and break its seals?" (Rev. 5:2, translation mine). This is the eye of the storm in Revelation.

God's story has no beginning and no ending, but the part of God's story that begins in Genesis ends in Revelation.

With reference to this scene Adela Yarbro Collins writes perceptively that "the heavenly council is faced with a serious problem."[19] The account drives home the seriousness of the problem by stating that "no one in heaven or on earth or under the earth was able to open the scroll or to look into it" (Rev. 5:3). John's reaction should also be noted: "I began to weep bitterly because no one was found who had what it takes to open the scroll or to look into it" (Rev. 5:4, translation mine).

What is the problem represented by the scroll that, in turn, carries the connotation of crisis? Yarbro Collins says that "the problem facing the heavenly council is the rebellion of Satan which is paralleled by rebellion on earth."[20] This is an excellent answer, and it is a much better answer than many of the ideas that have been proposed for the heavenly scene and the mysterious scroll. But even this is not the whole answer. Jumping ahead in the story for a moment, we move a step closer to the heart of the problem when the content of the scroll begins to unfold. Scenes of war, famine, death, and destruction roll across the screen, symbolized by the notorious horsemen of Revelation (Rev. 6:3–8). The import of these scenes is clarified when John hears the problem put into words.[21] What his eyes see at this point are martyrs "who had been slaughtered for the word of God and for the testimony they had in their possession" (Rev. 6:9, translation mine). What his ears hear is their cry, "How long, holy and true Lord, will it be before you act justly and vindicate us for our blood [shed] by those who dwell on the earth?" (Rev. 6:10, translation mine).

There is no better description of the plot that seeks its resolution in Revelation than this scene, rising from within the book and spoken by innocent victims of suffering. The cry, "how long," echoes the quintessential theodicy question in the Bible.[22] From the point of view of the martyrs, justice is denied or at least delayed. There is an intolerable discrepancy between what is expected of God and what God is actually doing. The content of the scroll reflects the most troubling facets of human reality. God appears not to take the requisite measures against evil. Indeed, the way God has chosen to address Satan's rebellion is even more disconcerting than the rebellion itself.[23] The charged heavenly scene seems rife with the questions that human beings find perplexing. Why did God permit evil? Why has God allowed evil to operate on such a long leash? Why, returning to William Butler Yeats's depiction of reality, have things developed to the point where "the falcon cannot hear the falconer," where "things fall apart," and "the centre cannot hold"?[24] When we understand this to be the problem facing the heavenly council, it is easy to appreciate why no one in the council feels up to the task of "breaking the seals."

It is in answer to this problem that Jesus makes His entry before the heavenly council (Rev. 5:1–6). In spine-tingling detail, He suddenly appears "in the middle" (5:6).[25] John reports that there, in the sacred *middle*, he saw "a Lamb standing" (5:6). The image of the Lamb is itself unexpected because the problem facing the council seems to call for a figure of power, and the voice announcing the entry of "the

Lamb" has reinforced this expectation (5:5). Already intense, the dissonance gets worse by orders of magnitude when John says that the Lamb appeared "as if it had been *slaughtered*" (5:6).

The significance of this description cannot be overstated. As Loren L. Johns has shown, the language describing the Lamb is the language "*of butchery and murder.*"[26] Jesus's death in Revelation is more a death by violence in the street than a dignified sacrificial death in the temple. Rather than posing as a figure of power, God's medium of revelation is the Lamb, and the Lamb, too, is a victim of violence. According to Revelation's unexpected logic, the Lamb is up to the task of breaking the seals of the scroll "precisely because it was slaughtered" (5:9).[27] In this capacity the Lamb has established credibility and authority of a kind that no opposing argument can withstand. Moreover, "*its having been slaughtered is an essential part of its identity* (5:12; 13:8)."[28] Whenever the Lamb is mentioned in Revelation, the fact of its slaughter is always to be included.

Of all the revelatory moments in Revelation, and there are many of them, this is the zenith and the decisive moment in God's story. The Lamb that appears in the middle is the medium of revelation. As Bauckham has shown, Christ's violent death "*belongs to the way God rules the world.*"[29] The high Christology that we find in this book, higher than in any other New Testament book except the Gospel of John, has a *theological* purpose. The Lamb is commissioned to reveal God and to tell God's story. Revelation's Christology is the handmaid of its theology. In Bauckham's words, "[t]he importance of John's extraordinarily high Christology for the message of Revelation is that it makes absolutely clear that what Christ does, God does."[30] In the simplest version, God brings an end to the cosmic conflict, but He prevails by means that are uniquely God's own. The deafening silence that precedes the breaking of the seals (5:3) and the amazed silence that follows (8:1) echo Isaiah's vision: "Kings shall shut their mouths because of him, for that which had not been told them they shall see, and that which they had not heard they shall contemplate" (Isa. 52:15).[31]

What are we to conclude from this? What are we to make of a story that seems to cast the victor as the weaker part and the victim of violence? At the very least we need to admit that God's story in Revelation confuses before it clarifies; it perplexes before it persuades. The seals that are broken by the Lamb are not only seals on the scroll "written on the inside and on the back" (Rev. 5:1). The *seal of incomprehension* must be broken, too, in the sense that the mind of the reader must be "unsealed" (cf. Isa. 29:10–11, 18: Dan. 12:9–10). Rather than serving primarily as the repository of coveted information about the future, Revelation also helps the reader see familiar realities in a new way. When, therefore, John reports that "no one in heaven or on earth or under the earth had what it takes to open the scroll" (5:3), it does not only mean that other potential candidates fall short because they cannot compete with Jesus's pedigree. Rather, as I have suggested elsewhere, "it means that *absolutely no one else would have solved the cosmic conflict this way*."[32]

God's story in Revelation confuses before it clarifies; it perplexes before it persuades.

The Lamb that appears in the middle "as if slaughtered" (5:6) sets the stage for the sealing that is to come. Looking ahead to the confrontation of signs that is to come, the Lamb has a sign. Those who are sealed will have the name of the Lamb "and his Father's name written on their foreheads" (14:1), and the Father has revealed His name in the Lamb.

THE DRAGON'S STORY

God, as noted, "is not the only one who is at work in this world,"[33] and the fault line in interpretations of Revelation runs right here: Who is the acting subject behind the calamities that are reported in this book? Already as the Lamb breaks the seals on the scroll sealed with seven seals, the story takes on a commanding quality, a demand to the other side to come forward and reveal its true colors (6:1, 3, 5, 7). "Showing colors" is precisely what follows, almost in a literal sense. Horses white, red, black, and toxic green gallop across the screen, symbolic of war, famine, pestilence, and death that devastate the earth (6:1–8). The calamities that are depicted in connection with the first four seals are not the result of divine agency any more than the martyrs crying out in connection with the fifth seal are at the receiving end of divine action (6:9–11). To the martyrs, it is the *absence* of the expected divine action that gives rise to their cry. The reality of the demonic is writ large on the entire sequence, perhaps nowhere in bolder print with respect to the rider on the horse that is toxic green, whose name is Death, who is followed by Hades, and to whom it is given "to kill with sword, famine, and pestilence, and by the wild animals of the earth" (6:7–8).

The dragon's story progresses and intensifies when the sequence of the seven trumpets begins (Rev. 8:1–11:19). As the fifth angel blows his trumpet, John says that he "saw a star that had fallen from heaven to earth, and he was given the key to the shaft of the bottomless pit" (Rev. 9:1). This is Revelation's shorthand "biography" of the opposing side and one of the loudest echoes of Isaiah's poem of Lucifer's fall from heaven (Isa. 14:12–20). Louis A. Brighton writes succinctly that "[t]he identity of this star is unmistakable, for it is the same personality that is embodied by the dragon in 12:3 and who is identified as the devil and Satan (12:9)."[34]

ALLUSIONS TO ISAIAH IN REVELATION'S FIFTH TRUMPET		
	Isaiah 14:12–20	Revelation 9:1–11
Subject	Star	Star
Place of Origin	Heaven	Heaven
Action	Descent	Descent
Descent to	Earth	Earth
	Pit	Pit
Characteristic	Destroyer	Destroyer

The fifth trumpet tracks the downfall of "the Shining One" spatially from heaven to earth, and from earth to "the bottomless pit" (Isa. 14:12, 19; Rev. 9:1). But the "inner" downfall vastly exceeds the spatial parameters: "the Shining One," the most illustrious of created beings, is now the fountainhead of darkness, suffering, and unnamable evil. He now bears a name that captures his essence. "They have as king over them the angel of the bottomless pit; his name in Hebrew is Abaddon, and in Greek he is called Apollyon" (9:11). God's antagonist is now, in plain English, the "Destroyer."[35] Even here, however, a host of leading interpreters do not bat an eye, reading it as though God is the acting subject in the sequence.[36]

Interpretations that make God the acting subject of actions that bear the signature of the demonic compromise the message of Revelation at its most important points. At this stage in the book, the author goes out of his way not only to show the demonic quality of the action but also to link the action and the acting subject with such clarity that the reader virtually finds the passport, the driver's license, the fingerprints, and copious amounts of DNA of the acting subject at the crime scene.[37] If we, too, have become confused regarding the identity and characters of the two acting subjects in Revelation, it is necessary to state clearly two additional features of this book before we proceed into more difficult terrain.

First, we should not expect the problems in Revelation to be worked out as they occur on our first passage through the book. The reader must get used to the idea that only a "veteran" reading will suffice;[38] that is, only on the second or subsequent passage through the text will the reader be attuned to the panoramic character of the author's story-telling ways. Being a reader is not enough; the reader must become a "re-reader," defined as a reader who "is informed by a prior experience of reading the entire work."[39] Anything less than this will leave the reader at a crippling disadvantage. There is a momentum in Revelation's story that trumps conventionality. What the writer sees, and what he sees coming, intrudes on his vision to the extent that he seems half-oblivious to the fact that he is not providing the requisite background for the reader to keep up. The reader must be aware of the whole before he or she can make the right call concerning the parts.

Second, we should heed the claim that "Revelation has been composed with such meticulous attention to detail of language and structure that scarcely a word can have been chosen without deliberate reflection on its relationship to the work as an integrated, interconnected whole."[40] John is a careful writer who does not deploy even the smallest word for no particular reason. Awareness of the whole and attention to seemingly minor details yield significant rewards. For instance, John says at one point that God's wrath will be poured out "*unmixed* into the cup of his anger" (14:10). The word *unmixed* may seem trivial until we realize that there is a *mixed* or *diluted* variety of God's wrath, a process in history that has been moving forward until it reaches its culmination. What comes to pass at the point when God's wrath is poured out *unmixed* must be understood in light of what has preceded this description. In connection with the seven last plagues, the story likewise reaches a point at which "the wrath of God is at its strongest" (15:1, translation mine). Here the reader must take into account the events described when "the wrath of God" was not at its most severe in order to put the scenes described into the proper perspective. The result that awaits the reader who heeds this advice is sure to come as a surprise.

There is a momentum in Revelation's story that trumps conventionality.

Even a tiny word like "woe" should not be despised (8:13; 9:12; 11:14; 12:12) because this word is yet another instance where awareness of the whole and attention to detail will show its worth. In the trumpet sequence, an eagle, or better, a *vulture*, appears in mid-heaven, crying out with a loud voice, "Woe, woe, woe to the inhabitants of the earth, at the blasts of the other trumpets that the three angels are to blow!"

(8:13). The "woes" are carefully marked in the text as they occur. "The first woe has passed," we are told after the fifth trumpet (9:12; cf. 11:14). The full significance of the woes will not sink in, however, until the reader gets to chapter 12, the chapter that constitutes the structural and narratival anchoring point for Revelation's message. At the point when Satan realizes his defeat, we hear the "woe" that electrifies all the other woes in the book. "But *woe* to the earth and the sea, for the devil has come down to you with great wrath, because he knows that his time is short!" a loud voice proclaims (12:12). Bracketing this chapter (ch. 12) as the starting point of Revelation's cosmic conflict story, the reason for the woe is Satan, the activity of whom leads the loud voice to exclaim "woe to the earth" (12:12). The re-reader of Revelation, aware of the whole, is enabled to hear the echo of this woe upstream in the text even though the trumpet sequence precedes the full description of the war in heaven. The woes are signifiers of demonic activity, additional forensic evidence pointing to the fallen "Shining One" as the cause of the calamities that are described. Listening again to the woes in the trumpet sequence, adjusted to the appropriate English idiom,[41] we hear the ill-omened threefold shriek of the vulture echo from mid-heaven over a progressively devastated earth, "How awful! How awful! How awful!" (8:13).

Awful, indeed! But the awful woe is also helpful and clarifying to interpreters. The person who heeds these clues will be in a good position to make sense of who is doing what in the book when the story moves into murkier terrain.

The confusion that bedevils the reader of Revelation with respect to who is doing what in Revelation is slightly less embarrassing when we discover that confusion on this point is not a problem of reading only. In the cosmic conflict of Revelation, the opposing side is hell-bent on promoting confusion with regard to the identities of the two sides. The opposing side is a deceiver as well as a destroyer, with as much emphasis on the former as on the latter. In both respects the zenith of demonic activity is yet to come.

Even though Satan is defeated by the child that was "snatched away and taken to God and to his throne" (12:5), he does not give up. John depicts Satan going forth "to make war against the rest of her children, those who keep the commandments of God and have in their possession the testimony of Jesus" (Rev. 12:17, translation mine). His aim is to defeat the followers of Jesus and to subvert the message that is in their possession. In order to accomplish this, Satan calls two surrogate powers to his side, the task of whom is to conceal the identity of the power that is moving behind the scene (13:1–18).

In the cosmic conflict of Revelation, the opposing side is a deceiver as well as a destroyer.

On the terms of Revelation, there are still two sides at work in the world, but it does not seem that way to those who live on the earth. To them, the demonic side seems to be melting away. Indeed, it seems as if there is only one story left, *God's* story. Just as Jesus appears as a slaughtered Lamb in the most revealing scene in Revelation (5:6), the deceptive power that arises from the sea in the service of the dragon has "a mortal wound" (13:3, RSV), a wound that is imitative of Jesus. Just as Jesus looks like a Lamb, the deceiving power that arises from the earth looks like a lamb although it speaks like the serpent (13:11). The images become blurred, the identities of the two sides indistinct. It is no longer easy to tell that there are two stories or to realize that "God is not the only one who is at work in the world."[42] The dragon's goal is to assume the identity of the Lamb and to imitate God's story with the intent of deceiving, and the scheme appears to be wildly successful because, as John sees it, "in amazement the whole earth followed the beast" (13:3).

Revealing details abound, however, to help the reader realize that there are still two powers at war in the story. The mouth and the faculty of speech stand out as the most conspicuous features of the powers that are opposed to God. Heinrich Schlier notes that a distinguishing mark of the first surrogate power "is its mouth."[43]

Jürgen Roloff likewise points out that the mouth is "the beast's most important organ."[44] This assessment is readily confirmed by the text (13:5–6). Speaking of the second of the two allies of the opposing side, Revelation says that it had the appearance of a lamb but "it spoke *like a dragon*" (13:11), or, in William Barclay's translation, it "spoke *like the serpent*" (13:11).[45] The prominence of the faculty of speech takes the plot into familiar territory, all the way back to Genesis. Speech is the most important faculty of the surrogate power and the mouth the most eye-catching organ because these are the features through which "the ancient serpent" instigated the initial subversion. Speech remains the *modus operandi*, in Revelation as much as in Genesis. The serpent is still *speaking*, wringing from the original misrepresentation of God the last toxic drops.

On the terms of Revelation, therefore, the view that God "is not the only one who is at work in this world" is understated.[46] In this part of the book (ch. 13), the dragon dominates the narrative. As David Barr astutely points out, the initiator and acting subject leading into the confrontation of signs is the demonic side.[47] "One of the most shocking things about this third story is that God is no longer the main actor," says Barr.[48] The focus is instead on Satan and the surrogate powers. Two acting subjects are preparing for the final showdown, one revealed in the reality of the slaughtered Lamb (5:6), the other attempting to sabotage this reality by an imitative subversion (13:3). The initiative even seems to shift to the opposing side. "The dragon acts and God reacts," Barr notes.[49] "This," he adds, "is the dragon's story."[50]

And "the dragon's story" is far from over.

FINALITY

Revelation's confrontation of signs takes place at a time when the opposing side is deploying its deceptive arsenal rather than showing itself to be the agent of destruction only. R. H. Charles's description of the sealing that happens on God's side of the story is unsurpassed because it is profoundly aware that the opposing side is preparing an unprecedented assault and because it offers valuable clues to the meaning of the sealing (Rev. 7:1–17).

> The sealing is to secure the servants of God against the attacks of demonic powers coming into the open manifestation. The Satanic host is about to make its final struggle for the mastery of the world. In the past their efforts had been restricted to attacks on man's spiritual being, and had therefore been hidden, invisible, and mysterious, but now at the end of time they are to come forth from their mysterious background to make open war with God and His hosts for the possession of the earth and of mankind. The hidden mystery of wickedness, the secret source of all the haunting horrors, and crimes, and failures, and sins of the past was about to reveal itself—the Antichrist was to become incarnate and appear armed, as it were, with all but almighty power. With such foes the faithful felt wholly unfit to do battle....And so just on the eve of this epiphany of Satan, God seals His servants on their foreheads to show that they are His own possession, and that no embodied (or disembodied) spirit of the wicked one can do them hurt.[51]

The seal symbolizes a reality that has been internalized on the part of the servants of God. "In its deepest sense," says Charles, "this sealing means the outward manifestation of character....In the reign of the Antichrist goodness and evil, righteousness and sin, come into their fullest manifestation and antagonism. Character ultimately enters on the stage of finality."[52]

The sealing precedes the efforts of the other side to put a mark on its followers, but we must not lose sight of the interaction and interplay of the forces that operate. As noted above, the story plays out in territory where "God is no longer the main actor"; where "the dragon acts and God reacts"; where, actually, it is "the dragon's story."[53] True to this scenario, the dragon acts by introducing the fateful "mark," threatening sanctions and death against those who resist the initiative (13:15–17). This is true to character because appearance and reality are not the same, seeing that the power behind this move looks like a lamb but speaks like the serpent (13:11).

While the "sealing" precedes Satan's initiative to put his "mark" on the entire human family, the sealing, too, can therefore be seen as a *reaction*. God anticipates the opponent's move, instituting measures that will prevent or limit its success (7:1–3).

It might be better, in fact, to scale back the temporal element and to view the confrontation of signs in Revelation as the expression of two radically different options. The two options are in this sense simultaneous and final more than they are sequential. God's story and the dragon's story are in the end so closely intertwined that the reader easily loses sight of what is action and what is reaction. Moreover, the stories seem virtually indistinguishable by the fact that the opposing side in the conflict seeks to advance its cause by appropriating the insignia of Jesus.

Indeed, while the values and aims of the two sides in the conflict could not be more different, the contrasts are attenuated by appearances. The final battle does not pit Jesus against the Roman Empire, or Jesus against Nero, as many critical interpretations have it,[54] or even Jesus against Satan. On the staggering terms of Revelation's narrative, the battle in John's account is a battle that pits Jesus against "Jesus." The Lamb "as if...slaughtered" (5:6) is deployed against an opponent whose exterior is a mirror image of itself: it looks "like a lamb" (13:11); it wears the stigmata of suffering and slaughter; and it even projects the prestige of being resurrected from the dead (13:3). To the extent that the selling point of the opposing side borrows luster from the most distinctive features of Jesus, it is to be expected that its sign, and the confrontation of signs that it is intent on implementing, will make the most of this connection.

In the context of this crisis, as the dragon prepares its final move, God *reacts* by commissioning a message to be given to the world. The reader of Revelation has already heard the vulture "crying with a loud voice as it flew in midheaven" the threefold message of destruction and doom, "How awful! How awful! How awful!" (8:13). Now the reader hears a second voice, also threefold, also coming from mid-heaven, and also proclaiming its message in a loud voice (14:6–11). This is the voice of the three angels, taking aim at the deceptive scheme of the other side. This voice, too, oscillates with finality, but this voice, unlike the voice of the vulture, is the voice of redemption and hope.

THE FIRST ANGEL

John calls the message of the first angel "good news," *euangelion*, addressed "to those who live on the earth—to every nation and tribe and language and people" (14:6). "Gospel" must be good news, and "an *eternal* gospel" must be good news of long duration, best expressed as "enduring good news" or even as "an eternally valid message."[55] In the simplest and most basic sense, this message should be heard as a message of hope.

The constellation of "news" and "eternal" is awkward because news in the modern sense is a matter of the moment. To meet the criteria of news the subject in question must refer to something recent and hot off the press. For this reason the expression in Revelation must be qualified. What John has in mind, invoking a voice from the Old Testament (Ps. 96:1–2),[56] is a point of view that has been contested. This will not come as a surprise to the reader of Revelation, already cognizant that the good news of this book is especially aimed at the misrepresentation of God that is the work of "the ancient serpent" (12:9; 20:2). What the messenger affirms has always been true, but it is newsworthy in the sense that it was not always seen to be true and now it is.

The message thus characterized, the first angel spells out the content in intriguing detail, "Fear God and give him glory, for the hour of his judgment has come; and worship him who made heaven and earth, the sea and the springs of water" (Rev. 14:7). As we have seen, the message is delivered in the context of what essentially is "the dragon's story." Humanity has another option that looks beguilingly similar to the undiscerning eye. The first angel urges "those who live on the earth" not to choose the other option no matter how enticing it looks.

Second, when the first angel proclaims "the hour of his judgment" (14:7), it is not as though "the dragon's story" suddenly has collapsed into God's story, or as though God at last is the only one who is at work in the world. The conflict is raging full blast, and "those who live on the earth" are in the throes of making a decision between two options that are impressed upon them with all the force of destiny and finality that each side is able to muster. Just as in the Gospel of John (John 12:31–32, 46–49), Revelation's notion of judgment retains a Johannine imprint: The hour of judgment is not perceived only as a moment in time when God will sit in judgment to review the choices that have been made and the deeds that have been committed. Judgment is also a matter of revelation, the time when forces and phenomena will declare themselves and be exposed for what they are. Anthony Tyrrell Hanson describes judgment (*krisis*) in this sense as the "culmination of the process," and the process in view has a revelatory intent.[57] There is unprecedented danger at this stage because "culmination" carries the connotation of intensification. But there is also hope, and hope is ascendant in the message. The long night of terror is coming to an end.

"The judgment being never juridical but revelatory, it is not the expression of the servile terror of men, but of their comprehension of the divine reality," says Jacques Ellul.[58] This statement may be too categorical and one-sided, but Ellul's emphasis on the revelatory character of the judgment has merit that is often ignored. At the hour of judgment, conceived in revelatory terms, "those who live in the earth" face a mortal danger by what the opposing side is attempting to do to them, and this danger must not be eclipsed by preconceived notions of a person's peril in the face of divine judgment, conceived in judicial terms.

Third, when the first angel calls on those who live on the earth to "worship him who made heaven and earth, the sea and the springs of water" (Rev. 14:7), he is deploying the language of the fourth commandment and the rationale given in the Old Testament for the significance of the seventh day (Exod. 20:11). This allusion is a devastating indictment of the dragon and *his* story on two levels. On the most obvious level, neither "the ancient serpent" nor his earthly surrogates can match *that*; nothing and no one on the opposing side has *created* "heaven and earth, the sea and the springs of water" (Exod. 20:11). The "size gap" between God and the pretenders that clamor for recognition is mind-boggling.

On the deeper and more important level, however, the allusion to the fourth commandment points beyond the fact that God is the Creator. Allusions are a form of verbal compression, intending to call to mind more than what is conveyed by the few words that are used. "The one who made heaven and earth and the springs of water" (Rev. 14:7; Exod. 20:11a) is also the Person who "rested on the seventh day," and who, leaving a permanent imprint on human time, "blessed the seventh day and consecrated it" (Exod. 20:11bc). "The character gap" that is implicit in the message is more critical than "the size gap" because it is "the character gap" that is the focus in the cosmic conflict.

When we hear the message of the first angel this way, it projects the relation of commitment more than the relation of power. God stands in relation to creation not only at the point of origin and not only as the Originator but also as "the God who responds to what has been created."[59] More than the memorial of an event, the Sabbath conveys the message of God's enduring and faithful participation in human reality. The first angel is on a revelatory mission, and the Old Testament substrate of the message of the first angel points to an ordinance that is revelatory in its most basic texture. God is indeed the Creator, but the One "who made heaven and earth and the springs of water" (Rev. 14:7) is also a Person of transparency and constancy, and, as the message of the first angel makes clear, the One who brings deliverance and hope. Above all, God's uniqueness is not limited to His superiority in the realm of power because the God of this book has His identity and character tied to the Lamb that was slaughtered (5:6).

If we now take a step back from the scene, imagining the voice of the first angel echoing in the distance, we might sense that the urgency in the angel's voice does not rise from the nearness of the end only. It has even more to do with the reality of the other side and its attempt to become the dominant influence. The imperative quality in the angel's voice should not be understood as an ultimatum to the human race that they are under obligation to worship God whether they think well of God or not. In the context of "the dragon's story," the imperative rises from the false reality that is revered by those who live on the earth. The dragon's ultimatum, insisting that those who live on the earth take its mark (13:16–17), rules out a purely secular alternative because those who do not choose God will not choose nothing. In light of the moves of the opposing side, the first angel's message offers an opportunity rather than a demand. It is the opposing side that makes the demand, and that on penalty of death (13:15).

The Sabbath conveys the message of God's enduring and faithful participation in human reality.

THE SECOND ANGEL

When the second angel proclaims the fall of "Babylon," crying out that "she has made all nations drink of the wine of the wrath of her fornication" (Rev. 14:8), we are still within the dragon's story. "Babylon" is a complex spiritual entity that in Revelation operates by appropriating the identity of the side to which it is opposed. Babylon has "fallen" in the sense that it has become what it once was not; it has lost what it could have been. Akin to the "falling away" that is Paul's preoccupation in 2 Thessalonians,[60] Revelation is most concerned about a phenomenon arising *within* the church rather than one attacking the church from without.[61] "At the end Satan's attack must be launched from a beachhead within the Church, where the earth-beast not only carries on priestly activities but displays the credentials of a prophet," says

Paul S. Minear of this part of Revelation.[62] Gregory Beale comes to the almost identical conclusion, stating that the imagery and background in John's portrayal "suggest deception within the covenant community itself."[63]

"She has made all nations drink of the wine of the wrath of her fornication" (Rev. 14:8). This language is not typically used of Babylon in the Old Testament. In prophetic lingo, Israel is the nation that is charged with the sin of fornication; Israel has "fallen" because of illicit relations with other powers, gods, and values (Jer. 2:20; 3:2, 9; 13:27). Babylon, on the other hand, is in the Old Testament charged with self-aggrandizement and conceit (Isa. 47:8; Jer. 50:24, 31), and it is called to account because of unspeakable cruelty (Isa. 47:6; Jer. 50:17). Fornication and adultery, however, are Israel's sins. When Revelation ascribes the sin of fornication to "Babylon," it conflates the characteristics of Israel and the record of Babylon in the Old Testament.

Bauckham's expansive view of Revelation's imagery is therefore worthy of notice. He contends that "Revelation's prophetic critique *is of the churches as much as of the world*. It recognizes that there is a false religion not only in the blatant idolatries of power and prosperity, but also in the constant danger that true religion falsify itself in compromise with such idolatries and betrayal of the truth of God."[64] The history of the Christian Church, with the union of political power and religion, its unapologetic justification of coercion and torture, its abysmal record with regard to the Jews, and its hostility to freedom of conscience, does not fare well in the light of Revelation's prophetic critique. On Patmos John sees a power that looks like a Lamb but speaks like a serpent in much the way that this scenario comes to fulfillment in the history of Christianity, and, it must be added, in a way that makes it necessary to apply John's climactic vision of Babylon to a horizon beyond the Roman Empire.

This sets the stage for the message of the third angel, the high point in Revelation's confrontation of signs.

THE THIRD ANGEL

> Then another angel, a third, followed them, crying with a loud voice, "Those who worship the beast and its image, and receive a mark on their foreheads or on their hands, they will also drink the wine of God's wrath, poured unmixed into the cup of his anger, and they will be tormented with fire and sulfur in the presence of the holy angels and in the presence of the Lamb. And the smoke of their torment goes up forever and ever. There is no rest day or night for those who worship the beast and its image and for anyone who receives the mark of its name." (Rev. 14:9–11)

Readers who have had reservations as to whether the messages of the first two angels belong in the context where "the dragon acts and God reacts"[65] will be less troubled to face this claim with respect to the message of the third angel.

THE DRAGON ACTS	Also it causes all, both small and great, both rich and poor, both free and slave, to be marked on the right hand or the forehead (13:15).
GOD REACTS	Those who worship the beast and its image, and receive a mark on their foreheads or on their hands (14:9).

The third message is nothing if not a reaction to the dragon's action, and, reading it as the final and most urgent intervention in the threefold sequence, it provides strong warrant for the view that the prior messages do indeed belong in the *action-reaction* framework. This is also the point where we not only see each of the two sides in Revelation represented by a sign but where it becomes explicit that there is a sharply focused *confrontation*.

Who, nevertheless, is doing what in the end-time confrontation of signs? What is action, and what is reaction? We are well advised to approach these questions in slow motion, step by step, listening closely to each element in the message of the third angel.

"Those who worship the beast and its image, and receive a mark on their foreheads or on their hands" (14:9b).

The "to-whom-it-may-concern" part of the message is the easy task. In the message of the third angel we are viewing the action of the opposing side through the lens of God's reaction. The initial action belongs to the dragon, executed by the closely knit triumvirate of the dragon, the beast that looked "as if it had been slaughtered" (13:3), and the lamb-like beast (13:11). As we have seen, the imitative aspiration of the triumvirate is revealed by the appearance of the beasts and by the signs and wonders they perform (13:13, 15). The signs (*sēmeia*) not only equal the greatest wonders in the Old Testament (13:13; cf. 1 Kings 18:24, 38), but they exceed anything ever seen in the past (13:15).[66] The imitation is itself a ruse, of course, because even where this triumvirate appears to approximate God's story, it is actually subverting it. It is not beyond the pale of John's vision to hear his voice join that of the Grand Inquistor in Dostoevsky's *The Brothers Karamazov* when the Grand Inquistor, with steel and fire in his eyes, explains to Jesus why the Church had to take the world down a different road than the one envisioned in the New Testament. The Church, the Grand Inquisitor tells Jesus, had to back off from the mystery of God's story and replace it with a mystery of its own.

> But if so, there is a mystery here, and we cannot understand it. And if it is a mystery, then we, too, had the right to preach mystery and to teach them that it is not the free choice of the heart that matters, and not love, but the mystery, which they must blindly obey, even setting aside their own conscience. And so we did. We corrected your deed and based it on *miracle*, *mystery*, and *authority*. All mankind rejoiced that they were once more led like sheep, and that at last such a terrible gift, which had brought them so much suffering, had been taken from their hearts. Tell me, were we right in teaching and doing so?[67]

In Dostoevsky's story, Jesus does not answer the Grand Inquisitor. If we let the third angel of Revelation in on this conversation, and if we grant that the story in Revelation accommodates Dostoevsky's concern, the answer is simple. "No, you were not right in teaching and doing so, and no, you were not right, certainly, in using coercion to bring about conformity to your scheme." Coercion, needless to say, is precisely the recourse of last resort of the opposing side against those who have not been enticed by its deployment of *miracle* and *mystery*, as when the opposing side in Revelation causes "those who would not worship the image of the beast to be killed" (13:15).

All of this belongs to the realm of "the dragon's story"; all the action so far is on the part of the opposing side. The difficulty begins when the angel proceeds to spell out the consequences to those who accept the mark of the opposing side and join forces with it. What will happen to them? Who is the source of the consequences that are brought to bear on those who make the fateful choice?

> ***"then he himself will drink the wine of God's wrath, poured undiluted into the cup of his anger" (14:10a, translation mine)***

Have we now moved from action to reaction, from "the dragon's story" to God's story? Is God at this point the acting subject, as leading interpreters aver? Beale, for instance, says that while "the intoxicating effect of Babylon's wine seemed strong, it is nothing in comparison with God's wine."[68] God, according to this line of thinking, is henceforth the acting subject. God's story and the dragon's story seem to converge on the deepest ideological level with respect to coercion and torture. In the dragon's version, according to the same logic, those who refuse to accept "the mark" will be ostracized and killed (13:15, 17). In "God's" version, those who take "the mark" will be subjected to excruciating torture, in some versions torture that has no end (14:10).[69]

The action and the object of the action are clearly stated in the text, but the subject of the action is not. Ambiguity on this point allows for a time-out that seems all the more necessary because of the implausibility that God's story, centered on a victim of torture in the person of the slaughtered Lamb (5:6), is now metamorphosing into a story that commissions violence on a large scale to be applied to the opposing side. Are both sides in the conflict ultimately committed to the threat of torture and its actual implementation, as the theology of the Christian Church has proclaimed for centuries?

The notion that "the wine of God's wrath" belongs to the realm of the dragon's action and not to the realm of divine reaction may on first suggestion only have a slim chance; but this, nevertheless, is the reasoning when Paul explains "God's wrath" in his letter to the Romans. Paul invokes "God's wrath" as the consequence that comes about when human beings turn away from the truth that is available to them. "Wrath" comes in the form of consequences of the choices people have made (Rom. 1:18–28), and the outcomes are part of a moral order that God actively upholds. In Paul's terminology, describing the reality of God's wrath, "God gave them up" to the demeaning practices to which people committed themselves (Rom. 1:24, 26, 28). God is depicted as the acting subject, but the reality for the person who is thus "given up" is God's absence. "By what things a man sins, by these is he punished," says Wisdom (Wisd. 11:16). Those who suppress the truth in Romans "are released from God's control and handed over to the control of their own desires."[70]

But the reader of Revelation does not need to call Paul to the rescue. God's wrath is fully explained in Revelation. At the climactic point in the story when "the wine of God's wrath" is "poured *unmixed* into the cup of his anger" (14:10), we are at the end of a process. The wrath is said to be *unmixed* because Revelation, in the sequences of the seals and the trumpets, has been long in the process of describing the *mixed* version of God's wrath.

This view is emphatically corroborated by the bowl sequence (15:1–16:21). Seven angels stand ready with the seven plagues, "which are the last, for with them the wrath of God is ended" (15:1). Whether we translate the verb that accompanies "the wrath of God" as "ended" or as "operating at full strength" is not decisive because in either case we are introduced to the conclusion of a process. It is the reality of a *process* that makes or breaks the deal for the interpreter. How the process works must be understood in light of the close parallel between the trumpet and the bowl sequence.

	TRUMPETS (8:7–11:19)	BOWLS (16:2–21)
1st	Hail, fire, and blood fall on the *earth*.	The bowl is poured on the *earth*.
2nd	A blazing mountain falls into the *sea*.	The bowl is poured on the *seas*.
	One third of the sea becomes *blood*.	The seas become *blood*.
	A third of *sea creatures die*.	Every living thing in them *dies*.
3rd	A blazing star falls on a third of *rivers and fountains*.	The bowl is poured on *rivers and fountains*.
4th	A third of *sun*, moon, and stars are struck, resulting in darkness.	The bowl is poured on the *sun*, resulting in suffering.
5th	Shaft of the bottomless pit opened.	
	Sun and air are *darkened* with smoke.	The bowl is poured out on the throne of the beast, plunging it into *darkness*.
	Locusts appear to *torture* people who are unprotected by the seal of God.	People "*gnawed their tongues in agony.*"

	TRUMPETS (8:7–11:19)	BOWLS (16:2–21)
6th	The four angels bound at *the great river Euphrates* are released.	The bowl is poured on *the great river Euphrates.*
	Cavalry numbering two hundred million kills a third of humanity.	Kings of the world assemble for battle on the great day of God the Almighty in a place called Armageddon.
7th		The bowl is poured into the air.
	Loud voices in heaven announce the coming of the kingdom of God and Christ.[71]	*A loud voice from the throne* announces "It is done."

Recalling that the acting subject in the trumpet sequence is unambiguously demonic, what will the interpreter say when he or she confronts the fact that the bowl sequence parallels the trumpets blow for blow with one major difference only? The bowls are worse, unfolding without any restraint.[72] Surely the close parallels between these two cycles suggest not only a scheme of recapitulation but also an ongoing process coming to completion. Again, whether we read that "the wrath of God is complete" (NKJV), "ended" (NRSV), "finished" (NASB), "completed" (NIV), or "operating at full strength" (15:1), the novelty is not the concept of "the wrath of God" but "the wrath of God" at the point when it is "finished." Still more important, of course, is the fact that Satan is the acting subject when "the wrath of God" is not yet finished and not yet manifested at full strength. What role does Satan have when "the wine of God's wrath" is poured out unmixed (14:10) and when "the wrath of God is finished" (15:1)?

It is the reality of a process that makes or breaks the deal for the interpreter.

The answer, no longer a surprise, is that Satan is hard at work bringing *his* story to completion. When most interpreters are confident that God is the sole acting subject, "the dragon's story" is not over. On the contrary, it is precisely when "the wrath of God" is let loose in full that the dragon unfurls its most spectacular feat. "The sixth angel poured his bowl on the great river Euphrates, and its water was dried up in order to prepare the way for the kings from the east. And I saw three foul spirits like frogs coming from the mouth of the dragon, from the mouth of the beast, and from the mouth of the false prophet. These are demonic spirits, performing signs, who go abroad to the kings of the whole world, to assemble them for battle on the great day of God the Almighty" (Rev. 16:12–14).

There is no hint here that the dragon has folded its tent and retreated from the conflict, leaving the field to God. The revelatory momentum is not only intact but is actually intensified and accelerated. God has now removed all restraint from the opposing side, but God has not become the acting subject of what the dragon, the beast, and the false prophet are doing. Far from it, we are in the thick of "the dragon's story" as it embarks on the penultimate offensive. Consistent with what we have seen earlier, the mouths of these creatures are again conspicuous and coordinated; they appear to speak with one mouth. If God is punishing in this sequence, He is punishing by what He permits. And what God permits, ultimately, is for the opposing side to reveal itself fully. As Revelation is careful to point out, this is something that *must* happen (1:1; 4:1; 20:3; 22:6). God is the acting subject in this interchange not as the One who makes it happen but as the One who sees evil unveiled in ways that are not anticipated even by the opposing side itself (cf. 1 Cor. 2:7–8).

What God permits, ultimately, is for the opposing side to reveal itself fully.

The foregoing concurs with the conclusion of A. T. Hanson's painstaking study of "the wrath of the Lamb" in the New Testament.

Indeed, "wrath" in Revelation is a more subtle and counterintuitive notion than imagined even by Paul.

> But closer investigation of how St. John the Divine uses his wrath vocabulary, and especially of the antecedents in the Old Testament of the phrases he uses, reveals that John, far from being a sort of throw-back to the Old Testament in his treatment of the wrath, presents us in fact with a more carefully thought out conception of the divine wrath even than Paul, one which is more closely related to the central message of Christianity, and which forms a completion and crown of all that is said about the wrath in the rest of the Bible.[73]

In Revelation, the characteristics of the two sides are the characteristics of one dying and the other killing, carrying over into the lives of the respective followers: "Christ and the saints conquer by dying; Satan and the powers of evil by physical force."[74] The calamities that are reported in Revelation "invariably refer, not to purely eschatological wrath, but to wrath worked out in the events of history."[75]

> ***"and they will be tormented with fire and sulfur in the presence of the holy angels and in the presence of the Lamb"** (14:10b)*

The acting subject is again left unstated, but it is hardly necessary to ask who is doing it: Torture has so far in this book been a signature statement of the demonic (9:4–5). Fire and sulfur, likewise, have until now in Revelation been the telltale sign of demonic activity (9:17–18), so much so that Jacques Ellul says that it is "the action of these Satanic powers that in every circumstance provokes death in the Apocalypse, and not at all, never directly, the action of God upon men."[76] Do fire and sulfur now carry the signature of God and the Lamb?

The interpretation that emerges within the framework of the dragon's action and divine reaction remains focused on the dragon as the acting subject, seeing "the holy angels and the Lamb" witnessing a scene that is entirely the creation and culmination of demonic activity. To the discerning eye John's panoramic vision reveals the logic of self-destruction working itself out on the demonic side all the way to the end.[77] Revelation's account of the cosmic conflict is in every important facet consistent with its antecedent in Isaiah, describing a power that destroys *its own land* and kills *its own people* (Isa. 14:20). What happens "in the presence of the holy angels and of the Lamb" (14:10) must therefore not be construed as though the Lamb and the angels are detached spectators to torment taking place under their active agency any more than Jesus in the Gospels is the One who brings disaster on the people who rejected Him (Luke 13:34–35; 19:41–44). The drama happens before the horrified eyes of "the holy angels and of the Lamb," but what happens is the Dragon's work, not theirs.

"the smoke of their torment goes up forever and ever" (14:11a)

Caird is quite right in saying that if we "cannot accommodate our minds to the idea of eternal torment, the answer is that neither could John."[78] The background of John's imagery is Edom and its demise, described as a fire that shall not be quenched; "its smoke shall go up forever" (Isa. 34:10). This background text curtails the notion of torture without an end, but the framework of the dragon's action and divine reaction has made the issue of eternal punishment a moot point. What is in view is the dragon's action—the smoke of its terror not to be blotted from the memory of those who have witnessed it.

"there is no rest day or night for those who worship the beast and its image and for anyone who receives the mark of its name" (14:11b).

At the beginning and ending of the third angel's message, Revelation takes care to specify that the warning is for those "who worship the beast and its image, and receive a mark on their foreheads or on their hands" (14:9), repeating it almost verbatim (14:11b).

Reading the entire message in reverse, the most telling feature of the group in question is that they have "no rest day or night" (14:11). Absence of rest goes to the heart of the experience of "those who worship the beast and its image and for anyone who receives the mark of its name" (14:11). This description is significant not only for the way it depicts the consequence that comes to those who take the mark but also for the light it sheds on our quest to identify the acting subject. Those who take the mark have "no rest" because rest is exactly what the opposing side is determined to take away. We are, as we have been all along, in "the dragon's story" where fear and apprehension are rampant and "rest" is nowhere to be found. By contrast, the initial call to worship God in this passage is couched in the language of rest, calling on people to "worship him that made heaven, and earth, and the sea, and the fountains of waters" (14:7), recalling, as we have seen, God's rest at Creation and the ordinance of rest for human and non-human creation alike (Exod. 20:8–11).

THE FAITHFULNESS OF JESUS

> ***What matters in this situation is the perseverance of the saints, those who hold on to the commandments of God as revealed by the faithfulness of Jesus (14:12, translation mine).***

The urgency and momentum of the messages of the three angels are not diminished or slowed by the prospect that the third angel may no longer be talking in the concluding admonition.[79] Whether we hear this text as the voice of the angel or the voice of John, it must be heard as "a scarcely hidden call to attention."[80] At this and similar points in Revelation (14:12; cf. 13:10, 18), there is to be direct eye-contact between the writer and the audience, the writer by necessity represented by the person who reads aloud the message of this book in the churches (1:3). In the person of the reader, John will look up from the letter to gaze directly into the faces in the audience. He must ascertain whether they look puzzled and perplexed, and, anticipating that they are likely to be as puzzled and perplexed as the living creatures and the twenty-four elders and all the other creatures "in heaven or on earth or under the earth" that have come face to face with God's baffling response to the cosmic conflict (5:3, 6), he must reconnect directly with them. He must know that they have understood and that they are on the same page. For this reason the closing admonition acts as a recapitulation of the entire message and as the take-home message itself.

Interpreters who are concerned that the present interpretation leaves too much to the category of "the dragon's story," too much in the column of demonic action, and too little to the realm of divine reaction are advised to listen carefully to the clarifying corrective that is implicit in the closing admonition. John's entreaty takes for granted that his audience hears the messages of the three angels as descriptions of demonic activity, bearing down on the world in appalling and increasing intensity. In the midst of a reality that allows the dragon to operate on a long leash, John falls back on the focal image that restores God's story to the center of the picture—indeed, the image that makes God's story hold up under the awful and mind-numbing pressure brought to bear on it. Using the attention-arousing word *hōde* as the lead word, translated "here" (NKJV, NASB, NRSV), "this calls for" (NIV), "this is why" (NJB), or "under these circumstances" (14:12), John signals unremitting awareness of the drumbeat of demonic terror that comes from the other side. "What matters under these circumstances," the circumstances being the climax of demonic activity, "is the perseverance of the saints, those who hold on to the commandments of God as revealed by the faithfulness of Jesus" (14:12, translation mine).[81]

The perplexity that reduces all creation to silence at the beginning (5:3) and ending (8:1) of the unveiling of God's story before the heavenly council has in John's closing exhortation lost none of its mind-shattering force. "The faithfulness of Jesus," understood as "the faithfulness of God in Jesus," distils and recapitulates God's entire story. While the setting for the urgent call belongs in the category of "the dragon's story," the focal image that lingers in the eye of the believer is the faithfulness of God. If persuasion (5:1–14), protection (7:1–3), and proclamation (14:6–12) seem altogether deficient in the face of the movements of the opposing side, the image of the slaughtered Lamb (5:6), recalled by John as "the testimony of Jesus" (12:17) and "the faithfulness of Jesus" (14:12), does not in Revelation meet the contemptuous response that God is doing nothing. Things do indeed seem to fall apart; it does seem like "the centre cannot hold." Mere anarchy does seem loosed upon the world, and with it the blood-dimmed tide,[82] but the image at the center of God's story shows a center that holds up under the terrible tide of "the dragon's story." Indeed, the puzzlement in Revelation is not that God is doing nothing, but that God is doing *that*; it is not that God is watching the drama from the sidelines but that God is commissioning those who follow the Lamb to take the mark of the faithfulness of Jesus (13:10; 14:1, 12).[83]

THE MARK AND THE NAME

We are striking close to bedrock when we read the Old Testament antecedent for the sealing imagery in Revelation. Speaking of God's commandments, the Israelites were told to "[b]ind them as a sign [*'ôt*] on your hand, fix them as an emblem [*tôtāpôt*] on your forehead" (Deut. 6:8; cf. Rev. 7:3; 13:16; 14:1, 9, 11). In the original context the "sign" and the "emblem" are symbols of the reality they represent; the New International Version cuts to the chase by using the word "symbol" for both words. Taken together, the terms combine the notions "revelation" and "perpetual remembrance." We have met the idea earlier (ch. 7), and now we meet it again, still with the meaning that "the sign steps in as the simplified filling-in and amplification of the revealing word of God."[84] In Revelation, therefore, God is revealed in the sign and remembered in terms of what is most contested and what the opposing side is most determined to subvert.

R. H. Charles moves well within the parameters of Revelation when he finds the imagery of the seal of God suggestive of the ancient Jewish practice that was designed to cement a person's relationship with God, here playing out in the context of conflict.[85] The one who bears the mark is protected because he or she knows the Name. "The faithful," says Charles, "received the mark of God on their foreheads [7:4; 9:4] and were henceforth secured against satanic assaults in the form of deception and temptation to sin. But the unbelieving world, which had received the mark of the Beast [13:16], were thereby just as inevitably predisposed and prepared to become the victims of every satanic deceit and to believe a lie."[86] God's sign enables discernment while the sign that expresses the dragon's name damages the faculty of discernment beyond repair.

The confrontation of signs in the end is thus expressive of the deepest characteristics of the two sides in the conflict, one side bearing a mark representing "the name of the beast or the number of its name" (13:17), the other side having the name of the Lamb "and his Father's name written on their foreheads" (14:1). While the imitative ambition of the opposing side manifests itself in its mark, it will not prevail against those who make the connection between God's sign and God's story. The signs, burnished in the crucible of conflict, have come home to their respective meanings.

What now of the sealing and the marking that "symbolizes the central dilemma of the Apocalypse"?[87] What of the most enduring biblical sign, the seventh day, instituted at the beginning of time by "the faithful and true witness," in Revelation characterized as "the beginning of God's creation" (3:14)? What now of the message of "the faithfulness of Jesus" (14:12) and of the sign that through the ages has held high the torch of God's enduring faithfulness? When, on Revelation's terms, the contest involves a sign that is to express the character and ways

What of the allusion to the fourth commandment in the urgent end-time message?

of God, what now of the sign that from the beginning was anointed to be God's signature statement? What now of "the commandments of God," understood in the broadest sense as a signifier of the kind of Person God is? What of the allusion to the fourth commandment in the urgent end-time message (14:7), precisely at the juncture where the confrontation of signs is most acute?

Revelation awaits the reader's response, looking for "the one who reads aloud the words of this prophecy" to complete the thought and to finish the pregnant sentence (1:3; 22:7).[88]

ENDNOTES

1. Fretheim, *God and the World in the Old Testament*, 9.

2. The hugely influential work of Hermann Gunkel (*Schöpfung und Chaos in Urzeit und Endzeit: eine religionsgeschichtliche Untersuchung über Gen. 1 und Ap Joh 12* [Göttingen: Vandenhoeck und Ruprecht, 1895]) is of value in demonstrating common ground between Genesis and Revelation even though its "history-of-religions" approach is inadequate.

3. Anton Vögtle, "Der Gott der Apocalypse," in *La Notion biblique de Dieu,* ed. J. Coppens (Gembloux: Éditions J. Duculot, 1976), 383.

4. Tonstad, *Saving God's Reputation*, 7–16.

5. W. C. van Unnik, "A Formula Describing Prophecy," *NTS* 9 (1962–63): 86–94.

6. Christopher Rowland's view (*The Open Heaven* [London: SPCK, 1982], 431) with respect to Rev. 13 is representative: "Most commentators would agree that the specific issue which lies behind this vision is the threat of an imposition of emperor-worship in Asia Minor." According to Charles (*Revelation*, I:xxi), "the object of the Apocalypse was to encourage the faithful to resist even to death the blasphemous claims of the State." Cf. also S. R. F. Price, *Rituals and Power: The Roman Imperial Cult in Asia Minor* (Cambridge: Cambridge University Press, 1984, [1998]).

7. Tonstad, *Saving God's Reputation*, 55–107.

8. Ibid., 41–54.

9. Bauckham, *The Climax of Prophecy*, xi.

10. An example that the city "Babylon the great" represents an ideological construct and not just the Roman Empire is found in the statement, "And in you was found the blood of prophets and of saints, and of all who have been slaughtered on earth" (Rev. 18:24). Even if Revelation is at pains to call the Roman Empire to account, it is grossly exaggerated to imply that the Empire is to blame for "all who have been slaughtered on earth." This indictment sees Babylon as an ideological construct.

11. James L. Resseguie (*Revelation Unsealed: A Narrative Critical Approach to John's Apocalypse* (Leiden: Brill, 1998), 56; cf. also Sigve Tonstad, "Appraising the Myth of *Nero Redivivus* in the Interpretation of Revelation," *AUSS* 46 (2008): 175–199.

12. David Aune, *Revelation*, vol. 2 (WBC; Nashville: Thomas Nelson Publishers, 1998), 767.

13. George Eldon Ladd, *A Commentary on the Revelation of John* (Grand Rapids: Eerdmans, 1972), 185.

14. Adolf Deissmann, *Bible Studies,* trans. Alexander Grieve (Edinburgh: T&T Clark, 1901), 246.

15. Ladd, *Revelation*, 246.

16. Tonstad, *Saving God's Reputation*, 55–107.

17. J. P. M. Sweet (*Revelation* [Philadelphia: The Westminster Press, 1979], 203) argues that Genesis 3:15–20 dominates Revelation 12; cf. also Paul S. Minear, "Far as the Curse Is Found: The Point of Revelation 12:15–16," *NovT* 33 (1991): 71–77.

18. Moberly, "Did the Serpent Get It Right?" 1–27.

19. Adela Yarbro Collins, *The Apocalypse* (NTM 22; Dublin: Veritas Publications, 1979), 39.

20. Yarbro Collins, *The Apocalypse*, 39.

21. The pivotal function of the fifth seal is recognized by a number of interpreters; cf. John Paul Heil, "The Fifth Seal (Rev. 6,9–11) as a Key to the Book of Revelation," *Bib* 74 (1993): 220–243; J. Lambrecht, "The Opening of the Seals (Rev. 6,1–8,6," *Bib* 79 (1998): 198–220. Giancarlo Biguzzi ("John on Patmos and 'Persecution' in the Apocalypse," *Est Bib* 56 [1998]: 212) writes that the cry of the martyrs "is the genetic nucleus of the whole narrative cycle of the scroll" (4:1–8:1).

22. Ps. 6:3; 74:9–10; 79:5; 80:4; 90:13; 94:3–7; Isa. 6:11; Jer. 4:21; 23:26; 47:5–6; Dan. 8:13; 12:6; Hab. 1:2–4; Zech. 1:12.

23. Tonstad, *Saving God's Reputation*, 124–143.

24. Yeats, "The Second Coming," 458.

25. Tonstad, *Saving God's Reputation*, 119–121.

26. Johns, "The Lamb," 780, emphasis added.

27. Ibid., emphasis added; idem, *The Lamb in the Christology of the Apocalypse of John* (WUNT 2.167; Tübingen: Mohr Siebeck, 2003), 159.

28. Johns, "The Lamb," 780, emphasis added.

29. Bauckham, *Revelation*, 64.

30. Ibid., 63.

31. Tonstad, *Saving God's Reputation*, 138–141.

32. Ibid., 141.

33. Vögtle, "Der Gott der Apocalypse," 383.

34. Louis A. Brighton, *Revelation* (St. Louis: Concordia Publishing House, 1999), 235–236.

35. Beale (*Revelation*, 503) holds that the "Destroyer" in this verse "is either the devil himself or an evil representative of the devil.

36. M. Eugene Boring (*Revelation* [Louisville: John Knox Press, 2003], 134–135), describing the trumpet sequence, is convinced that all the plagues coming from heaven are not caused by independent powers and proceed ultimately "from the sovereign hand of the one God." Noting how the water turns bitter under the third trumpet, Jürgen Roloff (*The Revelation of John,* trans. John E. Alsup [CC; Minneapolis: Fortress Press, 1993], 111) sees divine judgment on human disobedience "when God poisons the water and thereby destroys the place where these people live." To Aune (*Revelation 6–16*, 545), the purpose of the trumpet plagues "is not to elicit repentance but to exact punishment," with God acting as the executioner. According to Hans K. LaRondelle (*The End-Time Prophecies of the Bible* [Sarasota: First Impressions, 1997], 175–176), "the trumpets are in essence not natural disasters or general calamities, but God's covenant curses on His enemies." Beale (*Revelation*, 467) contends that the trumpets "are not intended to coerce unbelieving idolaters into repentance but primarily to demonstrate to them God's uniqueness and incomparable omnipotence."

37. Tonstad, *Saving God's Reputation*, 108–114.

38. The notion that a book demands a "veteran" reading has been proposed by Ehud Ben Zvi (*A Historical-Critical Study of the Book of Obadiah* [Berlin: De Gruyter, 1996], 4). I am indebted to James W. Voelz ("The Resurrection and the Ending of the Gospel of Mark," paper presented at the Society of Biblical Literature meeting in Washington, DC, in November, 2006) for awareness of the idea.

39. Voelz, "The Resurrection and the Ending of the Gospel of Mark," 7.

40. Bauckham, *The Climax of Prophecy*, x.

41. Barbara R. Rossing, "For the Healing of the World: Reading *Revelation* Ecologically," in *From Every People and Nation: The Book of Revelation in Intercultural Perspective*, ed. David Rhoads (Minneapolis: Fortress Press, 2005), 168.

42. Vögtle, "Der Gott der Apocalypse," 383.

43. Heinrich Schlier, "Vom Antichrist: Zum 13. Kapitel der Offenbarung Johannis," in *Theologische Aufsätze. Karl Barth zum 50. Geburtstag* (München: Chr. Kaiser Verlag, 1936), 117.

44. Roloff, *Revelation*, 157.

45. William Barclay, *The Revelation of John*, vol. 2 (Louisville: Westminster John Knox, 1976), 98; cf. William Hendriksen, *More Than Conquerors* (Grand Rapids: Baker Books, 1998 [1940]), 148.

46. Vögtle, "Der Gott der Apocalypse," 383.

47. David L. Barr, *Tales of the End: A Narrative Commentary on the Book of Revelation* (Santa Rosa: Polebridge Press, 1998), 101–103.

48. Ibid., 102.

49. Ibid.

50. Ibid.

51. Charles, *The Revelation of St. John*, I:205.

52. Ibid., I:205–206.

53. Barr, *Tales of the End*, 102.

54. Cf. Tonstad, "Appraising the Myth of *Nero Redivivus*," 175–199.

55. Aune, *Revelation*, II:826.

56. Bauckham, *Climax of Prophecy*, 286–287.

57. Anthony Tyrrell Hanson, *The Wrath of the Lamb* (London: SPCK, 1957), 164.

58. Jacques Ellul, *Apocalypse: The Book of Revelation*, trans. George W. Schreiner (New York: The Seabury Press, 1977), 172.

59. Welker, *Creation and Reality*, 10.

60. Cf. Sigve Tonstad, "The Restrainer Removed: A Truly Alarming Thought (2 Thess. 2:1–12)," *HBT* 29 (2007): 133–151.

61. Paul's message, in turn, echoes the Synoptic Apocalypse of Jesus; cf. David Wenham, "Paul and the Synoptic Apocalypse," in *Gospel Perspectives: Studies of History and Tradition in the Four Gospels*, vol. II, ed. R. T. France and David Wenham (Sheffield: JSOT Press, 1981), 345–375.

62. Minear, *I Saw a New Earth*, 119.

63. Beale, *Revelation*, 708.

64. Richard J. Bauckham, *The Theology of the Book of Revelation* (Cambridge: Cambridge University Press, 1993), 162, emphasis added.

65. Barr, *Tales of the End*, 102.

66. Cf. Ps. 135:16–17; 115:5; Jer. 10:14; 51:17.

67. Fyodor Dostoevsky, *The Brothers Karamazov*, trans. Richard Pevear and Larissa Volokhonsky (New York: Farrar, Straus and Giroud, 1990), 257.

68. Beale, *Revelation*, 759.

69. Grant Osborne, *Revelation* (BECNT; Grand Rapids: Baker Academic, 2002), 540–541.

70. Jewett, *Romans*, 167.

71. Adapted from Beale, *Revelation*, 808–810.

72. Jan Lambrecht, "A Structuration of Revelation 4,1–22,5," in *L'Apocalypse johannique et l'Apocalyptique dans le Nouveau Testament*, ed. J. Lambrecht (Gembloux: Éditions J, Duculot, 1979), 103.

73. Hanson, *The Wrath of the Lamb*, 159.

74. Ibid., 165.

75. Ibid., 160.

76. Ellul, *Apocalypse*, 65.

77. Cf. Sigve K. Tonstad, "Blood 'as High as a Horse's Bridle' (Rev. 14:20): The Devil Is in the Details," paper presented at the Society of Biblical Literature Annual Meeting in Washington, DC, November 5, 2006.

78. Caird, *Revelation*, 186.

79. Jan Lambrecht ("Rev 13,9–10 and exhortation in the Apocalypse," in *New Testament Textual Criticism and Exegesis. Festschrift J. Delobel,* ed. A Denaux [BETL 161; Leuven: Leuven University Press, 2002], 345) believes that "the angel no longer speaks. John himself addresses the readers."

80. Lambrecht, "Rev 13,9–10," 345.

81. Tonstad, *Saving God's Reputation*, 165–194.

82. Yeats, "The Second Coming," 458.

83. Charles, *Revelation*, I:356: Aune, *Revelation 6–16*, 731.

84. Keller, *Das Wort OTH*, 67.

85. Charles, *Revelation*, I:362.

86. Ibid., I:360.

87. Resseguie, *Revelation Unsealed*, 179.

88. See also Rev. 2:7, 11, 17, 29; 3:6, 13, 22; 13:9.

CHAPTER 27

THE SPIRIT OF THE SEVENTH DAY

A Song for the Sabbath Day.
Psalm 92:1

We can only learn the spirit of the Sabbath from those who recognize it as a blessing and who have experienced its blessing in their own lives. Those who dismiss the Sabbath as a temporary and burdensome ordinance from Old Testament times cannot help because to them the fault of the Sabbath is precisely that it has no "spirit." Others, believing that the shelf-life of the seventh day has expired for other reasons than that it lacks "spirit,"[1] will be similarly at a loss. But these views, for so long dominant, no longer hold sway with the degree of assumed self-evidence that they once had. The number of potential guides in the quest to retrieve the Sabbath may still be limited, but the number is growing. Voices speaking from a sense of loss and existential need, enticed by voices speaking from experience, are increasingly finding an audience inside and outside communities of faith. Above and beyond these voices is the voice of Scripture, holding forth its offer and projecting the offer as a gift even more than as a need. It is in the sense of the Sabbath as gift, recalling how the present study began, that the seventh day is stirring in the ruins, called forth more by the force of its enduring commission than by the longing of the wasteland underneath which it lies.

LOSS AND RETRIEVAL

Acknowledgement of loss is one reason to begin the journey of retrieval. Loss and need are both explicit in Jürgen Moltmann's stunning recognition of the Sabbath. "Without the Sabbath quiet," says Moltmann, "history becomes the self-destruction of humanity."[2] Marva Dawn, also quoted earlier, argues for a similar reason that a "return to Sabbath keeping is not nostalgia" but "a return to the spiritual dimension that haunts us."[3] In her view, too, the sense of loss is evident and the need to begin a pilgrimage of retrieval overdue. In recognition of merely one Old Testament meaning of the Sabbath, human time has been depleted of strength. The voices that now speak perceptively of the Sabbath as idea and practice recognize it as a missing zone of quietude and community, as time protected from commerce and commotion, and even as time set apart for worship. They welcome and urge a return to Sabbath rest as an antidote to human self-importance, overwork, and conspicuous consumption, highlighting the practical and spiritual benefits of the Sabbath concept.[4]

Nevertheless, these initiatives fail to make up for the discontinuity of God's story and for the disruption in the community of believers committed to the worship of the one God. The spirit of the Sabbath, its urgent revelatory mission, cannot be torn from its moorings in the seventh day. It is therefore not a coincidence that the Christian advocacy of the Sabbath is looking to the Jewish Sabbath experience for guidance and inspiration.[5] In the Jewish experience the Sabbath has been preserved as a day of profound significance in theological terms and as an exquisite enjoyment in actual experience. Rich theological meaning has been mined by leading thinkers in Judaism. "If we were to condense all of Judaism—its faith, thought, life, poetry and dreams—into a single word, there is but one word which could be used—*Shabbat*, or as it is referred to in English, the Sabbath," writes Pinchas Peli.[6] This conclusion is remarkable not so much for its belief that the Sabbath is important but more for its unstinting conviction that the Sabbath is a precious gift and a renewable source of meaning.[7] Peli uses words like "endearment" and "adoration" to express the Jewish sentiment, convinced that the seventh day is a day of delight that belongs to all humanity.

In many Jewish homes there is still an atmosphere of celebration when the Sabbath arrives at sundown Friday night. The table is set with special care, and the meal served highlights the sacredness of the occasion. Candles are lit, blessings pronounced, and toasts presented. Even in a Jerusalem hotel a visitor feels the contagious glow radiating from those who keep the Sabbath in this way. As the stillness of the Sabbath takes hold, the visitor may reflect on the cord that binds the present generation to those who have gone before, remembering their suffering and sharing in their hope.

The affirmation of continuity is just one of many reasons why Sunday struggles to shoulder the functions of the Sabbath. Nahum Sarna points out that the Sabbath is the only sacred day in the Hebrew calendar that is ascribed to pre-Israelite times.[8] It speaks to the continuity of the human story—pre-Israelite, Israelite, and beyond—and it affirms even more the continuity of God's intent. The roots of the Sabbath are sunk in the original soil of the divine-human relationship, enriched and nourished afresh by the encounters and visions of patriarchs and prophets who grasped God's purpose. Whether the Sabbath is eclipsed, according to the view of some, or replaced, as others see it, it signals discontinuity and disruption. This problem, of course—locating the Sabbath in an abstract idea, as if the "spirit" or the "soul" of the Sabbath can be dissociated from the seventh day and moved about freely at anyone's discretion—bedevils visions of retrieval that are committed to actualizing the Sabbath blessing apart from the body of the seventh day.

Many a secularized Westerner, stung by the discontinuities of his or her own existence, looks wistfully at the Jewish display of belonging—to God and to one another—and to the profound sense of destiny that goes with it. At times the modern believer, acknowledging the biblical roots of his or her faith and the untenable consequences of the long alienation, seems tempted to say to Jewish brothers and sisters, "Let the blessing of the seventh day be for me, too. Teach me how to experience the consecrated work-free zone. Show me how to celebrate the Sabbath."

The roots of the Sabbath are sunk in the original soil of the divine-human relationship.

But the greatest incentive and momentum rise from within Christian Scripture. This voice is heard in many places, but it takes on an unprecedented sense of urgency in the last book of the Bible. There, as we have seen already (ch. 26), a heaven-sent messenger appears "with an eternally valid message to proclaim to those who live on the earth—to every nation and tribe and language and people" (Rev. 14:6, translation mine).[9] The "eternally valid message," echoing one of the most important Old Testament texts concerning the seventh day, is pointedly couched as a call "to worship him who made heaven and earth, the sea and the springs of water" (Rev. 14:7; Exod. 20:11). Equally important, however, is the tenor of the message when we recognize that it is also drawing strength from one of the psalms (Ps. 96).

Probing its Old Testament background, the message is not only proclaimed with authority and confidence. The spirit of the message, as much as its urgent content, should be a focus of attention. Song, in fact, is its native medium. "Sing to the Lord, bless his name; tell of his salvation from day to day," begins the psalm that underlies it (Ps. 96:2).[10] This is not a song of mourning but a message of hope and confidence that must be distributed widely and urgently, implicit in the original Hebrew as well as in the Greek translation of the Old Testament, to "publish, preach, bear news, make glad with good news." As to the notion of "eternal good news," the source for this term originates in the expression "from day to day" which means "at all times," and what holds true "at all times" is eternal.

Should this affirmation take hold on a large scale, it will have far-reaching consequences. The Sabbath that has long been seen as a token of separation will at last unleash its pent-up ecumenical potential. To this end it holds a vast, untapped reserve, touching the deepest longings of human beings regardless of their background or profession. The need for belonging, the necessity of rest, and the encounter with something larger than oneself all find expression in the blessing of the seventh day. The Sabbath roots of our common humanity are beckoning all to join in the final homecoming. In the prophetic vision of the end, the Sabbath is put forward as a great unifier, transcending entrenched divisions, boundaries, and barriers (Isa. 56:1–7). It is to be a time for healing of the deepest wounds in the tortuous pilgrimage of mankind—of the loss of selfhood, of the person's separation from his origin, of the soul from the body, and of the alienated Jewish remnant from Christian believers and people of faith from other backgrounds. To this gathering believing Jews will bring the Sabbath that they have cherished and preserved throughout their experience of incredible suffering, and with it they will surely also bring the special psalm, the "song for the Sabbath Day" (Ps. 92:1).

A SONG FOR THE SABBATH DAY

According to Dan Vogel, observing Jews recite Psalm 92 "no fewer than three times during Sabbath: once at night, to usher in Sabbath, and twice the following morning, once within the preliminary service and once as the psalm of the day."[11] Jewish *midrashim*, creative and rather freewheeling musings on the biblical text, attribute the psalm to Adam, imagining that it was "composed by him on the first Sabbath of creation" and that it saved him from instant death after his sin. Alternatively, but still with Adam as the author, the psalm was composed in gratitude after being assured that Cain's life would be spared.[12] The psalm was then forgotten, to be reintroduced much later by Moses, an attribution that does not weaken its prestige.[13]

The Sabbath roots of our common humanity are beckoning all to join in the final homecoming.

It cannot be chance or mere serendipity that the "song for the Sabbath day" strikes the note of God's faithfulness. From the opening sentence the song rushes to affirm that God is faithful, proclaiming it by means of a duo of terms that are inseparable and mutually enriching in the Old Testament: God's steadfast love (*ḥesed*) and God's reliability (*'emûnâ*). The psalm does not at the beginning let us in on its point of reference, but the tenor is so confident that any reference may be assumed. No feature of human reality, no perplexity, and no voice to the contrary will succeed in overturning the validity of the psalm's affirmation.

> It is good to give thanks to the LORD,
>   to sing praises to your name, O Most High;
> to declare your steadfast love in the morning,
>   and your faithfulness by night,

to the music of the lute and the harp,
  to the melody of the lyre.
For you, O LORD, have made me glad by your work;
  at the works of your hands I sing for joy.
How great are your works, O LORD!
  Your thoughts are very deep! (Psalm 92:1–5)

The perception that the psalm "is a theodicy psalm" is as apt as the fact that it is precisely that—a psalm that concerns itself with God's ways in the face of the reality of evil.[14]

On this point, too, the psalm hews close to what this inquiry has found to be the persisting, pervasive, and overwhelming affirmation. How the psalm came to be seen as "a song for the Sabbath day" may never be known, especially since the text of the psalm does not mention the Sabbath except in the preamble, but the thematic concern is of one piece with the meaning and the message that the Sabbath from the beginning has poured into human existence.

The beginning of time is in view in the psalm, subtly hinted in the paired expression to "declare your steadfast love *in the morning*, and your faithfulness *by night*" (Ps. 92:2). Why would the writer resort to this term except as a reminiscence of creation, the *morning* and *evening* of the days of creation (Gen. 1:5, 8, 13, 19, 23, 31), culminating in the statement of God's faithfulness that brings the Sabbath into being (Gen. 2:1–3)?[15] The psalm thus takes a comprehensive view of human reality because, as to the past, the outer limit of its scope is Creation.

More is to come that will deepen the meaning of the psalm's initial affirmation and that will also bolster the tribute to God, "Your thoughts are very deep!" (Ps. 92:5). Aware that "the wicked sprout like grass and all evildoers flourish," the psalm insists that appearances are deceiving because the wicked "are doomed to destruction forever" (Ps. 92:7). It does not discount the fact that God has enemies wishing to subvert the divine government, but the subversion will fail; "all evildoers shall be scattered" (Ps. 92:9). In these verses the psalm knows more than it says, alluding to the cosmic conflict that runs deep in the biblical narrative.[16]

When, in verse 8, the psalm exclaims that "you, O Lord, are on high forever," the declaration is set against the context of combat. The psalmist has in mind "a specific event that has taken place in the past,"[17] a brazen attempt to overthrow the government of God. The attempted coup has failed, however; only God is "on high forever" (Ps. 92:8).

Having this as the reference point further deepens the meaning of the congregants' eagerness "to declare your steadfast love in the morning, and your faithfulness by night" (Ps. 92:2), anticipating the choir in Revelation that also, "day and night without ceasing," sing, "Holy, holy, holy, the Lord God the Almighty, who was and is and is to come" (Rev. 4:8). The affirmation is energized by the awareness that the conflict is not over because the subversive voice, accusing them "day and night before our God" (Rev. 12:10), is still at large. In the Sabbath liturgy of Psalm 92, therefore, Creation and cosmic conflict go hand in hand. The eyes are on God's ways in the conflict, and the psalm gives its attention to God's ways a pointed and peculiar assessment, "How great are your works, O LORD! Your thoughts are very deep!" (Ps. 92:5).

This is a crucial and liberating discovery. The eyes of the psalmist and those who sing this song have been illuminated. They see reality in a new light. Having grasped the complexity of evil, its hidden features, and its devious methodology, they are attuned to appreciate the finer points of God's remedial and healing intervention. "Your thoughts are very deep!" (NRSV); "How profound your thoughts" (NIV); or better still, "How great are your works, O God, how very subtle Your designs."[18] "Subtle" says it best, and it is God's subtlety that eludes the enemy and the disbelieving. "The senseless man does not know, fools do not understand" (Ps. 92:6, NIV), or, in the more crassly worded *New Jerusalem Bible*, "Stupid people cannot realise this, fools do not grasp it." It is kept from their sight because they are content with surface appearances. On the one hand, they underestimate the complexity of evil and overestimate its staying power. On the other hand, they fail to appreciate the subtlety of God's ways. Having misjudged the character of the problem, they also misperceive the solution. In important ways the uninitiated in Psalm 92 share a common perspective with the people in Yeats's twentieth-century poem, "The best lack all conviction, while the worst Are full of passionate intensity."[19] "Psalm 92 asserts that faith is not mere romantic dream; it is knowledge," says Vogel.[20] In this sense the brutish person, unwilling or unable to see and to respect nuance, is a person who "does not know" (Ps. 92:6).

While it is true that Psalm 92 has in mind "a specific event that has taken place in the past,"[21] its orientation is more toward the future than toward the past. Jewish readings of the psalm—and of the message of the Sabbath—emphasize that there is in the Sabbath an orientation toward the future and a yearning for the end that is also taken up by the "psalm for the sabbath day." Noting that the two renditions of the Ten Commandments offer different rationales for the Sabbath commandment (Exod. 20:8:11; Deut. 5:12–15), Pinchas Kahn probes the reason for this difference. He suggests that that Sabbath as a celebration of God's Creation of the world was "by itself basically insufficient."[22] The verdict pronounced in the Garden of Eden anticipates what is to come. "It *was* very good," says Genesis (1:31), but it speaks in the past tense of good that did not last. "Empirically speaking, however, life after Eden and to this day is frequently not 'very good,' and at times it is not even good. On the contrary, life can be replete with suffering and subjugation," says Kahn.[23] For this reason the emphasis shifts and expands, informing us "of a promise of an end to pain and suffering, of a vision of redemption."[24]

It is God's subtlety that eludes the enemy and the disbelieving.

The confidence in God's ways that is expressed in Psalm 92 presents a point of view that looks to the future. It sees reality from the vantage point of the end, factoring in the final outcome. The orientation of the Sabbath is forward-looking, expectant, and hope-filled, and its most resonant affirmation brings a foretaste of what will be in the end. In the Jewish legacy this has long been explicit because the psalm for the

Sabbath is seen as "a psalm for the future to come, to the day that is a complete Sabbath and rest for eternity (Siddur)."[25] The recurrence of the seventh day every week and the certainty that the next Sabbath will come have eschatological meaning. "The knowledge that each week eventually culminates in Sabbath reassures us that the 'Sabbath' of the hereafter will eventuate as well, regardless of all indications apparently to the contrary," says Vogel.[26]

Perhaps the most elusive part of the affirmations of the psalm is its emotional tenor, the shift from contemplation to proclamation all the way to exclamation. The rise in emotional tone must be underwritten by a matching convergence of the threads of evidence that lead to the convictions of the psalm. If even this fails to overcome one's reticence to join the affirming voices, afraid that emotion might override the reservations of reason, the psalmist has not opted out of the hard questions. The psalmist speaks, too, because there is a need for speaking, correcting the misperceptions concerning God that have accrued. Whoever joins in will discover that expression deepens impression. The evidence that has been persuasive to mind and heart will be energized by expression. "It is good" in more than one sense "to give thanks to the Lord" (Ps. 92:2), good for the one who hears it but even better for the one who says it. The dialogical character of the psalm prioritizes the benefit to the speaker because the believer is not talking to others or singing praises *about* God primarily for the benefit of a third person. The entire psalm, vocal and expressive though it is, unfolds as an "I-Thou" exchange. The speaking and singing "I" has the divine "Thou" as the partner in the dialogue. It is toward God that the entire outpouring is directed, complete with "the music of the lute and the harp...and the melody of the lyre" (Ps. 92:3).

The orientation of the Sabbath is forward-looking, expectant, and hope-filled.

GOD'S FAITHFULNESS IN JESUS

No matter how rich and rewarding in the Jewish perception, however, soundings in the "psalm for the Sabbath day" inevitably lead beyond the Jewish perspective. For the believer in Jesus the Sabbath experience cannot be the same as the Jewish legacy because God's revelation in Jesus impacts the message of the Bible in both directions, toward the past and the future. The psalm for the Sabbath day, affirming God's faithfulness, cannot sustain its claim apart from the revelation of God in Jesus. Jesus is etched into the narrative of the Old Testament, and the Old Testament story, in turn, continues into the New Testament so as to obliterate the distinction between "old" and "new." When we hear Jewish voices sing the "song for the Sabbath day," it is a beginning, but it is not the end. The dearth of Christian affirmations is troubling, of course, but we need not feel that we are in uncharted territory and entirely left to ourselves. If we sing the "psalm for the Sabbath Day" from the vantage point of "the faithfulness of Jesus," we will not be singing it alone.

I propose to conclude this inquiry into the lost meaning of the seventh day by urging that the rest of the journey need not be solitary, stumbling forward by trial and error in our wish to allow the Sabbath to reveal its most riveting focus or turn its experience into what it is meant to be. If we have been pointed in the right direction by the Old Testament and by Jewish mentors, and if the Jewish Sabbath experience has taken us part of the way, others stand ready to pilot us on from here. In addition to priceless input from the Jewish legacy—and I write this in all seriousness—we may be led onward by the hand of angels. I say this because, in the New Testament vision, it takes the input from angels to understand, affirm, and proclaim the connection between the faithfulness of God and the life of Jesus.

Karl Barth, who dismisses angels as "essentially marginal figures,"[27] can be excused on this point. His theological priorities lay elsewhere, ill at ease with the notion of cosmic conflict and more at home in a paradigm centered on divine sovereignty. His comment on angels echoes the prejudice of the twentieth century and is not the perspective of the Bible. At stake in the present context, however, is not only angels as a category of beings that have ceased to be considered theologically relevant. The larger question relates to the cosmic drama, bringing out into the open the problem that lies at the core of human existence. The angels, as they come to view in Revelation, act as though they have embraced the question that is most perplexing from the human point of view (Rev. 5:1–4).[28] Human experience is adopted as heaven's own. The reality of suffering and death, of hopes broken and deferred, of trials and tears, is not lost on the heavenly beings. Angels are fully as perplexed and troubled as human beings in the face of injustice and evil. The sense of God's absence that cuts to the bone of the human experience resonates in high heaven in the immediate presence of God. Angels do not doubt the existence of God; *that* perception of reality lies outside the purview of Revelation, but the question of God's faithfulness weighs heavily on the minds of the members of the heavenly council. The entire scene is suffused with a sense that God is not performing according to expectations. How long will the intolerable state of affairs be allowed to go on? "How long," we hear the slain martyrs cry in the most evocative scene before the heavenly council, "how long will it be before you judge and avenge our blood on the inhabitants of the earth?" (Rev. 6:10).

Jesus is etched into the narrative of the Old Testament.

In this context of animated suspense Revelation brings the final unveiling. We read of heavenly beings who lay down their crowns before God, saying, "You are worthy, our Lord and God, to receive glory and honor and power, for you created all things, and by your will they were created and have their being" (4:11). In the middle of the heavenly council we see the Lamb "looking as if it had been slain, standing at the center of the throne" (5:6). We realize that the impasse in the heavenly council is broken at this sight. God has, as it were, persuaded the angels that God has chosen the better way by which to overcome the rebellion. We hear heavenly beings make a new song ring through the universe, "You are worthy to take the scroll and to open its seals, for you were slaughtered and by your blood you ransomed for God saints from every tribe and language and people and nation" (5:9).

From heaven the final call goes out to all human beings to "worship him who made the heavens, the earth, the sea and the springs of water," carried, as it were, by the voice of an angel (14:7). The Sabbath allusion of this message has been noted; in Revelation this message has absorbed and appropriated the angelic perspective on the eternal good news. God's faithfulness is the cornerstone and foundation of this message. In the maze of conflicting, confusing, and distorted views regarding God's character there will be a gathering of people from "every nation and tribe and language and people" (14:6), responding in the context of fierce conflict to God's enduring faithfulness that has been revealed on earth through "the faithfulness of Jesus" (14:12).[29] The seventh day and God's faithfulness, linked from the beginning of human existence, remain linked, a blessing that will not be revoked except to indicate that God's faithfulness is in doubt (Gen. 2:1–3). The hero of this story, of course, as Revelation brings it to a close, and as the affirmation of God's faithfulness rings out in an ever-expanding circle (4:8; 5:8–14), is not the believer or anything that happens on the human side of the equation. The worthy One is God.

"Revelation," says Wolfhart Pannenberg, "is not comprehended completely in the beginning, but at the end of the revealing history."[30] This is a biblical idea, but it needs to be qualified by predictions and previews of the final outcome. According to Paul, even the most visionary believers see the worthiness of God in this life "in a mirror, dimly," only to be fully grasped when human beings at last will see God face to face (1 Cor. 13:12; Rev. 22:4). In Revelation, nevertheless, the line of demarcation between present faith and future reality, between the "already" and the "not yet," and between the seen and the unseen recedes. If we allow ourselves to see reality through the eyes of the angels, we are privileged to have a foretaste in this life of what the future experience will be.

What believing Jews have passed on through the ages, refined and enlarged in the perspective of angels, will be absorbed and further expanded in the Sabbath experience of all believers (Isa. 66:23). This, says Vogel, is the "granite-like belief in the Lord's perfection and justice, regardless of the prevalence of evil. This faith is renewed each Sabbath, suggesting a complete, never-ending cycle from Sabbath to Sabbath, from one recitation of Psalm 92 to the next. This geometric inevitability symbolizes the immeasurable faith that one day Creation will turn back upon itself and regain its original paradisal state."[31]

The vision of Psalm 92 confirms that the spirit of the Sabbath combines illumination and insight, understanding and joy, wrought out within an ever expanding circle of beings who trust God's subtle ways. What began at Creation will continue in the world to come. In this perspective the reason why God rested on the seventh day does not need to be argued because the reason is not hard to find. The seventh day was consecrated for the exquisite blessing and benefit of human beings (Mark 2:27).

Claiming that the seventh day represents a treasure of lost meaning is substantiated by the biblical witness. The Sabbath brings a message of togetherness instead of separation, permanence instead of transience, God's presence instead of God's absence, freedom instead of subjugation, continuity instead of discontinuity, wholeness instead of disintegration, other-centeredness instead of arbitrariness, and divine narrative more than divine imperative. The destruction that greets the eye in Revelation's frightful cycles and the Destroyer that appears on the opposing side of the cosmic conflict (9:1–11) come up short against the book's vision of healing and the Healer that makes right what went wrong (Rev. 22:1–4). In this context the composer of Psalm 92 is merely one voice in a long line of witnesses, augmented by those who have made the "song for the Sabbath day" their own throughout centuries of pain and sorrow. Preceding their witness is the song of the angels, heard first at Creation "when the morning stars sang together and all the heavenly beings shouted for joy" (Job 38:8). Preceding even the early witness of the angels, however, there is the witness of the Person who "blessed the seventh day and hallowed it" (Gen. 2:3).

We have read this line many times, but we do not read the first mention of the seventh day in the Bible correctly unless we are ready to entertain the possibility that God was singing at Creation. Creation is a work of unselfishness and unstinting magnanimity, and God's first word to human beings and even to non-human creation is a blessing.[32] The soul-stirring reality of love that seeks the good of others, the love that "does not seek its own" (1 Cor. 13:5, NKJV), is where the story begins and where it one day will end. As seen through the lens of the seventh day, the notion of "joy in heaven" is not a late invention in the Bible (Luke 15:7). We will have to set out for the sound of God's singing if we wish to know the spirit of the seventh day and the reality to which it points.

The seventh day was consecrated for the exquisite blessing and benefit of human beings.

ENDNOTES

1. Cf. Lincoln, "From Sabbath to Lord's Day," 344–412.

2. Moltmann, *God in Creation*, 139.

3. Dawn, *Keeping the Sabbath Wholly* (Grand Rapids: William B. Eerdmans, 1989), 50.

4. Ibid., 1–16; Dorothy C. Bass, "Keeping the Sabbath," in *Practicing Our Faith*, ed. Dorothy C. Bass (San Francisco: Jossey-Bass Publishers, 1997), 75–89; idem, *Receiving the Day: Christian Practices for Opening the Gift of Time* (San Francisco: Jossey-Bass Publishers, 2000); Lauren Winner, "Take the Day Off: Reclaiming the Sabbath," *Christian Century* 120 (2003): 27–31; Norman Wirzba, "Time Out: A Sabbath Sensibility," *Christian Century* 122 (2005): 24–28; Mark Buchanan, *The Rest of God: Restoring Your Soul by Restoring the Sabbath* (Nashville: W Publishing Group, 2006).

5. Bass, "Keeping the Sabbath," 79–81.

6. Peli, *The Jewish Sabbath*, 3.

7. The Jewish medieval philosopher Moses Maimonides thought that a Jew could transgress

all the laws of the Torah and still remain a Jew, though a sinful one, but one who desecrated the Sabbath would forfeit his Jewishness. Peli (*The Jewish Sabbath*, x) writes that "the Sabbath is thus the last trait of one's Jewishness."

8. Nahum H. Sarna, "The Psalm for the Sabbath Day (Ps 92)," *JBL* 81 (1962): 157.

9. Aune, *Revelation*, II:826.

10. Bauckham, *The Climax of Prophecy*, 286–287.

11. Dan Vogel, "A Psalm for Sabbath? A Literary View of Psalm 92," *JBQ* 28 (2000): 213.

12. Ibid.

13. Ibid.

14. Frank-Lothar Hossfeld, Erich Zenger, Linda M. Maloney, and Klaus Baltzer, *Psalms 2: A Commentary on Psalms 51–100* (Hermeneia; Minneapolis: Fortress Press, 2005), 445.

15. Ibid., 438.

16. Sarna, "The Psalm for the Sabbath Day," 161.

17. Ibid., 164.

18. Vogel, "A Psalm for Sabbath," 217.

19. Yeats, "The Second Coming," in *Poem a Day*, 458.

20. Vogel, "A Psalm for Sabbath," 217.

21. Sarna, "The Psalm for the Sabbath Day," 164.

22. Kahn, "The Expanding Perspectives of the Sabbath," 243.

23. Ibid.

24. Ibid.

25. Ibid., 244.

26. Vogel, "A Psalm for Sabbath," 217.

27. Barth, *Church Dogmatics* III.3 §51, 371.

28. Yarbro Collins, *The Apocalypse*, 39.

29. Tonstad, *Saving God's Reputation*, 165–194.

30. Wolfhart Pannenberg, "Dogmatic Theses on the Doctrine of Revelation," in *Revelation as History*, ed. Wolfhart Pannenberg, trans. David Granshou (New York: Macmillan Company, 1968), 133.

31. Vogel, "A Psalm for Sabbath," 220.

32. Tamarkin Reis, *Reading the Lines*, 22.

BIBLIOGRAPHY

Acton, Lord (Sir John). *Essays on Freedom and Power*. Selected by Gertrude Himmelfarb. Gloucester: Peter Smith, 1972.

Adams, Edward. "Paul's Story of God and Creation: The Story of How God Fulfils His Purposes in Creation." In *Narrative Dynamics in Paul*, edited by Bruce W. Longenecker, 19–43. Louisville: John Knox Press, 2002.

Akenson, Donald Harman. *Saint Saul: A Skeleton Key to the Historical Jesus* (Oxford: Oxford University Press, 2000).

Alexander, Loveday. "Ancient Book Production and the Circulation of the Gospels." In *The Gospels for All Christians: Rethinking the Gospel Audiences*, edited by Richard J. Bauckham, 71–112. Edinburgh: T & T Clark, 1998.

Alter, Robert. *The Pleasures of Reading in an Ideological Age*. New York: W. W. Norton & Co., 1996.

Alter, Robert, and Frank Kermode, ed. *The Literary Guide to the Bible*. London: Collins, 1987.

Andersen, Francis I. *Habakkuk: A New Translation with Introduction and Commentary*. Anchor Bible. New York: Doubleday, 2001.

Anderson, Bernhard W. *Contours of Old Testament Theology*. Minneapolis: Fortress Press, 1999.

______. "Abraham, the Friend of God." *Interpretation* 42 (1988): 353–366.

Andreasen, M. L. *The Sabbath*: Which Day and Why? Takoma Park, Washington, DC: Review and Herald Publishing Association, 1942.

Andreasen, Niels-Erik. "Festival and Freedom." *Interpretation* 28 (1974): 281–297.

______. *The Old Testament Sabbath: A Tradition-Historical Investigation*. Society of Biblical Literature Dissertation Series 7. Missoula, MT: Society of Biblical Literature, 1972.

______. "Recent Sudies of the Old Testament Sabbath: Some Observations." *Zeitschrift für die alttestamentliche Wissenschaft* 86 (1974): 453–469.

______. *Rest and Redemption: A Study of the Biblical Sabbath*. Berrien Springs, MI: Andrews University Press, 1978.

Andrews, John N. *History of the Sabbath and First Day of the Week*. 3rd ed. Battle Creek, MI: Review and Herald, 1887. Reprinted Sunfield, MI: Family Health Publications, 1998.

Aquinas, Thomas. *Summa Theologica* I. 2nd and rev. ed. Literally translated by Fathers of the English Dominican Province. Online Edition Copyright © 2006 by Kevin Knight.

Arnold, Clinton E. *The Colossian Syncretism*. Grand Rapids: Baker Books, 1996.

Artz, Fredrick B. *The Mind of the Middle Ages: A Historical Survey A.D. 200–1500*. Chicago: The University of Chicago Press, 1953.

Ashton, John. *Understanding the Fourth Gospel*. Oxford: Clarendon Press, 1991.

Asiedu-Peprah, Martin. *Johannine Sabbath Conflicts as Juridical Controversy*. Wissenschaftliche Untersuchungen zum Neuen Testament 2. Reihe 132. Tübingen: Mohr Siebeck, 2001.

Attridge, Harold W. *A Commentary on the Epistle to the Hebrews*. Hermeneia. Philadelphia: Fortress Press, 1989.

Auerbach, Erich. *Mimesis: The Representation of Reality in Western Literature*. Translated by Willard R. Trask. Princeton: Princeton University Press, 1953.

Aune, David E. "Dualism in the Fourth Gospel and the Dead Sea Scrolls: A Reassessment of the Problem." In *Neotestamentica et Philonica: Studies in Honor of Peder Borgen*, edited by David Aune, Torrey Seland, and Jarl Henning Ulrichsen, 281–303. Leiden: Brill, 2003.

______. *Revelation*. 3 vols. Word Biblical Commentary. Nashville: Thomas Nelson Publishers, 1997–1998.

Bacchiocchi, Samuele. *From Sabbath to Sunday: A Historical Investigation of the Rise of Sunday Observance in Early Christianity*. Rome: The Pontifical Gregorian University Press, 1977.

______."The Rise of Sunday Observance." In *The Sabbath in Scripture and History*, edited by Kenneth A. Strand, 132–150. Washington, DC: Review and Herald, 1982.

Baird, William. "Abraham in the New Testament: Tradition and the New Identity." *Interpretation* 42 (1988): 367–379.

Bakon, Shimon. "Creation, Tabernacle and Sabbath." *Jewish Bible Quarterly* 25 (1997): 79–85.

Barclay, William. *The Revelation of John*. 2 vols. Louisville: Westminster John Knox, 1976.

Barnes, Michael. "Paul, Context and Interpretation: An Interview with E. P. Sanders." *Journal of Philosophy and Scripture* 2 (2005): 37–42.

Barr, David L. *Tales of the End: A Narrative Commentary on the Book of Revelation*. Santa Rosa: Polebridge Press, 1998.

Barr, James. "Man and Nature: The Ecological Controversy and the Old Testament." In *Ecology and Religion in History*, edited by David and Eileen Spring, 48–75. New York: Harper & Row, 1974.

______. *The Semantics of Biblical Language*. Oxford: Oxford University Press, 1961. Reprint, Eugene: Wipf and Stock, 2004.

Barth, Karl. *Church Dogmatics*. Volume III, part 1. *The Doctrine of Creation*. Translated by J. W. Edwards, O. Bussey, and Harold Knight. Edinburgh: T. & T. Clark, 1958.

______. *Church Dogmatics*. Volume III, part 2. *The Doctrine of Creation*. Translated by Harold Knight, G. W. Bromiley, J. K. S. Reid, and R. H. Fuller. Edinburgh: T. & T. Clark, 1960.

______. *The Epistle to the Romans*. 6th ed. Translated by Edwyn C. Hoskyns. London: Oxford University Press, 1968 [1933].

Barth, Markus. "St. Paul—A Good Jew." *Horizons in Biblical Theology* 1 (1980): 7–45.

Barton, Stephen C. "The Epistles and Christian Ethics." In *The Cambridge Companion to Christian Ethics*, edited by Robin Gill, 63–73. Cambridge: Cambridge University Press, 2001.

Bass, Dorothy C. "Keeping the Sabbath." In *Practicing Our Faith*, edited by Dorothy C. Bass, 75–89. San Francisco: Jossey-Bass Publishers, 1997.

______. *Receiving the Day: Christian Practices for Opening the Gift of Time*. San Francisco: Jossey-Bass Publishers, 2000.

Bauckham, Richard J. *The Climax of Prophecy: Studies in the Book of Revelation*. Edinburgh: T. & T. Clark, 1993.

______. *God Crucified: Monotheism and Christology in the New Testament*. Carlisle: Paternoster Press, 1998.

______. "Joining Creation's Praise of God." *Ecotheology* 7 (2002): 45–59.

______."Sabbath and Sunday in the Medieval Church in the West." In *From Sabbath to Lord's Day*, edited by D. A. Carson, 299–309. Grand Rapids: Zondervan, 1982.

______. *The Theology of the Book of Revelation*. New Testament Theology. Cambridge: Cambridge University Press, 1993.

______. "The Throne of God and the Worship of Jesus." In *The Jewish Roots of Christological Monotheism*, edited by Carey C. Newman, James R. Davila, and Gladys S. Lewis, 43–69. Leiden: Brill, 1999.

______. ed. *The Gospels for All Christians: Rethinking the Gospel Audiences*. Edinburgh: T & T Clark, 1998.

Baur, F. C. "Die Christuspartei in der korintischen Gemeinde, der Gegensatz des petrinischen und paulinischen Christentums in der ältesten Kirche, der Apostel Petrus in Rom," *Tübinger Zeitschrift für Theologie* 4 (1831): 61–206.

______. *Paul the Apostle of Jesus Christ, His Life and Work, His Epistles and His Doctrine*. Translated by Eduard Zeller. 2 vols. London: Williams and Norgate, 1876. Reprint Eugene: Wipf and Stock, 2003.

Beale, G. K. *The Book of Revelation*. New International Greek Testament Commentary. Grand Rapids: Eerdmans, 1999.

Beker, J. Christiaan. *Paul the Apostle: The Triumph of God in Life and Thought*. Philadelphia: Fortress Press, 1980.

______. *Paul's Apocalyptic Gospel*. Philadelphia: Fortress Press, 1982.

Benedictow, Ole J. *The Black Death 1346–1353: The Complete History*. Woodbridge: The Boydell Press, 2004.

Ben Zvi, Ehud. *A Historical-Critical Study of the Book of Obadiah*. Berlin: De Gruyter, 1996.

Bergmeier, Roland. "ΤΕΤΕΛΕΣΤΑΙ: Joh 19:30." *Zeitschrift für die neutestamentliche Wissenschaft* 79 (1988): 282–290.

Bernard, J. H. *A Critical and Exegetical Commentary on the Gospel According to St. John*. 2 vols. International Critical Commentary. Edinburgh: T. & T. Clark, 1928.

Berry, Wendell. *The Unsettling of America: Culture and Agriculture*. New York: Avon Books, 1977.

Betz, Hans Dieter. *Galatians*. Hermeneia. Philadelphia: Fortress Press, 1979.

Bierma, Lyle D. "Remembering the Sabbath Day: Ursinus's Exposition of Exodus 20:8–11." In *Biblical Interpretation in the Era of the Reformation*, edited by Richard A. Muller and John L. Thompson, 272–291. Grand Rapids: Eerdmans, 1996.

Biguzzi, Giancarlo. "John on Patmos and the 'Persecution' in the Apocalypse." *Estudios Biblicos* 56 (1998): 201–220.

Bishop, Morris. *Petrarch and His World*. Bloomington: Indiana University Press, 1963.

Blackman, E. C. *Marcion and His Influence*. London: SPCK, 1948.

Blenkinsopp, Joseph. *Isaiah 1–39: A New Translation with Introduction and Commentary*. Anchor Bible. New York: Doubleday, 2000.

______. *Isaiah 56–66: A New Translation with Introduction and Commentary*. Anchor Bible. New York: Doubleday, 2003.

Boardman, John, Jasper Griffin, and Oswyn Murray, ed. *The Roman World*. Oxford: Oxford University Press, 1986.

Boccaccio, Giovanni. *The Decameron*. Translated by Leopold Flameng. London: Arthur W. Murray, 1888.

Boehm, Omri. "The Binding of Isaac: An Inner-Biblical Polemic on the Question of 'Disobeying' a Manifestly Illegal Order." *Vetus Testamentum* 52 (2002): 1–12.

Boman, Thorleif. *Hebrew Thought Compared with Greek*. Translated by Jules L. Moreau. Philadelphia: The Westminster Press, 1960.

Bonhoeffer, Dietrich. *Creation and Fall: A Theological Interpretation of Genesis 1–3*. Translated by John C. Fletcher. London: SCM Press, 1959.

Borg, Marcus. *Conflict, Holiness and Politics in the Teaching of Jesus*. New York: Edwin Mellen Press, 1984.

Borgen, Peder. *Philo of Alexandria: An Exegete for His Time*. Leiden: Brill, 1997.

Boring, M. Eugene. *Revelation*. Interpretation. Louisville: John Knox Press, 2003.

Botterweck, Johannes, and Helmer Ringgren, ed. *Theological Dictionary of the Old Testament*. Translated by David E. Green. Vols. 1–5. Grand Rapids: Eerdmans, 1974–1986.

Botterweck, Johannes, Helmer Ringgren, and Heinz-Josef Fabry, ed. *Theological Dictionary of the Old Testament*. Vols. 6–10. Translated by David E. Green. Grand Rapids: Eerdmans, 1990–1999.

Bowker, John. *Jesus and the Pharisees*. Cambridge: Cambridge University Press, 1973.

______. *The Targums and Rabbinic Literature: An Introduction to Jewish Interpretation of Scripture*. Cambridge: Cambridge University Press, 1969.

Boyarin, Daniel. *A Radical Jew: Paul and the Politics of Identity*. Berkeley: University of California Press, 1994.

Braaten, Laurie J. "All Creation Groans: Romans 8:22 in Light of the Biblical Sources." *Horizons in Biblical Theology* 28 (2006): 131–159.

______. "Earth Community in Joel 1–2: A Call to Identify with the Rest of Creation." *Horizons in Biblical Theology* 28 (2006): 113–129.

Bradley, James. *Flags of Our Fathers*. New York: Bantam Books, 2000.

Bright, John. *A History of Israel*. 2nd ed. Philadelphia: The Westminster Press, 1976.

Brighton, Louis A. *Revelation*. Concordia Commentary. St. Louis: Concordia Publishing House, 1999.

Brown, Peter. *Augustine of Hippo*. London: Faber and Faber, 1967.

______. *Authority and the Sacred: Aspects of the Christianization of the Roman World*. New York: Cambridge University Press, 1999.

______. *The Body and Society: Men, Women, and Sexual Renunciation in Early Christianity*. New York: Columbia University Press, 1988.

______. *The World of Late Antiquity AD 150–750*. London: Thames and Hudson, 1971. Reprinted 1991.

Brown, Raymond. *The Gospel According to John*. 2 vols. Anchor Bible. New York: Doubleday, 1966.

Brown, Raymond E., and John P. Meier. *Antioch and Rome*. London: Geoffrey Chapman, 1983.

Bruce, F. F. *Commentary on the Epistle to the Colossians*. New International Commentary on the New Testament. Grand Rapids: Eerdmans, 1957.

______. *The Epistle to the Galatians*. New International Greek Testament Commentary. Grand Rapids: Eerdmans, 1982.

______. *The Epistle to the Hebrews*. New International Commentary on the New Testament. Grand Rapids: Eerdmans, 1964.

______. *New Testament History*. London: Thomas Nelson, 1969.

______. *Paul: Apostle of the Heart Set Free*. Grand Rapids: Eerdmans, 1977.

Brueggemann, Walter. *A Commentary on Jeremiah: Exile and Homecoming*. Grand Rapids: William B. Eerdmans, 1998.

______. *Genesis*. Interpretation. Atlanta: John Knox Press, 1982.

______. *Isaiah 1–39*. Westminster Bible Companion. Louisville: Westminster John Knox Press, 1998.

______. *Isaiah 40–66*. Westminster Bible Companion. Louisville: Westminster John Knox Press, 1998.

______. *The Message of the Psalms: A Theological Commentary*. Minneapolis: Augsburg, 1984.

Bryan, Steven M. "Power in the Pool: The Healing of the Man at Bethesda and Jesus' Violation of the Sabbath (John 5:1–18)." *Tyndale Bulletin* 54 (2003): 7–22.

Buber, Martin. *Moses: The Revelation and the Covenant*. Atlantic Highlands, NJ: Humanities Press International, 1988; first published 1946.

Buchanan, Mark. *The Rest of God: Restoring Your Soul by Restoring the Sabbath*. Nashville: W Publishing Group, 2006.

Bultmann, Rudolf. "Die Bedeutung der neuerschossenen mandäischen und manichäischen Quellen für das Verständnis der Johannesevangeliums." *Zeitschrift für die neutestamentiche Wissenschaft* 24 (1925): 100–146.

______. *Existence and Faith: Shorter Writings of Rudolf Bultmann.* Edited by Schubert M. Ogden. London: Collins, 1964.

______. *The Gospel of John. A Commentary.* Translated by G. R. Beasley-Murray, R. W. N. Hoare, and J. K. Riches. Philadelphia: The Westminster Press, 1971.

______. *Theology of the New Testament.* 2 vols. Translated by K. Grobel. London: SCM Press, 1952.

Burridge, Richard. "About People, by People, for People: Gospel Genre and Audiences." In *The Gospels for All Christians: Rethinking the Gospel Audiences,* edited by Richard J. Bauckham, 113–146. Edinburgh: T & T Clark, 1998.

______. *Four Gospels, One Jesus?* London: SPCK, 1994.

______. *What Are the Gospels? A Comparison with Graeco-Roman Biography.* Society for New Testament Studies 70. Cambridge: Cambridge University Press, 1992.

Burrows, Millar. "The Origin of the Term 'Gospel.'" *Journal of Biblical Literature* 44 (1925): 21–33.

Burton, Ernest De Witt. *A Critical and Exegetical Commentary on the Epistle to the Galatians.* International Critical Commentary. Edinburgh: T. & T. Clark, 1921.

Byrne, Brendan J. "Interpreting Romans Theologically in a Post-'New Perspective' Perspective," *Harvard Theological Review* 94 (2001): 227–241.

______. *Reckoning with Romans: A Contemporary Reading of Paul's Gospel.* Good News Studies. Wilmington, DE: Michael Glazier, 1986.

Caird, G. B. "The Glory of God in the Fourth Gospel: An Exercise in Biblical Semantics." *New Testament Studies* 15 (1969): 265–277.

Calvin, John. *Institutes of the Christian Religion.* 2 vols. Edited by John T. Mc Neill. Translated by Ford Lewis Battles. Philadelphia: The Westminster Press, 1960.

Cantor, Norman F. *The Civilization of the Middle Ages.* Rev. ed. New York: HarperCollins, 1993.

______. *In the Wake of the Plague: The Black Death and the World It Made.* New York: Harper Perennial, 2002.

______. *Inventing the Middle Ages.* New York: Quill William Morrow, 1991.

Carroll, James. *Constantine's Sword: The Church and the Jews.* Boston: Houghton Mifflin Company, 2001.

Carroll, R., and M. Daniel. "'For So You Love to Do': Probing Popular Religion in the Book of Amos." In *Rethinking Contexts, Rereading Texts,* 168–189. Journal for the Study of the Old Testament Supplement 299. Sheffield: Sheffield Academic Press, 2000.

Carson, D. A. ed. *From Sabbath to Lord's Day: A Biblical, Historical, and Theological Investigation.* Grand Rapids: Zondervan Publishing House, 1982.

Cassuto, Umberto. *A Commentary on the Book of Exodus*. Translated by Israel Abrahams. Jerusalem: The Magnes Press, 1967.

______. *A Commentary on the Book of Genesis*. Part I. Translated by Israel Abrahams. Jerusalem: The Magnes Press, 1961.

______. *The Documentary Hypothesis and the Composition of the Pentateuch*. Translated by Israel Abrahams. Jerusalem: The Magnes Press, 1961.

The Catechism of the Council of Trent. Translated by the Rev. J. Donovan. New York: Catholic School Book Co., 1929. First published 1566 under Pope Pius V.

Cavaletti, Sofia. "The Jewish Roots of Christian Liturgy." In *The Jewish Roots of Christian Liturgy,* edited by Eugene J. Fisher, 7–40. New York: Paulist Press, 1990.

Chadwick, Henry. *Early Christian Thought and the Classical Tradition*. Oxford: Clarendon Press, 1966.

Charles, Norman J. "A Prophetic (Fore)Word: 'A Curse Is Devouring the Earth (Isaiah 24.6)." In *The Earth Story in the Psalms and the Prophets,* edited by Norman C. Habel, 123–128. Sheffield: Sheffield Academic Press, 2001.

Charles, R. H. *The Revelation of St. John*. 2 vols. International Critical Commentary. Edinburgh: T. & T. Clark, 1920.

Charlesworth, J. H. "Dualism in I QS III-IV and in John." *New Testament Studies* 15 (1969): 389–418.

Childs, Brevard S. *The Book of Exodus*. Old Testament Library. Philadelphia: The Westminster Press, 1974.

______. *Introduction to the Old Testament as Scripture*. Philadelphia: Fortress Press, 1979.

Chilton, Bruce. "Justin and Israelite Prophecy." In *Justin Martyr and His Worlds,* edited by Sara Parvis and Paul Foster, 77–87. Minneapolis: Fortress Press, 2007.

Choi, Hung-Sik. "ΠΙΣΤΙΣ in Galatians 5:5–6: Neglected Evidence for the Faithfulness of Christ." *Journal of Biblical Literature* 124 (2005): 467–490.

Cipolla, Carlo M. *Clocks and Culture*. New York: W. W. Norton & Company, 1978.

Clement of Alexandria. Translated by G. W. Butterworth. Cambridge, MA: Harvard University Press, 1919.

Clements, R. E. "The Unity of the Book of Isaiah." *Interpretation* 36 (1982): 117–129.

Cohen, I. Bernard. *Revolution in Science*. Cambridge, MA: Harvard University Press, 1985.

Collins, Adela Yarbro. *The Apocalypse*. New Testament Message 22. Dublin: Veritas Publications, 1979.

Conzelmann, Hans. *1 Corinthians: A Commentary on the First Epistle to the Corinthians*. Translated by James W. Leitch. Hermeneia. Philadelphia: Fortress Press, 1975.

Cook, Guillermo. "Seeing, Judging and Acting: Evangelism in Jesus' Way: A Biblical Study on Chapter 9 of the Gospel of John." *International Review of Mission* 87 (1998): 388–396.

Cootsona, Gregory S. "A Time for No." *Perspectives* 17 (2002): 24.

Copleston, F. C. *Aquinas*. London: Penguin Books, 1955.

Cousar, Charles B. *A Theology of the Cross: The Death of Jesus in the Pauline Letters*. Minneapolis: Fortress Press, 1990.

Cranfield, C. E. B. *A Critical and Exegetical Commentary on the Epistle to the Romans*. 2 vols. International Critical Commentary. Edinburgh: T. & T. Clark, 1979.

Crouzel, Henri. *Origen*. Translated by A. S. Worrall. Edinburgh: T. & T. Clark, 1989.

Cullmann, Oscar. *Early Christian Worship*. Philadelphia: The Westminster Press, 1953.

______. *The Immortality of the Soul, or the Resurrection of the Dead?* London: The Epworth Press, 1958.

Culpepper, R. Alan. *Anatomy of the Fourth Gospel: A Study in Literary Design*. Philadelphia: Fortress Press, 1987.

______. *The Johannine School: An Evaluation of the Johannine-School Hypothesis Based on an Investigation of the Nature of Ancient Schools*. Missoula, MT: Scholars Press, 1975.

Dahl, Nils Alstrup. "The Atonement: An Adequate Reward for the Akedah?" In *Neotestamentica et Semitica: Studies in Honour of Matthew Black,* edited by E. Earle and Max Wilcox, 15–29. Edinburgh: T. & T. Clark, 1969.

Darwin, Charles. *The Autobiography of Charles Darwin*. New York: W. W. Norton & Company, 1969.

Davidson, Richard M. *A Love Song for the Sabbath*. Washington, DC: Review and Herald Publishing Association, 1988.

Davies, Margaret. "Stereotyping the Other: The 'Pharisees' in the Gospel According to Matthew." In *Biblical Studie/Cultural Studies,* edited by J. Cheryl Exum and Stephen D. Moore, 415–432. Journal for the Study of the Old Testament Supplement 266. Sheffield: Sheffield Academic Press, 1998.

Davies, W. D., and Dale C. Allison. *Critical and Exegetical Commentary on the Gospel According to Saint Matthew*. 3 vols. International Critical Commentary. London: T. & T. Clark, 1997.

Davis, John J. *Moses and the Gods of Egypt: Studies in the Book of Exodus*. Old Testament Studies. Grand Rapids: Baker Book House, 1972.

Dawn, Marva J. *Keeping the Sabbath Wholly*. Grand Rapids: William B. Eerdmans, 1989.

de Boer Martinus C. *The Defeat of Death: Apocalyptic Eschatology in 1 Corinthians and Romans* 5. Journal for the Study of the New Testament Supplement 22. Sheffield: JSOT Press, 1988.

______. "The Meaning of the Phrase τὰ στοιχεῖα τοῦ κόσμου in Galatians." *New Testament Studies* 53 (2007): 204–224.

______. "Paul and Jewish Apocalyptic Eschatology." In *Apocalyptic and the New Testament: Essays in Honor of J. Louis Martyn,* edited by Joel Marcus and Marion L. Soards, 169–190. Journal for the Study of the New Testament Supplement 24. Sheffield: Sheffield Academic Press, 1989.

______. "Paul, Theologian of God's Apocalypse." *Interpretation* 56 (2002): 21–33.

de Vaux, Roland. *Ancient Israel: Its Life and Institutions.* 2 vols. Translated by John McHugh. New York: McGraw-Hill, 1965.

Dederen, Raoul. "Reflections on a Theology of the Sabbath." In *The Sabbath in Scripture and History,* edited by Kenneth A. Strand, 295–306. Washington, DC: Review and Herald Publishing Association, 1982.

Deissmann, Adolf. *Bible Studies.* Translated by Alexander Grieve. Edinburgh: T. & T. Clark, 1901.

______. *The New Testament in the Light of Modern Research.* London: Hodder and Stoughton, 1929.

DeMaris, Richard E. *The Colossian Controversy: Wisdom in Dispute at Colossae.* Journal for the Study of the New Testament Supplement 96. Sheffield: Sheffield Academic Press, 1994.

Descartes, René. *Discourse on Method and Related Writings.* Translated by Desmond M. Clarke. London: Penguin Books, 1999. First published 1637 by Descartes.

______. *Meditations on First Philosophy.* In *The European Philosophers from Descartes to Nietzsche*, edited by Monroe C. Beardsley, translated by Norman Kemp Smith, 25–79. New York: Random House, 1960.

deSilva, David A. *Perseverance in Gratitude: A Socio-Rhetorical Commentary on the Epistle "to the Hebrews."* Grand Rapids: Eerdmans, 2000.

Dibelius, M. "The Isis Initiation and Related Initiatory Rites." In *Conflict at Colossae,* edited by F. O. Francis and W. A. Meeks, 61–121. Rev. ed. Society of Biblical Literature Sources for Biblical Study 4. Missoula, MT: Scolars Press, 1975.

Diepgen, Paul. *Die Theologie und der ärtzliche Stand. Studien zur Geschichte der Beziehungen zwischen Theologie und Medizin im Mittelalter.* Berlin-Grunewald: Dr. Walther Rothschild, 1922.

Dies Domini. Apostolic letter proclaimed by Pope John Paul II, May 31, 1998.

Dillon, John. *The Middle Platonists 80 B.C. to A.D. 220.* Rev. ed. Ithaca, NY: Cornell University Press, 1996.

Dodd, C. H. *The Epistle to the Romans.* Moffat New Testament Commentary. London: Hodder and Stoughton, 1932.

______. *The Interpretation of the Fourth Gospel.* Cambridge: Cambridge University Press, 1954.

Dostoevsky, Fyodor. *The Brothers Karamazo*, translated by Richard Pevear and Larissa Volokhonsky. New York: Farrar, Straus and Giroud, 1990.

Doukhan, Jacques. *Hebrew for Theologians.* Lanham: University of America Press, 1993.

Dressler, H. P. "The Sabbath in the Old Testament." In *From Sabbath to Lord's Day: A Biblical, Historical, and Theological Investigation,* edited by D. A. Carson, 21–41. Grand Rapids: Zondervan Publishing House, 1982.

Driver, S. R. *The Book of Genesis.* London: Methuen & Co., 1904.

Duff, Nancy. "The Significance of Pauline Apocalyptic for Theological Ethics." In *Apocalyptic and the New Testament: Essays in Honor of J. Louis Martyn,* edited by Joel Marcus and Marion L. Soards, 279–296. Journal for the Study of the New Testament Supplement 24. Sheffield: Sheffield Academic Press, 1989.

Duhm, Bernhard. *Das Buch Jesaja.* Tübingen: Vandenhoek and Ruprecht, 1968. First published 1892 by Vandenhoeck & Ruprecht.

Dunn, James D. G. "4QMMT and Galatians." *New Testament Studies* 43 (1997): 147–153.

______."Did Paul Have a Covenant Theology? Reflections on Romans 9.4 and 11.27." In *The Concept of the Covenant in the Second Temple Period,* edited by Stanley E. Porter and J. C. R. Roo, 287–307. Leiden: E. J. Brill, 2003.

______. *Jesus, Paul and the Law.* Louisville: Westminster/John Knox Press, 1990.

______. "The Justice of God: A Renewed Perspective on Justification by Faith." *Journal of Theological Studies* 43 (1992): 1–22.

______. *The New Perspective on Paul.* Rev. ed. Grand Rapids: Eerdmans, 2008.

______. *Romans 1–8.* Word Biblical Commentary. Dallas: Word Books,1988.

du Preez, Ron. *Judging the Sabbath: Discovering What Can't Be Found in Colossians 2:16.* Berrien Springs, MI: Andrews University Press, 2008.

Durant, Will. *The Story of Philosophy.* New York: Pocket Books, 1953.

Durham, John I. *Exodus.* Word Biblical Commentary. Waco: Word Books, 1987.

Eastman, Susan G. "'Cast Out the Slave Woman and Her Son': The Dynamics of Exclusion and Inclusion in Galatians 4.30." *Journal for the Study of the New Testament* 28 (2006): 309–336.

Eichrodt, Walther. *Theology of the Old Testament.* 2 vols. Translated by John Baker. Old Testament Library. London: SCM Press, 1961.

Eisnitz, Gail A. *Slaughterhouse: The Shocking Story of Greed, Neglect, and Inhumane Treatment Inside the U.S. Meat Industry.* New York: Prometheus Books, 2007.

Ellul, Jacques. *Apocalypse: The Book of Revelation.* Translated by George W. Schreiner. New York: The Seabury Press, 1977.

______. *What I Believe.* Translated by Geoffrey W. Bromiley. Grand Rapids: Wm. B. Eerdmans Publishing Company, 1989.

Emmerson, Grace L. *Isaiah 56–66.* Old Testament Guides. Sheffield: JSOT Press, 1992.

Epstein, Isidore. *Judaism.* London: Penguin Books, 1959.

______, ed. *The Babylonian Talmud.* London: The Soncino Press, 1961.

Esler, Philip. *Conflict and Identity in Romans: The Social Setting of Paul's Letter.* Minneapolis: Fortress Press, 2003.

Eusebius. *Commentaria in Psalmos* 91. *Patrologiae Graeca* 23, 1172. Paris: J.-P. Migne, 1857–1866.

______. *The History of the Church.* Translated by G. A. Williamson. London: Penguin Books, 1989.

______. *The Life of Constantine.* Vol. I in *The Nicene and Post-Nicene Fathers.* Edited by

Philip Schaff and Henry Wace. Grand Rapids: Eerdmans, 1952 [1890–1899].

Evans, C. A., and J. A. Sanders, ed. *The Gospels and the Scriptures of Israel.* Journal for the Study of the New Testament Supplement 104. Sheffield: Sheffield Academic Press, 1994.

Evans, Craig A., and Donald A. Hagner, ed. *Anti-Semitism and Early Christianity.* Minneapolis: Fortress Press, 1993.

Farrer, Austin. *The Revelation of St. John the Divine.* Oxford: Clarendon Press, 1964.

Feldman, Louis H. *Jew and Gentile in the Ancient World: Attitudes and Interactions from Alexander to Justinian.* Princeton: Princeton University Press, 1993.

Fiensy, David A. *Prayers Alleged to Be Jewish: An Examination of the Constitutiones Apostolorum.* Chico: Scholars Press, 1985.

Finkelstein, Louis. *The Pharisees: The Sociological Background of Their Faith.* 2 vols. Philadelphia: The Jewish Publication Society of America, 1946.

Finley, Thomas J. "Dimensions of the Hebrew Word for 'create' (*bārā'*)." *Biliotheca Sacra* 148 (1991): 409–423.

Fish, Stanley. *Self-Consuming Artifacts: The Experience of Seventeenth-Century Literature.* Berkeley: University of California Press, 1972.

Fitzmyer, Joseph A. *Romans. A New Translation with Introduction and Commentary.* Anchor Bible. London: Geoffrey Chapman, 1993.

Flusser, David. "Tensions Between Sabbath and Sunday." In *The Jewish Roots of Christian Liturgy,* edited by Eugene J. Fisher, 142–147. New York: Paulist Press, 1990.

Foa, Anna. *The Jews of Europe after the Black Death.* Translated by Andrea Grover. Berkeley: University of California Press, 2000.

Forestell, J. Terence. *The Word of the Cross: Salvation as Revelation in the Fourth Gospel.* Rome: Biblical Institute Press, 1974.

Forster, E. M. *Aspects of the Novel.* New York: Penguin Books, 1962.

Fox, Robin Lane. *The Classical World: An Epic History from Homer to Hadrian.* London: Allen Lane, 2005.

Fredriksen, Paula. "Judaism, the Circumcision of Gentiles, and Apocalyptic Hope: Another Look at Galatians 1 and 2." *Journal of Theological Studies* 42 (1991): 532–564. Reprinted in *The Galatians Debate*, edited by Mark D. Nanos, 235–260. Peabody, MA: Hendrickson, 2002.

Frend, W. H. C. *The Rise of Christianity.* Philadelphia: Fortress Press, 1984.

Fretheim, Terence E. *Exodus.* Interpretation. Louisville: John Knox Press, 1991.

______. *God and the World in the Old Testament: A Relational Theology of Creation.* Nashville: Abingdon Press, 2005.

Frohnen, Bruce. *The American Republic: Primary Sources.* Indianapolis: Liberty Fund, 2002.

Gaston, Lloyd. "The Messiah of Israel as Teacher of the Gentiles." *Interpretation* 29 (1975): 25–40.

Gaventa, Beverly Roberts. "Galatians 1 and 2: Autobiography as Paradigm." *Novum Testamentum* 28 (1986): 309–326.

______. "The Singularity of the Gospel: A Reading of Galatians." In *Pauline Theology*, volume I. Edited by Jouette M. Basler, 147–159. Minneapolis: Fortress Press, 1991.

Gerstenberger, Erhard S. *Leviticus*. Translated by Douglas W. Stott. Old Testament Library. Louisville: Westminster John Knox Press, 1996.

Gilkey, Langdon. *Shantung Compound: The Story of Men and Women Under Pressure*. New York: Harper & Row, 1966.

Gnilka, Joachim. *Der Kolosserbrief*. Freiburg: Herder, 1980.

Gnuse, Robert. "Jubilee Legislation in Leviticus: Israel's Vision of Social Reform." *Biblical Theology Bulletin* 15 (1985): 43–48.

Goodenough, Erwin R. *The Theology of Justin Martyr*. Amsterdam: Philo, 1968. First published 1923 by Jena.

Gore, Al. *Earth in the Balance*. London: Earthscan Publications, 1992.

Gosse, Bernard. "Sabbath, Identity and Universalism Go Together after the Return from Exile." *Journal for the Study of the Old Testament* 29 (2005): 359–370.

Gottfried, Robert S. *The Black Death: Natural and Human Disaster in Medieval Europe*. New York: The Free Press, 1983.

Grassi, Joseph A. "'*Abba*, Father' (Mark 14:36): Another Approach." *Journal of the American Academy of Religion* 50 (1982): 449–458.

Greek-English Lexicon of the New Testament and Other Early Christian Literature. 3rd ed. Edited by Walter Bauer, Frederick William Danker, W. F. Arndt, and F. W. Gingrich. Chicago: The University of Chicago Press, 2000.

Green, Peter. *Alexander to Actium: The Historical Evolution of the Hellenistic Age*. Berkeley: University of California Press, 1990.

Greenberg, Irving. "The Shoah and the Legacy of Anti-Semitism." In *Christianity in Jewish Terms,* edited by Tikva Frymer-Kensky, David Novak, Peter Ochs, David Fox Sandmel, and Michael A. Signer, 25–48. Boulder: Westview Press, 2000.

Greene-McCreight, Kathryn. "Restless Until We Rest in God: The Fourth Commandment as Test Case in Christian 'Plain Sense' Interpretation." In *The Ten Commandments: The Reciprocity of Faithfulness,* edited by William P. Brown, 223–236. Louisville: Westminster John Knox Press, 2004.

Greenslade, S. L. *Church and State from Constantine to Theodosius*. London: SCM Press, 1954.

Grieb, A. Katherine. *The Story of Romans: A Narrative Defense of God's Righteousness*. Louisville: Westminster John Knox Press, 2002.

Guelich, Robert A. *Mark 1–8:26*. Word Biblical Commentary. Nashville: Thomas Nelson Publishers, 1989.

Guelzo, Allen C. *Abraham Lincoln: Redeemer President*. Grand Rapids: William B. Eerdmans Publishing Company, 1999.

Gunkel, Hermann. *Schöpfung und Chaos in Urzeit und Endzeit: eine religionsgeschichtliche*

Untersuchung über Gen 1 und Ap Joh 12. Göttingen: Vandenhoeck und Ruprecht, 1895.

Guy, Fritz. "The Lord's Day in the Letter of Ignatius to the Magnesians." *Andrews University Seminary Studies* 2 (1964): 1–17.

Habel, Normal C. "Introducing the Earth Bible." In *Readings from the Perspective of the Earth*, edited by Norman C. Habel, 25–37. Sheffield: Sheffield Academic Press, 2000.

Haenchen, Ernst. *John 1: A Commentary on the Gospel of John*. Translated by Robert W. Funk. Hermeneia. Philadelphia: Fortress Press, 1984.

Hahn, Scott W. "Covenant, Oath, and the Aqedah: Διαθήκη in Galatians 3:15–18." *Catholic Biblical Quarterly* 67 (2005): 79–100.

Hagner, Donald A. "Paul and Judaism: Testing the New Perspective." In Peter Stuhlmacher, *Revisiting Paul's Doctrine of Justification: A Challenge to the New Perspective*, 75–105. Downers Grove: InterVarsity Press, 2001.

———. "Paul as a Jewish Believer—According to His Letters." In *Jewish Believers in Jesus: The Early Centuries*, edited by Oskar Skarsaune and Reidar Hvalvik, 96–153. Peabody: Hendrickson, 2007.

Halsberghe, Gaston H. *The Cult of Sol Invictus*. Leiden: E. J. Brill, 1972.

Hanson, Anthony Tyrrell. *The Wrath of the Lamb*. London: SPCK, 1957.

Hanson, R. P. C. *Allegory and Event*. London: SCM Press, 1959.

Harink, Douglas. *Paul among the Postliberals: Pauline Theology beyond Christendom and Modernity*. Grand Rapids: Brazos Press, 2003.

Harkins, Paul W., ed. *Saint John Chrysostom: Discourses against Judaizing Christians*. The Fathers of the Church: A New Translation 68. Washington, DC: The Catholic University of America Press, 1979.

Harnack, Adolf. *Medizinisches aus der ältesten Kirchengeschichte*. Leipzig: J. C. Hinrichs'sche Buchhandlung, 1892.

Hauser, Alan J. "Gen 2–3: The Theme of Intimacy and Alienation." In *Art and Meaning: Rhetoric in Biblical Literature*, edited by D. J. A. Clines, D. M. Gunn, and A. J. Hauser, 20–36. Journal for the Study of the Old Testament Supplement 10. Sheffield: JSOT Press, 1992.

Hay, Malcolm. *Europe and the Jews: The Pressure of Christendom over 1900 Years*. Chicago: Academy Chicago Publishers, 1992.

Hays, John H. *The Eighth-Century Prophet Amos: His Times and His Preaching*. Nashville: Abingdon Press, 1988.

Hays, Richard B. "Christology and Ethics in Galatians: The Law of Christ." *Catholic Biblical Quarterly* 49 (1987): 268–290.

———. *The Conversion of the Imagination: Paul as Interpreter of Israel's Scripture*. Grand Rapids: Eerdmans, 2005.

———. *Echoes of Scripture in the Letters of Paul*. New Haven: Yale University Press, 1989.

______. *The Faith of Jesus Christ: An Investigation of the Narrative Substructure of Galatians 3:1–4:11*. Society of Biblical Literature Dissertation Series 56. Chico: Scholars Press, 1983. Reprint, Grand Rapids: Eerdmans, 2002.

______. "'Have We Found Abraham to Be Our Forefather According to the Flesh?' A Reconsideration of Rom. 4:1." *Novum Testamentum* 27 (1985): 76–98.

______. "'Here We Have No Lasting City': New Covenantalism in Hebrews." Conference on Hebrews and Christian Theology, St. Andrews, Scotland, July 19, 2006, 1–26.

______. "Is Paul's Gospel Narratable?" *Journal for the Study of the New Testament* 27 (2004): 217–239.

______. "Paul's Hermeneutics and the Question of Truth." *Pro ecclesia* 16 (2007): 126–133.

______. "'The Righteous One' as Eschatological Deliverer: A Case Study in Paul's Apocalyptic Hermeneutics." In *Apocalyptic and the New Testament: Essays in Honor of J. Louis Martyn,* edited by Joel Marcus and Marion L. Soards, 191–215. Journal for the Study of the New Testament Supplement 24. Sheffield: Sheffield Academic Press, 1989.

Hebert, Gabriel. "'Faithfulness' and 'Faith.'" *Reformed Theological Review* 14 (1955): 33–40.

Heil, John Paul. "The Fifth Seal (Rev 6,9–11) as a Key to the Book of Revelation." *Biblica* 74 (1993): 220–243.

Hendriksen, William. *More Than Conquerors*. Grand Rapids: Baker Books, 1998 [1940].

Hengel, Martin. *The Four Gospels and the One Gospel of Jesus Christ*. Translated by John Bowden. London: SCM Press, 2000.

______. *The "Hellenization" of Judea in the First Century after Christ*. London: SCM Press, 1989.

______. *Judaism and Hellenism*. 2 vols. Translated by John Bowden. London: SCM Press, 1974.

Heschel, Abraham Joshua. *The Sabbath: Its Meaning for Modern Man*. New York: The Noonday Press, 1975. First published 1951 by Farrar, Straus and Young.

Hirschberg, Peter. "Martin Luthers Haltung zu Shabbat und Sonntag im Horizont des Jüdischen Shabbatsverständnisses." *Luther* 69 (1998): 81–100.

Holleman, Joost. *Resurrection and Parousia: A Traditio-Historical Study of Paul's Eschatology in 1 Corinthians 15*. Novum Testamentum Supplement Series 84. Leiden: E. J. Brill, 1996.

Hooker, Morna D. "Were There False Teachers in Colossae?" In *Christ and the Spirit in the New Testament: In Honour of C. F. D. Moule,* edited by B. Lindars and S. Smalley, 315–331. Cambridge: Cambridge University Press, 1973.

Hossfeld, Frank-Lothar, Erich Zenger, Linda M. Maloney and Klaus Baltzer. *Psalms 2: A Commentary on Psalms 51–100*. Hermeneia. Minneapolis: Fortress Press, 2005.

Howard, George. "The 'Faith of Christ.'" *Expository Times* 85 (1974): 212–215.

Hughes, Philip Edgecumbe. *A Commentary on the Epistle to the Hebrews*. Grand Rapids: Eerdmans, 1977.

Hvalvik, Reidar. "Jewish Believers and Jewish Influence in the Roman Church until the Early Second Century." In *Jewish Believers in Jesus: The Early Centuries,* edited by Oskar Skarsaune and Reidar Hvalvik, 179–216. Peabody: Hendrickson, 2007.

Ignatius of Antioch. *To the Magnesians.* In *The Ante-Nicene Fathers,* vol I. Edited by Alexander Roberts and James Donaldson. Edinburgh: T. & T. Clark, 1867. Reprinted Grand Rapids: Eerdmans, 1987.

The International Standard Bible Encyclopedia. Rev. ed. Grand Rapids: Wm. B. Eerdmans Publishing Co., 1939.

Jacob, Benno. *The Second Book of the Bible: Exodus.* Translated by Walter Jacob. Hoboken, NJ: Ktav Publishing House, 1992.

Jacob, Edmond. *Theology of the Old Testament.* Translated by Arthur W. Heathcote and Philip J. Allcock. London: Hodder and Stoughton, 1958.

Jaeger, Werner. *Early Christianity and Greek Paideia.* Cambridge: Harvard University Press, 1961.

Jeremias, Jörg. *The Book of Amos.* Translated by Douglas V. Stott. Louisville: Westminster John Knox Press, 1998.

Jewett, Robert. "The Corruption and Redemption of Creation: Reading Rom 8:18–23 within the Imperial Context." In *Paul and the Roman Imperial Order,* edited by Richard A. Horsley, 25–46. Harrisburg: Trinity Press International, 2004.

______. *Romans: A Commentary.* Hermeneia. Minneapolis: Fortress Press, 2006.

Johns, Loren L. *The Lamb in the Christology of the Apocalypse of John.* Wissenschaftliche Untersuchungen zum Neuen Testament. 2. Reihe 167. Tübingen: Mohr Siebeck, 2003.

______. "The Lamb in the Rhetorical Program of the Apocalypse of John." *Society of Biblical Literature Seminar Papers* 37 (1998): 2:762–784.

Johnsen, Carsten A. *Day of Destiny: The Mystery of the Seventh Day.* Loma Linda, CA: The Untold Story Publishers, 1982.

______. *Man—the Indivisible.* Oslo: Universitetsforlaget, 1971.

Johnson, Luke Timothy. *Hebrews: A Commentary.* New Testament Library. Louisville: Westminster John Knox Press, 2006.

Johnsson, William. *In Absolute Confidence: The Book of Hebrews Speaks to Our Day.* Nashville: Southern Publishing Association, 1979.

Johnston, Robert M. "The Rabbinic Sabbath." In *The Sabbath in Scripture and History,* edited by Kenneth A. Strand, 70–91. Washington, DC: Review and Herald Publishing Association, 1982.

Jones, A. H. M. *Constantine and the Conversion of Europe.* Toronto: The University of Toronto Press, 1978. First published 1948 by Hodder & Stoughton.

Jörns, Klaus-Peter. *Das hymnische Evangelium. Untersuchungen zu Aufbau, Funktion und Herkunft der hymnischen Stücke in der Johannesoffenbarung.* Gütersloh: Gütersloher Verlagshaus Gerd Mohn, 1971.

______. "Proklamation und Akklamation: Die antiphonische Grundordnung des frühchristlichen Gottesdientes nach der Johannesoffenbarung." In *Liturgie und Dichtung*, edited by H. Becker and R. Kaczynski, 187–208. Sankt Ottilien: EOS Verlag, 1983.

Jospe, Raphael. "Sabbath, Sabbatical and Jubilee: Jewish Ethical Perspectives." In *The Jubilee Challenge: Utopia or Possibility?* edited by Hans Ucko, 77–98. Geneva: WCC Publications, 1997.

Justin Martyr. *Dialogue with Trypho*. In *The Fathers of the Church*, vol. 6. Translated by Thomas B. Falls. New York: Christian Heritage, Inc., 1948.

______. *First Apology*. In *The Ante-Nicene Fathers*. Volume I. Edited by Alexander Roberts and James Donaldson, 163–187. Edinburgh: T & T Clark, n.d. Reprint, Grand Rapids: Eerdmans, 1989.

Kafka, Frantz. *Amerika*. Translated by Edwin Muir. New York: New Directions, 1946.

Kahn, Isidoro. "Jewish Sabbath." In *The Jewish Roots of Christian Liturgy*, Edited by Eugene J. Fisher, 121–129. New York: Paulist Press, 1990.

Kahn, Pinchas. "The Expanding Perspectives of the Sabbath." *Jewish Bible Quarterly* 32 (2004): 239–244.

Kaiser, Otto. *Isaiah 1–12*. 2nd ed. Translated by John Bowden. London: SCM Press, 1983.

______. "The Law as Center of the Hebrew Bible." In *"Sha'arei Talmon": Studies in the Bible, Qumran, and the Ancient Near East Presented to Shemaryahu Talmon*, edited by Michael Fishbane and Emmanuel Tov, 93–103. Winona Lake: Eisenbrauns, 1992.

Kant, Immanuel. *Critique of Pure Reason*. Translated by Norman Kemp. London: J. M. Dent & Sons Ltd, 1934.

Käsemann, Ernst. "Die Anfänge christlicher Theologie," *ZTK* 57 (1960): 162–185. English translation entitled, "The Beginnings of Christian Theology." In *New Testament Questions for Today*, translated by W. J. Montague, 82–107. Philadelphia: Fortress Press, 1969.

Kee, Howard Clark. "The Social Setting of Mark: An Apocalyptic Community." *Society of Biblical Literature Seminar Papers 1984*, 245–255.

Keener, Craig S. *The Gospel of John: A Commentary*. 2 vols. Peabody: Hendrickson Publishers, 2003.

Keller, C. A. *Das Wort OTH als Offenbarungszeichen Gottes*. Basel: Buchdruckerei E. Haenen, 1946.

Kelly, Page H. *Amos: Prophet of Social Justice*. Grand Rapids: Baker Book House, 1972.

Kidner, Derek. *Ezra and Nehemiah*. Tyndale Old Testament Commentaries. Downers Grove, IL: Inter-Varsity Press, 1979.

Kierkegaard, Søren. *Attack upon "Christendom."* Translated by Walter Lowrie. Princeton: Princeton University Press, 1968.

______. *Frygt og Bæven. Dialektisk Lyrikk*. Kjøbenhavn: C. A. Reitzel, 1843; repr. Søren Kierkegaards Skrifter 4, København: Gads Forlag, 1997. English translation entitled, *Fear and Trembling: A Dialectical Lyric*. Translated by Walter Lowrie. Princeton: Princeton University Press, 1941.

———. *Practice in Christianity*. Edited and translated by Howard V. Hong and Edna H. Hong. Princeton: Princeton University Press, 1991. Original Danish version 1848.

Kimelman, Reuven. "Birkat Ha-Minim and the Lack of Evidence for an Anti-Christian Jewish Prayer in Late Antiquity." In *Jewish and Christian Self-Definition*, edited by E. P. Sanders, A. J. Baumgarten, and Alan Mendelson, 226–244. London: SCM Press, 1981.

Kittel, Gerhard. "πίστις Ἰησοῦ Χριστοῦ bei Paulus." *Theologischen Studien und Kritiken* 79 (1906): 419–436.

———. *Theological Dictionary of the New Testament*. Vols. 1–4. Translated by Geoffrey W. Bromiley. Grand Rapids: Eerdmans, 1964–1967.

Kittel, Gerhard, and Gerhard Friedrich. *Theological Dictionary of the New Testament*. Vols. 5–9. Translated by Geoffrey W. Bromiley. Grand Rapids: Eerdmans, 1967–1974.

Knierim, Rolf. *The Task of Old Testament Theology: Substance, Method and Cases*. Grand Rapids: Eerdmans, 1995.

Koch, Klaus. *The Rediscovery of Apocalyptic*. Translated by Margaret Kohl. London: SCM Press, 1972.

Koester, Craig R. *Hebrews: A New Translation with Introduction and Commentary*. Anchor Bible. New York: Doubleday, 2001.

Kraft, Heinrich. *Die Offenbarung des Johannes*. Handbuch zum Neuen Testament 16A. Tübingen: Mohr, 1974.

Ladd, George Eldon. *A Commentary on the Revelation of John*. Grand Rapids: Eerdmans, 1972.

Lambrecht, Jan. "The Opening of the Seals (Rev 6,1–8,6)." *Biblica* 79 (1998): 198–220.

———. "Rev 13,9–10 and Exhortation in the Apocalypse." In *New Testament Textual Criticism and Exegesis. Festschrift J. Delobel*, edited by A Denaux, 331–347. Bibliotheca ephemeridum theologicarum lovaniensum 161. Leuven: Leuven University Press, 2002.

———. *The Wretched "I" and Its Liberation. Paul in Romans 7 and 8*. Louvain: Peeters Press, 1992.

Landes, David S. *Revolution in Time*. Cambridge, MA: The Belknap Press, 1983.

Lane, William L. *The Gospel According to Mark*. New International Commentary on the New Testament. Grand Rapids: Eerdmans, 1974.

LaRondelle, Hans K. *The End-Time Prophecies of the Bible*. Sarasota: First Impressions, 1997.

Leepson, Marc. *Flag: An American Biography*. New York: St. Martin's Press, 2005.

Le Goff, Jacques. *Medieval Civilization*. Translated by Julia Barrow. London: Basil Blackwell, 1988.

———. *Time, Work, and Culture in the Middle Ages*. Translated by Arthur Goldhammer. Chicago: The University of Chicago Press, 1980.

Levenson, Jon D. *Creation and the Persistence of Evil: The Jewish Drama of Divine*

Omnipotence. Princeton: Princeton University Press, 1994.

Levine, Lee I. A. "Judaism from the Destruction of Jerusalem to the End of the Second Jewish Revolt: 70–135 C.E." In *Christianity and Rabbinic Judaism: A Parallel History of Their Origins and Early Development,* edited by Herschel Shanks, 125–149. Washington, DC: Biblical Archaeological Society, 1992.

Lewis, Alan E. *Between Cross and Resurrection: A Theology of Holy Saturday*. Grand Rapids: Eerdmans, 2001.

Lewis, C. S. *Mere Christianity*. New York: Macmillan, 1960 [1943].

Lightfoot, J. B. *St. Paul's Epistle to the Galatians*. London: Macmillan and Co., 1876.

Linafelt, Tod, ed. *Strange Fire: Reading the Bible after the Holocaust*. New York: New York University Press, 2000.

Lincoln, A. T. "From Sabbath to Lord's Day: A Biblical and Theological Perspective." In *From Sabbath to Lord's Day: A Biblical, Historical, and Theological Investigation,* edited by D. A. Carson, 343–412. Grand Rapids: Zondervan Publishing House, 1982.

______. *Truth on Trial: The Lawsuit Motif in the Fourth Gospel*. Peabody: Hendrickson, 2000.

Llewelyn, S. R. "The Use of Sunday for Meetings of Believers in the New Testament." *Novum Testamentum* 43 (2001): 205–223.

Lohse, Eduard. *Die Briefe and die Kolosser und an Philemon*. Göttingen: Vandenhoeck & Ruprecht, 1968.

Longenecker, Bruce W. *Eschatology and the Covenant: A Comparison of 4 Ezra and Romans 1–11*. Sheffield: Sheffield Academic Press, 1991.

______. *Narrative Dynamics in Paul*. Edited by Bruce W. Longenecker. Louisville: John Knox Press, 2002.

______. *The Triumph of Abraham's God*. Edinburgh: T & T Clark, 1998.

Longenecker, Richard N. *Galatians*. Word Biblical Commentary. Dallas: Word Books, 1990.

Löning, Karl. "Gottes Barmherzigkeit und die pharisäische Sabbat-Observanz. Zu den Sabbat-Therapien im lukanischen Reisebericht." In *Das Drama der Barmherzigkeit Gottes,* edited by Ruth Scoralick, 218–239. Stuttgarter Bibelstudien 183. Stuttgart: Verlag Katolisches Bibelwerk, 2000.

Loya, Melissa Tubbs. "'Therefore the Earth Mourns': The Grievance of Earth in Hosea 4:1–3." Paper presented at the annual Society of Biblical Literature meeting in Washington, DC, November, 2006.

Lührmann, Dieter. "Tage, Monate, Jahrezeiten, Jahre (Gal 4,10)." In *Werden und Wirken des Alten Testaments,* edited by Rainer Albertz, Hans-Peter Müller, Hans Walter Wolff, and Walther Zimmerli, 428–445. Göttingen: Vandenhoeck & Ruprecht, 1980.

Lull, David J. "'The Law Was Our Pedagogue': A Study in Galatians 3:19–25." *Journal of Biblical Literature* 105 (1986): 481–498.

Lundbom, Jack R. *Jeremiah 1–20: A New Translation with Introduction and Commentary.*

Anchor Bible. New York: Doubleday, 1999.

Luther, Martin. *Against the Sabbatarians. Luther's Works* 47. Edited by Helmut T. Lehman. Translated by Martin H. Bertram. Philadelphia: Fortress Press, 1971.

———. *The Bondage of the Will.* Translated by J. I. Packer and O. R. Johnston. New York: Fleming H. Revell, 1957.

———. *How Christians Should Regard Moses. Luther's Works* 35. Edited by Helmut T. Lehman. Translated by E. Theodore Bachmann. Philadelphia: Muhlenberg Press, 1960.

———. *On the Jews and Their Lies. Luther's Works* 47. Edited by Franklin Sherman. Translated by Martin H. Bertram. Philadelphia: Fortress Press, 1971.

———. *Vorlesung über den Römerbrief 1515/16.* In *Ausgewählte Werke.* Munich: Chr. Raiser Verlag, 1957.

MacGregor, G. H. C., and A. C. Purdy. *Jew and Greek: Tutors unto Christ.* Edinburgh: The Saint Andrew Press, 1959.

Mackay, Charles. *Extraordinary Popular Delusions and the Madness of Crowds.* London: Richard Bentley, 1841. Reprint, New York: Harmony Books, 1980.

MacMullen, Ramsay. *Christianizing the Roman Empire A.D. 100–400.* New Haven: Yale University Press, 1984.

Malherbe, Abraham J. *The Letters to the Thessalonians.* Anchor Bible. New York: Doubleday, 2000.

Marcus, Joel. *Mark 1–8: A New Translation with Introduction and Commentary.* Anchor Bible. New York: Doubleday, 2000.

Martin, R. A. "The Earliest Messianic Interpretation of Genesis 3:15." *Journal of Biblical Literature* 84 (1965): 425–427.

Martin, Troy. "Apostasy to Paganism: The Rhetorical Stasis of the Galatian Controversy." *Journal of Biblical Literature* 114 (1995): 437–461.

———. "'But Let Everyone Discern the Body of Christ' (Colossians 2:17)." *Journal of Biblical Literature* 114 (1995): 249–255.

———. *By Philosophy and Empty Deceit: Colossians as Response to a Cynic Crtitique.* Journal for the Study of the New Testament Supplement 118. Sheffield: Sheffield Academic Press, 1996.

———. "The Covenant of Circumcision (Genesis 17:9–14) and the Situational Antithesis in Galatians 3:28." *Journal of Biblical Literature* 122 (2003): 111–125.

———. "Pagan and Judeo-Christian Time-Keeping Schemes in Gal 4.10 and Col 2.16." *New Testament Studies* 42 (1996): 105–119.

———. "Whose Flesh? What Temptation? (Galatians 4.13–14)." *Journal for the Study of the New Testament* 74 (1999): 65–91.

Martyn, J. Louis. "Apocalyptic Antinomies in Paul's Letter to the Galatians." *New Testament Studies* 31 (1985): 410–424.

______. "The Apocalyptic Gospel in Galatians." *Interpretation* 54 (2000): 246–266.

______. "Events in Galatia: Modified Covenantal Nomism Versus God's Invasion of the Cosmos in the Singular Gospel: A Response to J. D. G. Dunn and B. R. Gaventa." In *Pauline Theology*, volume I. Edited by Jouette M. Basler, 160–179. Minneapolis: Fortress Press, 1991.

______. *Galatians: A New Translation with Introduction and Commentary*. Anchor Bible. New York: Doubleday, 1997.

______. *History and Theology in the Fourth Gospel*. New York: Harper & Row, 1968.

Mathewson, David. *A New Heaven and a New Earth: The Meaning and Function of the Old Testament in Revelation 21.1–22.5*. Journal for the Study of the New Testament Supplement Series 238. Sheffield: Sheffield Academic Press, 2003.

Matlock, Barry. "Detheologizing the ΠΙΣΤΙΣ ΧΡΙΣΤΟΥ Debate: Cautionary Remarks from a Lexical Semantic Perspective." *Novum Testamentum* 42 (2000): 1–23.

______. "'Even the Demons Believe': Paul and πίστις Χριστοῦ." *Catholic Biblical Quarterly* 64 (2002): 300–318.

______. "PISTIS in Galatians 3.26: Neglected Evidence for 'Faith in Christ'?" *New Testament Studies* 49 (2003): 433–439.

______."The Rhetoric of πίστις in Paul: Galatians 2.16, 3.22, Romans 3.22, and Philippians 3.9," *Journal for the Study of the New Testatment* 30 (2007): 173–203.

McCasland, Selby Vernon. "The Origin of the Lord's Day." *Journal of Biblical Literature* 49 (1930): 76–82.

McInerny, Ralph. "Ethics." In *The Cambridge Companion to Aquinas,* edited by Norman Kretzmann and Eleonore Stump, 196–216. Cambridge: Cambridge University Press, 1993.

McKenzie, John L. *A Theology of the Old Testament*. London: Geoffrey Chapman, 1974.

McPherson, James. *Battle Cry of Freedom: The Civil War Era*. New York: Oxford University Press, 1988.

Mendenhall, G. E. "Covenant Forms in Israelite Traditions." *Biblical Archaeologist* 7 (1954): 50–76.

The Midrash. Edited by H. Freedman and Maurice Simon. Translated by S. M. Lehrman. London: The Soncino Press, 1939.

Milgrom, Jacob. "Leviticus 25 and Some Postulates of the Jubilee." In *The Jubilee Challenge: Utopia or Possibility?* Edited by Hans Ucko, 28–32. Geneva: WCC Publications, 1997.

______. *Leviticus: A New Translation with Introduction and Commentary*. 3 vols. Anchor Bible. New York: Doubleday, 2000–2001.

Millard, A. R., and D. J. Wiseman, ed. *Essays on the Patriarchal Narratives*. Leicester: Inter-Varsity Press, 1980.

Miller, Patrick D. "Divine Command and Beyond: The Ethics of the Commandments." In *The Ten Commandments: The Reciprocity of Faithfulness,* edited by William P. Brown, 12–29. Louisville: Westminster John Knox Press, 2004.

Minear, Paul S. "Far as the Curse Is Found: The Point of Revelation 12:15–16." *Novum Testamentum* 33 (1991): 71–77.

The Mishna: A New Translation. Edited and translated by Jacob Neusner. New Haven: Yale University Press, 1988.

Moberly, R. W. L. "Did the Serpent Get It Right?" *Journal of Theological Studies* 39 (1988): 1–27.

______. "The Earliest Commentary on the Akedah." *Vetus Testamentum* 38 (1988): 302–323.

Moltmann, Jürgen. *God in Creation: An Ecological Doctrine of Creation.* Translated by Margaret Kohl. London: SCM Press, 1985.

Momigliano, Arnaldo. *Alien Wisdom: The Limits of Hellenization.* Cambridge: Cambridge University Press, 1990 [1975].

Moo, Douglas J. *The Epistle to the Romans.* New International Critical Commentary of the New Testament. Grand Rapids: Eerdmans, 1996.

Moore, George Foot. *Judaism in the First Centuries of the Christian Era: The Age of the Tannaim.* 3 vols. Cambridge: Harvard University Press, 1927–1930.

Morgan, George Campbell. *The Gospel According to John.* New York: Fleming H. Revell, 1933.

Morgenstern, Julian. "The Mythological Background of Psalm 82." *Hebrew Union College Annual* 14 (1939): 29–126.

Morris, Leon. *The Gospel According to John.* Grand Rapids: Eerdmans, 1971.

Mosna, C. *Storia della domenica dale origini fino agli inizi del V secolo.* Roma: Analecta Gregoriana, 1969.

Moxnes, Halvor. "The Social Context of Luke's Community." *Interpretation* 48 (1994): 379–389.

Moyers, Bill, ed. *Genesis: A Living Conversation.* New York: Doubleday, 1996.

Müller, Mogens. *The First Bible of the Church: A Plea for the Septuagint.* Journal for the Study of the Old Testament Supplement Series 206. Sheffield: Sheffield Academic Press, 1996.

Mumford, Lewis. *Technics and Civilization.* New York: Hartcourt, Brace & World, 1934.

Murphy, Nancey. "Human Nature: Historical, Scientific, and Religious Issues." In *Whatever Happened to the Soul?* Edited by Warren S. Brown, Nancey Murphy, and H. Newton Maloney, 1–29. Minneapolis: Fortress Press, 1998.

Murphy-O'Connor, Jerome. *Paul: A Critical Life.* Oxford and New York: Oxford University Press, 1997.

Myers, Jacob M. *Ezra·Nehemiah: Introduction, Translation and Notes.* Anchor Bible 14. New York: Doubleday, 1965.

Nebe, Gottfried. "Creation in Paul's Theology." In *Creation in Jewish and Christian Tradition,* edited by Henning Graf Reventlow and Yair Hoffman, 111–137. Journal for the Study of the Old Testament Supplement Series 319. Sheffield: Sheffield Academic Press, 2002.

Neufeld, Edward. "Hygiene Conditions in Ancient Israel (Iron Age)." *The Biblical Archaeologist* 34 (May, 1971): 42–66.

Newbigin, Lesslie. *The Light Has Come: An Exposition of the Fourth Gospel*. Grand Rapids: Eerdmans, 1982.

Newsom, Carol. "Common Ground: An Ecological Reading of Genesis 2–3." In *The Earth Story in Genesis,* edited by Norman C. Habel and Shirley Wurst, 60–72. Sheffield: Sheffield Academic Press, 2000.

Nilsson, Martin P. *Imperial Rome*. New York: Schocken Books, 1962.

Nohl, Johannes. *The Black Death: A Chronicle of the Plague*. Translated by C. H. Clarke. New York: J. & J. Harper, 1969.

O'Brien, Peter T. *Colossians, Philemon*. Word Biblical Commentary. Waco: Word Books, 1982.

Obeng, E. A. "Abba, Father: The Prayer of the Sons of God." *Expository Times* 99 (1988): 363–366.

Origen. *Contra Celsum*. Translated by Henry Chadwick. Cambridge: Cambridge University Press, 1965.

______. *First Principles*. Translated by G. W. Butterworth. London: Society for Promoting Christian Knowledge, 1936. Reprint, Gloucester, MA: Peter Smith, 1973.

______. *Homilies on Genesis and Exodus*. Translated by Ronald E. Heine. *The Fathers of the Church* 71. Washington, DC: The Catholic University of America Press, 1982.

Osborn, Eric. *Tertullian, First Theologian of the West*. Cambridge: Cambridge University Press, 1997.

Osborne, Grant. *Revelation*. Baker Exegetical Commentary on the New Testament. Grand Rapids: Baker Academic, 2002.

Oswalt, John N. *The Book of Isaiah. Chapters 40–66*. New International Commentary on the Old Testament. Grand Rapids: Eerdmans, 1998.

Pagels, Elaine. "The Politics of Paradise: Augustine's Exegesis of Genesis 1–3 Versus That of John Chrysostom." *Harvard Theological Review* 78 (1985): 67–99.

Pamment, Margaret. "The Meaning of *doxa* in the Fourth Gospel." *Zeitschrift für die neutestamentlich Wissenschaft* 74 (1983): 12–16.

Pannenberg, Wolfhart. "Dogmatic Theses on the Doctrine of Revelation." In *Revelation as History*, edited by Wolfhart Pannenberg, translated by David Granshou, 125–158. New York: Macmillan Company, 1968.

Parvis, Sara, and Paul Foster, ed. *Justin Martyr and His Worlds*. Minneapolis: Fortress Press, 2007.

Patterson, Charles. *Eternal Treblinka: Our Treatment of Animals and the Holocaust*. New York: Lantern Books, 2002.

Paul, Shalom M. *Amos*. Hermeneia. Minneapolis: Fortress Press, 1991.

Paulien, Jon. *Decoding Revelation's Trumpets: Allusions and the Interpretation of Rev 8:7–12*. Berrien Springs, MI: Andrews University Press, 1988.

______. *The Deep Things of God*. Hagerstown, MD: Review and Herald Publishing Association, 2004.

______. "Dreading the Whirlwind: Intertextuality and the Use of the Old Testament in Revelation." *Andrews University Seminary Studies* 39 (2001): 5–22.

Pedersen, Johannes. *Israel: Its Life and* Culture. 2 vols. London: Oxford University Press, 1926.

Peli, Pinchas. *The Jewish Sabbath: A Renewed Encounter*. New York: Schocken Books, 1988.

Philo. Volume 1. Cambridge: Harvard University Press, 1929.

Pidcock-Lester, Karen. "John 5:1–9." *Interpretation* 59 (2005): 61–63.

Plato. *Plato, Euthyphro, Apology, Crito, Phaedo*. Translated by Benjamin Jowett. New York: Prometheus Books, 1988.

______. *The Phaedo*. Translated by Raymond Larson. Wheeling, IL: Harlan Davidson Inc., 1980.

______. *Timaeus and Critias*. Translated by H. D. P. Lee. Middlesex: Penguin Books, 1971.

Popper, Karl. *Conjectures and Refutations*. London: Routledge and Kegan, 1963.

______. *The Open Society and Its Enemies*. 2 vols. London: Routledge, 1966.

Porter, Roy. *Flesh in the Age of Reason: How the Enlightenment Transformed the Way We See Our Bodies and Souls*. London: Penguin Books, 2004.

Posidonius. 2 vols. Edited by I. G. Kidd. Cambridge Classical Texts and Commentaries. Cambridge: Cambridge University Press, 1988.

Postman, Neil. *Amusing Ourselves to Death*. New York: Penguin Books, 1985.

Price, S. R. F. *Rituals and Power: The Roman Imperial Cult in Asia Minor*. Cambridge: Cambridge University Press, 1984.

Prior, Michael. *Paul the Letter-Writer and the Second Letter to Timothy*. Journal for the Study of the New Testament Supplement Series 23. Sheffield: Sheffield Academic Press, 1989.

Purcell, Nicholas. "The Arts of Government." In *The Roman World,* edited by John Boardman, Jasper Griffin, and Oswyn Murray, 150–181. Oxford: Oxford University Press, 1986.

Quaife, Milo M., Melvin J. Weig, and Ray E. Appleman. *The History of the United States Flag*. New York: Harper & Brothers, 1961.

Rappaport, Herbert. *Marking Time*. New York: Simon & Schuster, 1990.

Reichborn-Kjennerud, I. "Black Death." *The Journal of the History of Medicine* 3 (1948): 359–360.

Reim, Günter. *Studien zum alttestamentlichcn Hintergrund des Johannesevangeliums*. Cambridge: Cambridge University Press, 1974.

Reis, Pamela Tamarkin. *Reading the Lines: A Fresh Look at the Hebrew Bible*. Peabody, MA: Hendrickson Publishers, 2002.

Rendtorff, Rolf. *The Canonical Hebrew Bible: A Theology of the Old Testament*. Translated by David Orton. Leiden: Deo Publishing, 2005.

______. *Das Überlieferungsgeschichtliche Problem des Pentateuch*. Berlin: Walter de Gruyter, 1977.

______. "Zur Komposition des Buches Jesaja." *Vetus Testamentum* 34 (1984): 295–320.

Resseguie, James L. *Revelation Unsealed: A Narrative Critical Approach to John's Apocalypse*. Leiden: Brill, 1998.

Ridderbos, Herman. *The Gospel According to John*. Translated by John Vriend. Grand Rapids: Eerdmans, 1997.

Rius-Camps, J. *The Four Authentic Letters of Ignatius, the Martyr*. Rome: Pontificium Institutum Orientalum Studiorum, 1979.

Robinson, Gnana. "The Idea of Rest in the Old Testament and the Search for the Basic Character of the Sabbath." *Zeitschrift für die alttestamentliche Wissenschaft* 92 (1980): 32–42.

Robinson, James Harvey. *Petrarch: The First Modern Scholar and Man of Letters*. New York: Haskell House Publishers Ltd., 1970.

Robinson, John A. T. *The Priority of* John. Oak Park: Meyer-Stone Books, 1987.

Rodin, R. Scott. *Evil and Theodicy in the Theology of Karl Barth*. Issues in Systematic Theology 3. New York: Peter Lang, 1997.

Roloff, Jürgen. *The Revelation of John*. Translated by John E. Alsup. Continental Commentary. Minneapolis: Fortress Press, 1993.

Rordorf, Willy. *Sunday: The History of the Day of Rest in the Earliest Centuries of the Christian Church*. Translated by A. A. K. Graham. London: SCM Press, 1968.

Roshwald, Mordechai. "A Dialogue Between Man and God." *Scottish Journal of Theology* 42 (1989): 145–165.

Rossing, Barbara R. "For the Healing of the World: Reading *Revelation* Ecologically." In *From Every People and Nation: The Book of Revelation in Intercultural Perspective*, edited by David Rhoads. Minneapolis: Fortress Press, 2005.

Rouwhorst, Gerhard. "Continuity and Discontinuity Between Jewish and Christian Liturgy." *Bijdragen tijdschrift voor filosofie en theologie* 54 (1993): 72–83.

______. "Jewish Liturgical Traditions in Early Syriac Christianity." *Vigiliae Christianae* 51 (1997): 72–93.

______. "Liturgical Time and Space in Early Christianity in Light of Their Jewish Background." In *Sanctity of Time and Space in Tradition and Modernity*, edited by A. Houtman, M. J. H. M. Poorthuis, and J. Schwartz, 265–284. Leiden: Brill, 1998.

______. "The Reading of Scripture in Early Christian Liturgy." In *What Athens Has to Do with Jerusalem: Essays on Classical Jewish and Early Christian Art and Archaeology in Honor of Gideon Foerster*, edited by Leonard V. Rutgers, 307–381. Leuven: Peeters, 2002.

______. "The Reception of the Jewish Sabbath in Early Christianity." In *Christian Feast and Festival*, edited by P. Post, G. Rouwhorst, L. van Tongeren, and A. Scheer, 223–266. Louvain: Peeters, 2001.

______. "Table Community in Early Christianity." In *A Holy People: Jewish and Christian Perspectives on Religious Communal Identity*, edited by Marcel Poorthuis and Joshua Schwartz, 69–84. Leiden: Brill, 2006.

Rowland, Christopher. *The Open Heaven: A Study of Apocalyptic in Judaism and Early Christianity* London: SPCK, 1982.

Rowley, H. H. *The Rediscovery of the Old Testament*. Philadelphia: The Westminster Press, 1946.

Ruether, Rosemary Radford. *Faith and Fratricide: The Theological Roots of Anti-Semitism*. New York: The Seabury Press, 1974.

Ryle, J. C. *Expository Thoughts on the Gospels*. 4 vols. Grand Rapids: Baker Book House, 1977.

Sacks, Oliver. *The Man Who Mistook His Wife for a Hat and Other Clinical Tales*. New York: Harper & Row, 1970.

Safrai, Shmuel. "The Jews in the Land of Israel." In *A History of the Jewish People*, edited by H. H. Ben-Sasson, 307–342. Cambridge: Harvard University Press, 1976.

Saint Augustine, *The Immortality of the Soul*. Translated by John J. McMahon. *The Fathers of the Church* 4. New York: Fathers of the Church, Inc., 1947.

Sanday, William, and Arthur C. Headlam. *A Critical and Exegetical Commentary on the Epistle to the Romans*. International Critical Commentary. Edinburgh: T. & T. Clark, 1902. Reprint, 1992.

Sanders, E. P. *Jesus and Judaism*. Philadelphia: Fortress Press, 1985.

______. *Judaism: Practice and Belief 63 BCE–66 CE*. London: SCM Press, 1992.

______. *Paul*. Oxford: Oxford University Press, 1991.

______. *Paul and Palestinian Judaism*. Minneapolis: Fortress Press, 1979.

______. *Paul, the Law and the Jewish People*. Minneapolis: Fortress Press, 1983.

Sandmel, Samuel. *Anti-Semitism in the New Testament?* Philadelphia: Fortress Press, 1978.

Sarna, Nahum M. *Genesis*. The Jewish Publication Society Torah Commentary. Philadelphia: The Jewish Publication Society, 1989.

______. *The Jewish Publication Society Commentary on Exodus*. Philadelphia: The Jewish Publication Society, 1991.

______. "The Psalm for the Sabbath Day (Ps 92)." *Journal of Biblical Literature* 81 (1962): 155–168.

______. *Understanding Genesis: The Heritage of Biblical Israel*. New York: Schocken Books, 1966.

Sawyer, John F. A. *The Fifth Gospel: Isaiah in the History of Christianity*. New York: Cambridge University Press, 1996.

Schaff, Philip. *History of the Christian Church*. 7 vols. New York: Charles Scribner's Sons, 1910. Reprint, Grand Rapids: Eerdmans, 1970.

Schlier, Heinrich. "Vom Antichrist: Zum 13. Kapitel der Offenbarung Johannis." In *Theologische Aufsätze. Karl Barth zum 50. Geburtstag*, 110–123. München: Chr. Kaiser Verlag, 1936.

Schmid, H. H. "Creation, Righteousness, and Salvation: 'Creation Theology' as the Broad Horizon of Biblical Theology." In *Creation in the Old Testament*, edited by Bernhard W. Anderson, 102–117. Philadelphia: Fortress, 1985.

Schnackenburg, Rudolf. *The Gospel According to St John*. 3 vols. Translated by Cecily Hastings, Francis McDonagh, David Smith, and Richard Foley. London: Burns & Oates, 1979.

Schuster, M. Lincoln, ed. *The World's Great Letters*. New York: Simon & Schuster, 1940.

Schweitzer, Albert. *The Mysticism of Paul the Apostle*. 2nd edition. Translated by William Montgomery. Baltimore: Johns Hopkins University Press, 1998. First published 1931 byA. & C. Black (London).

Schweizer, Eduard. *Der Brief an die Kolosser*. Evangelisch-katolischer Kommentar zum neuen Testament. Neukirchen: Benziger Verlag, 1976.

Scully, Matthew. *Dominion: The Power of Man, the Suffering of Animals, and the Call to Mercy*. New York: St. Martin's Press, 2002.

Segal, M. E. "The Religion of Israel before Sinai." *Jewish Quarterly Review* 52 (1961): 41–68.

Selman, M. J. "Comparative Customs and the Patriarchal Age." In *Essays on the Patriarchal Narratives*, edited by A. R. Millard and D. J. Wiseman, 93–138. Leicester: Inter-Varsity Press, 1980.

Sherman, Robert. "Reclaimed by Sabbath Rest." *Interpretation* 59 (2005): 43–44.

Siegert, Folker. "Early Jewish Interpretation in a Hellenistic Style." In *Hebrew Bible/Old Testament: The History of Its Interpretation*. Volume 1.1. *From the Beginnings to the Middle Ages (Until 1300)*. Edited by Magne Sæbø, 141–162. Göttingen: Vandenhoeck & Ruprecht, 1996.

Sigerist, Henry. *Civilization and Disease*. Ithaca, NY: Cornell University Press, 1943.

Sigmun, Paul E. "Law and Politics." In *The Cambridge Companion to Aquinas*, edited by Norman Kretzmann and Eleonore Stump, 217–231. Cambridge: Cambridge University Press, 1993.

Singer, Isaac Bashevis. *The Collected Stories of Isaac Bashevis Singer*. New York: Farrar, Straus and Giroux, 1996.

Ska, Jean Louis, "Biblical Law and the Origins of Democracy." In *The Ten Commandments: The Reciprocity of Faithfulness*, edited by William P. Brown, 146–158. Louisville: Westminster John Knox Press, 2004.

Skarsaune, Oskar. "The Development of Scriptural Interpretation in the Second and Third Centuries—Except Clement and Origen." In *Hebrew Bible/Old Testament: The History of Its Interpretation*. Volume 1.1. *From the Beginnings to the Middle Ages (Until 1300)*. Edited by Magne Sæbø, 373–442. Göttingen: Vandenhoeck & Ruprecht, 1996.

______. "The History of Jewish Believers in the Early Centuries—Perspectives and Framework." In *Jewish Believers in Jesus: The Early Centuries*, edited by Oskar Skarsaune and Reidar Hvalvik, 745–781. Peabody: Hendrickson, 2007.

Skarsaune, Oskar, and Reidar Hvalvik, ed. *Jewish Believers in Jesus: The Early Centuries*. Peabody: Hendrickson, 2007.

Skinner, John. *A Critical and Exegetical Commentary on Genesis*. International Critical Commentary. Edinburgh: T. & T. Clark, 1910.

Slusser, Michael. "Justin Scholarship—Trends and Trajectories." In *Justin Martyr and His Worlds,* edited by Sara Parvis and Paul Foster, 13–21. Minneapolis: Fortress Press, 2007.

Smith, D. Moody. "Johannine Christianity: Some Reflections on Its Character and Delineation." *New Testament Studies* 21 (1975): 222–248.

______. "John." In *Early Christian Thought in Its Jewish Context,* edited by John Barclay and John Sweet, 96–111. Cambridge: Cambridge University Press, 1996.

______. *The Theology of the Gospel of John.* New Testament Theology. Cambridge: Cambridge University Press, 1995.

Smith, Gary V. *Amos.* Grand Rapids: Zondervan, 1989.

Smith, George Adam. *The Twelve Prophets.* Rev. ed. New York: Harper and Brothers, 1928.

Smyth, Geraldine. "Sabbath and Jubilee." In *The Jubilee Challenge: Utopia or Possibility?* Edited by Hans Ucko, 59–76. Geneva: WCC Publications, 1997.

Solzhenitsyn, Alexander. *A World Split Apart.* New York: Harper & Row Publishers, 1978.

Sonnenday, James W. "Unwrapping the Gift Called Sabbath." *Journal for Preachers* 2 (2000): 39–42.

Southern, R. W. *Western Society and the Church in the Middle Ages.* Middlesex: Penguin Books, 1970.

Spurgeon, Charles H. *The Treasury of David.* 7 vols. Grand Rapids: Guardian Press, 1976. First published 1870–1885 by Funk & Wagnalls.

Stanton, Graham. *The Gospels and Jesus.* Oxford: Oxford University Press, 1989.

______. "What Is the Law of Christ?" *Ex auditu* 17 (2001): 47–59.

Stauffer, Ethelbert. *Jesus and His Story.* Translated by Richard and Clara Winston. New York: Alfred A. Knopf, 1970 [1959].

Stendahl, Krister. *The School of Saint Matthew and Its Use of the Old Testament.* Philadelphia: Fortress Press, 1968 [orig. 1954].

Stettler, Christian. "The Opponents at Colossae." In *Paul and His Opponents,* edited by Stanley Porter, 169–200. Leiden: Brill, 2005.

Stevens, Marty. "The Obedience of Trust: Recovering the Law as Gift." In *The Ten Commandments: The Reciprocity of Faithfulness,* edited by William P. Brown, 133–145. Louisville: Westminster John Knox Press, 2004.

Still, Todd D. "*Christos* as *Pistos*: The Faith(fulness) of Jesus in the Epistle to the Hebrews." Paper presented at the Conference on Hebrews and Christian Theology, University of St. Andrews, July, 2006.

Stone, I. F. *The Trial of Socrates.* New York: Anchor Books, 1989.

Stowers, Stanley. *A Rereading of Romans: Justice, Jews, and Gentiles.* New Haven: Yale University Press, 1994.

Strand, Kenneth A. "A Note on the Sabbath in Coptic Sources." In *The Early Christian Sabbath,* edited by Kenneth A. Strand, 16–24. Worthington, OH: Ann Arbor Publishers, 1976.

______. "The Sabbath." In *Handbook of Seventh-day Adventist Theology,* edited by Raoul Dederen, 493–537 (Hagerstown, MD: Review and Herald, 2000).

______. "The Sabbath Fast in Early Christianity." In *The Early Christian Sabbath,* edited by Kenneth A. Strand, 9–15. Worthington, OH: Ann Arbor Publishers, 1976.

Strobel, August. *Untersuchungen zum eschatologischen Verzögerungsproblem.* Novum Testamentum Supplement Series 2. Leiden: Brill, 1961.

Stuhlmacher, Peter. *Historical Criticism and Theological Interpretation of Scripture.* Translated by Roy A. Harrisville. London: SPCK, 1979.

______. *Revisiting Paul's Doctrine of Justification by Faith: A Challenge to the New Perspective.* Downers Grove: InterVarsity Press, 2001.

Sumney, Jerry L. *Identifying Paul's Opponents: The Question of Method in 2 Corinthians.* Journal for the Study of the New Testament Supplement 40. Sheffield: Sheffield Academic Press, 1990.

______. *"Servants of Satan," "False Brothers" and Other Opponents of Paul.* Journal for the Study of the New Testament Supplement 18. Sheffield: Sheffield Academic Press, 1999.

______. "Studying Paul's Opponents: Advantages and Challenges." In *Paul and His Opponents,* edited by Stanley E. Porter, 7–58. Leiden: Brill, 2005.

Sweet, J. P. M. *Revelation.* Philadelphia: The Westminster Press, 1979.

Taylor, Barbara Brown. "Sabbath Resistance." *Christian Century* 122 (2005): 35.

Tcherikover, Victor. *Hellenistic Civilization and the Jews.* The Jewish Publication Society of America, 1959. Reprint, Peabody, MA: Hendrickson Publishers, 1999.

Terrien, Samuel. *The Elusive Presence: Toward A New Biblical Theology.* New York: Harper & Row, 1978. Reprint, Eugene, OR: Wipf and Stock Publishers, 2000.

Tertullian. *An Answer to the Jews.* In *The Ante-Nicene Fathers.* Vol. 3. Edited by Alexander Roberts and James Donaldson. Translated by S. Thelwall, 151–173. Edinburgh: T & T Clark, n.d. Reprint, Grand Rapids: Eerdmans, 1989.

______. *On the Flesh of Christ.* In *The Ante-Nicene Fathers.* Vol. 3. Edited by Alexander Roberts and James Donaldson. Translated by Peter Holmes, 521–543. Edinburgh: T & T Clark, n.d. Reprint, Grand Rapids: Eerdmans, 1989.

______. *On the Resurrection of the Flesh.* In *The Ante-Nicene Fathers.* Vol. 3. Edited by Alexander Roberts and James Donaldson. Translated by Peter Holmes, 545–595. Edinburgh: T & T Clark, n.d. Reprint, Grand Rapids: Eerdmans, 1989.

______. *Treatise on the Soul.* In *The Ante-Nicene Fathers.* Vol. 3. Edited by Alexander Roberts and James Donaldson. Translated by Peter Holmes, 181–235. Edinburgh: T & T Clark, n.d. Reprint, Grand Rapids: Eerdmans, 1989.

Thompson, Leonard L. *The Book of Revelation: Apocalypse and Empire.* Oxford: Oxford University Press, 1990.

Thompson, Marianne Meye. *The God of the Gospel of John.* Grand Rapids: Eerdmans, 2001.

Thompson, Michael B. "The Holy Internet: Communication Between Churches in the

First Christian Generation." In *The Gospels for All Christians: Rethinking the Gospel Audiences,* edited by Richard J. Bauckham, 49–70. Edinburgh: T & T Clark, 1998.

Tierney, Brian. *The Crisis of Church and State 1050–1300.* Englewood Cliffs, NJ: Prentice-Hall, 1964.

Tillich, Paul. *Dynamics of Faith.* New York: Harper & Row, 1957.

Toenges, Elke. "'See, I am making all things new': New Creation in the Book of Revelation." In *Creation in Jewish and Christian Tradition,* edited by Henning Graf Reventlow and Yair Hoffman, 138–152. Journal for the Study of the Old Testament Supplement Series 319. Sheffield: Sheffield Academic Press, 2002.

Tomson, Peter J. "Gamaliel's Counsel and the Apologetic Strategy of Luke-Acts." In *The Unity of Luke-Acts,* edited by J. Verheyden, 585–604. Bibliotheca ephemeridum theologicarum lovaniensum 142. Leuven: Leuven University Press, 1999.

Tonstad, Sigve K. "Appraising the Myth of *Nero Redivivus* in the Interpretation of Revelation," *Andrews University Seminary Studies* 46 (2008):175–199.

______. "'A Blessing in the Midst of the Earth': Traveling the Prophetic Highway in Isaiah." *Spectrum* 34 (2006): 46–53.

______. "Creation Groaning in Labor Pains." In *Ecological Hermeneutics,* edited by Norman Habel, 143–151. Atlanta: Society of Biblical Literature, 2008.

______. "The Father of Lies, 'the Mother of Lies,' and the Death of Jesus (John 12:20–33)." In *The Gospel of John and Christian Theology,* edited by Richard J. Bauckham and Carl Mosser, 193–208. Grand Rapids: Eerdmans, 2008.

______. πίστις Χριστοῦ: Reading Paul in a New Paradigm." *Andrews University Seminary Studies* 40 (2002): 37–59.

______. "The Message of the Trees in the Midst of the Garden." *Journal of the Adventist Theological Society* 19 (2008): 1–16.

______. "The Restrainer Removed: A Truly Alarming Thought (2 Thess 2:1–2)." *Horizons in Biblical Theology* 29 (2007): 133–151.

______. "The Revisionary Potential of 'Abba, Father' in the Letters of Paul." *Andrews University Seminary Studies* 45 (2007): 5–18.

______. *Saving God's Reputation: The Theological Function of* Pistis Iesou *in the Cosmic Narratives of Revelation.* London: Continuum, 2006.

______. "Theodicy and the Theme of Cosmic Conflict in the Early Church." *Andrews University Seminary Studies* 42 (2004): 169–202.

Torjesen, Karen Jo. *Hermeneutical Procedure and Theological Method in Origen's Exegesis.* Berlin: Walter de Gruyter, 1986.

Toynbee, Arnold. "The Religious Background of the Present Environmental Crisis." In *Ecology and Religion in History,* edited by David and Eileen Spring, 137–154. New York: Harper & Row, 1974.

Troeltsch, Ernst. *Zur Religiösen Lage, Religionsphilosophie und Ethik*. Tübingen: Verlag von J. C. B. Mohr (Paul Siebeck), 1913.

Tsevat, Matitiahu. "The Basic Meaning of the Biblical Sabbath." *Zeitschrift für die alttestamentliche Wissenschaft* 84 (1972): 447–459.

Tuchman, Barbara. *A Distant Mirror*. New York: Ballantine Books, 1978.

Vacherot, Etienne. *Histoire critique de l'ecole d'Alexandrie*. 3 vols. L'édition Paris, 1846–1851. Amsterdam: Adolf M. Hakkert, 1965.

van Unnik, W. C. "A Formula Describing Prophecy." *New Testament Studies* 9 (1962–1963): 86–94.

______. "The Purpose of St. John's Gospel." In *Studia Evangelica* I. Texte und Untersuchungen 73. Edited by Kurt Aland, F. L. Cross, Jean Danielou, Harald Riesenfeld, and W. C. van Unnik, 382–411. Berlin: Akademie-Verlag, 1959.

Veijola, Timo. "'Du sollst daran denken, dass du Sklave gewesen bist im Lande Ägypten'—Zur literarischen Stellung und theologischen Bedeutung einer Kernaussage des Deuteronioiums." In *Gott und Mensch im Dialog. Festschrift für Otto Kaiser zum 80. Geburtstag*. Edited by Markus Witte, 253–373. Beihefte zur Zeitschrift für die alttestamentliche Wissenschaft 345. Berlin: Walter de Gruyter, 2004.

Vermes, Geza. *The Dead Sea Scrolls in English*. 3rd ed. London: Penguin Books, 1987.

______. *The Religion of Jesus the Jew*. Minneapolis: Augsburg Fortress, 1993.

Voelz, James W. "The Resurrection and the Ending of the Gospel of Mark." Paper presented at the Society of Biblical Literature meeting in Washington, DC, November, 2006.

Vogel, Dan. "A Psalm for Sabbath? A Literary View of Psalm 92." *Jewish Bible Quarterly* 28 (2000): 211–221.

von Goethe, Johann Wolfgang. *Faust*. Part One. Translated by Philip Wayne. London: Penguin, 1949.

von Rad, Gerhard. *Genesis*. 2nd ed. Translated by John H. Marks. London: SCM Press, 1963.

______. *Old Testament Theology*. 2 vols. Translated by D. M. G. Stalker. London: SCM Press, 1975.

______. "The Theological Problem of the Old Testament Doctrine of Creation." In *Creation in the Old Testament,* edited by Bernhard W. Anderson, 53–64. Philadelphia: Fortress Press, 1984 [original German essay 1936].

Von Wahlde, Urban C. "The Johannine 'Jews': A Critical Survey." *New Testament Studies* 28 (1982): 33–60.

Wagner, J. Ross. "The Heralds of Isaiah and the Mission of Paul." In *Jesus and the Suffering Servant: Isaiah 53 and Christian Origins,* edited by W. H. Bellinger and W. R. Farmer, 193–222. Harrisburg, PA: Trinity Press International, 1998.

Wallace, Howard N. "Rest for the Earth? Another Look at Genesis 2.1–3." In *The Earth Story in Genesis,* edited by Norman C. Habel and Shirley Wurst, 49–59. Sheffield: Sheffield

Academic Press, 2000.

Wallis, Ian G. *The Faith of Jesus Christ in Early Christian Traditions.* Society of New Testament Studies Monograph Series 84. Cambridge: Cambridge University Press, 1995.

Watson, Francis. "Is Revelation an 'Event'?" *Modern Theology* 10 (1994): 383–399.

______. *Paul and the Hermeneutics of Faith.* London: T. & T. Clark, 2004.

Watts, John D. W. *Isaiah 1–33.* Word Biblical Commentary. Waco: Word Books, 1985.

Weinfeld, Moshe. *Deuteronomy and the Deuteronomic School.* Oxford: The Clarendon Press, 1972.

Weiss, Harold. *A Day of Gladness: The Sabbath among Jews and Christians in Antiquity.* Columbia, SC: University of South Carolina Press, 2003.

______. "'*Sabbatismos*' in the Epistle to the Hebrews." *Catholic Biblical Quarterly* 58 (1996): 674–689.

Welker, Michael. *Creation and Reality.* Translated by John F. Hoffmeyer. Minneapolis: Fortress Press, 1999.

Wenham, David. "Paul and the Synoptic Apocalypse." In *Gospel Perspectives: Studies of History and Tradition in the Four Gospels*, vol. II, edited by R. T. France and David Wenham, 345–375. Sheffield: JSOT Press, 1981.

Wenham, Gordon J. *Genesis 1–15.* Word Biblical Commentary. Waco: Word Books, 1987.

______. *Genesis 16–50.* Word Biblical Commentary. Dallas: Word Books, 1994.

Westerholm, Stephen. "On Fulfilling the Whole Law (Gal 5:14)." *Svensk exegetisk årsbok* 51–52 (1986–87): 229–237.

______. *Perspectives Old and New on Paul: The "Lutheran" Paul and His Critics.* Grand Rapids: Eerdmans, 2004.

Westermann, Claus. "Biblical Reflection on Creator-Creation." In *Creation in the Old Testament*, edited by B. W. Anderson, 90–101. Philadelphia: Fortress, 1985. Originally published 1971.

______. "Creation and History in the Old Testament." In *The Gospel and Human Destiny*, edited by Vilmos Vajta. Translated by Donald Dutton, 11–38. Minneapolis: Augsburg Publishing House, 1971.

______. *Genesis 1–11.* Translated by John J. Scullion. London: SPCK, 1984.

______. *Genesis 12–36.* Translated by John J. Scullion. Minneapolis: Augsburg Publishing House, 1985.

______. *Isaiah 40–66.* Translated by David M. G. Stalker. Old Testament Library. London: SCM Press, 1969.

Westphal, Jonathan, and Carl Levenson, ed. *Time.* Indianapolis: Hackett Publishing Company, 1993.

White, Ellen G. "God's Justice and Love." *Signs of the Times*, August 27, 1902.

White, Lynn, Jr. "The Historical Roots of Our Ecological Crisis." *Science* 155 (1967): 1203–1207.

Whitehead, A. N. *Process and Reality.* Cambridge: Cambridge University Press, 1929.

Wilken, Robert L. *John Chrysostom and the Jews: Rhetoric and Reality in the Late 4th Century*. Berkeley: University of California Press, 1983.

Williamson, H. G. M. *Ezra, Nehemiah*. Word Biblical Commentary. Waco: Word Books, 1985.

Willimon, William H. "Lord of the Sabbath." *Christian Century* 108 (1991): 515.

Wills, Garry. *Lincoln at Gettysburg: The Words That Remade America*. New York: Simon & Schuster, 1992.

Wilson, Jack H. "The Corinthians Who Say There Is No Resurrection of the Dead." *Zeitschrift für die neutestamentliche Wissenschaft* 59 (1968): 90–107.

Winner, Lauren. "Reclaiming the Sabbath: Take the Day Off." *Christian Century* 122 (2005): 27–31.

Wirzba, Norman. "A Sabbath Sensibility: Time Out." *Christian Century* 122 (2005): 24–28.

Wolf, Ernst. "The Law of Nature in Thomas Aquinas and Luther." In *Faith and Action,* edited by H.-H. Schrey, 236–268. Edinburgh: Oliver & Boyd, 1970.

Wolff, Hans Walter. *A Commentary on the Book of the Prophet Hosea*. Edited by Paul D. Hanson. Translated by Gary Stansell. Hermeneia. Philadelphia: Fortress Press, 1974.

Wolterstorff, Nicholas. *Divine Discourse: Philosophical Reflections on the Claim that God Speaks*. Cambridge: Cambridge University Press, 1995.

______. "God Everlasting." In *God and the Good,* edited by Clifton J. Orlebeke and Lewis B. Smedes, 181–203. Grand Rapids: Eerdmans, 1975.

Wrede, William. *Vorträge und Studien*. Tübingen: J. C. B. Mohr, 1907.

Wright, G. E. *The Old Testament Against Its Environment*. London: SCM Press, 1950.

Wright, Jacob L. *Rebuilding Identity: The Nehemiah-Memoir and Its Earliest Readers*. Beihefte zur Zeitschrift für die alttestamentliche Wissenschaft 348. Berlin: Walter de Gruyter, 2004.

Wright, N. T. "The Paul of History and the Apostle of Faith." *Tyndale Bulletin* 29 (1978): 61–88.

______. *Surprised by Hope: Rethinking Heaven, the Resurrection, and the Mission of the Church* (London: SPCK, 2007).

Wurst, Shirley. "Retrieving Earth's Voice in Jeremiah: An Annotated Voicing of Jeremiah 4." In *The Earth Story in the Psalms and the Prophets,* edited by Norman C. Habel, 172–184. Sheffield: Sheffield Academic Press, 2001.

Yeats, William Butler. "The Second Coming." In *Poem a Day,* edited by Karen McCosker and Nicholas Alberry, 458. Hanover, NH: Steerforth Press, 1996.

Yoder, John Howard. *The Jewish-Christian Schism Revisited*. Edited by Michael G. Cartwright and Peter Ochs. Grand Rapids: Eerdmans, 2003.

Zimmerli, Walther. *The Old Testament and the World*. Translated by John J. Scullion. London: SPCK, 1976.

Zinsser, Hans. *Rats, Lice and History*. Boston: Little, Brown and Co., 1934. Reprint, London: Macmillan, 1985.

SCRIPTURE INDEX

LEVITICUS

NUMBERS

DEUTERONOMY

ECCLESIASTES

ISAIAH

JEREMIAH

EZEKIEL

DANIEL

HOSEA

AMOS

HABBAKUK

MATTHEW

MARK

LUKE

JOHN

EPHESIANS

PHILIPPIANS

COLOSSIANS

1 THESSALONIANS

2 THESSALONIANS

2 TIMOTHY

HEBREWS

JAMES

1 PETER

2 PETER

1 JOHN

REVELATION

SUBJECT INDEX

E

F

G

H

I

J

N

O

P

R

S

T

U

V

W

Y

Z